МЭМО

New Soviet Voices
on
Foreign and Economic Policy

MЭMO

New Soviet Voices
on
Foreign and Economic Policy

Edited by

Steve Hirsch

The Bureau of National Affairs, Inc., Washington, D.C.

Library of Congress Cataloging-in-Publication Data

MEMO: New Soviet voices on foreign and economic policy/edited by Steve Hirsch.
p.   cm.
ISBN 0-87179-633-3
1. Soviet Union—Foreign relations—1985- 2. Soviet Union—Economic conditions—1976- 3. World politics—1985-1995. 4. International economic relations. I. Hirsch, Steve, 1952- II. Bureau of National Affairs (Washington, D.C.)
DK289.M46   1989
327.47—dc20   89-15907
                                                                                CIP

Published by BNA Books
1231 25th Street N.W., Washington, D.C.

Printed in the United States of America
International Standard Book Number 0-87179-633-3

Foreword

This book is an attempt to help break new ground in publishing and in the field of Soviet affairs. Sovietologists, Kremlinologists, and their brethren, like priests of an obscure and exclusive order, have for years been able to peruse the writings of Soviet thinkers in Russian or, in some cases, English. This situation was, until recently, fine, as far as the general public was concerned. The Soviet Union was far away and, to some, an Evil Empire; the musings of its intelligentsia were of little interest to most in the West. Moreover, tight control of the public pronouncements of Soviets dampened any nascent interest those outside the club might have had in going to the trouble of investing time and money to find out what was being published by the thinkers of the other superpower.

Since Mikhail Gorbachev's rise to power, though, both the diversity of publication in the Soviet Union and the breadth of Western interest in it have blossomed. Even beyond the sort of pop-Sovietology that sprang up in the wake of Gorbachev's ascension and the "Gorby fever" that has gripped many in the United States and Western Europe, it seems there is increased interest in the United States and elsewhere in the English-speaking world in what Soviets are saying, an interest that we would like to satisfy with this book.

New Soviet thinking on the rest of the world seems to be a good starting point for giving Western readers an insight into what is now happening in Soviet policy and intellectual circles. I was fortunate enough to make contact with a representative of the Institute of World Economy and International Relations during a conference in Kiev in 1987, whose suggestions eventually led to the publication of this book.

The Institute, known generally by its Russian acronym IMEMO, has presented some of the most forward-looking writing in the fields of foreign affairs and economics, an effort that will become evident to readers of this book. It should be mentioned that in April 1989 Yevgeny Primakov, IMEMO's director, was promoted to full membership in the Communist Party Central Committee during Gorbachev's shakeup of that body. Then in June, as we were completing work on the book, he was elected chairman of the new Council of the Union, one of the new Soviet parliament's two chambers. The Institute publishes a journal, *World Economy and International Relations*, known as *MEMO*. Thus a collection of articles from the last two years' issues of *MEMO* provides an obvious way to expose Western readers to new Soviet thinking.

The selection of articles, ranging from fairly general pieces to essays on such specific topics as cultural exchange through the electronic media and cuts in strategic weapons was worked out in Washington and Moscow in 1988. The pieces vary in format, including an interview, an exchange of letters, dialogues, statistical surveys, and straightforward essays. Some will appeal primarily to specialists while others will appeal to anyone with more than a passing interest in what is now happening in the Soviet Union.

This is a new sort of book for English-speakers and we largely left the selection of articles to the Soviet editors of *MEMO* because our goal is to present the views of Soviets to Western readers. Some of the articles contained quoted material translated into Russian from English or other foreign language sources. We attempted to reproduce the original wording of all of the quotations from English-language sources. Of those we could not locate, two were deleted, one was paraphrased, and one was included as retranslated into English with a note so indicating. Notes or comments by BNA's editors or translators appear in brackets to distinguish them from notes of *MEMO*'s editors.

As a journalist who has covered U.S.-Soviet relations over the last decade, I feel that these articles highlight areas of greatest concern to readers with an interest in the Soviet Union and its role in the world. As this project evolved from abstract concept to published book, I asked a number of Soviet specialists to look at the list of articles selected and was delighted to discover that they felt the selection would be useful to a wide range of readers.

I am quite certain that academics will find this book useful, as will journalists, and those in and out of government who contribute to developing Western policies toward the Soviet Union. I also hope, though, that people with no professional interest in the Soviet Union but a desire to learn more than they can from the general media about the important changes occurring in Soviet thinking will find this book a welcome addition to what has been available to date.

This book is a landmark effort for The Bureau of National Affairs, Inc., which is widely known in legal and business news and publishing, but not widely known in Soviet and East-West affairs. We hope that this book will be the beginning of an increasing BNA presence in these important areas, and that we will be able to contribute to knowledge of developments in East-West relations.

A great many people in the United States and the Soviet Union, at BNA, IMEMO, or outside, contributed a massive effort to produce this book. There is not room to thank them all here but I would like to recognize a number of them.

This project would not have been possible without the support of BNA's president, William Beltz, and its executive editor, Hugh Yarrington. They took what must have seemed like a fairly far-fetched idea at the time and committed both time and company resources to make it a reality. On the Soviet side, MEMO's editor in chief, German Diligenskiy, and his deputy, Ivan Tselichtshev, provided most of the Soviet input for the book. Following meetings in Washington and Moscow, Ivan put forward a Herculean effort to review BNA's translations on very short deadlines so that this book could be produced in a short time.

Naturally, a book of this sort could not be published without good translators. I believe we were extremely fortunate to have a superb translation team outside of BNA headed by Gordon Livermore and including Robert S. Ehlers, Bruce Collins, Elizabeth Hewitt, and Deborah Hunter. Gordon and his colleagues not only provided translation, but their expertise in Soviet foreign policy thinking was invaluable at various points along the way.

Within BNA Books, Timothy Darby helped with initial efforts to arrange for translating and editing and Camille Christie is as responsible as any other single person for publication of this book. She spent vast amounts of time editing copy and coordinating the transformation of the collected translations into the final product. Special thanks to Le T. Pham, of BNA's library, who provided a wealth of assistance in obtaining both English and Russian source materials from libraries throughout the Washington area.

Finally, there is one person who may deserve more credit than all of us. Sergei Stankovsky, a research fellow at IMEMO, during a meeting of U.S. and Soviet journalists in Kiev, suggested to me that there might be potential in a BNA-IMEMO project. It was Sergei's suggestion that led to the opening of talks between the two organizations and led, in fact, to the publication of this book. Thanks for the tip, Sergei.

June 1989   Steve Hirsch

Introduction

The journal *World Economy and International Relations* [*MEMO*] was founded in 1957 and has been published monthly since June of that year. *MEMO* is a publication of the U.S.S.R. Academy of Sciences' Institute of World Economy and International Relations [IMEMO], the U.S.S.R.'s largest research center for the study of problems in its field.

The 20th Congress of the CPSU, which exposed the personality cult and crimes of Stalin, can rightfully be considered the "godfather" of *MEMO*. That congress created a new political atmosphere in the country (sometimes called the "thaw"), and opened up possibilities for the free examination of problems in both domestic and international life, many of which had hitherto been considered forbidden topics.

In a situation characterized by a marked expansion of contacts with the external world, with the Soviet public showing increased interest in international problems, the journal rather quickly won readers' sympathies and acquired a readership of scholars, journalists, diplomats, and university instructors and students. Flattering comments about the journal have also been made by a number of prestigious economists and political scientists in the West, including Americans.

This interest has been evoked by the heated discussions that the journal has carried and the fact that it has raised and offered analyses of important current problems.

The journal gives special attention to questions of the world economy, the specific features of capitalism at the present stage of the scientific and technological revolution, integration processes occurring in the world, and the creative treatment of problems in political economy, sociology, and international relations. Articles developing the concept of the new political thinking occupy a central place in it.

MEMO regularly carries articles about the economies and foreign policies of the U.S.S.R. and the other socialist countries, their role and place in the world economy and world politics, and the state of, and prospects for, East-West economic cooperation.

Of course, the Brezhnev period of stagnation could not help but have a negative effect on the choice of topics for analysis and the very nature of research. For example, excessive emphasis was placed on the factors hobbling the development of productive forces and realization of the potential of the scientific and technological revolution in the West, and articles sometimes suffered from one-sidedness and dogmatism. At the same time, even then, innovative approaches to the treatment of a number of problems "broke through" in the journal's pages. That was the case in the 1960s, when, in connection with the explosive development of worldwide productive forces, the editors initiated a series of articles whose authors attempted to interpret the essence and historical role of the scientific and technological revolution. And a discussion of the place of the services sector in present day production corrected previous ideas about the nature of the work of service sector employees. For the first time, the conclusion was drawn that that work is productive.

Perestroika and glasnost have had an extremely beneficial effect on all of the journal's work. Now it is striving to become an outlet for the new thinking and to find adequate answers to the most urgent issues in world economic and social development and international relations.

The journal intensively criticizes obsolete ideological and theoretical stereotypes. The approach to the problems being investigated has become more realistic and objective. New, bold, and substantive studies have been written. Top priority is given to discussions, round tables, interviews, and dialogues among scholars. A number of conclusions that have been substantiated and developed in the journal have been taken into account in the process of developing state foreign-economic and foreign-policy decisions, and in the practical efforts to carry out radical economic reform in the U.S.S.R.

Lately the journal has given increasing attention to the publication of articles by well-known foreign scholars, politicians, and public figures (including Robert McNamara, former CIA Director Stansfield Turner, Sovietologist Seweryn Bialer, well-known economist Martin Feldstein, and others).

While carrying out a perestroika in the journal itself, the editors are trying to expand their readership, both within the country and abroad. The journal has been published in German for many years in the German Democratic Republic, and it is published quarterly in Japan. The editors' ties with journals in America, Europe, and Asia are expanding.

German Diligenskiy
Ivan Tselichtshev
Sergei Chugrov

April 1989

Contents

III. The U.S.S.R. and CMEA in World Economy

IV. The New Thinking in International Relations

V. The Third World

A Retrospective

Part One

Global Context of Perestroika

Capitalism, Socialism, and the Economic Mechanism of Present Day Production

Viktor Leonidovich Sheynis*

Many people who have taken the political economy course in our higher education institutions over the years have developed a deeply rooted critical attitude toward the political economy of socialism as an opportunistic and dogmatic discipline, and a respectful attitude toward the political economy of capitalism, which wins people over with the strict logic of its scientific categories and its seeming ability not only to explain but to predict the development of objective processes. Evidently the differences in the scholarly prestige of the two parts of the course are not solely determined by the merits of the author of *Das Kapital*, who expressed his own ethical creed in no uncertain terms: "A man, who tries to *adapt* science to a point of view that is drawn not from science itself (no matter how much science may err), but from the *outside*, a point of view that is dictated by interests that are *alien* to science and *external* to it—I call that sort of person *base.*"[1]

Starting in the 1960s some significant work was done on the political economy of capitalism, which was less constrained by limitations originating outside of science. Research by Soviet scientists meshed with work being done by foreign Marxists, who in a number of cases played a pioneering role in raising new questions.[2] The development of the theoretical potential amassed by various schools of non-Marxist theoretical thought was also of considerable importance, although the study of it was persistently forced into the procrustean bed of "criticism of bourgeois theories," and the criticism itself was generally rather primitive.

As the 20th century draws to an end, however, it is becoming increasingly obvious that the political economy of capitalism is also in

---

*Doctor of economics, chief research associate at the U.S.S.R. Academy of Sciences' Institute of World Economy and International Relations [IMEMO]. This article appeared in the September 1988 issue of *MEMO*.

[1]K. Marx and F. Engels, *Works [Sochineniya]*, Vol. 26, Part II, p. 125.
[2]See, for example, *V.I. Lenin's Teachings about Imperialism, and Today's World [Ucheniye V.I. Lenina ob imperializme i sovremennost]*, Moscow, 1967.

need of serious rethinking, that the corrections and refinements of older general propositions, the shifts in emphasis in the reading of the classics, and the enrichment of logical and historical categories are not enough. The method of simply incorporating "new phenomena in the economics of capitalism" in standard models is becoming less and less useful. The in-depth theoretical treatment of individual problems that has emerged in science must be used not to decorate the façade, but to rebuild the building's cornerstones. A new general theoretical paradigm is needed so we can see the world around us as it really is, imagine what it may be like tomorrow, and recognize what it obviously cannot become either tomorrow or in the more distant future.

But an updated concept of capitalism is also needed to understand our own society and its place both in history and in today's contradictory, but single and interconnected world, and in order to understand, in particular, that there are general features arising from the objective conditions of present-day economic and social development that should be characteristic of any developed society. And in order to make active use not only of the technology, but also of essential components of the economic mechanism that have demonstrated their effectiveness not just in the West, but also in some of the developing countries.

Yet the "ideas and models that were the result of different times and different opportunities for creativity," about which M.S. Gorbachev spoke at the Moscow meeting of representatives of parties and movements in November 1987, are still playing the role of "sacred cows" not only in ideology, but in much scientific thinking as well. I would go so far as to say that these include assertions about the decay, death, and general crisis of contemporary capitalism; assertions about the transition from capitalism to socialism as the main feature of the present era; claims about state planning as the main form for ensuring well-planned social production; the axiomatic approach to ownership under socialism, and the idea that state ownership enjoys preeminence over all other forms; and so forth. Unlike the actual "sacred cows" to which the Hindu tradition has assigned such a nonfunctional role by present-day standards, there is no use whatsoever for the myths that are burdening the social sciences. They must be cleared from our path.[3]

---

[3]The reader will see that I agree with some of the most important propositions in Ya. Pevzner's article that started the debate (see *MEMO*, No. 6, 1988, pp. 5-22) about the illegitimacy of erecting a wall between the political economy of capitalism and the political economy of socialism; about the universal nature of the laws and categories of commodity production; about the relationships between surplus value and profits, and between monopoly and competition, under the conditions of present-day capitalism; about the unsuitability of the concept of "state-monopoly capitalism"; and about the role of the market under the conditions of developed socialism, and the direction of transformations whose time has come.

I.

We are not far off from the 50th anniversary of the end of World War II, and a half-century is an immense period of time in terms of the current pace of the historical process. The conditions under which we have developed during these decades have been fairly difficult, but not extreme: Such a long period of peace is unprecedented in the history not only of the U.S.S.R., but of Russia as well, at least since the time of Peter I. Attempts to attribute our current lagging behind, economic imbalances, and social deformations to backwardness and hardships in the past for which we are not responsible carry less and less weight.

Without in any way understating our country's historic achievements, or the serious problems and difficulties that the capitalist economy and society are experiencing, one must admit that over the course of a fairly long period of time economic competition with capitalism has not gone as was predicted in either the prewar period or the early 1960s, when the Party Program that has just been revised was adopted. Although the U.S.S.R.'s economic potential has considerably expanded and has been renewed since that time, the problem is even more critical now than when it was first raised.

As we know, both directive and planning offices gave particular attention to gross economic indicators. But even in terms of those indicators, progress became increasingly difficult with each new five-year plan. According to data published by statistical agencies (which some knowledgeable economists believe to be seriously inflated),[4] the average annual rates of increase in the U.S.S.R.'s national income were as follows: in the 1950s—9.9 percent, in the 1960s—6.4 percent, in the 1970s—4.5 percent, and in the first half of the 1980s—3.1 percent.[5] This tendency toward falling rates of general economic growth has not been overcome in the first years of the 12th five-year plan, either.

As a result, the U.S.S.R.'s movement toward the United States in terms of both total national income and per capita income made a spurt in the 1950s, slowed down in the 1960s, and practically stopped altogether between 1970 and 1985, having reached 65 to 67 percent of the U.S. level for the first indicator, and 55 to 56 percent for the second.[6]

Calculations performed by American researchers using an alternative methodology for international economic comparisons (based on

---

[4]See V. Selyunin, G. Khanin. "Elusive Figures" (*Novy mir* [*New World*], No. 2, 1987).

[5]Based on *The National Economy of the U.S.S.R. over 70 Years* [*Narodnoye khozyaystvo SSSR za 70 let*], Moscow, 1987. pp. 7, 430.

[6]See *The U.S.S.R. National Economy: 1922-1982* [*Narodnoye khozyaystvo SSSR. 1922-1982*], Moscow, 1982, p. 91; *The U.S.S.R. National Economy in 1985* [*Narodnoye khozyaystvo SSSR v 1985 g.*], Moscow, 1986, p. 581.

parities of the purchasing power of currencies) show the same dynamics, but at a somewhat lower level. According to these data, the U.S.S.R.'s per capita income was 30.2 percent of the U.S. per capita income in 1950 (according to the Central Statistical Administration's data, this figure would be 26.2 percent), 40.1 percent in 1960, 47.4 percent in 1970, and 48.7 percent in 1980.[7] These highly aggregated indicators, however, still depict the situation in a relatively more favorable light for us, since they practically give no indication of the major changes in the course of economic competition.

Today we must compete not only with the United States, but also with the other capitalist countries, especially Japan, which has overtaken the capitalist world's leader in a number of important areas. According to calculations by Z. Brzezinski, in 1987 Japan had already surpassed the U.S.S.R. in GNP, thereby moving the latter into third place in the world.[8] In 1992 we are also going to have to deal with the reality of an economically united Western Europe (or more precisely, most of Western Europe). In addition, the sudden spurt of growth among the newly industrialized countries of the Third World deserves the very closest attention. They have demonstrated experience that is instructive for everyone by rapidly developing modern, research-intensive branches of industry, and by establishing fairly strong positions in promising industries in the world market. It is noteworthy that in the developed capitalist countries' market for high-technology products, a market which truly tests the competitiveness of products (i.e., not as our State Standards Committee and State Acceptance Procedures test their competitiveness), the U.S.S.R. is losing out even to developing countries. At the beginning of the 1980s the U.S.S.R.'s share of worldwide exports of all types of machinery products was just a little more than 2 percent, while the developing countries' share was 6 percent (naturally, the top firms accounted for almost the entire amount).[9]

The gap between us and the leading capitalist states (as well as some of the "newcomers") in terms of labor productivity,[10] efficiency in the utilization of production resources, and product quality is significantly greater than it is for gross economic indicators, and it is not changing in our favor. The U.S.S.R. economy is growing increasingly accustomed to seeing itself in the role of an Achilles who is forever chasing after the tortoise: Having overtaken all or almost all the world's

---

[7]Based on R. Summers and A. Heston, "Improved International Comparisons of Real Product and Its Composition: 1950-1980" (*Review of Income and Wealth*, No. 2, June 1984, pp. 207-262).

[8]*Moskovskiye novosti* [*Moscow News*], May 8, 1988.

[9]Based on *Handbook of International Trade and Development Statistics*, 1985 Supplement, New York, 1985, p. A-38.

[10]See B. Bolotin's data and commentary at pp. 375-390 in this collection.

countries in terms of the extraction and production of a number of basic types of intermediate products—petroleum, iron ore, steel, mineral fertilizers, cement, cotton—and even certain traditional consumer goods—footwear, cotton and wool fabrics, sugar, potatoes[11]—we repeatedly find ourselves falling behind in the technologically advanced, emerging industries, in the rapidly changing generations of production and household technology, in the efficient utilization of resources, and in terms of living standard and the quality of life.

Our economic *lag* behind the most developed capitalist countries has once again become *qualitative*, rather than *quantitative* if one views it in the context of the three technological methods of production that succeed one another in world history: hand-tool-based production, industrial production, and science-based industrial production. As a result of the industrialization of the 1930s and 1940s, the Soviet economy managed for the most part to rise to the second level, and to overcome the qualitative gap between Russia and Europe in the main, leading, and newly created industries (despite the persistence of a vast zone of manual labor in which the simplest implements were used). The qualitative gap in the new round of worldwide technological development has been recreated by the scientific and technological revolution.

Of course, in a number of branches of industry, mainly the defense and aerospace industries and several of those most closely related to them, the Soviet economy has made serious accomplishments. However, to conclude from this that it has, as a whole, reached the scientific-industrial stage of worldwide technological development would be just as wrong as saying that some African or Asian country has made the transition to the industrial phase merely because individual industrial enterprises using modern technology have been established there. The inadequate development of our economy manifests itself in many respects.

In the first place, we have not yet achieved the proper integration of science and production; a swollen network of research institutions operates, to a considerable degree, all by itself, while the production sphere adopts innovations only under the influence of strong non-economic pressure (the Ivanovo Machine Tool Association headed by V.P. Kabaidze is one of the few exceptions that have "broken out" of the system).

In the second place, our modernization of technology and products is limited, and sometimes even fictitious; the entire economy is oriented toward the stability of relationships, technology, and products, while the standard for the scientific and technological revolution

---

[11]See *The National Economy of the U.S.S.R. over 70 Years*, pp. 661-669, 672.

is mobility and continuous revamping of both production systems and consumption patterns.

In the third place, our current system for collection, processing, and systematic organization of information and its timely transmission to the proper place in the required form is in the embryonic stage. It is not just an inert management mechanism, but also a political and ideological system that tried to maintain absolute control over citizens' thoughts, that are to blame for blocking the transition to information technology at a time when the main thrust of the scientific and technological revolution lay in that direction.

The spurt of development that made it possible to complete the industrialization that had begun prior to the Revolution and to approximate, and even surpass, the performance of the developed capitalist states in certain areas is often credited to the administrative-command system of economic organization and to the political and ideological structures of Stalinism; when this is done, people ignore the fact that the price that society paid for all this was beyond measure. This is not the place to discuss the extent to which the establishment of this model was inevitable at that time, although it is difficult to agree with the widely held conviction that there was no alternative to that sort of development. One can hardly doubt, however, that the system of economic relations that took shape in the late 1920s and early 1930s, and the entire persisting legacy of Stalinism have been the main obstacle blocking development and dooming a great country to an unenviable role in the world economy.

Moreover, our own country has not been immune to the so-called demonstration effect of the higher and more diverse standards of mass consumption in the developed capitalist countries, an effect that has been described in detail in studies dealing with the Third World. As various forms of communications grow and the world information flow becomes more concentrated, this effect will grow stronger. The public perceives the benefits we have grown accustomed to as necessary and natural, but it increasingly refuses to accept the lack or shortage of things that a developed economy can provide today. The level of the standards set by the demonstration effect is rising all the time.

We need an up-to-date economy that generates scientific and technological progress, rather than rejecting it, and that is oriented not toward squeezing out performance indicators that have been calculated in the offices of central economic-management agencies, but toward meeting what are people's elementary needs by today's standards. We need an economy that delivers us from the humiliating pursuit of goods that are in short supply, from senselessly wasting our time standing in line, from the "difference in value" of the ruble in Moscow and Kaluga, and from many other well-known defects.

Our parting with the administrative-command system, however, is proceeding slowly and with difficulty. In the past year or two, quite a bit has been said in scholarly writing and, especially, public-affairs journalism about the reasons for this difficulty. Not the least of these reasons are the inertia of social,[12] political, and scientific thinking, and in particular, a fear of the phantoms of "market socialism," "revisionism," and "ideological sabotage"—an updated version of the medieval notion about the evil eye that the devil casts on unsuspecting people.

Although innovative research and bold approaches to controversial issues have recently done a great deal to clarify the situation,[13] far from everything has been said about two fundamental aspects of the problem. First, in terms of political economy and sociology, the potential for the development of the capitalist economy, the driving forces behind this process, and the depth and direction of economic and social changes have not been fully analyzed and understood yet; and second, the opposition between capitalism and socialism is still treated as an absolute in the sphere where the universal laws of market-based production [tovarnoye proizvodstvo] apply.

II.

It would be wrong, of course, to claim that there have not been any "minor shifts" in our notions about the historical evolution of the capitalist system in the 20th century. Over time, a transition was made from the political formula of the late 1940s, which stated that "the main danger for the working class now lies in the underestimation of its forces and the overestimation of the forces of the imperialist camp,"[14] to a more dialectical vision that tried to take into account not only the weaknesses and contradictions of the Western social and economic system, but also its strengths and considerable potential.[15] The devel-

---

[12]For greater detail, see I. Kon, "The Psychology of Social Inertia" (*Kommunist* [*Communist*], No. 1, 1988).

[13]First and foremost, one should mention a number of monographs that IMEMO has published on the developed capitalist economy, focusing on specific countries and problems; some of the latest controversial works are: Ya. Pevzner, *Controversial Issues in Political Economy* [*Diskussionnyye voprosy politicheskoy ekonomii*], Moscow, 1987; and "State Regulation and Private Enterprise in Capitalist Countries: Evolution of the Relationship (*MEMO*, Nos. 10-12, 1986; Nos. 1-4, 6, 7, 12, 1987); and articles by V. Kuznetsov (*MEMO*, No. 8, 1988), A. Anikin (*MEMO*, No. 11, 1987), Yu. V. Shishkov ("The Working Class and the Present-Day World," No. 1, 1986; No. 6, 1987), Ye. S. Popov ("The Working Class and the Present-Day World," No. 1, 1988), and others.

[14]*The Informational Conference of Representatives of Several Communist Parties in Poland in Late September 1947* [*Informatsionnoye soveshchaniye predstaviteley nekotorykh kompartiy v Polshe v kontse sentyabrya 1947 goda*], Moscow, 1948, p. 10.

[15]See *The International Conference of Communist and Workers' Parties. Documents and Materials* [*Mezhdunarodnoye soveshchaniye kommunisticheskikh i rabochikh partiy. Dokumenty i materialy*], Moscow, 1969, pp. 176-179.

opment of the Marxist theory of capitalism also made a contribution to the recognition of actual processes. The changes that capitalism was undergoing, however, were viewed primarily as a quantitative increase or decrease in its known characteristics.

Schematically, the notion of the historical dynamics of the capitalist method of production can be described as follows. The concentration and centralization of production and capital clearly prevail over deconcentration and decentralization. At a certain stage, concentration leads to monopoly. Monopolies break the economy up into a relatively small number of private economic domains, eliminate so-called free competition, undermine the mechanism of "normal" market price setting, and pump profits out of the nonmonopolized sector, since that sector remains both in that system's centers and on its periphery. The transition to monopoly capitalism sharply intensifies the tendency toward stagnation and toward the decay of the social and economic structure, and it speeds up the spread of parasitic phenomena.

At the same time, within the framework of private monopolies an apparatus for the management and control of production on a public scale begins to be formed. At the next stage, private-monopoly concentration also proves to be inadequate: a sort of "superstructure" emerges in the form of a powerful state sector, state capital, and state capitalism. The transition is made to state-monopoly capitalism, which is the direct precursor of socialism, since at this stage the preparation of the material conditions for the new social system is completed, all the contradictions of capitalism are aggravated to the extreme, a general crisis of capitalism develops, and only a socialist revolution can offer a way out of this crisis.

That is how—or approximately how—the main direction of historical development was described in the Marxist literature. This vision reflected the actual processes that took place in the late 19th and early 20th centuries, or at least some of them. The triumph of socialist revolutions, first in Russia, and later in Eastern Europe and a number of countries on the former colonial periphery, not only confirmed the certainty of prospects for the future, but also, it seemed, outlined the most likely scenario for the transition to the new social system on a worldwide scale: a progressive narrowing of the capitalist world, with more and more of its parts falling away from it.

The fact that this transition dragged out over a significantly longer period than was expected during the first years and decades following the October Revolution led at first to the invention of a fairly artificial theoretical scheme describing the stages of the general crisis of capitalism, and when the "third stage" turned out to be much too long, scientific thought reached a crossroads: either a new stage had to be conceived, or the "brakes" needed to be applied to the stages that had already been devised. Meanwhile, in the evolution of capitalism, processes that were increasingly difficult to reconcile with customary notions of capitalism's "over-maturity," "dying out," and "general crisis" were manifesting themselves more and more distinctly.

The scientific and technological revolution has begun, and it is continuing to pick up speed; the revolution in productive forces surpasses any technological revolution since neolithic times—this is becoming increasingly obvious today—in terms of its depth, totality, and diverse consequences in all spheres of social life. It is useful to relate this obvious statement of fact to Marx's well-known idea: "Not a single social formation dies out before all the productive forces for which it provides sufficient room have developed fully. . . ."[16] "The *tendency* toward stagnation and decay that is inherent in monopoly,"[17] which was not predominant at the beginning of the century, has not become, and is hardly likely to become in the foreseeable future, the dominant trend in present-day capitalism, and this is true of more than the technological sphere.

There is no question that serious contradictions are inherent in the capitalist economy and serious antagonisms are inherent in bourgeois society. But the recognition of this has nothing in common with a mechanical concept of the constant aggravation of all of capitalism's contradictions without exception, and especially of the main one—the contradiction between the public nature of production and the private nature of appropriation [i.e., of surplus value—*Trans.*]. Changes have taken place on both sides of this contradiction, and the private-capitalistic nature of ownership has undergone a certain degree of modification under the influence of social institutions. Internal economic and social stabilizers have gradually been built into the system, and over the course of several decades they have protected it from shocks that could have led to its collapse.

Periodic aggravations have occurred, of course, but not one of them has reproduced the drama of the revolutionary crisis of 1917 to 1920, or the hopelessness of the economic depression of 1929 to 1931, when it seemed that the reserves for preserving capitalism in the world were on the verge of being exhausted. Of course, with time some of these stabilizers have become shaky, and new contradictions have developed that could not be suppressed using previously proven means. But the system has "learned" to adapt many of them and turn them into sources of development, rather than degradation.

---

[16]K. Marx and F. Engels, *Works*, Vol. 13, p. 7.
[17]V.I. Lenin, *Complete Works* [*Polnoye sobraniye sochineniy*], Vol. 27, p. 397.

The elimination of the colonial system did not lead to a serious weakening of capitalism, either. For the most part, it was the old colonial-capitalistic structures that dated back to the period of original accumulation and the territorial division of the world and required noneconomic support that suffered damage. Contemporary high-technology and well-organized capital even benefited from the collapse of the colonial system. The narrower territorial sphere available for its activities, and national sovereignty restrictions placed on the "freedom of action" of foreign capital turned out to be more than compensated for by an expansion of economic space, an accelerated movement toward capitalism on the part of new countries that were in the rear echelons of historical development, and the growing integration of local forms of capitalism into world structures. And although the inclusion of these countries in the processes of capitalist transformation poses some difficult and unusual economic and, particularly, social problems, the majority of Third World countries are seeking solutions to these problems through development, and not through the elimination of capitalist structures. Some of them have managed to achieve definite social and economic progress along these lines, and world capitalism on the whole has acquired an additional base of development.

The "reserve" of social stability and vitality that capitalism has discovered has often been interpreted in a superficial way. Explanations in our literature usually involve its adaptation to new historical conditions, and concessions that it has been forced to make under pressure from the working people. Both formulas played a positive role in the interpretation of real processes at a time when theoretical thought was fettered by dogmatic prohibitions, and they made it possible to somewhat expand the boundaries set by nonscientific restrictions. Today, however, it would seem that their usefulness has been exhausted.

If capitalism has found an ability to adapt to a new, dramatically altered situation, then it evidently follows that it has undergone some fairly fundamental modifications at the level not only of its manifestations but of its laws, and in any case, that the established economic order is not on the brink of collapse. But the thesis about adaptation had the effect of moving the set of conditions that required change to beyond the limits of a given economy and society, and depicting them as something external to capitalism. It veiled the fact that it is, first and foremost, a society itself that forms the conditions of its existence and development. In retrospect, the investigator today can see with increasing clarity that it is not at the stage of free competition that existed only in the historical model of European and quasi-European societies, but at the present stage, that all the properties and potentials of capitalism, both negative and creative, are revealed to the greatest extent, and that its laws are realized most fully, and not in some distorted way.[18]

In Marxist literature contemporary capitalism is usually designated as state-monopoly capitalism. How adequate and sufficient is the characterization contained in this term?

In many works any large capitalist corporation is called a monopoly, without sufficient grounds for doing so. In reality, as Yu. B. Kochevrin wrote convincingly back in 1970, the structure of production and the market is more oligopolistic than monopolistic in nature.[19] But that is not all there is to it. In effect, we interpret an oligopoly as the most widespread form of monopoly, and one could accept this established, though somewhat semantically imprecise, use of the term. There is something else that is more important: the monopoly's replacement of free competition is often viewed as a modification of the competition mechanism in which it acquires a certain weakness and gives way to various forms of nonmarket regulation. But in the present-day capitalist economy, *competition*, although it has undergone certain changes, plays just as important a role as in the previous century, and it *has not been pushed aside into a secondary position in the economic mechanism.*

The bulk of the production of goods and services really is concentrated in the hands of a relatively small number of corporations. But, first, the relations among them are carried out in the market, where the laws of competition prevail.

Second, the evolution of the capitalist economy has not been one-directional, solely toward greater and greater concentration and monopolization. Relying on our customary gross indicators, we only belatedly noticed the increased role, like a second wind, that small- and medium-scale production had started to assume—and not on the periphery of capitalist production, but in the key areas on which scientific and technological progress depends. The stability of small-scale production today cannot be deduced merely from the premise that people there are prepared to be content with a lower profit rate, and therefore that it is supposedly maintained for the purpose of serving the monopolies. The effect of flexible production, which small autonomous firms turned out to be best equipped to use, often provides greater benefits than the effect of scale and concentration of resources. In many cases small and medium-sized firms have been considerably more capable of developing and introducing technological innovations than the cumbersome structures of large corpo-

---

[18]On this, see *Kommunist*, No. 2, 1988, p. 6.
[19]See *The Political Economy of Present-Day Monopoly Capitalism* [*Politicheskaya ekonomiya sovremennogo monopolisticheskogo kapitalizma*], Moscow, 1970, Vol. 1, pp. 119-125.

rations. Small venture firms have assumed a significant role. In many countries their contribution to scientific and technological progress is greater than their proportional place in the economy.

Third, corporations themselves, starting by delegating authority downward from the top of the management pyramid, have begun to move increasingly toward expanding the economic independence of individual units, coordinating them through the market and thereby monitoring the efficiency of each unit.

In other words, *present-day capitalism is no less competitive than monopoly capitalism. By the same token, the expansion of the economic role played by the state does not exhaust the essence of the transformations that capitalism has undergone.* It has truly become "state" capitalism since social reproduction can be carried out only under the condition that more or less significant sectors of economic activity are removed from the direct stimulating influence of the law of surplus value. If the law of capitalist appropriation is realized, it is only on the level of the society as a whole, and not the level of each individual item of capital. Other laws of capitalism have also undergone certain modifications.[20]

This does not mean, however, as some authors suppose, that state ownership is showing a tendency to crowd out all other forms of ownership.[21] In fact, the functions of ownership—control, disposition, and use—have been split up among the state, associations of capitalists, individual capitalists, and individuals participating in the economic process. After all, in the course of the scientific and technological revolution there has been a drastic increase in the importance of such factors of production as knowledge, inventiveness, and adaptability to the complex and changeable requirements of technology—that is, those properties that, unlike the means of production, cannot be alienated from the worker and turned into capital.

The rollback that began in the late 1970s in direct state control, which had expanded steadily in the preceding period, and the shift in emphasis from direct to indirect—from budgetary to credit and monetary—methods of state regulation, showed that the balance between the private-economy principles and state principles is neither permanently fixed nor changing in just one direction. The reason that cap-

---

[20]For greater detail, see S.I. Tyulpanov and V.L. Sheynis, *Current Problems in the Political Economy of Present-Day Capitalism* [*Aktualnyye problemy politicheskoy ekonomii sovremennogo kapitalizma*], Leningrad, 1973, pp. 145-189. It should be pointed out that in this book, the concept of which was developed in the 1960s, the trend toward increased state control was overestimated.

[21]This point of view was expressed in extreme form in the works of S. Mochernyy (see *The Mechanism of State-Monopoly Capitalism and its Contradictions* [*Mekhanizm gosudarstvenno-monopolisticheskogo kapitalizma i yego protivorechiya*], Kiev, 1986). It was the subject, in my view, of wholly justified criticism in an article by I. Osadchaya (see *MEMO*, No. 3, 1987, pp. 64-67).

italism has moved ahead of us in the scientific and technological revolution is because its economic mechanism has proved to be more flexible and mobile.

The "adaptation" or, more precisely, evolution of capitalism has also manifested itself vividly in the social sphere. The law according to which "the accumulation of wealth at one pole" is accompanied by the accumulation of "poverty, the torment of labor, slavery, ignorance, coarsening, and moral degradation at the opposite pole"[22] operates as a prevailing tendency only at the early stages of capitalist development, while in today's highly developed bourgeois societies it is blocked by a set of economic and social factors and manifests itself only under exceptional circumstances and in marginal spheres.

The thesis concerning the ruling class's concessions to its antagonist is also of limited use in explaining things. There are, of course, concessions by some and gains by others, but the relatively high living standard and civil rights of the working people are the result of a complex set of economic and social factors, and the expression of a balance among numerous social forces (incorporating different, sometimes opposing interests and aspirations), and not the result of an elementary confrontation of "class against class" in which one social agent, an "omnipotent" one, as is sometimes claimed,[23] prudently "concedes" something that is of little importance to itself, while the other—either because of a low level of social consciousness or inadequate organization—contents itself with only a piece of the pie, even though it could take it all.

Capitalism, of course, has not become either socialism, "a welfare society," or a society of "equal opportunities." It would hardly be reasonable to deny, however, that it has assumed as permanent and significant elements of its socioeconomic structure (and not just temporary and secondary elements) not only a high living standard for the majority of employed people, but also certain forms of social guarantees (albeit limited ones) and of protection for citizens (although this protection does not meet the aspirations of the disadvantaged segments of society), as well as public consumption funds, a developed system of cooperatives, consumers' societies, and so forth.[24] In other

---

[22]See K. Marx and F. Engels, *Works*, Vol. 23, p. 660.

[23]One of the favorite formulas in scholarly and popular literature, "the strengthening of the omnipotence of monopolies," is fundamentally illiterate, since "omnipotence," if it actually did exist in nature, could not "grow stronger."

[24]G. Diligenskiy rightly emphasizes that even "in the social sphere, too, socialism's advantages do not appear as unambiguous as they did in the 1920s or 1930s. . . . While perpetuating unemployment and material and spiritual poverty among broad strata of the population, it (capitalism—V. Sh.) simultaneously pursues a carefully developed and well-calculated social policy that objectively limits the scope of these phenomena. It would be naive, at the very least, to assert that even with conservative governments this social policy comes down merely to cutting back on social spending and encouraging mass layoffs. (*MEMO*, No. 3, 1988, p. 24; p. 42 in this collection).

words, it has turned what originally belonged to socialist and collectivist doctrine, not bourgeois-liberal and individualist doctrine, into sources of its own development and transformation. Evidently the time has come to reexamine the dogma according to which only the prerequisites for, and not the actual elements of, a higher type of social relations can emerge under capitalism.

Special mention should be made of the fact that, having suffered an attack of fascism at a critical stage, developed capitalist societies by no means embarked on a path of increased political reaction across the board, which seemed inevitable at the beginning of the century. To the contrary, democracy has become an adequate political form for present-day capitalism, and although it is far from the ideal model of democracy, it is qualitatively superior to what existed in the era of so-called "free competition."

A carefully weighed assessment of present-day capitalism, its profound contradictions, social defects, and parasitic outgrowths on the one hand, and its capacity for development and progressive transformations on the other, is necessary in order to see in an undistorted light the partner with whom socialism is going to be competing and cooperating "in a broader historical space than was previously envisioned."[25] The reference points for social progress along the path of evolution need to be defined correctly. The activities of forces that are working for the further transformation of capitalism, particularly the social democrats (although they are not the only ones), need to be viewed with understanding: their potential must not be overestimated, but neither must we forget our responsibility for such memorable formulas as "social democracy and fascism are not antitheses, but twins," and "right-wing socialists are serving warmongers," formulas which made a contribution first to splitting the workers' movement, and subsequently to the aggravation of the Cold War. We must not believe that any theoretical and ideological position that differs from our own represents a deception and betrayal of the working class. Those who are under the spell of eschatological expectations regarding the impending collapse of capitalism, no matter how just and sincere their protest, would do well to recall Lenin's words: "Illusions and self-deception are terrible; fear of the truth is disastrous."[26] But that is just one side of the story.

III.

For a long time the opposition between the economic systems of capitalism and socialism was viewed as a confrontation between the

---

[25]See *Kommunist*, No. 2, 1988. pp. 6-7.
[26]V.I. Lenin, *Complete Works*, Vol. 44, p. 487.

"anarchy of production," to which capitalism can supposedly be reduced, and the "principle of planning," which socialism supposedly embodies, although the deepest thinkers long ago pointed out the relative nature of such a comparison.[27] They are direct opposites only in the theoretical model. It is customary to associate economic imbalances, which sometimes assume threatening proportions, the plundering of resources, material and social losses for society, and economic and social crises with production anarchy and the randomness of the market. As we can see now, an economy with a suppressed market that supposedly develops solely on the basis of rational planning is not immune to all this either

In addition, as the scale of production grows and relations become more complex, alongside the centrally managed sector a shadow economy begins to develop that functions according to its own economic laws, circumvents juridical laws, and often gives rise to corruption and demoralization. It is impossible to eradicate this economy, because it meets established social needs (whether they are rational or irrational is another matter, and if they are irrational, so much the worse) that the planned subsystem cannot handle.

According to an estimate by sociologists, as of the mid-1980s about 2 million people (that is, approximately the same number as employed in the official system of cultural and arts institutions) were permanently employed in the U.S.S.R.'s shadow economy (the part of it involved in providing consumer services). Another 17 or 18 million (13 to 14 percent of all persons employed in the national economy) occasionally worked in the shadow economy. They produced goods and services valued at 14 to 16 billion rubles (representing approximately 28 to 32 percent of all paid consumer services, according to official statistics).[28] It is even more significant that the shadow economy provides for an important part of necessary ties among state enterprises that planning is incapable of providing for.

As for the effectiveness of the planning system, according to data cited by D. Valovoy, in the past 20 years, plan assignments for 170 of the most important types of products monitored by the state were not fulfilled once, while the production of some fell by as much as 20 to

---

[27]"A dogmatic distinction between either complete anarchy of production or a complete planned economy is nonspecific, non-Marxist, and incorrect" (Ye. S. Varga, *Essays on Problems in the Political Economy of Capitalism* [*Ocherki po problemam politekonomii kapitalizma*], Moscow, 1965, p. 48).

[28]Based on *The U.S.S.R. National Economy over 70 Years*, pp. 411, 412, 498; *Sovetskaya kultura* [*Soviet Culture*], July 9, 1988; and *Moskovskiye novosti* [*Moscow News*], April 26, 1987. Of total consumer services provided to the urban population, the following percentages are provided privately: 50 percent of shoe repairs, 43 percent of apartment maintenance and repairs, and 30 percent of household-appliance repairs. In rural areas, individual labor accounts for approximately 80 percent of all consumer services (*Planovoye khozyaystvo* [*The Planned Economy*], No. 7, 1987, p. 88).

30 percent or more below plan targets. A chain reaction of production interruptions inevitably resulted, and this created a situation of "planned anarchy" and caused plans to be modified to accommodate the actual situation, which aggravated the disproportions and forced an expansion of the list of products controlled from above. The vicious circle was closed. "We are having difficulty freeing ourselves from the illusion that everything in our economy goes according to plan," notes O. Bogomolov. "It is true that plans are drawn up and approved regularly, but life often takes its own course."[29]

All this forces us to take a new approach to evaluating legalized independence and autonomy for producers; the role of direct relations between enterprises, and between enterprises and consumers; the role of the market as the only possible signaling system, albeit not an ideal one, that reveals both the size of socially necessary outlays, and the scale of public demand for the countless different types of products that present-day production provides—in a situation in which all this is subject to continuous changes. *MEMO* and a number of other publications have carried criticism of the oversimplified view according to which restoring the rights of market-based production represents a return to capitalism.[30] In reality, it is not market-based production that finds its highest and ultimate expression in capitalism, but capitalism that is one variation of market-based production.

As Yu. V. Shishkov quite rightly stressed recently, the market and market-based production are the "offspring" and "one of the elements (one might add, one of the most important achievements—V. Sh.) of human civilization,"[31] and as such it is a constant with respect to both capitalism and socialism that is truly developed, and not still going through prolonged and agonizing birth pains. Various kinds of centralized orders for products, the direct exchange of products, a "transformed law of value," etc. represent not a step forward, but a step backward in social development, toward feudal-workshop regulation and primary accumulation.

Capitalism at the present stage is neither dismantling nor undermining market-based production, nor is it replacing it with monopolistic regulation; it is elevating it to a new level. The economic mechanism of present-day capitalism is a more or less adequate form for the functioning and development of science-based-industrial productive forces. It combines two contradictory principles—the "plan" (the deliberate regulating activity of central authorities) and the "mar-

---

[29]See *Pravda*, May 30, 1988; *Izvestiya*, July 16, 1988.

[30]See *MEMO*, No. 8, 1987, pp. 113-117; *Novy mir* [*New World*], No. 7, 1987, pp. 266-268.

[31]*Rabochiy klass i sovremennyy mir* [*The Working Class and Today's World*], No. 6, 1987, pp. 24-26. Yu. Shishkov singles out economic-management relations as one of the three subsystems of production relations.

ket" (the aggregate of automatic regulators, and the subsystem of direct ties and feedback among producers and between producers and consumers). Interruptions in production and disruptions are inherent in both of these principles; and it is no easy matter to bring them together, either. Nevertheless, each of the two basic components of the economic mechanism performs important functions, without which neither the economy nor the society could exist.

The market, the law of value, and the competition mechanism maintain the basic national-economic proportions (between production and all types of consumption, between consumption and accumulation, between savings and investments, among branches of production, and so forth); they supply incentives for producers, generate technical progress, establish criteria for production efficiency, "wash out" inefficient units, and maintain the general health of the economy. After all, the crises that shake the capitalist economy from time to time also perform important therapeutic functions. One ought to calculate which costs society more: the forced and socially painful removal of inefficient production, speculative credit, and adventuristic stockjobbing under capitalism, or the guaranteed existence of unprofitable enterprises,[32] interest-free (or even nonrepayable) credit, and price ratios that provide little incentive for production and create endless strains in the consumer market.

It should also be emphasized that identifying market relations with a lack of all planning and regulation [stikhiynost] does not reflect the realities of contemporary capitalism. The production and circulation of most goods and services are not a disorderly Brownian movement, and are not geared toward a totally unknown market. Of course, such activities as internal company planning, contract relations, work based on previous orders, or marketing cannot rule out various sorts of disruptions in the course of reproduction, or the appearance of unexpected interruptions at the micro- and macroeconomic levels (just as centralized planning cannot provide any guarantees against them, either), but they do substantially limit the development of uncontrollable, destructive processes.

The second component, centralized regulation on the scale of the national economy, plays an equally important role in the economic mechanism of present-day capitalism. It defines the "rules of the

---

[32]In 1986 unprofitable and low-profit (those bringing in revenue of less than 10 percent) collective farms and state farms accounted for 13 percent and 34 percent, respectively, of the total number of farms. The number of industrial enterprises operating at a loss reached 13 percent. For enterprises under the Ministry of Land Reclamation and Water Resources, whose "successful" activities involving the transformation of nature have been widely reported on in the press, and enterprises under the Ministry of the Building Materials Industry, financial losses were the norm (see *Sovetskaya Rossiya* [*Soviet Russia*], August 21, 1987; *Pravda*, August 19, 1987; *The U.S.S.R. National Economy over 70 Years*, pp. 287, 291).

game" that, in the interest of self-preservation and evolution of the system, all the participants in the economic process should follow. By changing these rules, it adjusts national-economic proportions within certain limits. It carries out a redistribution of the national income that makes it possible, for varying periods of time, to remove strategically important branches of production (basic research, new research-intensive types of production) and spheres of consumption (the social infrastructure) from the strict limitations of the value and market mechanism, and to use higher profitability to provide incentives for producers, and "free" goods or reduced prices to provide incentives for consumers. It provides the economic base for realizing the "goals of society"[33] (under capitalism, of course, these are goals whose nature is determined mainly by the will of the ruling class, but not only by it), goals which have passed through sociopolitical institutions where they have undergone a process of selection and redistribution according to "national priorities": military preparations, the set of social guarantees considered necessary under given conditions, environmental protection, and so forth. It erects barriers that provide the given national economy with varying degrees of protection against oppressive influences from without, and it lays paths that will foster the economy's outward expansion. It is also called on to maintain competitive conditions and to prevent monopolistic situations from developing in the markets, using noneconomic means, if necessary, to do so.[34]

IV.

Avoiding frightening ourselves with the specter of a "return" to capitalism is not the only reason that we need to recognize the constant nature and the socially neutral character of the economic mechanism that serves developed market-based production. It is extremely important to evaluate realistically the existing situation in our economy. Evidently, all the tested means for making it more efficient, for accelerating and expanding useful effects (improving labor discipline, introducing basic order in production, tightening administrative control over product quality, increasing work time, reallocating capital

---

[33]See J.K. Galbraith, *Economic Theories and the Goals of Society* [*Ekonomicheskiye teorii i tseli obshchestva*], Moscow, 1976.

[34]The direct equation of a large capitalist corporation with a monopoly not only obscures the diversity of the variations in which production units and markets work together, it also erases the boundary—which is sometimes quite mobile, but which nonetheless exists—between technologically well-equipped enterprises with modern methods of organization, marketing, social maneuvering, etc., and mafia associations that are oriented toward "easy," speculative income, and that establish their dominance in the market by relying substantially on noneconomic means and have no aversion to using gangster methods, up to and including "the use of dynamite against a competitor," as Lenin so graphically described it (see V.I. Lenin, *Complete Works*, Vol. 27, pp. 321-325).

investments among industries and territorial units), have exhausted their effectiveness or are on the verge of doing so. This realization is sinking in both at research institutions and at the level of the decision-making centers. In its statement of this problem, the 19th Conference of the CPSU made a major step forward, even compared to the 27th Party Congress, not to mention the first declarations about perestroika.

Yet the carefully planned economic reform is showing dangerous signs of spinning its wheels. Even enterprises that have been converted to economic accountability have not yet been given the rights that could ensure their genuine independence. The administrative infrastructure for the management of the economy, as represented by the economic ministries, has not yet undergone any fundamental changes. The dominance of the producer in a market characterized by shortages has not been shaken. So far, a certain expansion of space for nontraditional forms of economic activity (cooperatives, independent labor activity) has resulted not in satisfying the demand for priority goods and services or in lowering prices, but in the appearance— alongside the monopolistic state enterprises—of mini-monopolies that are taking advantage of distortions in the economy, and in an intensification of inflationary tendencies.

Foot-dragging and, sometimes, even attempts to turn back the economic reform in certain areas are due not only to resistance by those forces on whom its practical implementation depends, but also to a certain inconsistency in fundamental decisions. The transition from a high-expenditure economy to an efficient economy is extremely complicated for objective reasons, and it affects the interests of many people who are not to blame for the fact that their activity is inefficient or even harmful to society. Wrong or hasty steps can seriously aggravate the situation, but delaying reform can have equally dangerous consequences. Inconsistency in economic transformations is due, in part, to the fact that the theoretical concept of the reform and its place in the development of socialism have not yet been fully worked out.

It is typical that the vague euphemism "radical" is usually used to describe the reform itself in official documents, and it was only at the 19th Party Conference that such key concepts as market, competition, and intellectual property gained general recognition. It was stated loudly and clearly that the implementation of the reform required mobilization of forces outside the official apparatus, and that the Hungarian, Yugoslavian, and Chinese experiences are of general significance to socialism. Justifiably, criticism was leveled at attempts to use the once sure-fire label "alien ideas" to discredit the market. Attention was focused on the inseparable connection between economic democracy, whose ultimate expression is the freedom of the producer in the market, and political democracy, which is unthinkable without pluralism, glasnost, and competition among ideas.

A shift of priorities is on the agenda. Rather than relying on inflated state orders, rigid normative rates, central allocations, and the like to achieve absolute fulfillment of the five-year plan, which was adopted when even the contours of the new economic mechanism had been only vaguely sketched, it is immeasurably more important to make all economic proportions, ties, and relations rational and efficient, and to this end—to implement the Law on the Enterprise as quickly as possible in its full form (better yet, to bring this law, which is rather imperfect, as noted at the time it was ratified, up to at least the level of the more progressive Law on Cooperatives), and to bring the whole system of economic management into line with these laws.

What needs to be stepped up is not the growth in aggregate indicators in relation to "levels achieved," but the reorganization of the economic mechanism, which in its revamped form should be at least roughly introduced and tested before the 13th Five-Year Plan goes into effect. There is almost no time left for this, since a plan is already being drawn up now that threatens once again to crush initiative and the rights of producers. Ya. Pevzner quite rightly stresses that, although the socialist system provides opportunities for more effective regulation of the market in social respects than does capitalism, which has thoroughly developed the regulatory techniques, "it is necessary first of all to create that which is subject to regulation—the socialist market."[35]

So we are gradually discerning the meaning, in terms of political economy, of a task of truly top priority—the transition to consistently establishing the separate economic and legal identity of economic subjects, and the real independence of enterprises. Under capitalism, private ownership provides the basis for this sort of independence. But private ownership is just a special case, just one form of establishing separate identity. The economic independence of participants in production, without which it is impossible either to establish economic accountability or to objectively determine socially necessary outlays and the social usefulness of goods produced, is perfectly compatible with public ownership. This requires, however, that we reject the mythology that portrays the real relations of ownership in the administrative-command system in a distorted form.

In our literature the discussion of the problem of ownership is often not only opened, but closed, by contrasting ownership as a "real" economic relation to its legal and volitional expression. Granted, there is another point of view, according to which ownership is not a subject,

---

[35]*MEMO*, No. 6, 1988, p. 17. It would be better to say "the market under socialism."

an internal element of the system of political economy, but "a set of diverse legal, social relations, the scientific knowledge of which is reflected in the logical form of a system of legal categories."[36]

Without getting into a debate on this issue, it should be stressed that abstract arguments about ownership are not very productive when it comes to solving the urgent problems of economic perestroika.[37] Just as value is intangible apart from price, ownership cannot manifest itself except in the functions of control, disposition, and use. In any sort of developed market-based production (not just capitalist), these functions are increasingly divided up among various economic agents. The important task right now is this: after guaranteeing the necessary degree of public oversight and realization of the people's common interest (control), to deconcentrate the rights of disposition and use, and take decisive steps to do away with the monopoly of government departments in these spheres. But in order to do this in practice, it is necessary to overcome in theory the notion that the highest form of ownership and the one most suited to socialism is the maximum concentration of the prerogatives of both control and disposition (and to a significant extent, of use) in the hands of the administrative apparatus.

The idea that the actions of this apparatus correspond to the common interests of the people as a whole was introduced into political economy as an axiom, without taking at least two "correcting" circumstances into account. In the first place, this idea ignores the fact that the apparatus, including its upper echelon, develops its own specific, separate interests, in the absence of any sort of effective public control. In this connection, the boundary between the advancement of the interests of a given social group, as distinct from the public interests, and the rapacious intentions of individual mafia cliques naturally became fluid. In the second place, in a complex economic system, even a high degree of centralization and organization of economic management according to a strict hierarchical principle could not control the tendencies of individual localities and departments to advance their own specific interests and remove their own domains from the sovereignty of central economic authorities.

In the process of reorganizing our economic mechanism, both of its main components—the ties among enterprises (and between enterprises and the population) and central regulation—must be trans-

---

[36]V. P. Shkredov, *The Method for Studying Ownership in Marx's Capital* [*Metod issledovaniya sobstvennosti v Kapitale K. Marksa*], Moscow, 1973, p. 244.

[37]Chinese scholars are evidently ahead of us in the substantive discussion of the problems of ownership under socialism (see V.G. Gelbras, "Economic Reform in the P.R.C. and the Discussion of the Problems of Ownership of the Means of Production," *Rabochiy klass i sovremennyy mir*, No. 2, 1988).

formed in a radical way. The transformation of the enterprise into a genuine subject in the economic process is impossible unless it takes place in a truly universal market—universal in terms of both the assortment of goods traded in it, and the composition and type of its participants.

At this point we have, at best, only a consumer-goods market, which is seriously deformed by numerous shortages and price distortions. On the agenda now is the transition from central allocations through departments to wholesale trade—to the creation of a market in producer goods. Granted, this transition is not being carried out quickly and consistently enough, which is posing a serious threat to the entire economic reform. But both of these subdivisions of the market are attributes of simple market-based production. All factors, natural resources (including land and water), manpower resources, means of payment, and information should undergo selection and be evaluated through a market that is adequate to the conditions of present-day production. Cost-free access to all classes of limited resources should be the exception, not the rule. It is also time to reject the dogma according to which there can be no labor market under socialism. All that needs to be done is to rid this market of a powerful monopolist, the administrative bureaucratic apparatus that, in exchange for guarantees of full, albeit inefficient, employment, can dictate working conditions and standards of social behavior to the working people, and tell them which methods they have a right to use to protect their interests.

Since there is no prospect of moving beyond the limits of market-based production in even the distant future, such integral characteristics of its developed stage as profits, interest on loans, income from stock holdings, rent, and so forth, should not be regarded, even under capitalism, as merely transmuted forms of surplus value. In developed socialist production they cannot be merely formally recognized categories, either. (We must also reconsider our extremely vague concept of nonlabor income, a concept which encourages consumption rather than saving.) Freeing ourselves from theoretical stereotypes will also help us to give these categories, in practice, the role of automatic regulators of social production, regulators that are objectively determined and only within certain limits subject to arbitrary adjustments.

For this to happen, of course, the producer must be given freedom of economic maneuvering and freedom in the choice of partners, not to mention the choice of technology and the way production will be organized. The important thing here is for the owner [sobstvennik], once he has assumed his share of rights, to feel in reality that the reward for his labor is determined on the basis of its results as evaluated by the consumer, and not on the basis of quantity and quality as determined God only knows how and by whom.

The prerogatives stemming from the rights of ownership are a constant value at any given moment. An increase in them at one level inevitably leads to a decrease at another level. The directive-command functions of central economic agencies that dictate to enterprises the volume and types of production, the sorts of business ties they should form, charges, etc. (the "plan as law") should be reduced to a minimum; the rates at which percentages of profits are paid to the state budget should be standardized (at least at the level of individual industries); and state orders should be placed on a genuinely contractual basis, with the contracting parties enjoying equal rights and responsibilities that are regulated by civil law.

But this is just one side of the matter. An expansion of rights presupposes a drastic increase in the burden of responsibility—not in administrative offices, but in the market, since the meaning of competition lies not just in the possibility of large gains, but also in the introduction of a serious risk factor. As a result of the reform, participants in the economic process should no longer be confident that their income and very existence are guaranteed irrespective of the results of their own economic activities, and this is stipulated in the Law on the State Enterprise. All of us are now giving lip service to "overcoming the underestimation" of the market. But "prices, demand, and supply" are not simply "regulators of economic growth" that can be "mastered" by someone who is outside the boundaries of the market. Moreover, limiting the development of the market to the mandatory condition that there be "real growth in the living standard of all members of society," and portraying matters as though it were possible to bring the market into its own while avoiding the stratification of producers means that you are either creating illusions or projecting a fictitious market rather than a real one, and perpetuating the command economy while simply giving it a new name. For all the fundamental differences between socialism and capitalism, market mechanisms in and of themselves are socially neutral and can serve different class goals. Under capitalism the market exists by definition; under socialism the market either exists or does not exist (or, which is almost the same thing, drags out its existence in a "decaying state," and is "governed" by certain phantoms such as a "transformed law of value").

It goes without saying that the social consequences of this rather painful process, especially during the transitional period, should be at the center of attention. But only by moving along this path can we overcome the undermining of market-based production that defined the principal features of the economic model that was introduced in our country in the late 1920s and early 1930s, and that still exists today.

V.

By shifting responsibility for making the most important economic decisions from departments to enterprises and individuals, we are not moving away from socialism; what we are moving away from are early notions of socialism—notions which were determined entirely by historical conditions—as an economic system in which the movement of all production flows (of resources, manpower, output) is carried out on the basis of an ideal model worked out by a central planning office *ante factum* and implemented on the basis of direct orders to those actually performing the work. By no means are we returning to capitalism—on the contrary, capitalism, as it was at the turn of the century, has been profoundly influenced by socialism; what we are returning to is the main path of world development, since what is involved is both the economic mechanism and the redistribution of ownership rights.

Of course, practically everywhere now the economic mechanism is included in the broader mechanism of social development, in which society's priorities are identified and the means for realizing them are created, within the limits imposed by objective conditions. Here the differences between capitalism and socialism are truly great, just as, by the way, there are even greater differences between the early, undeveloped form of socialism (which was seriously deformed when compared to the ideal) and the model of socialism that we hope will grow out of perestroika. But in order to speed up and facilitate this transition, it is important to recognize the historically transient, extraordinary nature of the early model—the state-monopoly modification of socialism, which bore the imprint both of utopian ideas of leveling and of war communism.

The advocates of true economic reform have referred repeatedly to the works of Lenin in an effort to prove that the main contours of today's transformations in many respects have their origins in the days of the NEP [New Economic Policy], when a "transition from administrative socialism" to "the socialism of economic accountability" was carried out.[38] In turn, the "antimarketeers," who see "the economic separation of production collectives . . . [as] a distortion of the essence of socialism," and who are convinced that "a return to the market mechanism . . . is ruled out if one cares about the fate of socialism,"[39] have mobilized statements made by both Marx and Lenin at various times in defense of their own ideas.

The "battle of quotations" in today's scholarly discussion is rightly viewed as an inappropriate form for carrying out theoretical debate. There can hardly be any doubt, however, as to *the direction* in which Lenin's thought developed when theoretical ideas about the new

---

[38]N. Shmelev, "Advances and Debts" (*Novy mir* [*New World*], No. 6, 1987, p. 143).
[39]P. Ignatovskiy. "On a Political Approach to the Economy" (*Kommunist*, No. 12, 1983, pp. 69, 66).

society—ideas which were necessarily very general and approximate, which had taken shape in the bosom of European socialist thought, and which, as we can see today, had not yet fully detached themselves from the utopian dream—ran up against hard and cruel reality. Observing the "development of capitalism into a higher, planned form,"[40] and noting that the "mechanism of public economic management" had been "already prepared" within the framework of the major capitalist states' wartime economies,[41] Lenin concluded on the threshold of the October Revolution that "socialism is nothing more than a state-capitalistic monopoly *turned in the direction of benefiting all the people* and therefore ceasing to be a *capitalist* monopoly."[42]

In this vision of the future, consequently, the capitalistic, exploitative nature of the monopoly is supposed to be eliminated, but its principle, acquiring a qualitatively different social base, is preserved. This principle consists of the management of the economic life of tens of millions of people "from a single center,"[43] and the nonmarket, noncompetitive nature of economic decision-making.[44]

Commodity-money elements in the organization of the economy, which are traditionally associated with the NEP, had a difficult and complicated time entering the life of our country. Today it is an extremely important task of research in economic history to determine what happened in the first years of Soviet power as a result of the extraordinary conditions of war, ruin, and the destruction of economic relations,[45] and what was the result of the vision of socialism as an economic system in which the buying and selling of goods was to be displaced by "the planned distribution of products organized on a statewide scale," the bank was to be turned "into the central book-keeper of communist society," money was ultimately to be abolished, and the entire population was to be organized "into a unified network of consumer communes."[46,47]

---

[40]V.I. Lenin, *Complete Works*, Vol. 31, p. 444.

[41]See V.I. Lenin, *Complete Works*, Vol. 33, p. 50.

[42]V.I. Lenin, *Complete Works*, Vol. 34, p. 192.

[43]See V.I. Lenin, *Complete Works*, Vol. 30, pp. 219, 279, 347.

[44]Within the framework of the antithesis, which places "complete freedom of competition" in opposition to "complete socialization" (see V.I. Lenin, *Complete Collected Works*, Vol. 27, pp. 320-321).

[45]"We had no other alternative but to make maximum use of immediate monopoly, including the confiscation of all surpluses, even without any compensation," V.I. Lenin said at the 10th Congress of the RCP(b) [Russian Communist Party (Bolsheviks)] (see V.I. Lenin, *Complete Works*, Vol. 43, p. 79).

[46]These and similar propositions were formulated in the Program of the Russian Communist Party (Bolsheviks) that was adopted at the Eight Party Congress in 1919. See *The Eighth Congress of the Russian Communist Party (Bolsheviks). Minutes* [*Vosmoy syezd RKP(b). Protokoly*]; and V.I. Lenin, *Complete Works*, Vol. 38, pp. 121-122.

[47]Approaches to this sort of research in economic history are outlined by O.R. Latsis in his work, *Economic Centralization and Management Centralism: The Problems of Their Relationship* [*Ekonomicheskaya tsentralizatsiya i tsentralizm upravleniya. Problemy vzaimosvyazi*], Moscow, 1987, pp. 68-107.

There is no point in trying to be sly and make it seem as if in the first years of the NEP the buying and selling of goods, the economic accountability and independence of trusts, and cost levers of management were portrayed as basic principles inherent in the socialist economic system (rather than as transitional structures dictated by the predominance of peasant production in a backward country), and that the role of the market-competition factor in the survivability of capitalism was duly appreciated. But there is no doubt that theoretical thinking and practice were both moving in this direction at that time— toward a recognition of, and adaptation, to reality.

Lenin's political testament noted a truly "fundamental change in our entire point of view regarding socialism."[48] It was a change whose essence was understood far more deeply in the party in the first years after Lenin's death than in the period when Stalin and his successors held a monopoly on the interpretation of Lenin's theoretical legacy.[49] Now a "change" is needed once again, and probably a more thoroughgoing change that accords with today's realities, rather than simply a return to the "sources" of the theory. Ridding the classical legacy of its most recent encrustations and vulgarization is clearly not enough.

The dismantling of state-monopoly structures that have been introduced into socialism's economic mechanism and that have in many respects distorted public ownership itself does not require rejection of the centralized regulation of economic life. A flexible system of state goal-setting and indirect regulation needs to be set up that will provide all the participants in the reproduction process with sufficiently stable "rules of the game," and that will carry out, within the necessary limits, a redistribution of the national income by means of taxes, subsidies, loans, the currency exchange rate, and so forth.

We should, however, avoid creating new illusions. Setting up such a system and combining it with market processes, with enterprises that operate on the basis of genuine independence, cost-recovery and self-financing, and with the unleashing of economic initiative at all levels (including small-scale, decentralized production) is no easy or conflict-free matter. And in this regard the experience of present-day capitalism also has a great deal to teach us. The positive experience is instructive, since various alternatives and instruments of indirect regulation were originally worked out, modified, broken in, and rejected as defective on a market basis. And the negative experience is also instructive, since the imperfections of these instruments and the disruptions that they cause stem not only from private ownership, but

---

[48]V.I. Lenin, *Complete Works*, Vol. 45, p. 373.
[49]See, for example, N. Bukharin, "Lenin's Political Testament" (*Kommunist*, No. 2, 1988, pp. 93-102), and J.V. Stalin, *Economic Problems of Socialism in the U.S.S.R.* [*Ekonomicheskiye problemy sotsializma v SSSR*], Moscow, 1953, pp. 27-59, 122-131, 204-221.

also from the very nature, objective possibilities, and limits of this sort of regulation.

The categorical tone with which the advocates of socialist market-based production, who for the first time in many decades have the opportunity to expound their views freely, proclaim the advantages of their approach is perfectly understandable psychologically. One can go even further: without that sort of aggressiveness, which forms a certain social atmosphere, it would be impossible to break down either the deliberate resistance of the opponents of radical reform, or the "force of habit" of millions of people who have grown accustomed to a command economy. But in order for the switch-over to be not only accelerated (otherwise the undertaking risks being swallowed up by endless "clarifications" and accommodations, which have swallowed up more than one bold scheme), but also successful, we must recognize not only the advantages that it should bring, but also the accompanying problems that must be offset.

The transitional period is especially dangerous and difficult, and is fraught with the potential for serious economic imbalances and social tension. Along this path, crises can occur that divide society and feed both retrograde inclinations to restore the "old order" and adventuristic attempts to solve complex problems. It is important to approach these situations fully armed.

New political, economic, and sociological thinking; a renewed vision of the world; and a rejection of dogmatic stereotypes and "pseudo-theoretical prayer services" should serve the cause of accomplishing historically unprecedented tasks. During the years of perestroika, unprecedented cleanup work has been done in theory and ideology. But even more remains to be done.

Revolutionary Theory and the Present Day

GERMAN GERMANOVICH DILIGENSKIY*

The article raises some of the most difficult questions concerning the development of the Marxist-Leninist theory of revolution and stresses the need for its creative renewal in keeping with altered historical conditions. This renewal, the author notes, should be directed at a more concrete understanding of the role that various social forces play in the revolutionary movement and of its aims and methods; it should consider every aspect of both the experience of building socialism and the experience of social development under the conditions of state-monopoly capitalism. The creative development of theory demands bold revolutionary thinking and a repudiation of ideas that are firmly established but not corroborated by present-day social practice. The author does not consider his conclusions final and acknowledges that they are open to debate—the main purpose of the article is to call attention to problems that need further study. In upcoming issues of the magazine, the editors plan to publish a number of articles devoted to a more detailed analysis of these problems and to launch a broad scientific debate about them.

Under present-day conditions, there is a clear need for a fundamentally new interpretation of the direction and prospects for the revolutionary transition from capitalism to socialism. Fundamental changes in the dynamics and forms of the revolutionary process started to become evident sometime in the 1950s and manifested themselves even more fully in subsequent decades. In the 1970s and, especially, the 1980s, the pace of that process slowed considerably and the obstacles in its path grew larger. This trend showed in the serious weakening of revolutionary trends in the developed capitalist world; in the defeat of the revolution in Chile and the undermining of the results of the Portuguese revolution; and in contradictions in the development of countries that had freed themselves from colonial dependence, including those that embarked on the path of socialist orientation. The idea that was firmly established among Marxists that world social develop-

---

*Doctor of history, professor and editor in chief of *MEMO*. This article appeared in the March 1988 issue of *MEMO*.

ment consists mainly of the continual waning of capitalism's influence and the defection of more and more countries from the capitalist system seems increasingly out of touch with the new historical reality. It is becoming increasingly clear that the world has entered a lengthy historical phase in which opposing social systems coexist and compete peacefully, and that henceforth this peaceful competition will be the main form of conflict between socialism and capitalism. This does not mean a "fading" of the class struggle—either political or ideological—in the world arena, but it substantially alters the nature and content of that struggle.

An analysis of the current stage of the revolutionary process cannot be made by relying solely on theoretical propositions previously developed by Marxist thought. These propositions are, in part, inadequate and, in part, simply outdated.

Naturally, a new interpretation of the process of transition from capitalism to socialism does not mean that we should take a nihilistic attitude toward the historic achievements of Marxist-Leninist thought, or renounce its theoretical and methodological principles for obtaining knowledge of social phenomena.

Present-day social reality and the problems it presents, however, are so vastly different from the historical conditions in which the Marxist-Leninist concept of the revolutionary process was developed that not all of its past conclusions can serve as a theoretical basis for the efforts of revolutionary forces.

There is no reason to be frightened of this observation or to see something "revisionist" in it. It is common knowledge that the founders of Marxism-Leninism repeatedly revised their views on highly important questions when changes in the historical situation or new sociopolitical experience required it; moreover, they sometimes revised them very quickly and radically. Suffice it to recall, for example, how profoundly Lenin's idea of the NEP [New Economic Policy] changed the whole concept of building socialism.

We have always spoken of the need for the creative development of theory, but now we must raise this question anew in all its urgency and note the unsatisfactory state of our theoretical thinking. In the past, such development of theory often boiled down to more or less mechanically combining old propositions with new propositions that arose from certain pressing needs, without making any serious attempt to ascertain the effect that the new phenomena and assessments of them had on our whole system of theoretical ideas. This violated the integrity and the logical unity of revolutionary theory, and that theory did not so much develop as it superficially "adapted" to current social and political conditions and assumed an eclectic nature. The factors contributing to this tendency included a fear of critically reassessing outmoded propositions; the habit of keeping quiet about the most acute problems, especially if they were insufficiently clear, or of "solving" them on a purely declarative, verbal level; and last but not least, the lack of any self-critical analysis of our own practice, and the influence of apologist tendencies on theory. Such features are in many respects characteristic, for example, of documents from international conferences of communist parties held in the 1950s and 1960s, documents reflecting both the desire for a serious creative renewal of theory, and inconsistency in realizing that desire.

The demand for realism in theory and practice is one of the most urgent demands on today's revolutionary movement. This is especially true of the set of interrelated and high-priority problems having to do with the relationship between universal human interests and class interests, the relationship between the revolutionary struggle and the coexistence of opposite social systems, and the avenues of social progress.

A consistently scientific analysis of these problems is hampered by the deeply rooted, stereotyped idea of the bipolarity of the present-day world, and by a kind of one-sided tendency to turn the genuinely antithetical nature of the socialist and capitalist systems into an absolute. Our ideology has been speaking more and more distinctly lately about the unity of the present-day world, the growing interdependence of its various parts, and the priority of global interests and the needs of humanity as a whole. But it seems that this realistic idea has not yet been linked with theoretical concepts of general trends in world development, world social progress, and the revolutionary process.

The stereotyped notion of bipolarity is evident in the idea that the processes of social development in the socialist and capitalist worlds are completely mutually exclusive and totally opposite in nature. In capitalist countries this development is reduced solely to a deepening crisis, while in the socialist countries it is portrayed as nothing but steady, unceasing social progress. As far as the Third World countries are concerned, their only choice is between the established models of socialism and capitalism.

I think this picture is seriously flawed, and not just because it is an extreme oversimplification of the actual complexity, dialectical nature, and diversity of social development. No less important is the fact that it orients communists and other revolutionary and progressive forces not so much toward a creative search for strategies and courses of struggle that are in keeping with objective possibilities and tendencies, as toward an automatic adherence to ready-made models and a kind of fatalistic sense that both the content and the form of revolutionary transformations are predetermined givens.

All historical experience of the past few decades shows that this predetermination has nothing to do with real social development. Both the building of socialism in countries where revolution has triumphed and the activities of revolutionary forces in capitalist and developing countries constantly encounter situations in which previously accepted tenets and guidelines prove inadequate or irrelevant. Thus, it is now clear that the socialist transformation of ownership relations in the forms in which it was carried out after the Revolution proved incapable, in and of itself, either of creating a system of effective public management of economic and social development, or of providing for the comprehensive development of socialist democracy.

In capitalist countries tasks of revolutionary forces have proven far more difficult than once imagined, when it seemed that the masses could be rallied fairly quickly behind the slogans of the socialist revolution during a time of crisis when capitalism's inherent contradictions were aggravated. What has come to the fore is the problem of finding the goals and avenues of class struggle that accord with the level of economic, social, and cultural development of those countries, and with the social psychology of the masses. In other words, the revolutionary process in all its forms and manifestations is inseparably bound to the constant critical analysis and review of previous experience, and with the search for solutions to new problems; it is incompatible with the attempt to follow previously developed patterns.

The main cause of radical change in the conditions and course of the world revolutionary process is the invention and stockpiling of weapons of mass destruction, which have objectively made the survival of mankind the top priority of all social forces that are active in the world arena. Other factors contributing to this situation are aggravation of ecological and other global problems of human civilization, and the growing interconnection among complex technological, economic, sociopolitical, and cultural processes that determine conditions of the present and future existence of the world's peoples. Peaceful cooperation in the interests of averting thermonuclear disaster and resolving other global problems has become an inexorable imperative of international life.

These factors, however, do not stand alone. The conditions in which the revolutionary process develops have also been affected by changes in the nature of the socialist system's influence on economic and sociopolitical development in the nonsocialist world. On one hand, it acts as a powerful factor of positive change in the economy, social strategy, and politics of imperialism. Phenomena such as rapid development of the scientific and technological revolution and of state regulation of the economy in capitalist countries, increased material consumption by the majority of the working people, a certain expansion of their democratic rights, and progressive social reforms of the postwar decades have been due, of course, to the dynamics of capitalism's internal contradictions and to changes in the correlation of class forces. But at the same time, to a considerable extent they have also represented imperialism's reaction to the existence and development of the socialist system and the new balance of power in the world, and they have been stimulated by a desire for the preventive reinforcement of imperialism's social "home front." The same factor also intensified new tendencies in imperialism's neocolonialist strategy and prompted it to adopt measures capable of firmly binding the developing countries to the capitalist system.

On the other hand, the course of competition between the two systems has also been affected by the accumulation of problems and contradictions in socialism's development: stagnation and crises in its economy and political system, and the strengthening of bureaucratism and antidemocratic tendencies. As a result, the socialist example has lost some of its appeal, and the work of communist parties in capitalist countries has become much more difficult.

In analyzing the current problems of the revolutionary process, it is necessary, of course, to take into consideration the historical experience of victorious socialist revolutions. This consideration presupposes an understanding of the historical uniqueness of those revolutions, and of the concrete dialectics of the relationship between the general and the specific in them. But in order to gain such an understanding, one must avoid automatically elevating the specific historical features of revolution and socialist construction to the status of "universal laws." It is no less important to thoroughly master the Leninist approach to revolution as a vital creative process that inevitably contains elements of social experimentation and of the reappraisal of ideas that have not been confirmed by actual experience. Identifying the laws of the revolutionary process by no means entails either extrapolation of past experience into the present and future, or the idealization of that experience. It is primarily an analysis of past experience from the standpoint of, first, its dependence on specific historical circumstances, and second, its significance (positive and negative) for achieving the goals of the socialist revolution and realizing socialist values and principles.

Let us attempt to apply the stated methodological considerations to an analysis of two key aspects, two "problem clusters" of the contemporary revolutionary process.

These are, first of all, the problem of the concrete preconditions and driving forces of the revolutionary transition from capitalism to socialism; and the questions of who the social *subject* of revolutionary transformations is, under what conditions, and under the influence of what motives and interests, certain social groups can act as a revolutionary force, and by what means they are able to carry out the appropriate actions.

Second, there is the problem of the actual *content* of revolutionary transformations.

In analyzing these questions today, we are confronted with the need for a certain reinterpretation of our scientific and political language and our familiar theoretical concepts. After all, in our day even such fundamental Marxist concepts as the "working class," "class alliances," or "power of the working class" are hardly self-evident and axiomatic. The fact that these concepts often become ideological clichés and are used merely as theoretical abstractions in many respects hampers the creative development of Marxist thought; we do not always ask ourselves to what extent they reflect today's sociopolitical realities, the actual alignment of social forces, and the characteristics of the real subjects of mass social action.

The traditional notion of the direct causes of revolutionary crises and revolutionary situations also needs to be reinterpreted. By and large, these causes are reduced to the masses' growing outrage at their worsening condition and at governmental policies directed against their interests. To some extent, this idea continues to be relevant, especially for countries with a relatively low level of economic and social development and with tyrannical, dictatorial regimes. But under the conditions of modern, highly developed capitalism, it is becoming less and less relevant.

In many respects, the level of scientific, technological, and economic development reached by capitalism at the end of the 20th century, capitalism's social strategy, and the changes it has effected in the structure of the masses' needs and values, and in social consciousness, also provide a new perspective on the question of prospects for socialist revolution in the capitalist countries, and the question of which course developing countries should take. The exacerbation of the contradictions of capitalism, which occurred even during the relative economic prosperity of the 1950s and 1960s and assumed the nature of a crisis in the 1970s and 1980s, is increasing the potential for social protest, but it is becoming increasingly unlikely that this protest will develop directly into socialist revolution. This is the result of the specific, long-term, structural features of the socioeconomic, sociopsychological, and political situation that exists in the developed capitalist countries.

Let us list some of those features:

1. The level of economic development reached by contemporary capitalism and the social strategies it has developed enable it, even during severe economic crises, to avoid a marked deterioration in the

material status of the majority of the working people, and to localize the growth of dissatisfaction and protest in relatively limited social groups.

2. The structural alteration of capitalism on the basis of the latest scientific and technological advances makes the work of the organized workers' movement more difficult. Its revolutionary element, which even previously failed to achieve mass influence among the working class in the majority of capitalist countries, is now in danger of losing ground even where it once had become an influential political force.

3. Under the influence of the economic, social, cultural, and ideological evolution of capitalist society in the past few decades, serious changes have occurred in the needs and values of the masses, and in the structure of mass psychology and consciousness. Emotional motives for mass social behavior have weakened, while "rational" motives have grown stronger, and there has been a substantial increase in the desire for concrete knowledge of the real consequences of social and political actions, and their possible impact on the economic and social status of the mass social strata involved. The mass consciousness is less and less receptive to abstract and symbolic formulas for the radical transformation of society (so-called "isms"), while it shows more and more interest in concrete understanding and concrete methods of solving the problems that concern it. The ideals and values of socialism and anticapitalist feelings live on in the minds of working people in many capitalist countries, but their behavior in the sociopolitical arena shows no inclination on their part to take direct action to realize these ideals, or to carry out a "total" revolution in the sociopolitical system.

In the public, especially the mass, consciousness in capitalist countries, protest against capitalist relations is expressed not so much in a desire for such a revolution, for the replacement of capitalism with another social system, as in demands for a change in specific aspects of those relations and for their subordination to humanistic and democratic priorities. Without claiming to make any long-term forecast, one can still conjecture that in the foreseeable future the focus of the sociopolitical struggle in developed capitalist countries will be not the preservation or the abolition of the capitalist system, but the problems of humanizing and democratizing the existing relations and way of life.

4. The current "bloc" structure of international relations, the effective consolidation of most developed capitalist countries into a single political camp, international economic integration, and the trend, which has become firmly established in international life, toward the maintenance of a stable balance of forces between opposing political-military blocs—all significantly limits the possibility of a short (occurring in a matter of days, weeks, or months), victorious revolution in one of the developed capitalist countries (even if one allows the

extremely hypothetical possibility that internal conditions could become ripe for the outbreak of revolution in a given country).

This article does not deal specifically with the problems of the revolutionary movement in the developing countries, but it is worth noting that there, too, extremely profound changes have occurred in the objective situation over recent decades. Obviously, the diversity of the ways they can develop is even greater than in the citadels of capitalism, but the question of which way is best remains, for all practical purposes, unresolved. At the same time, the prospects for world social progress as a whole depend to a great extent on their choice. In any event, these problems also require detailed study free of preconceived notions.

In its ideological, theoretical, and practical activity, the international communist movement to some extent (although not fully, and not always consistently) takes the aforementioned changes into account. That is clear from new assessments and positions that have appeared in the programs of communist parties from the 1950s through the 1970s. They emphasize a more gradual development of the revolutionary struggle than was assumed in the past; its nonviolent, unarmed, "legal" forms (the "peaceful path" of revolution); and development of the movement for limitation of the monopolies' power and for real democracy into a movement for socialist transformations. But regardless of the forms, pace, and stages of the transition from capitalism to socialism, the question raised above concerning the social forces that are capable of carrying out that transition retains its full significance. Or, to be more specific, how does the proposition that the working class is the leading force of democratic and social reform and can overcome division in its own ranks in the course of struggling for those reforms, and can recognize its own vital interests and unite nonproletarian strata of the working people around itself, "work" under today's conditions?

An analysis of this question requires, at the very least, a well-substantiated assessment of the tendencies characterizing the current stage of development of the working class and other social groups in capitalist society, their ties and relationships, and their role in the social and political arena. A great many Marxist works have already been written on this subject, and their conclusions attest to a considerable increase in the complexity of the structure of social conflicts rending capitalist society, and to the impossibility of reducing those conflicts merely to the antagonism between the working class and the bourgeoisie. The boundaries of the working class, as we know, have expanded to include broad strata of office employees and persons engaged in mental work; this class now includes the overwhelming majority of the self-employed population. On the one hand, this potentially enhances the role of the working class as the principal mass subject of progressive transformations. But on the other hand, the growth and expansion of the working class are proving, in practice, to be a factor that in many ways hinders it from performing this role. Today the working class in capitalist countries acts less as a unified social community than ever before. Of course, in the past the proletariat was also split into groups differing in level of class consciousness and ideological and political orientation, but now this traditional stratification is increasingly interwoven with a deepening differentiation of immediate group interests within the class.

Marx emphasized the difference between a class as an objective socioeconomic category and a class as the subject of social action. Since that time, this difference has often been underestimated in theoretical Marxist writing. Yet today, under the influence of structural changes in society, this difference is growing considerably deeper. If one excludes the bourgeoisie proper, groups and strata that act as real social subjects (i.e., that are united by certain common sociopsychological attributes and pursue their own particular aims and interests), are usually of an intraclass or interclass nature, and the dividing lines between them cross the boundaries of class and "objective" (i.e., designated solely by socioeconomic criteria) strata.

Among such de facto communities there are, for example, employees in new and promising industries and occupations: the scientific and technical professionals; and some workers, as well as new types of small entrepreneurs, who are associated with these industries and occupations. They are inclined toward a kind of "conflicting cooperation" with the ruling class in the interests of technical and economic development, and they are interested in further raising their living standard and social status and are often influenced by neoconservative ideas.

Another large community is formed by the politically and ideologically amorphous mass of relatively low-skilled or unskilled workers; employees in the services sector; farmers; and office employees who are relatively unaffected by the negative consequences of crises. They show both dissatisfaction with certain aspects of their status, and a sociopolitical conformism fed by the fear of losing that status as a result of technological and structural changes. At the same time, there is a growing stratum of the so-called "unprotected"—the partially employed or unemployed, people on the fringes of the economy, the "new poor," bankrupt small businessmen—which is most widely represented in younger groups of the ablebodied population. They waver between a tendency toward irrational revolt and a fatalistic submission to their lot.

Workers in traditional industries and occupations that are declining because of technological progress form a special group. They generally represent the most militant and organized segment of the working class, but their ability to wage an active struggle and perform the role of the vanguard in class confrontation is limited by the threat that weighs on them of becoming unemployed and marginal.

A growing role in social and political life is being played by a segment of the intelligentsia, which is largely unconnected with material production, that shows a heightened interest in universal human and global problems and in the humanization of life, and that fills the ranks of the nontraditional democratic movements. Unlike in the past, the intelligentsia cannot be viewed today simply as an intermediate stratum that vacillates between opposing classes: its democratically minded segment acts as an independent social force and is becoming a center of attraction for members of other groups who are inclined to social and political protest.

Even the above list, which is inevitably brief and highly schematic, shows how difficult it is today to form a political opposition to the monopolistic oligarchy by acting solely on the basis of the traditional "class" principle—in other words, by counting on a working class that rallies other mass strata around itself to play the leading role in this process. Under conditions in which extensive social and sociopsychological differentiation has occurred in the working class, a one-sided emphasis on narrowly conceived class interests not only does not facilitate the growth of such an opposition, but can contribute to dangerous tendencies toward "collective egoism" and corporatism, which are already appearing. Proceeding from actual social reality rather than abstract theoretical formulas, it is extremely difficult, if at all possible, to find a system of immediate class interests that unites the entire working class and at the same time differs fundamentally from the interests of other mass strata. The class struggle of the working class is still the key factor in social progress, of course, but it is impossible to ignore the fact that under actual, present historical conditions, it is in real danger of being replaced by a struggle between narrow group and corporate interests.

These considerations show that in the development of an anti-monopoly opposition and, consequently, the revolutionary process, the organic combination of class, group, and universal human interests is especially urgent.

Such universal human interests, I think, should be understood not just as the solution of global problems, but as the general *interests of social progress* that are embodied in social aims and ideals capable of uniting the absolute majority of society. These are the ideals of peace, harmonious relations between human beings and nature, economic prosperity and social justice, personal liberty, healthy human relations, and a healthy way of life. It is important that these and similar ideals are shared by broad masses of people regardless of their socioeconomic status, political orientation, or ideological conviction. Clearly it is important for revolutionary forces to try to bring together group, including class, interests and subordinate them to these universal ideals. One can assume that it will be primarily the groups and communities that are most capable of mounting a practical defense of these ideals that can become the subject of the revolutionary process.

Such communities can hardly be identified with any "objective" social-class groups. In addition to objective socioeconomic factors, such cultural and psychological factors as people's cultural development and the breadth of their social outlook, the independence of their thinking, the level of development of their spiritual needs, and their types of values are playing an increasing role in the alignment of social forces in present-day capitalist society, and in the process by which a democratic opposition is formed. Moreover, depending on these factors, different and even opposite trends in thinking and social behavior will arise in one and the same objective socioeconomic situation. For example, whereas one segment of the relatively "privileged" strata of the working people is concerned with protecting and strengthening its privileges, another segment is inclined to protest against oligarchical power relations in the workplace and society, the antidemocratic policies of ruling circles, the cultural situation, the dehumanizing of the way of life, and militarism. A key objective for revolutionary forces is to support and develop these trends in all strata and groups of society.

The general humanism that is now coming to characterize the goals of the revolutionary struggle is, at the same time, consistent with its class nature. One has only to look at the objective, natural expansion of the working class's immediate and vital interests. Because it forms the overwhelming majority of society in the developed capitalist countries, today's working class is capable of uniting only around a program that is aimed at solving all of the problems of social development.

The political organization of the antioligarchy movement requires special analysis. It would hardly be right to unconditionally insist that communist parties take the leading role in this movement. It is unquestionably important for communists to try to enhance their role in the opposition movement and increase the significance of their contribution to its ideological and political platform, and to the unification of democratic forces. However, that is not the same as claiming political leadership of the movement. Such a claim is unrealistic, and not just because communist parties' influence over the masses has weakened. Even more important is the fact that the majority of the working masses in the capitalist countries are politically associated with diverse parties, currents, and movements, and that in those countries the ideal of political pluralism is by no means a fiction, but rather a deeply rooted value in the mass political consciousness. Under these conditions, the political organization of a democratic opposition is conceivable only as an alliance of participants who enjoy equal status—communists, socialists, other leftist parties and public organizations, and mass democratic movements.

Let us now discuss the second extremely important aspect of the revolutionary process—the problem of the *content* of progressive transformations. In analyzing this problem, we must thoroughly take into account the lessons learned from building socialism in countries where revolutions have triumphed. As we know, these revolutions in many respects turned upside down the relationship that Marxism revealed to exist between the economic base and the political and ideological superstructure of society. During the period in which socialism was being built, it was no longer the base that gave rise to a corresponding superstructure, but just the opposite, the party and state superstructure that created a new base and reorganized, at its discretion, both the system of production relations and the social structure of society. This course ensured the rapid pace of socialist transformation that was needed under certain historical conditions, and eliminated the possibility of a capitalist restoration. But at the same time it created the danger of arbitrary action and bureaucratic centralism, a danger that the socioeconomic system and economic culture would become the fruit of abstract, utopian concepts, and that overall economic development would be impeded.

Socialism's social accomplishments are great and indisputable. They include the provision of full employment, guarantees that the working people occupy a secure position in production, and the democratization of the public education system, which has created unprecedented opportunities for the working people's social and intellectual growth. They include new rights for the working people in the spheres of social security, health care, leisure and recreation, and culture. Historically speaking, socialism's achievements have marked a qualitatively new stage in world social progress. As noted above, they have had a powerful positive effect on the social situation in the capitalist world. In the economic sphere, socialism has provided an example of the unprecedentedly rapid and broad transformation of a semi-agrarian, backward country into a mighty industrial power; even now this example holds an attraction for countries that must solve the problem of overcoming economic backwardness.

At the same time, one cannot ignore the fact that the importance of a number of concrete aspects of socialism's positive experience has been changing along with changes in the concrete, historical global situation. Thus, in the context of the scientific and technological revolution, which gives rise to an intensive type of economic development, the extensive method of development and the related economic, social, and political structures and system of economic management lose their advantages. This applies not only to the developed countries, but also, to some extent, to many developing ones, since they too face the task of using the latest achievements of scientific and technological progress. In the social sphere, too, socialism's advantages do not appear as unambiguous as they did in the 1920s or 1930s; here too capitalism is forced to compete with socialism in areas such as social security, health care, and education. While perpetuating unemployment and material and spiritual poverty among broad strata of the population, it simultaneously pursues a carefully developed and well-calculated social policy that objectively limits the scope of these phenomena. It would be naive, at the very least, to assert that even with conservative governments this social policy comes down merely to cutting back on social spending and encouraging mass layoffs.

In analyzing the laws and the avenues of the transition to socialism, it is also very instructive to study the experience of state-monopoly capitalism and its characteristic methods of regulating economic and social processes. We know that this regulation has not done away with the anarchy inherent in capitalist relations, or rid the economy of crises. It remains a fact, however, that for all the economic and social contradictions of state-monopoly capitalism, it manages to achieve scientific and technological progress, a high degree of economic efficiency, and rather appreciable, if unstable, economic growth rates. One of the main reasons for this is its combination of purposeful centralized regulation with the independence of the subjects of economic activity.

The class nature of these subjects (capitalist enterprises, either privately owned or state-owned), together with their inherent motives and aims, makes them fundamentally different from the subjects of economic activity under socialism, but this by no means indicates that the transition from capitalism to socialism must entail repudiation of the principle of the independence of the economic subject (in this case, a socialist enterprise of one kind or another). After all, experience shows that such repudiation saps the vitality and effectiveness of the whole economic mechanism. It follows that many components of state-monopoly regulation can, as Lenin foresaw, be used in the process of socialist transformation.

In light of historical and contemporary experience, the demand that revolutionary transformations be based on objective economic and social laws and the laws of human psychology and social behavior is now assuming top priority. This type of transition from capitalism to socialism is incompatible with arbitrary and authoritarian methods, and in this sense it could be called the natural historical type. It presupposes, in particular, the use of the law of value, the necessity of market relations among producers and between producers and consumers, a mixed economy, and the combination of centralized planning and regulation with the independence of the subjects of economic activity.

We must also seriously reflect on the lessons of the revolutionary process that apply to the *political sphere*, the political organization of the society that is building socialism. Any revolution is essentially a democratic act, an act of the masses themselves. The entire process of revolutionary transformation should be just as democratic in its methods. This means that the society implementing those transformations should have not just a representative democracy, but the sort of democracy that presupposes the masses' real participation in political decision-making and in government. We know that Lenin's ideas on this matter were not sufficiently put into practice. Yet "participatory democracy" is one of the most important objective laws of socialist development, for without it there can be no feedback from the masses to the system of government, and without such feedback this system sooner or later ceases to serve the interests of the masses and begins to serve itself.

The question of defending revolutionary gains and suppressing internal counterrevolution becomes particularly complex in today's conditions. It seems that the method of dealing with this matter that is most compatible with socialist principles is to avoid turning methods such as the strengthening and toughening of punitive state agencies into absolutes, and to promote the development of autonomous public organizations and movements that are capable of isolating the counterrevolution and effectively defending revolutionary goals.

On the whole, one might conclude that under current conditions the very essence and nature of the problems that revolutionary forces must solve are undergoing a fundamental change. In the past, the main problem was how to lead the masses to struggle for socialism and to form the political army of the socialist revolution, whereas the goals of the revolution and the nature of socialist reforms seemed quite obvious. Today the problem of the revolution's prospects moves to a different plane, and the question "what kind of socialism?" becomes crucial.

The answer to this question can be found only along the path of creating a *concrete democratic alternative* to contemporary state-monopoly capitalism.

Obviously, one of revolutionary forces' most urgent tasks is becoming the search for strategies for the progressive transformation of society and for alternative types of economic, social, and political organization that are in keeping with trends in the development of productive forces, with the needs of modern man, and with the necessity of solving the global problems of human civilization. The main areas of this search are the creation of civilized international relations that eliminate military conflicts between countries; harmonious economic development that can subordinate scientific and technological progress to the interests of the working masses and preserve the natural conditions of human life on earth; a comprehensive humanization of the way of life that will create conditions for harmonious relations between society and the individual, and for the individual's material, moral and psychological well-being; the radical democratization of economic, social, and political relations; and the elimination of the hunger, poverty, barbarous living conditions, and economic and social backwardness of peoples in the Third World. In other words, this search is inseparably bound up with the practical struggle for *social progress*, which in today's world becomes the general avenue of the revolutionary process's development. It is clear that only through the development of this struggle can the necessary conditions be created for the direct advancement of socialist revolutionary goals, and for the understanding by both the revolutionary vanguard and the working masses of the actual content of those goals.

If one's vision is not obscured by a veil of primitive stereotypes, it is not hard to see that the search for the renewal and restructuring of society has a great deal in common in the two opposing systems. It is insufficient to say that in one system the concern is with improving socialism, while in the other the task is completely different—searching for the strategies for a socialist revolution. In reality, both the development of socialism and the activities of progressive forces in the capitalist countries are, in their internal content, aimed at solving certain problems and satisfying certain social needs, and these problems and needs are in some ways profoundly different and in some ways similar in the different systems. Thus, today most socialist countries do not face the problem of combating unemployment, which is a pressing concern for capitalist society; but the problems of putting the results of the scientific and technological progress to humanistic use, of humanizing the life of society and the individual, and of achieving real, and not just pro forma, democracy are urgent problems for both systems (despite all the differences in the concrete economic and sociopolitical conditions under which these problems are addressed). Of course, bureaucratism under state-monopoly capitalism and "socialist" bureaucratism have different social and class foundations, but it is highly symptomatic that in both systems the public perceives it as a hindrance to the normal functioning and development of society, and that in both an intensive search is under way for a democratic alternative to technocratic methods of management and to technocratic ideology.

Such facts, of course, in no way corroborate the once-fashionable theory of convergence, or diminish the fundamental differences between the opposing systems. But they do show that the unity of today's world is not confined to the interdependence of its various parts, or to the reality of civilization's worsening global problems. It also consists of the common nature of certain technological, economic, and social processes that are unfolding in the different social systems, and of the problems they engender.

This conclusion is essential to the efforts of the communist movement and other revolutionary and progressive forces. On the one hand, it is precisely in the course of the revolutionary renewal of socialism that is occurring today that, for all intents and purposes, we are resolving the question of whether the movement toward socialism is to be the general trend in world social development, and in particular, the question of just how realistic the prospect of socialism is for present-day, developed capitalist countries. The course of the struggle for social progress depends to a critical extent on the course of the revolutionary renewal of socialism. As in the previous historical period, the prospects for the socialist reconstruction of society on a world scale are inseparably bound up with what is happening in socialist countries and with the course and results of the constructive processes that were set in motion by the Great October Socialist Revolution.

On the other hand, the efforts to renew socialism should thoroughly and critically consider the whole experience of social development under capitalism. I think that such an approach to the problems of social progress significantly broadens the basis for creative international dialogue and cooperation both within the communist movement—among Marxists from the socialist, capitalist, and developing countries—and between communists and all other political forces and schools of social thought that share progressive, democratic values and ideals.

On the Threshold of a New Century

ALEKSANDR YEVGENYEVICH BOVIN* AND
VLADIMIR PETROVICH LUKIN**

The approach of the year 2000 has heightened interest in the history of the 20th century and in opinions as to what the 21st century has in store for us. The range of assessments is truly inexhaustible, both objectively, by virtue of their complexity and variety, and subjectively, by virtue of the inevitable diversity of views.

MEMO gives the floor to Izvestia political commentator Aleksandr Yevgenyevich Bovin and to Doctor of History and Professor Vladimir Petrovich Lukin. In doing so we proceed from the premise that the controversial nature of their individual opinions and conclusions should not be an obstacle to their publication.

Lukin: The end of the century and, at the same time, the end of the millennium are drawing near: "A time to gather stones. . . ." People have predicted anything from the end of the world to the coming of paradise by the end of the second millennium. And in the baggage of mankind, as it approaches this conventional milestone— but milestone nonetheless—three components are most apparent: the arms race, fraught with the threat of universal catastrophe; the mounting environmental crisis, precipitated by the technological sector's aggressive behavior toward the biosphere; and the sharpening contrast on a global scale between poverty and wealth and the growing social and international tension it entails.

Bovin: All that you've said sounds bleak. For behind each of the "components" you mentioned are people. Or, to be more precise, their suffering, their unhappiness. And death, the death of millions. It is a paradox of the century that never before has so much been said about peace as in the 20th century, but never have wars large and small reaped such a bountiful harvest.

Peace, like war, is divisible: zones of peace exist alongside, and alternative with, zones of war. According to the Stockholm International Peace Research Institute, there were 36 wars and armed con-

---

*Candidate of Philosophy and political commentator for the newspaper *Izvestia*.

**Doctor of History, international historian, public affairs commentator and prominent expert on the problems of Asia and the Pacific region. This article appeared in the December 1987 issue of *MEMO*.

flicts involving 41 countries last year alone. I don't think the figures have changed noticeably for this year. So one must admit that at the close of the century people have been fighting more and with greater frequency than at its beginning.

Lukin: Perhaps we should try to add some optimistic colors to the overall picture.

Bovin: One would like to, of course, but we should hardly shift our discussion to a plane of optimism versus pessimism. Things are far too complex, far too serious on all sides—far more complex and far more serious than any "sense of profound satisfaction." Mankind is approaching the third millennium amid crises, awash in contradictions and paradoxes.

In speaking of crises, contradictions, and paradoxes, of course, one has to see the differences between East and West, differences in the character and scope of their problems. But I wouldn't turn these differences into absolutes. The 20th century has been marked by the emergence of world socialism. This is an indisputable, unquestionable fact. But something else is indisputable and unquestionable as well. Socialism has yet to create an economy more effective than the capitalist economy. A number of socialist countries have encountered domestic crises, such as Hungary, Czechoslovakia, China, and Poland.

Lukin: Add to this the situation that arose in our country in the late 1970s and early 1980s, which the June plenary session of the Central Committee characterized as a precrisis state.

Bovin: Of course. And there is also the "experience" of sharp disputes on the international level, up to and including armed clashes, such as those between the U.S.S.R. and the People's Republic of China, and between Vietnam and the P.R.C. Bitter experience, but experience that cannot be neglected in a serious analysis.

Lukin: We are somehow still unaccustomed to discussing socialism's problems and difficulties in a sensible and matter-of-fact fashion. And it's high time we did so.

Bovin: In my opinion, your observation applies equally to the problems of capitalism and imperialism. You seem to understand this, but the concept usually slips into a well-trodden rut.

The crisis of capitalism, which engulfs all spheres of public life, is beyond question. Contradictions abound. There is a growing impression that what is happening is irrational. On the one hand, there is a genuine triumph of reason, of human thought. But on the other, there are mortal anguish, convulsions, and cultural perversions. The "old poor"—the birthmark, so to speak, of "pre-technological-revolution" capitalism—are being joined by the "new poor," and the number of déclassé and marginal groups and strata is growing—a concession to scientific and technological progress.

Lukin: Since mankind's advance from the ethnographic state to the social-and-historical state, this century has perhaps been the one most marked by advances and watershed developments.

And the drama of our civilization consists first and foremost in that objectively we have become completely different, while subjectively staying the same in many respects. We find ourselves in a century of totally new energy possibilities, a century of a previously unthinkable acceleration of technological change, a century of globalization of the worldwide process by which civilizations develop, a century of a fundamentally new level of involvement of the masses in world problems, a century in which various social and national ideas of the preceding centuries are being severely tested, a century in which much of what seemed quite realistic early in the century has proved illusory, and at the same time a century in which things that only recently seemed abstractions are on the verge of becoming reality. For example, worldwide apocalypse—nuclear, environmental, or demographic.

Never in recorded history has the gap between past and future been so great as for the people of the 20th century. This is one of the greatest tests for us all, it is truly a challenge to our history, to our civilization. And so far we haven't met this challenge all that well. The old and the traditional are rapidly being destroyed. But the destruction of traditions is outpacing the establishment of truly new and modern forms of societal life.

Bovin: In my view, the psychological atmosphere of the latter part of the century has been marked by a certain disaffection and disillusionment that have accumulated on the left. Not everything—far from it—has turned out as it was intended, as it was set forth in Party programs and political platforms. This applies, albeit in varying degrees, to both the social democratic and communist segments of the working class.

Social democracy promised to "ennoble" capitalism and to create a "state of universal prosperity." It has done much to improve the working man's life, but "universal prosperity" has not been achieved. By the same token, many goals proclaimed by the communists remain inaccessible, despite tremendous efforts over the course of seven decades.

Engels, following Hegel's lead, used the expression "the irony of history." History sometimes has an ironic fate in store for those who try to remake it. After carrying out a revolution, people may be surprised to see that they have not done exactly what they set out to do. For a long time we smugly took the view that this did not apply to communist parties, to socialist revolutions. Now we see we were mistaken, that history can also treat us with irony.

Progress has meant a sharp narrowing of imperialism's sphere of domination and the elimination of the most odious forms of political and economic oppression, such as "untamed" capitalism, fascism, and colonialism. What at the beginning of the century was the norm (Paraguay, for example, or South Africa) is now seen as the exception. However, none of capitalism's critics foresaw that capitalism would prove so viable or exhibit such adaptability to the new social and historical environment.

I wouldn't go so far as to say that each stage of capitalism's general crisis has brought closer or made more real the prospect of socialist transformations in the centers of world capitalism. At the start of the century, the prospect of the revolutionary collapse of capitalism was viewed as more realistic and imminent than it is today, at century's end.

Lukin: Here we have doubtless come to the main point of this analysis: to the possibility of remaining at once well informed and optimistic.

The source of optimism goes back to Russia in the year 1917, to the October turning point in Russian and world history—the most important event of the century. Today, social thinking sees that turning point as linked directly to our present restructuring, which could potentially play no less an important role.

Minerva's owl, well known to historians, was long overdue in this instance. Apparently, it too has trouble maintaining a 20th-century pace. An optimistic note, however, is sounded by the level and scope of the party's self-criticism, which is breaking through the wall between words and reality; by the rapid—considering the enormous difficulties—formulation at the January and June 1987 plenary sessions of the CPSU Central Committee of a concrete program of revolutionary renewal of all aspects of the life of Soviet society; by the explicit and unambiguous charting of the subsequent thrust of revolutionary reforms along the path of democratization; and finally, by the very first, but unquestionable, steps forward on this path.

Of course, all this is just a beginning. Of course, our generation's memory is burdened with the weight of unfulfilled aspirations. But these aspirations are the first of their kind—hence the optimism.

Bovin: We are perhaps living through a turning point, a watershed phase in the history of world socialism. The model of socialism rooted in the specific historical features that attended the formation of the world's first socialist state (Russia's backwardness, the hostile capitalist encirclement) was at an impasse and had exhausted itself. Rigid centralism, the administrative-command system of economic management, the lack of democracy, the dominance of a narrow dogmatism in science and culture—these are a few of the distinguishing characteristics of history's first model of socialism. The first attempts to move away from it, to revise it, date from the 20th CPSU Congress. Three decades of failures on that path had brought the U.S.S.R. to the brink of crisis. Hence the enormous significance of the decisions of the 27th CPSU Congress, which led the way to the renewal of socialism, to the creation of a new socialist model that combines a significantly more effective economy with full-fledged democracy.

Lukin: Don't you think there was an alternative, and that we missed that alternative somewhere during the 1920s and 1930s?

Bovin: Special research is needed here. At a glance, so to speak, it's hard to say anything definite. We were in the "clutches" of objective circumstances. Let me elaborate. The repressions under Stalin or, for example, the excesses of collectivization—these were phenomena of a subjective nature, they were not inevitable. As for the all-embracing centralism, the limited democracy, I see no alternative for that time.

Lukin: But I am certain that there was such an alternative. To have gone through a similar phase of development but with fundamentally different social costs—that was the alternative, in my view.

But let's talk about more topical matters today—especially since what is happening in our country is no longer ours alone. Perestroika, glasnost, democratization: it is simply impossible to say where their purely domestic significance ends and their international significance begins. For example, we must change our economic performance sharply for the better. And this is first and foremost an internal affair. But it has a direct bearing on both the material and psychological aspects of our country's actions in the world arena. For on one hand, we have attained parity with the United States in the military sphere in recent decades. But on the other hand, our ability to exert nonmilitary influence in world affairs has narrowed.

At the same time, the phenomena now referred to as a "lack of democracy" and stagnant tendencies in the social sphere—all these things have adversely affected the image of our country (and consequently of socialism) in the world. Thus, without any active resistance on our part, the objective preconditions were created for mass dissemination of the idea that a Soviet military threat existed.

In our by no means sentimental century, people are reluctant to believe declared intentions but are quite willing to explore realistic possibilities, using worst-case scenarios as a starting point. Our propaganda alone (or, to use the fashionable term, our counterpropaganda) is not capable of dispelling the image, deeply entrenched in the West, of an enormous country with very great military, but limited nonmilitary, capabilities. Even the most active foreign policy actions and initiatives are not enough. What we need here are real restructuring results and in particular a restored balance between military and nonmilitary capabilities for influencing international affairs—and on a reciprocal basis, as far as possible.

The initial steps of restructuring have already begun changing the situation for the better. Public opinion polls in various countries show that the Soviet leadership is trusted more than the American leaders. But we should hardly flatter ourselves. It's not clear yet which is the greater here—trust in us, or distrust of them. Evidently we are being greatly helped by the U.S. administration's preoccupation with "ideological pop-art" and with its potshots at primitive and timeworn targets. But while presidents come and go, the negative stereotypes grow more firmly entrenched in the public mind.

Only the first layer has now been stripped away from this anti-Soviet stereotype. And to prevent it from coming back, we have a great deal of work to do—and not just at the propaganda level, or even at the level of foreign-policy actions. Rather, this work must be done inside the country.

And so restructuring and democratization are two of the most important conditions for making optimistic foreign-policy forecasts a possibility.

Bovin: Generally speaking, depending on the progress and success of our restructuring, two alternative scenarios for the end of the century are theoretically possible. Let us examine the first scenario, the one we will strive to bring about. Restructuring encompasses and transforms all spheres of public life in the U.S.S.R. Modernization develops successfully in the P.R.C. The other socialist countries are able to solve their problems. In other words, the maturity level of world socialism rises.

And how will this affect the situation in the principal centers and citadels of capitalism? Let us pose the question in more concrete terms: what future is in store for conservatism?

Lukin: Neoconservatism is not eternal, at least not in its present Reaganite and Thatcherite forms. One can discern in it, however, two wavelengths, two types of waves—short and long. The first wavelength consists of specific leaders and their specific programs, positions, and political fates. Some, like Reagan, will go sooner; others, like Thatcher and Kohl, will depart the scene later, though also fairly soon in terms of the time frame we have elected. Modern conservatism's other wavelength, the long one, has to do with such factors as the distinguishing features of the scientific and technical revolution's present stage, with the crisis of liberalism and of social democracy, and with the serious difficulties confronting left-wing forces as a whole.

The new stage of scientific and technological progress has made the dilemma between social regulation and economic efficiency far harsher at century's end than at mid-century. The Reaganite response to this harsher dilemma has been a crude, egoistic and, from a class standpoint, restricted one, but a response nonetheless—a clear reaction to the change in objective reality. The same is true of Thatcher in Britain. But their liberal and reformist opponents have yet to offer a clear alternative to the neoconservative response. It's no accident that, to survive politically, the socialists in France and Spain have embraced a kind of "Reaganism with a human face"—embraced it while choking off their own tune, so to speak, and perfectly aware that they were doing so. Clearly, that tune was written long ago and is no longer to be heard at century's end.

Note that today, according to surveys, the conservatives in the United States and in a number of European states as well feel weakest in foreign policy. But in the economic sphere and even, strangely enough, in the social sphere, the situation is more complex and more contradictory. Of course, this long wave will also fade. The doctrine and practice of "improving" capitalism through an active social policy—i.e., social reformism—will become active once more. However, the reformists will have to find an answer to the question of how to combine their traditional methods with nontraditional solutions to the problem of economic efficiency in the new stage of scientific and technological progress.

Incidentally, in previous stages, social reformism has borrowed a great deal from socialism. I think that in the future as well, the more vigorous the development of restructuring in our country—and especially of the component dealing with effective and active social policy—the greater the scope and possibilities for the left-wing forces in the West, including their reformist segment.

Bovin: The end of the century has brought a new wave of scientific and technical revolution. Marx's prediction that the worker will cease to be the "main agent of the production process and will take his place at its side" (Marx and Engels, *Works* [*Sochineniya*], Vol. 46, p. 213) is coming true. The era of production without people is approaching. Given the synchronous development of social and scientific-technical progress, one can foresee tens and hundreds of millions of people moving to the service sector (culture, research, education, and public health). But it's too early to think about that. For the present, as I see it, mass unemployment remains and will remain the primary social problem of the scientific and technical revolution.

Last year, the countries of the Organization for Economic Cooperation and Development had more than 30 million unemployed. But what if that number should rise to 80 million or to 130 million? How will this affect political stability?

Lukin: Much is still unclear in this regard. Structural unemployment has indeed become a fact of life. At the same time, however, the number of jobs in completely new spheres is growing. Take the United States, where one of Reagan's main propaganda assets is his statement that 13 million new jobs have been created under his presidency. The number of people working in America today is greater than ever before, and there are fewer unemployed than in the early 1980s. What is this? A temporary distortion of the long-term process you mentioned, or a stable trend? It's difficult to say at this point.

Virtually all the new jobs have been in the service sector. What we are observing here is a process of social restructuring of perhaps roughly the same magnitude as the destruction of agrarian society and the channeling of the bulk of the population into industry. By its very nature, this process cannot help but be international and based on world interdependence. In order for the service sector to supplant industry in the United States or Britain, it is necessary that an agrarian society somewhere in the "newly industrialized countries" become an industrialized society and, consequently, that peasants become industrial workers, that urbanization take place, and so forth. Doesn't this mean that the economically interconnected world is becoming increasingly interconnected in social terms as well?

Generally speaking, what is involved, in my opinion, is no simple displacement of manpower, but processes of considerably greater complexity. But there is room in them for the sort of thing that you mentioned—namely, the fact that the working class is changing, both in terms of its working conditions and its goals in life. The number of retirees is growing, the number of people living on assistance is growing. In a number of capitalist countries, the labor unions are weakening markedly. New social ties are emerging, and old ones are growing weaker. In short, the entire social environment is changing.

Bovin: And if the social environment is changing, the perception of socialist prospects is apparently changing as well.

People often reason something like this: Objectively, capitalism matured long ago and is now overripe for socialist reforms. But the subjective force that could make this historical tendency a reality has been significantly weakened by the divisions within the workers' movement, by conflicts between social democratic and communist parties, and by the bourgeoisie's skillful ideological manipulation of the masses.

First, as concerns capitalism's having matured and become overripe. I think that framing the question that way fails to take into account and underestimates the possibility of restructuring under capitalism, which is to say the possibility of modification, transformation, and improvement of capitalist production relations. As for the subjective forces—particularly communist parties—we have often overestimated, for understandable reasons, their actual influence and actual role in the political life of their countries.

Unfortunately, the facts show that many communist parties in developed capitalist countries and in the Third World do not enjoy broad public support and that their political influence on the working people is weak. A study of the documents and materials of fraternal parties and of their internal discussions allows us to identify several causes of this situation. First are long-standing traditions of sectarianism, the tendency of some to distance themselves as "pure" political representatives of the working class from other, "impure" representatives. Second are the setbacks and difficulties on the path of developing real socialism, which naturally haven't drawn people to socialism but have alienated them from it. And third is the way that doctrine, political programs, strategy, and tactics have lagged behind the changing situation—lagged behind, not yesterday's demands but today's and tomorrow's.

Generally speaking, the communist movement is approaching the end of the 20th century in a complex and difficult situation that requires nonstandard solutions and, most important, a breakthrough to the masses, the winning over of the masses.

Lukin: Another paradox of century's end is that the masses in the capitalist countries are not supporting the political movement whose raison d'être is to fight for the masses' fundamental interests.

To the causes you cited I would add one more: The leaders of the bourgeoisie have succeeded in adjusting to the new situation more quickly than their political antagonists. They've managed to create a system of social shock absorbers and social counterweights that have enabled them to channel the masses' energy toward the reform, modernization, and "improvement" of capitalism. In other words, they have shown great political agility. This is the high price that many left-wing movements have paid for rigid doctrinairism—justified, as a rule, by an exclusive claim to "scientific" reasoning. Yet that doctrinairism didn't just appear out of thin air. On the contrary, it arose out of the airlessness that our restructuring is called upon to redress.

Bovin: Yes, the capitalists have learned a good deal and changed a good deal—in politics and in economics. It is therefore advisable to examine imperialism from the standpoint of its dynamics, to see the changes in its structures and mechanisms over time and to see its eventful history.

In Lenin's time, monopoly capitalism was dominant, and state-monopoly capitalism had only just emerged. The second half of the 20th century has been dominated by state-monopoly capitalism, with its bourgeois-reformist and social-reformist variant prevailing. Incidentally, the neoconservatives' policies have only modified this variant of state-monopoly capitalism, not eliminated it. It is theoretically quite possible that the state component will gradually come to outweigh the mere monopoly component, resulting in a relatively "pure" state capitalism.

The picture could be more complex. The enormous increase in the involvement of transnational corporations and transnational banks in the expansion process of world capitalism can be interpreted as the emergence of a transnational form, a transnational model, of state-monopoly capitalism.

Lukin: Can you project the five known attributes of imperialism onto this "transnational form," as you put it, of state-monopoly capitalism?

Bovin: The framework of our dialogue is too narrow to examine in detail the subject you propose. Let me confine myself to the basic approach to it. The five attributes of imperialism were formulated by Lenin 70 years ago. Imperialism was at the time all-powerful. Today it is no longer so. And to mechanically transfer or project the characteristics of that time to this fundamentally different time, or project them onto it, would be unscientific. Only a concrete analysis of concrete data can show which attributes continue to make up the "constitution" of imperialism, which have changed, which have receded into the past, and which have emerged anew.

In science, preconceived notions are ruinous. Last year, a respected scientist, describing the political division of the world, cited as a characteristic of imperialism, by way of example, the distribution of radio frequencies among states, as well as the "division" of shipping routes and air routes. Lenin hardly needs that kind of "defense."

Lukin: Let's return to the transnational corporation. The view exists that one of the general trends of world development is that conscious action plays a growing role in the life of society. One example of this trend is said to be the growing degree of organization and planning in the development of capitalism.

The transnational corporation, on the other hand . . .

Bovin: Is something akin to Reaganomics on a world scale.

Lukin: Not very precise, but you could put it that way.

Bovin: There is indeed a contradiction. The transnational corporation is a new—ultramodern, so to speak—organizational form of capitalist production, and yet in essence, in terms of its fundamental basis, it is a return to the old, an intensification of haphazard market relations in the world economic arena. However, experience has shown (and this experience has been assimilated by many capitalist theoreticians and leaders) that loosened control over the free interplay of market forces can run contrary to capitalism's interests and weaken capitalism as a whole. And so the transnational corporation and transnational bank will hardly be given carte blanche. Their operations will be circumscribed by general agreements on coordinating economic policies and by the existence of regulatory political mechanisms at the international level.

One such mechanism is the annual meeting of heads of states and governments of the seven leading capitalist countries. And again we see a paradox. To all intents and purposes, extremely few of the Seven's decisions—if we take specific recommendations on specific issues—have been implemented. So what's the purpose? Why do these extremely busy people, burdened with countless pressing concerns and worries, meet again and again?

The meetings of the Seven are an outward manifestation of one of the underlying trends of world development. Capitalism is adapting to the ever more complex historical conditions of its existence. To enhance capitalism's viability and its resistance to all manner of negative effects stemming from the "environment"—this, in short, is the purpose of these annual "shows" featuring selected political stars.

Lukin: And it becomes more understandable if one views what is happening from a broad historical perspective.

The history of the capitalist economy as an economy operating on the principle of self-regulation ended with the Great Depression and the world crisis of the early 1930s. Since then, the economic development of any given capitalist country has proceeded under the growing influence of the state and of government agencies and institutions.

Everything is relative. And the success of state-monopoly regulation is relative too. It cannot rid society of the fundamental, underlying sources of economic contradiction and social conflict. But it can, by redistributing national income, blunt the antagonism between labor and capital. Crises have not disappeared, needless to say, but they have, in response to anticrisis "therapy," taken on the more respectable form of "recessions."

To the ideologists of the "society of universal prosperity," it seemed that a recipe had finally been found for capitalism's eternal youth. It became apparent that the forms and methods of state-monopoly regulation that arose as a reaction to the shocks of the 1930s were no longer in keeping with the achieved level of socialization and internationalization of productive forces and the increasingly complex nature of economic ties. On the one hand, this has invigorated the activities of the neoconservatives, who see the root of all misfortune and evil in "excessive" state intervention in the economy. Hence Reaganomics, Thatcherism, and other forms of ideological desertion from our time to the time of free enterprise.

On the other hand, the shocks of the mid-1970s graphically demonstrated that the haphazard, uncontrolled development of world economic processes has a detrimental effect on the state of affairs within each country and impedes regulation of the economy at the national and state level. In the international arena, there is no central political regulator of economic processes that can play a role comparable to the role of the state. As a result, the world capitalist market and international economic relations in the nonsocialist part of the world are subject to uncontrolled forces to a far greater degree than the present level of state-monopoly regulation allows within individual countries. This entails permanent instability of world economic ties, which, given the ever-growing influence of foreign-economic factors on internal economic development, exacerbates economic crises. Consequently, the solution of internal problems has necessitated the transcending of state borders and undertaking economic regulation at the international level.

Bovin: Yes, that is the origin of the Seven. The first meeting of the powerful of this world was held in Rambouillet in November 1975. The circumstances have changed, but the task they are trying to accomplish is the same one undertaken 12 years ago: by joint effort, to strengthen capitalism's positions and learn how to regulate international economic ties.

Needless to say, each participant in this international economic directorate strives to uphold his own country's interests and acts in accordance with his understanding of the situation. The contradictions tearing at the thin fabric of agreement are obvious. The lesson that they should move in the same direction and march in step is being learned with enormous difficulty. Nevertheless, all indications are that there will be continued attempts to pool efforts, coordinate policies, and modernize and enrich the ways and means of influencing the world capitalist economy. The formation of an international capitalist mechanism to regulate economic activity will continue. To preserve and strengthen capital's sway in their countries, to preserve and strengthen the privileged status of the big league of industrial democracies in the world economy, and to put under conscious control the internationalization of production—these are the long-term objectives. And in its pursuit of them capitalism will bring to light and mobilize new potential for survival.

Lukin: I get the impression that we could still encounter some new variant of capitalism—for example, the variant once referred to as "ultra-imperialism." I don't want to conceal my apprehension: haven't we missed some very important—if not too "pleasant," from the standpoint of dogmatic thinking—intermediate stage in the development of capitalist society? And today we may be training all our fire on a place that the moving target has already left.

Bovin: I don't rule out that possibility. Granted, as concerns the concept of "ultra-imperialism," it was, as you know, compromised by [Karl] Kautsky some time ago. But let us recall the discussion at the time.

Kautsky put forward the proposition that the creation of a "world-wide united trust" and of "international united finance capital" was conceivable in the not-too-distant future. The imperialist powers, Kautsky posited, would stop fighting each other and would rely on their combined strength to plunder the rest of the world.

Lenin thought differently. He agreed that ultra-imperialism was "conceivable" in abstract terms as a new phase of capitalism following imperialism and that its development was moving in the direction of a single "world trust." However, Lenin termed the abstraction of ultra-imperialism a moot abstraction. First, because it turned the period of the "imperialist world" into an absolute and forgot that it would inevitably be followed by a period of "imperialist wars" that could not fail to explode any form of unity among the imperialists. Second, before things can reach the point of the creation of a "worldwide trust," imperialism "will inevitably collapse": Capitalism will become its antithesis.

Lenin's second argument, it seems to me, is still relevant today. The capitalists may simply lack the historical time to overcome their differences and to forge a single "worldwide trust." As for the first argument, history has left it in the distance. The emergence of world socialism and the supplanting of the colonial periphery by dozens of independent states have put imperialism in a position in which wars between imperialist states are an unaffordable luxury. And therefore, to take the long view, centripetal tendencies will prevail over centrifugal forces, and there will be a growing need to coordinate policies as an important means of enhancing capitalism's viability.

Lukin: In reflecting on the fate of capitalism, we must of course bear in mind that the situation at its centers and the relations among these centers will depend in large measure on the evolution of the Third World. And there, in the Third World, the picture is a very mixed one. Capitalism can be seen strengthening its positions in various and very important regions of the Third World. Take Asia and the Pacific, where in several major countries and subregions the question of path of development for the foreseeable future has been decided—and not in favor of socialism. With somewhat less certainty, but sufficient certainty nonetheless, the same can be said of a number of major countries and subregions of Latin America and Africa.

Why the relatively recent lack of clarity has sorted itself out in precisely this way is a complex question that requires careful research. One thing is clear: colossal difficulties have arisen on the path of noncapitalist development—far greater ones than were contemplated in the 1960s. Apparently, this was attributable both to objective problems—socioeconomic development's immanent resistance to any jumping over of natural stages—and to subjective circumstances having to do with the numerous mistakes and errors committed by the political leaders of the countries in question. Nor can one dismiss the effect of the difficulties that the world socialist system has encountered.

Bovin: One can hope that, as the restructuring of world socialism proceeds and as the international workers' movement and its political vanguard are invigorated, anticapitalist tendencies will intensify in the Third World, though the connection here is by no means either direct or clear-cut.

Lukin: Nor are the situation and vectors clearly defined. One noteworthy phenomenon in the Third World is the recent emergence of the region's own "power centers." Today India and Brazil, tomorrow Indonesia and Nigeria, and after that (at some point in the next century) other countries. The world of the future will be not only interdependent but also multipolar.

"Dependence/hegemony" relationships are still very strong today. We all see the developing countries' enormous debts, we all see the "second economy." This picture is not complete, however. Look at Brazil and the "newly industrialized countries" of Asia and the Pacific. They are by no means mere objects—they are subjects as well. They are offering increasingly fierce and effective competition to the developed countries, including competition in a number of high-tech fields. In general, it can be said that "dependence/hegemony" relationships are being joined and, in some places, supplanted by relationships of asymmetrical interdependence. The asymmetrical interdependence between North and South is one of the new, characteristic features of our time.

Meanwhile, in another region of the enormous Third World, we see mounting destructive tendencies of the most desperate kind. The death toll claimed by famine has exceeded that of the world wars; the demographic crisis is steadily growing; sown areas are shrinking. One gets the impression that the sum of human suffering is approaching a critical mass.

Bovin: An explosion can be averted. As it slowly and painstakingly strives to overcome its internal and external conflicts, the Third World is evolving in the direction of progress. We should also bear in mind that the Third World and the developed capitalist countries, for all their contradictions, have an objective interest in each other's dynamic growth, in cooperation. The developing countries' maximalist program is known as the new international economic order. The capitalist countries prefer other solutions. But time is nonetheless working on the side of justice—albeit slowly, very slowly.

Lukin: Do you believe, then, in the possibility of establishing a new economic order?

Bovin: Generally speaking, yes. Such an order is no less utopian than universal disarmament (or a nuclear-free world). If we intend to curb militarism, why stop at neocolonialism? Ultimately all history is a process in which utopian ideals become reality. For not so very long ago we considered the eight-hour workday, universal suffrage, and free medical care to be utopian dreams.

Lukin: Perhaps. But what can you say about the "nature of imperialism," which, as we all know, entails militarism and a drive for political and economic domination? I don't think I'm playing the devil's advocate to ask this question: Is the nature of imperialism a historical constant, something immutable, or can it be modified and altered?

Bovin: I have trouble with the phrase "historical constant." History is change, development, and movement that cannot leave some "constant" untouched. In Lenin's day, the "nature" of imperialism undoubtedly included the inevitability of wars between capitalist states, the inevitability of mother countries' political domination of their colonies. Today, however, wars between imperialist states are virtually impossible, just as a return to colonialism is impossible.

The fact of the matter is, apparently, that the "nature of imperialism" does not exist in and of itself, as some sort of abstraction. Or perhaps I should say that it is precisely as an abstraction that it can exist in and of itself. In real life it is subject to the influence—via a number of transmission mechanisms—of the social and historical environment. If imperialism finds itself in a situation in which war and the use of force cease to be advantageous, in which they would threaten the interests of imperialism itself, then militarism's possibilities are significantly narrowed. Though remaining aggressive by nature, imperialism will be unable to assert its aggressiveness in politics. The construction is somewhat intricate, but history has accustomed us to intricacies and subtleties.

Lukin: Especially since people have acquired the technical means to end their own history. Total nuclear war threatens total destruction. Meanwhile, the number and intensity of international crises are growing.

We can cope with the nature of imperialism by putting more pressure on militarism. But, for one thing, the mosaic of dangers is by no means monochromatic; and for another, we are still a long way from the ideal when it comes to mobilizing efforts to counter these dangers.

In my opinion, among the particularly alarming traits of modern international relations are a lack of will to combat international crises, a lack of will to combat the spread of nuclear weapons, and a lack of will to combat international terrorism.

Bovin: Isn't that statement a little too sweeping? For struggles are being waged on all three fronts. Perhaps not as consistently or energetically as we would like, but . . .

Lukin: That's just it. To avoid getting stuck by the problem's sharp edges, we wrap them in a verbal padding.

Of course, even the approach to these problems is enormously complex. And so for politicians who act according to the principle, "après nous le déluge," a lack of will in these matters is the best course. Meanwhile, the mass destruction of people in various parts of the world goes on. There are more and more nuclear weapons in identified and as yet unidentified underground emplacements. The geographical boundaries of terrorism are expanding. Terrorist methods are becoming increasingly refined and daring. And does the future hold the prospect of nuclear terrorism?

Meanwhile, politicians, diplomats, and journalists constantly argue over who was bad and wrong in a given situation and who was good and right. Now the situation is clearly beginning to change. However, genuine changes are visible only on our side. Washington is largely engaged in repackaging the same old stuff. It's still trying to prove to the world that mining Nicaraguan ports, for example, is right and good, while planting bombs on American passenger planes is bad and wrong. This approach is not only absurd in purely human terms, it is also bad in that it objectively limits the possibilities for reaching difficult and politically distasteful decisions—but decisions essential to all mankind—on the questions at issue.

Bovin: Learning how to manage international conflicts—or better yet, how to abolish them, preserve the values of civilization, and survive—are not only a class interest but a universal human interest as well. Common dangers compel all of us, all social strata and groups that are aware of what is happening, to see ourselves as fellow citizens and join forces to protect our future. For in order to argue which is better—capitalism or socialism—we need, at the very least, to exist.

Lukin: The threat of war is not the only danger that prompts us to emphasize universal human interests. The solution of other global problems also requires it. Of course, only an end to the arms race can provide the means with which to save us from overpopulation, famine, and ecological crises, which threaten all of us.

Man has been and remains a class and social being, of course. But in our day his social nature has become global and hence something common to all mankind. In the past, protecting one's home, one's status, one's tribe, or one's people meant protecting all these things from "others." Today it means protecting and saving mankind, the planet. At some point at the dawn of the historical process, the social and the national became estranged from the universally human. Today, toward the close of the second millennium of our era, these principles are drawing closer together once again. Powerful forces opposed to this process still exist and are actively at work. They exist and are at work everywhere. And these are precisely the stagnant and reactionary forces of the end of this century and the beginning of the next. In opposition to them, however, there are increasing symptoms of a truly new understanding of universal human values. Today these symptoms are manifesting themselves with the greatest clarity and in the most active fashion here in our country.

Bovin: I think responsible politicians in the West are aware of the destructiveness and catastrophic consequences of nuclear war. And this, in my view, makes the likelihood of deliberate, premeditated general war extremely slight. Nobody wants to die.

Lukin: But there still exists the danger of unpremeditated war. In a situation in which nuclear and nonnuclear thresholds are becoming increasingly blurred, in which the process of management (including military management) is becoming increasingly computerized, in which the danger zone is sharply expanding to encompass space and the ocean's depths, and in which the decision-making process, including that for possibly fatal decisions, is being decentralized and automated, the ability to control events that arms-race technocrats confidently speak of is becoming increasingly problematical.

Bovin: No matter what they say, only nuclear disarmament, the elimination of nuclear weapons, can provide a 100 percent guarantee of survival.

Lukin: We need to consider many other things in this regard. For the objective is not simply to reduce the quantities of arms. We want to lessen the danger of war. Let's suppose that all nuclear weapons have been eliminated, and so the danger of nuclear war has been eliminated as well. But what about the danger of conventional war? Thatcher is not alone in believing that removing the nuclear hindrances and nuclear deterrence can increase the danger of nonnuclear wars, including large (world) wars. Don't you think it is still difficult to give an unequivocal answer to this question?

Bovin: Obviously, movement toward a nuclear-free world must be seen not as an isolated process but as one of the components constituting a new phase of détente. The first phase of détente, which culminated in the 1975 Helsinki Conference, failed to go beyond agreements on nuclear arms limitations. These were important and necessary agreements. Although they did not stop the arms race (especially the qualitative arms race), that phase set a precedent and pointed us in the right direction, and for this reason it was ultimately overturned by the militaristic faction of the American bourgeoisie.

The phase of détente that must take the place of that bygone phase is based on the experience of past years and on a deeper appreciation of the unique characteristics of the nuclear age—in other words, on new political thinking. It is based on real and significant arms reductions, both nuclear and conventional, on a well-considered set of confidence-building measures, and on gradual progress toward a comprehensive system of security. And in such a program, which allays suspicion and fear and promotes greater trust among states, one can see a nuclear-free world as a realistic prospect.

At this point we must return to the Soviet Union. Only on condition that restructuring proceed successfully and that our international influence grow accordingly—only then can a solution to the problem of disarmament become a reality.

Lukin: And that influence must grow in tandem with the strengthening of mutual trust. I'd go even further than that: The growing trust that people place in us must be the main form in which our increased influence manifests itself. But the question of the nature and parameters of our influence is crucial in this regard. And in this connection we have much to do and much to change. But what if the conditions you cited are not met?

Bovin: Then the other scenario for the end of the century will be realized. Our influence in the world will decline, and the difficulties confronting world socialism will mount. Capitalism will become more insolent and more aggressive. Global confrontation will intensify.

Lukin: It's difficult, no doubt, to speak such words. But they must be spoken and spoken clearly, in order to remind ourselves again and again of the enormous responsibility—responsibility of world-historical significance—that we Soviet communists and Soviet people have assumed in undertaking the restructuring of our society and in embarking on the path of democratization. The fate of restructuring will determine the fate of our country, the fate of the century, and the fate of the world.

Cooperatives and Socialism

Yuriy Alekseyevich Vasilchuk*

"If we rid economic-growth indicators of these factors (high petroleum prices and income from mass alcoholism—Yu.V.), we find that over practically the past four five-year plans, we have experienced no improvement in the absolute growth of national income, and that it actually began falling in the early 1980s. Such is the true picture, comrades!" (M.S. Gorbachev)

The slogans of the October Revolution—"Factories to the Workers!" "Land to the Peasants!" and "All Power to the Soviets!"—were more than just propaganda ideas that were understandable to people. They were the real, principal goals of the socialist revolution, its vital soul and genuine meaning. Behind those slogans was the awakening of millions of people as independent and responsible creators of the historical process. It was that human factor that ensured socialism's advantage in growth rates (just as it forged the victory over fascism), despite all the stupidities, the blunders, and the incompetence of highly important economic decisions.

The years of the personality cult and the administered economy turned this mass of people into a passive "labor force" and, for all intents and purposes, alienated them again from the ownership of factories and land, and from power in society, thereby giving rise to economic stagnation, mass indifference, lack of initiative, apathy, cynicism, and corruption. As a result, the ministries and departments responsible for ensuring the public's requirements for food, consumer goods, superior products and services, and housing proved incapable of meeting their responsibilities. Over the span of four five-year plans, our production of useful output has grown in a purely statistical sense (without regard for the quality of the goods that make up our national income, or for the cost-plus methods used in determining their "value," and without regard for the way that the "growth" in national income has been "locked away" in the form of above-normative inventories, long-term unfinished construction, and the like).

---

*Doctor of Economics, sector head at the U.S.S.R. Academy of Sciences' Institute of World Economy and International Relations (IMEMO). This article appeared in the July 1988 issue of *MEMO*.

Do we have untapped potential for restoring the economy's dynamism? Average hourly labor productivity at independently operated cooperatives is two to two-and-a-half times that at state enterprises of the same type. There is no need for oversight, record-keeping is simpler, and the needs of the buyer and client get better consideration. Under the lease contract, which is closely related to the cooperative, the gain in labor productivity amounts to 30 to 40 percent, on average. Additional family labor resources are enlisted in production, and much better use is made of land and other resources.[1] In both cases one is spared the need to make new, ruinous 100-billion-ruble investments, or to increase prices. One simply has to avoid keeping people from working. That is what initiative, a sense of proprietorship, and the replacement of bureaucratic management methods with economic ones will do for an economy!

The Law on Cooperatives in the U.S.S.R. (together with the Law on the State Enterprise and the Law on Individual Labor Activity) is intended to create appropriate conditions for this new stage in our society's development and for restoring socialism's advantages. The CPSU Central Committee has proposed for discussion a truly innovative draft of that law—a draft containing many provisions that are vitally important to the development of the cooperative movement. The draft differs fundamentally from the version drawn up in 1987 by the U.S.S.R. Ministry of Justice. In late 1987, Soviet scholars brought persuasive criticism to bear on the attempt by the U.S.S.R. Ministry of Justice to maintain cooperatives, under the new law, as bodies devoid of rights and subject to the direction and tutelage of various agencies. Thus, at a session of the U.S.S.R. Academy of Science's Learned Council, chaired by Academician A. Aganbegyan, specialists from various organizations called attention to the harm caused by articles on mandatory deliveries and plan assignments for cooperatives, and on "recommendations" concerning payment of members and distribution of earnings; they called attention to bureaucratic procedures for "authorizing" or barring cooperatives that impeded development of a mechanism for competition, and to the need for developing higher forms of cooperation based on the issuance of stock—such forms as associations and cooperative banks. Key questions on providing legal and ideological foundations for the cooperative movement were posed in trenchant form.

The new draft law addresses the main issue: repeatedly, in various areas and matters, it protects cooperatives' autonomy and independence, and asserts their socialist character and equal status in the

---

[1]See T. Koryagina, V. Rutgaizer, Yu. Sillaste, and E. Truve, "Paid Services and the Law on Cooperatives" (*Kommunist*, No. 6, 1988, pp. 97-101).

socialist economic system. "Recognition of the cooperative sector as a component part of the country's single national economic complex is the foundation—one might say the heart—of the new document," M.S. Gorbachev has stressed.[2] It lays the foundation for its mass development and for mobilizing our economy's immense untapped potential for growth. Naturally, as in any major law, it has its contradictory provisions and "stipulations," which zealous administrators will use to slow the development of cooperatives.[3]

M.S. Gorbachev's speech at the collective farmers' congress, and remarks made during the discussion of the draft law by a number of major figures in both the scholarly and practical fields set forth completely new theoretical arguments and concrete proposals that require restructuring both our thinking and our practices. I would like to deal at greater length with certain of those questions.

Essence of the Mass Cooperative Movement and the Principal Condition for its Development

In all countries of the world, working people's families wage a daily struggle to get their children—the world's next generation—"on their feet," to lead honest lives, and to relay that baton to the future. That is why millions of people are banding together in cooperatives today, pooling their work time, knowledge, and talent, giving up their free time, and risking their hard-earned savings or plots of land. That fundamental factor also determines the essence of cooperatives and the policy of complete, unswerving support for cooperatives followed by communists and progressive forces in all countries. The cooperative movement plays a direct role in ensuring the working masses' material necessities of life. Two other traits of cooperatives (in the area of production) further strengthen their progressive character. The fact that the production process assumes a collective form is not the whole story. More important is that the process is organized, managed, and overseen by the membership itself—a group that has voluntarily joined forces—and that it is their creative act and a democratic form of work that they engage in of their own free will. Drawing attention to the importance of labor collectives' initiative and personal involvement, M.S. Gorbachev stresses that the creativity of the masses cannot be replaced by directives—not even the very best of directives. Finally, a third trait: the product of the labor involved becomes the property of the people themselves who are doing the work and is

---

[2]M.S. Gorbachev, "Enlist Cooperatives' Potential in the Cause of Perestroika," *Pravda*, March 24, 1988.
[3]See Ye. Primakov, "Economics and Cooperatives," *Pravda*, March 20, 1988.

distributed by them as proprietors, on the basis of existing legislation and contractual relations among them.

If we sum up these principal, "ideal" traits of cooperatives, which play a direct role in meeting the working people's vital interests in the areas of both what is produced and what is acquired (both are deformed under the conditions of capitalism), we reach the conclusion that cooperatives are of an unmediated social and socialist nature. Of course, cooperatives reveal their socialist content most fully in socialist countries.[4]

Karl Marx saw workers' cooperatives as a positive, or substantive, abolition of capitalist-type production "in the context of capitalist-type production itself"—a breach in the old form of production and a transition to a new form of production.[5] The difficulty in understanding this question lies in the fact that this breach is opened by the working people's individual ownership.

The voluntary nature of cooperatives (under capitalism, it is a crime to violate the principle of voluntary membership) means that ownership of the cooperative is voluntarily "put together" from the mass of individual ownership and, under certain conditions, once again "disintegrates" into individual ownership, revealing that to be its foundation and its "cellular" building blocks.

"With the necessity of a natural process, capitalist production gives rise to its own negation," wrote Karl Marx. "It restores not private ownership but individual ownership on the basis of the capitalist era's achievements: on the basis of cooperatives and common ownership of land and of means of production produced by one's own labor."[6]

Contemporary cooperative ownership is the sort of social ownership[7] that is based on individual ownership and that serves this individual ownership: otherwise, the cooperative itself falls apart. In this situation, each working person subordinates himself to the common interests only when the interests of each person are served, and only then are the interests of all served—to the extent that such is possible while still operating within a capitalist framework. Therefore, to understand the essence and dialectics of social cooperative ownership, one must see its basis—present-day individual family ownership and the individual labor activity (ILA) that arises on its basis.

In the context of the scientific and technological revolution, individual family ownership functions primarily in the form of an

---

[4]*Ibid.*
[5]See K. Marx and F. Engels, *Works [Sochineniya]*, Vol. 25, Part I, pp. 481-485.
[6]K. Marx and F. Engels, *Works [Sochineniya]*, Vol. 23, p. 773.
[7]*Ibid.*

increasingly complex household that owns expensive housing; increasingly satisfies its desire for complex household appliances, electronics, and personal transportation; utilizes a broad spectrum of services and semiprepared foods of various kinds; and provides for the sort of quality and conditions of everyday life that are necessary for the reproduction of a complex, active, and capable work force—a mass of enterprising people who are long on initiative and capable of changing the shape and nature of production processes. Only with a "human factor" of this kind is it possible to maintain high production standards and a quality of goods and services that meets world standards— possible, that is, to ensure development of the scientific and technological revolution.

Today's household is one of the most capital-, energy-, and science-intensive spheres of social production—a sphere, moreover, that is unprofitable and a "money-loser" for the employee himself. In the context of present-day capitalism, it is also the most labor-intensive sphere of human activity, adding 40 to 50 percent to the national income, as reported in official statistics. And the economic situation of today's working class cannot be understood without taking account of the quantity and quality of the work performed inside the family, and the requirements born of it.

The lack of sufficient income to meet the new requirements for the development of today's family is giving rise to an expansion, within the family itself, of the production of goods for the market, to an expansion of ILA; it is an autonomous form of economic activity that consists of voluntary participation by the able-bodied population in the production and sale of goods or services for the purpose of earning income within the framework of existing laws. The veiled or open commodity-money form of this activity on the part of the producer proper distinguishes it both from noncommodity activities within the family, and from paid work in the cooperative and state sectors.

Today, ILA forms the largest part of the rapidly growing unofficial sector of the economy, and the part with the greatest mass participation.[8] Thus, in the United States in 1981 about 80 percent of families were engaging in some form of activity in the unofficial sector, and its scope was the most significant in precisely the families with high income levels (and new needs). According to U.S. economists' estimates, in 1976 the unofficial economy produced an additional 22 percent of gross national product, and in 1978 it was already producing 33 percent. Even if its growth as a percentage of the whole had slowed

---

[8]According to our economists' and sociologists' estimates, as expressed at the Learned Council in October 1987, in 1984 there were already 18 million people engaged in ILA in one form or other (T. Koryagina). In 1988, according to official data, 300,000 people had permission to engage in ILA.

in the 1980s (which remains to be proven), it would substantially exceed 40 percent of GNP in 1988. To characterize the results of family and individual labor activity that is not accounted for in today's statistics, one could say that it is, in the context of the scientific and technological revolution, already a figure almost equal in magnitude to that of the national income. Such is the scale of the unrecorded economic activity alone that today gives rise directly to individual ownership and, consequently, also makes possible the mass development of public ownership—cooperatives—on its basis. This process of mass conversion of ILA into cooperatives normally goes through a number of stages.

Incidental ILA occurs when the rendering of services and the performance of some sort of work on a person's own initiative is of an episodic, irregular, and even unforeseeable nature, such as occasionally transporting people headed for the same destination, incidental repair work, various sorts of assistance, and mutual assistance in caring for the sick or for children. The requirement that ILA be reported is generally ignored in cases of this kind and has a number of negative consequences (it limits people's possibilities for obtaining services and earning money, fosters a complacent public attitude toward lawbreaking, and puts incidental labor earnings on a par with criminal gains).

Regular ILA in one's free time, as a rule, means an immense increase in workload and a loss of free time, and is generally occasioned by the inadequacy of basic earnings to provide for a family's needs. The employee has already met his economic obligations to society at his basic job and is at liberty to dispose of his free time, spending it in a manner that benefits his family and society. This additional work, freely undertaken, deserves particular recognition and support on the part of the state and society. This purpose should be served by simplified registration, assistance, and constant efforts to popularize this sort of ILA. The economic effectiveness of regular ILA in the U.S.S.R. manifests itself in the fact that the approximately 3 percent of farm land utilized for that purpose yields almost a third of the nationwide production of many agricultural crops. The new U.S.S.R. Law on Individual Labor Activity sanctioned this form of ILA in 30 types of crafts and services. However, the need for annual renewal of one's permit to engage in ILA, and the difficulties with raw materials and marketing limit the development of this sector, destroy the competitive mechanism, and often create a monopoly position for a "select" group of the self-employed.

In bourgeois society, the registration of such ILA serves only the purpose of taxing the earnings in question, not the purpose of assisting such labor activity.

Full-time ILA as basic employment, for the purpose of ensuring stable basic earnings for the family, differs fundamentally from regular ILA. In this case, we are dealing with working people making free, autonomous, and economically purposeful use of their working time in order to provide earned income to satisfy their family's needs.

In the 1960s and 1970s the scientific and technological revolution substantially restructured that mass form of individual labor activity. Previously, in the early days of the century, such work had been based primarily on a person's own modest capital (or land) and relied on knowledge and skills acquired on a purely empirical basis. This kind of ILA was conducted primarily in the oldest, traditional branches, which were experiencing economic difficulties. The cooperatives that grew out of it existed as a means of survival—as a way for people to extricate themselves from extreme need through joint labor, labor often akin to penal servitude.

The new ILA of the 1980s is based primarily on the individual provider's extensive information; his knowledge of science, technology, and the humanities; his artistic taste; his understanding of aesthetics and the dictates of fashion; his overall sophistication in dealing with customers and clients; and his attention to the client's opinion and to public interests. Its development in new and dynamic areas (repairing household appliances, electronic equipment, and motor vehicles; inventing; health care and education) eases the transfer of the needed labor resources to those areas, eliminates shortages of goods, and stops the upward spiral of prices. Many achievements in the area of general culture, many scientific and technical discoveries, and entire branches of production have arisen as a result of this type of ILA. Here the spontaneous growth of small capital is increasingly being replaced by ownership derived from individual labor, ownership which is close to that of the working family in terms of its reproductive role, and is distinguished by its surmounting (often only partially) capitalist exploitation while remaining within a capitalist framework. In our country, because of the "traditions" of the 1930s, this type of ILA is not permitted. A number of socialist countries, however, have actually created public associations of ILA employees with their own party cells, designation of leading production workers, competitions, and exchanges of experience.

Associated ILA, i.e., the cooperative, grows out of full-time ILA as a result of the economic expediency of joint sales of output or joint raw-materials supply, the need to expand operations, the joint work of specialists in different fields, and cooperation among an array of full-time and temporary employees, specialists, and unskilled workers.[9]

---

[9]The pharisaical methods of "defending" cooperatives in the 1930s consisted of defaming that basis—working families' individual ownership—by alleging that it would inevitably lead, not to

This vital tie between the cooperative on the one hand, and individual and family labor activity on the other, is shown with particular clarity in a number of specific types of cooperatives. They include the consumer cooperative, whose role is to provide families with the needed assortment and quality of goods; the housing cooperative, which is speeding solution of this most urgent social problem; the dacha-orchard cooperative, without which it would be difficult today to solve the problem of providing needed recreation for families and children; and others. It becomes obvious that cooperatives can be, and are intended to be, a means for solving not only large-scale *economic* problems of socialist society, but also its highly important *social*—and, at the same time, *political*—problems related to directly satisfying the constantly growing requirements of the working person's family.

The mass character of the free cooperative is generally based on the mass development of its economic cell—individual ownership—thanks to the principle of voluntary membership and the possibility for that ownership to "free itself" from one association, exist in the form of ILA, and then join another, or yet a third association that is more in keeping with the interests of the family and the working person, and with the interests of the working person's rapid development as the principal productive force and creator of the scientific and technological revolution. This kind of oversight by a united group of individuals—to use Marx's expression—over their combined production differs fundamentally both from arbitrary rule over those individuals by means of money, capital, and the terms of exchange, and from the "planned" distribution of such individuals among industries and spheres and types of activity by decision from above. Barriers impeding the development of full-time ILA not only "dry up" the environment in which cooperatives develop but also create a harmful coercion syndrome. The difficult beginnings of our cooperative movement during the 1986 to 1988 period have not been due entirely to the difficult and undeveloped state of family and individual labor activity, and to the immense difficulties of everyday life—such as waiting lines and daily commutes that consume people's free time and energy. To this day an equally important role is played by various legal provisions and economic measures, shaped over the course of decades, for putting a stop to ILA—arbitrary limits on the earnings of autonomous employees and cooperative members, and accusations of money-grubbing.

The law on cooperatives, which differed so strikingly from the

---

cooperatives but only to capitalism. For this purpose, the organic tie between individual ownership and vitally important collectivist, proletarian processes in the masses' family work was concealed.

initial draft prepared by the Ministry of Justice, had yet to be adopted, but as early as March 14, 1988 (concurrently with the publication of N. Andreyeva's article), the Ministry of Finance succeeded in getting the Presidium of the U.S.S.R. Supreme Soviet to adopt a decree imposing such a steeply progressive tax on cooperative members' earnings that, should a wealthy cooperative close down, almost nine tenths of its assets would be confiscated in taxes. And the right to close a cooperative was granted by law to local government agencies—the direct recipients of those tax monies. Normally, the Supreme Soviet automatically confirms decrees of the Presidium. But this time the nationwide public discussion of the law prevented the decree's presentation for confirmation. In addition, a resolution of the U.S.S.R. Supreme Soviet states: "The procedure and timetable for imposing a progressive tax on the earnings of people working in cooperatives are established by legislative acts of the U.S.S.R."—in other words, by decree of the Presidium of the Supreme Soviet.

"The contribution of our cooperatives is tens to hundreds of times less than that of cooperatives in the European socialist countries," the U.S.S.R. Council of Ministers' Social Development Bureau stated.[10] The blame here also lies with our economic science, which completely ignores the unity of family, individual, and cooperative labor activity in the development of the scientific and technological revolution, and their crucial importance for the rate of economic growth and the development of socialism.[11]

Economic Functions of the Working People's Cooperative Property[12]

Individual ownership, in taking the form of cooperative and public ownership, secures for itself (i.e., the given family collective) the right to participate in determining working conditions and in apportioning the product. The development of cooperatively pooled individual ownership (as opposed to the mere growth of monetary earnings under the conditions of shortages) thereby becomes the measure of the quantity and quality of work performed by the family, that is, *the measure of the human being's development as the chief productive*

---

[10]*Argumenty i fakty* [*Arguments and Facts*], No. 14, 1988, p. 1.

[11]Typically, this was precisely the major source of disagreement among the scholars who prepared the discussion of this question at the Learned Council: Specialists on cooperatives (G. Faktor, N. Lushina, and others) considered it unnecessary to discuss simultaneously the question of housekeeping and family work, i.e., the question of individual ownership.

[12]Making clear the economic functions of cooperative ownership by the working people requires, at the outset, an analysis of the "ideal case"—a situation of mass development of cooperatives that enjoy full rights. Against this backdrop, the scale of the tasks confronting us in this sphere today, at the inception of a "system of civilized cooperatives," becomes even more apparent.

force. Naturally, in the context of the cooperative movement, differences in the extent of that ownership (given a fair evaluation of the quantity and quality of work) should be incomparably greater than under the wage-leveling form of apportionment at the present time. Cooperatives make it possible to surmount wage-leveling—the principal social injustice under socialism. That is the effect of the first function.

Today, the true quality and level of development or completeness of a product or service depend greatly on such possibilities as joint, collective work by specialists in related fields, on the combined work of a specialist and his assistants, on his "team" (part of which the cooperative needs only temporarily), on joint marketing and joint raw-material supply. This is the basis on which the new type of cooperative arises, a cooperative whose success depends not on work akin to penal servitude, or on the pooling of lands or of small amounts of capital, but on the scientific knowledge and culture of its employees. In connection with the lack of equivalence among people's production roles in the new cooperatives, the latter can be organized only on the basis of unequal shares and differing authority on the part of its various participants, or on the basis of hiring additional employees to work in the cooperative. Cooperatives in the West generally utilize both these necessary organizational and legal forms of relations among the employees themselves, forms that overcome wage-leveling without giving rise, beyond certain limits, to antidemocratic manifestations or to exploitation.

Voluntary cooperation, like no other form of collective work, is capable of awakening in the masses a sense of proprietorship, of personal responsibility, and of having a personal stake; it is capable of restoring the work ethic and industriousness that form the principal moral foundation and economic basis of every dynamic society and that some people, so it seemed, had lost forever. It is no accident that so much urgency attaches today to the problems of introducing economic accountability and the collective contract in our industry, and the brigade and family contract in our agriculture: we are mobilizing this great creative power of the cooperative, and its economic and psychological "mechanism," to bolster the very foundations of our society and the foundations of socialism in the state sector as well.

The party's strategy in agriculture consists essentially in making both state farms and collective farms into "essentially cooperative-type associations of contractual, economic-accountability collectives operating on the basis of contracts concluded with the collective-farm board and the state-farm directorate."[13] How revolutionary it is to put the

---

[13]M.S. Gorbachev, "Enlist Cooperatives' Potential in the Cause of Perestroika," *Pravda*, March 24, 1988.

question in these terms, when one considers that today, "collective farms and state farms are not given the possibility of disposing of their above-plan output and improving local supplies."[14] Not even their above-plan output!

Elimination of wage-leveling opens the way to new goods and services, and to new technologies and inventions that are up against a blank wall today. Our present-day society has already built up immense potential in the form of a creative, thinking intelligentsia, researchers, specialists, inventors, organizers, people with a keen sense of excellence, connoisseurs and creators of fashion, and creators of remarkable handcrafted articles and highly artistic works in hundreds of spheres of human endeavor. Every year, this environment gives rise to hundreds of thousands of inventions, unexpected ideas, and models of products that would embellish the life of any family and any society, and that would improve the standards and efficiency of our production. The principal social injustice for these people is leveling, not even in the payment of their labor but in the drab way that the very content of their work has been leveled, and in the way that the scope for their creative powers has been curtailed.

We all know dozens of stories in which these inventions, new-model machines and mechanisms, and masterpieces of craftsmanship and art never make it into production or reach the public. And then, many years later, they reach us with the label "made elsewhere" and are paid for in foreign exchange. A major enterprise, burdened with orders, mandatory deliveries, and the need to utilize certain equipment, personnel, or raw materials, is in no hurry to revamp its shops' operations at an inventor's "request." Most often what is needed in such cases is the creation of a new, relatively small, flexible work force of employee-enthusiasts with prospects for major gains (both material and nonmaterial), but also the risk of serious losses. That is precisely when there is a need for economic autonomy—for cooperatives. It bears recalling that even under capitalist conditions, giant laboratories and research centers belong to major companies and corporations, but the bulk of inventions and innovations are produced by enthusiasts in charge of small groups of employees.

The Law on Cooperatives in the U.S.S.R. contains a series of articles providing incentives to cooperatives for research and development and for introducing new methods and products (Articles 26, 28, and others). But where is the guarantee that an inventor (or an artist, model-maker, or other specialist) who is a cooperative member will receive true compensation for his work, should it yield any sort of serious economic benefits? A new approach is needed to the entire

---

[14]*Pravda* editorial, April 19, 1988.

problem of assessing the results of intellectual and artistic labor—to the problem of intellectual property.

When freed from cooperative relationships in certain production spheres, individual ownership can quickly be applied in other, more promising spheres where demand from consumers or producers is great. This is quite a different thing from an employee's being fired against his will, as would be the case at a private or state-owned enterprise—it is an autonomous and responsible decision by the cooperative itself. Thus, in the context of a freely developing cooperative movement, individual ownership figures as a means of moving material and financial resources, and technical and other knowledge and abilities between spheres and branches of economic activity (the second function).

The paralysis of this process of moving people and resources to the production of useful goods and services most needed by society surfaces in the form of a "creeping spread of shortages."[15] Even under modern capitalist conditions there is an increasingly urgent sense of the need for cooperatives and a mass of self-employed people to exist alongside the giant private and state-run corporations. It might seem that these corporations can make everything better and for less money by taking advantage of the superiority of the larger production facility. However, in the 1970s and 1980s it has been precisely the largest corporations that have seen the growth—at the points where they intersect with other companies and other spheres—of "lacunae" of varied and individualized mass demand, both large and rapidly changing in relation to the range of products. As a rule, large corporations do not manage to take these changes into account. And in fact, for them, small production runs often fail even to recover their costs. Cooperatives (with self-employed individuals and small private firms) effectively supply this economic "risk sector" with production that does not lend itself to planning (as does production in the sector where monopolies prevail) or programming (as in the sector of large oligopolistic associations).

In our circumstances, the production and market sectors of the economy that are never penetrated by the sluggish associations and ministries, and where various shortages develop, are not just

---

[15]See V. Popov and N. Shmelev, "The Anatomy of a Shortage," *Znamya [Banner]*, May 1988, pp. 158-183. The authors rightly show the impossibility of an *administrative* solution to the problem of an optimal distribution of employees and resources among various production facilities in the context of a developed economy. However, they ultimately come to the conclusion that the autonomous movement of employees among the various sectors poses the danger of "rising prices and earnings differentials that are not always justified." In this case the costs of an insufficiently developed economic mechanism are found to be its organic defects. For does not this argument justify measures for regulating the economy and equalizing "unfair" earnings? Unrestricted trade is precisely what makes it possible to put an end to shortages—in other words, to rising prices.

lacunae—they are whole seas and oceans. It is the market sector—by nature an unplanned sector with constantly changing demand—that needs individualized, small-series production. No incantations or resolutions can remove it from our economy (or any other). It is important to see that these shortages do not only give rise to speculation, waiting lines, undue use of influence, and erode public morale: a shortage of one good in the state sector gives rise to a second shortage, and then a third—this time in the cooperative sector. The state sector is precisely where goods in demand find themselves getting "held back" for use in subsequent trades, or becoming the subject of allocations and ceilings, according to the law of chain reactions. And as a result, growing shortages undermine the entire economic planning mechanism. We have no small businesses to deal with shortages that can be eliminated by short production runs, and the all-out development of cooperatives that compete with one another is a way of fighting to maintain the principles of a planned economy, and of combating speculation and waiting lines—combating the shortages engendered not only by bad management in the state sector but also by the impossibility of planning everything in advance.

At the root of our shortages and waiting lines there lies a fundamental discrepancy between the present-day structure of employment and the requirements of developing the scientific and technological revolution. If the process of industrialization meant the transfer of more than a third of the working population from agriculture to industry, then the scientific and technological revolution means the need for an equally great shift of working people to the service sector, which constitutes the most dynamic part of the "risk sector." And this is understandable, since the scientific and technological revolution gives rise to a sharp increase in the importance of the human factor—of a sophisticated and knowledgeable employee. It is precisely to create that factor that 60 to 70 percent of the people working in the West's major economic centers are engaged in service-sector work today.

However, that sort of "civilizing of the economy" requires immense capital investment in the social and commercial infrastructure and means the inevitable loss of a significant portion of the industrial work force. Cooperatives ease the solution of both these problems. They go a long way toward freeing the state budget from setting aside additional funds for investment, and they significantly reduce industry's labor losses as a result of cooperatives' higher output and their enlistment of pensioners, students, housewives, and others, in the work process. In addition, in connection with the transition to full economic accountability and cost-recovery, many enterprises will inevitably discover a labor surplus. The working people themselves can ensure that it is used in an efficient and well-compensated fashion, if given the possibility of joining the new cooperatives and if the bureaucratic stumbling blocks are removed.

The amassing of public wealth in the form of "human capital" or the "human factor"—society's principal productive force—is the next function of individual ownership. Despite the large role that the service sector plays in these matters, the sole source of this process is individual property itself and the working person's family, which pays for all the services (including cost-free education and health care, which are supported by taxes). This third function is particularly important in the age of the scientific and technological revolution.

According to American economists' estimates, in 1982 it already cost an average of $237,000 to reproduce one employee (with two years of a state college behind him).[16] However, apart from financial outlays, that total includes only the lost wages of the mothers of the families in question, and not the entire "value added"—it does not take full account of the father's work in the home, and, most important, the regular everyday work of the young man himself, his many years of increasingly complex work on his own development. When all that is taken into consideration, the estimate has to be at least doubled. In addition, almost half of all young people now complete a full higher education.

Today, the baby-boom generations of the first stage of the scientific and technological revolution (the 1960s), when the annual birthrate exceeded the 4-million mark, are reaching the age of 25. Consequently, even with average expenditures of $400,000 per person, each annual contingent of the population entering the work force carries with it about $1.6 trillion worth of accumulated human labor, which surpasses in scale—and surpasses by a gigantic margin—the gross accumulation of material wealth.[17]

In addition, a central proposition of our political economy's treatment of capitalism (and a central thesis of textbooks on the subject) is still the thesis, descended from the age of industrialization, that the sole source of accumulation is surplus value. That being the case, it follows as well that the more one takes from the working people's individual property and turns over to banks and companies for investment, the higher the rate of economic growth. And the trade unions

---

[16]See *America in Perspective. Major Trends in the United States Through the 1990s*, Boston, 1986, p. 14.

[17]The earlier stages of this process have been examined: Yu. A. Vasilchuk, *The Scientific and Technological Revolution and the Working Class Under Capitalism* [*Nauchno-tekhnicheskaya revolyutsiya i rabochiy klass pri kapitalizme*], Moscow, 1980, Chap. 4; *Characteristic Features of the Process of Accumulation in Developed Capitalist Countries* [*Osobennosti protsessa nakopleniya v razvitykh kapitalisticheskikh stranakh*], Moscow, 1978; *Levels and Trends of Development of the Major Capitalist Countries* [*Urovni i tendentsii razvitiya glavnykh kapitalisticheskikh stran*], Moscow, 1977.

that oppose that are impeding the process of accumulation. In actual fact, the opposite is the case: under the conditions of the scientific and technological revolution, the principal source for the accumulation of public wealth is precisely the full-fledged functioning of individual ownership, on the basis of which individual labor activity and cooperatives grow.

Of course, the development of this process in capitalist conditions becomes possible only as the result of an intense class struggle and, in and of itself, merely creates the main *possibility* for the transition to a system of civilized cooperatives and forms a civilized employee.

Under our conditions, cooperatives, which have raised working families' earnings to a level sufficient for raising an average of two children, are also called upon to accomplish this central task—the formation of a new employee and consumer, and the transition to the scientific and technological revolution. At present, the state sector still does not provide earnings of that sort.[18] Cooperatives and individual labor activity can and must accomplish this task of raising earnings to 500 to 800 rubles a month without increasing prices, since an increase in monetary earnings in that system is based not on "paper" or unsalable output, but on real growth in the production of competitive goods and useful objects that are eagerly bought by the public.[19]

But that requires a *mass* development of these spheres of activity to a scale comparable to that of the "risk sector" in Western countries, where 50 to 60 percent of those employed presently work.

Economic-Law Problems of a "System of Civilized Cooperatives"

We have so far examined two elements that are necessary for the formation of a "system of civilized cooperatives": (1) the development of individual ownership and the formation of a civilized employee, and (2) the mass development of enterprises belonging to the working people themselves. A third, economic-law element is the development of a *joint-stock form* of these cooperatives. "Capitalist joint-stock enterprises, like cooperative factories, should be regarded as transitional forms in the progression from capitalist-type production to associated production," wrote Karl Marx, "only in the one, the opposition (between labor and capital—Yu.V.) is eliminated in a negative fashion, while in the other it is done positively"[20] (i.e., in the first case, in form only, while in the second, in substance). In a capitalist context,

---

[18]With two children, even the relatively high earnings of a shop supervisor and leading engineer (300 and 230 rubles a month) go primarily for food, clothing, and necessary minor expenditures. Families with two children are now considered "large" (see *Pravda*, April 6, 1988).
[19]Don't our political-economy textbooks so steadfastly resist the term "useful items" because it is dangerous for enterprises that operate perfunctorily, merely to fulfill their plans?
[20]K. Marx and F. Engels, *Works* [*Sochineniya*], Vol. 25, Part I, p. 484.

the functioning of the means of production in the form of individual ownership and that ownership's "transformation itself into the form of stock is still constrained by the capitalist framework."[21] The constraining factor in our country is the practice—descended from War Communism and still flourishing—of issuing direct commands both to state enterprises and to cooperatives. And the perception of this practice as the norm and as an advantage of socialism led to the rejection of the joint-stock form as "capitalist." To all intents and purposes, this attitude toward the joint-stock form of cooperative was fully preserved in the Ministry of Justice's 1987 draft. In this connection, the theses of the report discussed by the Learned Council of the Institute of the World Economy and International Relations in October 1987 stressed: "2.11. The highest forms of cooperative are by no means its most simplified forms. On the contrary, the highest forms, which entail the mastery of new technology; the application of new ideas, knowledge, and R&D results; people's assumption of reasonable business risks with their own funds, etc., require complex (and not simplified) monetary relations, both within the cooperative and between it and the tax, financial and other agencies."

After further substantiating the need for the joint-stock form of cooperative, the report went on to conclude that the draft law on cooperatives drawn up by the ministry blocked the development of the highest forms of cooperatives and the modernization of technology with cooperatives' own funds. It is very gratifying that the Law on Cooperatives in the U.S.S.R. that has now been adopted includes the basic provisions necessary for their development in joint-stock form. True, in this respect there are still a number of unclear questions that lend themselves to arbitrary interpretation and that hamper movement of stocks and mobilization of the public's funds. The civilizing significance of joint-stock forms of accounting for production assets also lies in the fact that it is directly related to the need for modernizing the entire credit and monetary system and for restoring both the economic role of autonomous state and cooperative banks, and the role of interest rates as an indicator of, and incentive for, effective investment and economic activities; it is also related to reducing inflationary pressures from the public's savings deposits and cash reserves.

When a cooperative mobilizes its own monetary resources through a system of shares or stock certificates, a reasonable and necessary risk becomes a risk "with one's own money" and not with funds borrowed from the state. Economic operations of this kind require the right to make rapid decisions (without first clearing them in detail) on such matters as setting prices, buying raw materials, making

---

[21]*Ibid.*, p. 483.

other business arrangements, paying labor (naturally, with subsequent accountability to shareholders and stockholders for the cooperative's assets, to employees for wages, and so on).

At the same time, the Law on Cooperatives in the U.S.S.R. requires that all such decisions be cleared with the general meeting, and it gives that body the right to check up, without limit, on every step taken by the board and the chairmen. What's more, the cooperative's management is accountable before the law for losses (eschew risks!), and large gains are also punishable ("wrongful enrichment"). If, in the normal course of business, economic measures are required in an area not stipulated in the charter, then a revised charter must be reconfirmed by the soviet executive committee—otherwise, there is a danger of dissolution of the cooperative. Cooperatives can buy things in stores only from a list of goods approved by the soviet executive committee. The draft law already contained a regular palisade of restrictions on cooperatives' economic initiative, which created conditions for administrative control of prices and for the imposition of departmental normative rates, state orders from agroindustrial committees, production plans, and more.[22] These restrictions are inevitably augmented with new instructions and resolutions by departments and local government bodies "in the interests of cooperatives' development." Take a look at this announcement-cum-threat that was published in *Zdravnitsa Kavkaza* [*Caucasus Health Resort*] in January 1988:

> FOR YOU, SKILLED CRAFTSMEN: "The management of the Goryachevodsk-settlement market has set up, on the market grounds, locations for the sale of consumer goods made by cooperatives and persons engaged in individual labor activity.
> Market hours are from 8:00 a.m. to 1:00 p.m. on Saturdays and Sundays.
> Persons selling goods in other than the established places will have their permits and licenses confiscated and will be subject to fines.

Naturally, cooperative members will soon learn to get around all such prohibitions. Naturally, those who do the checking will soon learn to expose all such violations, threatening the cooperatives with confiscation of their permits and licenses, and with abolition. The soviet executive committee has the right to close down a highly successful cooperative and receive almost 50 percent of its assets. The cooperative "can protest" to the courts or to the next higher soviet executive committee. The level of earnings of cooperative members (given their limited numbers and retention of a monopoly position in the region)

---

[22]Our periodical press and television have worked this topic over rather fully, and a number of such restrictions have been removed in the new law.

and of the multitude of people who check on them (burdened by concerns for their families' needs) are doubtless about 800 rubles and 200 rubles, respectively. The situation is by no means easy for either side.[23] The strict regulatory measures not only fetter the activities of cooperative members but also create an atmosphere of instability and uncertainty about the cooperative's future. Hence the attempt to "get everything they can" today, even if it means the violation of quality standards, high prices, and unhappy consumers. So much for "civilized cooperative members"! Even today, bureaucratic limitations cut off a lot of honest people wanting to engage in individual or collective labor; they thereby weaken competition in that area, create "cooperative monopolists," and at the same time, lay the basis for corruption of the administrative apparatus itself.

It would seem, however, that all parties (except the consumer) can feel satisfied. The cooperatives' members are not threatened by mass competition, the local soviets receive revenues from the cooperatives' earnings, the Ministry of Finance is spared the need to spend money on local communities' social needs, enterprises and the U.S.S.R. State Committee on Labor and Social Questions are not threatened with an exodus of manpower,[24] the trade network remains without competition (except for the morning hours of Saturday and Sunday), the economic-management departments have somebody to blame for price increases, the local authorities are no longer quite as responsible for the poor supply of consumer goods (there is another guilty party), the State Committee on Material and Technical Supply gets to keep its system of allocations and its apportionment of resources (try repairing motor vehicles and electronic devices, or making furniture, if you have no spare parts, or no wood), and the cooperatives are monitored by constant checks. What we have would seem to be a clear picture of yet another dying attempt to civilize the economy (many cooperatives that have already been "registered" are still inactive).

However, the actual situation is quite different, in that the law on cooperatives (together with the law on the enterprise and the law on individual labor activity) truly creates the possibility for a long-overdue

---

[23]On this question there was a major difference of opinion among specialists on the Learned Council. The report proposed maximum separation of cooperatives from the local administration, in view of collective farms' dismal experience. It proposed that cooperatives could be closed only through the courts, that there be close ties between cooperative members and the banks, and that the authority of local administrations be restricted to the simple registration of cooperatives, with recourse to the courts in cases where cooperatives break the law. Specialists on cooperatives in the service sector thought maximum "involvement" of the local soviets to be necessary.

[24]In the law itself, the development of individual labor activity and cooperatives is presumed to be based, as in the past, primarily on disabled workers, pensioners, and other persons who are either unneeded by the other sectors or who work in cooperatives in their free time from regular full-time jobs.

transfer of one fourth to one third of all employment to the service sector. The era of shortages, waiting lines, and administrative arbitrariness cannot continue under conditions of glasnost and democratization, conditions where it is possible to shift to individual or cooperative work with good earnings. Under such conditions the crucial question becomes the legal realm and the real guarantee of cooperative members' rights—*the transition to a socialist state ruled by law.*[25] The legal reform that is now on the agenda must bring the adopted legislation *in fact* into the lives of the millions.

What is particularly important in this regard? A *well-functioning system of full compensation for illegally caused damage* is vitally important for modern-day cooperatives. This requires not only development of appropriate legislation but, above all, creation of an economically competent people's court that is truly immune from outside interference and that is not bound by decades of accumulated departmental instructions and arbitrary administrative acts that are fettering economic initiatives in the state sector today. And of course, the state arbitration service, acting in place of the court, is quite unable to perform that role.[26] What is needed is restoration of a juridical culture in the state sector itself, and development of that process through the entire economy (the introduction of appropriate changes in the Criminal Code, the Code of Labor Laws, and other codes and legislative acts). What is needed is a legal guarantee of the rights and genuine autonomy of the leaders of perestroika at the local level.[27]

Creating a well-ordered environment of competing cooperatives and self-employed workers, Europeanizing the way that people interact and the external appearance of streets and cities, and getting the public to become more actively involved in work and in a cultured everyday life is a protracted and complex process of developing entire generations over a period of decades—a process that cannot be accomplished by short-term campaigns or by instructing enterprises each to set up two or three cooperatives of "their own." Meanwhile, a single decree by the central government is all it would take to destroy an environment of this kind. Therefore, what is needed here are constitutional guarantees and the creation of a body to ensure them—a Constitutional Court.[28]

---

[25]See the lead article in *Pravda*, May 12, 1988.

[26]See A. Vengerov, "Whose Side Is the Arbitration Service on?" *Sotsialisticheskaya industriya* [*Socialist Industry*], May 3, 1988. Judges' low salaries, their real dependence on local and higher bodies and officials and on the prosecutor's office, the controllability of the people's assessors (who must sign any and all verdicts)—all these have created "a truly unique judicial practice devoid of acquittals" (see *Kommunist*, No. 7, 1988, p. 94).

[27]See V. Savitskiy, "The 'Open Commission,' or Why the Bureaucrats Are Triumphant," *Literaturnaya gazeta* [*Literary Gazette*], May 11, 1988.

[28]See *Kommunist*, No. 7, 1988, p. 41.

The U.S.S.R. Constitution stipulates the CPSU's leading role. However, the draft Law on Cooperatives in the U.S.S.R. stated that the Party organization "directs the work of the entire collective" and "oversees the work of the board (or chairman) of the cooperative" (Art. 5, Pt. 3)—in other words, exercises direct management of the cooperative's business activities.[29] After the nationwide discussion of the draft, the Supreme Soviet removed that provision from the law. Even after that discussion, however, provisions were retained that need to be checked for their conformity to the Constitution—for example, Point 5 (p. 12), which specifies that cooperative members with any sort of conviction for "mercenary crimes" are deprived for life of their rights as producers.

However, the most serious legal problem is that of drawing up effective legislation to put a stop to monopolistic tendencies in cooperatives. In the United States, laws of this kind, which protect the consumer, came into being in the form of "antitrust" legislation. In Western Europe, they take the form of legislation dealing with limitations on commerce and competition, with consumer protection, and so on. In our situation, such legislation is particularly important in connection with the established monopoly position of the bulk of enterprises in the state sector. For example, "according to plan," our industry produces one blouse per year for every 10 women. This gives rise to shortages, to arrogance on the producer's part, and to high, monopoly-type prices (up to 50 rubles and more for a simple garment). The situation is exactly the same for such items as coats, or comfortable shoes. And the consumer is prepared to pay a great deal more for high-quality goods. As a result, after 10 years of economic stagnation, prices for children's shoes, for example—and for many other goods, as well— have risen 60 percent, while quality has deteriorated.[30] The cooperatives coming into being under those conditions are also monopolistic and find it possible to raise prices even higher and to skimp on quality even more (while reacting flexibly to fashion and to people's widespread, strong desire to eat without having to stand in line, to obtain needed information, and so on).

Of course, antimonopoly legislation to protect the consumer can work when what we are dealing with is the *exception*, and not the general rule. Therefore, the decisive factors are the mass nature of the cooperative sector and the creation, on that basis, of a healthy competitive environment that eliminates shortages. This process can be accelerated by offering the employees of many small enterprises the

[29]The power and authority of the Party are based not on its authority as established by law, but on its effective daily work among the masses. See V. Selivanov, "On the Party's Power and Authority," *Pravda*, March 31, 1988.
[30]See *Pravda*, March 31, 1988.

right to decide whether to shift to operating on the basis of a collective contract or as a cooperative, either leasing or buying out fixed assets. This would result in increasing society's income by producing a substantial growth in labor productivity, a new impetus to update equipment, an improvement in production efficiency, and the elimination of unprofitable enterprises; it would also bring about a real improvement in the state's financial health. This proposal (put forward in the report to the Learned Council) was also included in general form in the law.[31]

In this connection it would be well to recall that in the West, in the capital-intensive branches of production, the shift to collective worker ownership of an enterprise entails the buy-out of stock worth immense sums of money. In the 1970s, left-wing social democrats in a number of West European countries put forward programs for buy-outs of this kind through mandatory annual contributions to special funds managed by the trade unions. It is indicative that no other measure proposed by the reformist workers' parties that were in power at the time sent the rightists into such a rage. The bourgeois mass media regarded this policy of creating worker (or trade union) forms of collective stock ownership as a threat to the very economic foundations of their capitalist system. In our conditions, such measures would strengthen the foundations of our socialist system.

In presenting the new draft law to the Supreme Soviet, Chairman of the U.S.S.R. Council of Ministers, N.I. Ryzhkov, stressed with great disappointment the fact that we are still doing a poor job of repaying our debt to the peasantry: "If we want to be objective, then the price of all our industrialization, science, and culture, historically speaking, was paid by the countryside," but the village "remains, for the most part, poor and devoid of amenities." The prosecutors there "have still not cooled their ardor for combating 'nonlabor' earnings," the collective farms owe an immense, 88-billion-ruble bank debt, and measures were taken that, "objectively speaking, were aimed at destroying the village."[32] The new law raises the possibility of restoring social justice in our society.

The new law on cooperatives creates conditions for establishing whole systems of interactive organizations in the cooperative- and individual-labor sectors, including associations of producers (both individual and cooperative) or unions of cooperative members that monitor the quality of the goods and services being produced; con-

---

[31]T. Koryagina, V. Rutgaizer, Yu. Sillaste, and E. Truve raise the question of the need for the concrete elaboration of this provision of the law (see *Kommunist*, No. 6, 1988, p. 98). It is regrettable that all the questions that were in dispute at the Learned Council were found to be petty and insignificant by M. Antonov, who was so hard on us (see *Moskva* [*Moscow*], No. 3, 1988, p. 14).

[32]See N.I. Ryzhkov, "On the Role of Cooperatives in Developing the Country's Economy and the Draft Law on Cooperatives in the U.S.S.R.," *Pravda*, May 25, 1988.

sumer associations that research goods and services and inform buyers about them; and associations of persons engaged in individual labor (with their own party organizations and their own leading workers). The forms of activity of public organizations of this kind abroad are well known and quite effective. Adequate information and, above all, the development of high-quality economic statistics are an important condition for success of that sort in our country.

Cooperative and individual labor activity must become a *party matter*, with its own mass-information systems, newspapers, and magazines, and its own leading production workers, party organizations, and government awards. That is by no means to say that the administrative management methods of departments and state institutions must be transferred to this sphere.[33] I have in mind something quite different—public recognition of the full worth and social significance of any and all civilized work by people in a socialist society. This is the historical importance of the Law on Cooperatives in the U.S.S.R.

*   *   *

The internationalist importance of cooperatives is universally recognized. Cooperative members are organized today in the influential International Cooperative Alliance (ICA), which in 1986 already comprised national unions with a membership of over 500 million from 80 countries (membership was 350 million in 1972). In contrast to the international trade union movement, which has the same mass character but is politically divided, cooperative members from various social systems and of various political orientations have maintained, for almost 70 years now, a tradition of joint internationalist defense of the working people's interests.

As yet, cooperatives have established themselves as a truly powerful economic force primarily in the most developed capitalist countries. They comprise tens and hundreds of millions of "civilized cooperators," together with their own enterprises, trade networks, banks, training systems, common associations, and influential publications. These are active people confident of their capabilities.

Our foreign-economic relations are presently geared to major corporations. The new law, which grants cooperatives and unions of cooperatives the right and opportunity to conduct direct import-export operations and scientific and technological, production, and other joint activities with foreign organizations, will obviously permit an expan-

---

[33]"The work of the Central Union of Consumers' Cooperatives and of its organizations has essentially lost such important cooperative attributes as self-management, initiative, and enterprise. The cooperatives have essentially become bureaucratized," noted M.S. Gorbachev in addressing the Fourth All-Union Collective Farmers' Congress (*Pravda*, March 24, 1988).

sion of business cooperation with that sector of the world economy as well.

Under capitalism, cooperatives have to wage a difficult and constant struggle against three main adversaries. First, there are the monopolistic associations that strive either to destroy the cooperative sector or to subject the cooperatives to their power—to crush them under their subsidiaries or enterprises. Second, there are the political and even gangster-style mafias that will use any method to see that complaisant managers are put in charge of cooperatives, enabling them to utilize these collective undertakings in their own political or economic interests. It is characteristic that the fascist regimes in Italy, Germany, Spain, and elsewhere subjected the entire network of cooperative organizations to utter devastation. And third, there is the state bureaucracy, the functionaries who appropriate the right to interfere in cooperatives' internal affairs—the right to regulate their activities and distribute their earnings. Among the cooperatives' adversaries, high-sounding words about the public interest commonly used as a screen for venal class interests of an extreme-right-wing, even dictatorial type. Therefore, in the international cooperative movement, the principles of fighting against the monopolies, for democracy, against bureaucracy, and for social progress and internationalist economic and political cooperation are closely entwined. Now we will be able to participate even more actively in that mass, internationalist movement.

The creative force of cooperatives takes different forms in different production systems, and even in different sectors of one and the same system. To view these differences without prejudice, to understand their origins and consequences, and to properly assess cooperatives' capabilities and needs in differing conditions is to ensure the correctness of the decisions being taken and the correctness of communists' policy, both in our country and abroad. The new law creates the conditions necessary for that to happen.

Ideology in an Interconnected World

SERGEY VASILYEVICH PRONIN*

Invitation to a Discussion: With the publication of S. Pronin's and I. Osadchaya's articles, the journal begins the discussion of pressing problems involving the relationships between opposing ideologies, between Marxist and other scientific concepts in the context of the development of all-around cooperation between the socialist and capitalist countries and the establishment of the new political thinking. In opening this discussion, the editors proceed from the obvious need to overcome a number of obsolete stereotypes regarding the ideological struggle and non-Marxist social science, stereotypes which took root during the period of stagnation and in many respects impeded the creative development of Marxist-Leninist scientific thought. Let us hope that the journal's authors and readers will take part in the discussion that we are beginning.

The concept put forward by the 27th CPSU Congress of a contradictory but interdependent and, in many respects, integral world confronts Marxist social science with a good many tasks related to reinterpreting the theoretical aspects of the rivalry between the two systems. The new thinking demands the abandonment of rigid and fixed ideas about the most complex processes of our times, including ideas about the nature of the ideological struggle between capitalism and socialism under the conditions of peaceful coexistence between them. Considering the prospects for a historically lengthy period of such coexistence, it is important to answer the following questions:

• If the development of social relations is increasingly characterized by the existence of multiple variants, and the global requirements of present-day civilization are causing an intensification of material and cultural exchange between systems, should not the traditional confrontation between Marxism-Leninism and non-Marxist ideologies be complemented by contacts between them along certain lines?

• To what extent does the development of non-class-specific systems of values fit into the concept of the irreconcilability of class struggle, and is there a danger of "ideological convergence" as the

---

*Doctor of history, department head at the U.S.S.R. Academy of Sciences' Institute of the International Workers' Movement. This article appeared in the October 1988 issue of *MEMO*.

result of an exchange between ideas formed within the context of communist ideology on the one hand, and non-Marxist theories of social development on the other, or will such an exchange help strengthen Marxist theoretical positions?

By way of discussing the specific features of the ideological struggle between the two systems in the present situation, and the prospects for the future of that struggle, let us attempt to answer these questions.

The "Commonalities" of Socioeconomic Systems
Versus Class Struggle

The central idea of Marxism pertaining to the prospects for universal human civilization comes down to the notion that liberated labor should bring humanity freedom from the calamities engendered by class exploitation and antagonism among nations and states. That is, Marxism as an ideology claims to be not only the world view of a single class, but also a "universal human imperative," a theory of the development of the human being and humanity. It is Marxism that assumes the difficult task of searching for interconnections between the "engine" of history that the class struggle represents and the progress of universal human civilization.

Historical experience shows how complex the accomplishment of that task is. In the first place, the class struggle itself by no means guarantees inevitable, ubiquitous, and immediate progress.

In the second place, as experience indicates, the destruction of class oppression does not necessarily mean that the solution of universal human problems is imminent, since countries' specific national features and the diversity of peaceful and nonpeaceful paths of social development create a complex mechanism of interaction between the class struggle and historical progress.[1]

In the third place, the well-known thesis that capitalism is a brake on social progress, while true in a very general, world-historical sense, should not be interpreted in an oversimplified fashion as a kind of absolute truth that is always applicable everywhere. The facts show that the development of capitalism may contribute, albeit inconsistently, to the material and spiritual progress of humanity in a number of spheres of social life.

All these contradictions of the present-day world require theoretical interpretation, especially since many dogmatic, oversimplified, one-sided interpretations accumulated in Marxist social science during the long period of stagnation.

---

[1]*Pravda*, April 13, 1988.

The interpretation of class and ideological contradictions within capitalism and between capitalism and socialism that was characteristic of many of our writings from the 1930s through the 1970s can serve as an example. "In objective reality there is not and cannot be any merger of the interests of exploiters and exploited, any unification and synthesis between a society based on private capitalist enterprise and a society where public ownership prevails," noted one work from those years.[2]

In a general sense, this postulate is seemingly correct—the broad historical process of the replacement of capitalist production relations by socialist production relations can be viewed as confirming it. But every truth is concrete. Turning the most rational idea into an absolute without taking the dialectics of objective and subjective reality into account frequently leads to an impasse. A categorical assertion of the incompatibility of the two social systems, as we have in this case, ignores such a reality as the integral nature of the present-day world. Moreover, the incompatibility of the two types of ownership leaves aside a number of important questions: questions concerning the multisectoral nature [mnogoukladnost] of the systems, the socialization processes that take place regardless of forms of ownership or on the basis of private capitalist ownership, the possibilities of using public ownership as a means of exploitation, etc. The further development of the author's train of thought in the work just cited also leads to dubious and often incorrect conclusions. Thus, in order to sharpen the work's immediate sociopolitical thrust, the author categorically states that the socialist and capitalist "systems of ideas are antithetical and, consequently, irreconcilable throughout their entire content. No matter what urgent and important present-day issue we turn to . . . in every instance we discover, in the final analysis, diametrically opposed class positions and appraisals that are irreconcilable in the same way that science and pseudoscience, truth and falsehood, and progress and reaction are irreconcilable." This way of putting the question does not square with reality. It is also insupportable in a theoretical sense, since it ignores the philosophical law that the category of the specific is complemented by the category of the general, and that the two categories are interconnected. One can see how this occurs by analyzing the connection between ideologies, on the one hand, and the struggle and consciousness of the masses, on the other.

It is indisputable that class antagonism between labor and capital feeds the antagonism between the two ideologies. But the opposition between social subjects and their ideologies is a fairly lengthy process

---

[2]Ye. D. Modrzhinskaya, *Leninism and the Present-Day Ideological Struggle* [*Leninizm i sovremennaya ideologicheskaya borba*], Moscow, 1972, pp. 29, 31-32.

in which classes and ideologies not only mutually negate one another but also interact, take into account—in their own development—ideas developed by their adversary, and vie in solving the problems of their era.

Furthermore, it is important to keep in mind that the arsenal of means that the bourgeoisie uses to maintain its dominant position includes not only violence against the sociopolitical forces opposing it but also the co-option of its class opponents. There is yet a third condition for their coexistence. The class and ideological struggle unfolds against the backdrop of class-neutral, objective processes: scientific and technological progress, the progressive development of productive forces, the internationalization of production and social life, the rationalization of social structures and managerial functions, the exacerbation of the problems of environmental protection and public morality, etc. The partial, temporary, but diverse ways in which the interests of even antagonistic classes coincide in these areas are obvious. "Interaction exists in international life as it does in the internal life of peoples,"[3] G.V. Plekhanov noted.

With respect to the question of interclass "commonalities," V.S. Semenov formulates this idea as follows: "The matter should not be reduced simply to establishing the existence in society of several types of commonality among people and the existence of systems of differences; rather, one must clarify their common basis, which is the method of production, taken as a whole. . . . One and the same basis leads in one case to the development and manifestation of 'nonsocial' [nesotsialnyye] societal differences, while in another case it leads to 'social' [sotsialnyye] societal differences; in one case it leads to 'nonsocial' societal groupings, while in another case it leads to 'social' societal commonalities."[4]

In real life, as we know, ideologies are closely related to mass consciousness. The latter reflects the interests of individuals, the family, groups, organizations, classes, nations, countries and humanity; the further one goes, the more complicated things get in connection with the differentiation of economic and political institutions, the stratification of social, ethnic and sociocultural groups, etc. In this connection, the differentiation of mass consciousness comes to the forefront. But along with that differentiation, as G. Diligenskiy notes, there exist "certain general trends and tendencies in the development of mass consciousness as a whole. They stem, first and foremost, from the unity of the objective sociohistorical reality that consciousness

---

[3]G.V. Plekhanov, *Collected Philosophical Works in Five Volumes* [*Izbrannyye filosofskiye proizvedeniya v pyati tomakh*], Vol. I, Moscow, 1956, p. 660.
[4]V.S. Semenov, *Capitalism and Classes* [*Kapitalizm i klassy*], Moscow, 1969, pp. 31-32.

reflects. . . . Within the context of a given socioeconomic system, even the representatives of antithetical classes are 'part and parcel' of one and the same system of societal relations. The demands that each historical type of such relations makes on people's activity develop in them stable, 'systemwide' means of perceiving objective situations and reacting to them. . . ."[5]

While ideologies are class world views, at the same time they cannot help but reflect the "environment" of the mass consciousness and of the ideas, behavioral motives and interests of social subjects, i.e., the environment of various mass commonalities, both class and nonclass. On the other hand, the ideology of a given class itself influences the mass consciousness, and "the trends in mass consciousness that arise on the basis of that ideology often assume, within the framework of a given historical period, broader, 'intergroup' social dimensions and become indices of the state of the mass consciousness of capitalist society as a whole."[6] Thus, the general elements characteristic of any given types of mass consciousness and any given ideologies have national, state, cultural, political, religious, economic, and direct ideological bases.

A substantial number of these elements are of a class-neutral nature. This is why, along with the differences, there are also general regularities in the development of the two systems—capitalism and socialism. Those general regularities include the need for productive forces to correspond to the nature of production relations; they also include such laws as the laws of value, supply and demand, proportionality of production, and rising expectations. General regularities can be seen in the sociopolitical, ethno/cultural, and other spheres of the life of capitalist and socialist society. In the final analysis, the ideologies that crystalize class aspirations and interests reflect both the contradictions and the internal unity of a given system, as well as the differences between systems and the commonality of certain phenomena and processes on the global level.

What has been said does not mean that the class irreconcilability between bourgeois and communist ideology disappears. With regard to ultimate goals, it persists and is sometimes even intensified by the "competitive" struggle between the two ideologies for the most effective utilization of the class-neutral factors of socioeconomic and cultural progress for the purpose of advancing their own interests.

At the same time, it should be recognized that to a considerable extent this irreconcilability is a result of the stagnation in Marxist

---

[5]G.G. Diligenskiy, *In Search of Meaning and Purpose* [V poiskakh smysla i tseli], Moscow, 1986, pp. 81-82.
[6]*Ibid.*, p. 83.

theory over the past few decades. The internal methodological potential of Marxism has gone untapped in many respects—a potential which makes it possible to conduct a comprehensive, detailed analysis of the new processes and phenomena in social development, of their influence on the situation of the working class and the broad strata of working people, and of the paths and prospects for the socialist transformation of society. In the atmosphere of the decades of stagnation, real ideology was increasingly subordinated to the ephemeral interests of the political struggle, which dictated that any social processes be examined exclusively from the standpoint of antagonism between the systems.

As experience shows, dogmatism in ideology and underestimating or ignoring the objective causes of given processes and phenomena (such as the emergence of bourgeois reformism, of opportunism in the workers' movement, and of the concepts of "class peace" and the "historic compromise") will sooner or later lead the very policy of the revolutionary transformation of the world to an impasse. The Pyrrhic victories of revolutionary attempts to leap over historical stages, failures of political vanguardism and adventurism, the pseudorevolutionary "Verkhovenskyism" that Dostoevsky predicted, and the victims of the "personality cult" and the "cultural revolutions" are infamous. Dogmatism degrades Marxism to the level of a petit bourgeois ideology, which is characterized in principle by opportunism and the attempt merely to "ride the rhythm of history."

That is why it is extremely important, in the present situation, to see the dialectic of the "individual" and the "general" in class interests and ideologies, in social and universal human progress, and in socioeconomic systems.

It probably makes sense to make some adjustments in the schematic notion of "fundamental" and "partial" class interests that has predominated in our research, according to which "the fundamental interests of the proletariat and the bourgeoisie are diametrically opposed and cannot be reconciled," although "in the struggle, mutual concessions by the classes are admissible where individual issues are concerned."[7] Is it possible, for example, that the prevention of nuclear war or of global ecological disaster is not in keeping with the fundamental interests of all classes? Excessively categorical assertions to the effect that only "the progressive classes have a stake in the ascending development of society and in meeting the pressing requirements of social life"[8] appear doctrinaire and scholastic when viewed against the background of the realities of that life.

---

[7]See *Marxist-Leninist Philosophy: Historical Materialism* [*Marksistsko-leninskaya filosofiya. Istoricheskiy materializm*], Moscow, 1972, p. 133.
     [8]*Ibid.*

As for the class nature of ideologies, Lenin's well-known denial of the existence of any "nonclass or superclass ideology" in no way means that all contacts between Marxism and bourgeois ideology—and Marxism's use, in the interests of social progress, of various "products" of bourgeois ideology's historical development—are devoid of any objective basis whatsoever and inevitably give rise to the "ideological legerdemain" of convergence and lead to the "absorption" of socialism by the opposite system.[9]

Such "misgivings" and "warnings" stem from the same "childhood disease of leftism in communism" that Lenin once warned against. Unfortunately, despite that warning, it later exacted its bloody tribute. The practical application of Stalin's idea that the class struggle steadily intensified as progress was made toward socialism resulted in the substitution of a policy of totalitarianism for the ideology of social leadership of the working class. It was socialism, more so than the "class enemy," that fell under the gun, and that held up the establishment of a communist system on a global scale.

We must not fail to take such a cruel historical lesson into account today, when the dialectics of life have become much more complex, and it is mortally dangerous to try to fit the relations among social classes and their ideologies into the Procrustean bed of bipolar approaches.

The Peaceful Coexistence of the Two Systems and the Constituent Parts of Marxism

Perhaps in no area of social relations is the acute need for a dialectical approach to the opposition between the world's two main ideologies felt so keenly as it is in the area of international relations.

There is an urgent need for a further elaboration of concepts related to the problem of the interconnection between ideological confrontation and class struggle on the one hand, and international political relations on the other, and especially concerning the relationship between ideology and politics.

Until recently the predominant thesis in our literature was that "the main beachhead of the world class struggle . . . is the rivalry between the two systems—socialism and capitalism—and therefore the center of ideological battle has also shifted mainly to that plane."[10]

Of course, class and ideological struggle is "present" at all "stages" of social, national, and international relations. However, that does not mean that Marxism inherently regards international politics solely

---

[9]See Ye. D. Modrzhinskaya, op.cit., p. 29.
[10]V.V. Kortunov, Ideology and Politics [Ideologiya i politika], Moscow, 1974, p. 6.

from the standpoint of a class antagonism that presupposes a "fight for survival."

Just what such an approach leads to in practice is shown by the experience of the 1970s and 1980s, when attempts were made to implement the concepts of a number of ultraconservative bourgeois ideologists (Z. Brzezinski, A. Meyer and S. Huntington). The essence of their ideas is that, under modern world conditions, ideology should design a "pragmatic" social management and use political means to help defend the "spiritual values" of capitalism. As the principal means of such defense, they proposed using the established canons of the "religious and nationalistic" world view. Brzezinski, in particular, claimed that anticommunism would successfully perform its "international political function" by relying on religion and nationalism.

Of course, all this contributed in no small degree to the destabilization of an already unstable world political and economic situation. In the final analysis, the infamous thesis concerning the "evil communist empire" that was actively pushed during that period imperiled the existence of both opposing systems, and with them the whole world proletariat. But that means that the thesis concerning the exacerbation of ideological opposition between the systems has also come into irresolvable contradiction with the need for the survival of civilization and the historical progress of all humanity and socialism. That thesis did not accord with the theory of Marxism, either.

The new thinking that at present stimulates communist ideology as a whole reflects the diversity and underlying realities of life, rejecting the self-deception of our theorists of the periods of Stalinism and stagnation who imagined that economics, politics, human beings, and society would obediently and invariably transform themselves along the required lines under the influence of ideology. One result of the new approaches is the dawning recognition that extremely complex, reciprocal relations exist between ideology and the life of society.

This pertains especially to the reciprocal relationship between the class struggle and international relations. A number of articles that have appeared recently in our press have demonstrated the fallacy of the well-known formula "peaceful coexistence is a form of class struggle," whereby the class antagonism between labor and capital and the antagonism between ideologies that was adduced from it were extended to the sphere of international relations.[11] As has been noted correctly in this connection, this formula is flawed both theoretically and politically. Theoretically, because, as one author points out, "the 'addressees' of our policy of peaceful coexistence are states where the

---

[11]See, for example, *SShA—ekonomiki, politika, ideologiya* [*United States: Economics, Politics, Ideology*], No. 12, 1987, pp. 6-9; *Pravda*, Jan. 28, 1988; *MEMO*, No. 6, 1988, pp. 55-57.

bourgeoisie is in power, and the class struggle, if the words have any meaning at all, can be directed only against that same bourgeoisie."[12] And politically this formula provided an additional trump card for the forces in the West that call on people "not to trust the Soviets" and try to frighten them with the threat of the "expansion of world communism."

There are also other factors imposing the need to abandon attempts to view international relations through the prism of the ideological struggle, the need to de-ideologize them. In a world that is becoming internationalized, in which there are mounting dangers for the existence of the human species, and in which the broad masses are entering the political arena, the dialectics of combining the class principle and the universal human principle in world development consists of recognizing the objective role of universal human values and of each people's freedom of social and political choice; in the realization that socialism is the bearer of good will, dialogue, and trust; and in the understanding that within the other system and its ruling class there are a "peace party," a "pacifist camp," and rational social circles that espouse humanism and democracy.

Therefore, it seems to us, the opposition between the two ideologies does not mean that relations between systems are more antagonistic than relations between states, or that the former predetermine the latter. Experience demonstrates the opposite in most cases. There are a good many reasons for that.

In the first place, this is attributable to the fact that nationalist sentiments engendered by bourgeois society exercise a powerful influence in most parts of the world. In the imperialist era, contradictions between nationalities, which sometimes develop into conflicts between states, are intensified by the fact that it is not individual classes (the proletariat or the bourgeoisie) but larger associations—national communities—that are involved in such conflicts. This situation results from the fact that neither internationalism, in the form of solidarity among the working people of various countries in the struggle against imperialism, nor the internationalization of capital and the international bourgeoisie have yet reached the level at which class interests clearly predominate on a global scale in all cases. The opposition between the "aggregate worker" and "aggregate capital" is usually obscured in the mass consciousness by the clash of other interests within the context of planetary structures.

In the second place, the relative weight of the universal human imperatives mentioned above is increasing in relations between systems. In many respects, for extremely broad segments of the public,

---

[12]*MEMO*, No. 6, 1988, p. 55.

the objective need to solve global problems is assuming priority over the interests of individual classes. The historical process of the capitalist system's replacement by the socialist system is a lengthy, multistage, revolutionary—and simultaneously evolutionary—process that involves, in addition to social factors, nonsocial factors that operate within the contexts of both systems. In the future, this will result in a situation in which, as the influence of socialism grows and the policy of peaceful coexistence becomes stronger, the sphere of influence of the ideological component of relations between systems—a component dictated, in the final analysis, by class antagonism—will gradually be reduced, since this component increasingly will incorporate elements of universal values and priorities. The "explanatory," epistemological functions of ideology in our increasingly complex world will more and more clearly come to the fore, as opposed to the pragmatic, "mobilizing" functions that are most closely tied to politics. As public rationality and morality grow, the struggle between ideologies will start to manifest itself not so much in political struggle between countries, blocs, and systems, or in propaganda warfare, as in a dialogue among theories, the search for a balance of interests, and the interaction of mutually acceptable models of progress.[13]

So far, this prospect seems extremely remote. Nonetheless, one can predict with a high degree of certainty that the role of ideology as a propaganda weapon in relations between the two social systems will gradually decline, and its significance as a kind of strategic compass of social progress will grow.

Of course, this will require a serious reappraisal of many of the premises of the specific social science disciplines in order to bring about the sort of "link-up" between the two ideologies (and even the fusion of certain of their elements) that would make it possible to couple the two opposing systems' highest-level value concepts and their "philosophies of history" themselves. After all, the stability of their peaceful coexistence depends on it. Therefore the obvious—obvious, at least, to us—general values of differing ideologies need to be philosophically interpreted and logically connected with the integral content of each.

Of course, there are a good many obstacles here. Suffice it to mention, for example, differences in the methodologies and social orientations of Marxist and non-Marxist social science. But this circumstance should not stop us. In the search for points of contact we can make use of many ideas that were banished to "closed collections"

---

[13]In this connection one may recall Voltaire, who once observed that ignorance is the main reason for human misfortune, and that it was precisely the "spirit of dogmatism" that brought the "fury of the religious wars" (see F. Voltaire, *Annals of the Empire* [*Annales de l'Empire*], Paris, Vol. 13, p. 303).

during the Stalinist era and period of stagnation. What is important is an unbiased analysis of the latest accomplishments of Western scholarly thought. It may become apparent in the process that Marxism rests to a great extent on "traditionalist" processes of social development that were identified in the past. After all, the ideas on which its three sources were based were expressed in the 18th, 19th, and early 20th centuries. Obviously, the profound material and spiritual changes that have occurred since that time in connection with the internationalization of social relations, the influence of the scientific and technological revolution on social processes and the human personality, no longer fit into the three-part structural scheme that we know.

The time has come for the analysis of all these topics in our social science, for Marxism faces the need to comprehend the emergence of "those transitional forms that are encountered in all areas of nature and society."[14] In this case we are referring to those broad "global" currents of moral self-cleansing, cultural and spiritual development, and the recovery of historical and philosophical vision that are gaining momentum throughout the world, giving rise to a humanistic and universal-democratic consciousness. Denying the existence of this trend is equivalent to ignoring the laws of the objective evolution of living and of mankind that are presented in V. Vernadsky's theory: the transition of the biosphere, sociosphere, and technosphere into the noosphere, i.e., the sphere of reason, creativity, spiritual insights, and conscious physical and moral self-perfection. Vernadsky noted that the 20th century had already created the prerequisites for that transition in the form of the "universe of humanity" (its conquest of the biosphere), the "unity of humanity," the growing influence of the "popular masses" on social processes, and the emergence of a "morally responsible internationale of scientists."[15]

In the opinion of D.S. Likhachev, the elements of the "collective consciousness of humanity" that arise under these conditions (despite all the entropy-like forces disorganizing and disintegrating biological and social organisms) are already gaining momentum, eliminating dangerous hypertrophy in the power of man over nature and institutions over man, and also eliminating professional idiosyncrasy in human thinking. The building up of a cultural genetic stock and cultural milieu is paving the way for the establishment of a moral atmosphere and creating a "normal homosphere"[16] as a basis for the new vast sphere of a planetary world view. Culture, becoming increasingly integrated with ideology, is keeping pace with the social

---

[14]V.I. Lenin, *Complete Works* [*Polnoye sobraniye sochineniy*], Vol. 27, p. 379.
[15]Quoted from *Znamya* [*Banner*], No. 3, 1988, pp. 192-194.
[16]See *Inostrannaya literatura* [*Foreign Literature*], No. 1, 1988, pp. 212-213.

sciences—and frequently leading them—in going beyond national and social boundaries and actively addressing such persistently important "eternal problems" as the value dichotomies of "life-death," "freedom-oppression," "struggle-resignation," "knowledge-faith," and "love-hatred." The hierarchy of these values is mobile in the history and concrete life of countries.

It is obvious that our age, for the first time in history, has brought to the fore the problem of death in the form, not of individual tragedy, but of the actual possibility of the annihilation of man and the human species. This has become an extremely powerful incentive for recognizing universal human unity. In the offing are new changes in the correlation of these concepts and a new synthesis of the global, national, group, and personal significance of all the other "eternal problems," which will doubtless help shape planetary consciousness along the same lines.

Increasingly, the solution of the problem of the human individual is becoming the key to the solution of universal human problems. According to D.S. Likhachev's profound idea, "when we cease to notice the other individual, animosity and the misunderstanding of other nationalities arise. . . ."[17] Indeed, disregard for the individual is the source of extremely diverse interpersonal and social forms of alienation, including forms common to both systems.

In recent years the development of the Marxist foundations of global studies, which represent a synthesis of the philosophical, economic, ethnic, ecological and futurological approaches, has advanced considerably. This is apparent from documents of the 27th CPSU Congress and the works of V.V. Zagladin, I.T. Frolov, G.Kh. Shakhnazarov, E.A. Arab-Ogly, and other scholars. Evidently it is here, rather than in other areas of social science, that one should expect the first major breakthroughs in Marxist theory that will open up the possibility of building bridges to the future of a humanity freed from exploitation and war, the possibility of creating concepts in which social progress will be linked to the class interests of labor, to new notions about the relations between the two systems, and to universal human interests expressed in mass ideological and political tendencies.

In the process of developing Marxist global studies, it will quite likely be necessary to abandon the oversimplified ideas about the phase of worldwide communism that developed during the 19th and early 20th centuries.

It seems to us that the general theory of the succession of social systems that is being examined within the framework of global studies

---

[17]*Druzhba narodov* [*Friendship of Peoples*], No. 6, 1988, p. 223.

is assuming an increasingly clear-cut and finished form. Approaches to this can also be found in Marx's well-known six-books plan,[18] and in the numerous ideas put forward by the workers' and communist movement, especially during the 1920s.

A methodological basis for the development of Marxist theory is provided by Lenin's idea that communist ideology, "as the ideology of the class struggle of the proletariat," "is based on all the material of human knowledge, presupposes highly developed science, and demands scientific work."[19] Such "human knowledge" is by no means a monopoly of Marxist social science. Theoretical generalizations arise within the context of many ideological and political schools in the bourgeois world. That is why present-day Marxism, the new thinking, and the policy of glasnost in the U.S.S.R. are oriented toward creating an atmosphere in which a real comparison of views and a free exchange of ideas with those schools can take place.

Along what lines can that exchange be most productive?

By Cutting Away Anticommunism, Find the Rational Core

The development of comparative studies and forecasting in the West has been based on previously acquired experience in the economic and political integration of present-day capitalism. The methodological exchange of ideas here is mutually beneficial. What is now on the agenda is the more difficult task of expanding intellectual cooperation in identifying the latest trends in the internal development of the two systems. And that is possible only if there are contacts at the level of the individual social sciences. Here it is necessary once again to recall Lenin. In calling for comparing the "theoretical foundations of that philosophy (bourgeois philosophy—S. P.) and dialectical materialism," he had in mind the need not only for criticizing anti-Marxism, but also for identifying "new questions that dialectical materialism would have to 'deal with.'"[20]

Of course, the broadest such exchange can occur between Marxism-Leninism and the schools of social thought that determine the basic world view of the communist and social democratic movement and of radical leftist circles in the capitalist countries. For many decades a seemingly impenetrable and partly artificial barrier existed between our social science on the one hand, and "neo-Marxism,"

---

[18]As A.M. Kogan justifiably notes, "the methodology of Marx's six-books plan makes it possible to correctly approach the study of problems in the general theory of capitalism that are still unsolved, yet timely and important. . . . The six-books plan is of great importance not just for political economy, but also for philosophy" (A.M. Kogan, *In Karl Marx's Creative Laboratory* [V tvorcheskoy laboratorii Karla Marksa], Moscow, 1983, pp. 149, 166).

[19]V.I. Lenin, *Complete Works*, Vol. 6, pp. 362-363.

[20]V.I. Lenin, *Complete Works*, Vol. 18, p. 379; Vol. 20, p. 128.

"Western Marxism," and social reformism on the other. That barrier now is coming down, opening prospects for fruitful discussions that may give a powerful impetus to socialist theory and to the practice of democratizing social relations.

The exchange of ideas with bourgeois ideology—Marxism's opponent in principle—is a more complicated question. There are considerable obstacles on that path.

In the first place, we must evidently admit that for centuries our indigenous Russian social thought was unable to free itself from the burden of the distant past. It is worth recalling V.O. Klyuchevskiy's observations, which on the whole were fair: either "under Byzantine influence we were lackeys of a foreign faith and under Western European influence became lackeys of foreign thought"; or, being incapable of "correctly using foreign ideas" without prejudice to our "moral community," we feared them "like sin" and feared "the inquisitive mind like a seducer"; or, "we turned scientific truths into dogmas, made scientific authorities into fetishes, and turned the temple of science into a heathen temple of superstition and prejudice."[21] Naturally, all this was characteristic of the "cursed" past. But it is not easy to free ourselves, even now, from recurrences of such traditions, when they manifest themselves in some sort of present-day modifications of ancient disputes between the Slavophiles and the Westernizers.

In the second place, as previously noted, we must overcome the sectarian isolation and dogmatic ossification that presently typify even the branches of the social sciences.[22]

In the third place, there is a question that is irresolvable, a priori: Can the anticommunism characteristic of bourgeois ideology limit itself to a purely theoretical struggle?

One distinguishing feature of the second half of the 1980s is that since the 27th CPSU Congress the correlation of forces between bourgeois and Marxist ideology has been changing for the worse for our opponents and open adversaries. The perestroika and new thinking currently being established in our country are delivering a mighty blow to anticommunism's central nerve—anti-Sovietism. Whereas anticommunism was unable, even before, to work out even a minimally coherent "meta-ideology" as a "total" alternative to Marxism, now the scientific concepts of historical materialism will acquire more

---

[21]V.O. Klyuchevskiy, *Unpublished Works* [*Neopublikovannyye proizvedeniya*], Moscow, 1983, pp. 308, 309.
[22]In this connection one must note the groundlessness of criticism directed at the aforementioned work by A.M. Kogan, who has been charged with "reproaching . . . Karl Marx for his failure to deal fully with certain important problems in capitalist economics" (see I.M. Mrachkovskaya, *Toward the History of the Leninist Stage in Political Economy* [*K istorii leninskogo etapa politicheskoy ekonomii*], Moscow, 1987, p. 200). Denying the need to develop special areas of Marxism means limiting Marxism itself.

and more conceptual and real content. Before the 27th Party Congress, anticommunism actively employed the arsenal of the latest empirical studies of social processes for its purposes, now its monopoly in that area has been undermined. Sociology in the U.S.S.R. is now actively serving political theory and practice.

Anticommunists' hopes of deriving benefits from glasnost and the openness of socialism has ultimately proved unfounded, too.

The profound changes that are taking place in various spheres of socialist society, and the improvements they are bringing about in the Western public's perception of the U.S.S.R., cannot help affecting the tone and arguments of the proponents of anticommunism—at least in the realm of international relations. But for the improvement in the international ideological climate to gain momentum, we, too, must abandon certain dogmatic approaches and ideas.

In the first place, we must quit essentially equating bourgeois social science with anticommunist propaganda. Such an approach is plainly at odds with reality. In many works by Western scholars, criticism of the theory and practice of socialism is combined with a more or less objective analysis of capitalism itself and of global problems. In the second place, in underscoring the crisis of the capitalist world view, we unintentionally overlook the invigoration of the cognitive function in bourgeois social science. Yet thanks to it, Western scholars have managed in the past two decades to identify many fundamental changes in today's world.

Back in the 1970s, bourgeois ideologists started to repeat—in their own terms, but very persistently—Engels' well-known idea concerning the tremendous role of social theory in the political, class, and "historical" struggle. Thus, in the words of the prominent American sociologist A. Gouldner, "never before in a class society did the security of a ruling class depend so much on the presence of belief-systems appropriate to its rule."[23] The reason for this was also cited: the historical process has presently entered an especially intensive phase of the search for a general analytical basis. A "new ideological age" is beginning, declared R. Aron,[24] the patriarch of West European anti-Marxism, who died in the early 1980s. And the British bourgeois sociologist D. Wilhelm proposed working out "an alternative world-view," a "flexible" and "integrated" ideological system that would include "new ideas."[25]

---

[23]A. Gouldner, The Dialectics of Ideology and Technology: the Origins, Grammar and Future of Ideology, New York, 1976, p. 231.

[24]R. Aron, Comments on the New Ideological Age [Remarques sur le nouvel age idéologique], Paris, 1978.

[25]D. Wilhelm, Creative Alternatives to Communism. Guideline for Tomorrow's World, London, 1977, pp. 56, 76, 155.

Bourgeois ideologists have not succeeded in creating an integrative alternative to Marxism-Leninism. However, it is important to note that the bounds of bourgeois ideology's concerns have been expanding, and there has been a shift in methods to detailed, interdisciplinary analysis of problems. Of course, this change is aimed at identifying the objective laws of history and following them—primarily to the extent that this helps strengthen the positions of the bourgeois class, which is striving to "adapt" to those laws. Ideology has begun assuming the function of "spiritual renewal" and strategic "adaptation" to the world social situation and the scientific and technological revolution on the basis of philosophical, political-economic, and political programs. Since any ideology, bourgeois ideology included, represents a systematized body of theory that is a class-based reflection of reality in the form of a multidisciplinary set of philosophical, political, economic, social, legal, historical, and ethical views, it has managed to identify a good many fundamental trends in the social development of capitalism and universal human civilization in our time. And here one cannot fail to recall Lenin's well-known admonition to the effect that in the area of political economy and philosophy, for example, "Marxists' task . . . is to be able to assimilate and rework the gains that are made by those 'salesclerks' (you won't take a step in the study of new economic phenomena, for example, without relying on those salesclerks' works)."[26]

It would seem that the comparison of theoretical approaches in analyzing trends in the development of the socialist countries and the leading capitalist states is becoming no less important today. The fundamental differences between the two systems are changing with respect to how they satisfy the working masses' needs, their philosophical and organizational orientations toward collectivism and individualism, and so on. The development of scientific and technological progress, internationalization, and the increase in the role of the individual are giving rise to trends that are either common or similar.

It is now becoming increasingly obvious that many problems of "East and West" have been brought about by a sharp acceleration in the development of productive forces and the fact that production relations have lagged behind them. The replacement of technologies that has been gathering speed during the past 20 years in the industrially developed Western countries is already leading to fundamental changes in the rates of economic growth, bringing qualitative characteristics to the fore, and producing changes in the industrial organization of production and in the correlation between production and

---

[26]V. I. Lenin, *Complete Works*, Vol. 18, p. 364 (Lenin calls the professors of economics and philosophy the "salesclerks" of the class of capitalists and theologians).

consumption. All this requires an updating of systems of state regulation and of market relations; flexibility in production and distribution; and solution of the problems of deteriorating labor ethics, employment, social equality, and culture.[27]

A great many problems of a similar sort are presently confronting "reform theory" in our country in connection with developing the commodity-money economic mechanism, improving the system for distributing income and benefits according to work, decentralizing management structures, and designating consumption and culture as priorities, and also in connection with analyzing not only class contradictions but nonclass contradictions as well.[28] It is instructive that right now both the supporters of perestroika in the U.S.S.R. and many political figures in the West are citing the struggle against bureaucratism, dependency, inefficiency, bigness for its own sake, and so on, among their main goals.

A comparison of the methodological approaches of the Marxist and non-Marxist social sciences in the sphere of economic and political management can be especially mutually beneficial. Although the social essence of social production is different under capitalism than under socialism, one can find a great deal that is similar in the nature of current forms of regulating economic proportions. In both systems it is accomplished with the help of credit and monetary instruments, a policy of built-in tax stabilizers, and state regulation of prices, and by using budgetary means to reinforce the economic interests of the economic individual, the group, and the society in conditions of commodity production. The existence of points of contact here is inevitable, since the late 20th-century scientific and technological revolution confronts socialism and capitalism with common problems, for example, those related to the alienation of labor, the decisive role of skilled manpower, the new correlation between work time and free time, and new forms of income distribution and personal consumption. The time is passing when our country's administrative and economic-management system could brush aside these problems and the vital necessity of analyzing and solving them on the basis of the experience of not just the socialist countries, but the capitalist countries as well.[29]

---

[27]*MEMO*, No. 2, 1988, pp. 71-79.

[28]See *Kommunist*, No. 8, 1987, pp. 3-14.

[29]The beginning of a constructive approach to bourgeois research was made back in the 1950s by the Institute for World Economy and International Relations' [IMEMO] thesis concerning the two functions of bourgeois political economy. An important methodological step forward in the 1980s can be seen in Ya. A. Pevzner's work, *Debatable Issues in Political Economy* [*Diskussionnyye voprosy politicheskoy ekonomii*], which outlined a broad and detailed program of study of key theoretical problems (value, prices and profits, competition, inflation, the theory of equilibrium, marginalism), taking into account the most diverse nuances and ideas in bourgeois economic thinking. In the context of the present economic reform in the U.S.S.R., these ideas may receive not just theoretical but practical application.

A good many opportunities for the exchange of ideas are also opening up in connection with the need to activate the human factor. We are referring to the growing importance of the human individual and primary social groups, whose philosophical values and behavioral motivation are starting to play an unprecedentedly great role on both micro and macro levels of economic and political relations. The possibilities for individuals and groups to participate directly in management (in particular, by means of electronic communications), and the unsatisfactory nature, in both systems, of existing forms of public representation and state administration suggest that socialist democracy should not ignore the experience of democratic institutions in other countries. The task is not to take as a model and blindly copy everything that constitutes the concept of bourgeois democracy, but to seek optimal delimitations of representative, executive, legislative, and judicial power, and to develop effective mechanisms of democratic centralism within the framework of public institutions and unofficial associations. We know what great attention the 19th CPSU Conference gave to these matters.

The problem of individual freedom is closely entwined with the problem of political culture, without which neither social stability nor stable economic growth are possible.

If one looks at "foreign experience" in this connection, one cannot help noting that Western sociology plays an exceptionally important role in the management of social processes.[30] In identifying the key principles of the socialization of the individual (individual-society) and of group social relations, and in working out sociological interpretations of the scientific and technological revolution, it has accumulated extremely rich empirical material, which, as I.A. Butenko has correctly noted, makes it possible to detect certain objective processes, even though it retains the conservative meaning of attempting to justify the bourgeois way of life as the only possible one.[31]

Of interest, in particular, are the works of Western sociologists investigating incipient new forms of interpersonal and labor relations and the "new lifestyle" that is uninfected with the ethics of accumulation, or with alienation, individualism, nationalism, corporatism, and the degradation of culture. Even if the search for these new forms and styles of life expresses itself, for example, in the ideology of non-proletarian protest, or in a new natural philosophy, existentialism, neo-Freudianism, ecosocialism, ecomaterialism, Marxism can carry on a productive theoretical dialogue (not to mention engaging in joint

----

[30]See, for example, S. Lipset, *Revolution and Counter-Revolution: Change and Persistence in Social Structures*, New York, 1980, p. 3.

[31]I.A. Butenko, *Social Cognition and the World of Everyday Life* [*Sotsialnoye poznaniye i mir povsednevnosti*], Moscow, 1987, p. 10.

political actions) on these issues, because Marxism cannot conceive of itself without humanism, democracy, ecology, and culture, or without eliminating from real socialism the extremely harmful phenomena of de-ideologization, consumerism, social alienation, or throwbacks to feudalism. The advancement of the so-called "human factor" (it would be better to say the problem of the individual) to the foreground of socialist theory and practice categorically demands mobilization of every possible resource to provide for the psychological health of the individual, uncover his suppressed creative abilities, and define his biological limits. Therefore, for example, the searches being carried out in the West for a "new philosophy of life" and the "self-realization" of the individual in relation to other people, society, leisure, work, and nature are by no means of purely abstract interest.

A good deal that is interesting for us can also be found in the works of Western scholars that contain sociological generalizations of the laws of stratification, socialization, and communication in the developed capitalist countries in the 1960s through 1980s, and in those works that reveal new forms of conflict and interaction between the attitudes of social groups (strata, castes, nations, races, religious schools, occupational groups) on the one hand, and political attitudes (liberalism, conservatism, radicalism, social reformism, sociocultural forms of consciousness) on the other. The tasks that present-day sociology sets for itself in this area are (1) to identify the distinguishing features of the relationship between group and class idea formations, on the one hand, and the normative and value criteria of ruling social systems, on the other; and (2) to clarify the content of the comprehensive concept of the "sociocultural phenomenon," without which it is genuinely difficult under present conditions to understand the specific features of political processes and the way that the scientific and technological revolution is "perceived," not just by social, occupational, and cultural strata, but also by various social systems.[32] All this is very closely bound up with the problem of analyzing mass consciousness and its subsystem, the political consciousness of the masses, and the emergence under the conditions of the scientific and technological revolution of new sociocultural and functional groups.

Marxist political science and sociology, which presently face the task of developing the concept of socialist popular self-government, cannot ignore changes in the relationships between newly forming and traditional social strata on the one hand, and the rationalization processes engendered by the rising flows of information and "knowledge"

---

[32]Here Marxist methodology can be used to pare away constructive ideas from the bourgeois interpretation of the concept of "culture," according to which, specific ethnic and institutional features and the "social habits" and customs of population groups are portrayed as the basis of the ideologies of eras, countries, and peoples.

on the other. The West's experience shows the diversity of the social consequences of the decentralization and destandardization of those flows (for example, through computerization). Evidently, something of the sort is also inevitable under socialism. All this dictates a need for further development of the Marxist theory of social and political planning, and for a reappraisal of the essence, role, and interrelationships of such seemingly well-established categories as the family, national communities, social order, state and public institutions, authority, and so on.

Obviously, the "openness" of Marxism to ideas of a different philosophical origin is a delicate problem. What is required here is not just the renunciation of dogmatism and the ensuring of the conditions for broad glasnost, openness to debate, and an influx of information. It is no less important to determine what must be assimilated and what not, what represents a tool of cognition or action, and what undermines the prospects for progress. The explanation of the fact that blind anticapitalism and anti-Americanism are just as fruitless as anticommunism and anti-Sovietism should be a necessary step on this path. In general, ideologies with the stress on "anti" lead to an impasse. A clear-cut orientation toward defending the interests of the working masses and the universal values of the individual, and toward solving global problems through the joint efforts of both social systems, and a reliance on objective knowledge—therein lies the guarantee that Marxist social thought will exercise a greater influence on the subsequent development of human civilization.

Cultural Exchanges and Policy in the Era of the Scientific and Technological Revolution

VYACHESLAV GEORGIYEVICH IGOREV*

The fundamental changes now emerging in information and communication were characterized at the February (1988) plenary session of the Central Committee of the Communist Party of the Soviet Union as a factor assuming "decisive importance for modern world development."

On one hand, unprecedented possibilities are opening up for the rapid and free exchange of spiritual values and information on a global scale. It is already possible to transmit virtually instantaneously to any point of the globe an extensive volume of various types of communications via television, radio, and videocassette. The industrially developed countries of the West are in effect establishing interactive networks of personal computers (PCs) linked to various cultural, scientific, and general-information data banks. The household TV screen with attached microcomputer will evidently become a common means of national and subsequently international communication, opening storehouses of valuable information and works of culture to the broadest access.

On the other hand, these same technical means can be, and often are, used to spread ideas and morals that are detrimental to civilization, and thus pose the threat of an even greater estrangement of mankind along national, social, cultural, ideological, moral, and religious lines.

Given that, an analysis of trends in the development and use of new means of communication in international cultural ties assumes particular relevancy. An understanding of these trends that meets the demands of the time is essential to formulating a cultural policy consistent with the thrust of social progress, of the scientific and technological revolution, and of the broadening movement for a new

---

*Journalist and author of a number of works on problems of cultural and informational exchanges. This article appeared in the June 1988 issue of *MEMO*.

informational and cultural order. In performing such an analysis, it is important that we take a sober view of the realities of this century, whose imperative is coexistence among states with differing social systems and distinct systems of ideology and morality.

1. Underlying the use of recent technological advances in international cultural exchanges is the symbiosis between the computer and the TV screen, the computer and new generations of copying equipment, and the computer and the latest communication technology. The use of a compact laser printing device (laser printer) attached to a personal computer linked to a data bank makes it possible even today to print books and periodicals right in the home. Optical and magnetic discs in centralized data banks—electronic libraries—have the capacity to store exact copies of all books, newspapers, magazines, manuscripts, and other printed works, as well as all audiovisual materials, produced in the course of the many centuries of human history. The development of this equipment essentially raises the possibility of gaining access to the achievements of world science and culture without ever leaving the home.

In many developed countries, PC owners can, by subscribing to public electronic libraries that are opening, acquaint themselves with the major national and foreign periodical publications, news agency reports, scientific articles published in recent years, and so on in their homes. The creation of electronic depositories of audiovisual materials is on the horizon.

A qualitative leap in printing technology has led to the phenomenon of individual publishing in the West. The use of word processors makes it possible to replace the typewriter with a CRT and keyboard. As a result, it is possible to rework a text, change the page format, and insert graphics or illustrations quickly and without technical difficulties. Home desktop-publishing operations are putting out the widest variety of printed matter, from one-page newsletters to actual books with high-quality text and color illustrations.

The magazine *Publish!* has appeared in the United States, for example, a magazine for amateur publishers who exchange their print creations or try to sell them on the market for such publications. In this way, the marriage of the PC, the printer, and the data bank makes it possible not only to eliminate the "book famine" for masterpieces of world literature or popular printed works that are still in short supply but also to realize the long-standing dream of all amateur writers to see their works published.

One vivid example of the qualitative advances in publishing is the computerized publisher that launched the British newspaper *Today* in 1986. The staff writes and edits printed texts and composes photography and illustrations on PC display terminals at home or in the office.

The materials are then transmitted from the PCs over telephone wires to a computer that selects the best way to compose the text and illustrations, in accordance with a prescribed program. The pages composed in this manner are then transmitted over telephone lines directly to the typesetting devices in the print shop. All subsequent stages of the printing process also proceed under the direct control of the computer, with minimal human labor. In the developed capitalist countries there is an emerging trend toward the development and mass use of compact and inexpensive PCs coupled with printing and copying machines for home—not to mention commercial—use.

All of this compels us to raise in all seriousness the question of whether the current restrictions on access to copying and duplicating machines are essentially becoming an obstacle to cultural and scientific discourse, and whether, with the development and introduction of new equipment in the future, they will not prove downright senseless. It should also be pointed out that, despite the artificial constraints on the use of duplicating equipment and computer printers and on photocopying for private purposes, there is now widespread unauthorized use of departmental photocopiers to copy interesting articles, other printed works, and even major works of literature that our publishing houses have either published in insufficient quantities or failed to publish altogether. Without spending a kopek of their own money (using state-owned paper and copying machines instead!) enterprising underground operators are publishing or republishing works by Bulgakov, Vysotsky, and other Soviet and foreign authors in demand. And although a copy of such a book, which may bear the imprint "Night Worker Publishing House—press run 10 copies" in jest, costs from 50 to 100 rubles, there will be buyers for it as long as state publishing houses are unable to meet reader demand.

One cannot help asking: if existing restrictions on the use of copying equipment or of personal-computer printers to copy printed matter make no sense economically, and if they run counter to the increasingly pronounced, objectively determined, and essentially progressive world trends and to the imperatives of the scientific and technological revolution, does it make sense to keep them in effect any longer?

The experience of the leading countries in information science (the United States, Japan, Great Britain, France, the Federal Republic of Germany) shows that the regional trend of development in this area consists of creation of a network of diverse interconnected communications channels based on widespread use of inexpensive and readily accessible PCs and on advances in television, radio, video, and photocopying equipment and in printers. These countries have succeeded in attaining a severalfold intensification of production and creative endeavor through unimpeded cultural and informational intercourse via electronic, print, and other audiovisual means. Such intercourse is becoming a routine matter and a condition of further progress. Moreover, the process of decentralizing creative endeavor, the emergence of a great many new scientific and cultural poles of attraction for groups and associations that differ in interests and occupations, and indeed, the very logic of the democratization of public life inevitably raise the question of the need to recognize such associations' right to communicate among themselves nationally and internationally via all possible communications media.

The primary objections to framing the problem in these terms can usually be summarized as follows. Given unimpeded communication, won't splinter groups like Pamyat [Memory] and Glasnost have an excellent opportunity to promote their views? Yes, they will. However, it seems that in this day and age the most effective means of combating erroneous and even socially harmful ideas can and must be the power of persuasion and counterargument—certainly not the suppression of dissident views, much less their proscription.

Given these radical innovations in communication, it is becoming increasingly difficult, and in some cases downright impossible, to protect morality, ideological precepts, and purely human values by administrative methods. The choice of means for regulating public life—and for regulating the increasingly complex and varied system of communication, in particular—requires greater balance on the one hand, and greater flexibility on the other.

The basic principles governing the regulation of informational and cultural intercourse are assuming increasingly clear outlines. Of course, a good deal depends on various countries' specific national characteristics. But one can also discern universal principles that are recognized by most countries, such as a ban on the disclosure of military or state secrets or information that offends a citizen's honor and dignity. The socialist countries have worked for universal acceptance of the principle that making propaganda in favor of war, racial hatred, and ethnic strife is illegal, as is using communications media to the detriment of public health and morality.

Quite naturally, we by no means have complete answers to all the complex questions that have already risen or will arise in the foreseeable future as a result of the rapid qualitative improvements in communications media. It is important to correctly identify the thrust of objective trends of development, in order to formulate cultural and social policies that are consistent with them.

2. The rapid technological breakthroughs in television and video equipment—breakthroughs that in and of themselves have spawned a veritable revolution in international cultural exchanges in the second

half of this century—merit special discussion. More people are able to experience works of world culture audiovisually, and the selection available to consumers is expanding significantly. For example, the use of direct-relay satellites and receiving equipment (parabolic antennas and descramblers) will eventually allow people to choose for themselves which of various countries' television programs they want to watch.

In many countries, more and more people are using privately or commonly owned reception equipment. Since 1984, for instance, students at Columbia University in the United States have been using a parabolic antenna for daily reception of television broadcasts directly from the Soviet Molniya [Lightning] communications satellite. In July 1987, Japan's NHK television network began direct telecasting via communications satellite. Some 230,000 homes in the country had been equipped with individual antennas to receive the satellite's signal as of October 1987, and nearly 500,000 were by the end of that year. The number of subscribers is expected to exceed 1 million by mid-1988. (In the United States, 1.6 million homes were equipped with such antennas in 1987.) And whereas picking up the low-power signals has up to now required parabolic antennas of 1.3 to 1.5 meters in diameter, a new generation of satellites, among them the Japanese model, transmit such a powerful signal that antennas of much smaller diameter can receive it. Retail prices are coming down accordingly. An antenna with converter cost 135,000 yen ($940) in Japan late last year, while today the price is down to 100,000 yen (less than half the average monthly wage of a hired worker). It is estimated that nearly 300,000 such antennas will be sold to the public in 1988.

There are owners of homemade parabolic antennas in our country, as well. Many common materials are successfully used to fashion them.

Within a few years high-definition television and video equipment with 1,125 and more scanning lines is expected to appear on Western markets, equipment that will produce a television image of significantly improved quality. A TV screen using liquid crystals is in the final stages of development and will eventually supplant the picture tube. Its image will be generated by means of coded digital signals. Similarly, video cassette recorders will be transformed into microprocessors that will decode the digital signals into sounds and images. These technological advances will create realistic conditions for development of national and international electronic informational and cultural infrastructures employing a single type of signal. These infrastructures will be able to integrate today's largely unconnected channels of information processing, radio, television, video, and print. The United States plans to achieve such integration as early as the

1990s. Trying to peer still further into the future, the well-known Soviet science fiction writer Ye. Parnov foresees a time when the marriage of cable television and the personal computer will enable a viewer to change the plot of a television film at his own discretion, and even to insert himself in the picture as another character.

New technological advances in television and video will markedly intensify international cultural intercourse and speed its globalization. The "language barrier" will not impede this communication because it is becoming technically possible to broadcast television programs in all the planet's major languages simultaneously.

As television and other communications become globalized, states with advanced technical capabilities will naturally be in the best position to promote their culture and ideology. According to USIA Director C. Wick, the United States hopes that American pop-culture will be introduced in other countries, establishing a foundation for the penetration of other American values. The socialist countries hope to use the emerging possibilities to provide as many of the planet's people as possible with objective and exhaustive information about present-day socialism.

There is already a discernible tendency to turn the airwaves into an important field of competition for ideas, moral and cultural norms and scientific advances. The conclusions that French journalist A. Caunt has drawn in this regard are indicative. In Caunt's view, when it comes to television, all countries, regardless of their political line or ideology, constitute a single whole. However, the goal of their rivalry, as he put it, will be not to seize new lands but to colonize them via electronics and images; only countries that can compel others to listen to them will maintain their status as major powers. It is quite clear, Caunt concludes, that the first states to shift to global broadcasting via satellite will gain enormous advantages over all the rest.

Some phenomena anticipating the advent of the age of worldwide television have appeared and are making rapid headway in our country. They include, in addition to satellite broadcasting and the first homemade parabolic antennas, the rapidly expanding individual exchange of programs on video cassettes, which is virtually immune to administrative control.

According to very approximate data, there are now 350,000 VCRs in our country, only 52,000 of which are Soviet-made. Meanwhile, only a small percentage of VCR owners patronize the 140 video rental stores operating in the country. Of the 600 video cassettes they offer, 400 are in virtually no demand. The overwhelming majority (95 percent) of VCR owners use unofficial, "hand to hand" rental sources that have all the controversial foreign films that have not been released in our country.

Technical progress has already created conditions such that VCRs—and, in the near future, perhaps devices that can receive television programs directly from satellites, as well—will become household objects just as common as radios and television sets. Owners of VCRs and these other devices will also try to see films and television programs that cannot be rented by the public or seen on television. Obviously, maintaining effective administrative control over information and works consumed via such channels is technically impossible—and hardly warranted from the viewpoint of cultural policy.

It seems that the time has come to view this problem from a somewhat different standpoint, one that takes worldwide trends and practices into consideration. The spread of individual video in the world is assuming ever-broader scope. Hence the need to search for common approaches toward regulating the use of video equipment. There are already several established standards that have been adopted in many countries. For example, the principle of copyright on television and video programs is generally recognized; those who reproduce them without authorization or who organize public showings are subject to large fines. Using privately owned devices to receive satellite telecasts without authorization or without a legal subscription to them is considered "airwave piracy" and entails financial sanctions.

Another important issue concerns the purposes for which household video equipment is used in the developed capitalist countries, which have several years' lead on our video in terms of evolution. According to Swedish radio, for example, one in three Swedish families owned a VCR in 1986. Video rental stores offer all the most popular films of world cinema of the past 20 years, now totaling more than 6,000 titles. Adventure films are in the highest demand, with 50 percent of the total, followed by comedies (22 percent) and children's films (7 percent).

In our country, the expanding use of household video is accompanied by a number of negative phenomena. An atmosphere of suspicion sometimes grows up around VCR owners, many of whom have suffered unjustified prosecution or arbitrary actions on the part of certain officials of local administrative agencies. At the same time, the selection of films in video stores fails to reflect the achievements of modern foreign films, theater, or entertainment and does not offer popular Soviet theater or concert productions. The quality and quantity of Soviet-made VCRs are unsatisfactory. New capacity and assembly lines at the Voronezh VCR Plant that will allow the plant to increase annual VCR production to 200,000 units will be commissioned only in 1990.

Our technological lag in the video field, and with it our inability to meet modern cultural and aesthetic needs, risk becoming even greater with the emergence of the liquid-crystal TV screen, videoprocessors, and the further spread of personal computers, video and magnetic disks, and cable television.

Various countries throughout the world are reporting more and more advances in this area. In Paris, for example, a unique video store that is to become a kind of video archive in the French capital opened in early 1988. After a cable television system is put in place in the French capital in 1993, it will be possible to use the archive right in one's home. In other words, a significant step has been taken toward the creation of an integrated electronic informational and cultural infrastructure.

Obviously, the advent of an era of virtually unimpeded audiovisual cultural and informational exchanges on the international level is not far off either. It will clearly become more and more difficult for states to extend their sovereignty to such exchanges. Radio broadcasting and television, and with them information transmitted and stored by the latest computer, laser, video, and other technical innovations, will become an all-embracing means of cultural and informational intercourse.

In other words, the cultural and informational sphere, like other spheres of human activity, is exhibiting a sharp intensification of the trend, noted by Marx and Engels, for local and national insularity to be supplanted by comprehensive ties, and comprehensive interdependence, among nations. "This applies equally to both material and intellectual production. The fruits of the intellectual endeavor of individual nations will become common property. National one-sidedness and narrow-mindedness will become increasingly impossible."[1]

The development and globalization of communications in the era of the scientific and technological revolution naturally raise the question of protecting nations' cultural identity and countries' and peoples' spiritual values and traditions from negative external influences. It seems that this protection must be afforded by instilling in people an inner conviction of the virtues of their own culture, and that the guarantee of the effectiveness of efforts to counter undesirable cultural surrogates for a given society lies in enhancing people's overall culture, improving upbringing and education, mobilizing public opinion, cultivating good taste, and ensuring that the given culture's own works are high in quality, relevant, and incisive.

It is also beyond doubt that a commitment to socialist ideals, a deep conviction of socialism's historical rightness, and the choice of

---

[1] Marx and Engels, Works [Sochineniya], Vol. 4, p. 428.

moral guideposts consistent with the lofty criteria of humanism can endure only if they are grasped and assimilated by the individual himself. "In our view," Lenin emphasized, "the state is strong by virtue of the consciousness of the masses. It is strong when the masses know everything, can judge everything, and do everything deliberately.[2]

The wisdom of the folk proverb that a picture is worth a thousand words lies precisely in the fact that human beings have an innate need to think critically and independently, without accepting on faith ready-made assertions about objects and phenomena. For this reason, our search for knowledge cannot be satisfied, for example, by someone else's opinion of a work that we cannot acquaint ourselves with first-hand, especially in the age of communications media, as discussed above.

The Marxist precept that only practice can serve as the criterion for truth is wholly and completely applicable to the sphere of cultural exchanges as well: an individual can assess the correctness of judgments about a work only through practical knowledge of that work. Experience shows that, inevitably, prohibitive measures with respect to a foreign literary work and the impossibility of forming one's own opinion of foreign works that are criticized in the press frequently have the opposite effect from that intended and serve as publicity of sorts for those works, which are often mediocre but arouse curiosity only by virtue of the fact that they are hard to find or inaccessible.

There is still another aspect to the problem. We find ourselves in a curious position when we criticize works that we cannot read, see, or hear. Our Western opponents put themselves in the same position when they try to judge the fruits of Soviet culture with only a very superficial knowledge of them.

It would also make sense to rid ourselves of fears that a firsthand acquaintance with bourgeois ersatz culture will lead to an erosion of our moral and intellectual values. To fear this is, in effect, to doubt the strength of people's convictions and their spiritual health, and to abandon one's faith in the advantages that such universal human concepts as good, justice, common sense, morality, love of peace, and humanism—concepts that communist ideology has consistently championed—have over ignorance, immorality, and aggression. As I see it, as socialist society develops, the "shrinking reflex" that stems from a fear of subjecting ourselves to the degenerating influence of bourgeois culture and ideology will weaken rather than grow stronger. In reality, however, this is by no means always the case. As the journal *Kommunist* [*Communist*] rightly observed in an editorial, certain administrators "have insultingly underrated and belittled the ideological

---

[2]Lenin, *Complete Works* [*Polnoye cobraniye sochineniy*], Vol. 35, p. 21.

conviction, awareness, culture, and political and legal astuteness of the Soviet people, who are quite capable of sorting out for themselves what is suitable intellectual nourishment and what is not."[3]

3. Today it is essential to formulate new approaches to cultural policy—and especially to its foreign-policy aspects—that are consistent with the latest scientific and technological advances and with the processes under way in our country. The basis for this is being created by the policy of restructuring, glasnost, and democratization and by the new political thinking.

It seems we also need to take a fresh look at such seemingly established notions as the "culture industry" and the "entertainment industry," which until now have had largely negative connotations. It is sometimes forgotten that this industry can and must be used to popularize genuine masterpieces of world art. The question, then, regards the content and quality of the specific works it disseminates. The high professional level, say, of the pictures of many Hollywood film companies only does honor to these "industries." The well-known Soviet composer R. Pauls has observed with good reason that we are faced with the task of creating our own "entertainment industry," one that is consistent with our ideological, educational, and aesthetic traditions.

The inability of many of our works to compete on the international culture market is a serious problem. This problem stems in large measure from the extension to culture, art, and literature of the ideology and mentality of our stagnant period, as well as from less exacting criteria in evaluating artistic endeavor, a subject discussed in detail at the January (1987) plenary session of the CPSU Central Committee. To this day, however, some find it more convenient to attribute this problem to "cultural imperialism" and to the "domination of Western pop-culture" than to our own shortcomings.

American cultural expansion is undoubtedly real. At the same time, it primarily affects countries that are politically, economically, and culturally dependent on the United States. The Americanization of Western culture is discussed with alarm in all capitalist countries—especially the West European states—where U.S. cultural output predominates by virtue of its high profitability, technical level, and advertising budgets. But what about in the socialist countries, where this dependence is unquestionably absent? It so happens that here, too, American films, for example, have proven the biggest money-makers. But whereas in the West the American cultural invasion rests on a firm economic foundation (American capital controls film rentals, publishing, the press, private television programs, and so forth), in the

---

[3]*Kommunist*, No. 15, 1987, p. 10.

socialist countries the success of a given work depends above all on its artistic or technical quality, and in some instances on its scarcity as a result of arbitrary prohibitions. Furthermore, such measures have retarded the natural development of several modern schools in our art and, as a consequence, intensified derivative elements, especially in rock music culture.

Thanks to advanced technology, tendencies toward diversity, varied genres, and a multiplicity of individual choices will make themselves more and more strongly felt in cultural life in the modern world. The technical possibilities that modern equipment is opening up and the falling prices and miniaturization of that equipment are leading to a situation in which the means of creativity and of disseminating its fruits are becoming accessible to increasing numbers of people and groups. To a considerable extent, these media are ceasing to be mass media and are becoming group and even individual media. In other words, we are witnessing a certain "demassification" of the means of creating and disseminating works. It is demand that serves as the basic measure of popularity. Today, the relationship between supply and demand, including supply and demand where works of culture are concerned, is regulated chiefly through commodity-money exchange. Products of creative endeavor are treated as goods, with all the ensuing consequences.

One cannot help but ask whether the time has come to stop investing the notion of "commercialization of culture" with a purely negative connotation. Is it right to maintain that there cannot and should not be cultural commerce based on high quality, broad selection, and well-organized publicity of the products available to art lovers? Perhaps our contempt for the commercial approach—in the positive and truly professional sense of the word—and our resulting underestimation of what it takes to succeed in cultural exchange that such an approach entails are precisely what have caused the many unsolved problems facing Soviet culture. These include such problems as the exceptionally poor advertising of works of Soviet culture on the international book, music, film, video, and other markets; the lack of financial accountability, on the part of television and the makers of television programs, for producing uninteresting and artistically weak programing; the payment of honoraria for the mere production of a work, rather than for its actual sale on the market; and the oversupply of some books and records while others—those in high demand— remain in short supply. These shortcomings deprive our works of their ability to compete in international exchanges and, where our creative intelligentsia is concerned, erode its talented members' skill at competing in creative endeavors. Finally, we are coming to realize that in international cultural exchanges, sound commercial practices are the only way to achieve maximum ideological effect, to stimulate interest in works of socialist culture, and to disseminate these works on a broader scale.

I believe the time has also come to change our attitude toward foreign works that have enjoyed great financial success. Soviet audiences know only by hearsay of the Western world's biggest box-office hits of recent decades, which abound in films of record popularity that are unknown to us ("King Kong," "Jaws," "Star Wars," "The Exorcist," "E.T. The Extraterrestrial," recent films starring S. Stallone, such as "Rocky IV," "Rambo," and "Cobra," the James Bond film series, and several installments of "Superman"). In our country, these films are now being circulated among VCR owners. As new hits are released, they will also find their way to VCR owners.

Some—though by no means all—of these films have anti-Soviet overtones. And so the question of an adequate reaction arises once again. In this regard, the main argument cited at press conferences and in the press to substantiate the undesirability of allowing such anti-Soviet films as "Red Dawn," "Rambo: First Blood, Part II," and the television series "Amerika" to be shown to our viewers is that the release of such films could trigger a wave of hatred and negative feelings toward the United States. I daresay that this sort of reaction is less likely than one of adulation for the West's film, entertainment, and other idols, especially among young people. It therefore seems that we would only stand to gain from a graphic demonstration of the caricatured, implausible, and detrimental ways in which Western propaganda and certain "works" portray Soviet people. An objective knowledge of the stereotypes current in the West and an understanding of them can only promote our society's ideological and moral cohesion.

The arguments of those who oppose this approach can be summarized as follows: we cannot permit negative phenomena from the West to be propagandized in our society. That is undoubtedly true. On the other hand, as common sense suggests and existing experience indicates, by no means every showing of such phenomena is necessarily tantamount to propaganda in their favor. For example, the March 29, 1987, publication in *Moskovskiye novosti* [*Moscow News*] of a letter from 10 people who emigrated from the U.S.S.R. at various times and for various reasons does not amount to anti-Soviet propaganda—on the contrary, it exposes anti-Sovietism. The portrayal of violence and brutality in E. Klimov's film "Come and See" [Idi i smotri] or of immorality in L. Bunuel's "The Discreet Charm of the Bourgeoisie" is by no means tantamount to propaganda in favor of these phenomena. One could cite a number of other examples. It will always be a matter of concern, therefore, to competently distinguish between propaganda in favor of a phenomenon and the opportunity for anyone who so desires to observe it firsthand.

Developing this thought, I would like to say that the showing in our country, for example, of the aforementioned Bond films (classics, of sorts, of the Western spy-thriller), "The Exorcist" (the pinnacle of the horror-film genre), or even "Rambo" and "Red Dawn" ("masterpieces" of anti-Sovietism), when accompanied by qualified commentary from film experts, political scientists, psychologists, and other specialists, would hardly have the effect that some cultural administrators fear. It is not a question of circulating in our country the entire gamut of Western anti-Soviet and other mass-market output. The problem is of a different sort: modern civilized man must have the right and opportunity to personally acquaint himself with works that have become accessible to a majority of the world's population and are being discussed throughout the world. Without this, his understanding of the processes at work in world culture will be incomplete.

It has rightly been suggested that often those who warn the loudest of the pernicious effects of works of Western mass culture are the very ones who regularly go abroad and take every opportunity to get to know them—ignoring the degenerative effect that this has on their own morality and ideology.

Among other things, the very fact that more and more Soviet people are going abroad and experiencing various aspects of bourgeois culture firsthand argues in favor of the approach proposed in this article.

Needless to say, the recommended approach does not amount to acquiescence to harmful stereotypes. On the contrary, we must make exhaustive and tenacious efforts to destroy them.

As the sad experience of confrontational approaches shows, success in this endeavor is more likely through personal contact between cultural figures, members of the public, and the intelligentsia than through mutual recriminations, exposures, accusations, and visa refusals. What if Stallone, who has been rightly criticized in our press for the anti-Soviet films he has made, could visit our country, acquaint himself with the changes taking place in it, learn something—albeit just a smattering—about the centuries-old culture of our peoples, and have discussions with people who work in Soviet film, as was done by Kristofferson, who appeared in the film "Amerika"? Perhaps it would alter his stereotyped attitude and, who knows, perhaps even suggest to him other subjects for his creative pursuits.

It should be pointed out that just such bold, nontrivial approaches to cultural exchanges have won broader and broader acceptance of late. In an interview with the newspaper *Sovetskaya kultura* [*Soviet Culture*], for example, O. Rudnev, the chairman of the Soveksportfilm

[Soviet Film-Export] Foreign Trade Organization, expressed the view that "it would be useful to give the Soviet viewer a firsthand look at just what sort of ideological opponent we face today . . . and how he talks about us. It might well be worthwhile to show certain films with an antisocialist bent on television, albeit in excerpted form, for our mass viewer has no inkling of the vulgarity, cynicism, immorality, and falsehood with which our life is sometimes depicted!"

But there is another approach as well. N. Gilevich, the First Secretary of the Board of the Belorussian Republic Writers' Union, recommends, for example, that in order to protect the "young, upcoming generations from becoming infected with grave social and moral afflictions," we must "categorically stop the purchase and showing of ideologically and morally depraved foreign motion pictures and television films that have a pernicious effect on the minds and hearts of our young people. . . . The same goes for imported music and art. We cannot go on flooding this country with vulgar and harmful ersatz art and things that morally and aesthetically corrupt our young fellow citizens!"

As I see it, the question of which of these two policy approaches to foreign cultural exchanges is the correct one is resolved as the accuracy of their assumptions is tested in practice. One thing is certain: although the approaches are opposite, both pursue the same end result—protecting the interests of our society's healthy development. As was noted at a conference in the CPSU Central Committee that reviewed progress in implementing the resolution of the CPSU Central Committee and the USSR Council of Ministers "On Measures to Further Improve Concerts in the Country and to Strengthen the Physicial Facilities and Equipment of Concert Organizations," "the modern world is shrinking and becoming increasingly interconnected in terms of communication. To think it possible to create in this world some kind of niche or habitat insulated from outside influences and to wait there safely in meek submission is not simply to indulge in illusions but also to condemn oneself to defeat."[4]

One of our highly important policy tasks remains that of struggling for the observance of established rules of international communication and of sensible forms of coexistence among states and peoples. We must demonstrate again and again to our Western partners that, in our day and age, the use of "pseudocultural influences" to erode the moral and humanist principles of mankind, or those of the individual communities that make it up, is fraught with the gravest consequences—perhaps even universal destruction.

---

[4]*Pravda*, Oct. 22, 1986.

On the other hand, however, creating some sort of artificial, "sterile" environment by erecting administrative and technical barriers is impossible and unnecessary: In the long run, this leads to impaired social immunity and to weakened mechanisms of social self-regulation. We cannot imbue people with lasting political and moral immunity to the ideological opponent's propaganda by means of "bans," "prohibitions," "barriers," and other measures essentially impeding development of effective internal resistance to "pathogenic" phenomena.

It seems that given the growing internationalization in all areas of life and today's radical changes in means of communication, our state must find qualitatively new ways to accomplish the tasks of protecting its national culture. Obviously, the basic path must be one of shifting the emphasis from administrative and technical methods to ideological and moral ones. The policy of developing democratization, glasnost, and initiative is creating important preconditions for this.

In international cultural exchange, democratization is manifested in the diversity and, sometimes the opposition of viewpoints, loyalties, and creative schools and in the possibility of freely and openly seeking, discussing, and transmitting information and works of culture. The practice of enforced silence in regard to certain works or schools and of maintaining "topics closed to discussion" is becoming not only politically hopeless but also impossible in practical terms. In the past this has only put trump cards in our ideological opponents' hands.

The emerging objective situation demands ever more insistently the free competition of talent in the international cultural arena. As we know, serious imbalances exist in this area today: the developing countries remain unequal in status; audiences in the socialist countries are far better acquainted with Western film, literature, and music than the Western public is with socialist culture, and so forth.

Competition in equal conditions among works and talents on a worldwide scale will give the socialist countries new opportunities to advance the ideas of humanism and high moral standards, to protect these ideas from the effects of bourgeois culture's negative aspects, and to win new sympathies and adherents through the comparison of different world views. The high quality of our cultural works and their artistic merit, professionalism, and intellectual appeal guarantee this.

One would like to believe that the common sense and morals of "intelligent man" will help to find and establish an optimal order of world cultural exchange that will have no place for pseudocultural offerings, and that humanity will emerge even stronger from this test of intellectual maturity. The struggle for the triumph of universal human values will serve as a salubrious and cleansing factor in this test.

Editors' Note: Great efforts are being made under the auspices of the United Nations and the United Nations Educational, Scientific and Cultural Organization to draw up rules to govern international cultural and information exchange.

A basic principle of international intercourse is the right proclaimed in the Universal Declaration of Human Rights, adopted by the U.N. General Assembly on Dec. 10, 1948, to freely adhere to one's convictions and to seek out, obtain, and disseminate information and ideas by any means and irrespective of national frontiers (Art. 19). Differences between the socialist and capitalist countries on issues pertaining to norms of international intercourse stem from the way they view this right. The Western countries—first and foremost the United States—insist on the unimpeded movement of ideas and information, citing the formulation of the aforementioned article as justification for this demand. In the view of socialist countries and in that of most developing countries, however, such an approach would inevitably result in potential violations of the rights and freedoms of other citizens at whom offensive, immoral, or hostile information could be directed. The latter viewpoint is consistent with the provisions of the International Pact on Civil and Political Rights, adopted by the U.N. General Assembly on Dec. 16, 1966. The pact observes that the exercise of the stipulated rights imposes special obligations and special responsibility and, consequently, may entail certain restrictions that are established by law and are essential to respect for the rights and reputation of other persons, to the protection of state security, and to the maintenance of public order, health, or morality (Art. 19). The pact also calls for outlawing any and all propaganda in favor of war and of any and all statements advocating national, racial, or religious hatred that constitutes incitement to discrimination, hostility, or violence.

All the basic U.N. and UNESCO documents concerning these issues are suffused with the idea of the inadmissibility of using communications media to the detriment of other people and countries. Such documents include, for example, the "Declaration on the Dissemination Among Young People of the Ideals of Peace, Mutual Respect, and Mutual Understanding Among Peoples" of Dec. 7, 1965, and the "Declaration on Basic Principles Concerning the Contribution of the Mass Media to the Strengthening of Peace and International Mutual Understanding, to the Development of Human Rights, and to the Struggle Against Racism and Apartheid and Incitement to War" of Nov. 28, 1978.

It is noteworthy that, with increasing frequency, the United States is the only country that votes against U.N. decisions aimed at ensuring the use of communications media solely on the basis of a good-neighbor, friendly and correct attitude toward other peoples. For example, only the U.S. delegation voted against the resolutions on "Questions Concerning Information" at sessions of the U.N. General Assembly in 1982 and 1986 (131 and 148 delegations respectively voted for the resolutions). The United States continues to refuse to sign the International Convention on the Use of Radio Broadcasting in the Interests of Peace, adopted Sept. 23, 1936, whose signatories "mutually undertake to prohibit and, should it occur, to immediately put an end to the broadcast on their territories of any programs that, to the detriment of good international mutual understanding, are by their character aimed at inciting the population of any territory to actions that are incompatible with internal order or security."

Virtually all international documents on questions concerning the dissemination of information take note of the undesirability of maintaining existing imbalances in information flows to the detriment of the developing countries and of the need to achieve diversity in sources of communication. In 1978, the Ministry of Information of Tunisia, as a representative of the Nonaligned Movement, submitted to the U.N. Secretary-General a study on a "New International Information Order." The study substantiates the need for the early creation of such an order from the developing countries' viewpoint and offers specific recommendations for its establishment. The document emphasizes that the right of interaction must guarantee not only the right to be informed but also the right—which follows from it—to inform, to supplement incomplete information, and to correct erroneous information. The idea of establishing a new world information order is consistent with the Soviet approach to the problem of the need to democratize and humanize international relations.

In the Vanguard of History

Igor Yevgenyevich Guryev*

Great historical events always have many implications. One of the most important political outcomes of the October Revolution of 1917 was the emergence of Bolshevism as a world phenomenon.

Lenin's party of Bolsheviks, taking over the struggle of Russia's proletarian working masses and leading them to a revolution that became a turning point in world history, demonstrated in the most convincing manner—through practice—that when class struggle is raised to a revolutionary pitch and scope it leads to socialism. The force of this example gave rise to a wave of communist parties being formed in many countries that were embroiled in class struggles. The workers' movement split decisively into two main currents—the revolutionary and the reformist.

In 1918 communist parties were formed in Germany, Austria, Hungary, Poland, the Netherlands, and Finland. By the summer of 1920, delegates from 27 communist parties participated in the meeting of the Second Congress of the Communist International, which had been established in 1919. By the time the Seventh Congress was convened in July 1933, the Comintern consisted of 76 communist parties and organizations. They had 3,141,000 members, including more than 785,000 members in capitalist countries.

There are now active communist parties in 95 countries, including socialist countries, countries that have been liberated from colonialism, and industrially developed capitalist countries. Membership totals more than 80 million, compared to 400,000 in 1917. Over the 70 years since the October Revolution, the number of communists in the world has increased two hundredfold. Is this not eloquent testimony to the great vital force of the communist movement! But quantitative indicators alone do not paint a complete picture of how the communist parties' influence has grown. Communists are supported, their ideas are shared, and many hundreds of millions of people vote for their candidates in elections.

---

*Doctor of economics, deputy director of the Institute of World Economy and International Relations (IMEMO). This article appeared in the November 1987 issue of *MEMO*.

The successes are indisputable. But they were paid for with hard work, intense struggle, and the lives of hundreds of thousands, millions, of communists. History, of course, is not a simple stroll down Nevskiy Prospect, especially for those who blaze the trail into the future. In countries outside the socialist world, communists' perseverance and dedication to their cause is tested by hardship, privation, and even open harassment and persecution. Not all of them always prove capable of meeting that test. Hence the growth of the communist movement in that part of the world assumes all the more meaning and importance.

In documents of the 27th CPSU Congress the communist movement is characterized "as one of the most influential ideological and political forces of the present day." Communists are ideologically and politically leading the progress of hundreds of millions of people toward the creation of an essentially new, communist civilization. This fact alone, when viewed from the standpoint of its historical significance, places communist parties in an absolutely unique position vis-à-vis those social forces and organizations (including mass organizations that are universally recognized and highly influential) whose energies are directed toward preserving and "patching up" the old capitalist civilization.

Directing the actual building of new social relations is just one aspect of communists' activities. No less important, perhaps, is their most active participation in all the major historical events of the modern age, in all those battles whose results in many respects determine the political face of the world today.

Communists have led social revolutions of majorities of the working people in all countries where the revolutions have taken place and been victorious. Currently the socialist part of the world contains about a third of the planet's population.

Communists have taken the most active part in, and in some cases even led, national liberation revolutions. Countries that have been freed from colonial dependency make up a significant majority of the world community of nations today.

Communists always have been and continue to be on the leading edge of the struggle against the forces of imperialism and reaction. During World War II they made an outstanding contribution to organizing the resistance movement and, after that, to crushing the shock troops of international imperialist reaction—German fascism and Japanese militarism. Today, defending life itself on the planet against the threat of nuclear destruction, communists are playing an extremely active role in the mass peace movement.

In whatever battles they have participated, past and present, communists, guided by Marxist-Leninist theory, have invariably defended the interests, rights, and life aspirations of the working people. They strive to gain their support among the masses, and they back the working people's demands and struggle together with them. It is precisely this type of political activity that has allowed communists to have a marked influence on the course of events on both national and international levels, to significantly effect changes in the world historical situation as a whole, and to become one of the most influential political movements of the present day.

At the same time, it would be a dangerous error to think that the communist movement is always "doomed to succeed," or to perceive historical justification and correctness in all the actions of communist parties. Certainly, their belief in the historical inevitability that socialism will replace capitalism, their clear understanding of the objective laws of social development, and their high degree of organizational cohesiveness give communists a vanguard role in the workers' movement, enabling them to direct the struggle of the forces for social progress along the most proven paths, and to act as a kind of pathfinder of history.

However, all these distinguishing qualities, in and of themselves, are no guarantee against the severe ordeals of the objective situation and struggle, nor against communists' own weaknesses and mistakes. There are a number of factors and circumstances that occasionally may adversely affect a given party's situation. They include abrupt and sometimes unpredictable turns in social development; changes in the political mood, consciousness, or behavior of the masses; increased opposition from ideological and political adversaries; a party's own miscalculations in evaluating the overall situation, appraising major trends in changes that are occurring, and judging the interests and goals of its allies in the struggle; a party's mistakes in choosing the main directions and means of struggle; and disagreements within a party. These and other factors may cause a party to lose supporters, weaken its support from the masses, and temporarily reduce its influence.

In recent years problems of this sort have been encountered, in particular, by a number of communist parties in the West. Some of them have experienced a drop in the influx of new members, and sometimes even an absolute decline in membership. The Italian Communist Party lost more than 200,000 members from 1977 to 1986, though it remains the largest communist party in the nonsocialist world (according to April 1986 figures, the Italian Communist Party had about 1,596,000 members). Communists are concerned by the "aging" of many parties in the face of a marked decline in the entry of young people. For example, according to 1985 data, 10 percent of the

Italian Communist Party's membership consisted of young people of ages 18 to 30, while only 3 percent belonged to the 18 to 24 age group.

Growing difficulties are being encountered in distributing the communist press. The circulation of party newspapers and magazines has declined in a number of countries. The number of votes for communist candidates in parliamentary elections is declining. Communist Party candidates received more than 21 percent of the vote in the 1973 elections to the French National Assembly; in 1981 they received 16.8 percent, and in 1986—only 9.8 percent. In special parliamentary elections held in June 1987, Italian Communists received 26.6 percent of the vote, which was 3.3 percent less than in the 1983 elections.

The communist movement has long been an integral factor in world political development. That is why changes in the situation of a number of communist parties in the capitalist West—slowed progress in some, a retreat from achieved positions in others—have an importance that goes beyond these parties themselves. These changes cannot be measured solely on the scale of the political development of individual countries.

At the same time, when problems are encountered more or less simultaneously in not just one or two, but a whole series of parties, they indicate that the primary cause of difficulties lies not so much in the activities of any individual parties (though realities of this sort should not be ignored, either), as in the objective changes that present-day state monopoly capitalism is undergoing.

Changing Conditions

The ability to change is one of capitalism's constant properties.[1] Economic crises, especially those that possess the greatest destructive force, may play a special role in the process of change. By significantly worsening the working people's situation, embittering them, and causing waves of mass indignation, such crises pose a direct threat to the very existence of the capitalist system and force the ruling class to initiate various reforms and try to renew existing forms of social relations.

---

[1]This was obvious back in the 1860s, when Marx, in his preface to the first edition of *Capital*, wrote that "present-day society is not a hard crystal but an organism capable of transmutations and in a constant process of transmutation" (K. Marx and F. Engels, *Works* [*Sochineniya*], Vol. 23, p. 11). It is also obvious in our day. "Present-day capitalism differs in many respects from what it was like at the beginning and even the middle of the 20th century" (*Materials from the 27th Congress of the Communist Party of the Soviet Union* [*Materialy XXVII syezda Kommunisticheskoy partii Sovetskogo Soyuza*], Moscow, 1986, p. 130).

One of the most vivid examples of this is the New Deal and the series of socioeconomic measures undertaken by U.S. President F. Roosevelt in order to overcome the extremely severe consequences of the general cyclical overproduction crisis of 1929 to 1933. In practice, Roosevelt's actions paved the way for a liberal-democratic form of state interference in the economic and social development of society. At the same time, they accelerated the transition from monopoly capitalism to state monopoly capitalism.

In the 1970s and early 1980s, the state-monopoly economy, which by then was already developed, found itself at the mercy of a series of crises.

First, a period of currency disputes began that to one degree or another has continued to this day. They culminated in the failure of the Bretton Woods currency system, which was based on a fixed U.S. dollar exchange rate for gold and for all other national currencies. Then an acute energy crisis erupted: The developed capitalist countries "suddenly" encountered shortages of petroleum resources, followed by a sharp, almost tenfold increase, which hit two peaks, in prices for them. This crisis has had a serious impact on both national economies and the world capitalist economy as a whole. Inflation has become "Enemy No. 1" everywhere. Twice in a relatively short time span, from the mid-1970s to early 1980s, deep and prolonged (by standards of the postwar decades) cyclical overproduction crises have dealt staggering blows to the industrial life of all the developed capitalist countries almost simultaneously. Unemployment, the dimensions of which at least tripled over a period of just over 10 years, has become a genuine social disaster. The size of international capitalist indebtedness has grown by two orders of magnitude—from tens of billions of dollars to more than a trillion dollars. A number of basic material-production branches have found themselves in a state of chronic slump. They include the steel and textile industries, the former of which had served, until recently, as the basis for heavy industry, as the latter had for light industry.

A situation of multipolar, crisis-plagued instability that is practically unique in all of history has developed in the capitalist economy. It represents a glaring contrast to the situation of relative prosperity that prevailed in the 1950s and 1960s. The conditions for capital activity have greatly worsened, and the risk for new capital investment and entrepreneurship in general has increased. All of this has caused increased mass anxiety and discontent.

It was perhaps the monopoly bourgeoisie who announced their discontent most loudly. They leveled their complaints primarily against the state, viewing its liberal-reformist socioeconomic policies as the main cause of all woes, especially inflation and the difficulties of improving competitiveness. Almost everywhere (in some cases, with the help of the mass media) "crises of confidence" in the ability of governments to create the conditions for healthy economic development broke out. The economy became the politicians' enemy. But that was for liberal democratic politicians. Taking advantage of the dissatisfaction with those politicians' socioeconomic policies to advance their own interests, representatives of the ruling class's conservative wing strove for (and gained!) power.

It would seem that the growth of inflation and unemployment, and the conservatives' attack on the social rights and gains of the working people should have led to an explosion of indignation among the masses and the rapid development of immediate preconditions for profound, general democratic transformations, and should have brought the revolutionary prospects for the communist parties closer. However, that did not occur.

In all likelihood, there are several reasons it did not.

In the first place, in the course of the past five years the economic situation in the whole group of the developed capitalist countries has changed for the better. The pressure of inflation has eased. The energy situation has stabilized. The volume of social production has risen, though not at very high rates (2.6 percent in 1986).

At the same time, a number of obvious instability factors continue to operate. The situation in the currency markets sporadically deteriorates; the scale and dynamics of international indebtedness are causing great apprehensions; the possibilities for resolving unemployment by the methods of conservative economic policies look dim.

Nonetheless, the fact remains that in the mechanism of capitalist reproduction, in the bourgeoisie's economic activities, and in the state's economic policies, a potential has been found that has made it possible to get the ship of the economy off the sharp reefs on which it found itself in the mid-1970s to early 1980s. Moreover, capitalism's active utilization of the specific features of the new stage in the scientific and technological revolution has resulted in a relatively rapid development of advanced production processes and the services sphere, and in a structural reorganization of the economy. With the extremely active participation of transnational capital, international economic relations have been developing dynamically. All this could not help but affect the attitude of the relatively broad masses toward the economic potential of present-day capitalism, and could not help playing a political role.

In the second place, significant changes have taken place in the social structure of hired labor. Its boundaries have expanded, and the size of the working class has grown. The field of the basic class contradiction has become correspondingly wider. However, that does not mean that the pressure of anticapitalist—much less revolutionary—tendencies has risen correspondingly among hired labor. The processes of differentiation of the working class have intensified under the influence of crisis-related processes, capital's tapping of the potential of the scientific and technological revolution, and structural changes in the economy.

A reduction is occurring in the relative, and sometimes even absolute, size of the industrial proletariat—miners, steel workers, machinery-industry workers, and so on—who form the nucleus of the working class. At the same time, new detachments of that class employed in the vigorously expanding services sector have been growing rapidly. These detachments already conspicuously outnumber industrial workers. Equally conspicuous, however, is their inferiority to the latter in terms of organization, militancy, and consciousness of the ultimate interests of the workers' movement.

A watershed has also been created between those who have the opportunity to work in the "legal economy" and those who find themselves on the roadside—the unemployed, people employed in the "underground economy," foreign workers, a substantial number of retirees, and other categories of so-called marginal strata of the proletarian population. For the former, the main thing is to at least preserve what they have, especially their jobs. Under the conditions of mass unemployment, they often do not think about any sort of new gains. The latter are striving to break out of the critical situation in which they find themselves. What they need are precisely new gains, a struggle for improvement. But the former are in the majority, and this circumstance alone puts the latter in a certain isolation and throws them back into a kind of social and psychological ghetto.

Tendencies toward differentiation are also manifested in the working class's industrial nucleus. Its vocational and skill composition is changing. The proportion of skilled workers has been growing. In 1986 they already made up 43.9 percent of the total number of U.S. industrial workers.[2] In this group the substratum of specialists, who in level of education and training and in the nature of their work come extremely close to engineering and technical personnel, has been growing. This is obviously one form in which the natural process of the development of human society's main productive force manifests itself. That is the positive significance of that tendency. But one must not overlook the fact that this group of industrial workers manifests social passivity, and many of them are less inclined to rely on the strength of class solidarity and are more oriented toward personal

---

[2]*Unemployment and Earnings*, Jan. 1987, p. 177.

success. All this is by no means helping to increase the revolutionary potential of the working class's nucleus.

The same thing can evidently be said about the process whereby the composition of the industrial working class is renewed through the increasingly active addition of employees from the expanding information industry. These new strata represent a complex conglomerate that is substantially inferior to the traditional nucleus of the proletariat in terms of its level both of organization and class consciousness.

The decline in the concentration of workers in large and extremely large enterprises is yet another fundamental change in the traditional makeup of the proletariat's industrial ranks. The modernization of old enterprises (up to 80 percent of capital investments in the Western countries goes to modernizing production equipment) and adoption of labor-saving equipment and technologies are accompanied by a reduction in the number of people employed at such enterprises. In most cases new enterprises are geared from the outset to the use of the smallest possible amount of human labor. The decline in employment levels at industrial enterprises is causing a drop in the industrial proletariat's level of class organization and making it more difficult to achieve unity in its mass actions.

Thus, the changes that have taken place over the past 10 to 15 years in the structure of hired labor have by no means helped increase its social and political activism. On the one hand, the potential militancy of the working class's traditional nucleus has declined. On the other, the new members' protest against exploitation and oppression has not yet acquired its full scope. The situation is worsened by mass unemployment, which prompts workers and office employees to wage primarily defensive battles and, at the same time, by intensifying the competition between them, limits their ability to resist capital's offensive.

Under these conditions, the ruling class's right wing found it relatively easy to execute a conservative turnaround across the whole political front, especially where the working class's interests were most directly affected—in the sphere of social policy.

In the third place, the working masses' attitude toward capitalism has become more complicated. The level of mass protest in the developed capitalist countries is not declining. The working people are fighting against the closing of enterprises, employers' refusal to raise wages, huge military expenditures, environmental pollution, the inadequate state attention to higher education, and so on. Their protest takes various forms—rallies, demonstrations, marches, picket lines, strikes, sympathy strikes, the occupation of empty buildings and enterprises.

All this is evidence that the class struggle remains the dominant feature of political life in capitalist society, and that the masses are convinced of the efficacy of that struggle. At the same time, the high level of protests shows that capitalist reality itself continues to provide a fertile environment for mass discontent.

Still, broad strata of the working population of the developed capitalist countries have hardly risen, at least in the past few years, to the level of protest directly against capitalism as a whole, as a system of social relations. Acute discontent with the state of affairs in various areas of life does not turn into indignation at the system's general inability to solve vitally important problems. The idea is developing in the mass political consciousness that many fairly urgent problems of social development can be solved through struggle without overturning the social system as a whole.

This more complicated attitude toward capitalism reflects the experience both of the class struggle and of the development of capitalism over the entire postwar period. In class battles, through offensives and retreats, realizing success and suffering defeats, the working people on the whole have achieved a significant increase in real earnings compared to the early 1950s (an increase ranging from 30 percent in the United States to 300 percent in Japan). And capital has found it possible—naturally, by intensifying the exploitation of the workers themselves, first and foremost—to undertake that increase, although it has repeatedly counterattacked against earnings, relying, moreover, on the state's help in doing so. The growth in real earnings has contributed to a change in the quality and structure of personal consumption, as well as in the working people's lifestyle.

The policy of reforms that was followed fairly actively up to the mid-1970s and subjected to conservative restrictions in the 1980s played no small role in making the attitude toward capitalism more complicated. Even in a curtailed form, the system of social welfare created under pressure from working people has reduced the intensity of hardships engendered by capitalism. Functioning as a kind of shock absorber, it has made it possible in years of crisis to divert growing discontent away from the faults of the social system and direct it toward the shortcomings of current programs.

The attitude not only toward the socioeconomic system but also toward the political system of bourgeois society has grown more complicated. In evaluating its pluses and minuses, fairly broad masses of the working people consider first and foremost the fact that they have been able to make considerable social gains under that system. The increasingly pragmatic and rationalistic tendency in mass consciousness operates in the same direction. This tendency orients people primarily toward seeking the kinds of solutions to society's complex problems that, while affecting some of those problems' causes, leave basic social institutions unchanged.

In the vast majority, the working people in the developed capitalist countries have achieved relative material prosperity, rely on their social gains, and enjoy certain democratic freedoms. They count on the possibility of fighting to defend their interests, but at the same time they are afraid of subjecting what they have gained to the risk of serious social battles and upheavals.

All this attests to the survivability of present-day capitalism, its ability to adapt to the new conditions caused by its own contradictions, and the bourgeoisie's ability to temporarily strengthen its power, even in an unfavorable crisis situation, without resorting to extreme right-wing coups and fascist putsches, as happened in the 1930s.

The state of affairs in the developed capitalist countries indicates that a revolutionary situation is not among the possibilities for the near future of their social and political development.[3] The top echelons have demonstrated their ability to govern in the old way and keep the situation under control using neoconservative means and methods. The lower classes, on the whole, are demonstrating just as clearly that today they do not aspire to radical changes. In terms of its objective content, this sort of situation has always constituted the greatest difficulty for revolutionary parties. And it is creating difficulties for communists in a number of developed capitalist countries today, as well. At the same time, it is necessary to continue work among the masses and seek new opportunities and ways, because the whole objective course of capitalist society's development—the continuing process of the socialization of production, the expansion of the areas affected by crisis upheavals, the exploitation of hired labor by the owners of capital, and the class struggle as the sole means of defending the interests of the exploited—confirms the historical inevitability of the replacement of capitalism by a communist society.

Back in the late 1950s communist parties, taking the lack of a revolutionary situation into account, started making attempts to advance toward revolution by struggling for democracy. In the crisis-torn years of the 1970s, these attempts continued.

---

[3]"Relatively recently," it was noted at an international discussion meeting held in Prague on certain important problems of the present-day communist movement, "communists believed that the 20th century would be the century of the worldwide triumph of socialism. But now it is clear that, no matter how great revolutionaries' natural desire to bring the hour of victory closer might be, this goal is receding into the more distant future" (*Problemy mira i sotsializma* [*Problems of Peace and Socialism*], No. 10, 1986, p. 46). Essentially the same viewpoint is expressed by Alvaro Cunhal, General Secretary of the Portuguese Communist Party: "In some countries, for objective and subjective reasons, communist parties have lost the prospect of revolution for the near future" (*Pravda*, Sept. 4, 1987).

In Search of New Ways

The elaboration of programs of socioeconomic development as alternatives to state-monopoly programs has become part of the practice of all communist parties. Their primary objective is to reflect the direct interests of a given country's working people as fully as possible. The point of this objective is obvious: to attract the attention of as many of them as possible, rely on their support, and lead them to fight for the program's implementation. Naturally, programs should be specifically geared to the conditions of each country. In this connection, no two programs can be alike. Under different economic conditions—the relatively prosperous 1950s and the crisis-torn 1970s—state policies change. Correspondingly, different alternatives are also developed.

The greatest difficulty in drawing them up, much less implementing them, is to make them realistic. In a certain respect, a number of their provisions are knowingly doomed to failure. After all, these programs are supposed to secure the workers' interests and be an alternative to the interests of capital reflected in state programs, under conditions in which production is subject to the laws of capitalist entrepreneurship and the bourgeoisie holds command positions in both the economy and in politics.

Alternatives put forward during economic crises are extremely difficult to implement. In order to receive mass support, they should be aimed at overcoming the crisis and emerging from it. This requires increasing the efficiency of social production, something in which the bourgeoisie also has a considerable stake. At the same time, the democratic alternative should be aimed at radically improving the overall situation of the working class and the working masses, and subordinating the country's production potential to the needs of its working majority.

The complexity of the situation in which alternative programs are drawn up sometimes helps stir up among some party members a tendency toward various forms of reconciliation with capitalism and with certain shadings of reformism and opportunism. Certain efforts are also required to overcome the inclination to put forward demands that promote class interests but are understood in a purely dogmatic sense and are divorced from realistic possibilities. Quite often current demands pertaining to the working people's socioeconomic interests—employment, wages, social insurance—are put forward in a concrete form that, to all intents and purposes, implies the elimination of capital's economic and political power. This sort of sectarianism can only lead a party to become divorced from the real struggle of the masses. Many parties are familiar, to one degree or another, with such difficulties.

While seeking ways to solve problems affecting the working people's daily interests, communists at the same time pursue more general goals. First of all, they include the democratization of society by ensuring the working people's genuine participation in managing the economy at various levels. The process of democratization that communists advocate under the conditions of present-day capitalism is inseparably bound up, in its class essence, with the process of expanding and strengthening the working class's positions in the state. And this, in turn, may open the way to the creation of more favorable political conditions for the fundamental restructuring of social relations as a whole.

Naturally, the search for new ways to advance toward revolution by fighting for democracy is not limited solely to developing programs for a democratic alternative. The fundamental questions of revolution, especially its stages, forms, and means of accomplishment, occupy a significant place in parties' theoretical activities. On all these questions, communists have waged an active fight against pseudoleftist tendencies, whose slogans have been used by terrorist groups to carry out their actions in a number of West European countries.

The problems of the relationship between revolution and democracy have also been worked on. The lack of sufficient clarity on these questions and a certain enthusiasm for empty declarations "prepared the ground for the emergence of certain contradictions and vacillations in the theoretical and practical activities of some communist parties, and even for what amounted to a revision of experience-proven conclusions of revolutionary teachings. . . ."[4] S. Carrillo's book *Eurocommunism and the State* was a concentrated expression of such tendencies. As we know, the concept of "Eurocommunism" was adopted to some extent in a number of communist parties. In the final analysis, the concept's internal untenability caused it to fail. Nonetheless, considerable damage was done to the communist movement. The divided Spanish Communist Party suffered severe losses, and the prestige of certain other parties suffered in the eyes of the working class.

The question of creating broad alliances of democratic forces is an urgent matter in the practical political activities of the communist parties, even the largest ones. Cooperation with other political forces is essential to communists—among other reasons, in order to combat the threat of nuclear war and rebuff the right-wing conservatives' offensive.

---

[4]See *The International Workers' Movement: Questions of History and Theory* [*Mezhdunarodnoye rabocheye dvizheniye. Voprosy istorii i teorii*], Vol. 8, Moscow, 1985, p. 512.

An important element of communists' approach to accomplishing this task in the context of the developed capitalist countries is the arrangement of contacts and cooperation with socialists and social democrats at all levels—from low-level organizations to high executive bodies. In some of the most developed capitalist countries this sort of cooperation has reached the level of a relatively extensive experiment (the "alliance of leftist forces" in France and the "new parliamentary majority" in Italy). After the Franco regime's fall, relations between communists and socialists in Spain started to develop on a different basis than before. Other communist parties have also taken important initiatives in the direction of eliminating disagreements with the social democratic movement.

In a number of countries, especially where there are large communist parties, joint actions have successfully been carried out in local government bodies. This form of cooperation is especially important in view of the fact that, through the example of the daily practical activities of local, provincial, and city "governments," it persuades the masses that communists can effectively work together with socialists and social democrats in the national government as well.

However, cooperation with socialist and social democratic parties entails a good many difficulties and contradictions, some of which are hard to overcome. Social democrats and socialists continue to be parties that are mainly working-class in their makeup (and especially in their electoral base). At the same time, their following consists mainly of the reformist element of the working class, whose ideological and political outlook is relatively limited. In this connection, the task of overcoming anticommunist prejudices that have accumulated in social democratic parties and organizations is a very difficult one.

On the other hand, while according great importance to the alliance with socialists and social democrats and to pooling efforts in the struggle against the ruling class and its policies, communists do not aspire to "absorb" their allies, but nor do they permit themselves to be dissolved in them and slip into their ideological and political positions. The objectives that communist parties set for themselves can be successfully accomplished only if the role of the leading detachment in each such alliance is preserved for communists. All these are questions of fundamental importance. Their resolution does not depend strictly on the will and desire of communists, and it requires persistent, prolonged and extremely difficult work.

Circumstances may develop in such a way that socialists refuse to act in concert with communists. Thus, in 1978 in Italy an agreement was reached to create a parliamentary majority with the participation of the Italian Communist Party. For the first time in 30 years, the Italian Communist Party left the opposition and started supporting the government on the basis of a previously approved program that in many respects took the Communists' proposals into account. However, the Italian bourgeoisie's major political force, the Christian Democratic Party, plainly had no interest in carrying out many progressive measures, and the rightist forces within it tried to use the Italian Communist Party's membership in the parliamentary majority to demonstrate that the Communists' participation in governing the country should not necessarily be linked to any radical change in the socioeconomic situation. This period that was critical to the fortunes of social progress showed the effects of an absolutely inadequate coordination of actions between the Italian Communist Party and the Italian Socialist Party, which had also joined the parliamentary majority.

The unwillingness of the Italian Socialist Party's leadership to enter into closer cooperation with the Communist Party became the main reason for the lack of an alliance between these two branches of the Italian working class, although cooperation—and often, quite successful cooperation—had long been carried out in trade unions and local government bodies.

The experience of the French Communist Party's participation in an alliance of leftist forces also attests to the difficulties that may arise in relations between communists and socialists.

In 1981 a coalition of leftist parties—Communists, Socialists and Left Radicals—won the general elections in France. The Communists consented to join a majority government on the condition that a program of action developed jointly with the Socialists and calling for a number of progressive socioeconomic transformations be carried out. Socialists took the dominant positions in the government, but for a certain time the Communists gained the opportunity to defend the interests of the working class and strengthen their own influence. Joining the government, the Communist Party defended the masses' interests and, at the same time, oriented them toward constructive and independent-minded support of the governing majority. What the Communist Party had in mind was uniting government action with the mass struggle and the working people's participation in the management of society's affairs.

In February 1985 the 25th Congress of the French Communist Party pointed out the errors entailed in the practice and theoretical justification of an alliance of leftist forces like that of 1981 to 1983, which in actuality had come down to agreement solely on the level of the two parties' "headquarters." As a result, the idea that the Communists' and Socialists' goals were identical had started to take hold among the working people, even members of the French Communist Party. Illusions arose that the French Socialist Party was capable of abandoning its characteristic adherence to the ideas of bourgeois reformism. In the final analysis, all this could do nothing but weaken the Communists' positions both in the alliance of leftist forces and in the political structure of society as a whole.

The Socialists rather quickly put aside their election promises and, turning sharply to the right, set a policy of establishing a regime of "strict economy" and industrial "modernization" in the country. On the whole, this accorded with their patrons' interests. As for the Communists, their partners in the government coalition, the French Socialist Party, demanded that they honor their commitment to follow a unified political course, while simultaneously denying them any possibility of effectively defending the working people's interests.

In the summer of 1984, following elections to the European Parliament in which the French Communist Party and French Socialist Party lost a substantial number of votes because of constituents who stayed away from the polls, the Communist Party decided to withdraw from the government, and a little later moved into open opposition to it. At the French Communist Party's 25th Congress, the policy of "strict economy" followed by the Socialist government of L. Fabius was judged to be a model of the social democratic rule of the country in the interests of large capital. In opposition to that course, the Communists' congress put forward its own broad program of crisis-prevention measures. As for the sociopolitical force that might ensure accomplishment of that program's objectives, at the congress the idea was proposed of creating a "new union of the majority of the people": a broad coalition of forces favoring deep anticapitalist transformations. The main participant in the "new union" was to be the masses of working people themselves.

Communists have traditionally accorded great importance in their activities to relations with trade unions. The deterioration of the situation in the capitalist world connected with the conservative offensive, the growth of unemployment, and the intensification of anticommunism has weakened the political role of the trade unions. Disunity among various trade-union centers has increased. Relations between communist parties and the trade unions have also become more complicated and strained. But that means only that the communists must step up their work with trade unions.

The 1970s brought onto the scene of the developed capitalist countries' political life a mass of new nontraditional organizations forming, in their aggregate, a new protest movement against various forms of menace created and whipped up by present-day capitalism. We are referring to the antiwar movement, which attained an extraordinary scope and level of mass participation, numbering many tens and even hundreds of organizations in every country; the environmental protection movement (the so-called ecologists or Greens); the "civic initiative" movements, which are often governed by the principle that "citizens themselves should do what the state does not want to do"; as well as "alternative" movements that view the point of their actions as changing the forms of human community. Serious changes took place in the activities of women's, young people's, student, and other movements.

The principal breeding ground for the emergence of these movements or the increase in their activities was people's growing concern over such issues as the fate of the world and the state of their environment, callousness and bureaucratism of the state and its institutions, and with mounting, crisis-torn instability. By virtue of their mass membership and the continuous nature of their actions, these movements turned into a real social force.

Taking the protest movements' mass nature and democratic orientation into account, communists in the developed capitalist countries endeavor to cooperate with them. At the same time, the social heterogeneity of the movements' participants, the contradictory nature of their views, their alienation from existing political institutions, and their outright mistrust of parties, including communist parties, create considerable obstacles to establishing the alliance of democratic forces that communists advocate. The formation of such alliances is also hindered to no small degree by reactionary imperialist forces, which try to frighten the potential participants in such alliances by warning of the communists' "intrigues" and the prospects of "dependence" on them. At the same time, the communists themselves recognize that expanding and increasing the intensity of contacts with the nonproletarian strata that make up the main social base of the protest movements increases the danger that the communist movement will be infiltrated by views alien to the scientific, Marxist-Leninist world view.

Surmounting these difficulties requires considerable efforts to improve political practice, defend the purity of Marxist-Leninist theory, and develop it creatively. In trying to achieve greater cooperation and mutual understanding with the democratic movements, communists focus on the question of exactly what goal draws them closer to those movements. Such an approach makes it possible to unite the broadest strata of the population in the capitalist countries to tackle the most urgent problems, and to give that struggle a genuinely mass, popular scope and character.

The struggle for peace and disarmament has become the most important of all the vital issues. Communists in the developed capitalist countries regard ensuring peace as the indispensable condition of social progress. They do not rule out the possibility that, under certain circumstances, the problem of preventing war is even capable of becoming decisive in the question of power.[5]

In the struggle for peace, the communist parties are the most active force. But their real significance in this cause, as in others, is determined not so much by their independent actions as by their joint struggle with all participants in the antiwar front. Achieving effective cooperation among all the participants in that front requires surmounting considerable difficulties. In their goals and makeup, antiwar movements are of a general democratic nature. Their participants are united by a common interest in the prevention of nuclear war. At the same time, peace advocates may hold extremely diverse positions, even directly contradictory ones, on other highly important issues pertaining to international life and the internal life of the capitalist countries. In a number of countries the antiwar movement is weakened because of the working class's insufficiently active role in the struggle for peace. And the support that some workers—sometimes a sizable number—give in elections to political parties that follow a policy of increasing international tension and stepping up the arms race deals a direct blow to participants in the antiwar front, drawing an appropriate reaction from them. Surmounting contradictions and difficulties of this sort requires considerable efforts from communists, including efforts in the area of political ideology.

Antiwar movements conduct their activities in national arenas, attempting primarily to influence the foreign-policy decisions of the governments in question. But the problem of war and peace is international in essence. The objective of preventing war, especially nuclear war, can be accomplished only by strengthening the international solidarity of all peace-loving forces.

The unity of the international communist movement can become an extremely important precondition of such solidarity.

Great October opened a new era in the history of humanity—the era of the revolutionary renewal of the world. But the path of renewal is difficult and thorny, since the course of history is unpredictable, and the turns and changes in its course are capricious and unexpected. Every real step toward the complete liberation of humanity from all forms of social inequality and injustice requires tremendous effort.

Striving to sort out the intricate weaving of events, seeking true solutions, working to overcome difficulties and their own weaknesses, relying on the masses' support and leading those masses, communists—the pathfinders of history—continue their heroic path.

---

[5]See *Problemy mira i sotsializma*, No. 11, 1985, p. 46.

The P.R.C.: The Search for an Optimal Foreign Economic Strategy

ALEKSANDR IGOREVICH SALITZKIY*

Since the late 1970s the P.R.C. [People's Republic of China] has embarked on a path of far-reaching reforms whose main objective is the creation of an economic mechanism that would gradually modernize productive forces and bring the country's scientific and technical potential up to present-day requirements. Achieving this objective has required a significant expansion of ties with the outside world, ties that were seriously damaged during the Cultural Revolution.

The October 1984 Chinese Communist Party Central Committee resolution on the reform of the economic system noted that, since the time of the third plenary session of the CCP Central Committee of the second convocation (1978—*Ed.*), "the policy of expanding ties with the outside world . . . has proven successful in practice. We will continue . . . actively expanding the scope of technical-economic exchange and cooperation with other countries, do our utmost to make a success of the special economic regions, and open an even greater number of port cities to the outside world. The use of foreign capital investments and the attraction of foreign entrepreneurs to our country for the creation of joint enterprises based on Chinese and foreign capital, for the joint management of enterprises and for the creation of enterprises solely on the basis of their own investments—all this is also a necessary and useful addition to our country's socialist economy."[1]

Within the framework of the so-called "open policy" in China, a number of measures have been taken to visibly enhance the role of external factors in economic development. This policy brought to life new areas of foreign economic activity and promoted the dynamic growth of trade with other countries. Changes in foreign economic ties, the practice of providing for them within the economy, and the search for optimal ways for the country to participate in the interna-

*Candidate of economics, senior research fellow at the Institute of World Economy and International Relations (IMEMO). This article appeared in the September 1987 issue of *MEMO*.
[1]*Chinese Communist Party Central Committee's Resolution on the Reform of the Economic System*, Beijing, 1984, pp. 38-39.

tional division of labor are studied extensively by Chinese economists and are widely discussed in the scientific press. The achievements and problems of the "open economy" largely determine the course of economic reform and have a direct effect on study and assimilation of foreign experience and familiarization with advanced technological models. This idea is invariably stressed in the works of Chinese specialists, who assign a major role to the accelerated development of foreign economic ties in the socioeconomic progress of the world's most populous country.

Economic relations of the People's Republic of China with foreign partners are distinguished by a large number of unique features. At the same time, the more than eight years of experience that Chinese organizations have amassed in their cooperation with foreign entrepreneurs, banks, and international economic organizations is of definite interest in the context of improving socialist countries' foreign economic policy and introducing new forms and methods of that policy.

I.

The basis of the P.R.C.'s foreign economic ties is foreign trade. The average annual rate of its growth from 1981 to 1986 was high—10.5 percent—while its volume increased from $20 billion in 1978 to $73.8 billion in 1986, equal to roughly 20 percent of the gross value of its industrial and agricultural output. In the 1980s trade as a whole was balanced, but by mid-decade the rate of increase in exports—the main source of hard currency—had slowed. In 1984 it increased by 10 percent (imports by 37 percent), and in 1985 by 4.7 percent (54.2 percent). In 1985 the trade balance showed a large deficit of almost $15 billion. In 1986 the situation improved somewhat—the deficit was reduced to $12 billion by increasing exports by 12.8 percent and imports by only 1.6 percent.[2]

The geographic division of the P.R.C.'s foreign economic ties is weighted heavily in favor of the states and territories of the Asian-Pacific region. They account for roughly 70 percent of Chinese trade and for the overwhelming majority of nontrade operations. China has been rapidly developing ties with Western Europe and the countries of the Middle East, and, in the past few years, its relations with socialist states, as well. In turn, the relative importance of trade with the P.R.C. is especially great for Japan, Hsiang-chiang (Hong Kong) and the ASEAN countries, as well as Australia.

---

[2]*Jingji Ribao*, Jan. 12, 1986; *Renmin Ribao*, Feb. 27, 1987.

One is struck by the marked imbalance in China's trade ties with developed capitalist countries (see Table 1), which is not offset by its positive balance of trade with Hong Kong, Macao and the developing countries. As a result, the current ratio between the P.R.C.'s exports to and imports from capitalist countries is impeding the development of foreign trade with them, making a cutback in imports mandatory.

In 1985 and 1986 the problems of expanding exports were a serious topic of discussion in economics publications. The publications contain many interesting assessments of the results, problems, and future of the "open policy," as well as practical proposals for enhancing the hard currency and economic effectiveness of foreign economic ties. In the view of Chinese economists, one of the main means of increasing the influx of hard currency is to improve the structure of exports.

Industrial products presently account for over half of Chinese exports, and the output of light industry for about 40 percent.[3] This is still considered insufficient. Chinese specialists stress that when quantitative restrictions apply, which is the case for a substantial percentage of P.R.C. goods in the markets of developed capitalist countries, low prices are no longer effective as a means of competing and increasing

TABLE 1
Individual Countries' Share of P.R.C.'s Foreign Trade in 1985
(percentages)

	All Trade	Exports	Imports
Japan	30.5	22.2	35.8
Hong Kong and Macao	17.5	27.1	11.3
United States	10.6	8.6	11.9
F.R.G.	4.6	2.7	5.8
Singapore	3.3	7.5	0.6
U.S.S.R.	3.0	3.8	2.4
Brazil	2.0	1.6	2.3
Canada	2.0	0.9	2.7
Australia	1.9	0.7	2.7
Italy	1.7	1.1	2.1
Britain	1.6	1.3	1.8
France	1.4	0.8	1.7
Vietnam	1.3	1.0	1.4

Source: Guoji Maoyi, No. 4, 1986, p. 59.

---

[3]See Guoji Maoyi, No. 11, 1986, p. 61.

hard-currency income. In the majority of cases, it is more important, for example, that products conform to consumers' tastes and habits, and that their packaging and design meet modern standards. Improving quality and developing new export products becomes the chief objective. Chinese economists think this goal can be achieved by increasing the number of specialized enterprises and shops, which provide about 30 percent of state purchases for export, and by improving the technical level of local industry, which accounts for 15 percent of the goods marketed overseas.

Among the measures aimed at improving the sale of the output of light industry and the food industry on foreign markets, the "trade-industry-agriculture" chain proposed by Chinese specialists merits attention. This entails the creation of an economic mechanism by which foreign-trade companies familiar with conditions on foreign markets become the main "regulators"—they provide the orders (and the imported materials and equipment needed to fill them) to industry, which, in turn, adjusts the assignments given to agricultural enterprises for the production of a certain type of raw material.

One of the most pressing problems in the organization of foreign trade is the level of coordination. Since 1979 the right to conduct foreign-trade operations has been extended to a wide range of companies that are subordinate to branch ministries, provinces, or cities, as well as to certain industrial enterprises. This has significantly stepped up efforts to find export resources. In time, however, problems resulting from the decentralization of foreign economic activity came to light. Thus, companies of different subordination increasingly compete with each other on the foreign market, which leads to a lowering of the prices on many of their goods and to an increase in the number of unprofitable export operations for industrial enterprises.

This situation has led to measures to strengthen centralized control and to introduce the practice of issuing export licenses. Nevertheless, Chinese publications still carry many articles arguing for stricter regulation of the export policy of certain economic units. Thus, an article by well-known economist Xue Mujiao, in particular, stresses the need to reduce the number of companies engaged in foreign economic operations, and to establish a lower limit on the export prices of a number of goods. He also notes the unsatisfactory results achieved by the offices of a number of export-import companies in Hong Kong. Apart from their excessive number, these companies often evade taxes, manipulate hard currency in all sorts of ways, and so forth.[4]

---

[4]*Ibid.*, No. 3, 1986, pp. 4-8.

Price levers are assigned an important role in accelerating the growth of exports. Chinese economists point out that the current methods for pricing export and import goods does nothing to encourage export. Often enterprises that have fulfilled assignments for the production of export goods find it unprofitable to sell above-plan output on the foreign market, since their earnings in yuan are lower than if they sold the same goods on the domestic market. This fact, as well as an analysis of the relationship between domestic and world prices on export and import goods, lead Chinese specialists to the conclusion that the country's current pricing mechanism is geared more to import replacement than to export incentives. Unless this situation is remedied and unless a strategy backed by practical measures and reforms is found for the simultaneous development of exports and imports, it will be difficult for them to substantially increase the contribution that foreign economic ties make to economic development.[5]

Exports have been encouraged somewhat by lowering the exchange rate of the yuan with respect to foreign currency (the rate was last lowered in the summer of 1986). But it is obvious that this measure alone is not enough, especially since it causes inflation. A certain role can be played by the current partial exemption of export enterprises from taxes, a measure compensated for by the state's increased revenues from the sale of import goods at higher prices on the domestic market.

But perhaps the decisive factors will be the successful development of new goods and markets and the active search for additional opportunities to sell industrial products. The P.R.C.'s foreign economic strategy is geared to a gradual decline in the percentage of exports claimed by raw materials and fuel, especially oil. At the same time, agricultural production's successes have created the basis for a rapid increase in exports of agricultural raw materials and food—corn, cotton, raw silk, rice, and fruits and vegetables. Here emphasis is on raising the degree of processing and bringing the product up to world standards of quality.

In the 1980s, serious changes affected the P.R.C.'s import policy. At the beginning of the decade there was a substantial reduction in the importation of assembled sets of equipment and a gradual shift to varied forms of importing technology, such as licenses and engineering-consultation services. The circle of industries receiving imported technology and materials widened. In addition to heavy industry, they now include light industry, the food industry, and agriculture. One

---

[5]See *Jingji Yanjiu*, No. 12, 1985, pp. 22-23.

factor that contributed to the development of foreign-trade ties was the significant reduction in imports of food and agricultural raw materials.

At the same time, certain import trends are a source of concern for Chinese specialists. Because import functions have been dispersed among a wide range of companies and because proper coordination is lacking, the practice of importing outmoded equipment has become widespread, as have purchases at overstated prices and excessive importation of consumer goods that compete with local products. The Chinese press notes the need for strengthening the principles of planning and centralization when acquiring foreign technology and equipment and for strict monitoring of import operations by the Ministry of Foreign Economic Relations and Trade.

Saving hard currency and increasing exports of finished goods and imports of technology are the main features of the current stage of foreign-trade policy. In 1986 the P.R.C. expanded its purchases of technology after considerably reducing its imports of consumer goods. Exports were increased despite the reduction in exports of petroleum and petroleum products and the drop in their prices. The proportional share of mineral fuel in the value of Chinese exports declined from 26 percent in 1985 to 15 percent in 1986.

II.

One of the central issues of the P.R.C.'s foreign economic strategy is the problem of attracting and using foreign investment. Since the 1979 adoption of the law on joint enterprises, they have played an important role in modernizing the economy and developing foreign economic ties. At present the P.R.C. is completing its development of a legal basis for cooperation with foreign entrepreneurial capital. Its activity in the P.R.C. is already regulated by more than 80 laws and resolutions. Until just recently there has been a consistent liberalization of the terms governing this activity: tax rates on profits and lease payments were lowered and there were periodic extensions of the periods during which joint enterprises were exempted (either fully or partially) from taxation.

There is a preferential tax and customs system in four special economic zones (special economic regions)—Shenzheng, Zhuhai, Shandou and Xiameng. Since 1984, tax privileges have been extended to 14 port cities. In April 1986 a law allowing the creation of enterprises based entirely on foreign capital was ratified.

The concept of using foreign investments applied in the P.R.C.'s statistics and press encompasses a broad range of agreements covering the foreign partner's participation in economic activity. Moreover, "investments," in addition to the capital of entirely foreign-owned and joint (joint-stock) enterprises, include the foreign capital involved, without equity interest, in various forms of cooperation. The latter include contracts for management and servicing, production-sharing agreements, licensing deals combined with lease contracts, and compensation contracts that provide for investments to be repaid with a share of the output.

Out of foreign entrepreneurs' total capital investment of $4.6 billion at the end of 1985, no more than 20 percent comes from joint enterprises and less than 10 percent is from companies fully controlled by foreigners. Thus, the dominant forms are the nonequity participation, new types of investments that are being used more and more widely by monopolistic capital in its relations with developing countries.[6] Another specific feature of joint business undertakings in the P.R.C. is the leading role played by Hong Kong firms (roughly 70 percent of investments).

The dynamics of the influx of foreign business capital was characterized by its rapid growth in the 1984-1986 period (over $5 billion, as against $1.5 billion in the 1979-1983 period). The distribution among industries is distinguished by a large (over half) share of money going to nonindustrial areas—international tourism, trade, public food service, the service sector, and municipal construction. Roughly $1.5 billion is being used to explore offshore petroleum deposits, and to mine coal. The remaining investments are concentrated in the processing industry. The focus of cooperation here, as a rule, is on light-industry enterprises and producers of household electronics that receive technology, raw materials, assemblies, and components from abroad for a fixed percentage of their profits.

In evaluating the results of joint enterprise, Chinese specialists include among its positive aspects the appearance of a number of modern industries distinguished by their high labor productivity and the quality of their goods and services. Joint enterprises serve as a kind of guide for Chinese industry in the production of goods that meet top specifications, the organization and management of economic activity, the creation of well-paid jobs, and the training of key workers and office employees. Well-developed trade and industrial regions were created practically from scratch in the immediate vicinity of Hong Kong and Macao (the Shenzheng and Zhuhai special economic zones), helping to strengthen the P.R.C.'s economic ties with these areas that are so vitally important to the country's foreign economic relations.

At the same time, joint business undertakings have led to a number of problems and apparently have not fully lived up to the expectations of the open policy's initiators. Beginning in the latter half

[6]See MEMO, No. 1, 1986, pp. 121-126.

of 1985, the Chinese press has published many critical commentaries on the current practice of attracting business capital.

One of the main difficulties is that of providing enterprises with power, fuel, transport, and skilled personnel. As expected, attracting foreign investment has meant that the Chinese side has had to spend a great deal of money creating the necessary infrastructure. But in a number of instances, these expenditures have considerably exceeded planned amounts, especially in the special economic zones. In Shenzheng, for example, where some $800 million in foreign money had been invested by the end of 1985, outlays for capital construction from 1980 to 1985 exceeded 6 billion yuan.[7] Only one fourth of this money came from local and province budgets, while the remainder came from centralized subsidies and bank loans.

The low quality of many Chinese-made goods and their failure to meet international standards make it very difficult to supply joint enterprises with the necessary components, which have to be purchased on the foreign market. The foreign investors themselves often have a direct stake in this. As a result, roughly one third of the joint enterprises that were created proved unable to make profits in hard currency. In 1984 and 1985 the special economic zones, which have been geared mainly to exports, imported more than they exported and were forced to use $600 million in hard-currency loans from the Bank of China. The situation was aggravated by insufficient control by central bodies, resulting in use of joint business channels during this period for above-plan importation of producer and consumer goods, which incurred considerable hard-currency losses.[8]

This was the main reason for the regulations imposed on joint enterprises in 1986. Enterprises are required to balance their hard-currency accounts; those that have reached their currency ceilings are forbidden to spend profits abroad. New joint business undertakings have been restricted or terminated in a number of industries for which foreign technology imports have reached sufficient levels (for example, the production of picture tubes for color television sets, refrigerators and other household appliances). Foreign capital is not permitted in any industry in which state enterprises and foreign-trade companies have begun having problems selling in foreign markets (for example, in the clothing industry).

The creation of joint service enterprises geared to domestic demand—photo services, taxis, etc.—has been virtually halted. Limits have been placed on the construction of hotels. In the fall of 1986 additional benefits were extended to enterprises producing export

---

[7]The average exchange rate for the yuan during that period was $0.45.
[8]*Jingji Yanjiu*, No. 4, 1986, p. 55.

goods. Among other things, they have been granted a three-year, 50 percent reduction in the tax on their profits on condition that no less than 70 percent of their output be exported to foreign markets. These regulatory measures have made some investors unhappy. There was a considerable reaction in the Western press when a conflict arose and was settled at the enterprise operated jointly with American Motors (a plant for the production of cross-country vehicles in Beijing), which was temporarily denied the right to import spare parts from the United States. All this affected the volume of new investment on which agreement had been reached in 1986. They dropped to almost half of what they were in 1985. At the same time, a greater number of large companies geared to the creation of export industries in China were enlisted in cooperative ventures, and 76 percent of foreign investments were channeled into industry (the figure from 1979 to 1985 was only 45 percent).[9]

In its present state, the joint business enterprise is still not an important source of modern technology capable, to any significant extent, of replacing the customary importation of technology. This is also evident from the small amount of foreign capital invested in industrial enterprises and from the very terms of contracts on production cooperation. Through this channel the P.R.C. receives not the newest technology, as a rule, but mainly standard, proven technology. The Chinese side's role is often limited to the assembly of finished products from the client's assemblies and parts, or in other words, participation in the final stage of the production process. Chinese specialists estimate that only 40 percent of the technology brought into joint enterprises in Shenzheng is "comparatively up-to-date," and that only a small portion of it meets requirements of the 1980s.[10] Due to the Chinese side's limited role, the import component is excessive and the average value-added ratio of the joint enterprises' output is low. Thus, hard-currency and technological problems are interrelated here.

Nonequity forms of joint enterprise and "contract relations" are increasingly viewed by the P.R.C. as arrangements that fail to accomplish the aim of raising the economy's technological level to today's requirements. Chinese organizations show an obvious desire to attract big capital for the formation of joint enterprises so as to give the foreign partner a long-term interest in ensuring the successful operation of the facility and in the joint use of the most up-to-date methods of production, and at the same time to gain access to its sales network. Practical experience has shown that it is a good idea to cooperate with foreign

9*Renmin Ribao*, Mar. 7, 1987.
10*Jingji Yanjiu*, No. 6, 1986, p. 40.

companies in renovating existing enterprises (although foreign investors are still reluctant to do this).

A significant percentage of the conflicts that plague the creation of joint enterprises arises from foreign entrepreneurs' desire to maximize output for the domestic market, which naturally meets with resistance from Chinese organizations, resistance that has grown even stronger due to the worsening of the hard-currency problem. It is obvious that this will be one of the main obstacles to an increase in foreign investment. It is hardly possible to significantly increase the scale of joint enterprise by further liberalizing the legal terms of foreign companies' activity in the P.R.C. and lowering lease payments, taxes and the earnings of Chinese personnel.

The immediate hard-currency results of joint enterprise should be decisive. But they are still low, especially in cooperation with small and medium-sized firms in Hong Kong. The restriction of this area of joint enterprise is also necessary in a number of instances because the created enterprises compete with state foreign-trade companies, "knocking down" the prices for traditional Chinese export goods.

For the P.R.C., it is more promising to create joint enterprises with the participation of big Hong Kong capital, which is often linked to transnational corporations and transnational banks. The foreign side, as a rule, is interested in the successful operation of joint enterprises, which is aided not only by their joint-stock form but by the fact that stable business relations with China are viewed by that category of entrepreneurs as a certain guarantee of their companies' long-term interests in Hong Kong. At the same time, China's efforts to attract firms geared to the production of export products encounter keen competition from the "newly industrialized countries"—centers of expansion of transnational corporations and transnational banks in Southeast and East Asia.

Joint enterprise can now be seen only as an auxiliary element of the P.R.C.'s foreign-trade strategy in its key areas: an increase in goods export and hard-currency income for noncommercial items, plus the importation of advanced technology. Its role is somewhat greater in the development of the specific set of relations that is forming between the economies of the P.R.C. and Hong Kong.

It would be inaccurate, however, to view the problems and difficulties of attracting and using foreign investments as an indicator of the ineffectiveness or unsuitability of this form of foreign economic ties for China. It is obvious that many negative results must be seen as the inevitable outcome of the initial—the most capital-intensive and largely experimental—phase. With time the P.R.C.'s policy in this area is becoming more selective—with respect to both the technical level of the industries being created and their possible yield of hard currency. This is the purpose of measures to control hard currency, the increase in some cases of the minimum level of investment in joint enterprises, and the privileges granted to the partner for the transfer of advanced technology. Many plans for cooperation, including those that stipulate only the assembly of output or its sale solely on the domestic market, are already regarded as inappropriate for Chinese conditions.[11]

III.

No less important than concrete economic results is, in our view, the effect that China's new forms of economic cooperation with foreign countries have on formulation of domestic and foreign economic policy by encouraging both directly and indirectly the revision of outdated methods. In a broad sense the importance of joint enterprise is determined largely by its modernizing influence and the introduction of new ideas into economic theory and of up-to-date methods and forms of management into practice. These, like certain other trends in foreign economic policy established in the 1980s, are interrelated elements of the essentially progressive shift to the creative use of advanced foreign experience.

What is becoming more flexible, among other things, is the rate for the use of foreign loan capital, including loans from the governments of certain developed capitalist countries, as well as international financial institutions. Just 10 years ago the receipt of foreign loans was regarded as "bowing to the foreign," or "selling national interests." Since then not only the use of loans from companies, but large-scale borrowing of financial resources, have become a firmly established practice for Chinese organizations. Initially (in the late 1970s and early 1980s) the P.R.C. sought mainly "cheap" (low-interest) loans from governments and international banks. The chief creditors were the Japanese government and the International Bank for Reconstruction and Development [World Bank].

But in the past few years China has increasingly resorted to loans on the markets of private loan capital, which is due partly to the lowering of interest rates by commercial banks. In 1986 it received its first major long-term loan from a syndicate of Hong Kong banks. Since 1985 active efforts have been made to sell government bonds from the Bank of China and certain other Chinese organizations on foreign financial markets. The country's foreign debt at the end of 1986 totaled $20.6 billion, the rate at which it was serviced was estimated at 8 to 10 percent, and hard-currency reserves exceeded $10 billion.[12]

---

[11]See *Jingji Yanjui*, No. 2, 1986, p. 48.
[12]*Beijing Review*, Apr. 6, 1986, p. 16; *Far Eastern Economic Review*, Mar. 26, 1987, p. 53.

There has been a considerable increase in the activity of Chinese banks in Hong Kong, where they perform various operations including the acquisition of private banks' assets, insurance, real estate deals. One of the main aims of this activity is to maintain favorable economic conditions on that territory and prevent the possible escape of capital from transnational corporations and transnational banks because of the scheduled 1997 restoration of the P.R.C.'s sovereignty over Hong Kong.

One new area of foreign economic policy is business activity abroad. By the end of 1985, the P.R.C. owned fully or jointly 181 enterprises (mainly in developing countries) in which over $250 million was invested. They include restaurants and food-industry enterprises, as well as several mining operations for the extraction of iron ore, copper, diamonds, and gold. Chinese organizations are also showing a great deal of interest in the creation abroad of lumber mills that would subsequently export their products to the P.R.C.

Construction projects with Chinese contract firms as partners have become widespread abroad, and they employ 31,000 Chinese workers and engineers. In addition, brigades of Chinese workers, cooks, sailors, athletic trainers are sent abroad; as of the end of 1985, 27,000 people were employed in such brigades.

One of the main items in the P.R.C.'s noncommercial hard-currency income is revenue from international tourism, which got its start in the late 1970s. During the Sixth Five-Year Plan (1981-1985), this source yielded nearly $5 billion in revenues. The majority of the tourists are residents of Hong Kong and Macao, as well as ethnic Chinese from Southeast Asian countries. Some of them are being repatriated, acquiring homes in China and contributing money to joint enterprises, which is encouraged by the authorities. In 1986 revenues from tourism totaled $1.5 billion. But the Chinese press has expressed concern that the number of foreign tourists is not increasing fast enough.

The development of new areas of foreign economic cooperation has significantly increased the P.R.C.'s net income from noncommercial items—it totaled $3.8 billion in 1986.

The intensification of the P.R.C.'s ties with other states, its growing involvement in active international cooperation in many areas, and its use of foreign experience cannot occur painlessly for a country that until recently was almost isolated from foreign influence. The open policy has revealed quite a few acute problems by sharply outlining the boundaries between new and old and modern and obsolete. When it is implemented in practice it often fails to accomplish the established objectives. A great many pressing problems also arise from the increase in the influence on the P.R.C.'s economy of fluctuations in the world capitalist economy. One example is the drop in oil prices, which adversely affected China's export revenues and cast doubt on the prospects for joint enterprise in the extraction of shelf reserves of oil.

Nevertheless, in the opinion of Chinese economists, the P.R.C.'s growing involvement in the world capitalist economy is not tantamount to an increase in its dependence on developed capitalist states: "Under postwar economic and political conditions, the increase in countries' interdependence in the economic sphere does not necessarily lead to an infringement of political independence and economic self-sufficiency. On the contrary, only through active participation in the international division of labor, which stimulates the rapid development of society's productive forces, can political and economic sovereignty be strengthened."[13] Moreover, the P.R.C.'s foreign economic strategy is aimed at decreasing its dependence on individual partners.

This tendency is evident, in particular, in China's desire for multilateral economic cooperation involving international organizations. It can clearly be seen in its import policy, especially in its selection of suppliers of technology that the P.R.C. diversifies its sources as much as possible. Recently this was shown in increased importation of technology from West European countries, with a certain decrease in the percentage supplied by Japan and the United States. Thus, in 1985 the main supplier of technology was the Federal Republic of Germany, and purchases in France and Great Britain increased substantially. Chinese economists point to the possibilities for expanding the importation of technology from newly industrialized countries, as well as for acquiring "intermediate" technology from other developing countries.

IV.

One factor that ensured the relatively high rate of growth of the P.R.C.'s foreign economic ties in the 1980s was their orientation to the economies of rapidly developing Asian states—Japan, the ASEAN countries, and Hong Kong. Another important factor was the increase in the export of petroleum and petroleum products, whose volume in 1985 was nearly double the 1981 level. But it is obvious that in the next few years these factors will no longer be able to exert such a favorable influence. Therefore an important strategy for fulfilling the assignment set for the Seventh Five-Year Plan (to increase foreign trade by 40 to 50 percent) is to diversify the geography of trade and search for partners with whom ties could be expanded very quickly. Among the most

---

[13]*Waimao Jingji, Guoji Maoyi*, No. 1, 1986, p. 19.

promising markets are the socialist countries, who still account for a small share (slightly over 9 percent in 1986) of the P.R.C.'s foreign trade.

One considerable advantage of this type of economic cooperation is the fact that it can be done without direct hard-currency expenditures, on a barter basis. Moreover, the expansion of ties with other socialist countries could also alleviate some of the other problems involved in developing the P.R.C.'s foreign economic relations. It is clear that at present they are highly dependent on trends in world capitalist trade, whose negative effect is more easily overcome if one systematically and steadily increases barter with the CMEA countries. China is also faced with the acute problem of competing on the world market with the producers of labor-intensive goods. At the same time, it is obvious that the PRC's economy can complement the economies of the majority of other socialist countries, which creates new opportunities for increased trade.

One of the problems revealed in the course of the open policy's implementation is the uneven participation of various areas of China in relations with foreign states. The largest profits have been reaped by the coastal zone. Chinese economists believe that the country's northeast and northwest regions could considerably increase their "foreign contribution" to economic development through cooperation with socialist countries. Among other things, plans exist for the creation in the northwest of a special economic region similar to the zones in southern China.

"The creation of this region," Chinese specialists note, "could attract machinery and equipment from the U.S.S.R. and other European states. Industrial animal husbandry and the industry to process its products could be created in the region—changing the area's specialization, which is mainly raw materials . . . . After the normalization of Soviet-Chinese relations, the region could become one of the main transshipment points between Europe and Asia."[14]

The interest in cooperation is mutual. That is why the P.R.C.'s foreign economic ties with socialist countries, and especially the U.S.S.R., have developed rapidly in the past few years. They will continue to grow rapidly in the 1986-1990 period, in accordance with the concluded agreements. Cooperation is of an increasingly diverse nature: trade, including border trade, and the reconstruction of old enterprises and construction of new ones in China.

During the official visit to the P.R.C. of N.V. Talyzin, candidate member of the Politburo of the CPSU Central Committee and First Vice-Chairman of the U.S.S.R. Council of Ministers, it was noted that

---

[14]*Gexue, Jingji, Shehui* (Lanzhou), No. 1, 1986, p. 35.

it would be advisable in future to use such practices as industrial cooperation, the processing of raw materials on commission, deals in which investments are paid off in output produced by the facility in question, and the creation of joint enterprises. Sino-Soviet trade should total more than 12.5 billion rubles for the period from 1986 to 1990 and, by 1990, the annual figure should be nearly double that of 1985 (1.6 billion rubles).

The development of ties between the P.R.C. and the CMEA countries is accompanied by a growing mutual interest in many different areas. It is increasingly important for the two sides to trade experience in the resolution of social, economic, and foreign economic problems under the conditions of large-scale social reform. These kinds of exchanges between socialist countries are mutually advantageous and, moreover, free of a number of negative ideological elements that arise in their relations with capitalist partners.

Chinese economists are not ruling out the possibility that the increase in the country's foreign trade could slow in the next few years. But we think this fact should not be taken as evidence of a decline in the role played by foreign-trade factors and the open policy in economic development. Even within the current quantitative limits, the country's operations in foreign markets could very well step up their modernizing influence on the economy, science, and technology. The organization of foreign economic ties is becoming increasingly flexible and versatile, miscalculations and mistakes are regularly analyzed and corrected, and achievements are being developed and reinforced.

Bold experimentation in the search for efficient methods of expanding export production, using imported technology and engaging in new types of cooperation with foreign partners, together with an increase in coordinating and planning efforts, can ensure the continued improvement of the structure of trade and create more advantageous conditions for China's participation in the international division of labor and for the effective use of existing raw material, labor, and technology resources.

Even now it can be said that the open policy has significantly increased the contribution that foreign economic relations make to economic development. With the moderate increase in their percentage of the country's gross national product, economic ties with foreign states better reflect the needs of the economy as a multi-industry complex than they did in the 1970s, when foreign trade was subordinated solely to the development of two or three branches of heavy industry.

The rapid development of China's economy and foreign economic ties in the course of the current reforms is becoming an ever more visible component of the international division of labor. This makes it an urgent necessity to thoroughly study the theory and practice of the P.R.C.'s open policy—an important instrument for promoting economic construction and enhancing the country's role in the world economy.

Part Two

Present Day Capitalism, U.S. Problems

The Change in Regulatory Strategy in Capitalist Countries

IRINA MIKHAILOVNA OSADCHAYA*

Over the course of the 1980s there have been substantial changes in the mechanism and strategy of government regulation of developed capitalist countries' economies. A process of establishing a new system of ties between the state and private capital and between regulation and competition has been under way, and there has been a shift in economic-policy goals and priorities.

Under the influence of a complex mix of objective economic and political causes, the structure of state-monopoly capitalism that evolved in the 1950s through 1970s—with the state sector extending to many branches of material production, with the growing redistribution of national income through the budgetary system and the credit and monetary system, and with a ramified structure of normative regulation—has been undergoing reorganization, essentially on the basis of conservative principles of state intervention in the economy.

The class content of conservative restructuring is a desire for social revenge on the part of the ruling circles. However, the change in regulatory strategy in the economic sphere is by no means an unambiguous process. An assault on workers' rights and gains, a weakening of social guarantees, a deliberate intensification of risk factors and uncertainty in the lives of the working people, who have been called upon to strengthen labor discipline by typically capitalist methods, and a reduction in social spending backed by calls for "austerity" are being combined and intertwined with an improvement of relations between the state and capitalist enterprises, with more effective and less costly state regulation, and with a reduction in direct forms of intervention and bureaucratic activism. This latter factor is unquestionably promoting flexibility in the economic system and a further growth in productive forces. Conservative principles of economic regulation presuppose that priority will be given to competition, the market, and

---

*Doctor of economics, section head at the U.S.S.R. Academy of Sciences' Institute of World Economy and International Relations [IMEMO]. This article appeared in the October 1987 issue of *MEMO*.

also to private-monopoly elements of planning; for the purpose of forcing the pace of innovation, and in the interests of capitalist accumulation, the state is encouraging and developing market relations.

The causes that predetermined the changes in the nature of the relationship between the state and the economy; in the scale, forms, and methods of state intervention; and in the objectives of economic policy are many. These changes represent a reaction of the monopolistic bourgeoisie to a crisis in state regulation of the economy caused by a severe worsening of the conditions of economic reproduction in the mid-1970s. The specific forms of the changes taking place in large part stem from the present stage of the scientific and technological revolution, and the closely related expansion in the scale of international merging of capitalist countries' economies. All this makes new demands not only on the economic policy of the state, but also on the entire mechanism of state-monopoly capitalism.

A considerable role has also been played by the increasingly contradictory nature of the extensive growth of the state apparatus itself, and of its direct forms of intervention in the economy. Until recently, we devoted primary attention to the positive aspects of the state's influence on economic processes. Experience shows, however, that this influence is contradictory, and the "costs" that it entails can, in certain conditions, give rise to serious negative effects that retard economic development and require not so much a further expansion in state intervention, as a change in its forms and an increase in its effectiveness.

On the Limits of the Extensive-Type Growth of State Intervention in the Economy

The transition to the conservative variant of state-monopoly regulation in the majority of developed capitalist countries (the United States, Britain, the Federal Republic of Germany, Japan, and France) is taking place in the context of heated debates over such "reform"— debates in which the interests of monopoly capital, the broad masses of working people, and the middle strata clash, as do the political interests of the ruling and opposition parties. Opposing viewpoints are expressed by right-wing conservative economists and those of the radical school of bourgeois political economy; between them lies a gamut of views of moderate conservatism and moderate Keynesian economics. These debates reflect the contradictory nature of the state's very role in a capitalist economy, as well as a desire to define an "optimal" form of relations between the state and the economy—a form which the various political forces by no means see in the same way in particular periods of history.

The ideologists and representatives of private-monopoly capital are today's most avid opponents of "big government." They demand greater freedom from taxes and from the hobbles of microeconomic regulation, which impose certain social obligations on enterprises, and they demand a radical change in the balance of power between the entrepreneurs and the trade unions that defend workers' rights and interests.

However, the state is criticized not only by the ideologists of monopoly capital, but also by the traditional proponents of government regulation, including leftist forces. In this connection, a more balanced and comprehensive assessment of the state's role in state-monopoly capitalism's economic mechanism is needed. In particular, is it true, as widely asserted, that "a further expansion of the state's economic functions" is "a regular and irreversible feature of present-day capitalism, attributable to the objective need for the development of its immensely expanded productive forces," or that there is "a growing assumption of state control of productive forces"?[1] There is no doubt that the state plays a strategically important role under state monopoly capitalism. But can its economic functions expand indefinitely? After all, one has to bear in mind that state monopoly-capitalism, as a modern-day capitalist system (in developed countries) based on concerted action by the state and private-monopoly capitalism, has already taken shape. Changes within the system can take place (and do take place, as we see), but not necessarily only in the direction of enhancing the state's power and influence. After all, the forms of monopoly capital itself also change. Today, we are encountering particularly turbulent processes of private-monopoly socialization based on the growth of transnational corporations that are capable of solving technical and economic problems that previously only the state would have been capable of handling. Medium- and small-scale entrepreneurs, cooperatives, and other such entities, are assuming a new role.

The steady expansion of the state's economic functions under the conditions of state-monopoly capitalism has limits imposed by the growth of the internal contradictions themselves of state intervention in the economy. These contradictions form a kind of regulating mechanism that enables state-monopoly capitalism to maintain itself as a "mixed" system that is incapable, in our opinion, of evolving into a system that could be characterized as "state capitalism."

---

[1]See *MEMO*, No. 6, 1987, p. 85; No. 7, 1987, p. 95.

The character of the contradictions in question has to do with the dual nature of the bourgeois state. On the one hand, as a superstructure category and as a part of the economic mechanism of state-monopoly capitalism, it is called upon to protect and express the interests of the ruling class—above all, those of the monopolistic bourgeoisie. On the other hand, it is a relatively autonomous body capable of expressing the interests of society as a whole—insofar as these concern the development of productive forces, the mitigation of some social problems, the stabilization of economic reproduction, and so forth. From this standpoint the growth of state intervention in the economy in all forms—direct, indirect, administrative, legislative—is an expression of tendencies attributable to the socialization of production. In the final analysis, the state figures as the vehicle for introducing the public, rational principle of organized planning into capitalism's otherwise haphazard development.

The postwar restoration of the developed capitalist countries' economy, which took place in the context of a powerful upsurge in the democratic movement and was accompanied by the creation of many basic production and infrastructure branches, by the development of a system of social insurance and social security, by a growth in expenditures on education and health care, by the mastery of new technologies, and by the creation of a number of capital- and research-intensive industries, could not have been accomplished without a colossal increase in the state's power, without the formation of a state sector and a mechanism for the redistribution of society's material and financial resources by means of credit, financial, administrative, and legislative levers for influencing the economy.

Being relatively autonomous, the state can come into conflict with individual monopolies. Under pressure from the democratic movement (provided the situation develops as basically favorable to that movement), the state can take steps that are detrimental to monopoly capitalism as a whole and can limit its interests. The possibility of realizing the leftist forces' democratic alternative, in particular, is based on this circumstance.

As long as the expansion of state intervention conformed to the strategic interests of the ruling class as a whole or, in any case, did not infringe on them, capital not only went along with that expansion but did everything it could to use state power to bolster its own economic and political positions. But could the state's involvement in the processes of capitalist reproduction (on the basis of a growth in state enterprise, rapid increases in state expenditures and taxes, an increased state share of national income, increased legislative regulation of private enterprises) proceed at the rates characteristic of the 1960s and 1970s without coming into conflict with the interests of monopoly capital in the process? Gradually, that contradiction began to deepen. It was manifested above all in the growing limitation of capital's political power during the strong upsurge in the democratic and workers' movement of the 1960s. Implementation of liberal and social-reformist variants of regulation proceeded in tandem with an enhancement of the role of trade unions, which not only worked to achieve wage increases but also strove to limit capital's managerial power at the factory level.

Therefore, in analyzing the nature and causes of the conservative shift, it is essential to keep in mind, above all, the limits to the growth of state intervention that are imposed by the class nature of the state. "There is obviously a lot that we will not understand in present-day conservatism," notes S. Peregudov, "if we do not keep in mind the fact that an extremely important motivating factor for the bourgeoisie— and not just for the monopoly bourgeoisie—is the desire, if not to restore the fullness of entrepreneurial and managerial power, then at least to weaken intervention in economic life on the part of the state, the trade unions, and the workers' movement in general, when such intervention infringes on the 'sacred right' to dispose of one's private property."[2]

The limitation of capital's political power was intertwined in the second half of the 1970s with a sharp increase in economic difficulties. The conditions of economic reproduction changed substantially: inflation, structural and cyclical crises, a drop in the rate of growth of labor productivity,' a resumed growth in capital-intensiveness—all led to a slowdown in the rate of economic development and a drop in profit rates. For monopoly capital, improving efficiency and cutting costs assumed decisive importance as a condition for increasing the rate of capital accumulation and for breaking through to new frontiers in the scientific and technological revolution.

The most accessible means of resolving these problems was to limit the growth of wages by political means—by attacking labor unions' rights and abandoning the policy of full employment—and to cut costs related to the growth of state intervention in the economy (taxes), as well as expenditures (on social programs, environmental protection, occupational safety). Hence, the interests of capital accumulation required a reduction in state intervention in the economy and a change in its goals and methods.

Proceeding from this premise, one can conjecture that the state's relative autonomy had outstripped the role it was intended to play as an organization consonant with the interests of monopoly capital and embodying the power of the bourgeoisie as a whole, and as a part of

---

[2]*MEMO*, No. 12, 1986, p. 102

state-monopoly capitalism's economic mechanism. The foundation stones of that mechanism continue to be private enterprise, the monopolistic corporation, the market, and competition, which have assumed new dimensions under conditions of the internationalization of capital. For monopolies, the "cost" of regulation had begun to exceed its benefits.[3] But is expansion of the state's social and economic functions solely responsible for the costs against which monopoly capital launched an attack? No, it is not. The intensification of state intervention in the economy also entails other costs—costs from the standpoint not only of capital's private interests, but of the interests of society as a whole. And here we turn to another aspect of the state's relative autonomy.

Our idea of the state's relative autonomy, of its capacity to influence the economy in an effective and rational way, and of the limits to that capacity would be incomplete if we saw only the positive aspect of that autonomy and of the growth in state control. The relative autonomy of the state and the spread of its influence to more and more new spheres of economic and public life also mark a growth in the state bureaucratic system itself, which has its own laws of development.

We often speak of the exhaustion of extensive-type factors of economic growth and of extensive-type utilization of economic resources. However, there are limits to any system's ability to expand by extensive means. Has this limit not also been reached in the growth of state intervention in the economy of developed capitalist countries on the basis of a colossal increase in the bureaucratic apparatus?[4] The growing complexity of administrative agencies and their organization on hierarchical principles spawn tendencies toward bureaucratic usurpation of power and the loss of effective feedback from economic and social processes. Over time, the bureaucratic "costs" of state intervention become more than just a brake on the development of productive forces. They gut many of the working class's gains.

---

[3]The "costs" of state intervention are the subject of rather extensive research, particularly in the context of so-called cost-benefit analysis. In addition, to the concept of "market failure" that was previously elaborated, there has been added the concept of "government failure." This serves as the basis for a comparison of circumstances in which state intervention is more effective than the market mechanism, and vice versa.

[4]The topic of bureaucratization is studied in a number of works in the field of political science: "The immense expansion in the functions of the modern bourgeois state has led to an unprecedented development of the bureaucracy, which has turned into a gigantic machine with its own hierarchy, its own behavioral norms, its special discipline and privileges"; and further: "If the numerical growth in the state apparatus, occasioned by the expansion of its activities to new areas or by an expansion of its work in old areas, results in a differentiation of that apparatus, then the growth of its role in society will spawn an opposite tendency: the strengthening of corporate identity, bureaucratic exclusivity, elitism, and a sense of being independent of society" (F. M. Burlatskiy and A.A. Galkin, *The Modern Leviathan* [*Sovremennyy Liviafan*], Moscow, 1985, pp. 41, 48); see also *State and Administration in the United States* [*Gosudarstvo i upravleniye v SShA*], Moscow, 1985.

It is not just the capitalists' interests to which bureaucratization is hostile. It is even more alien to the interests of the broad working masses, for whom its consequences are similar to capitalist exploitation—only emanating, in this case, from bureaucratic officialdom. In studying the question of the bourgeois state's relative autonomy, the classical works of Marxism noted the possibility of its rise to a position of power over society—the transformation of its apparatus from a body serving society into a power that subordinates society to itself. "Bureaucracy," Marx wrote, "considers itself the ultimate goal of the state. Since the bureaucracy makes its 'formal' goals into its substantive goals, it comes into conflict with its 'real' goals at every turn. It is therefore compelled to pass off the formal as substance, and substance as something formal. Matters of state become office tasks and office tasks become matters of state. As for the individual bureaucrat, he transforms the state's objectives into his personal objectives—*into the drive for advancement, the making of a career.*"[5]

What do the colossal growth of the state apparatus and its bureaucratization mean from an economic standpoint? Decision-making and implementation are slowed down and drawn out; the feedback mechanism breaks down (after all, the work of state agencies does not depend on market conditions and the activities of the enterprises that they direct); there is a proliferation of administrations and agencies whose actions are often poorly coordinated; and, in the absence of a long-term and truly centralized coordination of economic policy (for want of the planning principle), these agencies often make contradictory and mutually exclusive decisions. Thus, for example, the policy of "fine tuning" the economy as a means of stabilizing the economic cycle has not worked out, not only because of the poor quality of forecasting (and indeed, the impossibility of precisely forecasting changes in economic conditions), but also because the bureaucratic instrumentalities of economic policy have been incapable of reacting quickly to changes in economic conditions, and decisions have been very late in coming. Such decisions do more harm than good.

Many American researchers feel that the rigidity of the state apparatus and the ossification of the old established forms of administration greatly impeded the implementation of a long-term growth strategy. The numerous organizational levels and the poor coordination among them made it difficult to reach prompt economic decisions and carry them out quickly; they produced decisions that were not only uncoordinated but often blatantly contradictory as well. "Beginning in the Sixties, the number of federal agencies and programs exploded into

---

[5]K. Marx and F. Engels, *Works* [*Sochineniya*], Vol. I, pp. 271-272.

the hundreds," the American economist T. Alexander has noted. "Most were created to deal with narrow issues. Few were coordinated with one another, many were crisis-oriented . . . and the outcomes have often been mutually conflicting or contrary to what was intended."[6]

Add to this the fact that for the many thousands in the bureaucratic ranks, government service often becomes a safe haven that guarantees steady earnings. And in this connection, corruption, bribe taking, influence-peddling, and other types of "white-collar crime" ensure them their own monopolistic "superprofits," which are every bit the equal of the private sector's superprofits.[7]

That is why increasing bureaucratization causes even the leftist forces to oppose excessive growth of the state apparatus. But while monopoly capital uses criticism of "big government" primarily to curtail those of its elements that perform social and economic functions, leftist forces draw different conclusions from bureaucratization. To counter the bureaucratization of state institutions, they advocate the ideas of democratic oversight at the center, at the local level, and at enterprises, as well as the idea of widespread worker self-management and initiative on an informal basis.

The Budget and Redistributive Processes

Continuous growth in budgetary redistribution of national income and increase in government spending (and not just military spending) have contradictory consequences.

The growth of spending means an increase in the state's financial needs, which are satisfied by tax revenues and by expanded governmental borrowing to cover deficits. Both means of covering government expenditures have a definite effect on the processes of economic reproduction.

By taking from the economy with one hand and giving back with the other, the state can alter the relationship between saving and

---

[6]*Fortune*, Mar. 1977, p. 149.

[7]"The study of U.S. government administration in the 1970s and early 1980s shows that the spectrum of current manifestations of bureaucratism is extremely wide. Among them one can cite, for example, the swelling of the government machine; a fondness for bigness for its own sake, and excessive centralization; excessive regulation; an abundance of all sorts of unnecessary forms, documents, instructions, etc.; inertia and resistance by government bureaucrats to any changes; stagnation, red tape, and a narrowly professional approach to the consideration of any issues; careerism and a low level of competence on the part of government employees, which result in serious mistakes in administration; and finally, embezzlement, corruption, and other forms of 'white-collar crime'" (*State and Administration in the United States*, pp. 140, 141). The same work cites eloquent data: by the end of the 1970s, 58 regulatory agencies were publishing annually about 7,000 rules and directives regulating the activities of private business, nonprofit organizations, and government departments themselves. The *Federal Register*, the annual compilation of all regulations, grew from 9,562 pages in 1960 to 71,120 pages in 1980. (The Reagan administration reduced it by one third.)

consumption of national income; it can stimulate an expansion of demand (consumer or military) or, on the contrary, it can increase savings and accumulation and change their structure. In certain circumstances these effects can work in the same direction: it is possible to increase the share of consumption by stimulating demand, and on that basis encourage a growth in capital investment (this premise is the basis of the Keynesian theory of regulating the economy by stimulating demand). But a situation can arise in which an expansion of demand (by means of budgetary redistribution that, with the help of a deficit, touches off inflation) comes into conflict with the interests of capital accumulation. In addition, contradictions between capital accumulation and budgetary redistribution can also arise in a case where such redistribution is carried out for the purpose of accumulation—for example, to subsidize state-owned enterprises or to help private capital—if the effectiveness with which this money is used declines for some reason or other. But in all cases the growth of state expenditures requires a tax increase, whose negative impact on the economy has been underestimated, and which quite obviously cannot be limitless.

The share of national income being redistributed through the state budgetary system (through taxes) has increased at a rapid rate in a 20-year period (see Table 1). In Japan (the lowest level for developed capitalist countries) from approximately 20 to 30 percent; the United States, from 27 to 32 percent; Canada, 26 to 39 percent; and the European countries, from 30-35 percent to 40-45 percent. Expenditures have grown even more rapidly because of the immense growth in budgetary deficits.

TABLE 1
Total Governmental Spending and Revenues as a
Percentage of Gross Domestic Output

| | 1960 | | 1982 | |
	Spending	Revenues	Spending	Revenues
United States	27.6	27.3	37.6	32.0
Japan	18.3	20.7	34.2	30.2
F.R.G.	32.5	35.1	49.4	45.3
Britain	32.6	30.3	47.4	43.7
France	34.6	34.9	50.7	46.9
Italy	30.1	28.8	53.7	41.5
Canada	28.9	26.0	45.8	39.0

Source: Revue économique de l'OCDE, No. 4, 1985, p. 31

In all countries, tax revenues have grown at a faster rate than domestic output, thus making them a larger share of national income (see Table 2). Taxes on individual income and social-insurance taxes have grown at a particularly rapid rate. It should be added that inflation has played an important role in increasing income-tax revenues. The nominal growth of incomes did more than just expand the taxpayer base. In a system of progressive tax rates, the rise in nominal earnings and the shift of earners into higher tax brackets automatically increased tax payments to the state.

Corporate taxes in such countries as France, Italy, Japan, and Britain grew at the same rate as did total tax revenues and exceeded the growth of domestic output to the same extent. But in the Federal Republic of Germany and the United States, their growth rate lagged significantly behind that of gross domestic output. This indicates that tax revenues declined as percentages of both government revenues and gross domestic output (in the United States, for example, corporate taxes dropped from 23.2 to 9.8 percent of the federal budget between 1960 and 1983).

The data cited enable us to draw certain conclusions.

As concerns corporate taxes, there is no serious evidence to support the thesis that high taxes constrained the rate of capital investment. The change in the structure of government budgetary receipts shows that corporate taxes accounted for a constant or a constantly shrinking percentage of government revenues. No small role in this was played by a multitude of tax breaks and loopholes, as well as by accelerated depreciation, which substantially decreased the tax burden on profits.

At the same time, the share covered by income taxes and, especially, by deductions for social insurance grew constantly. It is no accident that further increases in the tax burden were opposed especially by the "new middle class," which includes the petite and middle bourgeoisie, the managerial apparatus, and a percentage of the intelligentsia and of workers and farmers. It was precisely this broad stratum of the public that turned away from liberalism and became the principal social base of conservatism in the 1980s.

It is indicative that the 1986 tax reform in the United States met with fierce resistance from big capital, for while it significantly reduced corporate tax rates (from 46 to 34 percent), it eliminated many of the tax benefits that had been so widely enjoyed by monopoly capital. At the same time, the reform was aimed at a marked reduction in income taxes, together with a sharp cutback in the progressive income-tax rates, as a result of which the principal winners were the population groups belonging to the middle strata—particularly their top level. (Instead of 15 rates ranging from 11 to 50 percent, as of 1988 there will

TABLE 2
The Elasticity of Individual Components of Tax Revenues
in Ratio to Gross Domestic Output (1965-1982)

	All Tax Receipts	Income Tax	Corporate Tax	Social Insurance Deductions		Property Tax	Consumption Tax	Tax on Individual Goods
				Hired Work Force	Enterprises			
France	1.11	1.22	1.11	1.41	1.19	1.04	1.03	0.82
F.R.G.	1.14	1.26	0.87	1.37	1.37	0.67	1.12	0.70
Italy	1.12	1.50	1.19	1.05	1.16	0.75	1.19	0.59
Japan	1.19	1.26	1.13	1.42	1.47	1.25	....	0.87
Britain	1.05	1.06	1.07	1.07	1.24	0.97	1.46	0.78
U.S.	1.08	1.18	0.6	1.36	1.45	0.80	1.31	0.72

Source: Revue économique de l'OCDE, No. 4, 1985, p. 2

be only three—15, 28, and 33 percent.) The reform also calls for an increase in the minimum earnings that can be subjected to taxation. Of course, it is difficult to say on the basis of statistical data where the "limit" to the growth in the tax burden lies. In some countries the public "accepts" a 50-percent tax level, while in others, like the United States, a 30-percent redistribution of income touched off a widespread protest, which came to be called a tax revolt and which inspired the basic ideas of supply-side theory and contributed to the series of tax reforms launched by Reagan in 1981.

This limit is apparently the result of a multitude of factors, both economic and political.[8] Among the important economic factors are the nature of government expenditures and the extent to which the tax monies are returned to the basic mass of taxpayers in the form of transfer payments and social expenditures. The fact that, in the United States, a large part of government expenditures is swallowed up by the military (and therefore represents a clear reduction in people's earnings) may be one reason why the limit was lower there than in European countries.

In our opinion, the negative effects of the growth in the tax burden manifest themselves both directly, by affecting economic motives and incentives, and indirectly, by changing the general macroeconomic conditions of reproduction. Numerous phenomena point to the limits to continued growth of the tax burden, for example, the drop in the savings rate, the growth of the so-called shadow economy, and the existence of groups in the population that prefer to live on public assistance, rather than taxable income. It is quite obvious that raising taxes to provide for a further growth in state expenditures would be extremely difficult under these conditions.

While the growth rates in gross domestic output and individual earnings were still high, which was the case until the mid-1970s, the government was able to redistribute a growing portion of them. The amount of earnings that remained after taxes continued to grow. However, as economic dynamism declines, a further expansion of tax-based redistribution becomes increasingly difficult. It is not surprising that, when the growth of tax receipts slowed in conjunction with falling growth rates, the inertia of previous increases in state expenditures led to a colossal growth in borrowings and to swelling budgetary deficits.

---

[8]In the opinion of the British economist R. Klein, the size of the redistributed portion of national income is basically determined by political, rather than economic, factors. "What really matters, it seems," he writes, "is the ability of the political system to make given levels of expenditure—and the consequent tax rates—acceptable without provoking a backlash in terms of either votes or wage demands. Given strong labor movements effectively incorporated into the process of public decision-making, governments appear able to sustain much higher levels of spending than in Britain without either damaging economic performance or being voted out of office; the pattern in Sweden and Austria, for instance" (*Lloyds Bank Review*, Jan. 1984, p. 13).

The negative effects of deficits require special analysis. We will look at their impact on the process of economic growth.

Budget deficits in all countries have hit unprecedented levels. By the mid-1980s the aggregate government budget deficit (federal, state, and local) grew to 3.4 percent of gross national product (GNP) in the United States, while the federal budget deficit exceeded 5 percent of GNP; in France after 1981 it ranged from 2.7 to 3 percent; in Britain, from 3.4 to 3.9 percent; in Italy, from 12 to 14 percent, and in Canada, from 6 to 6.6 percent. Only the Federal Republic of Germany and Japan were able to gradually reduce their deficits over the course of the 1980s.[9] The very nature of budget deficits changed as well. The previously assumed cyclical nature of the budget deficit meant that it would inevitably rise and grow at times of recession, but would be reduced to a minimum or eliminated in an economic upturn.

From the mid-1970s onward, and particularly after the upturn got under way in the 1980s, the situation began to change. The fact that the deficit persisted in conditions of an economic upturn and a certain improvement in employment levels became an increasingly alarming phenomenon. That sort of deficit was given the name "structural." In contrast to a cyclical deficit, it does not disappear when the economy shifts from recession to upturn. It is precisely the structural component of the deficit that poses the most serious problem for public finances. In the 1980s the growth of a persistent structural component that sharply increased governmental indebtedness resulted in the long-term (negative) consequences of deficit financing, rather than the short-term (positive) ones. The accumulation of budget deficits increased governmental indebtedness and, accordingly, raised the proportion of government expenditure on interest payments.

As the data in Table 3 show, the amount of net interest payments as a percentage of federal government expenditures rose from 8.9 percent in 1980 to 13.7 percent in 1986.

Assessing the influence of governmental borrowing on the economy requires that many circumstances be taken into account. Attention commonly focuses on its potential inflationary effect, although no direct tie exists between loans and inflation, as the experience of the 1980s shows: The immense deficits persist amid falling inflation rates.

The inflationary impact depends in large measure on the methods of financing governmental borrowing (i.e., whether they are financed by the banks in their role as creators of credit, or by private-sector savings), and also on the degree to which the production capacity of a country's economy is being utilized.

---

[9]See *OECD Economic Outlook*, Dec. 1986, p. 10.

TABLE 3
State Indebtedness[1] (as a percentage of GNP or Gross Domestic Output;
and, in parentheses, Gross Interest Payments[2]
as a Percentage of Total Government Expenditures)

	1972	1975	1980	1983	1986[3]
U.S.	25.7 (3.3)	24.8 (3.3)	19.6 (3.9)	24.6 (5.5)	30.0 (7.1)
Japan	−6.5 (3.6	−2.1 (4.5)	17.2 (9.8)	25.8 (12.7)	25.8 (14.8)
F.R.G.	−5.8 (2.5)	1.0 (2.8)	14.3 (4.0)	21.8 (6.3)	22.6 (6.5)
France	9.1 (2.3)	11.1 (2.9)	9.1 (3.4)	13.3 (5.0)	18.2 (5.9)
Britain	64.8 (9.4)	57.6 (8.9)	48.2 (11.0)	47.4 (10.4)	48.0 (11.3)
Italy	50.0 (5.5)	59.9 (9.3)	60.0 (13.6)	84.1 (15.8)	99.0 (16.1)
Canada	4.3 (10.8)	4.3 (9.9)	13.3 (13.9)	23.9 (15.6)	37.0 (18.7)

Source: OECD Economic Studies, No. 7, 1986, pp. 109, 130.
[1]Net indebtedness of central and local governments.
[2]For the United States, the percentage of net interest payments.
[3]Estimate.

Today, the inflationary potential of governmental borrowing is
limited, thanks to a restrictive credit and monetary policy, and to the
impact of some favorable factors affecting prices (the drop in petroleum
and raw-material prices, the decline in the growth rate of wages, and so
on). But in these conditions a different question arises: To what extent
can governmental borrowing start to compete with the real amassing of
private capital? To answer this question it is important to clarify two
circumstances.

First, whether the economy is operating under conditions of high
or low savings, i.e., whether it would be useful for the state to drain off
private savings that would not otherwise find profitable application and
would cause stagnation.[10]

Second, the uses to which the borrowed money is put. If the state
uses it for productive purposes, then "in that case one can speak only of
a change in the structure of the real capital being amassed but not of a
decrease in the amount."[11]

The present-day economy is by no means "suffering" from excessively high savings rates—in most countries they have dropped, and in

---

[10]"If private accumulation is sluggish, if private savings exceed the requirements of real
private capital formation, then the syphoning off of capital by public borrowing—regardless of the
subsequent use of the funds thus mobilized (be it consumption or accumulation)—will most likely
have a stimulative effect on the economy. The arguments of those who champion the theory of
deficit financing commonly turn this property of public borrowing into an absolute" (*The Political
Economy of Present-Day Monopoly Capitalism* [*Politicheskaya ekonomika sovremennogo
kapitalizma*], Vol. 1, Moscow, 1975, p. 402).
[11]*Ibid.*

countries where they were high (Japan) they have been offset by an excess of capital exportation over importation. In the United States, the reduced rate of domestic private savings has been the object of particular concern to economists.

As for the utilization of public borrowings, it is quite apparent that it has less and less to do with productive accumulation and is increasingly geared to financing military expenditures and paying the growing burden of interest on the debt.

The colossal growth of budget deficits and of governmental indebtedness has forced bourgeois economists (including the Keynesians) and politicians to reexamine their previous ideas about the stimulative role of deficit financing. Hardly anyone disputes the short-term stimulative effect of budget deficits on demand. But today the accent is shifting to their long-term effects. These negative effects manifest themselves in three ways:

• because of the colossal growth in interest payments, the deficits become self-reinforcing;

• their persistence is a constant potential source of inflationary tendencies, should there be a relaxation of credit and monetary policy; this limits the possibility of utilizing them effectively for short-term stimulation of the economy;

• the competition between public and private borrowing in capital markets leads to the private sector's being "squeezed out" of the credit markets by the public sector, and consequently to a drop in the rate of growth of private capital accumulation, with all the negative consequences which that entails.

To what extent can one say that these negative effects have a serious impact on the economy?

Let us look at the relation of public borrowing to the volume of net private savings (without counting the influx of foreign capital) (Table 4). The data in the table show one group of countries—particularly the United States, but also France, Italy, and Canada—in which the state sector's claims on private savings show a tendency to rise, and another group—Japan, the Federal Republic of Germany, and Britain—where the opposite picture can be observed.

The influx of foreign capital can change the real situation. The connection between private investment (I), private savings (S), the public deficit (D), and the influx of foreign capital (A) can be expressed by the following formula:

$$I = S - D + A$$

It follows from the formula that as long as the influx of foreign capital compensates for, or at least mitigates, the impact of the deficit

TABLE 4
Ratio of Total Public Budget Deficit to Net Private Savings[1]

	1975	1980	1981	1982	1983	1984	1985[2]	1986[2]
U.S.	52.4	21.6	14.9	69.8	69.0	51.5	75.9	72.6
Japan	17.1	28.2	26.5	26.2	26.4	19.5	12.7	9.5
F.R.G.	55.2	35.0	49.0	45.4	31.7	24.9	15.3	11.9
France	20.2	−2.6	23.8	40.9	46.1	40.7	47.7	42.8
Britain	81.4	43.4	40.4	30.3	44.4	42.1	34.2	36.3
Italy	69.4	48.5	74.6	81.4	90.5	95.2	92.7	87.1
Canada	24.1	21.8	14.3	50.1	53.6	53.7	55.5	47.5

Source: OECD Economic Outlook, Dec. 1985, p. 5.
[1]Net private savings equals personal savings plus gross enterprise savings (net of write-downs on inventory), minus depreciation.
[2]Estimate

on private savings, then (other things being equal) private investment experiences no shortage of resources.

Government borrowing constituted the most serious competition to private accumulation in the United States (72.6 percent) and Italy (87.1 percent). However, while Italy was unable to mitigate that dangerous situation with an influx of foreign capital, the American government's policy (dubbed a "beggar-thy-neighbor policy") ensured almost total compensation for the impact of the public deficit on private savings and, consequently, on the accumulation of capital.

This is shown by the data in Table 5, in which the final result of current operations in the balance of payments is used to characterize the dynamics of net foreign investments (although they are not entirely equivalent).[12] In this connection, a deficit in current operations reflects a net influx of foreign capital, and a surplus reflects a net outflow. By subtracting the public deficit from gross private savings and adding the negative result of current operations (or subtracting if the result is positive), we get the real sum of accumulations that determined the extent of domestic investments in the country. In 1982 and 1983, when the budget deficit increased sharply and the influx of foreign capital (reflected in the deficit in current operations) barely

---

[12]"As a rule, in official publications," M. Portnoy writes, "the final result, or the balance of current operations, is determined as the sum of the balances of trade, services, and unilateral transfers. . . . It is thought that the balance of current operations reflects the quantity of real items of value that a country has transferred abroad or received from abroad as an addition to gross domestic output" (Payment Relations—A Hidden Knot of Interimperialist Contradictions [Platezhnyye otnosheniya—skrytyy uzel mezhimperialisticheskikh protivorechiy], Moscow, 1987, p. 31).

TABLE 5
Investments, Savings, Public Deficit, and Final Result
of Current Operations in the Balance of Payments
(as percentage of GNP, 1980s)

Year	Gross Private Domestic Investment	Gross Private Savings	Budget Deficit Federal, State and Local Government	Federal Budget	Final Result of Current Operations in Balance of Payments
1980	16.0	17.5	− 1.3	− 2.2	0.1
1981	16.9	18.0	− 1.0	− 2.1	0.2
1981	14.1	17.6	− 3.5	− 4.6	− 0.3
1983	14.8	17.7	− 3.8	− 5.3	− 1.4
1984	17.9	18.4	− 2.9	− 4.6	− 2.8
1985¹	16.8	17.5	− 3.3	− 4.8	− 2.8

Source: Economic Report of the President, Washington, 1986, p. 51.
¹Average data for first three quarters.

exceeded the capital outflow, gross domestic private investments in the American economy fell to an unprecedented level. In succeeding years, however, a rise in the influx of foreign capital helped to restore and even exceed the former rate of private accumulation.

At the same time, this solution to the problem of capital accumulation makes it very vulnerable and dependent on external factors; it reinforces the potential uncertainty and instability of economic development. That is why budgetary deficits are an urgent problem even in the United States, to say nothing of the countries that, for all practical purposes, have financed U.S. losses with part of their own domestic savings.

The Contours of Change

Thus, the tremendous extent of outright assumption of state control and redistribution of national income through the budgetary system have raised objective barriers to further extensive-type expansion of state intervention in the economy. That is one of the most important reasons why economic policy is being reorganized on a conservative basis.

The adaptation of state-monopoly capitalism to new conditions of reproduction and to internationalization of capital presupposes a change in economic policy—in its priorities, goals and instruments. M. Weidenbaum, the former Chairman of the President's Council of

Economic Advisors, formulated the conservatives' position as follows: "a major transformation of the economy is badly needed. But my prescription for change is hardly in terms of a further shift of power from the private sector to the public sector. . . . Rather, I urge what can be called the 'free market' approach—a greater reliance on the competitive forces of the business system to keep down inflationary pressures while providing higher levels of production, income, and employment."[13]

What general economic-policy contours can be seen at present in the context of the conservative shift? Above all, priorities are changing—scientific and technological priorities are taking precedence over social ones; and the primary goals of combating inflation, increasing efficiency and competitiveness, and significantly improving conditions for the profitable accumulation of private capital have replaced the goal of "full employment." Hence the shift in emphasis from a policy of stabilizing the economic cycle and of "full employment" to a medium- and long-term strategy of economic growth, and to the solution of structural economic problems. Increasing the rate of accumulation is replacing the expansion of demand as the chief strategic aim of regulation. While previous policy banked on using government to limit the operation of the market, today the priority goes to the market itself and to competition. "Government for the market" is the way that conservatism's ideologists formulate that reorientation.

On the whole, the new tendencies in economic policy assume the following form.

Reprivatization processes unquestionably play an important role. The effort to solve budgetary problems, enhance the effectiveness of public enterprises on the basis of purely capitalist management principles, deprive many leading segments of the working class of political power and reduce that class's numbers, and offer, as a counter to the idea of nationalization, the concept and practice of "people's capitalism" (by selling a portion of the stock in erstwhile public enterprises to workers and office employees)—all these and many other factors lie at the basis of the present process of reducing the public sector of the economy.

There has been a change in the character of macroeconomic regulation, whose basic instruments are the budget and the credit and monetary system. The role of the budget has decreased in the realm of current regulation. There has been a discernible effort to limit its role as a tool of social policy and as a tool for redistributing income in favor of the poorest strata of the population and mitigating capitalist society's sharpest contradictions.

---

[13]*Challenge*, Mar./Apr. 1978, pp. 40-41.

The policy of limiting the growth of social expenditures and reducing the number of social programs lies at the basis of all conservative governments' economic policy.

Primary emphasis is being placed on the broad use of fiscal policy—to be more precise, reducing income tax, particularly on high incomes, adopting less progressive tax rates, and lowering corporate taxes—to encourage growth in private savings and in the net profits that remain at firms' disposal. These measures are regarded as a general, long-term policy of stimulating capital investments and growth of production.

At the same time, emphasis has been placed on a medium-term credit and monetary policy whose principal role is to combat inflation and strengthen the monetary system.

Measures have been taken to limit direct forms of intervention in production and pricing, and to limit administrative and legislative controls on environmental protection and occupational safety.

In the context of the present stage of the scientific and technological revolution and of the internationalization of economic life, the interests of economic growth and structural reorganization of the economy have lent greater importance to industrial (or structural) policy. This concept is very broad. It encompasses, in particular, measures that limit the negative aspects of monopoly and that stimulate research and development, as well as certain forms of governmental participation in the structural reorganization of the economy—in developing certain industries and branches of the infrastructure. Today, the sharpest disagreements between advocates and opponents of state intervention in the economy involve industrial policy. The conservatives think that all problems of industrial development should be resolved on the basis of private-enterprise choice and competition, without assistance or subsidies from the state. The activities of the state should be limited to traditional areas—organizing education, training personnel, basic research, major scientific and technological projects (in which the state should participate as program organizer and partner to private capital), and the construction of roads and other infrastructure elements, although even in that area one finds a partial transfer of functions to private firms on a contractual basis.

The advocates of industrial policy consider it inevitable and necessary to carry out broad measures involving the state's direct participation in financing the development of leading industries, in reorganizing failing or stagnant production facilities, and in stimulating regional development.

Intensified competition, which is a consequence both of objective processes (the internationalization of the economy and structural shifts within it) and of deliberate policy on the part of capitalist countries' governments, is giving rise to sharp contradictions—particularly contradictions of an international nature. Trade wars, protectionist measures, fluctuating exchange rates, discord with regard to interest rates and a related inability to control the migration of international capital, the growth of indebtedness—these factors all undermine domestic forms of economic regulation and reinforce the instability of the capitalist system as a whole. Therefore, in speaking of the distinguishing features of the current reorganization of state-monopoly capitalism's structure, it is necessary to emphasize the special role played today by international aspects of the regulation of the capitalist economy. The need for such regulation is becoming increasingly persistent: it can be seen from the regular meetings among the heads of state of the largest capitalist countries to discuss economic problems, and from the increasingly active role of international organizations—their stepped-up role in economic analysis and forecasting, and in drawing up specific recommendations on the economic policies of particular governments. And at the same time, the inability of capitalism to work out coordinated economic-policy goals and methods at the level of the world economy is an extremely important factor in the growing instability and deepening contradictions of international capital.

* * *

Thus, one can conclude that, while the "dismantling of state-monopoly capitalism" has not occurred and is not in progress, fundamental changes involving not only decontrol and deregulation, but also the privatization of certain areas of economic life, are taking place in the economic mechanism and regulatory strategy. They are results of the search for a system of relations between the state and private capital, and between centralized regulation and private-monopoly regulation, that is more rational and optimal from the standpoint of the present-day requirements of the scientific and technological revolution and the internationalization of the economy.[14]

In the process of restructuring, monopoly capital is striving not only to limit the forms of state intervention and the types of state expenditures that were the result of democratic transformations, and not only to give greater scope to the market and private enterprise, but also to carry out a certain rationalization of centralized regulation, enhance its effectiveness and flexibility, and concentrate the state's energies and means in the decisive areas of economic development.

---

[14]See the materials on the discussion "State Regulation and Private Enterprise in Capitalist Countries: The Evolving Relationship" (*MEMO* for 1986 and 1987).

The United States: Problems of the Formation of a New State-Monopoly Structure

Vasiliy Pavlovich Volobouev*

The crisis in the postwar system of American state-monopoly capitalism that developed in the mid-1970s could not help but direct the attention of Soviet scholars to fundamental problems of the evolution of American imperialism. What direction will it take? What will be the role and the concrete functions of the bourgeois state in the state-monopoly economy of the late 1980s? To what extent did the current shifts result directly from the development of objective processes, and to what extent did they represent a subjective reaction to those processes? Finally, what were their possible and probable long-term consequences? These and many other questions have taken on exceptional relevance today with respect to the economy of the leading imperialist country—the United States of America. After all, it is the epicenter of socioeconomic disturbances that could lead to far-reaching changes in the structure of post-war state-monopoly capitalism. It is where the reaction to the crisis in the neoliberal (Roosevelt-Keynesian) system of state-monopoly capitalism, which held sway until the early 1980s, has given rise to powerful processes (and so far, the most radical processes in the capitalist world) of reorganization of the entire state-monopoly structure. In effect, what is involved here is the gradual crystallization of a new model of state-monopoly capitalism, in which both the role and mechanism of state regulation of the economy, and the form of that regulation's "linkage" with a monopolized market, which is now a global, worldwide market, are viewed differently than they were in the past.

I.

From the time of its consolidation in the 1930s and 1940s, a characteristic feature of U.S. state-monopoly capitalism has been its

---

*Candidate of Economics, senior research associate at the Institute of World Economy and International Relations [IMEMO]. This article appeared in the January 1988 issue of *MEMO*.

179

distinctive combination of the basic elements comprising the framework of the American model of a "mixed economy": a more or less monopolized, and therefore, more or less distorted, market[1] with a specific system of state regulation. This system, while preserving certain coordination functions for the market itself, nonetheless made it possible for the political regime to influence basic economic parameters without regulating the economy on the supply side. Thus the regulation of reproduction was carried out without any direct interference with capitalism's holy of holies—production proper, and the process of capital formation.

This system[2] included three main structural elements, which crystallized during the course of development of the laws and contradictions inherent in capitalism. First is the financial mechanism for regulating reproduction. Second is the subsystem of legal regulation, which is macroeconomic in function (although often it is also selective and microeconomic in its objectives). Third is the social infrastructure. For virtually the entire postwar period the financial, especially budgetary, mechanism occupied a dominant position among the instruments for influencing the dynamics of the national economy. The function of state-monopoly stabilization of reproduction as that function was understood following the Great Depression was primarily the prerogative of that mechanism. Given such premises, the nature of the functioning of the "mixed economy" and the concrete role of the financial mechanism can be described as follows.

The process of capital formation remains the monopoly of associated and individual capitalists. Its intensity determines the quantitative characteristics of economic development, especially the economic growth rate. The state performs traditional functions of maintaining a "rational" legal framework for the reproduction of capital and, when encountering cyclical fluctuations in private investments, tries to level them out through budgetary regulation and credit and monetary regulation of aggregate demand. Under certain circumstances that demand, as follows from a Marxist analysis of the reproduction of capital, is capable of actually exerting a short-term and medium-term influence on the rate of profitability (business income). Consequently, within certain limits the fluctuations in business activity are suppressed, and economic growth is stimulated, while

---

[1] "Monopolies," wrote Lenin, "growing out of free competition, do not eliminate it, but exist above it and alongside it, thus giving rise to a number of particularly acute . . . contradictions, frictions, and conflicts." (V.I. Lenin, *Complete Works* [*Polnyye sobranyye sochineniya*], Vol. 27, p. 386.)

[2] For more detail about its structure and evolution, see *Problems in American Studies* [*Problemy amerikanistiki*], Vol. 2, Moscow, 1983, pp. 169-190; *Criticism of Bourgeois Theories of State-Monopoly Capitalism* [*Kritika burzhuaznykh teoriy GMK*], Moscow, 1984, pp. 87-112; *The United States: State and Economy* [*SShA: gosudarstvo i ekonomika*], Moscow, 1976.

there is a higher degree of utilization of economic resources, including manpower. At the same time, steady economic growth makes it possible, without any fundamental change in distribution, to finance social programs, which the U.S. ruling class has long considered to be a fundamental guarantee of social stability—one more condition for the reproduction of capital.

Those aspects that have been enumerated here, which characterized the actual mechanism of reproduction in the postwar system of state-monopoly capitalism and were "captured" and reflected in the practical tenets of Keynesian regulation of the economy, tended, however, to turn particular, transient historical circumstances into absolutes. In effect, both the concept of regulation of a state-monopoly economy, and the related global concept of a "mixed" economy presupposed the linear development of the existing state-monopoly structure.[3] In particular, it was taken for granted that within the framework of the system, the means of state control would always effectively encompass the objects of that control. What's more, it was also postulated that those objects would respond in one simple and unambiguous way. For example, budgetary expansion of demand—a classic Keynesian prescription—was supposed to unfailingly stimulate real activity if it was not neutralized by a change in the positions of other state-monopoly instruments. Economic incentives, in this case offered by the central authorities, were thought to be so strong that they would always force economic agents to act in the direction expected by the state. In short, in the dialectics of the system, the creators of state-monopoly policies totally overlooked the fact that the system would undergo a qualitative change as it evolved in a "steady state"—that is, when the change in actual reproduction relationships[4] was predictable and quantitative in nature, and reproduction of the system was assured by manipulating the degree of intensity of state regulation.

Meanwhile, in essence the capitalist nature of the reproduction process remained unchanged. Therefore, the objective logic of accumulation could not help but advance the tendencies inherent in the movement of capital. The changes that had gained strength by the early 1970s started to mature. At the same time, the entire system of economic regulation, which was trying to keep this development within a state-monopoly framework, was oriented toward short-term or, at most, medium-term regulation of the conditions of reproduction. In principle, that system (and its chief distinguishing structural feature, the dominance of financial instruments of demand management)

---

[3]Even the most institutionalist interpretation of these concepts by J. Galbraith suffered from this flaw.

[4]They were the most thoroughly studied and formalized by American orthodox Keynesianism.

did not directly touch the epicenter of the changes—the investment process. Yet it is through that process and only through it, as Marx stressed repeatedly, that technological innovations can make any headway under capitalism.[5] This is especially true considering that, with the development of the scientific and technological revolution and its related new wave of concentration of capital, the primary subjects of that investment process—the monopolies—started not only to increasingly control national markets, but also to outgrow them, to move up to a global level, and thus to acquire greater independence from the national state-monopoly strategy, particularly from the national policy of demand management. At the same time, the formation of a truly worldwide market in borrowed capital gave global dimensions to the separation of monetary capital from real, productive capital, internationalizing—with extremely complicated consequences[6]—the financial aspects of the reproduction of national capital in the current era.[7]

Generally speaking, the tendency toward progressive development of the foreign-economic aspects of reproduction that Marx deduced from the logic of capitalist accumulation resulted in raising the internationalization of the capitalist economy to a new level by the late 1960s and early 1970s. Consequently, at the same time that the United States on the one hand, had become much more vulnerable to the influence of foreign economic forces than in the past, it became increasingly apparent on the other hand, that traditional state-monopoly means were inadequate to deal with these exogenous economic forces then taking shape in the contemporary, highly integrated world economy. Without at least a partial globalization of individual instruments belonging to the previous system, state-monopoly regulation proved incapable of controlling the national reproduction process.

Therefore, in a retrospective assessment of the evolution of the Roosevelt-Keynesian system of state-monopoly capitalism in the United States, one can only draw the conclusion that as long as the application of its regulatory instruments conformed with the objective trends in postwar economic development, and as long as the economic trends based on the material embodiment of the first round of the scientific and technological revolution fostered the accumulation of capital in the United States and in the world capitalist economy as a

---

[5]See K. Marx and F. Engels, *Works [Sochineniya]*, Vol. 25, Part 1, pp. 270-292.
[6]See, for example, I.S. Korolev, *Currency Relations under Capitalism: Economics and Politics [Valyutnyye otnosheniya kapitalizma: ekonomika i politika]*, Moscow, 1986, pp. 111-125.
[7]In this connection, the very development of technology, the quantitative expansion of the field of accumulation, and the growth in population raised specifically global problems of world development (resource problems, in particular), problems whose appearance completed the process of the internationalization of the objective conditions for reproduction within any individual country.

whole—as long as these things happened, the expansion and intensification of state regulation within the conceptual framework of this system made it possible to achieve certain positive results.[8] However, when these trends reached a point where they had not only completed the intensive technological and economic transformation of the prewar world capitalist system, but had also passed through the stage of developing "in breadth," a sharp discrepancy began to emerge between the capabilities of state-monopoly regulation and objective economic conditions. As a result, there was a sharp drop in the effectiveness of traditional methods, particularly budgetary methods, used by the state to influence reproduction. And later state-monopoly regulation itself, in its existing forms, became a factor in the deteriorating performance of the U.S. economy, aggravating a series of problems, which were global in nature and only partially related to national state economic functions.

Specifically, in the 1970s growth of production slowed considerably. Inflation accelerated, exceeding the 10-percent mark by the early 1980s. Unemployment assumed a scale unthinkable for the "age of Keynesianism." These events created complicated problems for financing the social infrastructure, raising doubts about its future as it had taken shape in the postwar period, as well as doubts about the traditional reformist views of accomplishing the social and political stabilization of American capitalism. In addition, the United States' foreign-economic balance deteriorated sharply.

At this stage previous systems and concepts of state-monopoly regulation suffered bankruptcy. They proved incapable of providing any serious movement toward the social and economic goals whose realization, in the opinion of the U.S. ruling class, had served and should serve as a guarantee of capitalism's adaptation to a changing world. In other words, these were goals that had justified, in the eyes of the imperialist bourgeoisie, the very existence of state-monopoly structures, and state interference in economic life. During these years of stagflation, of the reversal of the United States' foreign-trade balance, and of the instability of American currency, a deep and far-reaching crisis of the traditional system of state-monopoly regulation took shape, and by the end of the decade that crisis encompassed the entire structure of postwar state-monopoly capitalism. That crisis also

---

[8]Thus, in the 1950s and 1960s the development and complication of state-monopoly regulation, particularly the active utilization of Keynesian instruments to manipulate aggregate demand, contributed to a temporary, partial resolution of the economic contradictions of capitalism. It moderated the cyclical fluctuations in reproduction, stimulated relatively high growth rates, facilitated the solution of medium-range structural problems and the use of scientific and technological advances to make production more efficient, and on this basis contributed to the stabilization of the unemployment rate and a tangible improvement in the working people's economic and social situation.

initiated the process of a fundamental modification of state-monopoly capitalism and has become an important element in the gradual consolidation of its transnational form.

II.

One can identify two aspects of the American strategy for the transformation of the state-monopoly capitalism system: the short-term aspect that represents a response to temporary conditions and is known by the term "Reaganomics"; and the long-term, structural aspect, i.e., the one that actually reflects the policy of transforming the previous state-monopoly capitalism system. In real terms, of course, the two aspects are connected: some intermediate results are needed in order to implement a long-term reform strategy with the approval of the ruling class. However, the structural, long-term nature of socioeconomic programs in the United States, and the struggle to define and institutionalize the direction of change indicate that it is the second aspect that is of particular interest now, especially from the standpoint of analyzing the objective tendencies affecting it, and the objective conditions that, refracted in the consciousness of the bourgeoisie's ruling group, have brought about a clear departure from previous state-monopoly practice.

The central feature uniting all the fragments of U.S. conservative economic policy is the limitation (at the very least) of state interference in economic life. And whereas the concrete, interrelated goals of that policy still come down, in general, to some restoration of the favorable results of economic development that American state-monopoly capitalism managed to achieve in the 1950s and 1960s, the means for achieving those goals (in contrast to the practice of the past four decades) is a certain *relative* relaxation of state-monopoly regulation.

Reagan has said that the goal of his administration was to achieve new progress for America and new opportunities for all its citizens. He said there was one means of achieving this goal: free the individual, eliminate regulation of the market, and restrict the size of the government apparatus and the power of the federal government.[9] "My first and foremost objective," he stressed in this connection, "has been to improve the performance of the economy by reducing the role of the federal government in all its many dimensions . . . .We should leave to private initiative all the functions that individuals can perform privately."[10] Touching on the positive economic role of the state in this context, the president asserted that it consists only of creating "a

---

[9]*New York Times*, Nov. 19, 1982.
[10]*Economic Report of the President*, Washington, 1982, pp. 4, 5.

sound, stable long-term framework in which the private sector is the key engine to growth, employment, and rising living standards."[11]

Accordingly, the strategy aimed at realizing and reinforcing this role for the central government consisted, and still consists, of four main elements.

First is a far-reaching restructuring of the entire budgetary mechanism. This includes a radical transformation of the tax system, a change in the structure of spending (in particular, the proportion of military expenditures has been rising sharply), and a reorientation of the concept of budgetary influence on reproduction.[12] In this connection, the intention is first to limit and eventually to reduce the relative size of the federal budget in the economy.

Second is the deregulation of a number of sectors of the economy along with an overall relaxation of legal regulation of economic activities (including a change in antitrust legislation) and the privatization of various segments of the economy.[13] Since budgetary reform, to all intents and purposes, was completed, these aspects of Reagan's strategy are increasingly moving to center stage.

The third element directly related to the first element, is a serious reduction of the social infrastructure that had been created by the early 1980s as a result of the persistent struggle of the U.S. working class.

The fourth element is a certain expansion of the functions of credit and monetary regulation, particularly with respect to consistent management of the "noninflationary" growth of the money supply of bank lending.[14]

It must be emphasized that the Republican government also regards all the measures listed here as the core of foreign-economic policy. The President's Council of Economic Advisers stated that: "the administration's approach to international economic issues is based on

---

[11]*Ibid.*, p. 10.

[12]The key point here in the reorganization of the entire budget complex was, of course, the transformation of the tax structure. The heart of the reforms on the supply side, the London weekly *The Economist* pointed out, was the change in the tax system (see *The Economist*, Oct. 4, 1986, p. 14). The multiple-stage reform of the federal tax system in the United States in 1981-1986 once again confirms the accuracy of this assertion. In actuality—and this is the most important thing—during those years the Reagan government put an end to the progressive tax scale that had its roots in state-monopoly processes of the first half of the century; it replaced the graduated system of tax ceilings (which until 1981 ranged from 14 to 70 percent) with just two rates, 15 and 28 percent, virtually eliminating the existing differentiation in the taxation of individual income. In this context (together with a number of other serious changes) the base tax rate for business income was also lowered from 46 to 34 percent (for more detail see *MEMO*, No. 6, 1987, pp. 89-98).

[13]Like deregulation, government experts believe that privatization should be viewed as a "method for improving" the performance of the market economy in many of its sectors (see *Economic Report of the President*, Washington, 1986, p. 187). So far in the United States, in contrast to the leading Western European countries, this "improvement" has been limited and has affected only state companies involved in rail transportation and electric power production.

[14]See *Proceedings of the USSR Academy of Sciences. Economics Series [Izvestiya AN SSSR. Seriya ekonomicheskaya]*, No. 5, 1984, pp. 129-140.

the same principles which underlie its domestic programs: a belief in the superiority of market solutions to economic problems and an emphasis on private economic activity as the engine of noninflationary growth."[15]

Here one cannot help but notice the fact that in all aspects of economic policy—and they take on a definite character only when viewed as a whole[16]—the present U.S. administration is carrying out, or even completing, a deliberate transformation of the former structure of state-monopoly regulation. In fact, although specific tactical deviations and rhetorical tricks have occurred with some frequency, and although federal spending (and deficits) has increased substantially as a proportion of the GNP[17] (an increase due, in part, to the specific conditions of the crisis of 1980-1982), what we have before us is a set of strategic measures that could lead, in time, to development of a different version of macroregulation. This version is based on the need to exercise increasingly less "rigid" and more *indirect* government control of the economy, and it assigns market forces a fundamentally new and, generally speaking, leading role in realizing the goals of the development and sociopolitical stabilization of contemporary capitalism. As the specific structure of this system of state-monopoly regulation is defined, the model itself—the political economic structure—of U.S. state-monopoly capitalism may undergo fundamental changes, since the emphasis in the "state-monopolized market" relationship will shift from "state" to "market." Moreover, the preservation and, possibly, development of the open nature of the U.S. economy (unless, of course, there is a breakdown in conditions involving free trade and the movement of capital) will tend to reinforce a shift of this sort.

Here we come once again to its objective imperatives and subjective conditions.

III.

In terms of the influence of objective economic factors, the same domestic- and foreign-economic trends that had caused the bankruptcy of Keynesian regulation of the state-monopoly economy in the

---

[15]*Economic Report of the President*, Washington, 1982, p. 167.

[16]It is precisely the integrated, interconnected nature of these elements, as G. Skorov properly observes, that "gives them a certain new quality" (*SShA—ekonomika, politika, ideologiya* [*The United States—Economics, Politics, Ideology*], No. 9, 1981, p. 119).

[17]So here with regard to the problem of the colossal budget deficits that continue to put the future of Reagan's conservative experiment in great doubt, there was a glaring failure of the administration's medium-range financial strategy. As one of the creators of that strategy quite convincingly attests, this failure was, given the alignment of political forces in the country, inherent in that strategy from the outset, along with the ensuing economic consequences (for more detail, see D.A. Stockman. *The Triumph of Politics*, New York, 1986).

1970s played a decisive role. A qualitative metamorphosis became apparent in the sum total of conditions that in the 1930s and 1940s had determined the previous directions in the development of macroeconomic regulation and the structure of state-monopoly capitalism as a whole. Not much significance was attributed to the changes, and this initially led to attempts to compensate for the declining results of capitalist reproduction by strengthening and internationalizing the traditional instruments of regulation.

The consequences of these attempts, however, exceeded even the worst expectations. By the late 1970s and early 1980s, the American ruling class faced a dilemma. Either it had to try to correct the existing situation by expanding state regulation of the economy and making it even tighter (up to the point of undertaking the coordinated, global control of demand), while remaining within the general framework of the former structure and concept of state-monopoly capitalism; or it had to look for fundamentally different approaches. Such approaches not only had to offer "convincing" ways to solve the United States' most critical domestic economic problems, but also had to ensure a certain amount of harmony in U.S. relations with the world economy, where the Americans were continuing to lose ground and the growing impulses for internationalization and interdependence dictated the need for further integration of the U.S. economy into the world economy.

In the first option, the choice (despite the fact that it looked like a minimal departure from the status quo) would objectively result in significantly changing the previous structure of state-monopoly capitalism in the direction of strengthening the state-regulation principle on both the national and the global levels. (On the national level, the very nature of the Roosevelt-Keynesian synthesis would change.) In the second option, a more complicated scenario would develop, since the proposed form of limited state control and the further "opening up" of the economic system would increase the importance of the market factors, including exogenous ones, that were taking shape in the world capitalist economy. Objectively, the role of the state here would be less clearly defined.

Given these circumstances, the choice inevitably took on strategic implications, and the second alternative was chosen. The failure of the state-monopoly strategy in the 1970s—a failure so serious that for a significant part of the U.S. establishment it compromised the very idea of state interference in reproduction—tipped the balance in that direction.

By the end of the 1970s the maximum expansion in the state's economic role allowed by the Roosevelt-Keynesian system under the existing objective domestic and international economic conditions had probably been reached. Moreover, the development of internationalized capitalist reproduction, which had taken on global dimensions and risen to a new level of worldwide integration—"the international unity of capital," as Lenin wrote[18]—required not merely a change in the forms, instruments (and institutions), and methods of state regulation, but a rethinking of the actual concept of the economic function of the national state as such.

The rethinking began and is being carried out within the framework and on the basis of state-monopoly relations. But it immediately called into question the previous fundamental, "philosophical" arguments in favor of strengthening the state principle in a "mixed economy." However, certain political and ideological processes, which in their current form were brought to life by the crisis-induced adaptation of American state-monopoly capitalism to new realities, focused the thrust of this rethinking, this wholesale change, not so much outward as inward. In any case, in the thinking of the ruling class, the objective conditions that have been described were perceived and interpreted as hindering effective state interference and, conversely, as favoring a market solution to economic problems. Meanwhile, the conceptual foundations of Reagan's "conservative revolution" blossomed in the fertile soil of criticism of the genuinely distressing results of traditional state-monopoly regulation.

As a result, the contours of a new alignment of forces on key issues in economics and political ideology began to take shape. These were issues involving the formulation of the principles of state interference in economic life, the determination of the political-economic structure of state-monopoly capitalism, and the development of options for "effective" government policies. New schools and concepts whose economic philosophy fit into the course that had been defined for the restructuring of state-monopoly capitalism moved to the forefront of both theory and practice.[19]

Their common credo and central practical idea, which became firmly established in the official mentality, were the "emancipation" of the decentralized, coordinating matrix of the market, and the reduction of state regulation of the economy to the politically acceptable minimum. Accordingly, from this perspective it is state regulation and the Roosevelt-Keynesian policy of economic and political stabilization of postwar capitalism that are viewed as practically the universal cause of crises in the U.S. economy.

---

[18]See V. I. Lenin, *Complete Works*, Vol. 24, p. 124.
[19]For more detail, see I.M. Osadchaya, *Conservatism versus Reformism* [*Konservatizm protiv reformizma*], Moscow, 1984, pp. 66-100, 163-211.

With such an approach to the nature of the present crisis,[20] everything seemingly becomes clear and simple. For example, the decline in the rate of economic growth, the chronic sluggishness of the investment process, as well as the stagnation of productivity, have been and are being explained as the results of an excessive, "prohibitive" level of taxation of economic agents (entrepreneurs, in particular), the expansion and tightening of state regulations, and the "eating up" of profits and savings by the Keynesian policy of deficit-based stimulation of reproduction. Inflation was caused by decades of an irresponsible credit and monetary policy for regulating demand. The high unemployment rate is the synthetic result of the aforementioned causes, plus a growth in social programs that "exceeded realistic bounds" and supposedly weakened the incentives for people to work. The United States' loss of ground in the world economy is the natural result of destructive state "activism" in the domestic economy, and neglect of "healthy" growth in the private sector.[21]

The logical conclusion drawn from these propositions that each contains a grain of truth, is the interpretation of the current crisis of state-monopoly capitalism as a crisis of the state and a crisis of the state regulation of economic life, and not a crisis of capitalism itself.[22] Therefore, the policy of "reviving" capitalism seems like a promising response. Therefore, the limitation and reduction of state interference are viewed and recommended here as a "good in and of itself," as a means that is capable, through the market mechanism, of getting the growth engine started up, of cutting unemployment, and of simultaneously loosening the grip of inflation and foreign-economic restrictions, while stimulating intensive private formation of capital by attacking the working people's living standard. Hence the attempts to institutionalize a "neocapitalist" version of state-monopoly capitalism that is capable, in the opinion of its ideologues, of riding on the crest of a new wave of history.

---

[20]See the dubious "classic" of this approach: G. Gilder, *Wealth and Poverty*, New York, 1981; also J. Wanniski, *The Way the World Works*, New York, 1983.

[21]Arguments of this nature are summed up in the *Economic Report of the President*: "the vitality of the American economy and the prosperity of the American people have been diminished by inappropriate policies of the federal government: unnecessary government regulations that discouraged initiative and wasted scarce capital and labor; an inefficient and unfair tax system that penalized effort, saving, and investment; excessive government spending that wasted taxpayers' money . . . and created budget deficits that reduced capital formation and added to the burden of the national debt; and monetary policies that produced frequent business cycles and a path of increasing inflation" (*Economic Report of the President*, Washington, 1984, p. 3).

[22]What's more, capitalism is portrayed as some sort of universal, viable principle, which is destroyed step by step by the escalation of state control of the economy—destroyed in all of its elements, including the most subtle, motivational aspects of production relations. "The problem of contemporary capitalism," Gilder writes, "lies not chiefly in a deterioration of physical capital, but in a persistent subversion of the psychological means of production—the morale and inspiration of economic man . . ." (G. Gilder, *op. cit.*, p. 28).

However, this subjective and, to a great extent, exaggerated and distorted evaluation of the crisis and of the trajectory of historical processes contains a deep internal contradiction. An analysis of the problem shows with perfect clarity that what is occurring today is a profound crisis and the disintegration of the entire former state-monopoly structure, a disintegration that is a necessary result of capitalist development. It is another matter that this development has gone further along the lines of the internationalization of state-monopoly capitalism, which has led to the transformation of its national systems and supranational forms, and consequently, to a certain duality in contemporary state-monopoly processes.

On the one hand, these processes have come to be characterized by tendencies (explicable within their context) toward decentralization and the limitation of state interference on the national level as the open economy becomes increasingly integrated into the world economy, making it pointless to strengthen traditional control over economic forces that take shape beyond the boundaries of the national economy. On the other hand, the globalization of capitalist reproduction has given rise to powerful imperatives for a supranational centralization of macroeconomic stabilization functions. However, in the world capitalist system there is not, in principle, any international regulatory mechanism analogous and comparable to the previous national mechanism, and at the given level of economic and political development there probably cannot be. (Thus in any case, in the foreseeable future the consolidation of genuinely global state-monopoly regulation will to some extent be limited and will primarily affect the institutional structure of the world capitalist economy.) Consequently, the growing discrepancy between postwar systems of state-monopoly capitalism and the new conditions of historical evolution has created not only an urgent need to adapt to these conditions, but also an objective opportunity to make that adaptation by deliberately stimulating the development of a global, monopolized market by the transnationalization of monopoly capital.

This is also a form of "organization" of the world capitalist economy. It is a form, however, that is specifically capitalistic and that, at the present stage, acquires its coordinating aspects only in connection with the national and supranational elements of state-monopoly regulation. And it is this point that the Reagan plan for transforming state-monopoly capitalism overlooks, if not totally, then at least to an extent that is significant, even crucial, for current policies. Furthermore, in the strategic sense, this is that plan's *main contradiction*.

From the standpoint of political economy, the essence of the plan is that by altering the existing state-monopoly structure, it attempts to re-create, in light of new historical conditions, the atmosphere and structures of classical capitalist accumulation. In actuality, by orienting itself toward a predominantly market solution of economic problems, the Reagan administration is counting on the assumption that the market flexibility and discipline that are restored as a result of its economic program (a flexibility and discipline which are supposed to be even more effective because they will actually be imposed from without, through the global market mechanism) will be able to promote long-term growth in business income.[23] Consequently, there may be (and to some extent this is already happening) a significant acceleration in the accumulation of capital and an increase in private investment as a share of the GNP, and thus (assuming a substantial increase in productivity), it will become possible to respond in a positive fashion to the set of problems related to the foreign-economic aspects of the U.S. economy's development. And first and foremost, it will become possible to restore competitiveness, which would serve, in a way, to insulate the open economic system from serious disruptions of economic equilibrium.

This, incidentally, is the real meaning of the unified approach to domestic- and foreign-economic matters in the Republican administration's policies. Here we see once again the hidden motive force behind its course: to prepare the American economy for greater involvement in the world economy, but to carry out this integration from a position of strength.

We should point out that although, in many of its specific aspects, this extremely class-oriented, reactionary strategy is full of contradictions and is conceptually and politically vulnerable, it does contain elements of understanding of the new nature of economic space. And therefore, despite the fact that the poorest segments of American society are having to pay, and will continue to pay, a high price for Reagan's conservative course,[24] from the standpoint of the ruling class, this course can count on a certain degree of success. Generally speaking, if the formation of a favorable investment climate continues to result in fairly vigorous and stable, noninflationary growth that leads to at least a gradual decline in the unemployment rate, and in this respect does not conflict with the goals of maintaining social and political

---

[23]In this model, as in the "good old days" of classical capitalism, an improvement in the standard of living for hired labor takes place only through an increase in production efficiency, while wages are stabilized or even reduced as a share of the national income. A strict credit and monetary policy, squeezing out inflation, is supposed to lead gradually to a drop in the prevailing interest rate. According to the logic of things, the restructuring of the budget mechanism is supposed to work in this same direction. (For a detailed critical analysis of the Reagan administration's economic program, see V.P. Volobouev, *The Financial Dilemmas of the United States* [*Finansovyye dilemmy SShA*], Moscow, 1987, pp. 139-184.

[24]Bourgeois scholars who are even the least bit objective cannot help but acknowledge this fact.

stability in the United States,[25] then in the late 1980s at least the basic tenets of the "conservative revolution" will have a decisive influence on the consolidation of a new system of state-monopoly regulation and on the structure of American state-monopoly capitalism as a whole.

From all the evidence, however, it will be impossible to achieve this result without devoting a great deal of attention to the foreign-economic aspects of the development of the present-day U.S. economy, and without a more serious reorientation toward a global level of strategy for restructuring state-monopoly capitalism in the United States. In short, the external conditions for the institutionalization of the Reagan "reforms" will play an exceptionally important, even key, role. They already mark the objective boundary beyond which attempts to exert a deliberate influence on the economic organization of society become destructive in nature, and the further things go, the clearer that boundary will become.

Weighing all the pros and cons, and taking into account all the limitations that Reagan's strategy continues to encounter, one is forced once again to say that its main chance—and ultimately, its only chance—is for the capitalist economy to surge ahead to a new level of scientific and technological progress.

As noted in the Soviet literature of the early 1980s, the beginning of large-scale commercial exploitation of innovative scientific and technological advances really could give the U.S. economy an opportunity for the broad-scale renewal of productive capital on a qualitatively new technological basis. In the context of the government's present economic policies, this really could bring about a prolonged and intensive, relative reduction in manpower costs and, consequently (assuming that certain other conditions, mainly a drop in interest rates, were observed),[26] a certain increase in the business income rate. This would provide, through the feedback mechanism, an additional impetus for capitalist accumulation.

As wages experience a relative reduction and interest rates drop substantially, a trend toward a temporary increase in the business income rate is becoming increasingly apparent. And in this case if it gains momentum, there is only one possible outcome. We are talking

---

[25]And generally speaking, most of the bourgeois establishment has evaluated Reagan's program positively from this viewpoint. For example: "Despite the inadequacy of the ideas with which Mr. Reagan came into office," wrote H. Stein, who is known for his consensus views, "they contained elements of validity. We did need to put more emphasis on economic growth and price stability. We did need to reduce those taxes that bore most heavily on growth and these expenditures and regulations that were least productive. The private economy needed more breathing room, and more assurance of stability in government policy" (H. Stein, *Presidential Economics*, New York, 1984, p. 22).

[26]In functional, quantitative respects there is another important contradiction of Reagan's economic strategy here. Because of the special role of U.S. interest rates in the world capitalist economy, incidentally, it also has a supranational, global dimension.

about something more than just another cyclical upswing. Under certain conditions (having to do primarily with the presence of the necessary international state-monopoly instruments), it is possible to foresee the beginning of an ascendant phase in those long fluctuations, lasting 40 to 60 years, in the economic growth rate that are related to extremely long-term fluctuations in profitability and are based on underlying changes in the entire technological basis of the economy.[27]

One cannot close one's eyes to this possibility. The development of capitalism has not come to a standstill. And the current crisis in capitalism's economic forms contains within it the prerequisites for a partial correction. As Lenin pointed out, any crisis means (along with the possibility of temporary delay and regression) an aggravation of contradictions, the manifestation of those contradictions, the collapse of everything that is rotten, and an acceleration of development.[28] This fully applies to the current processes of restructuring of the neoliberal system of state-monopoly capitalism.

One of the most important tenets of Marxism-Leninism states that an acceleration of the progress of productive forces requires appropriate forms of organization of economic life and a renewal of outdated production relations, even if that renewal (as in the given case) does not affect the basic foundations of the ruling system. It seems that American capitalism, encountering colossal difficulties and the discrediting of the previous course of state-monopoly evolution, is once again experimenting with new forms of economic organization in an attempt to speed up the development of productive forces at any cost.

Therefore, in evaluating the changes of Reagan's conservative economic policies, it would be more correct to say that now, like "yesterday," its calculations are built not on sand, but on the perfectly definite and rational hope that a reorientation of the entire system of state-monopoly capitalism toward the stimulation of private capital formation will make it possible, in a situation in which the world is at the initial stage of a powerful new technological breakthrough, to translate this breakthrough into practice and turn it into an entire era of expansion, not only of the American economy, but of the world capitalist economy as a whole. In this connection, the U.S. President has stressed: "recovery alone is not good enough. Our challenge is far greater: lasting *worldwide* (our emphasis—V.V.) economic expansion . . . ."[29] Only under these circumstances can the investment process acquire an autonomous impetus that will be sufficient to carry out the consolidation that the rightists envision of the conservative

---

[27]See *Kommunist* [*Communist*], No. 6, 1983, pp. 36-37; No. 4, 1984, pp. 116-122; *Rabochiy klass i sovremennyy mir* [*The Working Class and Today's World*], No. 1, 1986, pp. 62-82.
[28]See V.I. Lenin, *Complete Works*, Vol. 26, p. 372.
[29]*New York Times*; Sept. 28, 1983.

model of state-monopoly capitalism. Only under these circumstances, from the standpoint of the U.S. ruling class, will the temporary failures of "Reaganomics" at the peak of the 1980 to 1982 crisis be offset in a "lasting" way by its longer-term results.

But is the scientific and technological renewal to which we have referred, a renewal which in its very essence is international, conceivable without a corresponding expansion of international state-monopoly regulation? In other words, will the power of the American economy alone, considering its now-reduced weight in the contemporary world, be sufficient to guarantee the long-term, stable ("sustainable," as U.S. government experts put it) world expansion of accumulation that is needed for the technological restructuring of the capitalist economy?

As if in response to the second question, leading American economists F. Bergsten and L. Klein once wrote that there is a tendency "to rely heavily on recovery in the United States to lift everyone (read: the capitalist countries.—V.V.) back to (at least modest) prosperity. Unfortunately, it is not very likely that this strategy will work."[30] Furthermore, Bergsten and Klein stressed, recent experience has shown that not a single country even has the capability of carrying out a unilateral expansion of reproduction.

The events of 1983 to 1987 indicate that this assessment was incorrect. Following the U.S. example, the spontaneous forces of the capitalist cycle, in conjunction with state-monopoly stimulation measures, began a phase first of revival, and then of upswing, throughout the entire world capitalist economy. But given its present approach to the international aspects of economic development, an approach which generally continues to have a national-egoistical bent, is the United States capable of maintaining a growing economy in some sort of shaky equilibrium over a long period of time? There is only one answer to this question, and thus to the first question, and that answer is *no*.

Without a far-reaching adjustment in current American policies, both in their more general, structural aspects and in their specific aspects (particularly budgetary and international financial aspects), stable expansion of the world capitalist economy is impossible. It is impossible primarily because of external, international factors.

The departure from traditional systems of state-monopoly regulation that is occurring simultaneously in the United States and a number of other capitalist countries is leaving a "gray zone"—an area of reproduction that today is hardly covered either by existing global instruments, or by altered national structures of state regulation. Yet

---

[30]*The Economist*, Apr. 23, 1983, p. 25.

that gray zone can be and is becoming a source of extreme instability in the world capitalist economy. This is true if only because of the sharp increase in competitive tendencies and greater decentralization of investment and pricing decisions that have been brought about by the growing "opening up" of national economies; the formation of a highly integrated world capitalist market; the growing international division of labor; and the appearance in the 1970s and early 1980s of new economic sectors in which, because of the specific technological features of their production processes, dozens of newly formed, relatively small companies that were independent of the monopolistic giants in terms of their pricing policies gained a foothold.

This potential instability is capable at any moment of ending the economic upsurge developing in the United States and other imperialist countries. And the macroregulation of the national economy in its present form is hardly capable of blocking such a course of events. This is especially true since that regulation is itself restricted by rigid limitations imposed by external, global conditions of development of the capitalist economy. Specifically, with the initial impetus for growth coming from the United States, it was precisely that country that found itself in a relatively unfavorable position both in terms of inflation (short-term), and—on a scale that no one could have predicted—in terms of its foreign economic position, with all the ensuing consequences for credit and monetary policies, and thus (through interest rates) for the U.S. government's entire program. Yet besides this, the problem of the United States' ensuring a "natural" expansion of world investment continues to be burdened by a number of factors, among which one must single out resource limitations, which have been aggravated by the unprecedented militarization of the economy, as well as the extreme vulnerability of world banking and currency systems, which are foundering under the weight of the colossal indebtedness. The stock-market collapse in October 1987 is an extremely graphic example of the economic danger posed by the further growth of that indebtedness.

Taken together, all this indicates the exceptional riskiness of the United States' current economic strategy and its relatively poor chances for any long-term success without a more serious attitude toward its foreign economic aspects, and without the simultaneous implementation of state-monopoly measures that are international in nature. As long as this sort of adjustment remains more a vague probability than a clearly defined policy, the Republican administration's intention to divert today's state-monopoly processes into the channel of limitation of state regulation of the economy on both the national and global levels will distort the objective logic of these processes and go beyond the limits of historical reality. And in this connection the fact that the relative weakening of state influence on national reproduction and the increase in the role of market factors are still not being offset by an adequate strengthening of international state-monopoly regulation only increases the vulnerability of the present conservative economic policy.

The Export of Capital and Internationalization of Production in the U.S. Machinery Industry

MIKHAIL VIKTOROVICH STEPANOV*

The present stage of capitalism is characterized by the interweaving of national economies, and an intensification of the influence of internationalization of economic life on the regular patterns of each country's economic and sociopolitical development. As was noted at the 27th CPSU Congress, "the direct result of the capitalist concentration and internationalization of production is the strengthening of transnational corporations."

The internationalization of production, which has undergone tremendous development in the past two decades, is fundamentally affecting the situation of individual corporations and monopolization as a whole. The present-day characteristics of the export of capital have manifested themselves most vividly in the research-intensive sectors of industry, especially the machinery industry, where the bulk of scientific and technological advances are implemented.

Conditions for the Export of Capital and the International Orientation of an Industry

Monopolies' drive for dominance, including dominance beyond the boundaries of national economies, is expressed through the export of capital. Here the tendencies toward concentration and centralization and toward the relative overaccumulation of capital are bound up in a single knot. Among American firms, the machinery manufacturers are distinguished by a high level of international activity. In 1950 they accounted for one third of all money invested by U.S. companies in the manufacturing industry abroad; by the early 1980s this figure had risen to approximately one half.[1] In terms of the degree of internationaliza-

*Candidate of economics, senior research fellow at the U.S.S.R. Academy of Sciences' Institute of World Economy and International Relations [IMEMO]. This article was published in the January 1987 issue of *MEMO*.

[1] Calculated on the basis of *U.S. Business Investment in Foreign Countries*, New York, 1976, p. 96; and *Survey of Current Business*, Aug. 1984, p. 29.

tion of production operations (which amounts, on the average, to more than 30 percent),[2] the following industries are especially prominent: electronic components and industrial electrical equipment, instruments, transportation machinery, and agricultural equipment.[3]

The expansion of foreign trade in the first postwar years only laid the foundation for formation of the present regional and branch structure of U.S. foreign investments, which are concentrated mainly in the high-technology machinery industries of the developed capitalist countries. The export of capital contributes, in turn, to commodity exports. It is no accident that export quotas have been increasing for types of machinery and equipment which are increasingly produced by U.S. corporations foreign branches: turbines and generators, pumps and compressors, electrical measuring instruments and computers, farm machinery, and lifting and transport equipment.

The dominant U.S. position in world goods markets, especially in high-technology products, delayed the broad-scale export of production capital in the 1950s and early 1960s, since such export entailed the difficulties of organizing production in a foreign country.[4] The growth in the concentration of production and capital in the other Western countries, and the strengthening of their corporations' positions forced U.S. firms to revise their forms and methods of external expansion. Direct investment became the main means of foreign activity. In the expanding export of equipment from the United States since the late 1960s, the leaders have been foreign branches of companies using their internal company channels not just for the relatively free movement of products to foreign markets (circumventing customs barriers, for example, or restrictions on imports) but also for transferring part of their profits "home," as well as for technology transfers. Since that period, the export of capital by machinery manufacturing companies has consistently and to an ever greater extent exceeded the export of machinery products (see Table 1).

In the 1970s the export of capital became one of the most monopolistic branches of economic activity. By the end of the past decade, the largest 50 machinery corporations accounted for more than 60 percent of total foreign assets of the industry's corporations conducting operations in foreign markets.

The concentration of the export of capital in the hands of a relatively small circle of machinery corporations is closely tied up with the

---

[2]Calculated as a ratio of the value of exports of goods from the United States and sales abroad to total U.S. industrywide production.

[3]See S. Lall, *The Multinational Corporation*, London, 1980, pp. 23-24.

[4]The main reasons here were the discrepancy between the United States and other capitalist countries in degree of economic development, the discrepancy between the technical level of the U.S. machinery industry and its facilities and equipment on the one hand, and the production infrastructure in the receiving countries on the other.

TABLE 1
Ratio Between Sales by U.S. Companies' Foreign Branches (I)
and Exports of Goods from the United States (II)
(in billions of dollars)

Industry	1957			1965			1977		
	I	II	I as % of II	I	II	I as % of II	I	II	I as % of II
General machinery	1.9	3.2	59	5.4	5.0	108	46.2	22.5	205
Electrical machinery	2.0	0.9	222	4.0	1.7	235	24.5	10.5	235
Transportation machinery	4.2	2.7	156	10.7	3.3	324	75.0	18.7	401

level of concentration of national machinery production and of the sphere of research and experimental design work. At the beginning of the 1980s more than 70 percent of U.S. firms with international operations belonged to machinery branches where the four largest companies produced more than 65 percent of the output. In 1980 in the most highly monopolized sectors of the American machinery industry—the automotive industry and the manufacture of computers and office equipment—the proportion of foreign involvement was about 60 percent.[5]

The internationalization of production operations is characteristic of many branches of the U.S. machinery complex, but it has become most widespread in the sectors that are distinguished by either higher capital- or labor-intensiveness, or by the complexity of technologies employed and the high technological level of production. In other words, what is involved are mainly the transport-machinery, electrical-equipment and electronics industries, instrument manufacturing and the aerospace complex. Many companies conduct operations abroad, but the preponderance of all foreign assets, sales, and profits is accounted for by a relatively small number of the largest transnational corporations.

The diversification of production is an objective condition contributing to the expansion of the export of capital. The modern company is becoming increasingly multibranch and diversified.[6] Corporations' utilization of differences in profit norms in interbranch transfers of capital is limited by the relatively narrow framework of national production operations, branches, and markets. The fact that differences in profit norms between countries are more sizable than differences within a single country inevitably means that diversification on the national level paves the way for turning a company into a transnational corporation. This is especially characteristic of the machinery complex, which includes a wide range of production operations and subbranches. In addition, the improvement of technology under the influence of scientific and technological progress has brought about radical changes in the production process, which has required transnational corporations to divide parts of the process among different countries and technologically related branches. For the large

---

5Calculated on the basis of "Transnational Corporations in World Development: Third Survey," United Nations, New York, 1983, pp. 357-363. The index of foreign participation is the ratio of the number of firms whose foreign operations constitute more than 25 percent of their total operations to the total number of firms in the industry.

6See N.I. Mnogolet, *The United States: Industrial Concerns* [SShA: promyshlennyye kontserny], Moscow, 1976; G.V. Polunina, *Multibranch Concerns in the System of Present-Day Capitalism* [Mnogootraslevyye kontserny v sisteme sovremennogo kapitalizma], Moscow, 1980; *MEMO*, No. 10, 1984, pp. 137-141.

machinery corporations, this lowered costs through optimal distribution of production factors.

There is a direct connection between diversification within the context of a national economy and internationalization of production. First, for capital to satisfy its urge to grow and increase its sphere of activities, a firm must do more than transfer capital within a single country. When limited by the confines of a national market, already monopolized to a considerable extent, large machinery corporations can use the export of production capital to expand diversification of production. Here it must be kept in mind that internationalization of production, which, on a corporate basis, combines the national resources of individual countries into a single production and technological complex, creates the preconditions for bringing the division of labor within a company (between the parent company and its foreign branches) closer to an international division of labor (among countries within the framework of an industry or group of industries).

In the second place, narrowly specialized firms account for only a minority of the largest U.S. transnational industrial corporations. In the mid-1970s to early 1980s, they amounted to only one fourth of U.S. transnational machinery corporations. In the third place, many affiliates abroad are in industries to which the parent company does not belong. At the end of the 1970s the percentage of total corporate sales accounted for by sales of products in the parent company's branch of specialization amounted to 74 percent in the transportation machinery industry, 63 percent in the general machinery industry, 56 percent in the instrument industry, and 54 percent in the electrical equipment (and electronics) industry.[7] Moreover, specialization is not at odds with diversification as a present-day form of the production concentration.[8] They are interrelated through the concentration, at machinery corporation's enterprises, of specialized production facilities (shops, or sectors) that are linked by cooperative production arrangements, often involving two or more branches of industry.

Thus, diversification and the export of capital, which represent independent forms of solving the problem of the overaccumulation of capital, are closely interconnected.[9]

In the postwar period, machinery corporations had numerous motives for expanding abroad. Among the most general motives were

---

[7]*Survey of Current Business*, Oct. 1981, p. 43
[8]Except for the expansion of conglomerate-type production.
[9]This view is held by a number of Soviet economists. See, for example, A.Z. Astapovich, *U.S. International Corporations: Trends and Contradictions in Development* [*Mezhdunarodnyye korporatsii SShA: tendentsii i protivorechiya razvitiya*], Moscow, 1978; A.V. Buzuyev, *International Monopolies: New Elements in the Struggle for Markets* [*Mezhdunarodnyye monopolii: novoye v borbe za rynki*], Moscow, 1982.

postwar restoration of the capitalist countries' economies, especially those of the European countries; the liberal attitude of those governments toward the growth in direct American capital investments; establishment of controls on the importation of goods in many capitalist countries; and improvement of conditions for the application of American capital as a result of the creation of common markets and associations, such as the European Community and the Latin American Free Trade Association.

These stimuli, however, create a need to export capital and explain its general regional focus, but do not explain an investor's choice of specific countries and industries. A firm making the decision to export capital endeavors to use to greatest advantage its strengths as well as the economic conditions in the countries and industries selected. This raises the problem of evaluating the production and scientific and technological potential of U.S. corporations investing abroad, as well as the existence in a given country or industry of specific economic incentives for the application of American capital.

Foreign Production: Incentives, Forms of Organizations, and Corporate Strategies

A basic distinguishing feature of the international movement of capital is the dominant position of the United States, which accounts for about 50 percent of developed capitalist countries' capital investments channeled abroad.

American superiority is based on the fact that the technical composition of U.S. capital and its capital-labor ratio are superior to that of Japan and the European Community, to say nothing of the developing countries, and this gives American investors advantages over local firms in the latters' national markets.[10] At the same time, compared with domestic enterprises, foreign affiliates are distinguished by lower labor costs. These factors allow U.S. companies to make more effective use of their production resources.

Important among the economic incentives for U.S. machinery corporations' foreign expansion during the 1950s and 1960s was their desire to achieve a higher profit norm (in comparison to the U.S. level). At the end of the 1970s this incentive for foreign investment ceased to be decisive for U.S. transnational corporations (see Table 2). Variations in the relative profitability of U.S. machinery corporations' domestic and foreign capital investments in certain years does not fundamentally alter the current general tendency toward an evening out of those indices.

---

[10]See A.V. Buzuyev, *op. cit.*, pp. 70-80; J.H. Dunning, *International Production and the Multinational Enterprise*, London, 1981, pp. 51-66.

TABLE 2
Profit Norms of U.S. Machinery Corporations*

In U.S.			Abroad		
1973	1977	1980	1973	1977	1980
10.1	12.0	12.5	16.9	12.3	10.1

Note: The profit norm is the ratio of net profits (after taxes) to the amount of capital advanced, or of foreign investments.
*Excluding metalworking and instrument manufacturing.

The existing relationship in levels of profitability for U.S. investments can be attributed to production costs and, above all, to national differences in wages. Whereas the difference in pay levels of American and foreign workers was very substantial until the mid-1960s, since the late 1960s and early 1970s this source of superprofits for U.S. machinery corporations has lost its significance in many countries, and chiefly in the most developed capitalist countries, while fundamental differences in pay levels continue to exist between the United States and the developing countries.

U.S. corporations are interested not so much in differences in production costs between the parent company and its subsidiaries as in the possibility of utilizing highly skilled production personnel, even if they are highly paid, and the latest foreign scientific and technological advances. Therefore even the technology transferred from the United States is characterized by a higher level of capital intensiveness, complexity, and research intensiveness, coupled with lower labor intensiveness.

The developing countries occupy a special place in the sphere of American monopolies' interests. The most profitable sphere for the application of capital in the 1950s and 1960s, they have now turned into sources of cheap materials and manufacturers of assemblies and parts for assembly plants in the United States and abroad.

In addition to U.S. transnational machinery corporations' principal motive for transferring production capacity to the developing countries—the persisting difference in national production costs—there are a number of specific reasons for investing in that region. In the first place, the marketing of developing countries' products is substantially easier, especially for American investors who supply the needs of the local market. In the second place, the degree of automation of assembly operations and the technical and technological level of production at enterprises of U.S. transnational machinery corporations in the developed capitalist countries are considerably higher than in the developing countries, since automation is a kind of countermeasure against high wages. For example, in the early 1980s the volume of capital investment per employee in machinery branches of U.S. corporations in the developed capitalist countries was 80 to 100 percent higher than in the developing countries. Hence there is a kind of savings in costs. In the third place, some developing countries (chiefly the "newly industrialized countries") have shown a rapid assimilation of new technologies and growth in the demand for research-intensive machinery products, and have followed a policy of promoting an export orientation in a number of industries or promoting the development of import-replacing production operations. State programs of this sort were introduced in 1969 in Mexico, 1971 in Argentina, and 1972 in Brazil. The policy of using foreign (primarily American) capital to solve the problem of industrialization and to raise the technical level of national machinery production creates objective preconditions that facilitate U.S. transnational machinery corporations' penetration of developing countries' economies. One of the first U.S. machinery corporations to sign an agreement to assist the development of export branches in the aforementioned countries was the Ford Motor Co. Such exporters in Brazil not only receive financial support but are freed from import restrictions (in addition to receiving compensation of 70 to 90 percent of the value of imported equipment and 50 percent of imported raw materials and other materials). The penetration of the largest U.S. electrical-equipment and electronics corporations into the newly industrialized countries was arranged in a similar fashion.

In the 1960s a situation developed in which outlays for manpower in the production of machinery and equipment became an important factor in the general increase in production costs.[11] This forced the transnational corporations to shift the production of many parts and components to the developing countries and territories. For many U.S. transnational machinery corporations, semiconductors, electric light bulbs, electrical instruments, sewing machines, and other goods were produced in Hong Kong, Brazil, Mexico, Argentina, Singapore, South Korea, the Philippines, among others, where labor-intensive and small-scale production operations were being transferred. Thus, the U.S. transnational corporations themselves create the opportunities and conditions in which "extra profits from privileged and monopoly sales offset the low profitability of 'normal' sales."[12]

At the same time, by the late 1970s to early 1980s, a trend was gradually developing that could subsequently reduce the attrac-

---

[11] For example, under the conditions of a drop in the cost of electronic circuits from $170 in the early 1960s to $5 in the 1980s.

[12] V.I. Lenin, *Complete Works* [*Polnoye sobraniye sochineniy*], Vol. 28, p. 171.

tiveness of investing in the developing countries for U.S. machinery corporations. This trend was connected with the growing importance of new high technologies in international competition among the three centers of imperialism. In a situation in which machinery product competitiveness was being achieved through comprehensive automation of production and use of new resource- and materials-saving technologies and construction materials, the traditional motivation for investing in the developing countries—cheap production resources—could prove secondary.

The general reasons and specific motives cited above for the export of capital predetermined a clear-cut geographical tendency in U.S. transnational machinery corporations' foreign investments: Canada, the most developed West European countries, Japan, and the newly industrialized countries of Latin America and Southeast Asia. In the early 1980s they accounted for 92 to 93 percent of all capital investments by U.S. machinery corporations in machinery manufacturing abroad (excluding metalworking and instrument manufacturing).

U.S. capital holds the strongest positions in the automotive industry and the production of computers, semiconductor instruments, and various types of electrical equipment. U.S. monopolies have cornered about 60 percent of the world computer market, including 75 to 80 percent of the market in mini computers. In passenger cars, in 1981 Ford Motor Co. alone controlled 15.2 percent of the Canadian market, 11.8 percent of the West German market, 30.9 percent of the British market, 23 percent of the Australian market, and 16.7 percent of the South African market (in trucks, the corresponding figures were 30.2 percent, 7.7 percent, 30.6 percent, 13.1 percent, and 10.7 percent).[13] British affiliates of General Motors and Ford produce one third of Great Britain's passenger cars, and in the Federal Republic of Germany, their affiliates belong to the four largest West German automotive firms. U.S. transnational corporations account for about 60 percent of semiconductor industry sales on the world capitalist market. American capital holds especially strong positions in the FRG, Great Britain, France, Singapore, Malaysia, Mexico, and Brazil.

Characteristically, the largest U.S. machinery corporations try to ensure complete or preponderant control of their foreign enterprises, regardless of where they are located, while the smaller firms prefer to establish companies associated with foreign capital (less then 50 percent participation) and to conclude licensing agreements. As for interregional differences in U.S. foreign investments in the industrially

---

[13]See *High Technology Industries: Profiles and Outlooks*, April 1983, pp. 19, 12; *Transnational Corporations in the International Auto Industry*, United Nations, New York, 1983, p. 205.

developed and newly industrialized countries, most U.S. machinery corporations organize enterprises like the affiliates of the largest transnational corporations. In other developing countries, U.S. companies (regardless of their size) do not try to become majority stockholders in the enterprises that are established. Frequently they, too, follow a policy of signing licensing agreements.

The explanation of such differences cannot be reduced completely to the problem of the size of the controlling block of stocks in a newly established or acquired company. The establishment of 100-percent or even predominant ownership in a subsidiary organization in the developed capitalist world is determined not so much by a parent company's desire to control the firm in question more fully (especially since a controlling block of stocks may now be measured not in tens of percentage points but in just several percentage points), as by legal motives. The point is that at that level of control it is possible to carry out the unimpeded transfer of technology, and the movement of goods and profits within the context of the entire transnational corporation. This is especially characteristic of machinery corporations.

The crisis that gripped the capitalist world's economy from the mid-1970s to early 1980s forced U.S. transnational machinery corporations to rethink their attitude toward joint ventures abroad. Since the situation in the world market has deteriorated for many American firms, they have been more willing to establish such enterprises abroad (while simultaneously taking advantage of any chance to become sole owner of a new firm). For example, lately the transnational automotive corporations have come to appreciate the advantages of cooperation with West European and Japanese companies. In the early 1980s General Motors acquired a block of stock in Suzuki Motor, and it is beginning to produce small cars jointly with it. Cooperation with Toyota is expanding for the same purpose. This way of organizing foreign production allows the parent company in the United States, in addition to expanding its sphere of influence, to ensure access to advanced foreign technology.

The growing scale of the transfer of production capacity abroad, especially to the developed capitalist countries, and the establishment by U.S. companies of joint ventures on foreign soil that are tied to the parent companies' domestic activities (deliveries of products, technology, and so on) attest to a significant increase in the internationalization of machinery production and the formation of a second U.S. machinery manufacturing complex abroad.

International Expansion and Integration Processes

While the formation and development of transnational corporations are a consequence of the high level of concentration and centralization of production and capital on the national level, they are, in turn, of considerable importance in strengthening the economic potential of individual concerns that conduct operations abroad. For many monopolistic associations in the industry, foreign activities have historically provided a source of considerable profit and a means of strengthening their positions in the national and world markets. Among these companies, one can single out the following (followed by the share of profits obtained from foreign operations, as a percentage of the corporation's total profits, in 1980): IBM (53.4), Ford Motor Co. (45, 1976), ITT (52), Xerox (45.2), Hewlett-Packard (43.9), and General Electric (42.2).

In increasing the scale of the socialization of production, transnational corporations obtain additional advantages beyond participation in the economic division of the world. Parent companies also derive substantial financial benefits from that method of organizing production. The export of capital from the United States largely boils down to providing no more than the initial amounts for setting up foreign ventures and, according to our estimates, amounts to only 25 to 30 percent of all foreign investments by U.S. machinery corporations abroad. At the same time, the cost reductions improve production efficiency throughout the whole corporation.

Despite its relative independence, an affiliate provides a steady flow of money to the parent company. In the past 10 to 15 years, the amount of repatriated money from foreign operations has been increasing. The dimensions of this process can be judged by looking at the change in the percentage of the total profits of the foreign branches of U.S. transnational machinery corporations that are reinvested; from 1970 to 1983, this figure dropped from 65 to 42 percent.

The transnational corporations' scientific and technical policies[14] are devised in such a way that their foreign affiliates turn into a source of revenue for the parent company from the transfer of licenses, know-how, technology and patents. In the late 1960s U.S. machinery corporations received about 60 percent of all payments from their foreign enterprises in the form of royalties.[15] In the late 1970s and early 1980s, this figure rose to 90 percent. For some companies, international transfers of technology—either through relocation of production facilities or through licensing—have become a matter of corporate survival and part of their global strategy to maintain cost competitiveness in the U.S. and in foreign markets," notes American economist J. Baranson.[16]

---

[14]For more details, see *MEMO*, No. 11, 1985, pp. 42-47.
[15]Royalty payments include payments for patents, trademarks, technology, and licenses.
[16]J. Baranson, *The Japanese Challenge to U.S. Industry*, Toronto, 1981, p. 116.

Many U.S. transnational machinery corporations use their foreign affiliates to improve competitiveness by relying on foreign companies' technological advances. Thus, the British affiliate of General Electric and the Japanese Hitachi Corp. formed a joint company to supply color television sets to the parent companies for marketing. This joint venture has unlimited access to the research, development work, and production technology of Hitachi, a world leader in that area. General Electric thereby has the opportunity, through its foreign affiliates, not only to obtain high-quality and competitive products to sell on the American market, but also to import advanced technology. According to the president of OPIC [Overseas Private Investment Corp.],[17] foreign investment is a two-way street which, as a result of access to new and growing markets, and the increased export of American products, gives a new impetus not just to other countries but also to the United States.

The 1970s substantially changed the relative positions of the three centers of imperialist competition. West European and Japanese monopolies became a real force that U.S. corporations had to reckon with not just in the world arena but in their own country.

Foreign capital holds its strongest positions in such sectors of U.S. machinery production as machine-tool manufacturing, semiconductors, home electronics and household appliances, and instrumentation. From 3 to 7 percent of total employment, fixed capital, and produced output are concentrated in those sectors. Only in the automotive industries does the expansion of foreign corporations rely mainly on the export of products. Whereas enterprises controlled by foreign capital produce less than 1 percent of that branch's gross output in the United States, foreign models of vehicles account for about 23 percent of car and truck sales in the U.S. market (of which approximately 80 percent are from Japanese producers).

Despite the increase in West European and Japanese companies' operations in the United States, their influence on the market in machinery products is still not so substantial when compared with chemical or petroleum products. The problems of technological competitiveness and management, marketing, and after-sale servicing under the conditions of severe competition continue to present them with serious obstacles to gains in the American market. In addition, the conformity of foreign products and technology to U.S. standards, which are considerably stricter in the machinery and electrical equipment industries than in other branches of industry, is also important.[18]

---

[17]OPIC is a private industrial corporation that finances foreign operations of American firms. [*Editor's note:* OPIC·is a U.S. federal agency that provides political risk insurance and finance services to encourage U.S. private investment in developing countries.]
    [18]See, for example, Yu.I. Yudanov, *The Export of Capital From Western Europe* [*Eksport kapitala iz Zapadnoy Yevropy*], Moscow, 1980, pp. 111, 113.

The substantial concentration of production and capital in a number of machinery branches,[19] and the economic potential of U.S. corporations have also determined the forms of foreign companies' penetration into the United States. The main such form has been the acquisition of controlling stock or a substantial amount of stock in existing U.S. companies. Dutch, British, and Swiss monopolies have been the most active. As of the beginning of the 1980s, stocks and other securities of enterprises operating in the U.S. machinery industry accounted for 92 to 94 percent of the total assets of foreign companies' U.S. affiliates. Stocks of newly established enterprises accounted for only 5 to 6 percent.

Foreign firms have obtained certain shares of participation in large, even the largest, U.S. corporations in the semiconductor and electronics industry; West German Siemens A.G. has a 20 percent interest in Advanced Micro Devices, and its Robert Bosch has a 12.5 percent interest in American Microsystems; Britain's Lucas Industries has a 24 percent interest in Siliconix, and several Swiss companies own shares in IBM and Eastman Kodak.

Another important form of foreign investment in the United States is the establishment of joint ventures. This is the course that has been followed, for example, by the Swiss company Brown, Boveri; West Germany's Siemens A.G. and Kraftwerk Union; and the Japanese Fujitsu and Toyota.

For many years foreign companies used American corporations' marketing channels to secure a foothold in the U.S. market. Their establishment of their own distribution and marketing networks is a relatively new form of marketing foreign products. In the second half of the 1970s about 15 machine-tool manufacturing companies from various capitalist countries established such enterprises. Moreover, they surpassed U.S. firms in their rate of expansion of facilities in the distribution and sales areas. Japanese machinery companies, which regard establishment of their own combined production and marketing enterprises as a basic means of selling products in the U.S. market, were particularly successful.

To assess the economic influence of foreign capital, it is necessary to compare the efficiency with which foreign and national companies operate. Such a comparison reflects the dual influence of foreign firms on the U.S. machinery manufacturing complex. On the one hand, the efficiency with which foreign firms utilize manpower from the production to the sale of products is 20 to 23 percent higher, on average, than

---

[19]For example, the four largest corporations account for 73 percent and 49 percent, respectively, of all shipped output in the U.S. transportation-machinery and instrument industries (calculated on the basis of *Census of Manufactures, 1977*, Vol. I, Washington, 1981, pp. 9 (41-58)).

for U.S. companies. This contributes to a relative reduction in the demand for manpower and a growing role for the machinery industries in swelling the ranks of unemployed. On the other hand, the efficiency with which foreign companies use fixed capital (the ratio of sales to the value of fixed capital) is 50 to 55 percent higher, on average, than for U.S. companies. This has the result of raising the return on capital and improving the efficiency of U.S. machinery production.[20] By enjoying such advantages within the United States, foreign capital is forcing U.S. firms to mobilize resources to fight the growing competition. At the same time, integration tendencies are growing stronger, and the organization of joint production with foreign companies is assuming an increasingly broad scope. On the other hand, by shifting a substantial amount of production capacity abroad, U.S. corporations compensate (more or less) for the loss of a certain share of the American market.

*   *   *

The ability to concentrate separate parts of the production process in different countries and link the enterprises together, under a corporation's control, in a single technological process with specific and detailed technological specialization, thereby minimizing production costs or getting closer to the principal commodity markets, is what accounts for the effectiveness of transnational corporations' operations and distinguishes them from "ordinary" national firms. A comparison of the effectiveness of a group of U.S. machinery companies (from the *Fortune* 1,000 list) shows that in the 1970s and early 1980s sales and assets per employee, and the rate of return on capital were 15 to 20 percent higher, on the average, for the 20 largest transnational machinery corporations than for 20 national firms.

The intensification of integration tendencies on the basis of the export of capital from the United States (and from other countries to the United States), and the operations of transnational corporations allow us to hypothesize that at the present time an international machinery complex is developing that operates on the basis of common technologies and the cooperative production and marketing of products among the leading corporations of the developed capitalist countries. Its scale can be judged by examining reciprocal deliveries of products between national producers and foreign affiliates. Thus, in

---

[20]Such advantages on the part of foreign, especially Japanese, companies in the United States are the result of a high level of the organization of labor and management of production processes, and the use of the most advanced technologies and equipment. For example, Japanese producers in the United States use five to six times as many robots per million cars produced as do American manufacturers. As a result, the production costs of American affiliates of Nissan, Toyota, and Honda Giken are 40 to 50 percent lower than those of U.S. automotive corporations (see J. Baranson, *op. cit.*, p. 155).

1983 U.S. imports from the foreign affiliates of U.S. transnational corporations amounted to 90 percent (compared to 70 percent in 1977) of exports by U.S. corporations to their foreign enterprises.[21] Enterprises founded in the United States by West European and Japanese parent companies have a similar significance for those companies.

Thus, the dimensions of the internationalization of production are growing, and simultaneously the conditions, forms, and actual content of international competition are changing. The international integration of machinery production is becoming an objective necessity. A growing number of corporations are taking part in this process regardless of their national affiliation. There is a growing tendency toward the optimization of production and economic relations on an international basis. This tendency, however, does not rule out the development of confrontation between individual producers and countries. All this is causing changes both in national machinery industries and in the organization of production on an international scale.

---

[21]Calculated on the basis of *Survey of Current Business*, Apr. 1981, p. 34. The amount of intracompany trade as a percentage of the total volume of exports of the products of U.S. machinery firms gives a measure of the dimensions of reciprocal goods flows. At present it comes to more than 50 percent.

Economic Crises and the Structure of Reproduction in Western Europe

Viktor Ivanovich Kuznetsov*

For more than 10 years (since the first half of the 1970s) the world capitalist economy has been experiencing considerable difficulties. On the average, the rate of overall economic and industrial growth has declined between two thirds and one half of what it was in the 1950s and 1960s. The dynamics of production and exchange have become less stable. Far from maximum use is being made of manpower resources and production capacity. Many Western economists, particularly adherents of the institutionalist, structuralist, and sociological schools, describe the state of capitalist reproduction in the 1970s and 1980s as a special kind of crisis.

Signs of this crisis can be seen in the steady deviation of several basic proportional relationships, such as the ratios between profits and wages, accumulation and consumption, and capital investments and labor productivity, from the trends that were predominant during the first 20 years after the war. If one looks at stable proportions [i.e., proportional relationships—Trans.] as structural characteristics of reproduction, then the disruption of their "usual" state can be called a structural crisis. Another characteristic feature of this peculiar, prolonged crisis, especially its second half, is that according to all calculations and observations, intensive technological and organizational transformations are taking place in most areas of the economy. A profound transformation of production processes is taking place on the basis of the widespread introduction of electronics and automation, other progressive technologies, and new forms of labor organization.

A reasonable question arises: under the conditions of a retarded and disproportional development of production and exchange, how were the mechanisms of scientific and technological progress and accompanying structural transformations of the economy put into

*Doctor of economics, chief research associate at the U.S.S.R. Academy of Sciences' Institute of World Economy and International Relations [IMEMO]. This article appeared in the September 1987 issue of *MEMO*.

motion, and what primarily motivated business owners to turn toward a more intensive type of economic development?

Types of Economic Growth and the Profit Rate

Structural changes are invariably a feature of any kind of economic growth, be it extensive or intensive. In the extensive type of development, production volume is typically expanded mainly by bringing in additional manpower resources and material production factors. In the intensive type of development, the predominant processes entail the technical and technological renewal of production equipment and materials, and improvements in the quality of the labor force, means which achieve an increase in production primarily through an improvement in the social productivity of labor.

With the extensive type of development, the need to change the proportions of economic reproduction as measured in monetary value and physical units stems from the simple fact that when new resources are continuously brought into production, sooner or later shortages of these resources will develop, and their prices will begin to rise. As Marx observed, "if the quantity of unpaid labor [surplus value—V. K.] . . . grows so fast that it can be turned into capital only through an extraordinary increase in additional labor, then wages will rise."[1]

With the extensive type of development, the impetus toward structural reorganization comes primarily from individual and public demand, which is stimulated by an increase in wages paid to the work force. Because of income-based differences in the elasticity of demand for certain goods and services belonging to the consumption fund, the demand for various types of products grows unevenly, and the speed with which production facilities expand in various industries is correspondingly uneven. Changes occur in the proportional relationships among the branches of industry, initially in the second subdivision of social production [i.e., the consumer-goods industries—Trans.], and then in the first subdivision [the producer-goods industries—Trans.].

For economies, like those of Western Europe, that participate actively in the international division of labor, the foreign-economic sphere is also a source of shifts in proportions and changes in supply and demand. Competition among capital that is foreign with respect to each individual country acts as a powerful factor in shaking up ossifying structures (those undergoing monopolization) in the reproduction of national capital.

With the intensive type of development, the main thrust of the forces stimulating structural reorganization comes from industries

---

[1] K. Marx and F. Engels, *Works* [*Sochineniya*], Vol. 23, p. 634.

belonging to the first subdivision, the sphere of research and development, and the political and ideological superstructure (if society, in the
person of its ruling class, recognizes the demands of the times and of its
productive forces).

In reality there are no "pure" types of economic growth. Nevertheless, in the case of Western Europe we can speak of predominantly extensive or predominantly intensive forms of production,
which have alternated during the postwar years. Thus, by many indicators, economic development in the period immediately prior to the
crisis (the second half of the 1960s and the early 1970s) can be classified
as predominantly extensive, while economic development in the
period since the mid-1970s can be classified as predominantly
intensive.

The extensive nature of development in the precrisis decade
showed in the decline, starting in the second half of the 1960s, in the
proportion of the GNP spent on research and development in most
capitalist countries, accompanied by continued high rates of growth in
production and, especially, accumulation; in the increase in the capital-intensiveness of production in some of these countries; in the
existence of materials-intensive and energy-intensive types of production in most industries; in the accelerated growth by the late 1960s (in
complete accordance with Marx's analysis) of nominal and real wages,
and the increase in their proportional share of the national income; in
the shift from relatively moderate increases in prices for finished
products to an inflationary rise in these prices; and in the prolonged
maintenance of relatively low unemployment, along with a steady

TABLE 1
Average Annual Rates of Growth in Production
(based on constant prices, percentages)[1]

	1961-1973		1974-1986	
	I	II	I	II
European Community	4.7	5.1	1.8	1.2
F.R.G.	4.6	5.1	1.9	1.1
France	5.6	5.4	2.1	1.1
Great Britain	3.1	2.8	1.3	0.8
United States	3.8	5.3	2.3	2.2
Japan	9.5	12.3	1.1	2.9

Based on: *The Economic Condition of Capitalist and Developing Countries. Survey for 1986 and Early
1987* [*Ekonomicheskoye polozheniye kapitalisticheskikh i razvivayushchikhsya stran. Obzor za 1986 g. i
nachalo 1987 g.*], Supplement to *MEMO*, No. 8, 1987, p. 7.
[1] I is the gross national product. II is industrial production.

expansion of employment and an increase in the ablebodied population entering the labor market.

Indeed, between 1955 and 1973 the capital-intensiveness of West German production, for example, grew by 39 percent (with an average annual increase of 1.8 percent). In Great Britain the increase over the same period was 13.4 percent (0.7 percent annually). These data are cited by the authors of the book *When Crises Are Prolonged* . . . [*Quand les crises durent* . . .]. As to the dynamics of wages as a proportion of national income, they write that since the early 1970s there has been an important change. Compensation for hired labor has been increasing as a percentage of the added value of production. This is especially characteristic of the Federal Republic of Germany, Italy, and Japan. In Great Britain this trend appeared earlier—starting in the mid-1950s, and in the United States it first appeared in the mid-1960s.[2]

European Community statistics show average annual increases in consumer prices for the 10 member countries of 3.3 percent between 1960 and 1968, and 6.0 percent between 1969 and 1973. The unemployment rate among the economically active population of "the Ten" fluctuated from 1.9 percent to 2.5 percent between 1960 and 1973, and only in 1974 did it start to climb steadily upward. At the same time, in the precrisis period employment expanded annually by 0.3 percent, while after 1973 (1974 to 1985) it suffered an overall decline.

Of course, the nature of the precrisis period is much more complicated than a strict interpretation of the concept of extensive type of development would imply. The features of extensive development are simply superimposed on a general, indisputably intensive type of postwar economy (intensive compared with earlier stages in the development of capitalism). It is as if they form a veil, behind which one can see unquestionable evidence of "basic" intensive development: high rates of labor productivity, an increase toward the end of the period in the proportion of the unused labor force, despite a continuing increase in the employment rate, and so forth.

The type of economic development that had taken shape by the mid-1960s was drastically disrupted by the crisis of 1974 to 1975. And although not only cyclical, but also structural, factors played a role in this crisis and the subsequent crisis of 1980 to 1982, the basic tenets of the Marxist theory of crises seem entirely applicable to both these crises.

Marx viewed a production crisis as the result of a crisis in the accumulation of capital. The latter develops every time the "stimulat-

---

2See J. Mazier, M. Basle, J.-F. Vidal, *Quand les crises durent* . . . , Paris, 1984, pp. 200-201.

ing effect of profit is dulled"[3] as the result of a drop in the profit rate. The basic, or ultimate, task of a crisis is to raise the profit rate to such a level (a precrisis level) that the expanded reproduction of capital and production once again assume meaning for its protagonists—the owners of capital or their authorized representatives, the managers.

During the course of a crisis, Marx writes, "the reason for the decline (in accumulation—V. K.), that is, the disproportion between capital and the labor force that is available for exploitation, disappears . . . . The price of labor once again drops to a level that corresponds to the needs of the growth of capital. . . ."[4] Thus, Marx speaks of a disturbance first in proportional relationships as expressed in monetary values, and only as a consequence of this first disturbance does a disturbance arise in proportional relationships in the reproduction of the social product as expressed in physical units.

Capital has two specific methods to put pressure on the price of labor: by changing the situation in the labor market in its favor—increasing the army of unemployed by reducing the volume of production; or by increasing the productive power of labor—replacing part of the white- and blue-collar workers employed in production with machines. Both methods take a certain amount of time, but the second also requires additional financial means or a radical qualitative and structural reorganization of the investment process.

It is not difficult to see that there is a close connection between the two methods. This connection does not rule out the possibility, however, that a "correction" of the profit rate can begin with one of the methods. Success at one end opens up the possibility of advancement at the other, and vice versa. Indeed, lowering the price of labor under the pressure of unemployment or by other means frees up additional financial resources for technical retooling. And by forcing labor out of the production process, retooling increases the number of unemployed working people and, thus, their pressure on the wage level.[5]

Once technical modernization has begun, if the prerequisites are there in the form of a scientific and technological foundation, this modernization encompasses not only newly created facilities, but existing ones as well. Thus the process of modernization goes beyond the boundaries of the crisis and continues in subsequent phases of the cycle, or even over the course of several subsequent cycles. A technological revolution in new capital is accompanied by a technical revolution in original capital. Of course, Marx's theoretical model does not touch on the problem of an "open economy." But it retains its

---

[3] See K. Marx and F. Engels, *Works*, Vol. 23, p. 633.
[4] *Ibid.*
[5] *Ibid.*, p. 642.

analytical force as concerns internal sources of contradictions and their development, and the effect of a drop in the profit rate on the formation of specific aspects of the production process. It is no accident that words written a century ago so precisely characterize the general features of recent decades: "a decline in the profit rate . . . promotes overproduction, speculation, crises, and the appearance of surplus capital along with surplus population."[6]

Now, with statistics and a large number of special research studies at our disposal, we can state the following with confidence. Long before 1974 West European capitalism began to experience difficulties maintaining the profit rate at a level necessary for the unimpeded expansion of accumulation according to the reproduction proportions that existed as of the mid-1960s. "The trend toward a decline in the profit rate," stresses one recent book on the 1970s and 1980s, "arose in most of the world's leading countries long before the crisis of 1974 broke. In the Federal Republic of Germany and Great Britain, for all practical purposes, this decline began even before 1960."[7]

Of course, the trend toward a decline in the profit rate in the late 1960s and early 1970s was not the cause of the crisis of 1974 to 1975. But it did contribute to the aggravation of contradictions in production and distribution and to increased tension in relations between labor and capital, and it deepened the crisis and the difficulties that occurred during the entire subsequent period. In turn, the crisis sharply accelerated the drop in the profit norm in industry and worsened the financial situation of West European companies for a long period of time. Only in 1981 did profitability somewhat begin to improve.

Analyzing the prospects for the 1980s, the authors of a report from the French Center for International Prospective Studies and Information correctly assert: "The question of the connection between profits and investments is a key one for European countries."[8] This question was just as important throughout the 1970s, when economic and, to a significant extent, social and political processes in the West European countries developed in a situation of low profitability. This weakened the motivation not only for additional accumulation of capital, but also, other things being equal, for the renewal and modernization of equipment.

West European capitalism was forced to mobilize all its financial and ideological reserves to take a number of measures in the face of a stepped-up trade and economic offensive on the part of American and Japanese capitalism. These measures were aimed on the one hand, at

---

[6]K. Marx and F. Engels, *Works*, Vol. 25, Part I, p. 265.
[7]J. Mazier, M. Basle, J.-F. Vidal, *op. cit.*, p. 202.
[8]*L'économie mondiale 1980-1990: la fracture?* Paris, 1984, p. 121.

reducing the price of manpower and on the other, at intensifying the restructuring of the production base so as to increase its efficiency, accelerate the growth in labor productivity, improve the competitiveness of products, and maintain its positions in the world economy.

The Foreign Economic Aspect

The development of the structural crisis of the 1970s and 1980s in the capitalist world, in general, and Western Europe, in particular, was unusual in that external factors combined with internal reasons for shifts in the monetary-value proportions of reproduction. Their influence was so significant that even taken independently of internal processes they could have prompted certain countries to initiate an active structural reorganization. The connection between national economies and the world market, which had been increasing throughout the entire postwar period, grew even stronger in the 1970s and 1980s (see Table 2).

The dependence of most West European countries on outside sources of industrial raw materials and energy, and the sharp fluctuations in world prices for these goods in the early and late 1970s upset the existing structure of production costs for practically all industrial and agricultural goods. This alone confused the picture for producers competing with one another, weakening some and strengthening others overnight.

Industries and firms producing goods that were, if not identical, at least interchangeable, were affected even more. The increase in the price of oil improved the positions of the coal and gas producers, and it made nuclear power plants, despite the huge increase in ecologically necessary expenditures, promising sources of energy. Synthetic and

TABLE 2
The Ratio of Exports to the Gross National Product
(percentages)

	1960	1970	1980	1985
OECD Countries	9.0	10.6	16.4	20.0
Western Europe	15.5	17.8	22.6	26.6
United States	4.0	4.4	8.5	5.7[1]
Japan	9.4	9.4	12.5	13.6

Based on: Main Economic Indicators, *Monthly Bulletin of Statistics*, for the corresponding years.
[1] In 1985 imports represented 9.4 percent of the U.S. GNP, as opposed to 4.1 percent in 1970 and 9.9 percent in 1980.

artificial fibers, various types of plastics, and generally speaking, all the products of the organic-chemical industry, which in the 1950s and 1960s had actively displaced traditional materials (metals, wood, brick, cement), suddenly found themselves in a considerably less advantageous position because of the high energy costs involved in their production. Also because of the rise in energy prices, energy-intensive equipment and technology started to be replaced by energy-efficient counterparts—not immediately, but at an increasingly rapid pace.

Thus, under the influence both of the factors that gave rise to structural crises[9] and of differences in the rates of growth in labor productivity among the various industries, the shift in relative prices and the gradual change in familiar monetary-value relationships led to a different pattern of growth rates among the various industries. Within the processing industry there was a sudden slowdown in the most rapidly developing group of industries—the chemical industries—and production in ferrous metallurgy and metalworking virtually came to a standstill. Average growth rates in the organic-chemical industry dropped by seven percentage points between the 1960s and 1970s; the production of paints, plastics and plastic products, and synthetic fibers lost six percentage points.[10]

Besides the significant shifts in relationships between costs and prices in various sectors, the majority of capitalist countries started to pay much more for imported fuels and several types of raw materials than they had in the 1960s. This meant that the amount of the importing countries' surplus value, transferred in monetary or commodity form as payment for petroleum, grew substantially in some cases.

In France, for example, the value of energy imports was approximately 1.5 percent of the GNP in 1970; in 1975 it had risen to 5 percent, and up to 1986 it fluctuated between 3.5 percent and 4.5 percent. Between 1974 and 1977, the average negative trade balance for goods and services consisting primarily of energy resources and agricultural products, reached 2.4 percent of the GNP in the Federal Republic of Germany, 2.5 percent in France, and 4.9 percent in Great Britain (in 1970 these countries had no negative balance).[11] For the 10 countries of the European Community, the average balance of payments turned out to be negative in the period of 1974 to 1976 and 1979 to 1982, that is, every time there was a sharp increase in world oil prices.

---

[9]Regarding the nature of the structural crisis, we are inclined to share the opinion of R. Entov, who views this crisis as an outbreak of specific contradictions, "generated by the prolonged operation of monopolies in key industries (complexes) of the world capitalist economy" (see *The Economic Cycle in the United States: The 1970s to Early 1980s* [*Ekonomicheskiy tsikl v SShA. 70-ye—nachalo 80-x godov*], Moscow, 1985, p. 20.

[10]*Economie mondiale: la montée des tensions*, Paris, 1983, p. 68.

[11]*Economie prospective internationale*, Jan. 1980, p. 86.

In this same period West European imports of energy resources, as expressed in physical terms, not only did not rise, they declined. This meant that part of the national income of West European countries was transferred to exporters of the higher-priced oil without a corresponding compensation in kind. It should be stressed, however, that the actual amount of this transfer ultimately proved to be much smaller than might have been expected, considering the huge dimensions of the price leap. Three factors were working in favor of the industrially developed capitalist countries.

First, to the extent that it occurred through a rise in the indebtedness of the importer countries, payment for the increase in energy prices was not something deducted from their national income or national product, but was limited to a simple increase in financial obligations. The transfer of real assets and real revenues is drawn out over time and takes place later as debts and interest on debts are paid off.

Second, it was the oil-exporting countries themselves that initially extended the loans. Since they were unable to use all of their export earnings immediately to purchase real assets, they placed a significant portion of these earnings in the capital-lending markets of the oil-importing countries, thereby restoring the total size, as it were, of those countries' effective foreign demand. Of course, the structure of countries involved in payments for oil and the structure of investments of recycled petrodollars did not coincide, but supply and demand nonetheless evened out through the world financial-capital market.

Third, from the standpoint of the redistribution of newly created value between oil exporters and oil importers, deferment of the "real" repayment of the increased value equivalent of purchased oil (through the export of goods and services), had another important effect. The oil exporters' deferred effective demand gradually eroded as the result of an increase in world prices for equipment and industrial and agricultural products.

Thus, on the average, among the 10 European Community countries, import prices for goods and services (including energy resources) increased by a factor of 3.3 between 1970 and 1981, while export prices increased by a factor of 2.8 (prices for industrial goods, which accounted for the bulk of the exports, increased by a factor of approximately 3.1).[12] This means that most of the increase in prices of imported raw materials and energy resources was compensated for, in the final analysis, not by a transfer of real assets, but by an increase in the price of exported products of the processing industry.

---

[12]*Economie européenne*, Nov. 1981, pp. 175-176; *Economie mondiale, op. cit.*, p. 87.

However, no matter how small the macroeconomic effect was from the redistribution of value between developed capitalist countries and oil exporters from the developing world, the fact itself of the price increases for imported raw materials cannot be disregarded. For every country taken individually, the processes involved in the breakdown of price relationships between products going into world circulation and products taken out of it proved to be an extremely important factor in restructuring domestic reproduction proportions both in terms of the structure of income (wages vis-à-vis profits) and the proportional relationships among branches of industry. The reorganization took place under the pressure of a sharply intensified competitive struggle in world markets.

And here Western Europe clearly did not come out on top. Figures show that it could not stand up to competition from other parts of the world. In 1967 Western Europe accounted for 42.4 percent of international trade (20.6 percent, not counting trade within Europe itself), and in 1985 this figure had dropped to 37.9 percent (16.8 percent).[13] It had lost about four percentage points, which had gone to Japan and the newly industrialized countries of Southeast Asia.

Thus, beginning in the first half of the 1970s the simultaneous effect of internal and external factors changed, once and for all, the monetary-value structure of the economy that had made it possible for a good quarter of a century to carry out the expanded reproduction of capital at a fairly rapid pace. The lead that Western Europe enjoyed over the United States in the 1950s and 1960s in terms of the indicators of GNP growth, industry, investments, and living standard seemed to presage a relatively slow, but steady strengthening of the positions of the West European power center vis-à-vis its main partner in the imperialist camp.

The crisis that arose in economic growth and the existing type of development not only upset the placidity of some political and business circles in Western Europe, it also raised a problem point-blank: either the region would overcome its difficulties and move once again into the trajectory of pace-setting development, or it would have to admit that all its postwar hopes of building a unified and economically independent alliance of countries were unfounded. "Europessimism" was the extreme manifestation of the anxiety of the "Europists" and the hidden malicious pleasure of the "Atlantists." The latter have always seen the fate of the Western part of the European continent as inseparably bound up with their American partner, even at the price of

---

[13]Based on: *Economie mondiale: op. cit.*, p. 92; *Les collections de l'INSEE*, Nos. 131-132, Paris, 1986, Vol. II, p. 13.

subordinating themselves to that partner, at the price of their assuming a secondary role. The success or failure of the radical structural reorganization of the economy along the lines of the intensive development of West European capital should decide this question about the two directions of development, the two alternatives for Western Europe's position in the world economic system.

The Redistribution Reaction

How has Western European capitalism adapted to the new conditions of reproduction, and how has it surmounted the weaknesses that were revealed? The adaptation process has gone through two qualitatively different stages. Their approximate boundaries can be marked by the crises of 1974 to 1975 and 1980 to 1982. The mechanism of adaptation at the first stage can be called primarily a redistribution, and at the second stage it can be called primarily a technological reaction on the part of economic agents. We will explain what this means.

For our aspect of analysis, the most important distinguishing feature of the first stage was a high and disorderly rate of price increases that was different for different industries. It began under the influence of differences in the energy, raw-materials, and labor costs of the products of various industries, and it also resulted from differences in the market positions of those industries (some were more monopolized than others).

Encountering an increase in unit production costs, corporate executives tried to maintain profitability at the previous level by including the entire increase in the prices of raw materials and other materials, energy, and manpower in the sale prices of their products. In other words, they attempted to pass the effect of cost changes on to the consumer (mainly other firms), and used the price mechanism to get out of their dilemma by redistributing the value that was being created in the economy to profit themselves. This was a spontaneous reaction shown by all economic agents at once. It was obviously a zero-sum game, but it could not help but intensify competition within and between industries, particularly price competition.

There was even more about it that was unusual: the historically unprecedented aspect of capital's redistribution reaction was that it started to take place during the period of the profound crisis of 1974 to 1975. This contradicted the theoretical models for the behavior of business owners in a cyclical crisis. Prices, which were supposed to drop, actually rose, and the relationships among them changed almost independently of the specific features of the movement of production, and independently of the phases of the cycle. The reason for this was not only the increase in energy prices. The universality and duration of the phenomenon were tied in an obvious way to a change in the nature of the capitalist economic mechanism that had taken place much earlier, and to the fact that free competition was being pushed into the background, and monopolistic and state-monopoly forms of competition were taking over the leading roles. The phenomenon that was called "stagflation" in the economic literature could appear, and did appear, only in a completely and thoroughly monopolized economy. And if one needed any special confirmation of the monopolistic nature of present-day capitalism, it would be hard to find a better argument than the existence of stagflation.

The stagflation of the 1970s was the result of an attempt to preserve the precrisis structure and methods of production through monopolistic control of the markets. It is obvious that not everyone could succeed on this course, but individual segments of the monopoly bourgeoisie and individual countries succeeded for a while in protecting their own interests. For example, the Federal Republic of Germany, taking advantage of its high level of international prestige in the machinery industry, was able to maintain its volume of exports and retain its traditional customers, despite a substantial increase in export prices.

In two instances the redistribution reaction made it possible to neutralize, at least partially, the distortions in macroeconomic proportions that arose because of the crisis. We have already mentioned the first instance in illustrating the process involving the transfer of newly created value between oil-exporting and oil-importing countries. We find the second in the sphere of relations between the working people and the owners of the means of production. The increase in consumer-goods prices led to a slowdown in growth, a stagnation, or even a decline in the real purchasing power of the broad masses of working people. The success of the monopolies resulted in slowing the growth of effective demand, consumption, and subsequently, production. The resolution of one contradiction using monopolistic pricing methods gave rise to a number of other contradictions, the elimination of which required other forms.

The redistribution reaction is organically related to inflationary processes. Inflation was a necessary means and, under the existing circumstances, practically the only means of mitigating the disproportions in reproduction. Its drawback was that, because of its spontaneous nature and unpredictability, the inflationary rise in prices contributed to a deterioration of the general conditions of reproduction and reduced the reliability of price information and investment decisions. Ultimately, it prolonged the low rates of economic growth.

The Transition to a Technological Strategy

Overcoming the trend toward a slowdown in economic growth required that the strategy of formal adaptation—through the circulation of goods and money, and the redistribution of income—be combined with a strategy aimed at intensification of the economy, that is, aimed at reducing unit costs by increasing the efficiency with which the means of production were used, or by carrying out a radical modernization of the means of production. This requirement stemmed from the structural nature of the negative processes of the 1970s.

Without a shift to the priority production of relative surplus value—the essence of the intensive type of economy—it would have been socially dangerous, particularly in the politically unstable countries of southern Europe, to try to restore the profit rate solely by putting pressure on the real income of the working people (that is, by trying to restore the rate of absolute surplus value to the precrisis level). Raising the productivity of social labor, on the one hand, and reorganizing the system for regulating reproduction on a more realistic basis taking into account the growing level of internationalization, on the other—these are two basic aspects of intensification that have moved to the forefront since the late 1970s and early 1980s.

The decisive motivating factor behind the rejection of the redistribution reaction and the shift to a strategy of scientific and technological progress was the sharp intensification of competition resulting from the breakup of the national and, in some cases, international monopolistic structures of production and distribution that had developed at earlier stages. With the rise in the level of internationalization and "openness" of national economies, and with the end of the era of relatively closed economies, the monopolistic power of the former "conductors" of a country's production disappeared. Possession of even 100 percent of national production was no longer a guarantee of retaining monopolistic regulation of an industry's supply and demand.

The increasingly close merging of industries' national markets into a single world market—and transnational corporations can achieve that sort of result even while national-state control is formally maintained over foreign trade—opened up the opportunity for large "world-class" companies and groups to measure their strengths against those of their competitors. This situation did not invariably allow the creation of a cartel on a worldwide scale, which is what happened in the synthetic fiber markets. More often, national concerns and financial groups entered into an open or veiled struggle for sales markets.

The distinctive nature of the competitive struggle in the 1970s and 1980s consists, among other things, of the following. Finding themselves in unfamiliar foreign markets that they have not mastered, where the consumers generally do not know their products or their reputation, large companies are forced to change their forms of competition. In new markets it is impossible to resort at the very outset to nonprice methods of competition. These markets first have to be penetrated using lower prices than those of domestic producers. Only after winning a sufficiently large share of the market is it possible to stress the quality and prestige of a product at the same price or higher than that of competitors.

Price competition is the most open form of rivalry, in which each party operates openly, and the level of costs and companies' financial power ultimately prove to be the main argument. Hence the natural desire of the participants in the competitive struggle to lead by using every possible method to lower costs, including the use of scientific and technological advances in the production and sale of products.

Some corporations realized the limited possibilities of the redistribution strategy relatively long ago. During the crisis of 1974 to 1975, attempts were made to expand the use of scientific and technological progress to modernize equipment, create new consumer goods, and employ fundamentally new technologies. Following unsuccessful attempts in 1974 to 1977 to apply the typical methods of the 1960s for expanding investment demand and effective consumer demand to stimulate and develop production, the economic activity of bourgeois governments started to develop in this direction. Granted, the drama of state policies was that, by the time governments recognized the nature of the new requirements, the possibilities for them to effectively influence the economy, including the process of modernizing production, had been reduced sharply.

The reserves of budgetary policy had run dry during the years of the mid-1970s crisis, from which all countries had emerged with government financial deficits unprecedented for peacetime (from 3 to 5 percent to 8 to 10 percent of the GNP, and more). Therefore, beginning in the second half of the 1970s, in Western Europe strictly financial considerations took priority in both spending and taxation: The aim was to return to a budget that was at least somewhat balanced. In the face of this task, it became necessary, if not to ignore deeper reproduction problems altogether, then at least to approach them with the utmost restraint.

The situation with respect to credit policy was no better. Here inflation became an obstacle to rational use of credit policy in the interest of the accumulation of capital. As the inflation fever dragged on, its negative consequences, especially its undermining of the process of capital accumulation, became increasingly evident. Inflation changed from the ally of monopolistic corporations into their enemy. By the second half of the 1970s anti-inflation slogans had been turned into concrete measures in a policy of "strict economy." Many countries started to wage a consistent and uncompromising campaign against inflation. Credit and monetary policies were chosen as the main instrument of anti-inflationary measures. Limits on the amount of money in circulation, increased interest rates, and cutbacks in favorable loan terms—all these steps, naturally, left little possibility for using credit to stimulate investments, scientific research, and the efficient restructuring of corporations and industries.

From the standpoint of its potential contribution to improving the efficiency of production, poor use was made of another instrument of economic policy, the state sector in the sphere of production, infrastructure, and services. In countries in which it accounted for a significant share of the production apparatus (for example, Great Britain, the Federal Republic of Germany, France, Italy, Austria, Sweden), with the onset of the crisis of 1974 to 1975, governments hastened to command executives of state companies to increase investments and thereby reduce the scope of the decline in investment demand and the production of investment goods.

Since a policy of budgetary economy was proclaimed at the same time, loans in national and international capital-lending markets became the main source of financing for state companies. By the late 1970s, with investments up by 50 to 100 percent (an increase that was far from always warranted by prospects for the development of markets and scientific and technological progress), the indebtedness of state enterprises and the size of deficits on their balance sheets had greatly increased. The acceleration of investments had to be stopped and more attention paid to their qualitative structure and to the selection of areas for investment, but the damage to the prestige of state business had already been done. Right-wing forces hastened to take advantage of this, unleashing a widespread campaign in the 1980s to reprivatize state property.

In analyzing the reasons for the replacement of Keynesian government economic policies with neoconservative policies, one must evidently take into consideration all three specific circumstances surrounding the weakening of the material foundation of government regulation. Combined with the intensified competitive struggle that resulted from the internationalization of economic life, they enable us to better understand the objective reasons for the triumphal march of neoconservatism since the late 1970s. The neoconservatives' emphasis on creating the best conditions for investment activities by entrepreneurs, and their interest in supply rather than demand represent an ideologically prepared response to the real demands of production, and to the urgent need to seek out new technical and technological solutions to the problem of increasing production efficiency.

The technological response, as the predominant type of activity among companies and government administrations in Western Europe, came in to replace the redistribution response relatively late—following the second "oil shock" (1979) and the first obvious commercial successes of Japanese and American competitors in new areas of technology.

A natural question arises: why did West European capitalism take so long to make the shift to the active use of scientific and technological advances to solve the problems created by the structural crisis? A whole series of peculiarities of the West European economy and sociopolitical structures evidently played a role here.

First, Western Europe was considerably more sensitive than the United States to the destabilizing blows of the first oil crisis, since it is more dependent on imported energy resources. Second, West European workers are better organized than workers in the United States and Japan. They put up strong resistance to the attack on their living standard. To a considerable extent, this resistance was also responsible for the long duration of companies' poor financial results, whose improvement could at first be expected only from a redistribution of the national income in favor of capital.

Third, the subordinate position of Western Europe with respect to the United States in the world economy had an effect. It often forced European capitalism to adapt, willingly or unwillingly, to American monetary and credit policy, currency policy, and trade and economic policies, and then to pay for the miscalculations of those policies with its own money.

The fourth and final factor is that the West European countries suffered more severely from the dismantling of traditional methods of macroeconomic regulation, since the state had always played a more substantial economic role there.

Theoretically speaking, the two reactions—the redistribution reaction and the technological reaction—could exist side by side. In practice, however, this coexistence encounters difficulties. The main one is the inflationary atmosphere that characterizes the former and conflicts with the latter. Inflation represents an instability in monetary-value relationships, uncertainty in investment prospects, and strong speculative incentives for the owners of monetary capital. The introduction of scientific and technological advances into production requires exactly the opposite: confidence in regular profits, which may be small, but must be stable; an abundant market in borrowed capital;

and minimization of the risk in capital investment that stems from uncertainty about the prospects for changes in prices, income, and so forth.

From this standpoint, the resolute campaign against inflation that the West European countries undertook following the U.S. lead was a necessary condition for the transition to a technological type of strategy. But the redistribution strategy, which was just producing its first results in Western Europe in the early 1980s, was thereby denied one of its most effective instruments. Granted, in the labor market unemployment took the place of inflation as a factor reducing real earnings, and in the commodity markets in trade with the developing countries, those countries' indebtedness took the place of inflation. The shift from an inflationary economy to a deflationary one, however, always means a decline in growth rates, and sometimes, as was the case in 1980 to 1982, it also means an economic crisis.

The active restructuring of monetary-value reproduction proportions (wages vis-à-vis profits, savings vis-à-vis consumption) entails large shifts in effective demand. At the first stage of the period in which we are interested, the basic structure-determining impulses moved from demand to supply. And since demand was formed under the conditions of a general contraction (slower growth) of income, structural shifts in production proceeded in the context of slow growth rates. The sluggishness of effective demand persisted.

At the second stage, the structure of production began to change under the influence of the modernization of the technical base and the updating of both producer and consumer goods. Generally speaking, we can proceed on the assumption that the main direction in which the structure-determining impulses are moving now is from supply to demand, from production to consumption.

The new technical and technological base of production and new forms and methods of centralized (state-monopoly) and decentralized (competition-monopoly) regulation of reproduction proportions, are forming the structure and qualitative nature of individual and public demand for the next 10 to 20 years. Within the framework of this process we are seeing individual industries "fitting in" with one another, the gradual formation of new proportional relationships among industries, an active search for adequate organizational forms for production units and complexes, and the occupation by individual national segments of the bourgeoisie of their own places in the international division of labor. In Western Europe these processes are developing no less intensely than in other centers of imperialism, although they are developing significantly later, in somewhat different forms, and with different results.

Japan: Scientific and Technological Progress and the Organization of the Economy

ALEKSANDR ALEKSANDROVICH DYNKIN
AND IVAN SERGEYEVICH TSELICHTSHEV*

From the Editors: In this issue, responding to readers' wishes, we are initiating a new regular section, "Reports on Research Trips." Its objective is to present the results with the greatest theoretical and practical interest from trips abroad by scholars from the U.S.S.R. Academy of Sciences' Institute of World Economy and International Relations and other institutes and institutions. The first contribution to this section is a dialogue between A.A. Dynkin, head of IMEMO'S Economics of Scientific and Technological Progress Section, and I.S. Tselichtshev, our journal's deputy editor in chief. They discuss the results of their research work in Japan.

Tselichtshev: The topics we worked on in Japan were very similar. You were concerned more with the questions of scientific and technological progress, and I was concerned more with economic organization and the evolution of the entrepreneurial structure at the present stage of scientific and technological progress.

I propose, Aleksandr Aleksandrovich, that we start with the question of the relationship between basic and applied research. It is known, for example, that, at least until recently, Japanese companies were very strong in applied research and development, while in basic research Japan largely depended on its partners. In talking with people from the country's academic and business circles, I repeatedly asked whether that situation would change and, if so, how. Would Japan continue to be primarily a country of applied research and development, or were any sort of serious changes possible? In this connection, my attention was drawn to the idea of a change in the very nature of research work and in the very organization of the whole research-development-production-marketing cycle. I have in mind both linear

*Dynkin is a candidate of economics and section head at IMEMO. Tselichtshev is a candidate of economics and deputy editor in chief of *MEMO*. This article appeared in the October 1987 issue of *MEMO*.

and nonlinear models of that cycle. I think that you, too, touched on that matter more than once in your conversations.

Dynkin: Absolutely. It's a very complex and interesting question. In addition to studying Japanese experience with scientific and technological development, the objectives of my trip included an attempt to compare it with the established model of scientific and technological development in the United States. Therefore, I was constantly trying to draw parallels between the distinctive features of scientific and technological progress in the two countries. It is true that Japan has traditionally lagged behind in basic research, and if we were to draw a line showing the stages in the research cycle that was typical of the 1960s and first half of the 1970s, at the point where basic research was represented in that line for the United States, for Japanese firms we would show a search for information in the external environment, mainly abroad. After that would come applied research; that is, at that time the Japanese managed, for all intents and purposes, to get by without basic research. Later they developed the following principle: do basic research only where applied research fails to produce some desired result, or when problems arise in the course of applied research requiring theoretical analysis. Later they transformed that principle, and the so-called nonlinear model of the innovation process was born. The gist is that, as progress is made toward the sale of output and toward the development of new technologies, basic and applied research, development work, and even pilot production runs are repeated over and over. And, of course, the results of the research stages are repeatedly evaluated. There you have the nonlinear idea, which is now evidently a universal principle for all major Japanese firms and helps save time in the innovation process.

Tselichtshev: Besides that, as I understand it, in accordance with traditional views that were correct for their time, the idea for an innovation is typically born at the stage of basic research. There it is duly "brought to fruition," and only then is it applied in practice, following the chain of steps through applied research, development, and production. But today it is said that the probability of an idea's surfacing is approximately the same at any stage in the chain—in production, for example, or possibly in development. That being the case, an assignment travels back through feedback channels to the area of basic research: Finish working out the idea and do certain theoretical research on the given set of problems, preparing for the effective introduction of the innovation in practice. This exchange of ideas really does happen quite often. It's called the "rugby principle."

And that's where the Japanese are strong—in the organizational aspect. It seems to me that so-called project teams perform rather effectively in Japanese firms. Take, for example, the Toray company.

You also visited it. More than 100 relatively small project teams, five to six people each, operate at the firm simultaneously. And what's important is that research people, production workers, and people from marketing work side by side in these groups. They have a definite objective—coming up with the concept of a new product. That means defining its user attributes (identifying something unique about them), figuring the unit cost and price, and indicating the market (domestic or foreign). On the basis of such a concept, the research units continue their work, but now with quite specific goals. This is also very important for the production and marketing units, since working together with the researchers allows them to see what is in store and to become directly involved in the innovation process. In short, what we have here is an effective means of interfacing research, production, and marketing.

I think that one can formulate a general conclusion as follows: granted, Japan still lags behind the United States in the scale of basic research, but in the overall Japanese research system, including its basic level, some very strong aspects are apparent. I would even say that one can see advantages over other countries. First, there is the orientation of all the research stages toward the final result, and the existence of adequate organizational forms that provide for the effective linkage of various units in the research-production cycle. I see factors of Japan's competitiveness here.

Dynkin: In speaking of the internal structural proportions of Japan's research potential, one should note that since around the early 1980s the relationship among spending for basic research, applied research, and development has been about the same as it has been for the past 20 years in the United States. In the United States these proportions have been stable and are as follows: 12 to 13 percent for basic research, 24 to 25 percent for applied research, and the rest for development. A similar relationship has also existed since the early 1980s in Japan, and I think this is no accident, since the stability of these proportions in the United States obviously indicates their "maturity" and conformity to the economy's needs for the assimilation of existing basic research. A sharp increase or reduction in the share of any one stage in the cycle would produce negative results, since either the system as a whole would be unable to cope with the initial research that had been done, or there would not be enough of that research. The fact that Japan has arrived at similar proportions is, in my view, extremely significant. In terms of absolute amounts invested in research and development, the U.S. figures today are approximately double those of Japan. But the figures on spending for research and development as a percentage of gross national product are practically identical. Of course, one must also keep in mind the efficiency with which research is utilized. In the United States more than three-fourths of public spending for research goes into military research (including military space research), while only 2 to 3 percent goes for that purpose in Japan. At the same time, in the past 20 years the amount of state budgetary funds as a share of total national spending for research in Japan has dropped from 31 percent in 1965 to 21 percent in 1985. Thus, forecasts in the late 1970s to the effect that the state's share in the financing of research would approach 50 percent (the level long since reached in other developed capitalist countries) by the early 1990s are not being borne out. The reason is the state budget deficit, and the active use of private business funds through a system of indirect regulation. However, if one excludes spending for military research from U.S. public expenditures for research, the amount of that spending as a percentage of total national investments in research drops from 48 percent to 22 percent (in 1987), which is consistent with the analogous Japanese figure.

Let's look at research intensiveness in the United States and Japan for specific industries. Statistics show that in the automotive and electronic industries the research intensiveness of Japanese products is just over half that of American products, yet everyone knows the competitiveness problems that the Americans have been encountering. In my view, this is a sign of the efficient utilization of scientific and technological potential. In particular, it is related to what you were talking about: the project teams, as well as to a high degree of cooperation among Japanese firms. Moreover, at the research stage the principle of cooperation, as I see it, is decisive, and the center of gravity of competition shifts to the production and marketing stages. There is competition to reduce costs, improve quality, and win customers. The Japanese are known for their ability to zero in effectively on the differentiated needs of the market. Firms themselves often create needs on the basis of their analysis of living conditions or, where it's a question of customers for producer goods, the nature of production. These are all, unquestionably, strong sides of the Japanese model of technological progress.

It should also be noted that competition in Japan is extremely fierce. For example, in every machinery industry (the automotive industry, the robot industry, the electronics industry, and so forth) there are more than 10 major firms that are more or less equal in their capabilities, while the degree of monopolization is much higher in the United States.

Tselichtshev: In my conversations with Japanese specialists, we frequently discussed the following issue. U.S. companies that do major military research have a firm financial base in the form of federal budget appropriations, and therefore they can wait fairly long for a practical outcome. Moreover, when this government support exists, when the federal budget is brought into play, I think that the commercial incentives grow weaker. Japanese companies, including firms engaged in military research, always adhere to the so-called cost-recovery principle. In their case, budgetary support from the government is minimal. Therefore, research is oriented toward a rather rapid return on investment. As Professor T. Isomura noted, for example, a U.S. firm is prepared to wait 10 to 20 years, whereas a Japanese firm won't wait more than five. That really is a very important aspect of the matter. And obviously, the principles that govern the expenditure of funds in Japan prove to be somewhat different.

Now for a word about cooperation and competition. That is a fundamental aspect. After all, in Japan the bulk of research and development work is done in private firms. This has its strong points. But it also has its minuses—for example, a certain deconcentration of research and development. A private firm, even the largest, can find it difficult to carry out large-scale research projects, which often require a pooling of many producers' efforts and a nationwide undertaking.

Dynkin: Of course, it's necessary to achieve a certain "critical mass" of resources here.

Tselichtshev: Unquestionably. And in that connection one notes the existence of research associations in such areas as the development of technology for very large integrated circuits (this association existed until the early 1980s), the basic technologies for production of fifth-generation computers, and a number of others. The associations have proved their effectiveness. They make it possible to pool the efforts of the leading producers; the government gets involved; and a certain unified, nationwide strategy is carried out. But all this is at the stage of research and establishing the basic technology. As soon as the point of development and modification of the basic technologies is reached, the association is dissolved, and its former partners become competitors. At this point an entirely different principle comes into play. Thus, it seems to me, highly effective forms are gradually being found for stimulating research work and rapidly applying research results in production. I have in mind some sort of optimal arrangements for combining cooperation and competition.

At the same time, of course, such associations by no means always function smoothly. The reason lies in the differing interests of companies, their reluctance to put their best personnel at the disposal of an association, and the difficulties of combining representatives of different companies into a team, so that they are working under a single leader and under the same roof. A great deal depends on who is in charge of the association, and so forth. In short, this form of organizing research does not always work, and sometimes, instead of forming associations, it is necessary to distribute the various research topics among a number of companies. That is something entirely different, and the results are much poorer. As for the associations, they are one of the most promising forms of organizing research activity.

Dynkin: Here I would like to add that one of the people I talked with assured me that 95 percent of Japan's research budget is allocated in a centralized fashion. That may be an exaggeration. But what did he have in mind? Above all, the committees that operate in the Ministry of International Trade and Industry and the extremely effective network of informal ties among major Japanese specialists employed at various firms and universities.

Here I would like to return to a matter that you have already touched on. It is true that firms in the U.S. military-industrial complex can wait decades to recoup their outlays. But one must also keep in mind that the modern firm is involved in more than one industry. Naturally, arms producers' business activities generally include civilian branches as well. And here, it seems to me, the difference between the United States and Japan is that the Americans are oriented toward short-term financial results, at least that is the way it was in the late 1970s and early 1980s. And that often undermined, so to speak, the long-range orientation of the scientific and technological process, whereas in Japan—and this is already a commonplace—firms are oriented more toward the long-range future and market share, rather than toward short-range profits and profitability. In addition, compared to the American corporation, the Japanese corporation is more closely tied to its existing work force, and it finds it more difficult than the American corporation to make decisions to drastically reduce or increase its personnel. In my view, this long-range policy can be counted as one of the advantages of the Japanese strategy of scientific and technological development.

Tselichtshev: I would even say, not just scientific and technological development, but the overall development of corporations. Indeed, inasmuch as juridical persons predominate among the stockholders of Japanese firms; inasmuch as a reciprocal stockholding system exists whereby corporations own each others' stocks within the framework of monopolistic financial groups, and the corporate executives, to all intents and purposes, delegate to each other the right to manage without interference; and inasmuch as there is a lack of tight control on the part of stockholders whose chief interest is in rapidly obtaining maximum profits, the Japanese manager is considerably less oriented than the American or West European manager toward short-range financial results. This makes it possible to formulate strategic plans and carry them out, I would say, in a more tranquil atmosphere and with a larger degree of autonomy on the executive's part. That is still another serious factor in companies' competitiveness.

But I would like to move on now to the question of diversification, which you just mentioned. In my conversations in Japan it was one of the key questions. Until recently—and this is well known—Japanese firms were considered highly specialized. By the standards of the Western business world, the extent to which they were tied to their basic industries was considerable. Now the situation is starting to change, and rather drastically so. This merits close attention, including attention, I think, from the standpoint of our own economy's prospects for development. There is growing recognition that under current conditions a large firm's orientation toward a single branch of industry, not to mention the production of a single product, has little future and is economically unjustifiable. Previously it was still possible to choose between the advantages of narrow specialization and the advantages of diversification. Today diversification has, to all intents and purposes, become an imperative. Almost every large company is engaged in a search for a specific diversified concept of development. It presupposes, first of all, a carefully considered set of products and industries that are related either technologically or in type and means of marketing. In Japan, unlike the United States, companies do not stray too far from their principal, basic industry. In the first place, this really does have to do with the low turnover of personnel. If we take, for example, a textile company, considering the extremely broad range of specialization of Japanese specialists, one can assume that a specialist in textile production will be able to work, with appropriate retraining, in certain branches of the chemical industry, or in the production of a number of new materials, but it will obviously be hard for him to work in data processing. And it is extremely, extremely difficult to find manpower outside a firm in the context of a system of long-term employment. And so, first we have a set of industries and production facilities that are interconnected in terms of technology and marketing. Here I would further like to note that industrial companies often get into service-sector industries that are related in one way or another to their principal production specialty (for example, food companies will get into the food-service sector, while automotive companies will get involved in tourism, and so forth).

But that is not all. There is a second extremely important aspect of diversification—the mandatory inclusion, in virtually any major firm's multibranch concept (or, as the Japanese now say, using the English term, in its CI or "corporate identity") of at least some products belonging to industries that are in the forefront of scientific and technological progress (electronics, data processing, biological engineering, new materials). This is an extremely important circumstance. First, because it provides a tremendous stimulus to the development of advanced industries, and second, because it results in intense competition in those industries, which also cannot be discounted when analyzing the dynamics and level of their development.

It seems to me that this gives us something else to think about on the theoretical level. To a certain extent, the development and realization of multibranch concepts (corporate identities) of this sort shift the center of gravity of competition from the level of individual industries to the level of the economy as a whole. To a certain extent, I would even say that monopolistic structures in particular industries are "undermined." It is not so much the producers in a single industry as it is the various corporate identities that are competing—on the level of the economy as a whole. This is also in many respects a qualitatively different situation from the one that existed, say, in the 1960s or 1970s.

And another fundamentally important point: a producer must form his own concept, his own corporate identity, independently. No instructions from above can work here. Yet the formation of such a multibranch concept is a decisive factor in improving the efficiency of resource utilization. In Japan and other capitalist countries economists are currently using the category "economy of scope"—economy in terms of the range and mix of products.

Dynkin: Economies of diversity.

Tselichtshev: Yes, of diversity. In other words, it is more efficient to produce numerous types of different products, even in small lots, at one large firm than it is to distribute the same types of products among a corresponding number of smaller, specialized firms. That, of course, is far from a universal rule, but such a tendency operates rather often.

Dynkin: Undoubtedly, that is an important fact. Economies of diversity are one of the most important components of the current strategy of economic development. The principle is to produce specialized products for a specific user while preserving the low level of costs that is characteristic of mass production. The material basis for doing so consists of the latest automation (flexible manufacturing systems, for example, or robots) and data processing. Incidentally, even today analogous trends can be seen in the United States. The well-known enthusiasm for forming conglomerates has been replaced by the establishment of supergroups, as the Americans call them, within companies. The basis of their formation is primarily technological, and they deal with all aspects of the process of putting innovations into production. Another example: firms that produce rolling-contact bearings follow the technological chain from the basic product in both directions—downward into the production of specialized steels, and upward into the production of special machine tools and measuring instruments. It is the connection with a single technology that links numerous independent and quasi-independent divisions today.

In my view, the stage of financial diversification, if one may put it that way, is to some extent already past in Japan. You were talking about cross-ownership of stocks. In the 1960s that was clearly the dominant feature. Today, that feature is unquestionably technology. You noted that nowadays all firms, even in the old industries, are trying to diversify in the area of advanced technology. In Japan, unlike the United States, that process is actively encouraged by the state. You probably recall our visit together to the Japan Development Bank, during which we were told about an interesting study. It showed that if one compares the 1980s with the mid-1970s, different industries have become more alike in terms of the structure of their research activities. For example, light-industry firms are actively conducting research and development work in the area of data processing and automation, and companies in many of the traditional basic industries are working along the very same lines. This is being accomplished thanks to the provision of governmental incentives, particularly through credit and financial policy, for research in the area of "fundamental technologies," as the Japanese say. And the list of such technologies is determined by the central government or local administrative agencies. To all intents and purposes, the state determines the areas of research and launches a structural reorganization of the economy along the lines it has determined. These principles of Japanese credit and financial policy ensure a so-called synthesis of technologies, since they encourage traditional industries to develop the latest areas of science and technology.

This is an interesting aspect of the Japanese model.

Tselichtshev: We have not yet touched on that important form of organizing research activities and technological entrepreneurship known as venture business.

How do you assess its prospects in Japan, and what about its specific features?

Dynkin: For the United States, venture business has become one of the main areas of scientific and technological development. Statistics indicate that small and medium-sized companies are much more active in terms of innovations than are large organizations with, so to speak, "ossified structures." In Japan the main level where scientific and technological advances are made is still the large corporation. I recall a meeting with one of the firmest believers in venture business, Mr. Yanagida, the president of the Nippon Tectron company. That firm is probably as well known in Japan as Genentech is in the United States. He believes in the future of venture business in Japan, but he sees circumstances objectively holding up the development of this form of entrepreneurship. What are those circumstances? The first, unquestionably, is the relative lack of mobility of talented specialists, especially young ones, since work in a large firm is still considered the most prestigious in Japan. Mr. Yanagida complained to me that he cannot recruit the number of first-rate specialists under the age of 35 that he needs. The second circumstance is a definite scarcity of sources of borrowed capital. I visited the Sumitomo Bank, where I was told that a group had been set up to finance venture businessmen, but when I tried to find out what were the principles and methods for allocating those funds, the people I was talking with evaded a clear answer, saying that there was no formal set of methods, just certain specifically Japanese relations. Those relations develop in quite different ways. For example, on the basis of family ties or regional loyalties. And that is the way venture firms are selected in the Sumitomo Bank.

Tselichtshev: I also got the impression that Japanese banks or, more precisely, venture capital—in Japan that comes mainly from subsidiaries of the largest banks and insurance companies—begins providing loans to business ventures only when they are already more or less established and have gained a reputation.

Dynkin: Of course.

Tselichtshev: And at the initial stage, when they need the money most, it is extremely hard to get it. In the United States there is no such problem.

Dynkin: And a third factor that Mr. Yanagida spoke of is Japan's lack of the necessary infrastructure for venture business. What did he have in mind? Primarily, inadequate access to data banks, and the lack of a well-developed system for leasing needed equipment and of a broad network of specialized courses where venture businessmen can receive advanced training and retraining. In Japan all this is still in the embryonic stage, whereas it has already undergone considerable development in the United States. To support that, let me cite figures indicating how much easier it is for a venture company to develop in the United States. At present the annual growth in the turnover of the 100 largest U.S. venture firms is about 110 percent, whereas for comparable Japanese firms it is 40 to 50 percent.

Tselichtshev: Several years ago a series of articles under the rubric "Venture Fever" started to appear in the Japanese economics magazine *Toyo Keizai*. Other publications also devoted a good many pages to the "venture boom." I have the impression now that even we got a little carried away at the time with accounts of the dynamic development and broad prospects for the venture business in Japan. On the whole, I agree with you. The U.S. version of venture business has no future in Japan; people don't believe in it. But at the same time, certain forms of economic organization that compensate for the inadequate development of that type of technological entrepreneurship can't help but exist. It seems to me, for example, that the functions of the classic venture in Japan are performed, to a considerable extent, by venture subdivisions that either operate within large corporations or have been set up by those corporations as new firms. In the first case, they are called internal ventures, in the second case, external ventures. Right now it seems that external ventures are preferred.

Dynkin: "External" according to the terminology accepted in Japan?

Tselichtshev: Yes. What is involved is that a large corporation, in order to develop some new line of business or other, sets up a small venture-type firm, gradually giving it more and more independence. An interesting questionnaire was distributed among a group of major businessmen. They were asked what type of venture they preferred, internal or external. Most said external. Why? Because a venture firm must, in any case, have a considerable degree of managerial independence and autonomy. It must take risks. When a venture operates within a large firm, the decisions that are made within it have to pass through numerous stages of approval and refinement. There's no getting around the traditional urge for consensus in Japanese firms. Therefore, it is more effective to place the venture outside the boundaries of the firm. But what is the strength of this form of organization? In the first place, the new firms acquire the ability to take risks, and without risk there are no major innovations today. In the second place, the principle of the small group or small organization applies, and flexibility, maneuverability, and responsiveness are achieved. In the third place, the new firms can use the resources—financial, technological, and personnel—of the large corporations.

In this connection, there is something else I would particularly like to mention. The practice of separating individual subdivisions from large corporations and making them independent firms for developing new lines of business has struck deep roots in Japan. And this is the method and form of organization that we ought to pay the closest attention to, especially from the standpoint of utilizing the human factor. First, the prestige and authority of the people who work in such firms increase substantially. It is one thing for a person to head a department or a section—even in a large corporation—but it is something else for him to become the president of a firm, even a relatively small one. Second—something I have already spoken about—a firm that has been split off this way functions as a compact organization. Decisions are made and carried out rapidly. There are no lengthy processes such as refining decisions or securing multiple approvals. And third, oversight. In this case one could say that the oversight function is performed directly by the market—by consumers, creditors, stock holders, and so forth—whereas for an internal company subdivision, even one with the highest degree of autonomy, oversight is always based more on its accounting books. In that case it can "hide" behind other subdivisions. It seems to me that this circumstance is very important. And in summing up this part of our conversation, I would like to emphasize the idea that the extensive use of the small organization and the small operational group to stimulate the innovation process is a universal principle for Japan, the United States, and I think, West European countries.

The only question is the framework in which such a group operates. It can function either within a large corporation or outside of it. But in my opinion there is no doubt that such groups are necessary, essential.

Dynkin: Now, Ivan Sergeyevich, I would like to put the following question to you: Everyone knows that "quality circles" function effectively in Japan. In my opinion, changes in the nature of present-day production, its specialization and differentiation, and reliance on the principle of economies of diversity or economies of optimal scale create certain problems for traditional quality circles, which are often associated with standard, assembly-line production. How do you see the prospects for the development of this method of organizing labor?

Tselichtshev: You know, my view on this question, by and large, had been formed—or, more precisely, altered somewhat—even before the trip. And I was once again convinced of the need to rethink stereotypes and approach the problem more broadly after a talk with Kadzuo Koike, a professor at Kyoto University, who is probably Japan's leading specialist on labor management. I think we somewhat exaggerate the importance of that form of organization among all the other forms, means, and strategies for stimulating quality, labor productivity, and efficiency. K. Koike puts it this way: Yes, the quality circles do exist, and they are of some use, but there is something else that is much more important. A worker in a production section performs two types of operations: routine operations, when the assembly line is started up and operates in a certain way, and a certain type of product is produced; and nonstandard operations, such as resetting equipment, preventing defects, and performing certain complicated repair work, if the need arises. The Japanese worker, the average worker, passes through various of his firm's shops and sections in accordance with the practice of personnel rotation. Extremely complex company programs of education and advanced training have been set up for him. As a result, he is well oriented in production as a whole and can perform both routine and nonstandard operations with equal success. At the same time, in the United States and Western Europe, say, there is a more rigid assignment of functions among workers and engineering and technical personnel.

Dynkin: A characteristic feature of American and West European management is the existence of a large number of fixed positions and corresponding job descriptions. In Japan that is not the case.
Tselichtshev: And that is also important. But the main thing, in my opinion, is still the fact that in the Western countries engineering and technical personnel perform mainly nonroutine operations, while workers perform routine operations. In Japan the worker sees, so to speak, the entire process as a whole and has greater opportunity to affect it in a purposeful way. Today, when the proportion of small-series production is growing, the product mix is expanding drastically, and technologies are being rapidly updated, this is especially essential. I am convinced that this aspect of the matter is somewhat more important than quality circles. As for the circles, they seemingly have retained their significance. I think that they can also be used in the small-series production of a broad mix of products.

Dynkin: It was no accident, Ivan Sergeyevich, that I asked the question about quality circles. I had a very interesting discussion about this problem with Kenichi Imai, a professor at Hitotsubashi University. He was saying that combining people engaged in creative work, such as specialists involved in research and development or computer programming, into circles has generally proven to be more difficult than it is with blue-collar workers. In general, the traditional division into white-collar and blue-collar employees is no longer adequate today. There are also so-called gold-collar employees—people who develop product concepts, highly qualified researchers, specialists in computer programming—in short, people engaged in individual creative work. They are less willing to take part in such group forms of labor organization. That is what I mainly had in mind. K. Imai suggests the idea of introducing more flexible forms. To use our terminology, he suggests organizing something like all-purpose brigades, which would include both people in development work—that is, people engaged in creative work—and certain production personnel. What is interesting is that he proposes that they include representatives of subcontractors and even customers. I think K. Imai's view that quality circles will eventually undergo such an evolution merits our attention.

Tselichtshev: That is probably the case, although there is another side, too. In Japan individual creative work is not based on any established, well-developed forms of incentives. Group work predominates in any case. An innovator who has developed a new technological process does not receive as great a material reward as in the United States. That may to some extent impede basic innovations, and no evolution of quality circles will save matters. But since we have started talking about K. Imai, I think we simply have no right to overlook the so-called network concept that so many of his writings are currently devoted to substantiating and developing. According to K. Imai, this is, so to speak, a universal principle of organization both within companies—which you have, in effect, just illustrated—and on the intercompany level.

In this connection, the following idea arises: to a considerable extent, the development of the Japanese economy in the 1960s and 1970s took place within the framework of fairly clearly defined vertical organizations. The famous six leading financial monopoly groups, the so-called shudan (Mitsubishi, Mitsui, Sumitomo, etc.), belong to this category. The same thing is true of the pyramidal subcontracting systems, where a large company is on the top, and it has its first-level subcontractors; they have their own subcontractors (the second level); and beneath them is the third level, and so on all the way down to the base of the pyramid. All relationships are long-term and rigidly defined.

Dynkin: Is that what is meant by the term "keiretsu"?

Tselichtshev: No, keiretsu is somewhat broader. Keiretsu can also apply to horizontal relations, to certain partnership relations in the production of a similar final product, and so forth. In a number of cases that term is also used to refer to financial groups. Subcontractors, on the other hand, are called "shitauke" in Japanese.

And so, right now the vertical organizations are being partially eroded. Take, for example, the financial monopoly groups (the shudans). Each of them used to have its own firms in virtually all the principal branches of the economy.

Dynkin: A kind of autarky.

Tselichtshev: A kind of "gentleman's set" of basic industries to which the shudan extends its sphere of influence. At the top of the association, of course, is a bank. Companies in each industry know who to turn to for loans. Also at the top is a so-called general trading company, which carries out middleman commercial operations. And also at the top, finally, are conferences of the presidents of the leading companies, which determine the strategies for a group's development. That's the way it used to be, but what is the situation now? First, the coordinating role of the banks is growing weaker, if only because the demand for credit, relatively speaking, is declining. The industrial companies and other companies have "enough" money. Second, the general trading companies are also going through an extremely difficult period, since they are geared primarily to marketing large lots of similar traditional products and are weak in the markets of the high-technology industries. As for the sessions of the presidential councils, they now engage primarily in exchanges of information. The center of gravity in the decision-making process is shifting further toward the company level. As we have already said, the firms are diversifying and going into new industries. Many of them lie at the juncture between old industries, and there is a need to combine the technologies, know-how, and production experience of companies with highly diverse specializations. In order to build a competent multibranch strategy that meets today's requirements, a firm needs to conclude contracts with a considerably larger number of parties than is possible within the framework of its own financial group. Therefore, if such groups are not breaking up, they are at least becoming interwoven with a growing number of other intercompany partnerships that lie outside their bounds. There you have the "network."

Dynkin: That is, a company is becoming more of an open system.

Tselichtshev: Absolutely right. One can put it that way. Exactly the same thing is happening with the subcontracting systems. On the average, every subcontractor in Japan fills orders for four to six head firms. Moreover, the head firm tries to keep a subcontractor from supplying it with more than 70 to 80 percent of its output. That would seem to be a paradox, but it's not at all. By encouraging a subcontractor to deal with other large companies, it helps that subcontractor acquire certain additional skills, knowledge, know-how, and technologies, that is, helps it become a more efficient supplier. And I am not even speaking of economies of scale and the corresponding reductions in costs. There you have another network.

Dynkin: But here there is also a negative aspect in the eyes, say, of the president of a large company. As people I talked with in Japan demonstrated, this form of subcontracting relations is the main channel through which technologies are transferred from one large producer to another. And here there probably needs to be a certain balance, since the leakage of technology takes place through such channels. But obviously relations of this sort are needed from the standpoint of raising the technological level of the economy as a whole.

Tselichtshev: In my opinion, given the present level of relations among companies and of cooperative production arrangements, a company is capable of monopolizing a technology for only a very short period of time, in any case.

Dynkin: Unquestionably, since the rate of change is very rapid.

Tselichtshev: And the rate of technology transfer is colossal.

Dynkin: And under those conditions, protection by patent is not always advisable, either.

Tselichtshev: Well, that's logical, although at first glance it's surprising. But let's return to the networks. As far as the head company is concerned, it endeavors to buy even the same part from several suppliers simultaneously. That is the so-called principle of multiple sources of supply.

Dynkin: Of course, price competition comes into full play here.

Tselichtshev: Now I am approaching a very important aspect of the matter, and one that I find extremely interesting. It is often said that relations among companies in Japan are rigid. Whereas a head firm and a subcontractor in the United States may conclude a contract for a year, say, and once the year is up, a new contract is often signed with a different firm. In Japan, to the contrary, relations are of a permanent, long-term nature. There is even a Japanese proverb that says, "A nodding acquaintance—no business." I would say this is a kind of guide to action in the economic sphere. But why does such a system operate? This, once again, is very important from the standpoint of our economy. The reason it works is that it is suffused with competition. Naturally, with multiple supply sources the head company changes and regulates the relative share of different subcontractors in accordance with their financial performance and innovation potential. Since a subcontractor also serves several clients, it, too, may have a certain freedom to maneuver.

Granted, to get a complete picture, one must also note the following circumstance. Japanese specialists in the area of economic organization agree that the network form of organization is the most efficient, but they differ in their assessments of the extent to which it has already become a reality. K. Imai claims that networks are the organizational basis of the Japanese economy today, while H. Okumura (Progress Publishers recently brought out his book "Corporate Capitalism in Japan" in our country), for example, says that so far that is only an unattainable ideal. His arguments are as follows: The manager of any corporation will tell you immediately what his principal bank is. Every subcontractor has a principal client who gets the bulk of his deliveries and who also serves as his creditor, consultant, and so forth. All the remaining relations just amount to a small makeweight. Moreover, suppliers by no means have unlimited choices. For example, a Toyota subcontractor will never become a subcontractor of its chief competitor Nissan. It seems to me that for the present the truth lies somewhere in between. One can compare the lines of subcontracting relations to trunks and branches. The trunks are dense, established relations, while the branches are relatively new, less intensive ones. But the branches have a tendency to become more numerous and "thicker," that is, ties outside the limits of established relations are becoming more active and richer in content.

In general, it is indisputable that scientific and technological progress today requires a considerable expansion of all sorts of partnership relations, an increase in the activities of producers within the framework of various associations, and freedom in the choice of partners. No regulating body can "draw" an economically rational network of relationships from above; only the producers themselves can define it. In other words, decisions defining the structure of relations both within and between industries are taken at the level of companies, and therein lies the prerequisite for the formation of economically effective networks.

But our discussion is drawing to an end, and I think it is time for us to move on to management within companies.

Dynkin: Then let us turn to comparisons again.

Starting in the mid-1970s, under the impact of Japan's foreign economic expansion, the thesis that there was a crisis in American management and that Japanese management was superior became widespread in the United States. In the second half of the 1980s both the theoreticians and practitioners of American management have essentially completed a period of intensive, in-depth study of the experience of Japanese management. The chief lesson that the Americans have drawn consists of recognizing the importance of the so-called "soft" component of management that is associated with an orientation toward personal social, psychological, and cultural traditions. In the United States today, people fully recognize the importance of providing incentives for quality and a nonmaterial motivation to work, of forming the values and principles of a corporation's activities, and of other methods of bringing the human factor into play.

Over a long period of time, problems were solved in American corporations by changing organizational management structures and the forms of financial control, and by shakeups in leadership. The Japanese, on the other hand, pay attention mainly to the style and methods of work, and the nature of interaction. Of course, they also reorganize management structures, but this is accomplished more smoothly.

I see the average Japanese firm as more centralized than the American. Its divisions, which specialize in production of various products, are more dependent on headquarters. That is indicated by the fact that a division of an American firm usually receives from headquarters estimates covering its various outlays, whereas a division in Japan receives a plan for its total list of products, its costs, its profits, its suppliers, and even its personnel. Of course, the plan is drawn up on the basis of input from the divisions, but headquarters approves it and sends it down.

In my view, one factor in the Japanese firm's greater centralization is the traditional weakness of theoretical research.

Tselichtshev: How is that?

Dynkin: The point is that the United States has a well-developed system for both the free and commercial transfer of the results of basic research from the universities and public research centers to private business. As yet, Japan has no such system, or almost none. Hence it is necessary for large companies to have strong research centers that do theoretical, as well as applied, work. This encourages centralization. In the United States it is easier to transfer research and development work to a company's divisions. And in general, divisions have broader rights in U.S. firms.

Tselichtshev: I recall my visit to Fuji Denki, a well-known electrical equipment company, and a candid talk with its managers. I asked, in particular, what the firm's executives saw as the main lines of reorganization aimed at stimulating scientific and technological progress and at putting technological innovations into production. The answer was unequivocal: drastically increase the divisions' independence and make them almost independent companies. That means, for example, that decisions in such areas as the structure of production (within the framework of established specialization) and investments, prices, marketing organization, relations with suppliers and customers, hiring blue-collar employees, and eventually, possibly even wages are to be made within the divisions. As for headquarters, it is expected to perform three extremely important functions: provide strategic planning (which naturally includes technological policy); serve as a financial center; and provide for training, advanced training, and assignment of highly skilled specialists.

But that is not all; the most interesting is yet to come.

At Fuji Denki I was told about research that the Mitsubishi Institute did on commission for the company. The question was put as follows. What system of organization best accords with the present conditions of scientific and technological progress: a centralized system with strong headquarters, or a decentralized system with strong divisions? And here are the results: the Japanese firms in the top international class, so to speak, that have shown the best performance have traditionally been firms with strong divisions and relatively weak headquarters. That includes Matsushita Denki, Toyota, Hitachi, and certain others.

Dynkin: And Honda, probably.

Tselichtshev: Honda, too. But the system of strong divisions with relatively weak headquarters is good when production is standardized and when the functions of each subdivision are defined in a more or less clear and straightforward fashion. In that case they work independently with a high degree of autonomy, and headquarters performs the role of a kind of holding company, or financial center. But when the time comes for a major investment decision on the level of the company as a whole, for some sort of changes in strategy, or for moving into new industries, the centralized system is preferable. Then headquarters needs to actively guide the company as a whole and actively intervene in the subdivisions' affairs, right down to the details. For example, Matsushita Denki was trying to break into the production of the latest data-processing equipment. It launched an "Action-1986" campaign, but it did not succeed in breaking into that field. I think this was largely because the company was unprepared to operate in a centralized fashion. What ideas do the results of the Mitsubishi Institute's research suggest? First of all, most likely, the idea that some sort of combination of the centralization and decentralization principles is needed. This idea may even seem banal. But the task of management at present is to find nonbanal ways to implement it. I thought one idea that was formulated in the course of a talk with Prof. Hiroyuki Itami of Hitotsubashi University was extremely interesting: the idea that there are waves of centralization and decentralization. Waves of decentralization, when the divisions work under conditions of considerable autonomy, within a set framework and a given specialization, for 10 to 12 years, say, should alternate with shorter periods of active and rather drastic centralization, when headquarters takes everything into its hands, actively intervenes in the divisions' work, tells them what to do and how to do it, and carries out certain strategic changes connected with the development of new production processes, product areas, and technologies on the level of the company as a whole. That is followed by a new wave of decentralization. In Japan, from every indication, that approach is gradually gaining acceptance. In short, decentralization as such, in and of itself, is no panacea. On the other hand, under present conditions the centralization principle is undergoing serious changes.

Dynkin: I would like to end this part of our discussion with the following generalization.

For now, it is understood that the divisions are satisfactorily coping with market risk, with economic risk, so to speak. But when you add innovations to the picture and an additional sort of risk arises—technological risk—that is when centralization is needed. That is probably the answer to the question of what is effective and when.

On the whole, I think that one can conclude that there has been a certain mutual enrichment of the Japanese and American approaches in both the theory and practice of management. With a view to the Japanese experience, in the United States the concepts of "rational management" and "organizational humanism," which were regarded for the past few decades as antithetical, are undergoing a rather agonizing process of synthesis. As a result, a new management strategy is being formed—entrepreneurship as a style of economic behavior. It is basically geared to traditional American sociopsychological values: dynamism, risk, and individualism. The Japanese are also borrowing American approaches, but they are substantially modifying them with reference to their own specific national features. In this regard I would like to discuss the organization and management of research and development.

The Japanese understand the danger of the scientist's anonymity, his attachment to the group, and group conformism. Their understanding of these problems is making them take countermeasures aimed at individualizing scientific creativity. I have in mind the program of research in promising technologies. Projects in this program are named for leading scientists. They invite specialists who are up to 35 years of age to take part in the projects. Half of the financial rights to patents that may arise in the course of carrying out a project will belong to its leaders.

Tselichtshev: It seems to me that there will be no radical venturing beyond the confines of group conformism. The provision of incentives for research activity is bound up primarily with a certain lifestyle, working conditions, the creative and intellectual content of work, the degree of independence in work, prestige, and opportunities for promotion. But no more than that. In my opinion, Japan isn't "threatened" with the emergence, to put it crudely, of rich researchers who will receive big money for their research and stand out sharply against the general background. The individual will be rewarded within the framework of a group. The results of his research and the profits and revenues it brings in will still be regarded, as they are now, as the property of the organization.

Dynkin: That is, you see definite limits to the development of the basic component of the country's research potential?

Tselichtshev: I think that the basic component will develop primarily within the framework of the group, and motivation will be mainly group motivation. T. Isomura, for example, says that at present even major basic ideas are the result of people working side by side within the framework of a large organization, and that trend will be borne out in Japan. That is, the individual will be rewarded within the framework of the group, and no further.

Dynkin: That, of course, is debatable. I often encountered the claim that the "not invented here"—that is, "not invented in Japan"— syndrome is very strong in the country. Japanese specialists often receive recognition by working abroad and creating a reputation for themselves there. I see yet another circumstance supporting your point of view. Japanese researchers, Masanori Moritani in particular, note that the present stage of scientific and technological progress accords with the proclivities of the Japanese. What they have in mind is the orientation toward miniature, elegantly made products. At the same time, according to this view, the growing importance of software in the economy demands individualization and an orientation toward certain nonmaterial factors. Such an orientation is not characteristic of Japan.

At the same time, it is very important that a certain consensus exists in the country regarding the need to activate the creative potential of the Japanese.

The traditional weakness of theoretical research in Japan is the most difficult problem for independent scientific and technological development. One of the ways cited for overcoming Japan's lag in the area of theoretical research is to enhance the social prestige of the Japanese theoretical scientist and reorganize the higher-education system in the direction of encouraging the development of students' creative abilities. Great hopes are being placed on new forms of borrowing the accomplishments of foreign research.

Japanese firms' numerous victories over American and West European competitors have forced the latter to change their attitude toward traditional means of transferring technology in the form of patents, licenses, and know-how. More and more often the Japanese are running into a tightening of access to scientific and technological developments abroad. In this connection they are making flanking maneuvers aimed primarily at obtaining basic research results. The most common maneuvers are to invite foreign scientists and specialists to work in Japanese research centers and give lectures, to finance and organize international research programs, and to finance research at American universities and small high-tech companies in exchange for the right to commercial use of the results obtained. A number of Japanese scholars believe that the internationalization of science involves primarily theoretical research, therefore making it more difficult at present for the United States and Western Europe to isolate Japan from access to scientific advances. On the whole, I am not inclined to assert categorically that in the foreseeable future, say over the next 15 to 20 years, Japan will be a second-rate power in terms of basic research.

Tselichtshev: No way. In this connection one can mention the "human frontiers" program that was recently made public, and a great deal more.

Dynkin: That is a very vivid example. Obviously, this program will become one of Japan's extremely important scientific and technological undertakings in the 1990s. In comparison to other major governmental programs, it is distinguished by its focus on theoretical and basic research, the involvement of practically all the key government departments, and its orientation toward extensive enlistment of foreign specialists in carrying it out. The nationwide and, possibly, international nature of the program allows one to compare it to the

Eureka program or the SDI. It has unquestionably a foreign-policy goal—to eliminate charges from the United States and other countries that Japan underfinances basic research but utilizes other countries' results. The economic goals are to create the research bases for developments in the areas of biotechnology, sixth-generation computers, new generations of robots, health care, and ecologically clean production processes, with a view to the 21st century.

Tselichtshev: Well, Aleksandr Aleksandrovich, the time has probably come to draw some conclusions, although I am afraid that we have raised more problems than we have found answers. Let me submit a conclusion for your judgment. Today scientific and technological progress is impossible anywhere without major changes in the organization of the economy. Japan is no exception. The ways to carry out this reorganization are not simple, and their consequences are ambiguous. Nonetheless, the Land of the Rising Sun provides many examples of effective adaptation to the current conditions of production, the market, and scientific and technological activity. Much of the Japanese experience of economic organization reflects the objective requirements for the growth of productive forces in an industrially developed country.

Dynkin: I agree. And I want to make a small addition. In the past 20 years Japan has made a great scientific and technological leap, gearing itself primarily to civilian production. The borrowing of foreign advances has not turned into the borrowing of foreign priorities or methods for implementing them. The Japanese principles for the organization of economic life cannot be viewed apart from the country's general social and cultural context and specific national features and traditions. That is one of the basic methodological principles for studying both the theoretical and practical aspects of Japanese management.

Part Three

The U.S.S.R. and CMEA in World Economy

Problems of Improving the Effectiveness of the U.S.S.R.'s Foreign Economic Relations

VIKTOR BORISOVICH SPANDARYAN AND
NIKOLAY PETROVICH SHMELEV*

The years of stagnation seriously distorted our foreign economic relations. Instead of being an effective instrument for promoting intensive economic development by extracting advantage from the international division of labor, they were used mainly as a means of reducing current and chronic national economic shortages.

As a result, efforts to radically eliminate existing imbalances dragged on and the shortages even increased due to bureaucratic pressure for imports (since the state was paying for it all). Accordingly, the development of foreign economic relations was defined mainly by import requirements, while exports were increasingly regarded merely as a means of paying for purchases, as a compulsory phenomenon, especially since enterprises gained virtually nothing from exports but additional worries. The rise in price of energy resources in the 1970s made it possible to restrict our exports (especially for freely convertible foreign currency) to two main products—oil and gas. The percentage of other export items, including machinery and equipment, declined, while many traditional goods ceased to be exported at all, increasingly emphasizing the "monoculture" aspect of our exports. Machinery and equipment exports declined from 23.6 percent in 1972 to 12.5 percent in 1984. In 1986 that figure rose to 15 percent, not from an increase in the physical volume of deliveries, but from the decline in the percentage of energy resources exported because of the drop in petroleum and gas prices. When it comes to the percentage of exports accounted for by machinery and equipment, a number of developing countries already surpass the U.S.S.R.

---

*Spandaryan is a candidate of economics and senior research associate at the U.S.S.R. Academy of Sciences' Institute for the United States and Canada; Shmelev is a doctor of economics and section head at the institute. This article appeared in the August 1988 issue of *MEMO*.

To a great extent foreign economic relations have ceased to serve the country's socioeconomic and political goals. They are in urgent need of a radical restructuring. This is precisely the object of the important decisions that have been taken to improve the U.S.S.R.'s foreign economic activity. Work in this area is continuing. A businesslike discussion of the prospects for developing foreign economic relations with an eye to our own experience and that of other countries should facilitate the implementation of these decisions.

Under current conditions, prospects for economic progress, not only of small countries but of the largest states, as well, are determined to an ever greater extent by their level of active participation in the international division of labor. Export of industrial goods and services has become a strong factor in the economic, scientific, and technical development of all developed capitalist states and, in the past 15 or 20 years, of the so-called newly industrialized countries, as well.

In capitalist economies increasing attention is being paid to development of foreign economic relations, including the factor of foreign competition (in both foreign and domestic markets) as a crucial catalyst for restructuring economic potential.

The increase in the "openness" and interdependence of national economies has virtually become a worldwide trend. Our country is still the least affected by this trend, however.

For decades we have underestimated one of the key functions of foreign trade, which is to compare national and world levels of production, national and world costs, and the scientific and technical sophistication of output. Meanwhile, the experience of leading industrial countries shows that this kind of comparative assessment through international competition is a necessary condition for dynamic scientific and technical progress.

Soviet industry has been largely removed from participation in world competition in both domestic and foreign markets. Many Soviet enterprises and economic managers are still virtually insulated from the realities of the modern world economy with its "iron law" that industrial potential and output must continually be improved (under threat of an economic "death penalty"). This predictably results in higher material and labor costs than in other developed countries, in an excessively energy-intensive economy, and in goods and services of poor quality. Remaining outside the competitive struggle with foreign producers (especially on the domestic market) seriously hampers scientific and technical progress in the economy. The reform of foreign activity now under way is meant to eliminate this artificially created defect in the Soviet economy and to ensure effective use of external factors of development.

Today the most important economic criterion for the efficiency of foreign economic activity is the extent to which these factors help to accomplish the main strategic economic objective—accelerating scientific and technical progress and elevating Soviet enterprises and associations to world standards in equipment, technology, and product quality. It is assumed that this will be achieved by restructuring the domestic economic mechanism, by developing direct ties with the CMEA countries, and by increasing cooperation with the West and with developing countries. But if the elements of the new economic mechanism developed thus far (including its foreign economic component) have achieved anything, it has been only to somewhat accelerate scientific and technical progress in the Soviet economy. They by no means guarantee that progress will rise to the highest world standards.

Indeed, one can hardly expect this to happen merely as a result of the universal spread of economic accountability, self-covering of costs and self-financing, or granting enterprises and associations the right of access (even unlimited access) to the foreign market. These are all necessary but not sufficient conditions to achieve solid status among world leaders in scientific and technical progress. It is just as incorrect to assume that, in order to solve the problem, it is enough to use the reform's principal present-day foreign economic methods—countless foreign-currency coefficients and foreign-currency entitlements. Moreover, the incentive effect of these economic levers depends on attaining a certain level of export, and that is precisely the central and most difficult problem of foreign economic activity.

Thus, it must be admitted that *economic levers* designed to achieve the strategic aim of raising the Soviet economy to the highest world standard are still not sufficiently developed. Attempts are still being made to compensate for missing elements of the economic mechanism with administrative methods (for example, passing resolutions that make the attainment of world standards of technology and quality in the production of machinery and equipment an absolute requirement). But these purely administrative decisions are basically part of the old, rejected management practices and can yield only limited results.

It seems that what must be done under current conditions is to define more clearly the ultimate goals of the foreign economic restructuring and the methods by which they can be achieved. It is apparent that the main guide for reform should be the guarantee that the Soviet economy is as open as it can be at any given time to the world market. That is the only way to make optimal use of the advantages of the international division of labor and the only possibility we have of gradually reaching world standards of production in a wide range of industries. Until Soviet enterprises are forced to gear themselves daily to the standards of the strongest foreign producers, it is economically unrealistic to expect our country to mass produce competitive products.

It is often thought that this function of outside stimulus can be performed by and large by the market of the CMEA, which, in implementing the Comprehensive Program for the Scientific and Technical Progress of the CMEA Member Countries, will increasingly approach the level of the world market. In the future this undoubtedly can and should happen. But at present the socialist commonwealth's market is characterized by low standards and by the often inferior technological level of goods exchanged. Under such conditions, excessive dependence on the limited potential of the CMEA market could prolong the current problems.

These statements do not mean that the success of the reform will depend entirely on the expansion of economic ties with the West. It is a question of creating an economic mechanism that will constantly weigh the production costs of Soviet producers against those of the best foreign (socialist and capitalist) producers.

To solve this problem, we think that, apart from making economic changes on the home front, it is also necessary to consistently implement a specific program for restructuring foreign economic activity that envisages effective economic incentives for exports, changes in the way exports are structured, creation of an optimal organizational system for foreign economic activity, extensive use of advanced forms of foreign economic relations, and other needed measures. In other words, it is a question of switching from a passive to an active stance, to an offensive policy in foreign economic relations, to a strategy for "breaking into" world markets that is in keeping with our economic, scientific, and technical potential.

The Development of Export Potential

The development of export potential is the basis of effective foreign economic activity and a guarantee of the country's economic security as it moves toward greater openness toward the external market. Foreign experience shows that the success of export activity is determined primarily by its specialization and the measures taken to provide incentives for it. In the first stage of economic restructuring— in other words, until foreign economic activity becomes a natural element of many enterprises' and associations' daily economic life— the responsibility for determining the most effective areas of export specialization and the appropriate incentives should probably be assumed by central economic agencies.

In the CPSU Central Committee and U.S.S.R. Council of Ministers' well-known resolution on improving the management of foreign economic relations, the drafting of a program for developing the country's export base is assigned to the U.S.S.R. Council of Ministers' State Foreign Economic Commission and the U.S.S.R. State Planning Committee, with the participation of standing bodies of the U.S.S.R. Council of Ministers and ministries and departments.

While implementing this program, which is of crucial importance to the fundamental restructuring of foreign economic relations, it is necessary to take resolute leave of the old, stereotyped methods, and especially the principle of allocating goods for export on a "residual" basis, and the deeply rooted view of export production as an ancillary function of economic development. This does not mean merely drawing up target figures for development of production of certain export goods for specified years. This has already been done, without visible success. It is important to put the export program on a sound material footing and to create, first and foremost, a variety of economic (and even nonmaterial) incentives for development of export production. This simply cannot be accomplished without investing substantial resources, drawing on the most advanced achievements of Soviet and foreign scientific and technical progress, enlisting the most highly trained personnel, and making skillful use of our country's natural advantages (for example, large-scale production of many types of machinery and equipment, industrial energy and raw-material self-sufficiency, the geographic factor).

The experience of many other countries shows that the development of export production is a powerful impetus to economic development, the growth of national income, and the effective utilization of advantages offered by the international division of labor, and that it repays the resources and efforts invested in it a hundredfold. In view of the size of our country's economy and its huge domestic market, we are not saying that the economy should be geared solely to exports. The point is to use exports as an accelerator of development and a dependable means of achieving advanced world standards.

It is clear that, for the foreseeable future, fuel and raw materials will continue to be an important part of our export industry—particularly in our relations with the CMEA countries and with a number of industrially developed capitalist states with which we have long-term agreements and joint projects. But it is no less clear that this "specialization" does not have long-term prospects.

The way to improve the structure of Soviet exports is to diversify them, to shift from the sale of raw materials to the sale of products processed from them, and to do everything possible to develop, and provide incentives for, the export of manufactured goods, especially machinery and equipment.

In developing the country's export base, we should not lose touch with reality and attempt to skip over successive stages through sheer willpower. It was stressed at the 27th Congress that "in posing the task of actively utilizing foreign economic activity to speed our development, we plan to restructure foreign trade step by step and to make exports and imports more effective."

Any radical change in the structure of our exports depends on implementation of a program for developing Soviet machine building. It is obvious that the interests of fundamentally restructuring the national economy and effectively developing the country's export base coincide. In order to achieve both objectives, a program for developing Soviet machine building should organically combine the satisfaction of domestic needs and exports. This offers the most reliable guarantee that Soviet machine building will attain the highest world standards. But this task is by no means simple.

The Soviet share of world exports of machinery and equipment has declined from 3.2 percent in 1970 to 2.1 percent in 1985. By way of comparison, the Federal Republic of Germany accounts for 14.8 percent; the United States, 16.5 percent; and Japan, 20.9 percent. To restore and strengthen the Soviet position, the rate of growth of our exports of machinery and equipment should, by the year 2000 at least, exceed that of world trade in these products by 50 to 100 percent.

All this again emphasizes the importance of developing Soviet machine building as a key strategic objective. There is vast potential for this in the development of specialization and cooperation, as well as in direct interbranch ties with the CMEA countries.

In our efforts to ensure Soviet manufacturing broad access to the world market, it is important, however, to remember that no one is waiting for us in this market, that the market is saturated, and that international trade is developing in the context of an intensifying competitive struggle. That is why any attempt by new Soviet exporters of manufactured goods to significantly expand exports or to enter the market will inevitably encounter competition, as well as trade and political barriers, from both developed capitalist countries and newly industrialized states that are actively entering the world market with their comparatively cheap products.

Under these conditions, the Soviet strategy for an export drive should proceed mainly from the clear-cut, economically substantiated selection of enterprises and industries that are capable of making sufficiently broad and sustained inroads in the world market. It is possible that initially they will be the same enterprises and industries that are currently being granted the right to conduct independent foreign economic activity. Obviously, it is also necessary to determine the export specialization of certain regions whose location and export potential are most favorable from a general economic standpoint (the Far East, Leningrad, and the Baltic republics, for example). In so doing, it must be kept in mind that the reverse side of export specialization is the mothballing or curtailment of certain secondary industries whose products are more profitably imported, primarily from socialist and developing countries. An effective customs policy should help to ensure export and import specialization. The customs tariff should make economically unjustifiable imports unattractive while encouraging import of goods that are more profitably imported, utilizing the advantages of the international division of labor. It makes sense to channel revenues from import duties mainly into the development of export industries.

The development of foreign economic relations (as well as any other sphere of economic activity) presupposes the concentration of financial, hard-currency, and material resources on priority areas, including capital investments in modernizing export industries and strengthening the necessary infrastructure (service facilities, stocks of spare parts, advertising, transport, communications, modern office equipment, and so forth).

An important condition for expanding exports is the implementation of effective incentive measures. Virtually all foreign countries, including the United States, the Common Market countries, and Japan, are implementing long-term special programs to provide the utmost assistance to national exporters by creating favorable trade, political, and economic conditions for them. Government agencies in these countries grant exporters various subsidies and preferential loans, give them tax breaks and insure exports (including insurance against losses resulting from inflation and fluctuations in currency exchange rates), try to maintain a rate of exchange for the national currency that favors exports, assist in the organization of exhibits and in sending and receiving trade delegations, supply economic and commercial information, and help them choose markets and partners. It is with these practices in mind that we must create equally favorable conditions for Soviet exporters and—as far as possible—even more favorable ones.

To this end, we think that it is above all necessary to establish an economically substantiated and uniform rate for converting the ruble into principal foreign currencies. Such a measure, which does not entail large material outlays, will sharply improve the effectiveness of our exports (in rubles) and economic organizations' interest in them. At the same time, it would be an additional means of keeping economically unjustified imports in check (the present rate does just the reverse by encouraging purchases abroad). A uniform rate would enable us to escape a situation (one that also threatens to get out of control) in which, due to the existence of virtually thousands of currency coefficients, almost every industry, and now essentially every type of product, has its own exchange rate. The question of introducing an economically based rate for converting the ruble into convertible currencies requires serious study, of course, but this must be done if we truly intend to put the advantages of the international division of labor to effective use. Establishment of an economically based rate for converting the ruble into foreign currency will also be an important prerequisite for the gradual transition of our economy (as the country's export potential increases) to ruble convertibility.

A very important step in this direction can and should be the switch to the convertibility of the so-called transferable ruble [the CMEA accounting currency—*Trans.*], which still plays the limited role of an accounting unit in relations between CMEA countries. The convertibility of the transferable ruble is a mandatory, indispensable condition for the deepening of economic integration and the introduction of direct ties and other advanced forms of bilateral and multilateral economic cooperation within the socialist commonwealth. We must finally realize that nothing will work without this. One cannot do violence to economic laws indefinitely. The administrative levers of integration are already worn out.

Second, we must obviously be bolder about granting foreign-currency loans to business organizations and we must grant them more widely, not only to create and develop export-industry facilities but to finance their activities in other areas having to do with development of foreign markets (such as advertising, customer service, the granting of credit to agent firms), as well as in cases where, in order to compete, they have to permit buyers to pay in installments or, in other words, grant so-called supplier credit.

Third, we think it is necessary to provide exporters, on preferential terms, with insurance against the risks in supplying under long-term export contracts, including losses from exchange rate fluctuations and inflation.

Fourth, it is necessary to grant additional tax privileges to organizations that export mainly machinery and equipment, finished goods, and services, particularly by increasing the funds that remain at their disposal (foreign-currency entitlements, for example, or bonus funds), and by accelerating depreciation allowances. In certain cases, where domestic prices are considerably higher than world prices, it is probably a good idea to provide government assistance to increase the competitiveness of items that are particularly important to the Soviet export industry. Such assistance should not be endless, however.

To provide effective aid to economic organizations that have been granted the right of direct access to foreign markets, it would make sense to create a single service for promoting exports. Considerable assistance could be given by the U.S.S.R. Chamber of Commerce and its branches in the republics and in major economic regions through consultation, sponsorship of seminars and courses, or organization of exhibits and fairs. The services of a consulting center operating under its direction could also be very helpful. In this connection, it is very important to step up efforts to gather, process, store, and distribute commercial information on markets, firms, and so forth. At present our exporters and importers must still constantly operate in the dark, without knowing anything about the market, especially when it comes to products of the machine building industry and other advanced industries.

One urgent task is to step up the activity of the foreign-trade firms being set up in union republics and to see that they quickly get local products onto foreign markets. This will promote the enlistment of additional export resources and help to better satisfy local demand with imports. In attempting the serious and difficult task of altering the structure of foreign trade and mobilizing all export sources, we must leave no stone unturned. This area could also be one of the channels through which the influence of world standards of quality spreads to every aspect of our daily lives.

At the same time, we must look the truth in the eye: Until we manage to establish a direct link between domestic and foreign prices and until we make the transition to a ruble that is at least partially (if not fully) exchangeable, all our attempts to radically invigorate the foreign economic sphere will be on very shaky ground. This applies to both foreign trade proper and to all new forms of cooperation (both within the CMEA and with our partners in the capitalist world). It is our firm belief that *the question of ruble convertibility is the crucial, central problem in the entire reform of our foreign economic system and, accordingly, in the entire matter of the Soviet economy's "openness."*

Organizational Restructuring of Foreign Economic Activity

The reform of the organizational structure of foreign economic activity has already encountered serious obstacles. Still evident, and often stronger than ever, is the arbitrary approach to the planning of exports, which hinders the search for optimal solutions. The difficulty of planning and keeping records on foreign economic activity is exacerbated by the sizable differences between domestic and foreign-trade prices. Dozens of enterprises that have won the right to enter the foreign market are hampered, in setting up their own foreign economic operation, by personnel problems and the problem of high costs that often are not justified by the relatively small amounts of goods exported. All this impedes development of foreign economic relations and leads to undermining established business relations with foreign partners, loss of the already modest Soviet gains in world exports of machinery and equipment, and sometimes even to direct foreign currency losses from incompetent and ill-considered deals.

There is no doubt that in the initial stage of reform certain costs are inevitable. But attempts to resolve conflicts by using administrative levers and drawing up hundreds and thousands of new normative rates and foreign-currency coefficients distorts the essence of the reforms outlined by the party and turns the right to operate on the foreign market and the resulting profits into an imposed and sometimes burdensome duty for many enterprises and associations.

Under these conditions, it is necessary to ensure the clear legal interpretation of the laws and resolutions that have been adopted. Enterprises' right to foreign economic activity *should be just that—a right—and not an obligation.* In accordance with the U.S.S.R. Law on the State Enterprise (Association), it should be universal and regarded as an integral part of full economic accountability. At the same time, the methods by which this fundamental provision is carried out can be varied and determined by the enterprises (associations) themselves on the basis of economic advisability. They include, for example, various forms of production cooperation, joint enterprises, the creation of one's own sales network, and the use of intermediaries.

An analysis of the types of enterprises that have won the right to operate on the foreign market shows that their output (tractors, excavators, automobiles, household refrigerators, universal machine-tools) is, by today's international standards, mostly average or poor from a technological standpoint and encounters keen competition on the foreign market from Western producers who have flooded the international channels through which such goods are marketed. Under these conditions it is hardly realistic to expect that the creation of our own foreign-trade firms will, in and of itself, lead to a substantial increase in the export potential of the majority of enterprises. At the same time, for many of them the costs of such reorganization are too high.

In a number of instances, it might be more effective, from an organizational standpoint, for producers to avoid creating many relatively small foreign-trade units and instead, to use the services of *major economically accountable foreign-trade associations* that have a universal product list and their own working capital. By centralizing import-export operations for a rather wide range of products, these intermediaries could have considerable influence on foreign-trade prices, lower the cost of commercial operations, handle the job of finding markets and advertising, and ensure effective presale preparation and postsale servicing. Economically accountable trade associations could also serve as intermediaries in finding partners for joint production, as well as perform other services. The system of organizing foreign economic activity through major, multipurpose trade firms has proven highly effective in Japan, which has become a leading power in world trade in a short time.

Foreign-trade intermediaries' relations with industrial enterprises should be built on the principles of full economic accountability, on an equal footing, and on a voluntary basis. With the transition to wholesale trade in the means of production, the concentration of purchases of certain types of goods would enable these foreign-trade brokers to put imported equipment on the domestic market as competitors of Soviet producers of such goods, creating a real counterbalance to the producer monopoly that still exists here. Unlike the current foreign-trade associations of the U.S.S.R. Ministry of Foreign Economic Relations and some other ministries and departments, these intermediaries in the form of economically accountable associations would not be strictly limited in their product list, but would offer a wide array of goods and services.

As an increasing number of enterprises, associations, or foreign-trade intermediaries enter the foreign market, it is necessary to reinforce the principle of centralization to protect national interests, determine a uniform, long-term trade policy, develop a contractual-legal basis for intergovernmental agreements and a system for monitoring their observance, ensure that the U.S.S.R. has a well-balanced trade and payments balance, provide incentives for exports and regulate imports, issue licenses for operations on the foreign market, and provide consulting services and advice on methods. These matters cannot be scattered among separate departments. They should be handled by the U.S.S.R. Ministry of Foreign Economic Relations.

The widespread entry of Soviet enterprises into the foreign market is impossible without the psychological restructuring of management personnel and a change in the way they assess the role and importance of foreign economic activity. It is time that we resolutely overcame the psychology of all-encompassing economic self-sufficiency as a good thing that justifies self-isolation and that is, in effect, the ideological reason for a Soviet economy "closed" to the influence of all world economy trends, including progressive ones. It is necessary to convince many economic managers that assertions such as "we aren't Singapore" belong to yesterday's international economic relations, that they really do need to copy from capitalists many of the methods used to operate in foreign markets, and that improper trade practices (expressed in the form of a failure to honor the terms of contracts and in attempts to blame one's own mistakes and shortcomings on the "machinations" of foreign suppliers and to accuse them of failing to deliver equipment that in fact has been lost or squandered) do not promote businesslike cooperation.

In view of the fact that the U.S.S.R. accounts for an extremely small percentage of the international division of labor, it is still difficult to count on being able to dictate to international business circles the conditions under which we will operate. Moreover, from the standpoint of Western firms, the Soviet market is largely closed and unpredictable at present, if only because they have not yet had direct access to it. Under these conditions, we apparently need (especially at first) not only to adopt many of the "rules of the game" that have become established in international trade, but to take certain other steps (tax, administrative, credit measures, and others) that would make our market sufficiently attractive to foreign partners from all groups of countries, including the CMEA countries.

Use of New Forms of Foreign Economic Relations

Modern-day international business cooperation is based on various forms of industrial, scientific, and technical cooperation.

In its economic content, cooperation is an intensive method of participation in the international division of labor. Unlike trade, which is based mainly on interbranch specialization of production, cooperative relations rely primarily on intrabranch specialization. "And this specialization," said Lenin, "is by its very nature endless—just like the development of technology."[1]

In relations with both the CMEA and the West, cooperation creates a considerably broader base for economic cooperation than do trade relations. This is where, even in the near future, we can expect tangible results in achieving objectives such as:

• assimilating advanced methods of organizing and managing production and improving the quality and competitiveness of output;

• attracting needed investments in the form of advanced technologies, machinery, and equipment;

• reducing the time needed for industry to adopt technical innovations;

• producing goods important to the national economy that are still being imported;

• acquiring foreign currency through the development of exports of manufactured goods, especially machinery and equipment;

---

[1]V.I. Lenin, *Collected Works* [*Polnoye sobraniye sochineniy*], Vol. 1, p. 95.

● utilizing foreign partners' marketing network and mastering modern marketing methods;

● obtaining regular information on trends in the development of foreign production.

The realization of this potential does not require large material, labor, or foreign-currency outlays. But it does require an effective system of tax, credit, customs-tariff, and other advantages that would encourage Soviet enterprises to engage actively in cooperative production with foreign partners.

Many forms of cooperative relations with foreign firms have been rather well proven in socialist countries and have produced positive results on the whole. Their experience shows that the most effective forms of international industrial cooperation are, as a rule, those based on direct production relations between partners. In this way their interests coincide to the greatest possible degree and they can establish close cooperation, particularly in the continuous improvement of production technology and updating of products. In this connection, it would be a good idea to pay special attention to certain types of production cooperation, such as:

Joint production on the basis of specialization that provides for exchange of specific aggregates and assemblies with the subsequent assembly of finished items at enterprises of either one or both cooperatives. The list of goods that the partners are to supply one another is usually stipulated for each side in a contract that defines the terms of deliveries, sales of output on the foreign market and financial settlements with one another, as well as ways of continuously improving the production process and the quality of output. This form of cooperation is already being used effectively in branches of the machine-building complex including machine tool and automotive production, the production of road-building equipment, production farm machinery, and equipment for light industry, the food industry and the service sphere.

Scientific-technical and production cooperation that encompasses the entire production cycle—from research and development to actual production and sales. The combination of partners' scientific and technical, production, and marketing potential with the opportunity for each of them to concentrate on a narrower product mix with a view to their production experience and the specific features of the production equipment being used makes it possible, in a short time and with fewer outlays, to develop and begin production of new, technically sophisticated items, effectively expand the volume of production and exports, and jointly work on the continuous improvement and modernization of products. This form of cooperation guarantees the greatest profits in such high-tech areas as electronics, instrument making, the aerospace industry, high-precision chemical engineering industries, and the tool industry.

Cooperation on the basis of unutilized Soviet inventions and designs—an area that our foreign partners are showing great interest in—could become one of the most promising areas of research and production cooperation. It was noted at the 27th CPSU Congress that the U.S.S.R. Academy of Sciences has 300 major development projects that have never been used in industry. To these one might add thousands of other inventions that go unused every year. Actively utilizing this resource, which at present is essentially worthless, as our side's contribution to a cooperative arrangement with foreign partners for rapid, joint industrial mastery and subsequent sale of new products on the world market could yield solid results in production and in foreign-currency earnings.

Joint enterprises that use foreign capital could play a significant role in the development of foreign economic relations. It has already been a year and a half since the decision was made public on the procedure for the creation and operation in the U.S.S.R. of joint enterprises with the participation of foreign partners. Despite the interest shown by many representatives of foreign business circles, however, the practical implementation of this new and important undertaking is proceeding rather slowly. So far only a few dozen joint enterprises have been created, and their viability has yet to be proven in practice. (By comparison, the People's Republic of China has over 10,000 joint enterprises that represent a total of nearly $9 billion in foreign investments.)

We must be aware that the foreign partner's main interest in creating joint enterprises in the U.S.S.R. is to gain broad access to the vast and growing Soviet market, with the expectation of earning and taking home, without restrictions, its profits (which must be at least as great as the profits it makes in its own country or in third countries from the operation of similar enterprises).

We are gearing the activity of joint enterprises to the foreign market (the development of the export base) and are giving our foreign partner, for all practical purposes, just one real way of getting its share of the profits—out of earnings from the sale of goods and services (once again, on the foreign market) and also (so far only in isolated cases) out of foreign-currency savings from the replacement of imports, or in other words, out of reductions in the foreign firms' share of the Soviet market. Of course, this stems from such fundamental causes as the nonconvertibility of the ruble, the gap between our domestic prices and world prices, and the rigid system of supply and distribution that still prevails in our country). Under these conditions, joint enterprises created on Soviet territory are essentially extraterritorial economic units, since they do not have direct access to the Soviet market in either the sales or purchase of goods and services. It is clear that the genuine development of joint enterprises' activity and their organic inclusion in the Soviet Union's economic turnover are possible only through an intensification of the economic reform in our country. Moreover, it is then that joint enterprises will bring to our economy the element of competitiveness that is so badly needed.

When joint enterprises are set up in any country, without exception (capitalist, developing, or socialist), the same legal models (forms) are used. The overwhelming majority are joint-stock companies or companies with limited liability, whose advantage lies in the fact that participants' liability is limited to their contribution to the joint enterprise's capital. The aforementioned legal models are carefully regulated in every detail by the laws governing joint-stock companies. The violation of these laws entails serious consequences, including even criminal penalties.

The joint enterprises created in our country are not joint-stock companies, even though this is the most understandable, suitable, and flexible model for enterprises of this type. Today, when our country is seriously considering the prospects for the broad introduction of the joint-stock type of enterprise, it makes even greater sense to extend it to joint enterprises that have foreign partners.

The Soviet Union has no law on joint-stock companies as yet. The 1927 statute on joint companies was repealed in 1962, and the Jan. 13, 1987, resolution contains neither provisions on the two aforementioned models nor the norms that would define the legal status of joint enterprises, and limits itself to stating that joint enterprises are legal entities under Soviet law. In fact, it appears that joint enterprises should be a separate subject under Soviet law. A paradoxical situation has arisen—the legal status of the state enterprise is defined by law, but the legal status of the enterprise that uses foreign capital is undefined. Therefore it is necessary to draw up a normative act on joint-stock companies and companies with limited liability.

The array of problems that arise during the organization of joint enterprises does not disappear with the drafting of a law on what legal forms they may take. Foreign capital and a foreign partner-investor participate in the joint enterprise. Its legal status is also in need of regulation. The terms of investment for foreign companies differ from country to country. The developed countries encourage foreign investments with almost no restrictions. The developing states have adopted investment codes that define the terms of access of foreign capital, the spheres of its application, and the advantages and guarantees granted to the foreign investor.

Such a law is needed in the Soviet Union, as well. We believe that in this respect, as well, it would be useful to familiarize ourselves with the regulation of foreign investments abroad. Among other things, it would be a good idea to provide several sets of regulations for foreign investors that would be applied depending on our interest in specific investments, their size, and so on. The spheres of application of foreign capital should also be defined. Many things are still unclear with regard to the personnel of a joint enterprise and the terms of their employment and dismissal, their salaries, and so forth. The stipulation that all executive positions at joint enterprises must be occupied by Soviet citizens is too rigid.

It should be noted that current legal regulations, while permitting the creation of joint enterprises in the U.S.S.R., at the same time contain a series of restrictive, if not prohibitive, provisions concerning their operation. [A number of changes pertaining to joint ventures were made by the U.S.S.R. Council of Ministers in December 1988—Trans.]

One obstacle, in particular, is the unconditional requirement that the Soviet side retain no less than 51 percent of the joint enterprise's capital. Considering that most of the value of a modern plant's fixed assets is comprised of technology and equipment that, under the terms of many negotiations currently under way, are the foreign partner's contribution, our share cannot be provided at the aforementioned level primarily through the construction of buildings and other structures and through the allocation of land and other natural resources. In fact, ready cash must be found to balance the amount of capital contributed by the other contracting party. This provision has an especially tangible effect on the possibilities for cooperation in machine-building industries, i.e., precisely where cooperation is most productive and desirable from the standpoint of our economic interests.

It should be noted that the laws in a number of socialist countries permit, when necessary, an increase in the foreign partner's percentage of joint enterprises' basic capital.

Controlling the quality of the output produced by the joint enterprise is considered a difficult problem by Western firms. Foreign business circles—and not without reason—express their doubts about the effectiveness of our system of quality control and the possibility of applying the international standards that have been adopted. It is not clear how basic Soviet laws on labor and wages should be applied to the work of joint enterprises. By the way, these laws, like statutes on the protection of Soviet workers' social rights, are unknown to the absolute majority of potential Western partners, and their superficial interpretation is based on the stereotype created by the Western media.

If we truly wish to develop such new forms of foreign economic cooperation as joint enterprises, we need to ensure appropriate economic and legal conditions for that purpose. In this connection, it is very important to create an atmosphere in which the decisions taken in the sphere of foreign economic activity are irreversible, especially in regard to the operation of joint enterprises. This can be accomplished by concluding:

• bilateral agreements with foreign states on mutual guarantees for the return of invested capital in the event of nationalization or other changes in the political or economic situation in one of the contracting countries;

• bilateral intergovernmental agreements on the procedure for taxing the profits of joint enterprises so as to avoid double taxation.

The fact that the personnel of our business organizations are so poorly prepared for foreign economic activity in general and for work with foreign partners on joint enterprises in particular is a serious problem. The lack of experience in such work; the negative mental conditioning resulting from the fact that for so many years questions having to do with foreign economic activity, as the domain of a narrow circle of specialists, were virtually "taboo" for the middle-level industrial managers; the system of management by directive that was cultivated for decades; and the executive's total material dependence, with no alternative, on a higher organization have produced a manager who has neither the desire nor the right to take risks.

Many representatives of foreign business circles believe that in most cases Soviet organizations are negotiating in a lackluster fashion that lacks initiative and professionalism, often changing their positions for no reason and shifting responsibility onto a higher organization. All this creates the impression that the Soviet side is reluctant to work toward practical results and is impeding the development of foreign economic cooperation.

This lends special urgency to the question of stepping up the foreign economic training of specialists and managers, including preparation for work in joint enterprises, and not only by training people here, but by sending them abroad and recruiting skilled foreign specialists to come to the U.S.S.R. The decision on training personnel for foreign-economic ventures opens up serious possibilities in this area.

Foreign experience leads us to conclude that it makes sense to study and use such organizational models as the *free trade zone*, which are meant to increase foreign firms' initiative in the production of goods and services, in trade and in other types of activity on Soviet territory. The production and assembly of products using foreign equipment and materials and Soviet electric power, raw materials, and manpower could be organized in such zones. Subsequent export of the finished product would make it possible to earn additional foreign currency income. Moreover, foreign firms might be interested in using free trade zones for the duty-free storage (until sale) of their products; the exhibition of their products in special facilities in the zones; and the presale preparation and subsequent servicing of output.

In world practice, free trade zones—which are located, as a rule, near sea ports, river ports and airports, at the intersection of transportation arteries, and in border zones—ensure exporters a number of advantages. Among other things, their goods in the zones can be stockpiled, stored, destroyed, transshipped, and re-exported without the imposition of customs duties. Moreover, the shipment of substandard goods is permitted, as is the above-quota importation of goods into the zone. No customs duty is imposed in the zone for losses from shrinkage, evaporation, leakage, defects, or errors in accounting. Within the zones one may carry out drying, sorting, mixing, and other such operations, making it possible to bring goods up to standards that qualify them for lower customs duties. The demands of the local market and buyers' tastes can be taken into account during processing. The use of free trade zones makes it possible to reduce the time between order and delivery, to reduce transportation costs as well, since the product can be delivered in bulk and subsequently assembled and packaged in the zone. It is also possible to avoid increases in the amount of duty caused by changes in the rate of exchange for foreign currency.

The stated advantages of free trade zones show the advisability of their active use in both the import and export activity of the U.S.S.R. and other CMEA countries. So far only Bulgaria (in July 1987) has adopted a decree on the creation of such zones in that country. Meanwhile, the United States, for example, has over 120 free trade zones, whose turnover is constantly growing. Recently free trade zones have been attracting foreign investors who are interested in building industrial enterprises in the vicinity. At the present stage of economic reform, such zones could become ideal proving grounds for trying out joint enterprises that are specially geared to exports.

The idea of *special economic zones* is also promising, in our view. By using such zones, China, in particular, has succeeded—in a comparatively short time—in attracting substantial direct foreign capital investments. Generally speaking, these zones operate successfully because of their special allure for foreign firms—minimal taxes, advantageous loan rates, and a guaranteed supply (in some cases at preferential rates) of power, raw and other materials, and skilled manpower. All this in exchange for freely convertible foreign currency, of course. Such terms ensure a rapid influx of foreign capital.

Special economic zones can help accomplish such economic objectives as mastery of modern methods of industrial management, development of the production of high-quality goods, accelerated economic development of certain areas, and an increase in foreign-currency income. It seems to us that special economic zones, or "economic confidence-building zones," could be set up in various areas of our country (the Baltic republics, the Black Sea coast, the Far East) and in the future perhaps also in interior regions, and become not only a suitable and mutually advantageous form of cooperation and a powerful stimulus to socialist countries' economic integration, but a factor in the continued improvement of political relations with developed capitalist countries.

Finally, a few words about our credit policy. The attraction of foreign resources is a necessary factor in the modernization of the economic potential of the majority of the world's countries, and the United States is no exception. Unfortunately, it is still thought here that the use of foreign loans is something extraordinary, and needed mainly because of failures in economic policy. This attitude is based on the experience gained from borrowing abroad in the 1970s, when, as a result of mistakes and miscalculations, the borrowed money often failed to produce the necessary results, or in other words, was actually eaten up.

If this state of affairs continues, it will hamper the implementation of long-overdue economic reforms for want of the needed domestic resources for this purpose. It will also inevitably mean continued emphasis on raw materials in our exports and even greater isolation from the main trends in international economic cooperation and from the incentives for scientific and technical progress that it provides.

The profound, qualitative changes now occurring in our economy justify the efforts to obtain funds on international credit markets provided, of course, that such money is used effectively, and provided the debtor's credit-worthiness meets accepted criteria in international practice. Our credit-worthiness is quite solid in international financial markets. This was proven, in particular, when Soviet bonds were successfully offered in Switzerland recently. A possible increase in the Soviet Union's borrowing is perceived in Western financial circles as something completely natural at a stage in which all aspects of economic life are being significantly restructured.

Until now we have also underestimated the great potential of Soviet banking institutions abroad. Expansion of their operations and the fuller and more effective use of modern international financial practices could help not only to reduce our real indebtedness but to postpone its repayment painlessly.

It goes without saying that the bulk of the money borrowed over the long term should be channeled into the purchase of modern imported equipment so as to organize production in machine building and other promising industries that is up to world standards and geared to both the domestic and foreign markets. If such a move is to make economic sense, the borrowed money must be used with the utmost effectiveness. For example, in borrowing foreign capital in the 1980s, the United States paid its foreign creditors interest at the market rate of 8 to 10 percent per annum, while the return on the capital invested in the American economy was 15 to 20 percent.

There is no doubt that what we need more than anything else is a real guarantee that the loans will be used effectively, a guarantee that our economic mechanism is still unable to provide. Therefore, it would be a good idea to first attract additional credit resources mainly within the limits of scientific and technical and production cooperation with Western partners for the financing of joint projects. In so doing, perhaps we should abandon our do-or-die efforts to obtain loans at below-market rates. As a rule, this "cheap" money actually costs us very dearly as a result of the overstated prices of the goods purchased with it. Incidentally, these long-term loans could eventually (given the necessary effort on our part) be transformed into stocks and bonds of the joint enterprises. This is already becoming a widespread international practice, and there is no reason we should not take advantage of it.

The trends of the past few years also warrant the switch from a passive to an active policy on world trade, and on the foreign currency and financial system and its chief institutions. Here we must also overcome certain stereotypes that have long existed both in our country and in the West. "We take a positive view of the General Agreement on Tariffs and Trade. The Soviet government is prepared to continue the process of conforming increasingly to the agreement, with the aim of full membership as the end result," said V. Kamentsev, Chairman of the U.S.S.R. Council of Ministers' State Foreign Economic Commission.[2] Things are more complicated in regard to the International Monetary Fund and the International Bank for Reconstruction and Development [World Bank], however. But it appears that here too positive international trends must eventually prevail. Socialist countries are full-fledged members of the international community, and without their active participation, the resolution of any economic problem of a global nature would ultimately be impossible. And the foreign currency-finance question is just such a problem.

---

[2]*Kommunist* [*Communist*], No. 15, 1987, p. 34.

National or collective economic self-isolation is no more possible today than is the policy of imposing an economic blockade for any period of time. The domestic and foreign aspects of the Soviet Union's economic restructuring should be organically interrelated. And restructuring cannot be totally successful until our country can achieve a status in the world economy that is in keeping with its real industrial, scientific, technical, and human potential and with its political weight in the world.

Socialism: Choice of World Economic Strategy

ALEKSEY VLADIMIROVICH KUNITSIN*

The scientific and technological revolution marks the transition from the extensive type (primarily across industry lines) to the intensive type (primarily within individual industries) of internationalization of production. Unquestionably, this process, which is essentially just getting under way, will have far-reaching economic and political consequences and affect the fundamental interests of socialism. Changes in the conditions of production are already radically changing the criteria for economic performance and reorienting producers from a national to an international value that reflects the most advanced world level of the technical outfitting and organization of labor. The role of the external factors of economic development—foreign competition, the international division of labor, cooperative production arrangements—is increasing. At the same time the costs of "independence" from the world market are rising; such independence puts the national economy in objectively worse conditions and ultimately leads to its reverse—economic and technical dependence.

In comparison to most regions of the world, the socialist countries remain, to a considerable degree, an isolated part of the world economy and do not experience the full force of international competition. The negative consequences of the "hothouse" model of development are fully manifested in the increased materials- and labor-intensiveness of production, and the poor quality of products and services. The lack of sufficient economic competition results in shortages of goods and has a ruinous effect on scientific and technological progress in the socialist countries.

The improvement of the international situation is contributing to greater openness to the world economy among the socialist countries. However, movement in this direction depends on the solution of complex problems. Central among them is the problem of economic

*Candidate of economics and senior research associate at the U.S.S.R. Academy of Sciences' Institute for the United States and Canada. This article appeared in the January 1989 issue of *MEMO*.

security, the essence of which lies in determining the optimal conditions for interaction with the world capitalist economy.[1] Given the existing gap between the levels of productive forces in the East and the West, there continues to be a real danger that, increasingly, socialist countries will become technologically and financially dependent on the capitalist "power centers," and that the world socialist economy will turn into a periphery of the Western economy. Under these conditions, working out a balanced world economic strategy emerges as an important scientific and practical task.

I.

The basis of the changes taking place in the world economy is the transformation of national value (production price) into international value. As we know, there are certain differences between the mechanism by which the law of value operates in the world market and that by which it operates in the internal market of a goods-producing country. Karl Marx pointed out three modifications of the law of value in international exchange: "more intensive national labor, in comparison to less intensive national labor produces, at a time when all else is equal, greater value . . .";[2] "more productive national labor is also taken into account as more intensive labor . . .";[3] and "the work days of different countries may relate to one another as skilled, complex labor relates to unskilled, simple labor within a single country."[4] As a result, "a country that finds itself in favorable conditions receives, in an exchange, more labor for a smaller quantity of labor. . . ."[5]

The specific features of the operation of the law of value in the world market appear outwardly as a consequence of limited possibilities for international migration of production factors—labor and capital. In reality, however, the ultimate reason for modifications in

---

[1]At the present time, for example, 24 million types of products are produced in the U.S.S.R., and a significant number of them are directly or indirectly linked to imports. As the country experiences economic, scientific, and technological development, the import component of national reproduction rises in both absolute and relative terms. The aggregate list of products produced also expands. Under these conditions, improving competitiveness and increasing the export of goods and services that provide the necessary foreign-currency resources for imports become increasingly important prerequisites for the uninterrupted functioning of the national economy. The inability to guarantee the proper level of export income (for example, in the case of a sharp change in world economic conditions, as happened in 1986 with respect to deliveries of Soviet energy resources to the West) may result in the disturbance of reproduction connections and, in the event that exports become chronically uncompetitive, in paralysis of the national economy. On the whole, the essence of the concept of "economic security" can be defined as the maintenance of a level and structure of national production that make it possible for it to adapt to changing world economic conditions without the danger of developing long-term, one-sided dependence on external resources for economic development.

[2]K. Marx and F. Engels, *Works* [*Sochineniya*], Vol. 23, p. 571.

[3]*Ibid.*

[4]K. Marx and F. Engels, *Works*, Vol. 26, Part III, pp. 104-105.

[5]K. Marx and F. Engels, *Works*, Vol. 25, Part I, p. 261.

the law of value lies in different production conditions among countries, especially in the development of productive forces, which determine different possibilities for the redistribution of resources among
branches and within branches of the economy under the influence of
world competition. When the redistribution of resources is more
difficult, the difference in production conditions becomes a source of
differences between national and international value, and the regulating influence of the latter on national production is limited by the
framework of foreign economic relations.

The drastic change in means of production brought about by the
scientific and technological revolution is changing the mechanism for
the formation of international value, the substance of which continues
to be the socially necessary abstract labor expended on the manufacture of a given product under world-average, socially normal production conditions, with a world-average level of productivity and
intensiveness. As long as technological progress takes place in an
evolutionary fashion, international value is formed on the basis of the
average expenditures of work time of the bulk of world goods producers. But when revolutionary changes in the development of the
means of production take place that raise labor productivity many
times—sometimes tens or hundreds of times—over (something that
happens initially in one country or several countries), that not only
reduces the world-average socially necessary expenditures of labor,
but also changes the world-average production conditions and the
world-average level of labor productivity and intensiveness. World-
average conditions approach the national production conditions of the
country or group of countries that have made a breakthrough in a given
area.

Until a technical innovation becomes widely adopted, the international value of a product is formed primarily on the basis of its
national value in the group of leading countries. Thus, any major
change in production technology depreciates expenditures of social
labor in the countries that lag behind in using it. That, in turn, is
directly reflected in the international economic position of those
countries.

Under present conditions, the revolutionary renewal of the
means of production has assumed a mass scale. New technologies affect
a wide range of industries and are continuously developing, making
continuous changes in world-average production conditions. While it
is national in form, the development of productive forces is becoming
international in content, since it relies on the totality of worldwide
scientific and technological advances and is set in motion by international competition. An increasingly significant portion of productive
forces is losing its national identity and taking on international forms of

ownership, organization, and management. Technological progress is removing obstacles to the intrabranch and interbranch redistribution of resources within national borders and between countries under the influence of world competition, accelerating the process of turning national value into international value.

The widening sphere of international competition is leading to an even more dynamic growth in the mass of goods and services whose value reflects not national but world production conditions and gravitates toward expenditures of social labor in countries with higher labor productivity. Expansion of international value is realized not only directly—through exchange value—but also indirectly—through consumer value that reflects the level of national production. Thus, both goods participating in international exchange and goods intended exclusively for internal use are being drawn into the sphere where international value mechanisms operate.[6] The intensity of international influence on the national economy increases accordingly.

Turning national value into international value fundamentally changes the conditions of economic operation. In the internal markets of many countries, especially the most developed countries, exchange proportions for an increasing range of goods are no longer determined by the national production price (production costs plus profit), but by the international price, which reflects the most advanced level of equipment, technology, and labor organization. This forces producers with higher individual costs, under the threat of financial failure, to raise production to the world level or seek other areas to apply their capital. As a result, the structure of the national economy is improved, and the productivity of social labor rises.

Washing out uncompetitive industries and types of production from national economies intensifies the international division of labor, which, in turn, improves the efficiency of national production. The international division of labor means the division of production conditions among countries, the specialization of countries in the production of a certain array of goods, and consequently, the need for complementary economies. The growing interconnection and interdependence among national economies are reinforcing the unity of the world economy.

---

[6]The mechanism for the transfer of international value criteria to a national economy through consumer value is as follows: A country that produces products for internal use that are inferior to comparable foreign products in consumer properties (quality, productivity, economy, reliability, ergonomic properties, environmental impact, weight, size, and possibly even aesthetics) is also more wasteful in its national expenditures of social labor, including expenditures in the production of export goods. The imported equivalent of such an export that reflects more efficient international production conditions represents a smaller amount of socially necessary labor and brings about a reduction of national value to the level of international value. Quite understandably, this mechanism begins to play a significant role only when a country's economy has become sufficiently involved in world economic relations.

Countries that for whatever reasons limit their participation in this process end up in a disadvantageous position. Because their producers are more oriented toward the national production price (rather than the international price), these countries, through the value mechanisms that have been considered, lag behind economically and technologically, and this weakens their international positions.

II.

The new world economic conditions are making more stringent demands on states' economic policies. The dialectics of the objective and the subjective in economics were once studied in depth by Engels. His observation that "the reciprocal action of governmental authority on economic development can be threefold in nature. It can act in the same direction—then development goes faster; it can act against economic development—then . . . it will suffer failure after a certain period of time; or it can erect barriers to economic development in certain areas and encourage it in other areas. This case ultimately leads to one of the first two. However, it is clear that in the second and third cases the political authority can cause the greatest harm to economic development and bring about a massive squandering of manpower and materials."[7]

The problem of coordinating politics and economics is especially urgent for the U.S.S.R. and other socialist countries, whose national economies are still predominantly closed in nature and for the most part operate in isolation from the world economy. Nearly three fifths of all national income today is created in the developed capitalist countries, which are leaders in most branches of scientific and technological progress. Seven or eight of the leading capitalist countries account for about four fifths of the sales of "working" technologies (actually embodied in equipment) and nine tenths of world license exports. That means that production conditions in the Western countries exert a determining influence on the formation of international value and production price. To the extent that a direct comparison between national and international value takes place in the process of exchange, the degree of stimulating influence that international value exerts on the development of a national economy proves to be directly dependent on the scale of economic interaction with the world capitalist market.

The intensiveness of economic relations of the U.S.S.R. and other socialist countries with the capitalist economy is substantially lower than the world average. Thus, Western imports account for an average of about 3 percent of the socialist countries' gross domestic product (in

---

[7]K. Marx and F. Engels, *Works*, Vol. 37, p. 417.

Hungary and, especially, Yugoslavia, this figure is considerably higher). For comparison, in the nonsocialist countries the analogous figure is about 11 percent, including 10.8 percent in the developed capitalist countries and 11.9 percent in the developing countries. For individual countries and regions, deviations from the average figures are rather substantial: The figure is 7.8 percent for the United States, 9.6 percent for Japan, 22.2 percent for the European Community, and 31.5 percent for the European Free Trade Association.[8] In this connection, the fact that their internal markets are also part of the world capitalist economy must be taken into account. Moreover, services account for an extremely high proportion of the developed capitalist countries' GNP (in the United States, about half); accordingly, the dependence of material production on imports in such countries is usually about twice as high as the figure given for the economy as a whole.

Although it is not an exhaustive index, a comparison of the proportion of Western imports in the gross domestic products of various groups of countries nonetheless makes it possible to fairly adequately evaluate the comparative intensiveness of the influence of international value on their economies. According to the author's calculations, the intensiveness of that influence in the socialist countries is approximately only one fifth to one tenth as high as in the other industrial countries (that is also indicated by the figures cited above). The missing economic stimuli must be compensated for in some fashion, otherwise the countries that lack them inevitably find themselves with inferior conditions for economic operations, which also inevitably results in their lagging behind.

Traditionally it has been believed that the socialist countries' lack of forced regulation of national production through world competition could be indirectly compensated for by means of special-purpose planning, socialist economic integration, and improvement of internal economic mechanisms. How correct is that approach?

Special-purpose planning organizes production for the attainment of the most advanced world levels in critical areas. It presupposes a balance between production programs, on the one hand, and material and labor resources, on the other, and coordination with the development of related industries. However, as experience shows, comprehensive balance in special-purpose plans can be achieved only for an extremely narrow set of objectives, usually having to do with the development of individual production processes.

---

[8]Calculated on the basis of *MEMO*, No. 6, 1986, p. 151, and No. 11, 1987, pp. 148-149; and *OECD Monthly Statistics of Foreign Trade*, Aug. 1987.

At the level of an entire economic branch, it is immeasurably more complicated to solve the problem of balancing plans, since it requires providing for changes in tens, even hundreds, of related production processes. And that, in turn, presupposes adjustments in the production programs of second-level and third-level suppliers, and so forth. As a result, the fulfillment of even a relatively narrow special-purpose program requires coordinating the production of tens of thousands of types of output, which is practically impossible. Moreover, any single breakdown in fulfillment of the program causes disorder throughout the production chain and requires an additional adjustment in plans. Therefore, it is obvious that the mechanism of special-purpose planning does not make it possible to attain the world production level in even a moderately wide range of economic branches, much less the economy as a whole.[9]

The stimulating effect of socialist economic integration has objective limits determined by national production conditions in the countries involved in integration. To the extent to which they are inferior to world-average socially normal production conditions, "integrated" national value differs from international value. Exchange proportions established on its basis prove less effective than exchange proportions determined by the world market. And their regulating function with respect to technical progress and the structure of production is correspondingly weaker. Thus, integration, by itself, is incapable of eliminating the existing gap between the level of production in the integrated countries and world-average socially normal production conditions.

As for improving the internal economic mechanisms of the CMEA countries, that is an essential but also insufficient condition for attaining the world production level. Current trends in the development of productive forces presuppose decentralization of management, democratization of economic operations, and flexible organizational forms. The adaptation of the economic mechanism to new demands is reducing expenditures of social labor, and improving the structure and technical level of production. However, as long as the consumer cannot choose freely between domestic and foreign goods, national producers will remain oriented toward the national production price.[10]

---

[9]In light of what has been said, the fact that many Western countries have made successful and fairly wide use of special-purpose programs may seem paradoxical. One must consider, however, that these programs rely on a more developed spectrum of related economic branches (both within the national framework, and on the scale of the world economy), and on the existence of reserve capacity, raw materials, and manpower. That makes it possible to plan only the key objectives and indices, leaving it to the market to take care of maintaining an ongoing balance in production. The socialist countries' access to such resources is limited because of the insufficient competitiveness of their exports.

[10]It is legitimate to ask how strongly, in general, value levers and stimuli have been set in motion in the national economies of the socialist countries and, especially, the U.S.S.R. On this subject, one can say that the centralized planning and distribution of resources substantially alter

Because of the economic laws described above, that price inevitably will be inferior to the international production price, which reflects a higher level of efficiency. Understandably, under such conditions the world level will not be reached.

"To be as modern—that is, competitive in quality and efficiency— as our global competition requires," the American economist J. Hardt quite rightly notes, "industrial nations must be open to the best and the cheapest products regardless of where they orginate. In a technologically changing world, the costs of adjustment and restructuring are substantial. However, the costs of closing one's economy are even greater . . . . Judging from the experience of advanced industrial countries, in order to modernize effectively, not only domestic restructuring but international interdependence is necessary."[11]

Thus, the general conclusion is that attaining the most advanced world levels of production efficiency is impossible without a constant comparison of national and international value through competition with the goods of the developed capitalist countries. The broader the dimensions of such competition, the stronger the stimulus exerted by higher world criteria of efficiency on the development of national production. For the U.S.S.R. and other socialist countries, this means that the problem of opening their economies to the world economy must be solved without delay.

III.

Movement toward world-economic openness presupposes improving the competitiveness of socialist countries' goods in the world market. However, the present state of their productive forces makes that task difficult to accomplish. Thus, in the U.S.S.R. more than half of the machining equipment is more than 10 years old. Yet specialists claim that the equipment becomes obsolete after eight years of service.[12] The percentage of new production capacity (under five years) declined from 46 percent in 1974 to 35 percent in 1985. However, even that equipment does not always ensure the production of competitive products.

Only one in ten of industrial projects built corresponds to the world level. Modernization of existing enterprises does not inspire optimism, either. At the Urals Heavy Machinery Plant, the flagship of

---

the intensiveness and contours of "value fields," but they cannot cancel the operation of the law of value in the socialist economy. To the extent that the socialist countries' world economic activities are accelerated, internal value proportions will gravitate toward international proportions.

[11]J.P. Hardt, "Perestroika and Interdependence: Toward Modernization and Competitiveness," Comments for Panel of the U.S.-U.S.S.R. Trade and Economic Council Meeting, Moscow, Apr. 1988, p. 15.

[12]See *MEMO*, No. 5, 1986, p. 29.

heavy industry, 10 to 12 percent of machine tools, or about 600 units of equipment, need to be replaced annually to maintain the proper level of technical re-equipment. Yet only about 120 machine tools a year are replaced.[13] And that situation is fairly typical. It is with good reason that the warning was voiced from the rostrum of the 19th Party Conference that in the sphere of scientific and technological progress, our "lag behind the world level is growing and assuming an increasingly ominous nature."

The situation is aggravated by the fact that up-to-date, competitive production can function only on the condition of a fairly high level of technical development across the whole range of related industries. They should be able to react promptly to needs that arise for new types of raw materials and other materials, semimanufactures, instruments and equipment. In the U.S.S.R. national economy, as we know, this extremely important condition is lacking. Therefore, any attempts to organize up-to-date, competitive production processes inevitably come up against the problem of supplies from subcontractors, and the more ambitious such attempts are, the greater the difficulties.

It is impossible to fully solve this problem within the context of the CMEA (for the same reasons that apply within the U.S.S.R.), and in practice, imports from the West are becoming the only solution. But since our ability to pay is limited, the number of competitive production processes is extremely modest. The most persuasive evidence of this is the commodity structure of Soviet exports to the West, four fifths of which are fuel and raw materials, and only 3 percent of which is machinery and equipment.

Until now the contradiction between the noncompetitiveness of Soviet products and the need for convertible currency to purchase imports has been resolved mainly in two ways—by increasing exports of fuel and raw materials, and by taking out foreign loans. However, it has not been possible to bring the country up to advanced positions in world industrial production by these means. The basic flaw of the fuel-and-raw-materials model of "cooperation" with the West is that it undermines our own scientific and technological efforts and creates a one-sided dependence on the developed capitalist countries. The U.S.S.R. has long since crossed the safe limits of such dependence, and proceeding any further along this path would be tantamount to gradual technological suicide—the import-provided "breakthrough" of individual production processes would increasingly be offset by an overall economic lag.

---

[13]*Kommunist*, No. 11, 1988, p. 26.

As for foreign loans, the evaluation of their possible role in the improvement of Soviet economy should be approached with the greatest circumspection, taking the state of the country's production base into account. There are considerable grounds for doubting the feasibility of proposals to reinforce perestroika in the U.S.S.R. by taking out large-scale loans of several tens of billions of dollars in the West to speed modernization of the economy and create a powerful export potential.

First, previous experience indicates that Western loans are not always used efficiently enough. That is due both to subjective factors and to the objective discrepancy between our domestic conditions of economic operation and the demands that the market-credit mechanism makes. Those demands include the existence of a developed industrial infrastructure and related production processes that are on a fairly high level, or, if they are in unsatisfactory condition, the possibility of compensating for both with imports; optimal time periods for bringing production facilities up to rated capacity; the strict observance of technological requirements; and so forth. The inability to satisfy these demands inevitably results in increasing the one-sided dependence of national reproduction on foreign credit.

Second, it is impossible to guarantee that the products of enterprises built on credit will be successfully marketed in the West and, consequently, that the loans will pay for themselves. The experience of a number of CMEA countries (especially Poland) that in the 1970s underestimated the danger associated with exceptionally tough and unpredictable competition in the world market and the likelihood of unfavorable market conditions, while simultaneously overestimating their own production potential, should serve as a warning against new foreign-economic miscalculations. Any failure of loans to pay for themselves necessitates the expansion of deliveries of nonrenewable natural resources—the country's sole, and by no means unlimited, export reserve. Moreover, the marketing conditions for those commodities are by no means always favorable. And considering that interest practically doubles the amount of a loan by the time it is paid off, if borrowing assumes a fairly wide scale, the need to increase exports of fuel and raw materials can assume catastrophic dimensions, and whether all those commodities will find a market is unknown.

Third, a large, multibillion-dollar importation of Western technology on credit would inevitably cancel out our own engineering efforts in the industries involved. Moreover, any technological import from the West always lags behind the most advanced production level by at least two or three years, and usually more. Thus, while receiving an essentially one-time (albeit extended over a long period) "injection" of what is less than the latest technology, the Soviet economy ends up back where it started, with an industrial base that is rapidly growing obsolete and a research potential that has been undermined.

What has been said, of course, does not signify some sort of taboo on foreign sources of financing. Attracting foreign loan money is an inseparable element of modern foreign-economic practice. The problem is to use it efficiently. The imperatives of the U.S.S.R.'s economic security require that the scale of foreign borrowing be kept carefully in line with the growth in competitiveness of Soviet goods and services on the world market.

Lately great hopes have been placed on "cost-recovery" forms of industrial cooperation: joint ventures, cooperative research and production arrangements, joint production, and other forms. This is unquestionably a promising area of foreign-economic "breakthrough." The question, however, is whether cooperative production arrangements with the West can reach the level of development that will provide the impetus needed by such a large-scale economy as the Soviet Union's to overcome its substantial lag behind the developed capitalist countries with their high rates of scientific and technological progress.

International cooperative production arrangements that are oriented toward internationally competitive products fit in poorly with rigid centralized planning, centralized supply of materials and equipment, administrative-command interference in the economic operations of enterprises, the low level of maneuverability of production factors, and interruptions in deliveries. The distorted structure of domestic prices and the nonconvertibility of the ruble are serious obstacles. In short, the scope of the cooperative-production "breakthrough" to the West will depend to a critical degree on the pace of economic reform in the Soviet Union.

Thus, a vicious circle has been created: efficient development of the economy is impossible without openness to the world economy, and vice-versa. The country can break this circle only if there is a net influx of foreign-currency revenues. The rate of the U.S.S.R.'s integration into the world economy and, in the final analysis, the possibility of reducing our lag behind the developed capitalist countries depend on the intensiveness of initial foreign-currency accumulation. Since most branches of the Soviet processing industry are not in a position to provide net foreign-currency revenues, and increasing our exports of fuel and raw materials is counterproductive and dangerous, the areas of foreign economic activity where realistic prerequisites exist (assuming that proper conditions are created) for accomplishing this task will be of critical importance. The range of such activity can be fairly wide and will depend mainly on the conditions under which those who engage in it operate, and the degree of their economic stake in such activity.

Taking into account the dimensions of the foreign-currency "famine" in our country and the powerful role of foreign-currency incentives, in our view it would be highly advisable, for the period needed for an initial accumulation of foreign currency, to take the following steps: remove restrictions on use by economic organizations and individuals of the foreign currency in their possession; completely free their foreign-currency income from taxation; and eliminate all foreign-currency deductions that go to higher agencies. Such measures would unquestionably give state enterprises and cooperatives a vastly greater economic interest in exporting, and would invigorate efforts aimed at obtaining foreign-currency income.

However, for such measures to be effective, it is necessary to abandon the practice of requiring authorizations in the area of foreign economic activity and move to one of simple registration, whereby the economic units alone would determine the advisability, scope, and forms of cooperation with foreign partners, and higher agencies would merely be informed of activity, but would not have the right to interfere in the decisions of production collectives. When enterprises are fully self-financing in terms of foreign currency (including through the use of domestic foreign-currency loans and purchases in foreign-currency auctions), the income obtained from exports of energy resources will be fully sufficient for the central government's purposes.

In our opinion, if such measures are implemented, a realistic possibility of a net influx of foreign currency exists in such areas as production and export of a wide range of labor-intensive industrial products that do not require a significant Western component; filling foreign companies' production orders on the basis of subcontracts; provision of various services (production, engineering, consultative, middleman, medical, transportation, and others); foreign tourism; and sale of intellectual property abroad. It seems that a vigorous driving force in this work could be provided by the collectives of enterprises that have adopted lease contracts and by cooperatives, if they are freed from excessive supervision on the part of state agencies and are not crushed by taxes. It is important to emphasize that the proposed course for expanding the sphere of openness to the world economy would not damage the U.S.S.R.'s economic security, but would actually strengthen it, since the growth of ties with the West would take place within the limits of the foreign-currency capacity of the Soviet participants in cooperation. Democratization of foreign economic activity, of course, does not remove the need for special-purpose state programs, or for special measures to develop exports. It is intended to facilitate and accelerate implementation of such programs and measures.

An important aspect of the analysis of the problem of openness to the world economy is a critical evaluation of the existing geographic structure of the U.S.S.R.'s foreign economic relations. Today it looks like this: 67 percent with the socialist countries, including 61 percent with CMEA countries; 22 percent with the developed capitalist countries; and 11 percent with the developing countries. Yet the structure of world national income is substantially different: 15 percent in the socialist countries (not counting the U.S.S.R.), including 6 percent in the CMEA countries (not counting the U.S.S.R.), 57 percent in the developed capitalist countries, and 14 percent in the developing countries. Thus, from the standpoint of the world economy, only the developing countries occupy an economically justifiable place in the U.S.S.R.'s foreign economic relations, which show a clear disproportion to other parts of the world.

It might be objected that this situation has in many respects developed for objective reasons, and that it reflects the political and economic integration of the socialist countries and has its advantages. That is indisputably correct. But it is impossible not to see that the existing practice is coming into increasingly strong contradiction with the no less objective process of the internationalization of production. Moreover, the damage from such a discrepancy is borne by the Soviet economy, as well as by our CMEA partners.

The underestimation of present-day world economic realities in the economic strategy of the U.S.S.R. and the socialist commonwealth as a whole is dooming socialism to lagging economically behind capitalism. Attempts, for political reasons, to cover up the problem of the inadequate structure of our world economic ties seem short-sighted, at the very least. Would it not make more sense to finally admit the objective state of affairs, no matter how harsh, unfamiliar, and frightening it might be, and to reckon with it, rather than with "convenient" stereotypes of the prospects for the economic development of socialism? We are not, of course, talking about cutting back our economic relations with the fraternal countries—they will continue to deepen. At the same time, the starting level of the CMEA countries' participation in the world division of labor is still extremely low and makes it perfectly possible to combine progress in socialist economic integration with a rationalization of the geographic structure of the CMEA countries' world economic activity.

And one more critical observation that seems trivial at first glance but is essential. By assigning total priority to cooperation among themselves, the CMEA countries thereby, willy-nilly, subject their partners from the capitalist states to de facto discrimination. That is easy to see if one looks, for example, at recent [party and government] resolutions pertaining to restructuring the U.S.S.R.'s foreign economic activities. In them, contacts with the West (and the developing countries) continue to be more strictly regulated than relations with socialist partners. To a certain extent this is attributable to and, partly, justified by the trade policies applied by Western states to the U.S.S.R. and the other CMEA countries. However, the preservation of such a practice is not in the economic interests of the socialist countries.

IV.

Proceeding on the basis of trends in the development of the world economy and the economic potential of the U.S.S.R. and other CMEA countries, one can imagine three options for their future world economic strategy.

Option I (optimistic) consists of the intensive integration of the socialist commonwealth into the world economy through the stepped-up accumulation of foreign currency. It presupposes the maximum liberation of economic initiative and strong state incentive measures, especially the aforementioned restructuring of foreign-currency regulation and taxation. Essential elements of such a strategy in the U.S.S.R. would be a substantial limitation of the sphere of centralized planning and a shift to market self-regulation of the bulk of the economy; abandonment of party and administrative interference in the current economic activities of enterprises; transfer of a substantial percentage of state enterprises to the ownership of labor collectives (leased ownership, cooperative ownership, or corporate ownership); creation of a securities market (such as stocks, bonds, promissory notes); deregulation of the foreign economic activities of enterprises and individuals; removal of unwarranted restrictions on entry into and exit from the country; development of domestic bank and commercial lending in foreign currency; and introduction of free convertibility for the ruble.[14]

The full set of these and other essential measures would be capable of sharply stepping up foreign economic activity and providing growth in foreign-currency revenues. Initially this growth might take

---

[14]It seems that an optimal solution of the problem of ruble convertibility might be a mechanism for contractual convertibility. It would presuppose endowing Soviet juridical persons entering into economic ties (primarily cooperative production arrangements) with foreign partners with the right to set and establish, in contracts, a currency exchange rate that is mutually acceptable to the contracting parties, as well as other conditions for bilateral transactions in foreign currency. That would make it possible to institute ruble convertibility gradually and painlessly, in organic connection with the expansion of foreign economic activity. Moreover, the state budget would be freed of the burden of covering a negative foreign trade balance, yielding that "privilege" to the direct participants in foreign trade operations.

place mainly through labor-intensive, non-research-intensive branches of production, the services sector, foreign tourism, intellectual activity, and the arts. At the same time, the redistribution, in loans, of part of the foreign-currency revenues would create the prerequisites for expanding foreign economic activities in other areas.

The difficulties and drawbacks of such a course are substantial; they are associated mainly with the need for a drastic internal restructuring, and with the inertia of a society that is psychologically unprepared for the necessity and inevitability, at the given stage in the development of socialism, of intensifying economic inequality and social stratification, or for the strict criteria for labor activity dictated by world production conditions. On this course one would need to be prepared for vigorous resistance and sabotage by a substantial part of the bureaucratic apparatus and those segments of the population that ideologically reject social competition. At the initial stages of the implementation of the aforementioned changes, an exacerbation of internal social tension, and conflicts among group interests would be unavoidable. However, there is evidently no other way to eliminate our economic lag behind the leading industrial countries.

Option II (pessimistic) consists of slowing down perestroika and preserving the existing model for the participation of the U.S.S.R. and other socialist countries in the international division of labor. In economic terms, this would result in further lowering the level of competitiveness of their exports, weakening their import potential, increasing their technological and credit dependence on the West, increase their selling off of natural resources, and a net outflow of national income. Attempts to eliminate the lag in the decisive areas of science and technology by relying on our own forces will require an excessive concentration of resources and their diversion from other spheres of the economy. In the final analysis, these attempts would be undermined by the nonproportional structure and generally inadequate level of development of the national economic complexes of the U.S.S.R. and other socialist countries.

Unsatisfactory economic efficiency would result in a further lag behind the developed capitalist countries, increase the attractiveness of the Western way of life, and revive sociopolitical apathy and cynicism in society. Along this path, intensification of centrifugal tendencies within the socialist commonwealth, and reorientation of certain East European participants in the CMEA toward economic, cultural, and political ties with Western Europe would be inevitable. The economic basis of the U.S.S.R.'s relations with the developing countries would be narrowed. And there is a great danger that the relative weakening of the Soviet economy would activate forces in the West that have an interest in military superiority and in wearing our country down through an arms race. In the final analysis, further isolation from world competition would inevitably result in economic and social stagnation, the rehabilitation of administrative-command methods of state administration, and the undermining of the domestic and international security of the U.S.S.R. and other socialist countries.

Option III (compromise). Both the first and second options are hardly possible in the near future. The first—since social conditions are not yet ripe for such radical changes. The second—by virtue of its objective economic inadvisability and the irreversibility of certain aspects of perestroika. Therefore, what seems most likely is a compromise option that combines the need for radical reforms with a desire to protect the sociopolitical status quo. Under these conditions, the prospects for economic development of world socialism would be determined by the correlation of reform and conservative principles in its domestic policies.

It should be emphasized that the compromise variant does not provide conditions for completely eliminating the economic lag and its negative consequences in the internal life and foreign policy of the socialist countries. At the current pace of the scientific and technological revolution, any slowing down, especially in the initial stages, could have irreversible consequences in the economic competition between the two systems.

Therefore, an extremely urgent task for the CMEA countries is the acceleration of perestroika and the utmost activation of social forces that are capable of accepting the historic challenge and bringing about the elevation of socialism to the highest world levels.

* * *

No matter what course the further development of socialism may take, the prospects for changes in the other industrially developed regions of the world appear fairly definite. Bringing about a drastic change in the means of production, the scientific and technological revolution will create the prerequisites for humanity's movement to a higher economic civilization, an important distinguishing feature of which will be the gradual removal of international economic barriers. This movement is not perfectly linear and not without conflict, and it will be mediated by a struggle among contradictory social interests and occupy a long historical period. But it is irreversible, since it is brought forth by the objective requirements of productive forces and can be cut short only by the disappearance of the corresponding material conditions of production—as the result, for example, of a devastating war. The internationalization of the economic base signifies movement toward a more rational organization of the worldwide economy on the basis of increased productivity and savings of social labor. The prospects for the socialist countries' participation in this historically progressive process will depend on the extent to which their economic policy accords with the objective requirements of present-day production.

As for the internal social "price" of perestroika, it is appropriate to recall M. S. Gorbachev's words at the ceremonial meeting on the 70th anniversary of the October Revolution: "but how long can we be intimidated, comrades, with reference to all sorts of drawbacks! Of course, drawbacks are inevitable in any undertaking, especially a new one. But the consequences of marking time, stagnation, and indifference are far more substantial and costly than the drawbacks that come up temporarily in the process of the creative establishment of new forms of the life of society."

Certain Questions Concerning the U.S.S.R.'s Economic Cooperation With the Developing Countries

LEON ZALMANOVICH ZEVIN*

The rapid growth of trade and economic, scientific, and technical cooperation between the U.S.S.R. and other socialist states and the developing countries in the postwar period has marked the emergence in the world economy of a new type of international economic relations among states with different levels of development. These relations are helping former colonies and semicolonies to overcome backwardness, to speed social and economic progress, and to strengthen political and economic independence. Mutual interest has spawned high rates of growth of trade and of economic, scientific, and technical cooperation between the Soviet Union and this group of countries. In the late 1970s and early 1980s, however, this cooperation began to lose its former dynamism, and since the mid-1980s the volume of reciprocal trade has declined as well.

What accounts for the onset of negative phenomena in this sphere of relations between the U.S.S.R. and the newly independent states? In the context of the new world economic situation and the radical reform of our country's economic mechanism, where should we look for solutions to the problems that have accumulated? What can lend new impetus to cooperation with the developing countries? The following article offers some answers to these questions.

Differences in levels of development in the world capitalist economy give rise, in economic relations, to inequality, to exploitation, and to a concentration of the benefits of international exchange and the international division of labor primarily in the hands of the more developed partners. Graphic manifestations of this pattern, which is inherent in capitalism, include a persisting gap in per capita gross national product, the existence of vast, stagnant zones of famine and poverty, the growing gap between the scientific and technical potentials of two groups of countries—the developing and the developed—and the conversion of the international monetary and financial system

*Doctor of economics, professor, and lead research associate at the U.S.S.R. Academy of Sciences' Institute of the Economics of the World Socialist System. This article appeared in the March 1988 issue of *MEMO*.

into a mechanism by which resources are pumped from the periphery of that economy to its centers.

The transnationalization of the nonsocialist world's economy modifies somewhat but does not fundamentally alter the character of relations between countries with varying levels of development: The "force lines" of exploitation and inequality are displaced to some extent from the international level to the branch, interfirm, and interbank levels. The introduction of transnational corporations in the Third World economy has reached unprecedented proportions. It is estimated that these corporations account for 40 percent of the developing countries' entire industrial output and half their foreign trade. Transnational corporations carry on 90 percent of world trade in technology, and operations with their subsidiaries in the countries of the developing world account for half the volume of all deals.[1]

One can therefore well understand the desire of former colonies and semicolonies, as soon as they become independent states, to find partners with which they can establish relations that will help them diminish their one-sided dependence on capitalist centers, to put those relations on an equal footing, to obtain moral and material support in their efforts to overcome economic and cultural backwardness, and to strengthen their positions in the international arena. They have found such partners outside the Third World in the U.S.S.R. and the other socialist countries. Thanks to their support, the developing states have gained a certain freedom of maneuver in their foreign economic activities, while the establishment of political cooperation with the socialist world has narrowed the potential for outside interference in the process of national rebirth.

This circumstance merits special emphasis, for attempts are often made in the West—and, in some instances, in the newly independent countries themselves—to reduce the effect of cooperation with the socialist states solely to the quantitative side, ignoring its qualitative aspects.

Basic Results of Cooperation

The Soviet Union's economic ties with the countries now referred to as the developing countries began in the 1920s and 1930s. But both then and in the early postwar years, the volume of those ties was small, and they were confined, as a rule, to sporadic trade operations and individual projects to assist the neighboring countries of the East. The ties began to undergo intensive development in the mid-1950s.

---

[1]See, for example, N. Shmelev, *The Third World and International Economic Relations* ["*Tretiy mir*" i mezhdunarodnyye ekonomicheskiye otnosheniya], MEMO, No. 9, 1987, p. 21.

From 1956 to 1984, trade with the developing countries was among the most dynamic, not only in the foreign trade of the Soviet Union but in world trade as well. Machinery and technical equipment accounted for a large share of our exports, and within that output the proportion of equipment supplied in complete sets remained high (roughly half the total). This trend served the needs of our partners, especially those of countries just embarking on industrialization. Mutual interest, the growing technical potential of the Soviet economy, and a policy of independent economic development in many Third World countries gave constant impetus to expansion of economic and technical assistance. It can be said that, on average, the volume of cooperation increased by 50 to 100 percent every five years.

The concurrent high rates of growth in both trade and economic and technical assistance reflected an important feature of cooperation with this group of countries: The increase in the volume of trade, especially in the initial stage of the establishment of relations with a given developing country, was to a significant degree a result of economic and technical assistance from the Soviet Union. In other words, this cooperation, in addition to direct material support in overcoming underdevelopment, became an important stimulus to the growth of trade in both directions and to the increasingly complex structure of that trade.

Regarding the qualitative aspect of our assistance, the overwhelming majority of it is aimed at strengthening the production potential of our partner countries and at establishing in them modern industrial branches and groups of interrelated production facilities. In

Dynamics of Soviet Union's Trade With the Developing Countries

	1956-1960 = 100			Growth Over Previous Five-Year Period		
Year	Total	Exports	Imports	Total	Exports	Imports
1961-1965	194	246	150	1.94	2.46	1.50
1966-1970	312	413	226	1.61	1.68	1.51
1971-1975	641	805	500	2.05	1.95	2.22
1976-1980	1,240	1,671	869	1.93	2.08	1.74
1981-1985	2,395	2,982	1,890	1.93	1.78	2.18

Calculated on the basis of: *Foreign Trade of the U.S.S.R.: 1918-1966. Statistical Collection* [*Vneshnyaya torgovlya SSSR za 1918-1966. Statistichesky sbornik*], Moscow, 1967, p. 63; *Foreign Trade* [*Vneshnyaya torgovlya*] for the relevant years.

this way the preconditions are created for modernization of the entire economic and social structure and for the establishment of an integrated national economy.

As for the quantitative aspect, under existing agreements and in cooperation with Soviet organizations—including cooperation based on extending long- and medium-term government and commercial credits—capacity is being built in the developing countries to smelt 28 million tons of steel a year (capacity to smelt 17 million tons had been built as of January 1, 1987); to extract 124 million tons of coal (22 million tons as of that date); to refine 30 million tons of petroleum (20 million tons); to generate 41 million kilowatts of electric power (15 million kilowatts); to produce 5.4 million tons of cement (4.3 million tons); to produce 192,000 tons of various types of equipment (172,000 tons); to manufacture 31,000 tractors (11,000); and to irrigate and put into production 2.4 million hectares of land (1.9 million hectares). In addition, 6,094 kilometers of railroad are being built (5,239 kilometers), 2,638 kilometers of highway are being laid (2,200 kilometers), and so forth.[2]

Even a cursory analysis of the dynamics and structure of this trade and economic and technical cooperation supports the statement that the Soviet Union has provided and is providing assistance to newly independent countries in their efforts to solve vitally important problems facing them. In its relations with these countries, the Soviet Union is not guided by narrow commercial considerations. While seeking to ensure for themselves the level of profitability that is universally accepted in international economic relations, Soviet organizations adhere to the principle of mutual benefit and promote the technical progress of their partners, the strengthening of their economic independence, and the conquest of backwardness.

The almost 2,200 facilities constructed or under construction in the developing countries with the Soviet Union's assistance include such enterprises and installations of key importance to their national economies as the Aswan Hydroelectric Complex and the Helwan Metallurgical Plant in the Arab Republic of Egypt; a hydroelectric complex on the Euphrates River, oil wells, and railroads in Syria; oil wells and irrigation structures in Iraq; metallurgical and machinery manufacturing plants, petroleum refineries, power stations, coal mines, opencut coal mines, and oil wells in India; metallurgical plants in Algeria, Iran, Nigeria, and Turkey; a bauxite-extraction complex in Guinea; dozens of enterprises, including a natural gas industry, in Afghanistan; and so on.

---

[2]*The U.S.S.R. National Economy in the Past 70 Years* [*Narodnoye khozyaystvo SSSR za 70 let*], Moscow, 1987, p. 652.

With the Soviet Union's assistance, modern economic complexes are being established in the Socialist Republic of Vietnam, the Republic of Cuba, the Korean People's Democratic Republic, the Lao People's Democratic Republic, and the Mongolian People's Republic, which have set about building socialism with poorly developed productive forces and with national industry either lacking or extremely weak. Three of the aforementioned countries are members of the Council for Mutual Economic Assistance. This enables them to employ forms and methods typical of socialist economic integration in their cooperation with the Soviet Union and other CMEA member states. This cooperation has resulted in significantly increased trade and in the execution of large-scale economic projects within the framework of economic and technical assistance, for the purpose of "accelerating the process of gradually equalizing the levels of economic development of the CMEA member countries and, first and foremost, of bringing the levels of economic development of Vietnam, Cuba, and Mongolia into line with the levels of the European CMEA member countries."[3]

The 43rd extraordinary session of the CMEA (1987) adopted a decision to draw up special comprehensive programs for multilateral cooperation between the European CMEA members and these three countries, programs that stipulate concrete measures to deepen reciprocal scientific, technical, production, economic, and trade ties. The Soviet Union has already concluded bilateral and long-term programs with these countries—programs to develop economic, scientific, and technical cooperation up to the year 2000. Such effective tools as coordinated economic plans and granting credit on preferred terms are used in assisting Vietnam, Mongolia, and Cuba, and, in a number of instances, incentive prices are used, which helps speed their social and economic progress and promotes their active inclusion in the international socialist division of labor.

The Soviet Union's foreign economic policy with respect to developing countries with differing social and economic systems, though distinct in the range of forms and methods and the relationship among them, *is essentially the same from the viewpoint of assisting these countries to overcome underdevelopment and of creating favorable external conditions for accomplishing this important task.*

The Soviet Union's internationalism in this area of foreign affairs is confirmed by the fact that, in the 1980s—despite serious complications in the world economic situation and the need to mobilize reserves to restructure its own economy and major social programs—the volume of Soviet economic and technical assistance to the developing coun-

---

[3]See *The Economic Summit Meeting of the CMEA Member Countries* [*Ekonomicheskoye soveshchaniye stran-chlenov SEV na vysshem urovne*], Moscow, 1984, p. 11.

tries has continued to grow, thereby creating the material basis for overcoming the adverse trends that have emerged in the recent past.

Problems of Cooperation

The stagnation phenomena that have accumulated in the U.S.S.R.'s economy in the past 15 to 20 years could not help but have an impact on foreign economic activity as well, including relations with the developing countries.[4] As of the mid-1970s, and especially the first half of the 1980s, alarming signs began to appear in this sphere. The problems surfaced and began exerting an increasingly negative effect on the dynamics and volume of trade, its structure, and the state of economic and technical cooperation. In scholarly literature, as well as in the assessments of Soviet foreign-trade organizations, a stereotype took hold, attributing these negative phenomena chiefly to the deterioration of world economic conditions and of the economic and financial condition of most developing countries. No doubt these and related factors do have an effect on this sector of international economic relations. But such a one-sided interpretation overlooks other reasons for bottlenecks in our cooperation with the developing countries.

In our view, one of the main causes of the definite instability and slowdown in the rate of growth of that trade—and of the absolute decrease that it has registered since the mid-1980s—is that the U.S.S.R. has yet to formulate a scientifically sound, long-term concept for developing trade and economic, scientific, and technical cooperation with the developing countries; a concept translated into a program of specific actions. Such a concept could encompass questions of the development of relations with various regions of the Third World, with the developing states' major business entities, and with certain large partner-countries, and define the role in this cooperation of major Soviet industrial complexes (such as the machinery-manufacturing, fuel-and-power, agroindustrial, and consumer goods complexes, for example). It could also provide for improvements in the mechanism of cooperation, to include—in addition to forms and methods of cooperation common to the overall system of foreign economic activity— various specific forms and methods of cooperation between countries at different levels of development. Until recently, attempts to assess the prospects for cooperation with this group of countries were distinguished by their lack of a comprehensive view of the problem and their failure to adequately coordinate the approaches of practical and research organizations.

---

[4]On problems of the Soviet Union's foreign economic activity, see *Kommunist* [*Communist*], No. 15, 1987, pp. 25-34.

The present situation is largely attributable to the predominance of the residual approach in determining the scope of our relations with the developing countries. We often turn to this sector of foreign economic relations not with a view to long-term economic benefit but only after identifying a shortage in output of one type or another. As a result, economic relations with a number of countries still take the form of numerous operations that bear little connection to one another—a means of accomplishing immediate or at best current tasks facing the economies of the Soviet Union and its partners in the developing world. This naturally slows the establishment of long-term ties based on a stable division of labor, specialization, cooperative production arrangements, and other forms of cooperation in the realm of production.

Hence the incomplete use of even existing potential for mutually complementary structures. Our partners, uncertain about the stability of the market and the possibility for selling their output on a long-term basis, are reluctant to invest capital in modernizing production to adapt its output to the needs of Soviet customers. This, in turn, fails to stimulate the search for new avenues of cooperation or efforts to draw into the orbit of cooperation branches and enterprises that remain outside it.

Current forms and methods that served, when the economic-cooperation mechanism was first taking shape, as powerful accelerants of that cooperation have now exhausted their potential to a considerable degree, and the sides find themselves facing a kind of *structural barrier*. This is borne out by, among other things, a trend toward a weakening of both sides' positions on reciprocal trade. The developing countries' share of Soviet trade has declined in the 1980s from 15 percent to 11 percent. By the same token, the Soviet Union's share of these countries' foreign trade now stands at less than 4 percent.

Even more alarming, from the standpoint of long-term prospects, is the way the structure of the U.S.S.R.'s economic cooperation with the developing countries is diverging from world trends in production and trade and from the nature of the economic processes under way in our Third World partners. In world trade, machinery output accounts for nearly a third of the total trade volume, while in Soviet exports the figure is no more than 15 percent, and something on the order of 20 percent in its exports to the developing countries. The proportion of machinery manufacturing in our economic and technical assistance is unjustifiably low, and the situation has not significantly changed in many years. Moreover, the provision of spare parts for exported equipment is unsatisfactory. Soviet suppliers apparently use specifications designed for our own country and fail to take into account severe climatic conditions in their customers' countries and inadequate skills on the part of these countries' labor forces. Nevertheless, the situation largely reflects unsolved problems with the supply of spare parts and replaceable equipment in the Soviet economy.

Insufficient knowledge of local market conditions often results in a situation in which exported equipment, including equipment provided in the context of economic and technical assistance, often goes unused for long periods of time and sits idle in warehouses. The other side of the coin is Soviet imports from the developing countries. Machinery and equipment are very poorly represented in these imports, despite the fact that these countries have made substantial improvements in the structure of their production and exports in recent years.

The developing countries gained firm footholds in world markets for textiles, ready-made clothing, footwear, leather goods, jewelry, toys, sporting goods, and several other types of consumer goods back in the 1970s. By 1985, their share in developed capitalist states' imports ranged from 10 to 30 percent in electrical components, telecommunications equipment, machinery and equipment (of both medium and high complexity), ferrous metals, and ferrous-metal, stone, clay, and glass products. The total annual volume of exports of machinery and equipment from the developing countries amounted to $47.2 billion, including $28.7 billion to the developed capitalist states, $14.1 billion to the developing countries, and $4.4 billion to the socialist countries.[5]

There are no firm assurances that substantive changes will occur in this sphere until we overcome the stereotype of viewing the developing countries primarily and almost exclusively as suppliers of raw materials and foodstuffs. Incidentally, the inordinately high proportion of foodstuffs and raw materials—including products we could produce ourselves—in Soviet imports has objectively impeded and continues to impede the process of optimizing the structure of our imports, without which we cannot expect steadily increasing trade or an increase in processing industry products in that trade.

An analysis of the state of international trade shows that one of the chief conditions for achieving competitiveness on foreign markets is the fullest possible integration of production and related services. A study of the operations of 200 leading transnational corporations (1982) showed that the ratio between their revenues from sales of finished goods and revenues from services was approximately 1.6 to 1.0 ($1,853 billion and $1,192 billion respectively).[6] Services occupy a very mod-

    [5]See *Trade and Development Report 1987*, United Nations, New York, 1987, p. 118; and *Monthly Bulletin of Statistics*, May 1987, p. 290.
    [6]See *Revitalising Development Growth and International Trade. Assessment and Policy Options*, Report to UNCTAD-VII, United Nations, New York, 1987, p. 151.

est place in the Soviet Union's foreign trade ties, and no network of specialized, export-oriented engineering and consulting organizations has been set up.

A discrepancy is emerging between the structure of the U.S.S.R.'s economic and technical assistance and the development strategies of the countries that receive it. Two branches—metallurgy and power engineering, which account for substantially more than half the total volume of our technical assistance—occupy an inordinate place in that assistance. As was pointed out, cooperation in the establishment of these branches has promoted and is promoting creation of the foundation of modern industry in a number of countries, and so its positive impact cannot be underestimated. However, these branches entail major installations that require large capital investments with lengthy recoupment time.

Meanwhile, the situation of most developing countries is such that it is difficult to count on the possibility of substantially expanded assistance in these branches in the medium-term. Given the developing countries' critical demographic and food situations, growing foreign debt, and unemployment, their national strategies typically concentrate on agriculture, areas of production that serve it, and the construction of medium-sized and small enterprises. They are counting on earning a rapid return on investments and on significantly expanding employment.

Nevertheless, research circles and business organizations in the Soviet Union have not been able to forecast or to promptly and fully assess changes in the developing countries' economies or the effect of these changes on the developing countries' place and role in world trade and in the international division of labor. The gap between the sequence in which branches are established under the Third World states' new strategy and the present structure of cooperation also impedes the development of cooperation because the shift in national priorities complicates mobilization of internal resources to cover local outlays for joint projects. In this context, there is no denying that, by virtue of a number of factors, ties have been inhibited with certain so-called "newly industrialized countries" that have become major producers and exporters of finished products, including sophisticated equipment.

Assistance in import-substituting branches predominates in our cooperation. This undoubtedly promotes the development of our partners' economic potential, but it fails to create any significant incentives to maintain stable ties on a long-term basis, to increase the developing countries' exports (something to which they are now devoting much attention), or to improve the repayment of Soviet credits. In our view, the Soviet Union's comprehensive program for increasing production and improving the quality of consumer goods fails to take sufficient account of the possibilities for cooperation with the developing states, which have become major exporters in world markets.

Finally, we have also failed to take prompt notice of the tendency for equipment supplied in complete sets to decline as a percentage of Third World countries' machinery imports as many of them—the Soviet Union's traditional partners included—move ahead in their industrial development. Demand is rapidly growing in these countries for "narrower" sets and for technically complex individual pieces of equipment, since their internal capabilities enable them to produce other types of equipment themselves. In the industrially more developed countries of this group—countries with sizable domestic markets—assemblies and parts now account for between 50 percent and 75 percent of all machinery imports. The American economist P. Desai, who studies Soviet economic problems, has published a book entitled *The Soviet Economy: Problems and Prospects.*[7] On balance, the monograph expresses high regard for Soviet assistance to the developing countries, in particular to India. However, it points out that a shortcoming of this assistance is a tendency to supply technology in a complete package at a time when many developing countries are capable of producing on their own a sizable number of components, as well as the required machinery for that technology. The author also discusses our low level of activity in licensing, our technical lag behind transnational corporations in a number of branches, and our poor knowledge of the specific characteristics of local markets.

All this allows us to say that the present mutually complementary nature of the economic structures of the Soviet Union and its partners in the Third World, which serves as the basis for their cooperation and gives impetus to its further development, is of a predominantly *interbranch* character. Under the conditions of scientific and technical progress and structural changes in the international division of labor, the maintenance of this model of cooperation cannot ensure high rates of growth in the long term or the extension of this cooperation to new avenues and fields. Both sides are faced with the need to develop to the greatest possible extent *intrabranch* specialization and cooperative production arrangements in machinery manufacturing, chemicals, and the agroindustrial sector, as well as in the consumer-goods branches.

The mechanism of Soviet cooperation with the developing countries established over the past three decades did accomplish the tasks before it for a certain period of time. The greater part of this economic cooperation is carried out under intergovernmental agreements on trade and on economic and technical cooperation. The institution of

---

[7]See P. Desai. *The Soviet Economy: Problems and Prospects*, Oxford, 1987.

bilateral joint commissions has arisen. These commissions assess the prospects for cooperation, organize it, monitor the implementation of agreed-upon decisions, set up working groups, and propose mutually acceptable forms and methods for implementing joint initiatives.

Here too, however, the years of stagnation were marked by inertia, an attachment to fixed patterns, and a lack of desire or incentive to search for new approaches and to react promptly and effectively to changes in international economic relations and in our partners' economies. One manifestation of the internationalization of the economy and of growing interdependence is the expanded practice of multilateral cooperation involving firms and organizations from several countries, including countries belonging to different social and economic systems. Soviet organizations are entering into cooperative relationships with organizations from other socialist countries to carry out joint projects in developing states. Thus far, however, this promising and effective form of relations has undergone almost no development. Soviet organizations continue to act as general contractor (supplier) and to make unsatisfactory use of the potential for subcontracting. In our view, this results from the fact that the parties to such dealings on the Soviet side are primarily government agencies and large organizations and enterprises. The present mechanism fails to encourage the independent participation of small and medium-sized enterprises in international cooperation: in most cases they simply supply assemblies and components to the principal Soviet enterprise on a basis of internal cooperative arrangements and specialization.[8]

Meanwhile, Soviet enterprises make poor use of the possibilities for international cooperative arrangements, the establishment of direct links, and the creation of joint enterprises in the production sphere. Cooperative arrangements in their present forms are for the most part not the result of some carefully planned project but a consequence of difficulties experienced in selling the output of cooperative facilities on a developing country's domestic market.

Trilateral forms of cooperation that involve firms and enterprises of the U.S.S.R., the developing countries, and the developed capitalist countries are also being assimilated at a slow pace. This is due, among other factors, to the low level of operational flexibility of Soviet

---

[8]There are estimates that more than 80 percent of all Japanese firms that make production investments abroad are small and medium-sized enterprises. For the leading developed capitalist countries as a whole, the figure is 50 percent. A typical way in which small and medium-sized firms participate in foreign investment activity is through subcontracting with transnational corporations. Using the ties they establish and the knowledge they acquire of a local situation, these firms subsequently shift to making independent investments. In France, for example, small and medium-sized firms have increased their share of the total volume of direct investments abroad to roughly 20 percent of the total. Often the investments result in the establishment of joint enterprises. Small and medium-sized firms are most active in metalworking, electrical machinery manufacturing, and chemicals (see *Trade and Development Report 1987*, 1987, pp. 94-95).

organizations, the lack of standard designs, and the lengthy process required to obtain approval for the assumed commitments to be included in the internal system of material and technical supply. Incidentally, trilateral projects—like many bilateral ones—often involve competition for contracts, which makes it particularly important to evaluate the commercial and technical aspects of a project properly, in conditions of stiff competition from Western companies and, of late, from firms in the newly industrialized and certain other developing countries.

The persisting fragmentation of export and import operations—and, in a number of instances, the insufficient coordination of foreign trade and economic and technical cooperation—have a constraining effect on the Soviet Union's foreign economic activity. This gives rise to different approaches to evaluating effectiveness on the part of certain entities engaged in foreign economic activity and to difficulties in dovetailing various measures and in applying the criterion of national economic effectiveness. Despite certain decisions taken of late, the sort of interest that direct producers have in stepping up their export activities remains a very serious problem. This is in large part a result of the administrative-command methods of economic management that were employed for several decades, the lack of experience in entering foreign markets independently and lack of skilled personnel who have mastered this new type of activity for the producers, insufficient information on marketing questions, and incentives that do not always offset the increased risk of operations in unfamiliar markets.

New Impetus

How can trade and economic, scientific, and technical cooperation between the U.S.S.R. and the developing countries be expanded, and how can its effectiveness and positive impact on the economies of the U.S.S.R. and its Third World partners be enhanced?

The Soviet economy's shift to intensive-type development, the radical reform of its economic mechanism, and its more active participation in the international division of labor entail accelerated development of the branches responsible for scientific and technical progress, particularly machinery manufacturing. Such a course must undoubtedly provide for an increase in the proportion of machinery and equipment in exports and for their gradually assuming a leading export position. The developing countries are already the chief market for the sale of our machinery and equipment in the nonsocialist world. It seems likely that these countries' needs for imports of machinery and equipment will grow in the long term.

The concept of cooperation, then, should apparently proceed from the need to prepare potential markets jointly with our partners and to take into account the specialization of Soviet machinery manufacturing within socialist economic integration and the possibility of mutually complementary and coordinated undertakings with enterprises from other CMEA countries. The search for new markets and the expansion of existing ones should be organically linked with giving our partners in the developing world a reciprocal opportunity to sell their finished products in the Soviet Union—including their machinery products—on a long-term and stable basis. This will require active use of joint-production forms of cooperation and establishment of direct links and joint enterprises. Extension of compensation-type arrangements—i.e., arrangements whereby investment capital is repaid in the form of a percentage of the given facility's output—to the processing branches of industry could make a sizable contribution.

Economic and technical assistance plays a special role in establishing markets for Soviet machinery and equipment in the developing countries. To ensure a significantly greater role for the machinery-manufacturing branches, a fundamental restructuring of our assistance is essential, in our view. It seems that particular attention will have to be devoted to assistance in the construction of medium-sized and small machinery-manufacturing enterprises that are well equipped and capable of prompt retooling. The narrow character of most developing countries' domestic markets makes the construction of these types of enterprises the most expedient.

Experience shows that marketing problems prevent large machinery-manufacturing facilities built in cooperation with the U.S.S.R. from reaching rated capacity for long periods of time. In building such facilities, it is therefore essential to design them for the possibility of cooperation with Soviet enterprises and to codify this through corresponding agreements and quotas for output distribution, including output distribution on the markets of third countries. Since medium-sized and small firms in developing countries are usually found in the private sector, broad cooperation in the machinery-manufacturing branches and increased exports of such products from the Soviet Union will apparently require expanded relations with national capital.

In our opinion, another essential shift in the structure of our economic and technical cooperation has to do with significantly increasing the role played in it by agriculture and other spheres of the agroindustrial complex. Profound agricultural backwardness and rapid population growth have severely intensified the food problem in a large group of developing countries. For this reason, increased food production is being emphasized, resources are being redistributed, and import priorities are being shifted in those countries' strategies for social and economic development. For the present, however, changes in the structure of Soviet assistance, despite having accelerated somewhat, lag noticeably behind the shifts in the structure of capital investments carried out by our partners, who have made solution of the food problem a top-priority task. In addition, we should bear in mind that the unsolved food problem imposes ever-greater constraints on the development of other spheres of their national economies and narrows their possibilities for importing machinery and equipment for industrialization.

Various forms of association between the intellectual and material resources of small industrial enterprises and research and design organizations of the Soviet Union (they presently have almost no *direct* involvement in foreign economic activity), could make a sizable contribution to increased volumes of trade and economic cooperation and to efforts to extend that cooperation to new branches and areas of production. Such associations in the form, say, of joint-stock companies and councils of directors could operate on a permanent basis within the framework of a single production process or as independent suppliers of various types of equipment for subsequent assembly into a single product. When necessary, interested enterprises and organizations could form a temporary consortium to carry out a specific cooperative project. As interbranch scientific and technical complexes are set up in the U.S.S.R., it would probably be useful to orient them increasingly toward foreign activity. The inclusion of new participants in our economic cooperation with developing countries would promote its diversification, establishment of direct ties between enterprises and organizations, and more stable trade and economic relations.

The need for a detailed *concept* of trade, economic, scientific, and technical cooperation with developing countries has already been mentioned. This concept should be used to assess the possible physical volume of purchases of basic goods in these countries and the export resources required for covering their cost, and to make provision for the materials and credits that projected areas of cooperation will require. A search for organizational and economic ways of tying our relations with the developing countries into the various programs that have been adopted in the Soviet Union—such as the fuel-and-energy, food, machinery-manufacturing, and consumer-goods production programs—would be extremely useful in efforts to lend greater dynamism and stability to our mutual dealings. From all indications, in the drawing up of at least certain of these programs, far from full account was taken of the possibilities for a division of labor with the developing countries that would ensure greater effectiveness of capital invest- ments and would enable us to concentrate in our country on areas of production with the most favorable conditions for growth and to gear our efforts to mutually beneficial imports from the aforementioned countries.

Such cooperation, it would seem, could find broader application to such goods as raw materials of certain types, petroleum, nonferrous metals, ready-made clothing, footwear, textiles, sporting goods, cer- tain types of electronic equipment, machines, household appliances, assemblies, parts, automobile spare parts, paints and varnishes, medi- cines, raw plant materials, tropical foods, and so forth.

In a number of instances we could avoid having to expand (or could even partially curtail) our production of certain types of output and meet our needs for them with imports that cost less to buy than to produce domestically. The resulting gain could serve as a basis for expanding such cooperation. In other words, in a number of cases such cooperation could be viewed as an alternative to domestic capital investments allocated to meet the country's needs (or some part of them) for a given product. A comparison of the alternative solutions— with due regard, of course, for the increased economic risk entailed in choosing a foreign supplier—will enable us to select the best one.

Unfortunately, owing to the practices of the past and to ster- eotypes that persist from those times, such calculations are hardly ever made, though their results could suggest a number of interesting alternatives. That would promote the more effective accomplishment of certain of the U.S.S.R.'s national-economic tasks, would serve to increase the production potential of its partners in the developing world, and would help to neutralize factors that impede expanded trade, economic, scientific, and technical cooperation between the Soviet Union and a large group of developing countries.

On the Role of Foreign Economic Relations in the Development of the U.S.S.R.'s Pacific Coast Regions

VLADIMIR IVANOVICH IVANOV AND
PAVEL ALEKSANDROVICH MINAKIR*

In accordance with decisions of the CPSU Central Committee and the Soviet government, Maritime Province and the Far East are to be turned into a highly developed economic complex that is an integral part of the system of unionwide and international division of labor. That complex needs its own major resource base, an optimal economic structure, and a developed social sector.

The recently adopted Long-Term State Program for the Comprehensive Development of the Far Eastern Economic Region's Productive Forces is aimed at implementing those decisions. Obviously, these plans have not only domestic economic significance but great international political significance as well. In the final analysis, their fulfillment will determine our country's position in the Asian-Pacific zone—a world economic center that is taking shape and growing rapidly. In light of these circumstances, the question of using foreign economic ties to resolve structural and long-term problems, as well as urgent social questions, and to expand exports and improve their distribution, is becoming extremely important.

In setting forth their views on the prospects for the development of the U.S.S.R.'s Pacific coast regions, the authors of this article devote special attention to the role of foreign economic relations as an important source of untapped potential for accomplishing the planned economic transformations.

The area's very name—the Far East—expresses the long-dominant Eurocentric view of the surrounding world. Essentially, this major economic region is still just being opened and settled, its potential developed, and its rich natural resources put into circulation. In the future, its resources and general economic potential can become an immense reserve for the entire Soviet economy. In addition, the

*Ivanov is a candidate of economics and department head at the U.S.S.R. Academy of Sciences' Institute of World Economy and International Relations [IMEMO], and Minakir is a doctor of economics and deputy director of the Khabarovsk Economics Research Institute of the U.S.S.R. Academy of Sciences' Far Eastern Division. This article appeared in the May 1988 issue of *MEMO*.

realization of this potential has more than economic significance. The dynamic and comprehensive development of the U.S.S.R.'s Pacific coast regions should ensure that our entire country, two thirds of whose territory is located in Asia, enjoys a vital and natural interaction with the Asian-Pacific region—the area to which the center of world economics and politics will most likely shift in the next century.

This obvious fact is making difficult headway and is still conflicting with the inertia of established views. Vladivostok remains a "closed city." And the very approach to the notion of security for these "peripheral" eastern regions, which are in many ways isolated from the country's basic industrial and economic centers, still remains narrow and continues to bear the stamp of dramatic events in our history and acute and painful problems of current international relations. It is appropriate to recall here our territorial disputes with Japan, the Russo-Japanese War, and the protracted struggle for the establishment of Soviet power—a struggle complicated by imperialist intervention. Events on the eve of World War II, including the trial of strength imposed on the U.S.S.R. at Lake Khasan and in the Khalka River region attested to the real threat of a second front against our country, at least until the major turning point in the Great Patriotic War.

Postwar events in the countries in close proximity to the U.S.S.R. and large-scale revolutionary changes have strengthened the position of socialism on the Asian continent. But because of the high level of military tension and political rivalry, East and Southeast Asia have remained zones of confrontation, instability, and crises. Suffice it to mention the wars in Korea and Indochina, U.S. attempts to encircle the Soviet Union from the east with military bases and alliances, the tension in Soviet-Chinese relations, the unsettled nature of relations with Japan, that country's territorial claims, and the intensity of the military confrontation in various regions of Asia.

In addition, as a result of vigorous processes of economic development in the postwar period, the place that East Asia and the entire Pacific region occupy in the world has undergone a qualitative change. A highly important center of economic activity has developed there with uncommon speed, even by today's standards, and there, as nowhere else, there has been a clear display of "modern-day capitalism's ability to rise to new levels in the socialization of production, to push back the limits on the growth of productive forces, and to adapt to the global challenges of the age."[1]

To date, the correlation of economic potentials among states in the western Pacific has not been evolving to the Soviet Union's advantage.

---

[1] *Kommunist* [*Communist*], No. 2, 1988, p. 5.

Among other things, the gap between the development rates of the Soviet Union's eastern regions and those of a number of neighboring countries has been growing, along with the gap in the extent of their integration into the system of regional economic ties. Trade relations are for all practical purposes the U.S.S.R.'s sole channel for interacting with the region. The extent to which the U.S.S.R.'s foreign trade is oriented toward the Pacific region (including China and the other socialist countries) is insignificant—about 8 percent of its overall trade (9 percent of exports and almost 8 percent of imports), while for the majority of the region's countries these indicators reach levels of 50 percent to 80 percent.[2]

The socialist states (the People's Republic of China, the Korean People's Democratic Republic, the Mongolian People's Republic, the Socialist Republic of Vietnam, the Kampuchean People's Republic, and the Lao People's Democratic Republic) are the Soviet Union's principal foreign-trade partners. Soviet aggregate exports to those countries vary between 4 billion and 5 billion rubles, while imports amount to 2 billion. Exports to the region's developed capitalist countries (excluding the United States and Canada) are at a level of approximately 1 billion rubles, while imports amount to about 2.8 billion. There is an even greater imbalance in trade with the ASEAN countries: in 1986, exports came to 55 million rubles, while imports totaled 265 million.[3] The U.S.S.R. does not maintain trade contacts with South Korea, Taiwan, or Hong Kong—which, together with Japan, are the most dynamic participants in regional ties. To all intents and purposes, Soviet exports to the Asian-Pacific region's developed capitalist countries and developing countries did not increase at all in the 1980s, and imports actually fell.

Intensive business contacts are a significant factor in political relations and in international confidence building, although it is also obvious that broad and productive economic cooperation is hampered without the normalization of international relations. The U.S.S.R.'s limited trade and economic involvement in regional processes often engenders distrust toward our foreign-economic initiatives, which results once again in limiting our possibilities for developing trade and other business contacts. This closed circle makes it significantly more difficult to activate Soviet foreign policy and to step up mutually advantageous economic cooperation in the Pacific region.

Foreign economic relations—a natural extension and organic part of the economy—are often formed under the influence of political, as

---

[2]*Pacific Economic Community Statistics, 1986*, Tokyo, 1986, p. 43.
[3]*U.S.S.R. Foreign Trade in 1986. A Statistical Collection* [*Vneshnyaya torgovlya SSSR v 1986. Statisticheskiy sbornik*], Moscow, 1987, pp. 11, 12, 14.

well as economic, requirements. However, the reason for giving priority attention to such relations in the Pacific region is not only to untie political knots, but above all, to make fuller use of external possibilities for meeting the needs of economic and social development. In that sense the U.S.S.R.'s Pacific-coast regions are called upon to become both the objects of expanded foreign economic relations with the region, and a link connecting the country's entire economy with the world economy's most dynamic zone.

M.S. Gorbachev's trip to the Far East in July 1986 and his speech in Vladivostok provided the impetus for rethinking our priorities in the region and the Soviet Union's status as a Pacific power. However, even the Soviet press often commented on the speech in a rather one-sided fashion. Principal attention was devoted to the foreign-policy part of the speech, while the sections devoted to perestroika and the economic development of that vast region were left in the shadows, as it were.

If one were to attempt to briefly summarize the points made in Vladivostok with respect to both domestic and international affairs, what clearly comes to the fore is the task of "compressing the time required to solve problems," sharply increasing the Far East's contribution to the country's economic potential, devoting priority attention to developing the eastern regions, and carefully assessing the Far East's economic prospects with a view to that area's special significance—natural resources, social and economic potentials, and great international prospects. As was noted in the Vladivostok speech, "The Far East is traditionally called the country's outpost on the Pacific Ocean. That is no doubt true. But today that view can no longer be deemed adequate. Maritime Province and the Far East must be turned into a highly developed economic complex."

As is known, a Long-Term State Program for the Comprehensive Development of the Far Eastern Economic Region's Productive Forces has been adopted. As a first task, the text virtually recapitulates that part of M.S. Gorbachev's Vladivostok speech where, speaking of the need to envision the area's long-term development within the framework of a unified state regional policy, he formulated the goal of a comprehensive program to create a highly effective economic complex in the Far East that is organically incorporated in the system of the nationwide and international division of labor, and that has its own major resource, research, and production base; an optimal economic structure; and a developed social sector. Thus, the program poses the problem of giving the Soviet Far East's economy the goal of "dual integration"—something that it clearly does not have now.

The Far East's situation in both the Soviet and the international division of labor is determined chiefly by its raw-material resources and the extractive industries, which account for about 30 percent of the region's total volume of industrial production, while the extent of the processing of raw materials remains quite low. In the 1960s and 1970s the relative cheapness of the raw materials brought about a lag in the processing industry and put areas that had already been developed on the verge of exhausting their resources. New facilities that went into production in the 1980s required major material and financial expenditures, which were also primarily aimed at maintaining the level of extraction of raw materials.

For a long time the Far Eastern economic region's orientation toward maximum, heedless use of fish, mineral, and timber resources maintained the illusion that the foreign-currency problem could be solved by accelerated growth of the raw-materials branches. In the process, insufficient attention was paid to the requirements of developing the Far Eastern region's own economy and ties with the world economy. As a result, the area's industry found itself cut off, as it were, from the needs of the region. A large percentage of its machinery output goes to the European part of the country, whence a counterflow of machinery arrives to meet local needs. The infrastructure, including its social components, has followed along behind the raw-material branches' specific needs and has been determined not by the needs of the area's comprehensive development and settlement, but by the tasks of developing the raw-material reserves as rapidly as possible and maximizing gross exports.

As a result, the Far East's overall economic potential, which determines the intensity and quality of both its internal and its foreign economic ties, has proved to be both inadequately developed, and deformed in its basic proportions. These disproportions, as V. Chichkanov notes, "are in large measure due to subjective causes and have resulted, in particular, from a lack of coordination between industrial-branch decisions and overall national goals for the region's comprehensive development.[4]

The industrial-branch approach to the Far East's development has led, in particular, to a slowdown in its rate of economic development and to a drop in its share of national production; and it has been precisely the priority branches—the timber, fishing, and extractive industries—that have found themselves most heavily hit by stagnation. There has been a lag in the development of nonferrous metallurgy, where the result of the narrowly departmental approach is that only five or six of some 20 to 30 highly valuable components are being extracted from certain types of raw materials. It has been estimated

---

[4]V. Chichkanov, "The Development of the Far East's Productive Forces: Problems and Prospects" (Kommunist, No. 16, 1985, p. 100).

that merely processing the dumps of nonferrous-ore tailings could triple the volume of marketable output. The "unprofitability," from the standpoint of narrowly construed branch interests, of developing processing facilities is the reason why immense quantities of raw materials are hauled beyond the region's borders, which has put the Far East in the position of a "raw-materials appendage."

The raw-materials specialization of production has become a serious limiting factor not only for internal development, but also for the Far East's business contacts with adjoining countries. It is slowing improvement in the effectiveness of foreign economic relations. Thus, the virtual stagnation of Soviet exports to Japan at the level of about a billion rubles a year for the past 10 to 15 years is due in no small part to the fact that exports consist exclusively of raw materials: timber (principally in the form of logs, four fifths of which are felled in the Far East), anthracite coal, fish, fish products, and rare and nonferrous metals. In all, the Far East's share in Soviet exports to Japan is estimated at 70 to 80 percent.

The application in practice of the "export-specialization" concept (based on gross-output figures), which for all practical purposes has become a component of the industrial-branch approach to the area's development and to the exploitation and utilization of its resources, has led to a virtual impasse not just in foreign-economic activity, but in the economic development of the Far East as a whole. In the 1980s the extractive branches sharply cut back their rate of expansion, and no other industries capable of taking on the role of generating economic growth could be found in the Far East.

Under these conditions, the need to turn the Far East economic complex into a system with elements of "dual integration" is becoming increasingly obvious. It is important that it be an organic part of the overall national economy and also that it be organically integrated into the system of the international division of labor. Obviously, only in that case will it become possible, first, to turn the Far East into a region that is fully up to national socioeconomic development standards, and, second, to create a foreign-economic and scientific-technical "contact zone" there. On that basis it is possible to overcome the notion, still applied in practice, of the Far East as an area with an export specialization or, to be more precise, a raw-materials export specialization—a concept that has caused exports of raw materials to be increased exclusively by expanding the scale of extraction.

It would seem quite natural to expect the foreign-economic section of the Long-Term State Program to offer concrete proposals for the Far East's organic inclusion in the system of national and international division of labor. However, even the title of the relevant section— "Strengthening the Export Orientation of the Far East and Transbaikal

Economic Complexes"—clearly indicates a bias toward the old approaches.

A threefold increase in the volume of exports is to be achieved, according to plan, primarily from deliveries of energy resources, from expanded cooperation with Japan in developing the region's timber resources, including production of more highly processed output, and from increased exports of machinery to socialist and other countries. According to forecasts, by the year 2000 lumber exports, by volume, will be no more than 10 percent of exports of logs. Exports of industrial woodchips will have the same ratio to exports of unprocessed timber. Given the fact that plans call for exporting coking coal to Japan at the present level (5.5 million metric tons a year) and for sharply increasing exports of natural gas, petroleum, and gas condensate to the region's countries, one can assume that by the year 2000 unprocessed raw material will continue to be the Far East's basic export, and that it will determine the export structure and the nature of the U.S.S.R.'s participation in the regional division of labor.

Speaking of internal economic parameters, then, for example, the production of lumber as a percentage of total timber harvested is practically unchanged and will remain for the entire period at a level of 16 to 18 percent, although the production of pulp will double, and the production of industrial chips will quadruple. The program makes no provision for the production of lumber in Maritime Territory, in Amur, Kamchatka, or Sakhalin provinces, or in the Yakut Autonomous Republic, although timber exports are planned at existing, or somewhat higher, levels.

Using these facts and figures exclusively as an example, it should be pointed out that the problem is not only in the fact that in the period from 1990 to 2000 the ratio of lumber to logs in exports will remain unchanged, and that this will result in major lost opportunities for earning foreign currency, and in additional material, human, and environmental costs to us. A situation could also very well arise in which selling logs at a profit to Japan, for example, will be impossible, while the requisite funds will have already been invested on our part— in other words, the requirements of the program will have been formally met.

Even now our Japanese partners are expressing highly selective demand for imported timber and wood products. More than 80 percent of their purchases consist of high-quality logs of coniferous species. Japan's growing demand for such products as cardboard, paper, plywood, particle board, and lumber is being satisfied under fiercely competitive conditions by both local and foreign producers, including North American ones. This presupposes that export products will meet the highest standards of quality and conform to the requirements, often highly specific, that are imposed by Japan. These limiting factors could be neutralized by organizing joint enterprises with the participation of Japanese capital and the use of Japanese technology, but as far as one can ascertain, no such plans are under discussion.

Evidence of due consideration for the foreign-economic component—consideration that reflects the increased complexity of ties with foreign partners and presupposes establishment of closer mutual relations at the production stage, including the necessary financial, technical, and commercial support—is also missing when one analyzes certain other sections of the program where its presence would be highly desirable. This is especially true of the sections that have to do with the resolution of social questions. Speaking in Vladivostok, M.S. Gorbachev noted: "If addressing social questions is vitally necessary for the entire country, it is doubly and triply so for the Far East."

For a long time the problem of developing the Far East was resolved with virtual disregard for the human being, since it clearly did not pay the ministries to invest in the socioeconomic infrastructure—especially since the cost of construction there is two to three times as high as in the central regions. Quite often the absence of normal living and working conditions was "compensated for" by providing pay increments—and from time to time, by supplying scarce consumer goods. Nevertheless, deposits in savings banks in the region are 14 to 35 percent lower than the average for the Russian Republic, and earnings are 20 percent lower than in the central areas of the country, even when the pay increments are taken into account. The level of consumption of goods and services is lower, and the selection of foodstuffs is worse. For every thousand people who come to live in Khabarovsk Territory, for example, there are 800 who leave. Of every 10 families that resettle on farms in Amur Province, only three are left after five years. The outflow of skilled personnel trained in the region, and the chaotic migration cause losses in the billions.

The acute labor shortage and personnel turnover severely damage the most vulnerable elements—the agrarian sector of the economy (more than half of all the food consumed in the Far East is shipped in from the country's western regions) and the building industry, including housing construction (in certain cases people have to spend 10 to 15 years on a waiting list before obtaining an apartment). Under existing benefits for people resettling, every family consisting of at least two working members is entitled to receive housing—a separate cottage, for example. However, the scale of resettlement is at odds with housing-construction capabilities, which, in turn, constrain the recruitment of labor for work in the Far East, and that limits possibilities for new construction. The region has an average of seven workers per construction site, and at this moment every second project would have to be "frozen" for the others to meet normative deadlines for completion. Yet more construction is needed in the region if its development is to proceed at a more dynamic pace.

It would seem that both housing construction and solution of the food problem could be areas of intensive foreign-economic cooperation. As one of its aspects, one might propose creating a network of enterprises to produce structural components for prefabricated buildings—panels and modules for building one- and two-story wooden houses of modern design. Construction of new comprehensive wood-processing enterprises and reconstruction of existing ones with the participation of foreign firms, and creation of facilities for producing building materials, finishing materials, floor coverings, and furniture would help to overcome the housing problems more quickly. At the same time, opportunities might arise for exporting a broad assortment of wood-processing products.

To proceed: the Far East accounts for 40 percent of the fish caught and canned in the U.S.S.R. However, there is an acute shortage of processing capacity, warehousing and production facilities, refrigerators, equipment and, finally, packaging, of which Far Eastern enterprises supply only enough to meet one third of the processing industry's demand. The additional packaging that is required is purchased in the Baltic region!

While fish catches have risen significantly in recent decades, the quality of the catch has shown a consistent tendency to deteriorate: Alaska pollock and sardines account for up to 75 percent of all output. The low level of technology used in processing this raw material has led to an overall drop in the quality of fish products, contributed to a further narrowing of the fish assortment, and caused a certain stagnation in export receipts. The degree of processing of the fish earmarked for export is low. In particular, the processing of Alaska pollock neglects the immense potential for preparing filets and chopped fish, for which a demand exists in neighboring countries. The enlistment of foreign capital, technology, and experience would not only speed the untying of these knots and increase the saturation of the domestic market—particularly that of the Far East—with fish products and partially prepared fish dishes, but could also help expand the fish assortment and improve its structure. In this connection, it would be a good idea to make provision for the use of foreign firms' production and marketing capabilities at the earliest possible stages in the development of the branches in question, particularly since Japanese business circles have shown considerable interest in projects of that sort.

The technical refitting of fishing operations and the construction of new fish-processing enterprises could become an area of joint enterprise. According to some assessments, the shortage of fish-processing capacity could reach critical levels in the next few years, and ship repair is still in difficult straits. Thus, during the past five-year period, large-displacement ships belonging to one Khabarovsk Territory collective fishing farm stood in port for 500 ship-days longer than the required time awaiting the cleaning of their hulls prior to repairs—in other words, to all intents and purposes, two ships stood idle for the entire five-year period.

Enlisting foreign companies and resources in this sphere on a compensation basis—i.e., under an arrangement whereby investments are repaid out of a percentage of the output—could substantially enhance the efficiency with which equipment is used, increase the degree of processing, improve product quality, and increase export earnings in trade not just with Japan but with the United States, Canada, the People's Republic of China, the Korean People's Democratic Republic, and South Korea. Modernizing shore facilities with the participation of foreign firms, refitting the small-craft fleet for coastal fishing, and providing mariculture enterprises with the necessary equipment are actions that could, in time, open qualitatively new opportunities for penetrating external markets.

The weak spot in the program, whose implementation still makes no provision for the least extensive use of external possibilities (such as the importation of labor), has to do with creating a modern construction industry. By the year 2000, the Far Eastern Economic Region has to use about 200 billion rubles in capital investments, including the performance of 80 billion rubles' worth of construction and installation work, and 101 million square meters of housing construction. Successful fulfillment of such a major investment program will require the organization of a new, modern, building-materials industry, a change in construction technology, and the comprehensive industrialization of building methods.

Obviously, in creating a construction complex, as opposed to the fishing or wood-processing industries, there is virtually no way of recouping foreign-currency expenditures. But without developing a modern construction industry, there is no way to solve the problems of providing the area with workers and engineers, and no way to achieve a thorough reconstruction and modernization of industry. A lag in developing the construction complex can result in the sluggish, incomplete fulfillment of the entire program, and threatens to cause major foreign-currency losses in other areas, and for a protracted period of time, at that. Thus, for example, of the 200,000 people working in the Dalryba [Far Eastern Fishing] Association, 45,000 are on waiting lists for housing. Although the fishermen produce 37 percent of Maritime Territory's gross output and provide a significant share of receipts from exports, their housing allocation is limited to 3 to 4 percent of the Chief

Vladivostok Construction Administration's output plans. The under-development of the construction complex potentially means sizable foreign-currency losses in the form of unrealized earnings from foreign tourism, the production of industrial output, and so forth.

The program calls for extensive economic cooperation with the socialist countries of Asia, including the creation of joint enterprises for production of agricultural products and consumer goods from Soviet raw materials, with the products and goods to be imported by the Soviet Union. Economic cooperation based on the use of Soviet raw materials to produce finished goods for import by the Soviet Union could also be supplemented by transferring part of the Soviet Far East's light-industry enterprises to the Socialist Republic of Vietnam and the Korean People's Democratic Republic, with their surplus labor resources. That makes even better sense in that the supply of consumer goods to the Soviet Far East presently comes mainly from the European part of the U.S.S.R. The local consumer-goods enterprises, for their part, work in conditions of acute labor shortages and labor turnover, and frequently rely on raw materials shipped in from elsewhere. Cooperative projects of this kind could enlist medium-sized and small firms from a number of countries in the region—firms capable of providing for the technological updating of products,[5] which could then be exported and, in particular, cover the significant deficit that the region's socialist states run in trade with the U.S.S.R.

Use of foreign-economic capabilities and foreign-currency resources in areas that promise no direct foreign-currency yield should evidently be accompanied by creation of a kind of Far Eastern regional system of priorities for foreign-currency expenditures, regularization of import purchases, and creation of mechanisms that would rule out the kinds of errors that have been made in the past. Thus, for example, imports of expensive Japanese equipment used at timber-felling sites grew year after year, and apparently no attempt was made to attract the necessary technology and machinery to produce such equipment our-selves. In view of this experience, one could—in creating joint wood-processing ventures, for example—avoid that sort of "compensation" model and gear foreign economic relations to the production of the necessary equipment by enterprises in the Soviet Far East.

In like fashion, it would make sense, for example, to gear our thinking not to the importation of refrigeration and fish-processing equipment but to creation of the necessary conditions for its produc-tion. That could open up new export prospects for Far Eastern indus-

---

[5]The problems of the Soviet Far East's ties with the socialist countries of Asia are analyzed in detail in M. Ye. Trigubenko and N.A. Shlyk's article, "On the Question of Stepping Up Direct Cooperation Between the U.S.S.R.'s Far Eastern Regions and the Socialist Countries of Asia," (*Problemy Dalnego Vostoka* [*Problems of the Far East*], No. 4, 1987).

try and help it to define its role both in the national economy and in relations with the entire region, especially with the socialist and developing countries.

In view of the region's remoteness from the country's principal automotive production centers and its proximity to the markets of China, the Korean People's Democratic Republic, and Vietnam, the Soviet Far East's machine-building complex could also include cooperative projects with foreign automotive companies. Such projects would give an impetus to the development of the whole machinery industry, expand export possibilities, and increase the saturation of the domestic market. A project for a joint automotive plant (Soviet-Japanese, for example) could be viewed, in the context of a special economic-cooperation zone, as one alternative, nontraditional approach to establishing advanced forms of economic ties with foreign countries.

In the Far Eastern Economic Region there has been virtually no progress in the area of organizing joint ventures with foreign firms. Under such circumstances, there has to be interest in the proposal by a group of Japanese insurance companies to set up a special joint-venture zone on a plot of Soviet territory near the border with the P.R.C. and Korean People's Democratic Republic. The lessee of this ground for 50 to 60 years could be a Soviet-Japanese consortium that would begin construction of a modern commercial port, international airport, thermal power plant, roads, and other infrastructure facilities. The Japanese side's investment in the project's implementation might amount to $5 billion to $6 billion. A fixed profit would be paid from the revenues obtained from renting fully developed plots of ground, ready for business use, to companies and organizations.

The implementation of such a project could give a powerful impetus not only to Soviet-Japanese trade and economic relations, but to the whole complex of Soviet foreign economic relations in the Asian-Pacific region. One cannot rule out the possibility that even China, which has no major ports on the Sea of Japan, would have an interest in the project. Participation in constructing the special zone's facilities might also be attractive to the Korean People's Democratic Republic.

It is not the authors' intention to draw direct analogies with the "export-production zones" and "special economic zones" that exist in certain of the region's developing countries, as well as China. In the majority of cases, the formation of these zones has to do with opportunities for using cheap labor, favorable geographic location, or special tax or investment advantages, and with the host countries' interest in increasing exports. In the final analysis, it is a question of specific national priorities and possibilities for attracting foreign partners. At the same time, although China's experience in this area may not, on the whole, be a model to be copied, it is nevertheless of considerable practical interest in many respects.

In the special economic zones, Chinese legislation grants foreign investors conditions comparable to those that exist in the countries of Southeast Asia. To attract foreign investments in industry, preferential tax and customs arrangements are extended to 14 "open" coastal-area cities and the island of Hainan.[6] Within the bounds of China's special economic zones, all foreign-trade transactions are duty-free. Producer goods are not subject to duty in the "open" cities, and in certain ones economic conditions for joint entrepreneurial activities are more favorable than in the special economic zones. In a number of cases, in the second half of 1986 the Chinese side substantially lowered rents and wage rates for local personnel, and rescinded the tax on repatriated profits. In the special economic zones, income tax rates are only half those provided for in the 1979 law on joint entrepreneurial activities.

More than a fourth of all foreign investment, which totaled about $7 billion in 1987, is concentrated in the zones. Roughly another fourth is accounted for by the three "open" cities (Canton, Shanghai and Tientsin), which are at the forefront of efforts to assimilate foreign experience. In 1986 aggregate exports of output produced on their territory reached $1 billion, and export goods account for a steadily growing share of overall production. Various forms of cooperation with foreign companies are being tested, and enterprises with foreign participation are becoming a kind of bellwether for China's industry and services sector, and are promoting the application of new approaches to organizing production, attracting foreign capital, and establishing long-term ties with foreign partners.

In reviewing the Soviet Far Eastern Economic Complex's prospects for development of foreign economic relations, one could, in our opinion, propose even more radical variants of territorial-administrative methods of attracting foreign investments, technology, and experience. Since individual economic zones obviously cannot promote solution of the entire range of problems, the Soviet Far East as a whole might be regarded as a natural zone of economic cooperation with foreign countries, aimed at creating a diversified economic structure and improving the quality of the social sector.

Trade in services is becoming an increasingly important area of economic exchange in which the Soviet Far East could participate more actively. Accelerated development of the U.S.S.R.'s Far Eastern regions and their broader involvement in foreign economic relations will require development of the merchant-marine fleet, increased

---

[6]For details, see A. Salitskiy, "The P.R.C.: The Search for an Optimal Foreign Economic Strategy," (*MEMO*, No. 9, 1987 [pp. 141-156 in this collection]).

cargo-handling capabilities at ports, and reconstruction and expansion of the ports themselves. As of now, marine transport capabilities lag behind the growing requirements of foreign trade and the market for transport services. A significant percentage even of Soviet export cargoes is carried in foreign bottoms, which means foreign-currency losses.

The onshore infrastructure (especially port facilities) on the Soviet Pacific coast is inadequately developed in comparison to that of other Pacific-basin countries. Of the main ports—Nakhodka, Vladivostok, Vostochnyy, and Vanino—only two are open to foreign shipping. Interested foreign firms could be enlisted in improving and expanding port facilities and the onshore infrastructure, including the construction of container terminals, warehouses, automated loading complexes, and processing enterprises.

Among other things, all this would help make more intensive use of the trans-Siberian container link, which, to all intents and purposes, serves only the port of Vostochnyy. The problem of containerization needs to be solved with respect not only to import-export cargoes but also to domestic cargoes in which the Far East is involved, and land-transportation capabilities need to be brought up to the current level of organization of container and unitized-load shipping and lighterage. It is noteworthy in this respect that the P.R.C.'s Seventh Five-Year plan for development of the national economy calls for intensive development of the production infrastructure, including power engineering, transportation, communications, and construction of hydroelectric stations and ports.[7]

Insofar as the structure of consumer demand in the region's developed countries is shifting toward a greater role for services, it would be incorrect to concentrate exclusively on the "industrial" approach to the Soviet Far East's economic development. It is a known fact that the area offers considerable possibilities for tourism and for attracting, on that basis, significant sums in foreign currency from Japan and the region's other countries. The expediency of enlisting foreign firms in the development of that branch is particularly apparent from the experience of China, where more than half of all foreign investments are in areas other than material production—in the construction of tourist complexes and hotels, restaurants, and municipal-service and consumer-service enterprises. As a result, the P.R.C.'s foreign-currency earnings from foreign tourism have been steadily increasing and exceeded $1.8 billion in 1987.

---

[7] "Foreign Direct Investment in the People's Republic of China," U.N. Centre on Transnational Corporations, New York, 1988, p. 23.

In developing a tourist industry in the Soviet Far East, the area's specific features can also be taken into account, including the fact that the inhabitants have virtually no place in the region where they can spend their vacations. The inhabitants of the Far East spend eight to ten times as much money getting to their summer-vacation locations as do people living in the country's European areas. To solve this problem and to create an all-purpose system for serving tourists—both Soviet and foreign—we will evidently have to abandon narrowly departmental approaches and seek out nontraditional solutions.

Specifically, under conditions in which there is a shortage of construction capacity and an inadequate infrastructure, it would scarcely make sense to create separate tourist and vacation facilities for serving Soviet and foreign tourists, as is presently the custom. On the other hand, where we are moving to a cost-recovery system with regard to foreign currency, which will make it clearly "unprofitable" for Intourist to earn rubles from Soviet tourists, a number of "compensation" mechanisms could be provided.

One of them is to raise foreign currency by selling fishing and hunting licenses, for example. In Canada and the United States, the commercial organization of sport fishing (principally for fish in the salmon family) has led to the emergence of a highly profitable form of international tourism. Thus, in Canada the value of the entire commercial catch of salmon is estimated at $145 million, while the sale of licenses to amateur salmon and trout fishermen yields $120 million. While the commercial value of a single salmon has remained practically unchanged at the level of $6 to $7 for the past 25 years, the yield from a salmon caught by a sport fisherman—including, of course, payment for all services rendered him—rose from $158 in 1956 to $333 in 1980.

The existence of an adequately skilled work force and of managerial personnel prepared to work in the rapidly changing conditions of the international market is of decisive importance for the creation of a reliable export base. Let us turn to China once again. The shortage of qualified personnel is one of the principal problems which that country's cooperation with foreign firms brought to light. In efforts to solve it, widespread use was made of foreign as well as domestic potential, including foreign universities and research centers. Commercial channels were also used to obtain appropriate vocational or educational training.

A highly important condition for implementation of the Long-Term State Program for the Comprehensive Development of the Far Eastern Economic Region's Productive Forces is the existence of an adequate and effective mechanism for making adjustments in it. In this connection, it must obviously contain a unit for management of foreign economic relations. The program as such reflects a new approach to planning and presupposes a combination of the industrial-branch and territorial approaches. At the same time, its work assignments are scattered across the various ministries and departments. And the departmental approach continues to be discernible in the section devoted to foreign economic relations.

One can assume, therefore, that if some supradepartmental coordinating agency is needed for implementing the program proper, such an agency is doubly needed to fully achieve the foreign-economic goals as formulated by M.S. Gorbachev in Vladivostok, since even under reconstruction of the system for organizing foreign economic relations, import-export operations are being transferred to the level of ministries, departments, enterprises, and associations.[8] Given the situation in the Far East, that can serve to reinforce the departmental approach. Moreover, the development and adoption of the program for the Far East attest to the need for purposefully "boosting" the area to a certain level, and for admitting that its potential for "self-development" has yet to be formed. This makes it all the more important that implementation of the program lead to qualitative advances, and to a change in precisely the situation that is in large part attributable to the departments' unchecked activities.

Maintaining the present organizational approaches to the program's implementation can only reinforce the orientation of the Far East's leading branches toward earning revenues from the export of raw materials. If that is the case, then traditional foreign-trade forms of economic relations will obviously be used. The customary "foreign-trade" approach to the U.S.S.R.'s participation in the international division of labor in the Asian-Pacific region is hopelessly out of date. The sizable gap in export potentials between the U.S.S.R. and neighboring countries is not just a matter of quantitative limits, but has to do particularly with qualitative and organizational characteristics. Therefore, banking on increasing Soviet exports by traditional methods will evidently change very little, and an "export base" predicated on specialization in raw materials cannot be in keeping either with the economic processes taking place in the region, or with the directions that changes in the structure of the Soviet economy are taking.

Hence the urgency of a fundamental restructuring of the entire Far Eastern regional economic complex, of moving it qualitatively closer to the economies of the leading states in the Asian-Pacific region, and of using every opportunity for forming qualitatively new "growth points" that would provide the stimulus for the Far East's

---

[8]V. Kamentsev, "Problems of Foreign-Economic Activities," *Kommunist*, No. 15, 1987, p. 26.

balanced and dynamic development and would ensure an expansion of its foreign economic relations.

To make the Far East a full-fledged economic partner of the leading Asian-Pacific countries, we need a well-conceived strategy aimed at its phased inclusion in the structure of the international division of labor, at setting both industrial-branch and geographic priorities, and at using a wide array of methods and forms of foreign economic relations. The development of such a strategy entails not only searching for a model for the Far Eastern region's long-term development and finding methods of using external factors in its structural revamping, but also cooperating with foreign countries to solve priority problems—particularly social and infrastructure problems.

Making purposeful and extensive use of external possibilities along the lines that have been indicated not only can supplement the measures set forth in the program, but can also play the major role in achieving the goals set forth in its important sections. In working to solve the urgent long-term and immediate problems of developing the economy of the U.S.S.R.'s Pacific regions, one cannot fail to consider that "the development of civilization is assuming an increasingly energetic character in the East, in Asia and the Pacific area. Our economy is also shifting to Siberia and the Far East. Therefore we have an objective interest in enriching Asian-Pacific cooperation."[9]

[9]M.S. Gorbachev, *Restructuring and the New Thinking for Our Country and the Whole World* [*Perestroyka i novoye myshleniye dlya nashey strany i dlya vsego mira*], Moscow, 1987, p. 187.

The U.S.S.R.'s Foreign Economic Relations in the Process of Perestroika*

The restructuring of foreign economic relations is an integral part of the radical economic reform being carried out in the U.S.S.R. Resolutions adopted by the CPSU Central Committee and the U.S.S.R. Council of Ministers in August 1986 laid the foundation for this effort.[1] They defined the basic areas of the perestroika—the creation of an effective foreign-economic complex; the direct entry of a broad range of enterprises and associations into the foreign market; a transition from predominantly trade relations to the organization of specialized and cooperative production, primarily with partners from the CMEA countries; the creation of an effective mechanism for foreign economic relations based on the improved planning of these relations, and on the development and strengthening of other economic levers and stimuli; and improvements in the organizational structure for the management of foreign economic relations.

A New Mechanism for the Management of Foreign Economic Activities

During the recent period, measures that were carried out were chiefly of an organizational and legal nature. For example, in order to manage the foreign-economic complex and provide effective coordination of its participants' work, the U.S.S.R. Council of Ministers' State Foreign Economic Commission was established, headed by a deputy chairman of the U.S.S.R. Council of Ministers. The commission is the highest collective body of state administration of the foreign-economic complex. It includes the U.S.S.R ministers of foreign economic relations and of finance, the chairman of the U.S.S.R. State Committee for Science and Technology, a U.S.S.R. deputy minister of foreign affairs,

---

*The survey was prepared by associates of the All-Union Research Institute on Foreign Economic Relations of the U.S.S.R. Council of Ministers' State Foreign Economic Commission: T. Artemova, G. Bulanov, A. Bulatov, S. Diykov, V. Korneyev, V. Krasnoglazov, V. Lavrov, S. Lavrov, N. Petrova, N. Simonov, N. Stomakhina, and N. Sheremeteva. It was compiled by A. Bulatov. This article appeared in the September 1988 issue of *MEMO*.
[1]These are the Aug. 19, 1986, resolutions, "On Measures to Improve the Management of Foreign Economic Relations," and "On Measures to Improve the Management of Economic and Scientific and Technical Cooperation with Socialist Countries."

and deputy heads of central economic departments and permanent agencies of the U.S.S.R. Council of Ministers.

In place of the U.S.S.R. Ministry of Foreign Trade and the U.S.S.R. State Committee on Foreign Economic Relations, which were eliminated, the U.S.S.R. Ministry of Foreign Economic Relations was created. It helps all Soviet participants in foreign economic relations to carry out their activities, monitors them to ensure that they serve state interests in the foreign market, and provides methodological and informational support and consultant services.

New subdivisions set up under the U.S.S.R. Ministry of Foreign Economic Relations—the Chief Combined Administration for Foreign Economic Policy, the Chief Administration for the Coordination and Regulation of Foreign Economic Operations, and the Chief Administration for the Competitiveness of Export Products—are concerned with all of these activities. The functions of the ministry itself include current management of export-import operations involving goods classified as being of statewide importance, provision of economic and technical assistance to foreign countries, and organization of the construction of facilities abroad and within the U.S.S.R. in which foreign firms are involved. As a result of the consolidation of foreign trade associations that were previously under various departments, there are now no more than 25 such associations within the ministry's system.

A great deal of work is being done to restructure the foreign-economic apparatus abroad, to carry out advertising and promotional activities, and to organize the training, retraining, and advanced training of personnel.

One of the main directions of the restructuring of the foreign-economic mechanism is that of granting U.S.S.R. ministries and departments, republics, and enterprises and organizations the right to enter the foreign market directly. They can create branch and territorial foreign trading associations, as well as foreign trading firms made up of enterprises and organizations. As of now, approximately 60 ministries and departments, all the union republics, and about 90 enterprises, interbranch scientific and technical complexes, and other organizations have been granted the right to enter the foreign market directly, so altogether there are approximately 200 Soviet foreign trading organizations (including associations and firms) operating on the foreign market.

In this connection the role of branch and territorial management of foreign economic relations is growing considerably, and special administrations (commissions) on foreign economic relations are being created in ministries, departments, and under union-republic councils of ministers.

The June 1987 U.S.S.R. Law on the State Enterprise (Association) provides a new definition of the role of the enterprise. Specifically, it significantly broadens its right to participate in the organization and execution of export-import operations, and in establishment of direct ties with enterprises and organizations in other CMEA countries; its right to make independent decisions on questions of cooperative production and research-and-development arrangements (including signing economic agreements and contracts for delivery of products and services connected with cooperative production arrangements and development of production); and its right to determine the best conditions for the export of its products when signing economic agreements with foreign trading organizations of other ministries and departments.

A number of other measures are also helping to increase the economic interest and accountability of enterprises with respect to development of foreign economic relations. Now the results of enterprises' foreign economic operations become an integral part of the overall results of their economic activities and directly affect the formation of economic-incentive funds. Foreign-currency funds are being created at enterprises. They are comprised of deductions (based on stable long-term rates) from money received from the export of finished products, as well as the entire foreign-currency receipts from operations involved in cooperative deliveries and the sale of licenses.

To create an export base, an enterprise can use foreign-currency loans granted by the U.S.S.R. Bank for Foreign Economic Affairs. An enterprise uses its foreign-currency fund to pay off such loans, as well as to pay fines, forfeits, and other forms of compensation in foreign currency. Foreign-currency funds contribute to modernization and technical retooling of enterprises, and to developing and updating their production.

A transition from centralized allocation of material resources to wholesale trade in producer goods on the basis of customers' orders, without limits and central allocations, will do a great deal to give enterprises a greater economic stake in developing foreign economic relations. Starting in 1989 wholesale trade in producer goods, using transferable rubles [the CMEA accounting currency—*Trans.*], will be initiated through the U.S.S.R. State Committee for Material and Technical Supply's All-Union Vneshpromtekhobmen Foreign-Trading Association [which deals with exports and imports of metallurgical, chemical, and petroleum products, and other raw materials—*Trans.*].

In order to give enterprises a greater interest in profitable exports and to reduce inefficient imports, differentiated foreign-currency coefficients are being introduced. They make it possible to evaluate import-export activities (on the basis of actual contractual prices) in

Soviet rubles, and thus to determine the contribution of foreign-trade activities to the overall results of an enterprise's economic performance. In order to increase the production and delivery for export of products that entail a high degree of processing, foreign-currency coefficients for these goods have been set at a level that is higher than the established ratio between foreign-trade and domestic prices.

These coefficients, however, do not affect the export of raw materials or the production of products that replace imports. Moreover, the level of coefficients and the size of actual foreign-currency deductions fail to create the conditions for complete implementation of the principles of cost recovery and self-financing in operations involving foreign currency. A gradual transition from differentiated foreign-currency coefficients to a single foreign-currency exchange rate will make it possible to resolve this and many other issues.

The development of economic accountability in foreign economic activities is being hindered by timidity in making the transition from the reliance on central export orders and import assignments to a system of contractual relations based on economic accountability. Regulations have now been drawn up regarding contractual relations between enterprises and foreign-trading organizations. Their implementation will mean that, in addition to the types and assortment of products, the amounts and dates of deliveries, quality, and the type and duration of contracts, contractual relations will also encompass domestic wholesale prices and contractual foreign-trade prices, the size of commissions paid, bonuses for the enterprises and foreign-trading associations involved, terms of delivery and payment, and the contracting parties' mutual financial liability. With the help of such contractual relations, an enterprise will become a participant enjoying equal rights in foreign economic relations.

Direct Ties

In the course of restructuring the management of foreign economic activity, a great deal of attention is being given to development of traditional and new forms of cooperation. The CPSU Central Committee and U.S.S.R. Council of Ministers' August 19, 1986, resolution "On Measures to Improve the Management of Economic and Scientific and Technical Cooperation with the Socialist Countries," identified the main goals and objectives of establishing direct ties, and it granted Soviet enterprises and organizations broad rights to develop such ties.

The U.S.S.R. Law on the State Enterprise (Association) gave enterprises and organizations the right to establish and conduct direct relations with partners from CMEA countries. In December 1986 the

U.S.S.R. Council of Ministers' State Foreign Economic Commission approved "Procedures for the Conducting by U.S.S.R. Associations, Enterprises, and Organizations of Direct Production and Scientific and Technical Relations with Enterprises and Organizations of other CMEA Member Countries" (amendments were made to this document in July 1987), which made it considerably easier to establish direct contacts with foreign partners. In addition, direct relations are regulated by a whole series of departmental documents. Bilateral intergovernmental agreements on the development of direct relations have been signed with the German Democratic Republic, the Hungarian People's Republic, the Mongolian People's Republic, the People's Republic of Bulgaria, the Polish People's Republic, the Socialist Republic of Romania, the Czechoslovak Socialist Republic, the Korean People's Democratic Republic, and Laos.

Soviet associations, enterprises, and organizations are showing an interest in establishing direct relations with partners from socialist countries. For example, cooperation is developing effectively within the framework of direct relations between the Leningrad Elektrosila [Electric Power] Production Association and partners from Bulgaria. Specialists from the Soviet association believe that it would cost two and a half to three times as much for them to produce themselves the products they are now receiving from Bulgaria.

Currently more than 1,500 direct relations have been formalized in protocols and agreements. Poland has been the most active of the CMEA member countries in setting up relations of this sort—more than 380 agreements have been established with enterprises and organizations in that country. There have been positive changes in the establishment of direct contacts with partners from Romania.

For the majority of Soviet enterprises and organizations direct relations with partners from socialist countries are something new. And as in any new endeavor, certain difficulties arise. Therefore, a great deal of attention is being given to improving the normative acts and guidelines that have been adopted. For example, in July 1987 the U.S.S.R. Council of Ministers adopted a resolution "On Procedures for the Transferring and Obtaining of Documentation Containing Inventions and 'Know-How' by Soviet Associations, Enterprises, and Organizations in Implementing New Integration Forms of Cooperation with Enterprises and Organizations of the Other CMEA Member Countries." As a result, Soviet participants gained the right to agree independently on the conditions for transferring and obtaining documents containing inventions and "know-how," and also to sign contracts, pacts, and agreements.

The CPSU Central Committee and the U.S.S.R. Council of Ministers' September 1987 resolution "On Additional Measures for the

Improvement of Foreign Economic Activity under the New Management Conditions" gives Soviet enterprises and organizations the right to sign contracts for one-time deliveries of products; prototypes of products; instruments; accessories; tools; and recyclable raw materials freed in the process of producing materials, machinery and equipment; as well as the right to provide services regardless of whether contracts and protocols on direct relations have been signed. The resolution also gives enterprises the right to obtain foreign-currency loans from the U.S.S.R. Bank for Foreign Economic Activity for a period of two to eight years. Measures are also being taken to provide assistance to Soviet enterprises and organizations in setting contractual prices for assemblies and parts delivered within the framework of cooperative production arrangements.

The procedures for sending specialists abroad on business trips have been made considerably easier for enterprises participating in direct relations, and customs formalities in the transport of cargo across Soviet borders have been simplified. In documents accompanying such cargo, it is sufficient to indicate the date on which an economic contract (or protocol) was signed, or the contract number, and this serves as the basis for allowing cargo across the U.S.S.R. state border. Special permits from the U.S.S.R. Ministry of Foreign Economic Relations are not required for shipping cargo within the framework of direct relations. Nonclassified technical documentation is allowed across the border on the basis of letters from the executives of the associations, enterprises, and organizations participating in direct relations.

Despite the considerable work that has been done to prepare an organizational and legal base for the development of direct relations, our enterprises and organizations are still encountering a series of difficulties in their practical activities. Specifically, the role of the branch ministries and the limits of their responsibility in the conduct of direct relations have not been clearly defined, and in practice this sometimes results in restricting the independence of enterprises in establishing and developing such relations.

The development of direct relations is being hindered by the large volume of state orders and the insignificant scale of wholesale trade. Problems are also arising with the balancing of deliveries within the framework of direct ties, and there is a shortage of specialists in foreign economic affairs.

Joint Ventures

One new form of cooperation is the joint venture within the U.S.S.R. involving foreign partners. The establishment of these enterprises is regulated by a Decree of the Presidium of the U.S.S.R. Supreme Soviet[2] and also by resolutions of the U.S.S.R. Council of Ministers.[3] Important amendments simplifying the procedures for establishing these enterprises and the system for selling their products were spelled out in the aforementioned September 17, 1987, resolution.

In the creation of joint ventures with partners from socialist countries, participants' shares in the enterprise's initial capitalization are not limited, while in joint ventures with partners from developed capitalist countries or developing countries, the Soviet share must be no less than 51 percent [this latter limitation has since been removed by a Dec. 10, 1988, resolution of the U.S.S.R. Council of Ministers, which also revised many other conditions pertaining to joint enterprises and to the involvement of Soviet enterprises in export-import operations.—*Trans.*].

Profits are distributed in proportion to the partners' shares of the initial capitalization. Partners from socialist countries carry out inter-state transactions in transferable rubles. Part of the profits can be received in freely convertible currency only when a joint venture exports products to appropriate markets. The principle of cost recovery of foreign-currency expenditures has been established for joint ventures with partners from developed capitalist countries and developing countries. This means that the profits distributed to the foreign partner in foreign currency come from export earnings.

As a rule, foreign partners have a special interest in enterprises that produce goods that replace imports. In this case the transfer of profits can also be carried out by a foreign partner's purchase of goods in the U.S.S.R. equal in value to the profits due him.

A major step in the development of joint business ventures was the organization of Soviet foreign-economic and American trade con-sortia for the establishment, in various branches of the Soviet econ-omy, of groups of joint ventures that sell goods both for export and on the U.S.S.R.'s domestic market, and that ensure foreign-currency cost recovery for each group of enterprises as a whole. The Soviet foreign economic consortium consists of enterprises and associations under the U.S.S.R. State Agroindustrial Committee and the U.S.S.R. Minis-try of the Medical and Microbiological Industry, Ministry of the

[2]"On Questions Related to the Establishment Within the U.S.S.R. and the Activities of Joint Enterprises and International Associations and Organizations Involving Soviet and Foreign Organization, Firms and Management Agencies," adopted Jan. 1, 1987.
[3]"On the Procedures Governing the Establishment Within the U.S.S.R. and the Activities of Joint Enterprises, International Associations and Organizations of the U.S.S.R. and other CMEA Member Countries," and "On the Procedures Governing the Establishment Within the U.S.S.R. and the Activities of Joint Enterprises Involving Soviet Organizations and Firms from Capitalist and Developing Countries," adopted Jan. 1, 1987.

Petroleum Industry, and Ministry of Instrument Making, Automation Equipment, and Control Systems, among others; and the American consortium includes seven large companies specializing in these same areas. [One of the firms, Ford Motor Co., has dropped out—Eds.]

A total of 61 joint ventures involving firms and organizations from 20 countries have been created within the U.S.S.R. (as of June 25, 1988), including 53 with companies from developed and developing countries (11 from the Federal Republic of Germany, 9 from Finland, 7 from Italy, 5 each from the United States and Austria, 3 from Japan, and others) and 8 with partners from socialist countries (5 from Hungary, 2 from Yugoslavia, and 1 from Bulgaria). For the most part these are enterprises specializing in machine building, light industry, the food industry, and the production of software programs and personal computers. Of all the joint ventures that have been created, 9 have initial capital totaling more than 10 million rubles, 13 have initial capital of between 5 and 10 million rubles, and 20 have initial capital of between 1 and 5 million rubles.

There are still some unsolved problems regarding the establishment and activities of joint ventures. These problems are associated particularly with some uncertainties in the organization of material and technical supply. Joint ventures are not included in the state planning system, and therefore the Soviet partner experiences difficulties with material and technical supply through the regular branch system. The problem of supplying joint ventures cannot be resolved through wholesale trade in its present, inadequately developed form in the U.S.S.R. What is more, legislation indicates that the U.S.S.R. Ministry of Finance has the right to lower the tax rate [for joint ventures], but it fails to specify the concrete cases in which this occurs. Therefore, at the stage of making technical and economic feasibility studies, the partners cannot accurately estimate a joint venture's financial potential.

Finally, there are serious difficulties in hiring employees. Normative documents stipulate that the terms of pay, the work and rest schedule, and social security and social insurance for the employees of joint ventures are determined by Soviet legislation, with the exception of matters pertaining to pay, vacations, and pensions that are resolved in contracts with each foreign citizen. However, legislation naturally does not cover all aspects of the activities of joint ventures. There are still some matters awaiting clarification by the U.S.S.R. State Committee on Labor and Social Questions, such as the wage and salary rates for Soviet personnel, and the procedures for hiring and firing.

Engineering-Consulting Services

The volume of engineering-consulting services exported from the U.S.S.R. is relatively small.[4] Over the course of the 11th Five-Year Plan their value was approximately 120 million rubles. Exporters of complete sets of equipment and of capital construction projects accounted for about 70 percent of this total.

Engineering-consulting services provided by specialized organizations have been negligible, and for the majority of foreign trade organizations this type of activity has been of minor importance. Engineering-consulting activity has been hindered because provider organizations (design and research institutes, enterprises) have had no economic interest in stepping up its development.

Serious steps are now being taken to expand the export of engineering-consulting services from the U.S.S.R. In the past this type of export was carried out by only a limited number of foreign-trade associations. Now virtually all the ministries, associations, and enterprises that have been granted the right to enter the foreign market independently have the right to provide engineering services independently to foreign clients. Subdivisions (associations, firms for the export of engineering-consulting services) are being established, so that in the future engineering-consulting services can be singled out as a specialized sphere of foreign economic activity.

Engineering firms have been set up to provide services of this sort within such all-union foreign-trading associations of the U.S.S.R. Ministry of Foreign Economic Relations as Tekhnopromeksport [which deals with exports related to the construction of power plants—Trans.], Selkhozpromeksport [exports related to the construction of agroindustrial enterprises—Trans.], and Tekhnostroyeksport [which deals with exports related to the construction of enterprises in the building-materials and construction industries—Trans.]. Attention is now being given to the question of creating similar specialized firms in a number of industrial ministries, including the U.S.S.R. Ministry of Railroads, the Ministry of Agricultural and Heavy Machinery, and the Ministry of the Maritime Fleet, among others.

An important factor in accelerating the entry of Soviet exporters into the international market in engineering-consulting services is the establishment of joint engineering ventures with companies from foreign countries. The organization of such firms makes it possible to take

---

[4]These include the set of production-related services provided in connection with construction of industrial and other facilities, and organization and management of production and product sales.

advantage of the commercial and technical experience, as well as the international status, of foreign partners.

With the aim of increasing the economic interest and expanding the financial and technical capabilities of Soviet exporters of engineering-consulting services, attention is being given to improving the system of pay and economic incentives for exports in this area. A substantial increase in contributions to the foreign-exchange funds of organizations that provide such services (including design institutes), and the provision of greater economic incentives for their employees could accelerate development of this promising form of foreign economic activity in the U.S.S.R.

Border Trade

Restructuring the system for managing foreign economic activity requires a new approach to evaluating the role and place in foreign economic relations of border (or coastal) trade, which is a traditional form of trade. In essence, it represents a decentralized form of foreign trade operations, the goal of which is to mobilize the additional local resources of border regions to expand exports to neighboring countries. Imported products that are received in exchange contribute to the social and economic development of both those regions and the country as a whole.

For a long time, however, border trade experienced considerable pressure from the central government. Protracted efforts were required to gain the consent of central departments as to the amounts and assortment of goods delivered, and there were also direct restrictions on a number of goods. At the same time, exports within the framework of border trade were often carried out using specially earmarked central allocations of materials, and the involvement of local resources was very limited.

Recently conditions of border trade have changed considerably, especially with traditional partners (Japan, the People's Republic of China, the Korean People's Democratic Republic, Finland, Sweden, and Norway). It is now carried out by republic foreign-trading organizations, and not the U.S.S.R. Ministry of Foreign Economic Relations, as in the past. Border relations involving consumers' cooperatives are carried on directly between local (republic, province, territorial) unions of consumers' cooperatives in the U.S.S.R. and cooperative organizations in socialist countries. Border operations involving the exchange of goods are also carried out by trade enterprises (or department stores). An active search is under way for new forms of foreign economic relations—joint ventures, cooperative production arrangements, border tourism, cooperation in the area of joint agricultural and environmental-protection activity, and so forth.

Reorientation toward local resources is proceeding extremely slowly, however. Questions involving the division of several types of export allocations between republic and central foreign-trade associations have not been resolved, and because of this, undesirable competition among Soviet suppliers is arising. It is not clear how the question of union enterprises' deliveries of products produced over and above the levels required by state orders and contractual commitments is going to be resolved.

At the same time, border trade fits in well with the new mechanism for managing foreign economic relations, since it is based on promptly and efficiently meeting the interests of the chief production units—the enterprises. It also makes an important contribution to the social development of territories, frees the initiative of the direct participants, and forces them to seek out new, additional potential for exports. The circle of foreign partners is being widened. For example, in 1987 Austria entered into border trade with the Ukraine. Relations are being established between the Central Asian republics and Afghanistan, and their trade with the P.R.C. is being expanded.

Cooperation with Various Groups of Countries

In 1987, despite measures to improve the management of foreign economic activity, the development of economic, scientific, technical, and trade relations between the U.S.S.R. and foreign countries continued to be determined by the structure that had been established in previous years. The country's foreign trade turnover declined by 1.5 percent in 1987 (it had declined by 8.2 percent in 1986), and totaled 128.9 billion rubles. This was the result of a continuing decline in world prices for raw materials and fuel (primarily for fuel and energy commodities, which accounted for more than 46 percent of Soviet exports in 1987), and a drop in the value of the dollar.

The drop in export revenues was partially offset by increasing the physical volume of exports, which rose by 2.1 percent in 1986 prices, due primarily to an increase in the export of fuel and energy commodities. In terms of value, Soviet exports declined by 0.2 percent, totaling 68.1 billion rubles (in 1986 exports had declined by 6.1 percent). Machinery, equipment, and means of transportation continued to account for a relatively small share of exports (15.5 percent).

In 1987 imports totaled 60.7 billion rubles, which represented a 3 percent decline in current prices, and a 1 percent decline when expressed in constant prices. The positive balance, which rose to

7.4 billion rubles, was partly used to pay off foreign debts, and partly went into the foreign-trade debt owed by other countries to the Soviet Union.

In the 1980s the number of countries with which economic and technical cooperation is being developed on the basis of intergovernmental agreements has risen from 81 to 85 (agreements were signed with Grenada in 1982, with Lesotho and Zimbabwe in 1985, and with Bolivia in 1987). They include 14 socialist countries, 68 developing countries and 3 capitalist countries. Countries in the socialist commonwealth account for the greatest percentage of the U.S.S.R.'s economic and technical cooperation. In 1987 their share was approximately 64.5 percent, as compared to 61 percent in 1985.

There was a marked increase in the export of complete sets of equipment and materials for projects being built abroad with the technical assistance of the Soviet Union, although the peak level attained in 1985 was not reached in 1987. On the whole, the value of exports in this area increased by 5.9 percent, whereas it had dropped by 10.8 percent in 1986. Exports of equipment and materials to socialist countries for investment projects grew by 6.8 percent (they had declined by 10.4 percent in 1986), and similar exports to developing countries rose by 6.3 percent (compared to a 13.1 percent drop in 1986). Deliveries to developed capitalist countries declined by 3.5 percent (in 1986 they had risen by 14.6 percent).

Cooperation with the *socialist countries* remains the top priority in the U.S.S.R.'s foreign economic relations. In 1987 those countries accounted for 67 percent of the Soviet Union's total foreign trade, with the CMEA countries accounting for 62 percent. As a consequence of changes in foreign trade prices that were unfavorable for us, in 1987 exports declined by 3.1 percent in value terms (to 44.2 billion rubles), while in physical terms they rose by 0.1 percent. Imports from the socialist countries rose by 0.7 percent (to 42.1 billion rubles).

Measures to improve the structure of goods involved in trade between the U.S.S.R. and the socialist countries failed to produce any significant changes, since the proportions and volumes of basic flows of goods and services had been agreed upon earlier in multilateral and bilateral documents. The main goal is still to increase the proportion of finished products (mainly machinery products) in the U.S.S.R.'s exports, and the primary method for doing this, besides mobilization of internal reserves, is to move from relations based predominantly on trade to in-depth specialization and cooperative organization of production, and to development of new forms of cooperation.

In 1987 our major foreign trading partners were still the German Democratic Republic, Czechoslovakia, Poland, Bulgaria, and Hungary (trade with them totaled 14.7 billion, 13.7 billion, 12.9 billion,

12.8 billion, and 9.7 billion rubles, respectively). In the past year, of all the CMEA countries, only Soviet trade with Czechoslovakia, Hungary, and Vietnam exceeded 1986 figures. Following a rapid increase in foreign trade with the P.R.C. and Yugoslavia, there was a decline in 1987.

Measures to improve national economic mechanisms and the mechanism of multilateral and bilateral cooperation are of great importance for the development of foreign economic relations with the socialist countries. In 1987 long-term concepts of bilateral economic, scientific, and technical cooperation between the U.S.S.R. and individual socialist countries were worked out for the first time. In 1988 the first documents spelling out such concepts were signed with Cuba. This work has been carried on in close connection with the preparation of a collective concept of the international socialist division of labor among the CMEA countries for 1991 to 2005, a document which was approved in July 1988 at the 44th CMEA Session.

The collective concept will provide the foundation for coordination of economic policies by the fraternal countries in areas of mutual cooperation. The session also approved special long-term comprehensive programs for cooperation between the European CMEA countries and Vietnam, Cuba, and Mongolia, which are aimed at solving those countries' most pressing problems and at expanding their participation in the international socialist division of labor. The CMEA session also approved proposals calling for the step-by-step restructuring of the mechanism for multilateral cooperation. Bulgaria, Hungary, Vietnam, the German Democratic Republic, Cuba, Mongolia, Poland, the U.S.S.R., and Czechoslovakia approved an agreement calling for the gradual creation of conditions for the eventual formation of a unified socialist market.

The primary instrument for the formation of stable economic, scientific, and technical relations among the CMEA countries is the coordination of national economic plans. From now on, coordination will be carried out at three interconnected levels: the level of the basic production unit, especially among enterprises involved in direct relations; the branch level; and the intergovernmental level. The participation by direct producers—enterprises and economic organizations—in the coordination of plans will open up new possibilities for deepening integration processes directly in the production sphere.

In 1987 the U.S.S.R. and six CMEA countries reached a general agreement on the use of national currencies for the settling of accounts in direct economic relations on the basis of the reciprocal convertibility of these currencies and their convertibility into transferable rubles. Interbank agreements have been signed with these countries on procedures for settling and keeping accounts in direct relations and other new forms of cooperation among enterprises. The first such inter-governmental agreements have been signed with Czechoslovakia, Bulgaria, and Poland.

The Comprehensive Program for the Scientific and Technological Progress of the CMEA Member Countries up to the Year 2000 is the core of multilateral relations. The shift of multilateral cooperation into the area of science and technology is a characteristic feature of the past year. On the Soviet side alone, more than 700 research organizations, including nearly all the interbranch research and technology complexes, are participating in the efforts to fulfill the assignments of the Comprehensive Program. As of the beginning of 1988, the countries participating in the program had signed 285 multilateral agreements, contracts, and protocols. A number of new products have been developed through their joint efforts. The development of more than 130 types of machines, equipment, and instruments, including new types of industrial robots, has been completed.

At the same time, there have been instances in which a pro forma approach has been taken to the Comprehensive Program. Specifically, its framework has in some cases merely been mechanically expanded by including work in it that is already being done under existing contracts and agreements. This sort of approach can lead to a repetition of previous mistakes: the dissipation of forces, rather than their concentration in accomplishing the main tasks that define the essence of the program. CMEA agencies have not set plan targets for assignments related to the development and introduction in production of new technology and new materials. That makes it difficult or even impossible to monitor the course of fulfillment of the Comprehensive Program's assignments.

In addition, cooperation needs to be put on a new technological footing. Instead of developing individual components of technological systems, the participating countries need to develop systems as a whole, including materials and technologies for their processing. In this connection, it would be a good idea to carry out the Comprehensive Program on the basis of special-purpose technological plans, which will require a serious change in the management and resource-supply system.

Radical changes have still not taken place in the amounts and structure of economic, scientific, and technical cooperation with *developed capitalist states*. Measures taken over the past two years to improve foreign economic activities are still just creating the prerequisites for improving cooperation. Under certain conditions these prerequisites can be realized in the next few years.

The primary conditions here are the structural reorganization of the Soviet economy, including its export sector, improvement in the quality and innovativeness of exported goods, greater responsiveness and breadth in the selection of forms of cooperation, elimination of bureaucratism in foreign economic activities, and enhancement of enterprises' economic interest in working for the foreign market. In addition, the guarded approach taken by many developed capitalist countries to economic, scientific, and technical relations with the U.S.S.R. needs to be overcome.

In 1987 Soviet exports to developed capitalist countries rose by 8.2 percent over the previous year (to 14.2 billion rubles). This was still much lower than the record figure reached in 1984. Low export earnings forced the U.S.S.R. to reduce its imports from those countries (15.8 billion rubles in 1986 and 13.9 billion in 1987). Consequently, total trade with Western countries in 1987 was almost one third lower than in 1984, and accounted for 21.8 percent of total Soviet foreign trade, compared to 33.6 percent in 1980. The considerable fluctuations in the volume of Soviet trade with the West reflects its main weakness—excessive dependence on the export of raw materials, particularly energy resources, for which world prices have drastically changed over the past decade and a half.

Joint companies operating in the West, in which the Avtoeksport [export and import of motor vehicles and farm machinery] and Traktoreksport [export, import, and servicing of tractors, agricultural, and other machinery] all-union associations, among others, are participating, are making a considerable contribution to cooperation with the West. They account for approximately half of Soviet exports of machinery, equipment, and vehicles paid for in freely convertible currency. Their role could be enhanced if more energetic efforts were made to bring in as shareholders Soviet enterprises and associations that have the right to enter the foreign market directly. Business cooperation associations that are being set up in our country and that operate on the basis of commercial principles are helping to make these enterprises and associations more familiar with the conditions of operating in Western markets, and to acquaint Western businessmen with the specific features of operations in the U.S.S.R.

On the whole, however, the majority of Soviet participants are just beginning to set up forms of cooperation with companies from developed capitalist countries that, for the Soviet participants, are nontraditional. Overcoming inertia is becoming one of the main tasks in the restructuring of business relations with the West.

The Federal Republic of Germany and Finland are still the leading economic partners in that group of states. For more than 15 years the Federal Republic of Germany has been the U.S.S.R.'s primary trading partner among the capitalist countries, although since 1985 total trade with that country has been declining (this is due primarily to the drop in prices on the world market for petroleum, petroleum products, and other energy resources). In 1987 the U.S.S.R.'s exports to the Federal Republic of Germany dropped to 2.3 billion rubles (from 2.7 billion in 1986), and imports dropped to 2.6 billion rubles (from 2.9 billion).

Within the framework of the U.S.S.R. and F.R.G. Commission on Economic, Scientific and Technical Cooperation, long-term and stable cooperation has continued in a number of traditional areas (chemistry and power engineering, including the delivery of Soviet natural gas to enterprises in the Federal Republic of Germany and deliveries to the U.S.S.R. of equipment, pipe, and materials for the construction of main gas and oil pipelines). There are approximately 50 current agreements on scientific and technical cooperation between Soviet departments and organizations and firms in the Federal Republic of Germany.

Industrial cooperation has become a promising area. More than 20 agreements are in the process of being carried out, including agreements for the production of high-efficiency models of concrete-pumping machines and concrete mixers (with the Stetter Company), metal-cutting machine tools and semiautomatic machinery (Elb-Schlif and Gildemeister), presses (Kieserling und Albrecht), industrial sewing and knitting machines (Pfaff and Meier), among others. Cooperation with firms from the Federal Republic of Germany in the construction of projects in third countries occupies an important place. Relations have been developing successfully with West German firms that have provided equipment for thermal electric power stations in Iran and Greece, metallurgical mills in Nigeria and Turkey, gas pipelines in Algeria and Libya, oil pipelines and oil tank farms in Iraq, nickel plants in Cuba, geological prospecting operations on the coastal shelf of Vietnam, and other projects. Experience in joint participation in projects of this nature has made it possible to move to more complex forms of cooperation—the establishment of joint companies, enterprises, and consortia. The intergovernmental agreement on scientific and technical cooperation that was signed in 1986 opened up broad opportunities for scientific, technical, and technological exchange between the U.S.S.R. and the Federal Republic of Germany.

Thus, in addition to traditional trade ties, in economic relations between the U.S.S.R. and the Federal Republic of Germany there has been a shift toward deeper industrial cooperation and the use of cooperative production arrangements. Negative elements in the Federal Republic of Germany's foreign economic policies with regard to the regulation of trade with the U.S.S.R., especially the use of lists of "strategic goods" (COCOM) [the Coordinating Committee on Multilateral Export Controls, through which the Western allies control shipments of high technology to the Soviet Union and its allies—*Eds.*], continue to be a factor hindering development.

In recent years negative tendencies associated with unfavorable conditions on the world market in energy resources manifested themselves in trade with the other important partner—Finland. A serious imbalance has developed in Finland's favor. The two sides have been making energetic efforts to eliminate this imbalance, as a result of which Soviet exports increased by 7 percent (to 1.7 billion rubles) in 1987. At the same time, traditional Soviet exports to Finland substantially exceeded the volumes called for in the current five-year agreement. Moreover, new goods started to appear for the Finnish market: fabrics, synthetic fibers, and some food products. At the same time, there was an unwarranted decline in the exports of Soviet machinery and equipment. The import of goods and services from Finland in 1987 declined in practically all groups. The drop in purchases was also due to the need to balance clearing accounts. On the whole, Soviet-Finnish trade was balanced in 1987.

In order to reduce the influence of world market conditions on Soviet-Finnish economic relations, it is important to develop new forms of cooperation, especially forms based on cooperative and specialized production arrangements. Cooperative arrangements involving component parts have undergone the most extensive development, although it is true that they still account for an insignificant share of the value of Soviet machinery and equipment imports from Finland. For example, Soviet components did not account for more than 8 percent of the total value of Finnish ships delivered in 1987. Within the framework of cooperative production arrangements, the largest deliveries from the U.S.S.R. consisted of communications equipment, special railroad cars, electronic equipment, and equipment for special ships.

In light of the initiatives put forward by M.S. Gorbachev in October 1987 in Murmansk, a program for the acceleration and expansion of economic and social development of Murmansk Province up to the year 2000 has been drafted and submitted to the government for consideration. The program assigns special importance to large-scale international projects, especially the Kola project. Within its context, 17 projects are specified for possible cooperation with Finnish firms. Work on these projects will begin after 1990.

In the area of economic cooperation with the United States and Japan, the figures are not high. Soviet-American trade in 1987 dropped once again—to 1.2 billion rubles (compared to 3.1 billion in 1984), primarily as the result of a reduction in grain imports. Soviet exports also declined—to 279 million rubles (from 312.5 million in 1986), which to a great extent is due to American trade legislation that is unfavorable to the U.S.S.R.

The 11th annual meeting of the American-Soviet Trade and Economic Council (ASTEC) in April 1988 and the summit meeting this June provide evidence that both sides understand the importance of expanding mutual trade and economic ties, especially since the potential here is great.

Trade with Japan dropped sharply in 1987—to 2.6 billion rubles, as against 3.2 billion in 1986. In large part this was due to the position taken by official Japanese circles: at the end of 1986 the cabinet approved a list of restrictions on exports to socialist countries. In addition, in March 1987 an anti-Soviet campaign was launched in connection with alleged violations by the Toshiba corporation of COCOM regulations in delivering metal machining equipment to the U.S.S.R. This affected the volume of Soviet imports from Japan, which totaled 1.6 billion rubles (compared to 2.2 billion in 1986).

During this same period, however, the fourth meeting of the Intergovernmental Commission on Scientific and Technical Cooperation was held (in December 1987), along with the 11th Conference of National Committees on Economic Cooperation. They outlined new areas for the mutually beneficial development of diverse trade and economic ties. The first Soviet-Japanese joint enterprise for the production of lumber has been in operation since April 1988, and an agreement has been signed for the establishment of a joint tourist and health spa complex on Lake Baikal.

Soviet exports to Japan have been characterized by a certain degree of stability (approximately 970-980 million rubles over the past two years), although there have not yet been any radical qualitative changes in their structure. Unprocessed raw materials continue to form the basis of these exports, and therefore the main task is still to increase the level of processing of goods exported to Japan, partly through the development of new forms of cooperative research and production arrangements, joint enterprises, and so on.

Developing countries occupy an important place in the Soviet Union's foreign economic relations. They account for 11.2 percent of the U.S.S.R.'s total foreign trade, and for more than one third of its trade with nonsocialist countries. In 1987 trade with this group of states rose by 0.4 percent to reach 14.5 billion rubles (in 1986 prices the volume rose by 3.6 percent). As in previous years, India, Iraq, and Afghanistan were the main trading partners (they account for more than one fourth of the U.S.S.R.'s trade with developing countries).

In 1987 special attention was given to making cooperation more mutually advantageous, and to expanding the interaction of economic structures in light of the changes taking place in the U.S.S.R. national economy and its foreign-economic complex. Cooperative production arrangements underwent further development, and the possibilities were studied of organizing more extensive cooperation in which assistance in construction of production facilities is repaid in the products of those facilities. Efforts were begun to work out other new forms of cooperation, including direct ties between Soviet enterprises and organizations and companies from certain developing countries, especially India.

Meetings between the two countries' leaders from 1985 to 1987, during the course of which a number of major agreements were signed setting the basic guidelines for economic and technical cooperation and development of scientific and technical ties and trade up to the year 2000, have been an important factor in expanding and deepening relations between the U.S.S.R. and India. Plans call for providing Soviet assistance to India in the construction of large new power-engineering facilities projects, including the Teri hydroelectric power complex, which will be the largest in the country, a number of large coal strip mines and underground mines, and a petroleum refining plant in Karnal, as well as in the reconstruction and modernization of a metallurgical mill in Bokaro, and in comprehensive geological prospecting for oil and gas in the districts of Northern Cambay and Kaveri, and in West Bengal state.

Special attention has been given to the further development of cooperative production arrangements between the two countries' machinery enterprises on the basis of the Long-Term Program for Cooperation Between the U.S.S.R. and India in the Area of Production, which was signed in April 1987, and to establishing other forms of ties between Soviet production associations, enterprises, and organizations, on the one hand, and Indian state-owned and private companies, on the other.

The expansion of Soviet-Indian scientific and technical cooperation that is called for in the Comprehensive Long-Term Program for Scientific and Technical Cooperation between the U.S.S.R. and India (1987) will serve the interests of accelerating scientific and technological progress in both countries. In accordance with this program, cooperation will be carried out in top-priority areas of basic and applied sciences and modern technologies. Agreements reached at the highest level call for Soviet-Indian trade to be increased by 150 percent by 1992 over the 1985 level, and for steps also to be taken to improve its structure.

At the same time, the principle of mutual benefit is still not being applied vigorously enough in the U.S.S.R.'s economic relations with India, or with other developing countries. Administrative-command methods and narrow departmental interests are continuing to interfere with the development of these ties.

Substantial adjustments need to be made in the financial mechanism for providing economic and technical assistance to developing countries, in order to achieve an optimal ratio between state and commercial loans granted to them. The very approach to selecting the areas and forms of development of economic and technical cooperation needs to be radically changed with a greater view to the interests of the U.S.S.R.'s national economy, so that cooperative projects are more strongly oriented toward the Soviet market. This will make it possible not only to avoid the establishment of unprofitable enterprises, but also—and this is especially important—to protect our country's long-range economic interests in a situation in which the developing world is in the grips of a protracted payment crisis.

* * *

The preliminary results of the recently begun restructuring of the U.S.S.R.'s foreign economic relations are contradictory. Although the basic areas for their improvement have been defined and a great deal of work is being done in these areas, it is encountering many difficulties. The chief difficulty is that the desired radical qualitative change has not yet occurred in the U.S.S.R.'s economic development. The radical reform of the Soviet economy is proceeding with great difficulty, structural changes in industry are taking place slowly, and there have been no noticeable changes in the quality and assortment of goods and services produced for the domestic and foreign markets. In short, the restructuring of foreign economic relations still has little reinforcement from changes in the national economy.

Changes in the mechanism for managing foreign economic activity have not yet produced any tangible results, although there has been some success in slowing the decline in exports, stimulating the development of new forms of economic relations, and giving enterprises a greater economic interest in the foreign market. The results of foreign economic activities in 1987 and early 1988 once again confirm the fact that the state of affairs in the foreign-economic complex depends on the country's overall economic situation, and on progress in restructuring the Soviet economy.

The Work of the Moscow Narodny Bank

The Moscow Narodny Bank (Moscow Narodny Bank Ltd.) has been in London for over a decade and is well respected in international banking circles. But in the Soviet Union it is perhaps known only to specialists. Meanwhile, now that Soviet enterprises, associations, and ministries have gained the right to enter foreign markets, the bank can be extremely useful to them in many respects—in the granting of loans, the study of probable market conditions, and so forth.

Since May 1987 the bank has been under the management of its new chairman, Aleksandr Stepanovich Maslov. He is 51 years old. He graduated from the Moscow Institute of Finance in 1958 and since then has worked in the banking system. Below we have published A.S. Maslov's answers to our journal's questions.*

MEMO: When and for what purpose was the Moscow Narodny Bank created, who owns its capital, and how many people does it employ?

Maslov: The Moscow Narodny Bank was founded in Moscow in 1911 to finance cooperative trade with foreign countries. In 1916 it opened an office in London, which served as the basis for the creation in November 1919 of an independent bank in the form of a British joint-stock company with foreign (Soviet) capital. One of the bank's important functions is to provide credit and payment services for British-Soviet trade. But its current tasks (as for all Soviet banking institutions abroad) are to provide a broad range of banking services for our country's foreign economic activities.

The bank's main stockholders are the U.S.S.R. State Bank and the U.S.S.R. Bank for Foreign Economic Activity; the stockholders also include a number of Soviet foreign trade organizations. As of January 1, 1988, it had 206 British and seven Soviet employees.

MEMO: How is the bank structured and what are its main functions?

Maslov: Our organizational structure is typical of commercial banks. The bank's board (six Soviet bank officials) serves as its executive body. Its activities are approved by a supervisory council repre-

---

*This article appeared in the July 1988 issue of *MEMO*.

senting the chief stockholders. Once a year the bank's performance and future plans are discussed at a general stockholders' meeting, when a board is elected for the next term. The administrative structure also includes credit, currency, and administrative committees, which submit the most serious questions to the board for approval. The bank's day-to-day activities are conducted by functional, analytical, and support sections (departments and groups) that handle specific types of operations. In 1971 the bank opened a branch office in Singapore, and since 1975 it has had an office in Moscow.

MEMO: What is the scope of the bank's activities?

Maslov: The bank's resources are continually growing, reflecting a general trend toward the development of the U.S.S.R.'s foreign economic relations. At the end of 1958 they totaled £ 8.6 million, in 1960—£ 55.6 million, in 1975—£ 1.2 billion, and in 1987—£ 2.1 billion. As of January 1, 1988, the bank's own capital totaled £ 103 million, and on the basis of this figure, *Euromoney* magazine's economic service included the bank in its annual list of the world's 500 largest commercial banks [*Euromoney*, June 1987, p. 152].

MEMO: Legally the bank is British. What is its place in the system of Soviet financial organizations?

Maslov: Our bank is inseparably linked with the U.S.S.R.'s banking system. We participate actively in resolving a number of basic problems in currency and credit relations between our two countries. Among other things, in January 1987 the bank participated in the signing of an intergovernmental credit protocol under which credit agreements have been signed with eight British banks for the financing of specific projects. In June 1987, the bank organized a seminar for Soviet banking and commercial organizations on the currency and credit aspects of cooperation. In December 1987, at the joint initiative of the British council to promote the export of capital and services (the British Invisible Exports Council) and our bank, a roundtable was held in Moscow with the participation of executives of a number of Soviet organizations and British banks. We are presently discussing with the British-Soviet Chamber of Commerce our plans for organizing an exhibit representing Britain's industry and financial sector in 1989 in Moscow. We plan to use this opportunity ourselves to advertise our bank's services.

MEMO: What role does the bank play in advancing loans to joint enterprises in which Soviet organizations and foreign firms participate?

Maslov: This is undoubtedly a promising area. On the bank's initiative, in June 1987 the first Soviet-British agreement was signed between the U.S.S.R. State Bank and the U.S.S.R. Bank for Foreign Economic Activity (at that time known as the U.S.S.R. Foreign Trade

Bank), on one hand, and the Bank of Scotland and Morgan Grenfell, on the other, on the creation of a joint bankers' consulting group. The group's purpose is to aid Soviet and foreign partners in organizing joint commercial companies in the U.S.S.R. (in areas such as taxation and ensuring profitability).

MEMO: How has the restructuring in our economy and particularly in the sphere of foreign trade affected your bank's activities?

Maslov: The restructuring of the U.S.S.R.'s foreign economic relations has expanded the circle of potential partners among Soviet organizations. The number of Soviet clients (including joint enterprises in Great Britain) with whom we already have a certain amount of experience in cooperation (NAFTA-U.K., the Russian Timber Agency, Razno-U.K., Bominflot, Intourist) have been joined recently by a number of export-import associations of some of the U.S.S.R.'s ministries and departments. In the near future we plan to establish direct business ties with certain industrial enterprises and republic executive bodies to explore the possibility of financing the development of their export base.

While channeling the bulk of its resources (up to £ 1 billion) into servicing our country's foreign economic relations, the bank also cooperates actively with foreign-trade and branch banks of fraternal socialist countries and with a number of production associations in the German Democratic Republic and Czechoslovakia. One example of this cooperation is the organization, together with National Westminster Bank, of a medium-term syndicated loan of $200 million to the Bulgarian Foreign Trade Bank. Contacts have also been established with the Bank of China's London office.

Our geographic location presupposes the existence of good relations with British banks and companies. We take a positive view of business relations with the country's leading clearing banks and with certain trade banks. Among others, Lloyds Bank, in 1986, and Midland Bank, in 1987, organized the sale of the bank's medium-term bonds in the form of a multicurrency renewable line of credit (a multioption note-issuance facility, or NIF)[1] and a credit that trades in the secondary market (a transferable loan facility, or TLF).[2]

The bank is trying to step up its cooperation with Great Britain's major companies: Imperial Chemical Industries, John Brown, Kertolds, GKN (metal industry), and IAD (automotive technology). The desire for cooperation is also shared by our partners, which we had a

---

[1]A type of loan that can be used in several currencies and that is financed through the periodic issuance of Euronotes. Euronotes are short-term, bank-guaranteed securities that are issued outside the borrower's country and freely traded on the market.—*Ed.*

[2]Negotiable international bank loans granted on the basis of the issuance of special securities.—*Ed.*

chance to confirm, in particular, during our recent meetings with Mr. Gormly, the head of John Brown, and with Mr. Varde, director of the GKN.

But in today's world a reputable commercial bank cannot limit its activity to its country of residence, especially since the Soviet Union's volume of trade with Great Britain is still smaller than its trade with a number of other industrially developed capitalist countries. Investments in the U.S.S.R.'s export-import operations with the Federal Republic of Germany, Italy, and Japan account for a substantial share of the bank's credit portfolio. Some of our proposals have aroused the interest of a number of major U.S. companies. We have some positive experience of cooperation with Canadian firms.

The new level of relations with clients demands that the bank advance loans not only for the sale and subsequent use of goods or services already produced, but for the production process itself. Among other things, specific talks are being conducted to negotiate such loans to several Soviet industrial enterprises in exchange for future hard-currency earned from the export of part of their output (gas cylinders, motor vehicles, lumber products, tea, local-industry products).

MEMO: Since we're on the subject of restructuring, I'd like to know how it affects the bank's own operations.

Maslov: You've touched on an important issue. Improvement of the "infrastructure" is a factor in the bank's profitability. This includes our personnel's level of professional training, their knowledge of the market and ability to work with clients, the optimal distribution of human and material resources in various areas with an eye to the future, and technical support (the capacity of the bank's main computer and how effectively it is used, the availability of microcomputers and the efficiency with which they are utilized, and the dependability of telecommunications equipment).

By way of illustration, in December 1987 the Moscow Narodny Bank concluded an agreement with the London office of Security Pacific Bank on the joint financing of Soviet-British trade in the form of "factoring."[3] This a relatively new and effective method of servicing international operations. At the same time, in order to effectively implement this agreement, personnel must persistently and skillfully market this service, adapting the general terms of the agreement to the structure of specific deals.

Another example: the contribution made by each branch of the bank is currently assessed in a rather approximate fashion. This year

---

[3]Factoring is a practice by which a bank acquires from industrial and trade companies claims against third parties and then recovers the necessary sums.—*Ed.*

we plan to install a more modern system for processing bookkeeping and statistical data with the help of a new computer, thereby introducing real economic accountability in our Bank.

The Moscow Narodny Bank and Other Financial Institutions in Great Britain

Rank[1]	Financial Institution	Own Shareholders' Capital[2]	Net Income[2]	Total Assets[3]
1	National Westminster Bank	6,608	907	123
2	Barclays Bank	5,485	911	116
3	Lloyds Bank	4,049	693	70
4	Midland Bank	2,980	357	78
5	TSB Group	2,179	168	19
6	Standard Chartered	1,910	223	47
7	Royal Bank of Scotland	1,388	173	29
8	Bank of Scotland	795	103	14
9	Kleinwort Benson Lonsdale	538	75	13
10	Morgan Grenfell & Co.	518	81	8
11	S.G. Warburg & Co.	340	61	4
12	Shroders	326	31	4
13	Yorkshire Bank	308	59	3
14	Hambros Bank	294	42	4
15	Hill Samuel & Co.	255	39	4
16	Saudi International Bank	209	15	5
17	Moscow Narodny Bank	208	16	3
18	Scandinavian Bank Group	186	25	5

[1]According to size of own shareholders' capital.
[2]Millions of dollars.
[3]Billions of dollars.

Statistics: The Soviet Union in the World Economy (1917-1987)

Part I[*]

The 70th anniversary of Great October turns us again and again to thoughts about the world-historical significance and complexity of the path that the Soviet people has traveled over these years. "Our revolution is the 20th century's most outstanding event, which heralded the beginning of a new era in the life of humanity. Time has thoroughly revealed its lasting significance and has illuminated the huge possibilities opened up by socialist social development," states the CPSU Central Committee's anniversary message to the Soviet people.

The revolution took place in an economically backward country that, by the standards of the theoreticians of the Second International, dared not even think about socialism. It was born as the result of an explosion of popular despair, the indignation of the working people, and the anger of the soldiering masses, exhausted by a 40-month war, famine, and the senseless death of millions of people. Not many of those who rose up in revolution had a clear idea of socialism. But the confluence of historical circumstances—the ruling classes' inability to suppress the people's discontent, the working people's intolerable situation, and the existence of a highly organized and purposeful Bolshevik party that had assumed leadership of the mass movement for peace, bread, and land—resulted in the socialist revolution's victory in none other than Russia.

The theoretical basis of the revolution was Lenin's doctrine of the uneven nature of the economic and political development of capitalism. Lenin demonstrated that, at an extremely high overall stage in the development of productive forces—at the stage of imperialism—capitalism turned into a single worldwide system torn by contradictions, the apogee of which—world war—could lead to the emergence of a revolutionary situation in a single, even economically backward country. Granted, in this connection it was initially assumed (until

---

*This article appeared in the November 1987 issue of *MEMO* and was continued in the December 1987 issue (see following article).

1922) that the revolution, having begun in one country, would turn into an international revolution that would lead to the establishment of socialism, if not in all states, at least in those that were economically advanced in their level of economic development and were materially ripe for it. The workers in the advanced countries would take advantage of the fruits of victory not only to improve their own lives but also to provide extensive economic assistance to those who had paved the way.

However, the path of humanity's social progress proved to be more tortuous and complicated. Experienced in political maneuvering, the European bourgeoisie managed to suppress revolutions in the countries where they took place (Germany, Hungary) and to prevent them in others. And although the solidarity of the West's working people with the people of Russia thwarted the imperialist powers' large-scale direct intervention and forced them to limit themselves for the most part to aiding the internal Russian counterrevolution, the absence of organized state support from the working class abroad increased the difficulties on our path tenfold.

In the years of World War I and the Civil War, the country lost about 19 million people—mainly of working age, 16 to 50—who were killed at the front or died from epidemics and famine. Economic ties among individual regions and among enterprises were severed. By 1920 industrial output had fallen to less than a sixth of the 1913 level, and grain harvests had declined by a third. In the words of H.G. Wells, who was well-disposed toward our revolution, Russia had plunged into darkness.

Nonetheless, it was not only backwardness, devastation, and famine that gave rise to the debate that unfolded in the party's ranks in the 1920s, debate over whether we would be able to build socialism in one isolated country, even if it occupied a sixth of the globe. The danger of the restoration of capitalism from without, by military force, was not the only question. Now, returning to those remote times, one can see that the discussion had to do with something else, as well— with whether, in a hostile encirclement, in the position of a besieged fortress, we would be able to preserve the principles of socialist democracy, the loss of which could not be offset by mere strengthening of our economic and defense potential, however great.

History itself gave an affirmative answer to that question, and it could have been even more persuasive if it had not been for the deviations from Lenin's principles and methods for building the new society, the violations of socialist legality and of democracy in party and society, and later, dogmatism in thinking and inertia in practical actions.

The building of socialism changed the face of our country and our people beyond recognition. Thanks to socialism, once-backward Russia became the world's second mightiest economic power. In 1913 Russia occupied fifth place—behind the United States, Germany (within its borders at that time), Great Britain, and France—in total national income, while it exceeded the United States in population by 50 percent and the other countries by 200 to 300 percent. By 1920 the situation had deteriorated catastrophically. But by 1940—just a little more than 10 years after the beginning of socialist industrialization— the Soviet Union already found itself in second place in the world in total national income.

It was during this decade that the "Russian miracle" was forged, a miracle that astonished all humanity with high economic growth rates and the depth of structural transformation in the economy. It is clear, however, that such a "time compression" could not take place smoothly, without consequences for the future.

In submitting the draft of the first five-year plan to the judgment of the party and the economic-management community, G.M. Krzhizhanovskiy, who headed the State Planning Committee in the 1920s, wrote: "The intransigence of the whole capitalist encirclement toward us forces us to pay particular attention to . . . building the sort of economic complex that will both ensure our defense and enable us to accomplish our continued economic upswing 'with our own hands.' Hence the inevitability of our pressing on heavy industry as the central point in our overall labor and defense capability."[1]

In this connection, the draft five-year plan pointed out, "we have no resources available from the countryside for carrying out our plan of industrialization. . . . With low labor productivity and a low per capita income, the countryside lives on the threshold of the physiological norms of existence and cannot serve as any sort of significant source of socialist accumulation."[2]

In actuality, however, it was precisely the countryside that bore a substantial part of the burden of industrialization on its shoulders. Thorough collectivization carried out long before the peasant masses could see the advantages of highly mechanized collective farming for themselves (and that, after all, was what Lenin's cooperative plan envisaged) was subordinated to a single goal—granted, one that decided the entire fate of industrialization. The establishment of collective farms provided for the uninterrupted flow into state granaries—with minimal budgetary outlays—of the grain necessary to

---

[1]*Prospects for the Development of the U.S.S.R. National Economy* [*Perspektivy razvertyvaniya narodnogo khozyaystva SSSR*], Moscow, 1927, p. xxii.

[2]*Ibid.*, p. 30.

feed the growing population of the old and new industrial centers and to obtain foreign currency in the external market to pay for imports of machine tools and other machinery.

According to recently published data, 80 to 85 percent of the equipment installed in Soviet plants during the first five-year plan period was purchased in the West. And the main source of foreign exchange was provided by grain, which accounted for 40 percent of the U.S.S.R.'s entire export earnings at the time. In the course of the five-year plan period alone, 13 million tons of grain—almost 15 percent of its total commodity output—was exported. It would be no exaggeration to say that the Soviet people paid for imported machine tools not with grain but with the famine of 1932 to 1933, which cost many lives. That was the true price of industrialization, which one party document has justifiably called one of the Soviet people's greatest heroic exploits.

But it was during the first five-year plan that the industrial foundation was laid for the defensive might that enabled us, within a matter of years, to repulse the Hitlerite aggression and save the world from the fascist plague. During the first five-year plan about 1,500 large enterprises went into operation, mainly in new branches of industry—the aviation, automotive, tractor, chemical, and machine-tool industries. A large number of these enterprises were sited in regions that were considered inaccessible to the enemy.

During the second five-year plan period, new plants were already outfitted, as a rule, with Soviet equipment produced at the new enterprises built from 1929 to 1932. Importation of equipment and exportation of grain to pay for it were reduced to a minimum. The third five-year plan gave Soviet people the first opportunity to taste the fruits of their efforts. Supplies to the cities improved, and the real incomes of the working people started to grow (after a 10-year decline). But that development was cut short by the war.

The Soviet Union emerged from the war with immense losses. On the territory that had been temporarily occupied by the enemy, thousands of enterprises, which in 1940 had accounted for about half of the country's entire industrial output, were destroyed. We lost one third of our national wealth. Total material damage, war expenditures, and losses of income during the years of the Great Patriotic War came to 2.6 trillion rubles in 1941 prices. In current prices this is about 300 billion rubles, which is equal to the U.S.S.R.'s total national income from 1924 through 1941. The war turned the results of 15 years of labor to dust, and that was only the direct material loss.

In the war against Hitler's Germany the Soviet Union lost 20 million of its sons and daughters. Highly approximate calculations, based on estimates of the potential contribution that each of them would have made to the national income over a period of 20 to 25 years show that the indirect material damage associated with the death of the working age population, which damage is usually not taken into account, was approximately equal to the direct losses.

And after the victory the country, which had barely healed its wounds, was forced to divert considerable amounts of its best resources to countering the military danger. From 1950 through 1985, expenditures from the U.S.S.R.'s state budget for defense exceeded 500 billion rubles in constant 1965 prices. Over the same period (and in the same prices), capital investments in industry were 975 billion rubles; in agriculture, 500 billion rubles; and in housing, 430 billion rubles. It is not hard to calculate that factors of foreign policy forced us over these 35 years to spend an amount of money on defense equal to half of our investments in industry and to all of our investments in agriculture, and exceeding all spending (state, cooperative, and individual) on housing construction.

One must not fail to take these facts into account in evaluating the present state and problems of, and the prospects for, the U.S.S.R.'s economic development and its competition (together with the other socialist countries) with capitalism. But even under these far from optimal conditions, the rates and scale of our economic growth have been rather impressive.

If one takes the average annual volume of national income during the first postwar five-year plan (the fourth) as 1, then for the following five-year plans the national income comes to 2 (fifth five-year plan), 3.2 (sixth), 4.5 (seventh), 6.5 (eighth), 8.7 (ninth), 10.8 (10th), 12.6 (11th), and 15 (12th, assuming the plan is met). The rates and scale of economic growth were especially great in the 1950s and 1960s. During this period widespread use was made of extensive factors—approximately 10 million new employees per five-year plan were enlisted in the production of goods and services, and accessible deposits of relatively inexpensive mineral raw materials were developed in inhabited European regions of the country.

As these extensive factors were exhausted, the Soviet economy's rates of development dropped off, and starting with the 10th five-year plan, the absolute growth in national income also began to decline. That, understandably, limited material possibilities for solving many social problems, including acute ones, such as housing, the development of public education, and health care. Under these conditions, improving the efficiency with which production resources were used, and shifting to a predominantly intensive type of development became especially important.

However, the policy of intensive economic development proclaimed by the 24th Party Congress in 1971 went largely without implementation. Half-measures were substituted for urgent radical transformations. In the 1970s the rate of return on assets continued to decline (by approximately 5 percent a year), as did the coefficient that characterizes correlation between capital investments in a given five-year period and the growth in national income in the subsequent five-year period (in the 11th five-year plan period that coefficient was only slightly better than one third of what it had been in the seventh).

The bitter experience of the past 15 to 20 years spoke eloquently of the fruitlessness of half-measures and the need for a radical economic reform capable of harmonizing the productive forces and production relations of socialism and ensuring dynamic development. The principles of that reform were gradually worked out after April 1985. The decisions of the 27th Party Congress and the CPSU Central Committee's January and June (1987) plenary sessions erected the framework of a new economic mechanism, on which the building itself must now be built.

The set of statistics offered here makes no claim, of course, to presenting a comprehensive picture of the Soviet economy's development from 1917 through 1987. Its purpose is to show the strengthening of the U.S.S.R.'s positions in the world economy. As far as we know, systematic worldwide statistics covering such a long period had not been published before.

General indicators characterizing changes in the balance of power in the world economic arena are provided by the figures on national income (Tables 2 to 6), as well as final industrial output (Tables 7 to 12) and final agricultural output (Tables 13 to 18). National income figures are calculated in accordance with the methodology employed in Soviet statistics, at the stage of its end use. They include only material goods that go for consumption (personal and collective) and accumulation. Collective consumption is composed of material outlays in the nonproduction sector—enterprises and organizations operating in the areas of social, cultural, and consumer services, management, and research.

In contrast to gross-output indicators, the final-output indicators used in the statistics offered here do not include the portion of output that goes for current production needs in industry itself (in the form of raw materials, semimanufactures, fuel, or component parts and assemblies), or correspondingly, in agriculture (feed, fodder, seed, and organic fertilizers). The internal turnover that is thereby excluded from a given industry's final output is determined from input/output tables. For countries where such statistics do not exist, the method employed was that of analogy to countries having a similar production structure and approximately the same level of scientific and technological development (judging from indicators of production efficiency).

Absolute figures characterizing production volumes were calculated first in national currencies (in 1980 prices), and were then converted to U.S. dollars, not at official exchange rates but purchasing power parities (actual price ratios) in that same year.

It should be emphasized that the translation of national indicators into any "foreign" currency—in this case dollars—substantially changes the statistical reflection not only of the structure of production, but also of its dynamics. When recalculated in another country's prices, the output of individual branches, as well as individual elements of the consumption and accumulation funds of national income, acquire entirely different "weights" in the total volume than they do when calculated in the national currency. Correspondingly, in a number of cases particular indices taken from national statistics but applied to different "weights," yield overall dynamics of national income and industrial and agricultural production that differ sharply from those cited in the national statistical sources.

The differences thereby obtained are directly proportional to the differences in the structure and principles of pricing between each given country and the United States. At the same time, it is generally acknowledged that in international comparisons involving not just the volume but also the structure and dynamics of production, it is necessary to use indicators expressed in a single currency. Only in that case does one get the required agreement between the rates of economic growth of individual countries and the change in the relationships among them in terms volumes of production and utilization of their national product. These observations should be kept in mind when examining the parameters of economic dynamics (Tables 3, 8, and 12), where some of the data given do not agree with figures of the U.S.S.R. Central Statistical Administration.

But even when recalculated in dollars, the growth rates of the Soviet economy prove substantially higher than those for all the developed capitalist countries. Our preeminence in rates over the long period under consideration is especially significant if one excludes from the calculation the wartime period and the period of postwar economic recovery. In the 1921 to 1938 and 1951 to 1987 periods the average annual rates of growth of national income were (percentages): U.S.S.R.—6.6, United States—2.3, Federal Republic of Germany—4.2, France—3, Great Britain—1.9, Italy—3, and Japan—5.6. The growth rates of Soviet industrial and agricultural production were also considerably higher. Thus, for industry they were (percentages): U.S.S.R.—9.5, United States—2.4, Federal Republic of Germany—4.3, France—3.4, Great Britain—2, Italy—4.6, and Japan—8; and for agriculture: U.S.S.R.—3.2, United States—1.4, F.R.G.—1.5, France—1, Great Britain—1.5, Italy—1.3, and Japan—1.4.

The calculations rely on publications of the U.S.S.R. Central Statistical Administration (*The U.S.S.R. National Economy* [*Narod-*

DIMENSIONS OF THE SOVIET ECONOMY
Totals for Years of Five-Year Plans[1]

Years (5-year Plans)	Utilized National Income	Gross Industrial Output			Gross Agricultural Output	Capital Investments	Foreign Trade	Fixed Assets at End of Period[2]	
		Total	Group "A"*	Group "B"*				Production	Nonproduction
1918–1923	10	8	2	6	230	...	2	25	35
1924–1928[3]	35	22	8	14	300	10	7	30	40
1929–1932[4] (1st)	40	35	15	20	250	15	12	35	45
1933–1937 (2nd)	100	85	40	45	300	30	6	55	50
1938–7/1/41 (3rd)	115	110	55	55	225	40	3	75	60
7/1/41–1945	120	130	80	50	180	25	4	65	55
1946–1950 (4th)	210	195	120	75	340	55	20	90	70
1951–1955 (5th)	415	410	270	140	400	105	45	135	100
1956–1960 (6th)	675	700	475	225	575	190	85	225	170
1961–1965 (7th)	945	1,100	775	315	640	280	140	360	250
1966–1970 (8th)	1,360	1,640	1,190	450	780	400	200	530	330
1971–1975 (9th)	1,825	2,375	1,735	640	880	565	365	805	450
1976–1980 (10th)	2,265	3,150	2,335	815	955	720	500	1,150	590
1981–1985 (11th)	2,650	3,780	2,800	980	1,010	845	625	1,570	765
1986–1990 (12th)[5]	3,170	4,640	3,400	1,240	1,155	1,040	725	1,865	1,000

*"A" represents producer goods; "B" represents consumer goods.
[1]Billions of rubles in constant 1983 prices.
[2]Billions of rubles in constant 1973 prices (based on full value, without taking depreciation into account).
[3]Not counting fourth quarter of 1928, when first five-year plan began.
[4]Counting fourth quarter of 1928.
[5]Planned.

noye khozyaystvo SSSR], *U.S.S.R. Industry* [*Promyshlennost SSSR*], and *U.S.S.R. Agriculture* [*Selskoye khozyaystvo SSSR*]); United Nations statistical agencies (including the specialized agencies—FAO, UNCTAD, UNIDO, and others), and statistics of individual countries. The estimates were prepared by B. Bolotin, senior researcher at the U.S.S.R. Academy of Sciences' Institute of World Economy and International Relations [IMEMO].

TABLE 1
World Population (millions of people)[1]

	1913	1920	1929	1938	1950	1986	1987
World	1,700	1,850	2,025	2,300	2,565	4,920	5,000
Developed capitalist countries	410	430	470	500	560	770	775
United States	97	107	122	130	152	240	242
Western Europe	230	235	250	265	285	355	355
F.R.G.	37	38	40	43	50	61	61
France	37	38	39	40	42	55	55
Great Britain	42	43	45	48	50	57	57
Italy	36	38	41	45	47	57	57
Japan	51	56	64	71	83	121	122
Developing countries	615	690	770	915	1,060	2,600	2,660
Socialist countries	675	730	785	885	945	1,550	1,565
CMEA*	250	260	270	300	300	463	470
U.S.S.R.	159	166	170	188	180	280	283
Other European CMEA countries	71	72	76	82	89	110	112
Non-European CMEA countries	20	22	24	30	31	73	75
China	400	440	485	550	607	1,045	1,055

[1]Here and thereafter—in the present composition, and within present borders.
*Council for Mutual Economic Assistance.

TABLE 2
National Income[1] (in 1980 prices, millions of dollars)[2]

	1913	1920	1929	1938	1950	1986	1987[3]
World	925	900	1,240	1,450	2,000	7,500	7,775
Developed capitalist countries	655	650	900	1,000	1,350	4,270	4,400
United States	225	260	355	350	650	1,600	1,650
Western Europe	350	300	415	480	525	1,650	1,685
F.R.G.	63	40	67	105	100	356	365
France	63	52	90	75	90	308	315
Great Britain	72	77	82	100	115	240	245
Italy	38	40	50	55	60	216	220
Japan	35	41	62	80	70	700	720
Developing countries	115	125	140	170	240	1,070	1,100
Socialist countries	155	125	200	280	410	2,160	2,275
CMEA	100	65	130	200	320	1,540	1,610
U.S.S.R.	55	20	62	120	200	1,050	1,100
Other European CMEA countries	40	39	60	70	110	450	465
Non-European CMEA countries	5	6	8	10	10	40	45
China	50	57	65	75	80	500	535

[1]According to the methodology of Soviet statistics (net output, or newly created value in the material-production sector, excluding services)

[2]Recalculated in dollars on the basis of comparable purchasing power (actual ratios of prices) in 1980.

[3]For the U.S.S.R. and the other socialist countries—as planned; for all other countries—estimates.

TABLE 3
Growth in National Income (1913 = 1)[1]

	1920	1929	1938	1950	1986	1987
World	0.95	1.35	1.55	2.15	8.10	8.40
Developed capitalist countries	1.00	1.35	1.50	2.05	6.50	6.70
United States	1.15	1.60	1.55	2.90	7.10	7.30
Western Europe	0.85	1.20	1.35	1.50	4.70	4.80
F.R.G.	0.65	1.05	1.65	1.60	5.65	5.80
France	0.80	1.45	1.20	1.45	4.90	5.00
Great Britain	1.05	1.15	1.40	1.60	3.30	3.40
Italy	1.05	1.30	1.45	1.60	5.70	5.80
Japan	1.15	1.75	2.30	2.00	20.00	20.50
Developing countries	1.10	1.20	1.50	2.10	9.30	9.55
Socialist countries	0.80	1.30	1.80	2.65	14.00	14.65
CMEA	0.65	1.30	2.00	3.20	15.40	16.10
U.S.S.R.	0.35	1.10	2.20	3.65	19.00	20.00
Other European CMEA countries	0.95	1.50	1.75	2.75	11.25	11.65
Non-European CMEA countries	1.20	1.60	2.00	2.00	8.00	9.00
China	1.10	1.30	1.50	1.60	10.00	10.70

[1]See notes to Table 2.

TABLE 4
Share of World National Income (percentage of total)

	1913	1920	1929	1938	1950	1986	1987
World	100.0	100.0	100.0	100.0	100.0	100.0	100.0
Developed capitalist countries	70.8	72.2	72.6	69.0	67.5	56.9	56.6
United States	24.3	28.9	28.6	24.1	32.5	21.3	21.2
Western Europe	37.8	35.0	33.5	33.1	26.3	22.0	21.7
F.R.G.	6.8	4.4	5.4	7.2	5.0	4.7	4.7
France	6.8	5.8	7.3	5.2	4.5	4.1	4.0
Great Britain	7.8	8.6	6.6	6.9	5.7	3.2	3.1
Italy	4.1	4.4	4.0	3.8	3.0	2.9	2.8
Japan	3.8	4.6	5.0	5.5	3.5	9.3	9.3
Developing countries	12.4	13.9	11.3	11.7	12.0	14.3	14.3
Socialist countries	16.8	13.9	16.1	19.3	20.5	28.8	29.2
CMEA	10.8	7.2	10.5	13.8	16.0	20.5	20.7
U.S.S.R.	6.0	2.2	5.0	8.3	10.0	14.0	14.2
Other European CMEA countries	4.3	4.3	4.8	4.8	5.5	6.0	6.0
Non-European CMEA countries	0.5	0.7	0.7	0.7	0.5	0.5	0.5
China	5.4	6.3	5.2	5.2	4.0	6.7	6.9

TABLE 5
Per Capita National Income (in 1980 prices, in dollars)[1]

	1913	1920	1929	1938	1950	1986	1987
World	550	485	615	630	780	1,525	1,550
Developed capitalist countries	1,600	1,500	1,925	2,000	2,400	5,550	5,675
United States	2,325	2,425	2,900	2,700	4,275	6,675	6,825
Western Europe	1,525	1,285	1,650	1,800	1,850	4,650	4,750
F.R.G.	1,700	1,050	1,675	2,450	2,000	5,825	5,975
France	1,700	1,370	2,300	1,875	2,150	5,600	5,725
Great Britain	1,700	1,800	1,835	2,075	2,300	4,200	4,300
Italy	1,050	1,050	1,220	1,220	1,275	3,800	3,850
Japan	700	725	960	1,125	850	5,775	5,900
Developing countries	180	180	180	185	225	400	415
Socialist countries	230	170	250	315	435	1,400	1,450
CMEA	400	250	480	665	1,065	3,325	3,425
U.S.S.R.	350	120	365	640	1,100	3,750	3,900
Other European CMEA countries	550	550	800	850	1,235	4,100	4,150
Non-European CMEA countries	250	270	330	330	330	550	600
China	125	130	135	135	130	475	500

[1]See notes to Table 2.

TABLE 6
Comparison of Average Per Capita National Income
(percentages; average figures for all developed capitalist countries together = 100)

	1913	1920	1929	1938	1950	1986	1987
World	33	33	33	30	33	27	27
Developed capitalist countries	100	100	100	100	100	100	100
United States	145	160	150	135	180	120	120
Western Europe	95	85	85	90	75	85	85
F.R.G.	105	70	87	120	85	105	105
France	105	90	120	95	90	100	100
Great Britain	105	120	95	105	95	75	75
Italy	65	70	65	60	55	69	69
Japan	45	50	50	55	35	105	105
Developing countries	about 10	12	about 10	9	9	7	7
Socialist countries	14	11	13	16	18	25	26
CMEA	25	17	25	33	44	60	60
U.S.S.R.	22	8	19	32	46	68	69
Other European CMEA countries	33	37	42	42	51	74	74
Non-European CMEA countries	16	17	17	17	14	10	11
China	8	9	7	7	5	9	9

TABLE 7
Industrial Output[1] (in 1980 prices, billions of dollars)[2]

	1913	1920	1929	1938	1950	1986	1987
World	550	530	830	885	1,300	5,950	6,150
Developed capitalist countries	475	450	700	680	1,000	3,400	3,475
United States	165	200	300	235	485	1,200	1,225
Western Europe	270	205	325	355	420	1,400	1,430
F.R.G.	65	38	76	97	95	360	370
France	46	32	66	53	65	246	250
Great Britain	75	69	75	88	118	222	225
Italy	13	13	24	26	32	189	192
Japan	7	12	23	40	25	510	525
Developing countries	25	35	50	80	135	850	875
Socialist countries	50	45	80	125	165	1,700	1,800
CMEA	40	26	53	85	130	1,250	1,310
U.S.S.R.	20	3	23	50	90	870	910
Other European CMEA countries	19	22	28	33	38	360	378
Non-European CMEA countries	1	1.5	2	2.5	2	20	22
China	10	15	24	33	25	375	400

[1]Final output, which is gross output, minus output used for current production needs in industry itself (machinery, equipment, and producer and consumer goods intended for other branches—agriculture, construction, and transportation).
[2]See notes to Table 2.

TABLE 8
Growth in Industrial Production (1913 = 1)[1]

	1920	1929	1938	1950	1986	1987
World	0.95	1.50	1.60	2.35	10.80	11.20
Developed capitalist countries	0.95	1.45	1.40	2.10	7.15	7.30
United States	1.20	1.80	1.40	2.95	7.25	7.40
Western Europe	0.75	1.20	1.30	1.55	5.20	5.30
F.R.G.	0.60	1.15	1.50	1.45	5.55	5.70
France	0.70	1.45	1.15	1.40	5.35	5.45
Great Britain	0.90	1.00	1.15	1.55	2.95	3.00
Italy	1.00	1.85	2.00	2.45	14.50	14.75
Japan	1.70	3.30	5.70	3.55	72.80	75.00
Developing countries	1.40	2.00	3.20	5.40	34.00	35.00
Socialist countries	0.90	1.60	2.50	3.30	34.00	36.00
CMEA	0.65	1.35	2.10	3.25	31.25	32.75
U.S.S.R.	0.15	1.15	2.50	4.50	43.50	45.50
Other European CMEA countries	1.15	1.45	1.75	2.00	19.00	20.00
Non-European CMEA countries	1.50	2.00	2.50	2.00	20.00	22.00
China	1.50	2.40	3.30	2.50	37.50	40.00

[1]See notes to Table 7.

TABLE 9
Share of World Industrial Output (percentage of total)

	1913	1920	1929	1938	1950	1986	1987
World	100.0	100.0	100.0	100.0	100.0	100.0	100.0
Developed capitalist countries	86.4	84.9	84.4	76.9	76.9	57.1	56.4
United States	30.0	37.7	36.1	26.6	37.3	20.2	19.9
Western Europe	49.1	38.7	39.2	40.1	32.3	23.5	23.2
F.R.G.	11.8	7.2	9.2	11.0	7.3	6.0	6.0
France	8.4	6.0	8.0	6.0	5.0	4.1	4.1
Great Britain	13.6	13.0	9.0	10.0	9.1	3.7	3.7
Italy	2.4	2.4	2.9	2.9	2.5	3.2	3.1
Japan	1.3	2.3	2.8	4.5	1.9	8.6	8.6
Developing countries	4.5	6.6	6.0	9.0	10.4	14.3	14.3
Socialist countries	9.1	8.5	9.6	14.1	12.7	28.6	29.3
CMEA	7.3	4.9	6.4	9.6	10.0	21.0	21.3
U.S.S.R.	3.6	0.6	2.8	5.6	6.9	14.6	14.9
Other European CMEA countries	3.5	4.1	3.4	3.7	2.9	6.1	6.1
Non-European CMEA countries	0.2	0.2	0.2	0.3	0.2	0.3	0.3
China	1.8	2.8	2.9	3.7	1.9	6.3	6.5

TABLE 10
Per Capita Industrial Output (in 1980 prices, in dollars)[1]

	1913	1920	1929	1938	1950	1986	1987
World	325	285	410	385	500	1,200	1,230
Developed capitalist countries	1,150	1,050	1,500	1,350	1,785	4,415	4,485
United States	1,700	1,875	2,450	1,800	3,200	5,000	5,050
Western Europe	1,175	875	1,300	1,340	1,475	3,950	4,025
F.R.G.	1,750	1,000	1,900	2,250	1,900	5,900	6,065
France	1,250	840	1,700	1,325	1,550	4,475	4,550
Great Britain	1,785	1,600	1,665	1,825	2,350	3,900	3,950
Italy	360	340	575	575	680	3,315	3,370
Japan	135	215	360	565	300	4,515	4,300
Developing countries	40	50	65	85	125	325	330
Socialist countries	75	60	100	140	175	1,100	1,150
CMEA	160	100	195	285	435	2,700	2,800
U.S.S.R.	125	20	135	265	500	3,100	3,215
Other European CMEA countries	300	300	370	400	775	3,275	3,375
Non-European CMEA countries	50	60	70	85	70	275	290
China	25	35	50	60	35	360	380

[1]See notes to Table 7.

TABLE 11
Comparison of Average Per Capita Industrial Output
(percentages; average figures for all developed capitalist countries together = 100)

	1913	1920	1929	1938	1950	1986	1987
World	28	27	27	28	28	27	27
Developed capitalist countries	100	100	100	100	100	100	100
United States	150	180	165	135	180	115	115
Western Europe	100	85	85	100	85	90	90
F.R.G.	150	95	125	165	105	135	135
France	110	80	115	100	85	100	100
Great Britain	155	150	110	135	130	90	90
Italy	30	30	40	40	40	75	75
Japan	12	20	25	40	17	95	95
Developing countries	about 3	about 5	about 4	about 6	7	7	7
Socialist countries	about 6	about 6	about 7	10	10	25	26
CMEA	14	9	13	21	24	60	62
U.S.S.R.	11	about 2	9	20	28	70	72
Other European CMEA countries	26	29	25	30	43	75	75
Non-European CMEA countries	about 4	about 6	about 5	about 6	4	6	6
China	about 2	about 3	about 3	about 4	2	8	8

TABLE 12
Production of Some Types of Industrial Products

	1913	1920	1929	1940[1]	1950	1987[2]
Electric power (gross output)[3]						
World	60.5	220.0	485.0	555.0	990.0	10,200.0
U.S.S.R.	2.0	0.5	5.5	48.6	91.2	1,660.0
% of world total	3.3	0.2	1.1	8.8	9.2	16.3
Petroleum (including gas condensate)[4]						
World	53.5	145.0	220.0	290.0	520.0	2,825.0
U.S.S.R.	10.3	3.5	12.5	31.7	37.9	625.0
% of world total	19.2	2.4	5.7	10.7	7.3	22.1
Coal (bituminous and lignite)[4]						
World	1,335.0	1,125.0	1,350.0	1,685.0	1,825.0	4,335.0
U.S.S.R.	28.5	10.0	35.0	163.0	255.0	655.0
% of world total	2.2	0.9	2.6	9.7	14.0	15.1
Steel[4]						
World	76.0	68.0	120.0	142.0	192.0	680.0
U.S.S.R.	4.3	0.2	5.0	18.3	27.3	161.0
% of world total	1.8	0.3	4.2	12.9	14.2	23.7
Cement[4]						
World	40.0	45.0	70.0	87.0	134.0	910.0
U.S.S.R.	1.8	0.25	2.0	5.8	10.2	138.0
% of world total	4.5	0.01	2.9	6.7	7.6	15.2
Synthetic resins and plastics[5]						
World	*	*	*	570	1,630	65,500
U.S.S.R.	*	*	*	11	67	5,500
% of world total	*	*	*	1.9	4.1	8.4
Chemical fibers and threads[5]						
World	*	*	*	875	2,150	20,000
U.S.S.R.	*	*	*	11	24	1,550
% of world total	*	*	*	1.3	1.1	7.7

*Insignificant production.

[1]Data for the nonsocialist countries included in world total are for 1938.
[2]Estimate based on results of first six months.
[3]Billions of kilowatt-hours.
[4]Millions of tons.
[5]Thousands of tons.

TABLE 13
Agricultural Output[1] (in 1980 prices, billions of dollars)

	1913	1920	1929	1938	1950	1986	1987
World	460.0	490.0	560.0	620.0	735.0	1,550.0	1,590.0
Developed capitalist							
countries	255.0	280.0	300.0	315.0	370.0	620.0	630.0
United States	70.0	82.0	86.5	90.5	118.0	175.0	177.0
Western Europe	140.0	150.0	165.0	170.0	180.0	310.0	316.5
F.R.G.	17.0	18.3	22.4	25.5	25.5	40.5	41.5
France	24.0	26.6	28.9	26.0	26.5	44.5	45.5
Great Britain	8.0	8.9	9.1	9.9	12.2	24.5	25.0
Italy	14.2	14.4	15.3	15.6	17.7	31.5	32.0
Japan	18.8	19.6	21.4	23.4	32.5	57.5	58.0
Developing countries	100.0	110.0	127.5	155.0	200.0	470.0	480.0
Socialist countries	105.0	100.0	132.5	150.0	165.0	460.0	480.0
CMEA	55.0	47.5	72.0	82.5	87.0	220.0	227.5
U.S.S.R.	35.0	25.0	45.0	50.0	50.0	135.0	140.0
Other European							
CMEA							
countries	16.9	19.0	23.0	27.9	31.5	70.0	72.0
Non-European							
CMEA							
countries	3.1	3.5	4.0	4.6	5.5	15.0	15.5
China	46.5	49.0	53.2	61.0	71.0	220.0	230.0

[1]Final output, which is gross output minus output used for current production needs in agriculture itself (for example, for seed, feed, etc.). See also notes to Table 2.

TABLE 14
Growth in Agricultural Output (1913 = 1)[1]

	1920	1929	1938	1950	1986	1987
World	1.05	1.20	1.35	1.60	3.35	3.45
Developed capitalist countries	1.10	1.20	1.25	1.45	2.45	2.50
United States	1.15	1.25	1.30	1.70	2.50	2.55
Western Europe	1.05	1.15	1.20	1.30	2.20	2.25
F.R.G.	1.05	1.30	1.50	1.50	2.40	2.45
France	1.10	1.20	1.10	1.10	1.85	1.90
Great Britain	1.10	1.15	1.25	1.50	3.05	3.10
Italy	1.00	1.10	1.10	1.25	2.20	2.25
Japan	1.05	1.15	1.25	1.75	3.05	3.10
Developing countries	1.10	1.25	1.55	2.00	4.70	4.80
Socialist countries	0.95	1.25	1.45	1.55	4.40	4.55
CMEA	0.85	1.30	1.50	1.60	4.00	4.15
U.S.S.R.	0.70	1.20	1.45	1.45	3.85	4.00
Other European CMEA countries	1.10	1.35	1.65	1.85	4.15	4.25
Non-European CMEA countries	1.15	1.30	1.50	1.75	4.85	5.00
China	1.05	1.15	1.30	1.55	4.75	4.95

[1]See notes to Tables 2 and 13.

TABLE 15
Share of World Agricultural Output (percentage of total)

	1913	1920	1929	1938	1950	1986	1987
World	100.0	100.0	100.0	100.0	100.0	100.0	100.0
Developed capitalist countries	55.5	57.0	53.5	50.8	50.3	40.0	39.5
United States	15.2	16.7	15.4	14.6	16.0	11.3	11.1
Western Europe	30.4	30.6	29.5	27.4	24.5	20.0	19.9
F.R.G.	3.7	3.7	4.0	4.1	3.5	2.6	2.6
France	5.2	5.4	5.2	4.2	3.6	2.9	2.9
Great Britain	1.7	1.8	1.6	1.6	1.7	1.6	1.6
Italy	3.1	2.9	2.7	2.5	2.4	2.0	2.0
Japan	4.1	4.0	3.8	3.8	4.4	3.7	3.6
Developing countries	21.7	22.5	22.8	25.0	27.2	30.3	30.3
Socialist countries	22.8	20.5	23.7	24.2	22.5	29.7	30.2
CMEA	12.0	9.7	19.9	13.3	11.8	14.2	14.3
U.S.S.R.	7.6	5.1	8.1	8.1	6.8	8.7	8.8
Other European CMEA countries	3.7	3.9	4.1	4.5	4.3	4.5	4.5
Non-European CMEA countries	0.7	0.7	0.7	0.7	0.7	1.0	1.0
China	10.1	10.0	9.5	9.8	9.7	14.2	14.5

TABLE 16
Per Capita Agricultural Output (in 1980 prices, in dollars)[1]

	1913	1920	1929	1938	1950	1986	1987
World	270	265	275	270	285	315	320
Developed capitalist countries	620	650	640	630	660	800	815
United States	720	765	710	700	775	730	730
Western Europe	610	640	660	640	630	870	890
F.R.G.	460	480	560	590	510	665	680
France	650	700	740	650	630	810	825
Great Britain	190	200	200	200	245	430	440
Italy	400	380	375	350	375	550	560
Japan	370	350	335	330	390	475	475
Developing countries	160	160	165	170	190	180	180
Socialist countries	155	135	170	170	175	300	305
CMEA	220	185	265	275	290	475	485
U.S.S.R.	220	150	265	265	275	480	495
Other European CMEA countries	240	265	300	340	350	635	645
Non-European CMEA countries	155	160	165	155	175	200	205
China	110	110	110	110	115	210	220

[1]See notes to Table 2.

TABLE 17

Average Per Capita Agricultural Output

(percentages; average figures for all developed capitalist countries together = 100)

	1913	1920	1929	1938	1950	1986	1987
World	43	40	43	43	43	39	39
Developed capitalist countries	100	100	100	100	100	100	100
United States	115	115	110	110	115	90	90
Western Europe	100	100	105	100	95	110	110
F.R.G.	75	75	85	95	75	85	85
France	105	105	115	105	95	100	100
Great Britain	30	30	30	30	35	55	54
Italy	65	60	60	55	55	70	70
Japan	60	55	50	50	60	60	60
Developing countries	26	25	26	27	29	22	22
Socialist countries	25	21	27	27	26	37	37
CMEA	35	28	41	44	44	59	60
U.S.S.R.	35	23	41	42	42	60	61
Other European CMEA countries	40	40	47	54	53	79	79
Non-European CMEA countries	25	25	25	25	26	25	25
China	18	17	17	17	17	26	27

TABLE 18
Production of Key Agricultural Products (average annual figures)

	1909–1913	1924–1928	1936–1940	1951–1955	1981–1985
Grain[1]					
World	535.0	600.0	640.0	731.5	1,740.0
U.S.S.R.	72.5	69.3	77.4	88.5	180.3
% of world total	13.5	11.6	12.1	12.1	10.5
Meat (dressed weight)[1]					
World	32.0	42.0	50.5	63.5	150.0
U.S.S.R.	4.8	4.2	4.0	5.7	16.2
% of world total	15.0	10.0	7.9	9.0	10.8
Milk[1]					
World	170.0	200.0	235.0	270.0	500.0
U.S.S.R.	28.8	29.3	26.5	37.9	94.5
% of world total	16.9	14.7	11.3	14.1	18.9
Eggs[2]					
World	105.0	125.9	155.0	191.5	525.0
U.S.S.R.	11.2	9.2	9.6	15.9	74.4
% of world total	10.7	7.4	6.2	8.3	14.2
Raw Cotton[1]					
World	12.5	15.5	21.0	26.5	43.5
U.S.S.R.	0.7	0.6	2.5	3.9	9.1
% of world total	5.6	3.9	11.9	14.7	20.9

[1]Millions of tons.
[2]Billions of eggs.

Statistics: The Soviet Union in the World Economy (1917-1987)

Part II*

The first part of this statistical collection cited figures reflecting how the U.S.S.R.'s relative share of the world economy (in the national income and industrial and agricultural output of the world as a whole) has increased, as well as how the U.S.S.R. has narrowed the gap with the developed capitalist countries in average per capita annual production volumes.

To a certain extent, average per capita figures can also characterize individual countries' levels of economic development. However, the decisive criterion here is labor productivity. That is what ultimately determines the strain on labor resources, their relative distribution among the sectors of material production and social services, the division of the public's time between work and leisure time, and so forth. The growth of labor productivity, and the change in the relationships between the U.S.S.R. and other countries with respect to this indicator constitute the principal content of this second part of the statistical collection.

Over the Soviet Union's 57 years of peacetime existence (1921 to 1940 and 1951 to 1987, i.e., excluding the war years and the period of postwar recovery), we have achieved a 19-fold increase in the productivity of social labor. During these same years, labor productivity has increased by a factor of only 5.5 in all the developed capitalist countries taken together (by factors of 13 in Japan, 9 in the Federal Republic of Germany, 7 in France and Italy, and 3.5 in Great Britain and the United States).

But the productivity of social labor in the U.S.S.R. is still 60 percent lower, on the average, than for all the developed capitalist countries (including 50 percent lower than that of Western Europe). According to the "Basic Guidelines for the U.S.S.R.'s Economic and Social Development in 1986-1990 and for the Period up to the Year 2000" that were adopted by the 27th Party Congress, the produc-

---

*This article appeared in December 1987. It is a continuation of the preceding article (Part I) begun in the November 1987 issue of *MEMO*. [Tables are numbered consecutively from Part I.]

374

tivity of social labor is supposed to be increased by a factor of 2.3 to 2.5 by the end of the century. That will represent an important step toward reaching the highest world levels in this critical area. By the year 2000 the U.S.S.R. is supposed to achieve a level of labor productivity equaling the present level for the developed capitalist countries as a whole, and equaling 75 to 85 percent of the level anticipated for them by that time. In that case the U.S.S.R. will be practically on a par with Western Europe with regard to this index.

The present level of labor productivity in Soviet industry (as well as in construction, for which estimates are not given here) is approximately 60 percent of the average index for all Western countries. Let us note that in our industry the level of productivity of labor engaged in basic production operations equals no less than 75 percent of the Western level. The lower overall index reflects the fact that we have a larger percentage of employees than the West in auxiliary production shops, where productivity is often extremely low because of widespread manual labor, a low degree of specialization, and the small-scale production (output in relatively small lots).

The improvement in the organizational structure of industry, and the establishment of branch and interbranch territorial "socialist corporations" relying on regional production infrastructures—and this is what the decisions of the CPSU Central Committee's June 1987 plenary session call for, in part—are intended to change radically the existing situation. In combination with the introduction of the latest scientific and technological advances and the activation of the human factor, the organizational restructuring of the economy will help the Soviet Union practically reach par with the West in terms of industrial labor productivity by the year 2000.

A considerably less favorable comparative level exists (and is expected to last even until the end of the century) with regard to labor productivity in agriculture. We have more than 24 million people employed in this sector—more than in all the developed capitalist countries taken together. However, the labor of all these millions produces less than 25 percent of the Western countries' output. In our country the productivity of agricultural labor is 80 percent lower than in those countries, which also goes a long way toward explaining our overall comparisons to them (for all material production sectors) with regard to labor productivity.

The fact that the levels of productivity of agricultural labor and social labor as a whole in the U.S.S.R. are interconnected and interdependent is obvious. A substantially larger percentage of employees in the material-production sector are employed in agriculture in our country than in the West (29 percent in the U.S.S.R., 20 percent in Japan and Italy, 14 percent in France, 9 percent in the United States and the Federal Republic of Germany, and 5 percent in Great Britain). The gap between output levels in agriculture on the one hand, and industry on the other, is far greater in the Soviet Union than in the developed capitalist countries (taking the productivity of industrial labor as 100, in 1986 the productivity of agricultural labor was 25 percent in the U.S.S.R., 100 percent in the United States, 75 percent in the Federal Republic of Germany, 65 percent in France, 130 percent in Great Britain, 40 percent in Italy, and 30 percent in Japan).

Until recently one could encounter the assertion in economics literature that the Soviet Union's lag behind the West in the productivity of agricultural labor was almost entirely attributable to unfavorable weather conditions. One cannot agree with that assertion. The intensification of farming techniques sharply reduces the significance of "initial" soil fertility. It is no accident that the highest grain yields in the world are obtained by the West European countries, whose soil and climate cannot be called propitious (in 1986, those yields were 60 centners per hectare in Great Britain, 53 centners per hectare in the Federal Republic of Germany and France, 50 centners per hectare in Denmark, 40 centners per hectare in Sweden, 30 centners per hectare in Finland, and 39 centners per hectare for the developed capitalist countries as a whole). In the U.S.S.R., however, the "average hectare" yields less than half as much grain (18 centners), while 150 percent more workers are employed on it (which is what accounts for the fact that our agricultural productivity is only one fifth of the West's).

An attempt to attribute our lag to the present inadequate mechanization or, more broadly, insufficiently high capital-labor ratio in the U.S.S.R.'s agriculture are equally groundless. It is true that the Soviet Union still lags behind the leading capitalist countries with regard to these indicators. But in the first place, the gap between us in terms of the capital-labor ratio is approximately half the size of the gap in labor productivity. In the second place, to a considerable extent the gap with respect to the capital-labor ratio is due to the same causes that underlie the relatively low productivity of agricultural labor in the U.S.S.R. The chief cause, it seems to us, is the attitude toward the land and toward work, and employees' relatively low stake (in the past) in improving their performance results.

During the previous, 11th five-year plan, for example, agriculture in the U.S.S.R. received 1.85 million tractors, 1.5 million trucks, 560,000 grain combines, and 210,000 silage harvesters. However, over these five years the number of operating tractors in agriculture increased by only 235,000, the number of operating trucks by 255,000, and the number of operating grain combines by 110,000; and the number of operating silage harvesters actually decreased by 10,000.

Let us point out that in the United States the increase in the total amount of farm machinery was even somewhat higher, while deliveries were only one fourth to one third of what they were in the U.S.S.R. In our country, 85 percent of the new tractors and vehicles, 80 percent of the grain combines, and more than 100 percent of the silage harvesters went to replace excessive numbers that had gone out of service, not only because of the poor quality of the machinery, but also because of people's careless attitude toward it.

The mighty potential of the U.S.S.R.'s socialist agriculture still awaits full utilization. The new economic mechanism in the agroindustrial complex that has been worked out in accordance with the decisions of the 27th Party Congress and subsequent Central Committee plenums should put an end to bureaucratic and administrative diktat in agricultural production, where it is particularly intolerable because this sort of production, by its very nature, demands maximum flexibility and maneuverability in accordance with changing conditions. Even in its initial phase, this economic mechanism has been fairly successful in passing the test of this year's difficult weather conditions.

In examining the figures on labor productivity that are given in this collection, one must keep in mind that they pertain to annual output and may substantially differ from the comparisons based on hourly output that are usually cited in official Soviet statistics. Whereas the difference between the two series of figures is not great in industry (the average annual work time per employee in industry is approximately 2,000 hours in all the economically developed countries), the situation is different in agriculture. Annual work time per agricultural employee is approximately 1,500 hours in the U.S.S.R., 2,600 hours in the United States, and as high as 2,800 hours in Western Europe. Understandably, the comparison between the U.S.S.R. and the United States in terms of annual output in agriculture is more than 40 percent lower (and between the U.S.S.R. and Western Europe, nearly 50 percent lower) than it is for hourly output.

The calculations rely on publications of the U.S.S.R. Central Statistical Administration (*The U.S.S.R. National Economy* [*Narodnoye khozyaystvo SSSR*], *U.S.S.R. Industry* [*Promyshlennost SSSR*], and *U.S.S.R. Agriculture* [*Selskoye khozyaystvo SSSR*]); United Nations statistical agencies (including the specialized agencies—FAO, UNCTAD, UNIDO, and others); and statistics of individual countries. The estimates were prepared by B. Bolotin, senior researcher at the U.S.S.R. Academy of Sciences' Institute of World Economy and International Relations [IMEMO].

TABLE 19
Number of Workers Engaged in Material-Production Branches[1]
(millions of people)

	1913	1920	1929	1938	1950	1986	1987
World	590.0	635.0	685.0	775.0	890.0	1,350.0	1,360.0
Developed capitalist							
countries	135.0	140.0	145.0	140.0	152.5	140.0	140.0
United States	26.5	30.5	32.0	28.0	30.5	36.5	36.8
Western Europe	77.0	80.0	80.5	78.5	81.5	66.0	66.0
F.R.G.	12.0	13.0	13.5	14.5	15.2	14.4	14.4
France	14.5	15.0	15.0	13.0	12.5	10.8	10.8
Great Britain	11.5	12.0	12.5	13.0	14.8	11.5	11.5
Italy	14.0	14.0	13.5	12.5	14.3	11.6	11.6
Japan	19.5	19.5	21.0	22.0	25.0	26.3	26.5
Developing countries	220.0	240.0	265.0	325.0	402.5	645.0	650.0
Socialist countries	235.0	255.0	275.0	310.0	335.0	565.0	570.0
CMEA	80.0	83.5	87.5	96.5	96.0	142.0	144.5
U.S.S.R.	48.5	50.5	52.0	57.5	55.0	83.0	84.0
Other European							
CMEA							
countries	24.5	25.0	26.5	28.5	30.0	35.0	35.5
Non-European							
CMEA							
countries	7.5	8.0	9.0	10.5	11.0	24.0	25.0
China	150.0	165.0	180.0	205.0	230.5	407.5	410.0

[1]Excluding trade.

TABLE 20
Productivity of Social Labor
(national income[1] per worker in the material-production sector,
in 1980 prices, in dollars)[2]

	1913	1920	1929	1938	1950	1986	1987[3]
World	1,570	1,415	1,800	1,870	2,250	5,550	5,725
Developed capitalist countries	4,850	4,650	6,200	7,150	8,850	30,500	31,425
United States	8,500	8,525	11,100	12,500	21,300	43,825	44,825
Western Europe	4,550	3,750	5,150	6,115	6,450	25,000	25,525
F.R.G.	5,250	3,075	4,950	7,250	6,575	24,725	23,350
France	4,350	3,465	6,000	5,775	7,200	28,500	29,150
Great Britain	6,250	6,425	6,550	7,700	7,770	20,875	21,300
Italy	2,715	2,850	3,700	4,400	4,200	18,625	18,965
Japan	1,800	2,100	2,950	3,625	2,800	26,600	27,175
Developing countries	525	525	525	525	600	1,660	1,690
Socialist countries	660	490	725	900	1,225	3,825	4,000
CMEA	1,250	780	1,485	2,075	3,330	10,850	11,150
U.S.S.R.	1,135	400	1,200	2,085	3,635	12,650	13,100
Other European CMEA countries	1,630	1,560	2,265	2,450	3,665	12,850	13,100
Non-European CMEA countries	715	750	900	950	1,000	1,665	1,800
China	335	345	360	365	350	1,225	1,300

[1]According to the methodology of Soviet statistics (net output equals newly created value in the material-production sector, excluding services).
[2]Recalculated in dollars on the basis of comparable purchasing power (actual price ratios).
[3]For the U.S.S.R. and the other socialist countries—based on plan targets; for all other countries—estimates.

TABLE 21
Growth in Productivity of Social Labor (1913 = 1)

	1920	1929	1938	1950	1986	1987
World	0.90	1.15	1.20	1.45	3.50	3.65
Developed capitalist countries	0.95	1.30	1.45	1.80	6.30	6.50
United States	1.00	1.30	1.45	2.50	5.15	5.25
Western Europe	0.80	1.15	1.35	1.40	5.50	5.60
F.R.G.	0.60	0.95	1.40	1.25	4.70	4.85
France	0.80	1.40	1.35	1.65	6.50	6.70
Great Britain	1.05	1.05	1.25	1.25	3.35	3.40
Italy	1.05	1.35	1.60	1.55	6.85	7.00
Japan	1.15	1.65	2.00	1.55	14.75	15.00
Developing countries	1.00	1.00	1.00	1.15	3.15	3.20
Socialist countries	0.75	1.10	1.35	1.85	5.80	6.00
CMEA	0.60	1.20	1.65	2.65	8.70	8.90
U.S.S.R.	0.35	1.05	1.85	3.20	11.15	11.50
Other European CMEA countries	0.95	1.40	1.50	2.25	7.90	8.00
Non-European CMEA countries	1.05	1.25	1.35	1.40	2.35	2.50
China	1.05	1.05	1.10	1.05	3.65	3.90

TABLE 22
Comparison of Levels of the Productivity of Social Labor[1]
(percentages; average figures for all developed capitalist countries together = 1)

	1913	1920	1929	1938	1950	1986	1987
World	32	30	29	26	25	18	19
Developed capitalist countries	100	100	100	100	100	100	100
United States	175	185	180	175	240	145	145
Western Europe	95	80	85	85	75	80	80
F.R.G.	110	65	80	100	75	80	80
France	90	75	95	80	80	95	95
Great Britain	130	140	105	105	90	70	70
Italy	55	60	60	60	45	60	60
Japan	35	45	50	50	33	85	85
Developing countries	11	11	8	7	7	5	5
Socialist countries	14	10	12	13	14	13	13
CMEA	26	17	24	29	38	36	35
U.S.S.R.	23	9	19	29	40	41	42
Other European CMEA countries	34	35	36	34	41	42	42
Non-European CMEA countries	16	15	14	13	11	5	6
China	7	7	6	5	4	4	4

[1]Taking into account the degree of accuracy of existing statistics, in cases where the rounded-off result differs from the basic result by no more than 5 percent, the relationships between countries in terms of labor productivity are rounded off to the nearest 10 or 5.

TABLE 23
Number of Workers in Industry (millions of people)

	1913	1920	1929	1938	1950	1986	1987
World	76.0	85.5	100.0	113.0	141.5	312.5	315.5
Developed capitalist countries	45.0	52.5	56.5	57.5	66.0	85.0	85.0
United States	10.9	13.9	15.3	13.9	17.7	23.1	23.0
Western Europe	27.4	30.5	31.8	32.7	36.7	37.3	37.2
F.R.G.	5.8	6.9	7.4	8.4	9.2	8.8	8.7
France	4.3	4.7	4.8	4.4	4.6	5.5	5.5
Great Britain	6.6	7.0	7.4	7.7	8.9	6.6	6.6
Italy	3.6	4.0	4.0	3.7	4.5	5.5	5.5
Japan	4.0	5.1	6.3	7.3	7.7	14.1	14.2
Developing countries	11.0	12.5	16.5	21.5	33.5	102.5	103.5
Socialist countries	20.0	20.5	27.0	34.0	42.0	125.0	127.0
CMEA	13.4	11.4	16.4	20.0	26.0	59.5	60.0
U.S.S.R.	7.5	5.0	9.5	12.5	16.6	37.5	37.5
Other European CMEA countries	5.0	5.2	5.5	6.0	8.4	18.0	18.2
Non-European CMEA countries	0.9	1.2	1.4	1.5	1.0	4.0	4.3
China	6.0	8.5	10.0	13.0	14.9	62.0	63.5

TABLE 24
Productivity of Labor in Industry
(annual production of final output per worker,
in 1980 prices, in dollars)

	1913	1920	1929	1938	1950	1986	1987
World	7,225	6,200	8,300	7,800	9,200	19,050	19,500
Developed capitalist countries	10,550	8,575	12,400	11,825	15,150	40,000	40,875
United States	15,125	14,400	19,600	16,900	27,400	51,950	53,250
Western Europe	9,850	6,705	10,225	10,850	11,450	37,525	38,450
F.R.G.	11,200	5,500	10,275	11,550	10,325	40,900	42,525
France	10,700	6,800	13,750	12,050	14,130	44,725	45,450
Great Britain	11,365	9,850	10,125	11,425	13,250	33,635	34,100
Italy	3,600	3,250	6,000	7,025	7,100	34,365	34,900
Japan	1,750	2,350	3,650	5,475	3,250	36,170	36,975
Developing countries	2,275	2,800	3,025	3,700	4,000	8,300	8,450
Socialist countries	2,625	2,200	2,950	3,675	3,925	13,600	14,175
CMEA	3,000	2,275	3,230	4,250	5,000	21,000	21,825
U.S.S.R.	2,625	600	2,425	4,000	5,425	23,200	24,250
Other European CMEA countries	3,800	4,225	5,100	5,500	4,525	20,000	20,775
Non-European CMEA countries	1,125	1,250	1,450	1,665	2,000	5,000	5,100
China	1,650	1,765	2,400	2,550	1,700	6,050	6,300

TABLE 25
Growth in Labor Productivity in Industry (1913 = 1)

	1920	1929	1938	1950	1986	1987
World	0.85	1.15	1.10	1.25	2.60	2.70
Developed capitalist countries	0.80	1.20	1.10	1.45	3.80	3.85
United States	0.95	1.30	1.10	1.80	3.45	3.50
Western Europe	0.70	1.05	1.10	1.15	3.80	3.90
F.R.G.	0.50	0.90	1.05	0.90	3.65	3.80
France	0.65	1.30	1.15	1.30	4.20	4.25
Great Britain	0.85	0.90	1.00	1.15	2.95	3.00
Italy	0.90	1.65	1.95	1.95	9.50	9.70
Japan	1.35	2.10	3.10	1.85	20.65	21.00
Developing countries	1.25	1.35	1.65	1.75	3.65	3.70
Socialist countries	0.85	1.10	1.40	1.50	5.20	5.40
CMEA	0.75	1.10	1.40	1.65	7.00	7.25
U.S.S.R.	0.25	0.90	1.50	2.00	8.70	9.10
Other European CMEA countries	1.10	1.35	1.45	1.20	5.25	5.45
Non-European CMEA countries	1.10	1.25	1.45	1.75	4.35	4.50
China	1.05	1.45	1.55	1.05	3.65	3.80

TABLE 26
Comparison of Labor Productivity in Industry
(percentages; average figures for all developed capitalist countries together = 100)

	1913	1920	1929	1938	1950	1986	1987
World	68	72	67	66	61	48	48
Developed capitalist countries	100	100	100	100	100	100	100
United States	145	170	160	145	180	130	130
Western Europe	95	80	80	90	75	95	95
F.R.G.	105	65	85	100	70	100	105
France	100	80	110	100	95	110	110
Great Britain	110	115	80	95	85	85	85
Italy	35	40	50	60	45	85	85
Japan	15	25	30	45	20	90	90
Developing countries	22	33	24	31	26	21	21
Socialist countries	25	26	24	31	26	34	35
CMEA	28	26	26	36	33	52	53
U.S.S.R.	25	7	20	34	36	58	59
Other European CMEA countries	36	49	41	46	30	50	51
Non-European CMEA countries	11	15	12	14	13	13	13
China	16	21	19	22	11	15	15

TABLE 27
Number of Workers in Agriculture (millions of people)

	1913	1920	1929	1938	1950	1986	1987
World	470.0	500.0	530.0	585.0	655.0	875.0	875.0
Developed capitalist countries	72.5	69.5	67.5	61.5	60.5	23.0	22.50
United States	11.5	11.3	10.9	8.8	6.0	3.2	3.20
Western Europe	38.5	37.5	36.0	33.0	32.5	11.5	11.15
F.R.G.	5.4	5.2	5.1	5.0	4.8	1.3	1.28
France	8.0	8.0	7.8	6.5	5.6	1.6	1.55
Great Britain	1.4	1.3	1.2	1.2	1.2	0.6	0.57
Italy	9.4	9.0	8.5	8.0	8.6	2.4	2.33
Japan	14.5	13.1	13.0	12.8	15.3	5.7	5.55
Developing countries	200.0	223.0	244.5	290.0	352.0	492.0	495.00
Socialist countries	197.5	207.5	218.0	233.5	242.5	360.0	357.00
CMEA	58.0	62.0	63.0	63.0	62.0	53.5	53.30
U.S.S.R.	35.0	38.3	37.3	35.0	32.1	24.5	24.20
Other European CMEA countries	16.5	16.7	17.7	19.0	19.9	12.0	11.80
Non-European CMEA countries	6.5	7.0	8.0	9.0	10.0	17.0	17.30
China	135.0	140.0	150.0	165.0	175.0	300.0	300.00

TABLE 28

Labor Productivity in Agriculture (final output per worker in agriculture, in 1980 prices, in dollars)

	1913	1920	1929	1938	1950	1986	1987
World	980	980	1,050	1,050	1,125	1,770	1,815
Developed capitalist countries	3,500	4,025	4,450	5,125	6,115	26,950	28,000
United States	6,100	7,250	7,925	10,275	19,650	54,700	55,300
Western Europe	3,625	4,000	4,575	5,150	5,550	26,950	28,400
F.R.G.	3,150	3,500	4,400	5,100	5,300	31,150	32,425
France	3,000	3,325	3,700	4,000	4,725	27,800	29,350
Great Britain	5,725	6,850	7,575	8,250	10,150	40,825	43,850
Italy	1,500	1,600	1,800	1,950	2,050	13,125	13,725
Japan	1,300	1,500	1,650	1,825	2,125	10,100	10,450
Developing countries	500	510	520	530	570	050	970
Socialist countries	530	480	610	640	680	1,275	1,350
CMEA	950	765	1,150	1,300	1,400	4,100	4,270
U.S.S.R.	1,000	650	1,200	1,425	1,560	5,500	5,775
Other European CMEA countries	1,025	1,140	1,300	1,470	585	5,830	6,100
Non-European CMEA countries	475	500	500	510	550	880	900
China	340	350	355	370	405	730	765

TABLE 29
Growth of Labor Productivity in Agriculture (1913 = 1)

	1920	1929	1938	1950	1986	1987
World	1.00	1.05	1.05	1.15	1.80	1.85
Developed capitalist countries	1.15	1.25	1.45	1.75	7.70	8.00
United States	1.20	1.30	1.70	3.25	9.00	9.10
Western Europe	1.10	1.25	1.40	1.55	7.45	7.85
F.R.G.	1.10	1.40	1.65	1.70	9.90	10.30
France	1.10	1.25	1.35	1.60	9.25	9.80
Great Britain	1.20	1.30	1.45	1.75	7.10	7.65
Italy	1.05	1.20	1.30	1.35	8.65	9.00
Japan	1.15	1.25	1.40	1.65	7.75	8.00
Developing countries	1.00	1.00	1.05	1.15	1.90	1.95
Socialist countries	0.90	1.15	1.20	1.30	2.40	2.50
CMEA	0.80	1.20	1.35	1.45	4.30	4.50
U.S.S.R.	0.65	1.20	1.45	1.55	5.50	5.80
Other European CMEA countries	1.10	1.25	1.45	1.55	5.70	6.00
Non-European CMEA countries	1.05	1.05	1.05	1.15	1.85	1.90
China	1.00	1.05	1.05	1.15	2.15	2.25

TABLE 30
Comparison of Levels of Labor Productivity in Agriculture
(percentages; average figures for all developed capitalist countries together = 100)

	1913	1920	1929	1938	1950	1986	1987
World	28	24	24	20	18	7	6
Developed capitalist countries	100	100	100	100	100	100	100
United States	175	180	180	200	325	200	200
Western Europe	105	100	105	100	90	100	100
F.R.G.	90	90	100	100	85	115	115
France	85	85	85	80	75	105	105
Great Britain	165	170	170	160	165	150	155
Italy	45	40	40	40	35	50	50
Japan	35	37	37	36	35	37	37
Developing countries	14	13	12	10	9	4	4
Socialist countries	15	12	14	12	11	5	5
CMEA	27	19	26	25	23	15	15
U.S.S.R.	26	16	27	28	25	20	21
Other European CMEA countries	29	28	29	29	26	22	22
Non-European CMEA countries	13	12	11	10	9	3	3
China	10	9	8	7	7	3	3

Familiar Ideas and Actual Facts

In connection with the publication of the statistical collection "The Soviet Union in the World Economy" (MEMO, Nos. 11-12, 1987),* the editors received a letter from I. Zvyagintsev, a reader from Izhevsk. In his letter he expresses a number of considerations about the problem in question and cites his own calculations that reflect doubts as to some of the figures in the collection. The editors believe that the author's reply to I.I. Zvyagintsev's questions may also be of interest to a broad range of the journal's readers.

Esteemed editors:

I assume that your journal, despite its theoretical orientation, is not intended only for professionals. I am one of those nonprofessionals. I do not acquire your journal often, but when I saw the title "The Soviet Union in the World Economy" in the table of contents for issue No. 11 for 1987, I bought that issue and read it with interest. This is the only attempt I have seen to compare certain economic indicators in human terms.

However, I developed certain doubts. Let me say from the outset that you may suspect me of having a certain instinct that demands that it simply be taken for granted that the U.S.S.R. is superlative in every respect.

Yes, I want us to look better. Of course, it is possible to understand perestroika as dragging our dirty laundry out from every possible corner in order to argue: look at the dirt—that means we need perestroika. And in some people's opinion, if there is not enough dirt, it has got to be invented so there will be something to undergo perestroika.

That was a long digression. Of course, one cannot force figures to conform to emotions. But in fact, just how accurate are your figures?

1. As I understand it, industrial and agricultural output are evaluated as value-added conditional net output [uslovno-chistaya produktsiya], without material outlays (to all intents and purposes, it can be considered net output, that is, the contribution to national income),

---

*See the two preceding articles. This exchange of letters appeared in the July 1988 issue of *MEMO*.

but in that case doubts arise as to whether the figures cited agree among themselves and are reliable.

By subtracting the contribution of industry and agriculture from national income, for 1987 we receive a "remainder" that, one must assume, characterizes the contribution of the other material-production branches—construction, transportation, communications, and trade: for the United States—$248 billion, for Japan—$137 billion, and for the U.S.S.R.—only $50 billion. Is it possible that the United States produces five times our net output in those branches?

2. The figures for 1913 elicit disbelief. Is it possible that Russia in those days was so backward that it was in the position of Vietnam, Mongolia, and Cuba in terms of per capita indices? If that was the case, then it was Karl Kautsky, and not Lenin, who really was right. At least one can draw such conclusions from that.

3. You compare defense expenditures for the 1950 to 1986 period (500 billion rubles) with other capital investments—in industry (975 billion), agriculture (500 billion), and housing (430 billion). Altogether, that makes 2,405 billion rubles. According to the table "Dimensions of the Soviet Economy," total capital investments for those years came to 3,105 billion rubles. It works out that 700 billion went for other purposes. Yet according to the same table, the growth in fixed nonproduction assets for the period in question was 785 billion rubles. And yet there were also capital investments in transportation, communications, construction, and trade.

The figures for 1938 are very dubious. How could we win the war if our industrial output for that year really did come to just over half of what was produced on the part of German territory that now constitutes the Federal Republic of Germany (not to even mention the output produced on the territory that now forms the German Democratic Republic, the western lands of Poland, and Kaliningrad Province of the Russian Republic)? In general, according to your figures it works out that before the war the U.S.S.R. occupied fifth place, after the United States, Germany, Great Britain, and France, in terms of industrial output. Yet it is known that as of the beginning of the 1940s we had attained second place in the world and first place in Europe in terms of this index.

4. Fairly recently it was stated in *Argumenty i fakty* [*Arguments and Facts*] (Nos. 42-44) that the U.S.S.R. occupies practically 24th place in the world in per capita consumption of goods and services (and there are only about 30 industrially developed countries). That is an outright insult to the people of 1905 to 1945, the people who died and lived then.

5. How is one to understand the indications that from 1921 to 1938 and 1951 to 1987 average annual rates of growth in national

income came to 6.6 percent in the U.S.S.R.? Were they identical in both the 1921 to 1938 and 1951 to 1987 periods? Or are these figures averages for the two periods mentioned?

Igor Zvyagintsev, 22 years old, Izhevsk.

* * *

Dear Igor:

(I am forced to address you by your first name, since I cannot tell your patronymic from your initials, and anyway our age difference allows such a form of address.)

Your letter made me very glad. Surprisingly many inquisitive, searching, and deeply concerned young people have made themselves known just recently, and that is the main result of our changes, of perestroika and glasnost. Your letter is also especially important to me for the fact that it makes it possible to identify the author's slips: places where my explanations were not clear enough, or where they were simply missing altogether. Before moving on to answer specific questions, let me say the following:

It is strange that a person of your intellectual makeup perceives perestroika as "dragging our dirty laundry out from every . . . corner," and considers that "inventing dirt" to be the grounds for the need for perestroika. Perestroika is not an "insult to the people of 1905 to 1945, the people who died and lived then." It is dictated by a profound respect for their heroic exploits, and by a desire to fully utilize, for the benefit of the people, the might of the socialist state whose foundation was laid by those people at the price of unparalleled effort and deprivation. And yet to pretend that everything is fine and that the economy is performing efficiently, while we are actually, because of an obsolete economic mechanism, using only half of what has been created by the people—that really would be showing shameful disrespect for the "people of 1905 to 1945."

And now let me move on specifically to your calculations, which have been occasioned by your doubts.

1. You compare the indices, expressed in monetary values, that I cite for national income and industrial and agricultural output, and you thereby attempt to prove that they disagree among themselves and are erroneous. Such comparisons are incorrect, since the volumes of industrial and agricultural production given in the tables are not net output, from which national income is made up, and not even conditional net output (as you suppose), but *final* output [konechnaya produktsiya]. Final output does not take into account the processing within an industry of raw materials, or semimanufactures and compo-

nents that are manufactured *within that given* branch of the economy, but it does fully take into account those same materials and component parts that come into the production process from *other* branches of the economy.

Let me recall the basic concepts used in statistics.

Net output [chistaya produktsiya] is gross output, less the value of raw materials and other materials and the depreciation of fixed production assets.

Conditional net output is net output plus depreciation.

Final output is conditional net output plus the value of the materials that a given branch receives from outside. For example, final industrial output includes the value of agricultural raw materials that are received for industrial processing, transportation costs, trade markups, the value of production services, and so forth. In terms of its physical substance, and in a functional sense, final output is what the given branch provides to the national economy (not counting its own output used in the production process).

Now do you understand that the connection between the figures given in the tables for industrial and agricultural production, on the one hand, and national income, on the other, is much more complicated than your calculations would indicate?

National income equals the sum of the final output of all the material-production branches, less the intrabranch turnover of raw materials and other materials, and the depreciation of fixed production assets. Let me illustrate this using the concrete example of the link between these indices for the U.S.S.R. and the United States in 1987 (all figures are in 1980 prices, in billions of dollars, with Soviet figures recalculated in dollars on the basis of the actual ratios of prices, rather than the official exchange rate).

	U.S.S.R.	U.S.A.
National income	1,100	1,650
equals the final output of:		
industry	910	1,225
agriculture	140	177
construction	250	280
transportation and communications	225	225
trade[1]	185	370
Total final output		
of all material-production branches	1,710	2,277
minus:		
interbranch turnover (usage) of raw materials and other materials	470	487
minus:		
depreciation of fixed production assets	140	140

[1]Trade markup on output of other branches.

These figures already bring out both our achievements and our shortcomings. Thus, in 1987 the ratio of the U.S.S.R. to the United States was much higher in terms of the total final output of the material-production branches (75 percent) than in terms of national income (66 percent). The reason for the differences between these ratios is also clear from the figures cited: while its total material-production outlays are practically equal to those of the United States, our country receives 33 percent less national income. If you consider, in addition, the intrabranch turnover (shifting from the index of final output to the index of gross output of the material-production branches), the coefficient of the materials-intensiveness of national income in the U.S.S.R. turns out to be nearly twice as high as in the United States. These are the figures that M.S. Gorbachev cited in his Murmansk speech.

Returning to your calculations, let me say that the high materials-intensiveness of the final output of Soviet agriculture and industry explain precisely the result that puzzles you. By subtracting the total industrial and agricultural output from the capitalist countries' national income given in the tables, you obtained a substantially larger "remainder" than in the U.S.S.R., a remainder which supposedly reflects the output of the construction and transportation industries and trade. Perhaps it bears repeating that, in any case, your calculations are incorrect because of the disparate nature of the indices you use of national income and final output of the material-production branches.

2. The figures given in Tables 5, 10, and 16 for average per capita national income and the industrial and agricultural output of individual countries in 1913 agree with the results once obtained by experts of the League of Nations and subsequently confirmed by calculations of the U.S.S.R. State Statistical Administration. As for the comparisons between Russia, on the one hand, and Vietnam, Cuba, and Mongolia, on the other, in terms of these indices—and they are what seem improbable to you—they fully agree with one another and explain one another. If the average figures for Vietnam, Cuba, and Mongolia combined are taken as 100, for Russia in 1913 you get 150 for national income, 250 for industrial output, and 130 for agricultural output (in this case I am using for calculations the original figures, which were rounded off, according to accepted rules, for use in the aforementioned tables, but that does not change anything fundamentally).

You will agree that the conclusion you draw that before the Revolution Russia was "in the position of Vietnam of that time, Laos, the Mongolian People's Republic, and Cuba" in no way follows from these figures (if you believe my calculations). In per capita industrial production, Russia surpassed those countries' combined total by 150 percent. As for the correlation in national income, it mainly reflects the low level of development of agriculture, which is common knowledge. Incidentally, the figures in the second part of the collection (*MEMO*, No. 12, Tables 24 and 28) even more vividly show the substantially higher level of Russia's economic development (higher than that of the aforementioned countries). In terms of labor productivity in 1913, it surpassed them by 140 percent in industry and 110 percent in agriculture. Russian industry in 1913 had 7.5 million employees—they were the ones who provided the main driving force of the Revolution.

Of course, in comparison to America, Germany, Great Britain, and France, Russia's level of economic development was extremely low, as evident from the second part of my collection. But can it be that you find anything surprising in that fact?

Now, with respect to the "correctness" of Kautsky, which my calculations supposedly confirm (which you take as self-evident proof of the erroneousness of those calculations). Of course, one can understand the doubts of that "orthodox" Marxist, who completely identified the readiness of any given country for socialism with the level of development of its productive forces. But history did not proceed according to Kautsky, so there is no point in mentioning him in vain.

3. You oppose the comparative figures I give [see Part I in this collection] for defense expenditures and capital investments in industry, agriculture, and housing to the figures given for total capital investments and the increase in fixed assets in the table "Dimensions of the Soviet Economy," and you reveal, you believe, that they do not agree.

The comparison of defense expenditures to capital investments by no means indicates that defense expenditures consist entirely of capital investments (capital investments account for less than half of them; the remainder goes for the maintenance of personnel and current material outlays of the armed forces). Further, you try to determine "capital investments in the nonproduction sphere, minus housing" on the basis of the growth in fixed nonproduction assets for 1951 to 1985.

First of all, where you get your figure for the growth in fixed nonproduction assets over that period (785 billion rubles) is incomprehensible. According to the table, the *total amount* of fixed nonproduction assets as of the end of 1985 came to 765 billion rubles (in 1973 prices), and their growth from 1951 through 1985 was 695 billion (765 minus 70). To this one should add that the table gives capital investments in 1983 prices and fixed assets in 1973 prices (which makes the simple addition and subtraction of figures from the two different series senseless), and that the growth in fixed assets is always less than capital investments by the amount that offsets the physical attrition of assets.

4. Your doubts as to the figures for the U.S.S.R.'s industrial production in 1938 and 1950 are very serious, but alas, they too are based on a misunderstanding.

It follows from Table 7 that in 1938 the U.S.S.R. occupied fifth place in the world in terms of final industrial output. You oppose that to the well-known fact that before the war the Soviet Union reached second place in the world in terms of total industrial production. You see a contradiction here that attests to the incorrectness of the figures given in Table 7.

At first glance your objections are persuasive, but only at first glance. Why?

a) When we say "by the end of the 1930s" we have in mind 1940 (the 1930s begin with 1931 and end with 1940, although that is not the way the layman customarily thinks of it);

b) To this day we measure industrial production in terms of gross output. Yet Table 7, I repeat, gives the figures for *final output*. What distinguishes them from gross output is the amount of materials of industrial "origin" that are used in the production process. And that use as calculated per unit of final output varies widely among different countries—and not just because of the differing efficiencies of technologies employed, for example, or the relative frugality of workers). Very important here are differences in the industrial structure of production, combined with the differing degrees of materials-intensiveness of the various industries, and so forth.

In order to show how important both factors are in this case, I will cite the 1938 and 1940 figures for the U.S.S.R. and the four countries that were ahead of us in 1938 in terms of final industrial output (in billions of dollars, in 1980 prices).

	1938		1940	
	Final Output	Gross Output	Final Output	Gross Output
U.S.S.R.	50	106	63	132
United States	235	280	245	290
Germany[1]	108	123	114	130
Britain	88	100	90	103
France	53	60	48	54

[1]Within its borders at that time.

It is not hard to see that the shift to the index of gross output (and to 1940) substantially changes the ranking of the countries. In terms of gross industrial output, in 1940 the Soviet Union already occupied first place in Europe and second place in the world (in terms of final output, it held third place in Europe and fourth place in the world). Also noteworthy in this case is the fact that in Soviet industry the intra-branch turnover [intermediate consumption] of materials is substantially greater than in the other countries considered. Let me remind you that this reflects primarily the incomparability of the branch structures of industrial production of the U.S.S.R. and the other countries, and the historically explicable orientation of our industrial development during the years of the first five-year plans toward heavy (primarily defense) industry, where the materials-intensiveness of output and the number of separate manufacturing processes are much greater than in light industry. Let me add that in 1940 the proportional share of the group "A" [producer-goods] branches in Soviet industry was three times as great as in the United States and more than twice as great as in Germany.

Let us particularly dwell on the comparison, for prewar 1940, of the U.S.S.R. and Germany. Having taken the lead over Germany, albeit by only a little, in terms of gross industrial output, we really were behind it by nearly half in terms of final output. You deny the possibility of such a correlation, asking how the U.S.S.R. could have won the war under such circumstances. There is one answer to this legitimate question: the Soviet people's readiness to endure material sacrifices, deprivations, and hardships for the sake of victory, and the ability of the planned Soviet economy to concentrate production on the needs of the front were unprecedented (and in that respect, there can be no comparison with Germany). Here is what is stated, for example, in a special section of a Central Statistical Administration reference book on the U.S.S.R.'s economy in the years of the Great Patriotic War: "While smelting approximately one third as much steel and mining just over one fifth as much coal as fascist Germany (counting what was shipped in from occupied countries and annexed territories, and imports), the Soviet Union created nearly twice the amount of arms and military equipment during the war years" (*The U.S.S.R. National Economy Over 70 Years* [*Narodnoye khozyaystvo SSSR za 70 let*], Moscow, 1987, p. 44).

5. Concerning the U.S.S.R.'s place in the world in terms of the per capita consumption of goods and services. Here, to be sure, you get angry (and seriously so, attempting once again to link perestroika to the defamation of our reality, rather than to the desire to tangibly improve the Soviet people's life) not at me but at *Argumenty i fakty*. Unlike *Argumenty i fakty*, I would not write that we are somewhere between 20th and 24th place in terms of this index. The point is, in many cases several countries at once have practically the same per capita consumption of goods and services. Here is how this looks for the recent period (the results of the author's calculation in dollars, in

1980 prices and according to the purchasing power parities of currencies for that year; the U.S. figure for that year is taken as 100):

1. United States	100
2. Canada, Sweden, Switzerland, France, Federal Republic of Germany, Belgium, Luxembourg, and Japan	86-90
3. Austria, Denmark, Iceland, Norway, Finland, Australia, Netherlands	81-85
4. Britain, Italy, Spain, New Zealand	76-80
5. German Democratic Republic, Czechoslovakia	71-75
6. Hungary, Bulgaria, Ireland, Greece	66-70
7. U.S.S.R., Poland, Yugoslavia, Israel	61-65
8. Portugal, Romania	55-60

You understand, of course, that the class differentiation of incomes and, correspondingly, of the level of consumption in the capitalist countries is very great. Therefore, if one compares the average consumption of goods and services per person in U.S. *working people's families*, the socialist countries' comparative indices rise by approximately five percentage points (in particular, the U.S.S.R.'s index is 67). Let me add that the level of consumption, although important, is by no means the sole yardstick of a people's well-being, and in terms of many other indices, especially those that characterize the degree of a person's social security (guarantee of work, access to education, medical care, old-age benefits, and so forth), the Soviet Union is ahead of the United States.

Indisputably, however, we could also be much closer to the first echelon in terms of the level of consumption if it were not for the burden of the arms race that imperialism has dumped on us and—and this is our own fault—our inefficient use of the resources that remain at our disposal once the urgent needs of defense have been met. Achieving the maximum efficiency in order to implement social programs is the main task of perestroika in the area of the economy. By accomplishing that task, we will *know* for sure that we are among the first in terms of the level of consumption (and that is better than *thinking* that we are among the first).

6. You are right, of course—the average annual rates of economic growth cited in the text for peacetime pertain to the entire period of 1921 to 1987 (not counting 1938 to 1950), and not just to 1951 to 1987.

Dear Igor! Let me add in a perfectly friendly way: I gave up my Sunday leisure time in order to answer you, and I am glad of it. People like you are our hope and our strength.

I wish you health, happiness, and the full use of your efforts and abilities for the good of the people.

Respectfully,

B. Bolotin,
Senior Researcher, IMEMO

Part Four

The New Thinking in International Relations

The New Thinking and Soviet-American Relations

Lev Lvovich Lyubimov*

The stable, positive nature of Soviet-American relations depends to a critical extent both on the general intentions of both sides to reduce the overall danger of war and normalize their relations in all aspects, and on their actual recognition of each other's mutual interests and their efforts to see guarantees of their own respective interests in the search for mutually acceptable solutions. The restoration of unity in the goals and practice of Soviet foreign policy—a unity that Lenin fought for back in the immediate postrevolutionary period—represents an important characteristic of the foreign policy component of perestroika today. The well-known Americanist Lev Lvovich Lyubimov shares his views on the past, present and future of Soviet-American relations.

The U.S.S.R. and the United States are the leading powers of the two sociopolitical systems that embody the unity and conflict of antitheses in the present-day world and the nexus of contradictions in its dialectical development. Soviet-American relations have an extensive history, whose results it would be appropriate to sum up in connection with the 70th anniversary of the Great October Socialist Revolution and the forthcoming 55th anniversary of the establishment of diplomatic relations between the two countries.

The establishment of a new social order in Russia began with the [1917] Peace Decree, the granting of independence to Finland and Poland, the repudiation of imperialist and colonial ambitions and claims, and the advancement of the idea of the peaceful coexistence of states with different social structures. In this same period, U.S. imperialism was taking the first real steps towards world dominance. For the world's two leading states, a new record of their policies and roles in the fortunes of humanity in the 20th century had begun.

The history of Soviet-American relations contains truly invaluable experience, and an examination of this experience makes it possible to

*Doctor of History, head of the Department of North American Research of the Institute of World Economy and International Relations (IMEMO). This article appeared in the March 1988 issue of *MEMO*.

interpret a long-standing dilemma of Soviet foreign policy, namely: whether the philosophies behind the Treaty of Brest-Litovsk and the Peace Decree were mutually consistent or artificially contradictory.

The Peace Decree set out the fundamental foreign-policy goals of the Soviet state for many decades to come and declared our long-term intentions and the fundamental principles of our foreign policy. On the other hand, the Treaty of Brest-Litovsk was precisely an example of the practical application of those principles in a specific, extraordinarily difficult situation, as well as evidence of the unity of word and deed. In his address to the Second All-Russian Congress of Soviets, Lenin declared a willingness to discuss any practical proposals to achieve an immediate end to the war. The bitter conflict surrounding the signing of the Treaty of Brest-Litovsk showed how hard it is sometimes to achieve that unity of word and deed in practice, and how difficult this dilemma is.

It is fundamentally incorrect to consider, in the specific situation surrounding the conclusion of the Treaty of Brest-Litovsk, only the most complicated features of that time—economic devastation, the lack of a combat-ready army, and the resulting difficult compromise. Certain characteristics of long-term significance in the concept of the Treaty of Brest-Litovsk stand out especially clearly today: the repudiation of empty, abstract peace slogans that are unsupported by action; the surmounting of the paralyzing, self-destructive complacency that stems from the conviction that one is invariably right; the repudiation of any form of state "missionary work"; the determined search for a common basis for cooperation in the name of peace; and finally, the understanding that peace is an extremely important condition for building socialism. The Treaty of Brest-Litovsk allowed the Soviet Republic to survive its most critical period. Lenin's line on this issue became an unconditional expression of the new political thinking that the Bolsheviks had demonstrated since the first months following the Revolution.

Russia's economic situation in 1917 was catastrophic. The fact that the country found itself in a gloomy situation was evident from the extensive devastation, the enormous scale of the physical destruction of industrial means of production, the total breakdown of the financial system, the damage to agriculture, and the near-total disintegration of transportation, as well as the appearance of millions of unemployed, homeless, disabled, and orphans. Such was the state of affairs that befell the Soviet regime at its starting point.

As for the United States, it had assumed a leadership position in the world economy even prior to World War I. The war's results had widened the gap between the United States and the remaining imperialist countries, since those results had, in many respects, created a favorable environment for cultivating the unique competitiveness of American products. The Open Door Doctrine was put into action, and claims to world hegemony increased. However, an American-centered structure did not in fact arise in the imperialist camp after the Treaty of Versailles. While suffering enormous economic and human losses in the war, Great Britain and France nonetheless retained substantial political influence on the course of international affairs. They retained and, in some areas, even increased their colonial holdings and economic territories.

Imperialist Japan, which had made its claims in China and was actively expanding into other regions of the Pacific Basin, was gaining strength. The Wilson plan for a "new political order" was rejected by the U.S. partners, while the Open Door Doctrine never did become part of the Versailles system. Attempts to use political methods to accomplish the expansion of American capital into the colonial empires proved unsuccessful, as did attempts in global politics to turn the League of Nations into a tool of American world dominance (its decision-making procedures gave obvious advantages to the European countries).

The United States' unpreparedness to assume, in actual practice, the role of political—much less, military—leader of the capitalist world was also reflected in the fact that from a military standpoint it was weaker than its rivals at the time in both the makeup of its armed forces and its experience using them in combat. Without a network of foreign military bases and strongholds, the United States could not establish the desired global infrastructure or regional infrastructures in Europe, Asia, or Africa. The European victor countries and, to a lesser degree, Japan, continued to possess all the trappings of political influence.

President Wilson's defeat at Versailles failed to be offset by the results of the Washington Conference of 1921 to 1922. The isolationist wing of the American ruling echelon preferred not to tie its hands with commitments to joint actions with the European countries, but rather to hold on to traditional leadership in Latin America. This wing saw the formation of the League of Nations as representing a tendency toward expansion of the European powers' influence on world politics, and a threat to the Monroe Doctrine.

The response of U.S. ruling circles to the revolution in Russia was an exception to this isolationist line. This response was extremely aggressive and tolerated any form of joint action with the European states, including intervention against the young Soviet Republic. U.S. ruling circles started to exhibit particular hostility toward the new Russia when the Republican Party came to power in 1921. They also made a contribution to suppressing the revolution in a number of European countries.

Following the end of the Civil War in Russia, the U.S. government ruined every possibility of establishing diplomatic relations with that country. In 1923 U S. Secretary of State C. Hughes demanded that the U.S.S.R., as "payment" for the possibility of establishing such relations, renounce the principal elements of its foreign policy and even its general goals of building socialism. Hughes' fanatical anti-Sovietism was later inherited by F. Kellogg, who succeeded him as Secretary of State in 1925. At this time an extremely hard-line policy was established toward the U.S.S.R. Experience has shown that only the U.S.S.R.'s strengthening of its economic and defense positions or the United States' own economic or political failures could cause this policy to undergo a certain reconsideration.

Economic successes in the Soviet Union in the late 1920s and early 1930s, coupled with the crisis in the U.S. economy between 1929 and 1933, forced American business to embark on a path of developing business relations with the U.S.S.R. (while maintaining a negative position on the issue of political recognition). The period of so-called "trade without recognition" began.

The importance of the 1930s in the history of Soviet-American relations is extremely great and cannot be reduced to the mere fact that the two countries established diplomatic relations in 1933. This was the time when more accurate perceptions of each other emerged, while inaccurate and sometimes caricatural stereotypes came to be replaced with images corresponding more closely to reality. The global political context in which these relations developed had a positive influence on them. The development of centers of aggression in Europe and Japan had already made it clear who should take to the barricades to defend civilization against the new barbarism. A gradual consolidation of forces against aggression, dictated by objective necessity, provided an impetus for mutual attraction between the U.S.S.R. and the United States (despite a certain loss of trust in the U.S.S.R. stemming from the flagrant errors and violations of socialist legality that occurred during the period of collectivization and in subsequent years). To some degree the development of Soviet-American relations in the 1930s laid the groundwork for the subsequent alliance in the fight against fascism.

The invasion of the Soviet Union by Hitlerite Germany led to the beginning of Soviet-American cooperation in World War II. After the Japanese attack on Pearl Harbor, the United States also became an actual participant in the anti-Hitlerite coalition. During the war, cooperation among the U.S.S.R., United States, and Great Britain withstood the test, in spite of our coalition partners' repeated efforts to deviate from the common line and their insistence on advancing unilateral American or British interests. The relations and joint actions of the U.S.S.R. and United States represented a stabilizing and consolidating element in the alliance. This was true both in coordinating military operations and in addressing the questions of the postwar world order. Unquestionably, to a considerable extent the policy of cooperation with the U.S.S.R. was supported both by F.D. Roosevelt personally and by a number of figures in his administration. At the same time, the United States still had forces that took rigid class positions and aspired to disrupt the favorable trend in relations between the U.S.S.R. and the United States. They were embodied in Vice President Harry Truman. Unfortunately, after Roosevelt's death zealous opponents of Soviet-American cooperation assumed power in the United States under Truman's leadership.

Following the end of World War II, in which the U.S.S.R. and the United States were allies, the Cold War, marking an extended period of Soviet-American confrontation, began almost immediately. Once the defeat of fascist Germany and militaristic Japan had been completed, the narrowness of the mutual basis for political cooperation became apparent. The Soviet Union's development into a real power and serious rival in the international arena resulted in a decisive parting of the ways, something that had been delayed solely by the inertia of the countries' having had a common strategic goal in World War II. Other objective causes of the sharp deterioration in Soviet-American relations include the time it took to recognize the consequences and realities of the nuclear age and the mutual inertia of established military and political concepts and doctrines (the thesis of the inevitability of a military confrontation between capitalism and socialism; the idea that it was possible to wage a nuclear war and obtain unilateral military advantages; the notion that a new world war, by analogy to the results of World Wars I and II, would inevitably have revolutionary consequences). Undoubtedly, subjective circumstances, such as the views of specific leaders, a distorted interpretation of the other side's actions, also played a negative role.

From the vantage point of the present, it seems that, for our part, an interweaving of objective and subjective factors manifested itself in a widening of the gap between the Peace Decree and the philosophy of the Treaty of Brest-Litovsk. In contrast to the United States, the Soviet Union was prepared, of course, to continue cooperation in the postwar period. But the concept of such cooperation that we put forward had been rejected previously, in the 1930s, and it did not move Washington to abandon its policy of hard-line confrontation.

In the prewar period the United States' interest in cooperating with us had been motivated, in the first place, by the benefits that trade with the U.S.S.R. provided to the U.S. economy, and in the second place, by the desire to maintain a certain balance of power in

Europe and Asia. Since that time fundamental changes had taken place in the world that demanded a serious theoretical interpretation and adequate reflection in practical policies. A clear-cut watershed on the European continent had been created between the states belonging to the two opposing systems. We regarded Soviet-American commercial and economic relations as a factor obliging us to work on further strengthening our power. The changes that had taken place in the international situation were viewed through the prism of the victory that had been won over fascism, a victory which had stimulated, in particular, the collapse of the colonial empires and the establishment of a military balance in our favor. These changes were perceived in an oversimplified fashion as proof that a radical transformation of the correlation of forces had occurred that supposedly presented us with hitherto unprecedented opportunities. Our increased self-confidence asserted itself in the idea that the philosophy of the Treaty of Brest-Litovsk had been temporary, had stemmed exclusively from our weaknesses at that time, and was now over and done with.

Indeed, the time of compromises stemming from our weakness had passed irrevocably into oblivion; the Soviet-German nonaggression pact of 1939 had been the last tribute to that policy. However, the great-power status that the Soviet Union had acquired, on which any solution of the problem of war and peace to a great extent depended, made the question of prioritizing our principles and objectives in international affairs perhaps even more urgent than in the prewar period. The Cold War was probably unavoidable. At the same time, it could have taken on somewhat more moderate forms if the sides had not been guided exclusively by the tug-of-war concept that constantly led to an impasse.

The struggle of the Cold War era became the engine of races in both nuclear and conventional arms, which resulted in squandering of vast resources on both sides. In the United States the strategy and policies of confrontation were institutionalized in the establishment and rapid growth of the military-industrial complex, which became an extremely important component of the domestic political and economic structure. Mutual stereotypes also took root in public and political thinking and became a barrier that was to stand for many years in the way of any constructive efforts in the sphere of Soviet-American relations. The adherence to these stereotypes resulted in numerous crises, starting with the Korean events and ending with the West Berlin and Caribbean crises in 1961 and 1962.

In the late 1950s and the 1960s Soviet-American relations slowly began to emerge from a state of political anabiosis. The basic impetus to this process was provided by the U.S.S.R.'s new political approaches developed at the 20th CPSU Congress. Many entrenched stereotypes underwent radical reexamination, and certain premises that had interfered in the U.S.S.R.'s development of a constructive policy in the international arena were discarded.

The rethinking of the premise concerning the inevitability of wars between socialism and capitalism gave dynamism to Soviet policy. The realities of the nuclear age came to be increasingly well recognized in both Moscow and Washington. The Eisenhower-Dulles hard line toward the U.S.S.R. and the other socialist countries not only failed to produce results but caused growing criticism of the United States in Western Europe. The Suez crisis and the revolution in Cuba, the defeat of the counterrevolution in Hungary, events in Lebanon, the launchings of the first Soviet space satellites, the crisis in relations between the United States and Latin America following U.S. intervention in Guatemala—all this led, in the final analysis, to certain changes in U.S. policies on a number of international problems.

The resumption in 1959 of the Geneva conferences of the foreign ministers of the U.S.S.R., the United States, Great Britain, and France on the German question, and the conclusion of the Antarctic Treaty that same year marked a certain stabilization in Soviet-American relations, which was subsequently developed in the diplomacy of the Kennedy administration. Starting with a worsening of relations and experiencing the lessons of the Bay of Pigs and Caribbean crisis, the U.S. leadership at that time was forced to recognize the impossibility of nuclear war, the fact that the U.S.S.R. and the United States had a number of coincident interests, and the necessity of ending the Cold War. One result of those changes was the 1963 Moscow Treaty banning nuclear tests in three environments.

The Soviet Union's attainment of parity with the United States in strategic arms (which created a qualitatively new basis for Soviet-American relations), and the military defeat of U.S. imperialism in Vietnam, along with the weakening of the United States' world economic positions, forced the American leadership to begin to reexamine its policies both toward the Soviet Union and on other problems. It should be noted that the new situation for the United States was, for the most part, correctly assessed by the U.S. leadership, which stopped the aggression in Vietnam, acknowledging defeat, and agreed with the need to limit the arms race and take a number of other positive steps in foreign policy.

The détente period began; it ended the first cycle of postwar Soviet-American relations, a cycle that had passed through the Cold War stage and a transitional stage toward a more stable and positive model. The negotiation method came to replace the policy of military pressure, which proved to have been substantially undermined. The

United States, albeit not without vacillation, recognized its own role as a party to such negotiations, rather than their presiding officer.

The détente years were marked by major accomplishments in Soviet-American strategic-arms-limitation negotiations and in preparations for solving a considerable number of global problems, and by a sharp increase in the role of multilateral diplomacy. Relations between the United States and the U.S.S.R. embarked on a course of ensuring greater security for each one and its partners, saving or using the national resources spent for military purposes more efficiently, and developing bilateral contacts on a broad range of issues. But the main result of détente was a certain movement away from confrontation and toward peaceful coexistence. The United States' readiness to undertake fundamental steps aimed at reducing tension and creating stable relations with the U.S.S.R. was an important feature of that period. In showing such readiness, the United States was by no means contemplating the development of those relations on the basis of equality and partnership. Its concept of "participation in détente" included such components as restricting the quantitative growth of the U.S.S.R.'s strategic arms (with a view to subsequently shifting its own efforts to a race in the qualitative aspects of arms), weakening or at least stabilizing the U.S.S.R.'s influence in the developing world, and ideologically "softening up" the countries of the socialist commonwealth.

Of course, the Soviet Union had no intention of following the rules of the game proposed by Washington. After achieving strategic parity with the United States, it showed a persistent desire to maintain it. The Soviet Union, of course, was no passive observer of events taking place in the developing countries, although events in Angola had already proven to be a severe trial for the U.S. maintenance of a positive attitude toward détente. Finally, the Soviet thesis concerning the exacerbation of the ideological struggle was taken by Washington as evidence that its intention in that area had no serious chance of being realized. On the other hand, the U.S.S.R. regarded the United States' inability to realize its plans as a natural result of changes in the correlation of forces in favor of the forces of peace and progress, and it saw this both as proof that the policy of détente was correct and as a pledge that it was irreversible.

At the same time, the fact that experience continued to confirm the inability to attain all the goals that the United States had set for itself when it became involved in the détente process reduced to nil that country's interest in continuing the process. Our policy failed to duly take this circumstance into account. And once again the failure to observe the correct relationship between the philosophy of the Peace

Decree and the philosophy of the Treaty of Brest-Litovsk "did its work"—this time it contributed to the fading of détente. I would like to emphasize that in the 1970s the question of the relationship between the actual content of détente and the limits within which the Soviet Union was prepared to make its compromise-based contribution to that content became especially pressing. Today that question has become even more important. After all, it is now that we are beginning to give adequate answers to it. For example, in the concrete conditions of the 1970s, notions of the relationship between détente and the ideological struggle that were based on the thesis concerning the exacerbation of that struggle and the "intensification of ideological confrontation between the two systems" resulted in our being unprepared to take a new approach to the so-called humanitarian problems. Moreover, in interpreting the thesis concerning the exacerbation of the ideological struggle, a certain bias had developed toward depicting that process as one that took place on the level of propaganda and "psychological warfare." Yet in the atmosphere of détente it more clearly and openly reflected the historical dispute over which system was more effective in economic, social, and political terms.

Or consider the following example. An academic approach was taken toward the Third World as a zone that was supposedly characterized throughout by the "growth of socialism," and as our natural ally in all cases in the struggle against imperialism without taking differentiation into account. This approach caused us to be drawn into regional conflicts. After Angola came events on the Horn of Africa and then—Afghanistan. This sharply intensified Soviet-American rivalry and polarized the two powers' positions on an issue to which they should have sought and, evidently, found mutually acceptable solutions.

Finally, a whole series of our established legal doctrines pertaining to the international sphere failed to accord with the emerging tendency in the mid-1970s to deal with certain issues on the basis of international law. Thus, the objective requirement that the functions of binding regulation of some types of states' activities be turned over to certain international organizations came into conflict with our doctrine, developed back in the prewar years, that denied any such right to international organizations on the grounds that it was a violation of state sovereignty, in all cases without exception. This put us in a situation where, while putting forward urgent and objectively necessary disarmament proposals, we simultaneously denied the right of effective mutual verification of disarmament measures. The concepts of verifying implementation, liability for violations (e.g., damages), and the mutual presentation of reliable information fared particularly badly. Yet the problems of international law that arose in huge numbers in the 1970s were an important part of the overall political context in which the détente process developed. Providing for the stable support and expansion of that context meant ensuring one of the basic conditions for détente, peaceful coexistence, and cooperation among states. And we cannot rule out the possibility that in the 1970s, and later, the United States took direct advantage in its policies of its knowledge of our stereotypes and its confidence that we would rely on them in any given instance. The United States' present maneuvers on verification issues, now that we have proposed radical steps in that area, show this theory's validity.

The period of détente proved short-lived. In the mid-1970s Soviet-American relations began to worsen, and by the first half of the 1980s there was already talk of a second Cold War. A new cycle set in that was characterized by higher costs of confrontation, with unprecedented amounts of money being spent on the military, political, and diplomatic "servicing" of confrontation. For the first time, a constant— not just crisis-related—threat of global nuclear disaster arose. A whole set of regional crises arose in which the symmetrical interests of the two great powers became involved.

The transition to this cycle resulted from a number of factors. The strengthening of conservative forces in the United States that began in the second half of the 1970s and brought the Reagan administration to power in the 1980 elections did not just accompany but supported this process. The uniting of the positions of the new rightists, traditional right-wing Republicans, and right-wing Democrats, and their attainment of power at the beginning of the 1980s in both Congress and the White House brought about major changes in U.S. foreign policy as a whole and its policy toward the U.S.S.R. in particular. If the factors contributing to the "departure" of détente from international relations were created by all sides, albeit to differing degrees, the return to confrontation was carried out exclusively by the United States, which bears political and historical responsibility for doing so.

At the end of the 1970s U.S. ruling circles for the first time recognized their advantage when the dynamics of the economic growth of their country and the Soviet Union were compared. Stagnation-related phenomena in the Soviet economy and social development, which led in the mid 1980s to the emergence of economic contradictions that were pre-crisis in form, interrupted an almost 50-year trend under which the Soviet national economy had shown faster growth rates than that of the United States.

In the United States these events were taken as a signal to add the burden of a new spiral of arms expenditures that, in its view, would be "critical" to undermining the Soviet economy. In the late 1970s and early 1980s, U.S. policy toward the U.S.S.R. consisted of efforts to restrain Soviet exports, prevent the import of medium- and high-technology products into the U.S.S.R., and undermine any form of economic cooperation between the U.S.S.R. and developed capitalist countries or developing countries. To all intents and purposes, the United States was trying to bring about the U.S.S.R.'s economic isolation. By sharply exacerbating regional conflicts and throwing hundreds of millions, even billions, of dollars into them, the United States attempted to force the Soviet Union, too, to shoulder the burdens of additional expenditures in those regions.

The Reagan administration's intention to change the existing correlation of forces in its favor was also demonstrated by such actions as its rejection of disarmament negotiations and of ratification of agreements that had already been achieved, as well as its attempt to revise those agreements; its revival of doctrines aimed at the attainment of military superiority; its adoption of the concepts of "acceptable losses," "limited" nuclear war, and the possibility of victory in a nuclear clash; its sharp increase in the military budget; its unbridled "psychological warfare" against the U.S.S.R. and the other socialist countries; and its outright interventionist actions in Grenada, Libya, and Lebanon.

The United States' policy toward the U.S.S.R. became an element of its policy of global revenge and a part of its efforts to restore its world standing, including its standing with the developing countries, Western Europe, and Japan. Whereas American diplomacy had showed a readiness in the mid-1970s to accept certain compromises in the North-South dialogue, as apprehensions regarding a raw materials shortage disappeared, that readiness diminished and ultimately gave way to the policy of a hard-line reexamination of American stands on all the problems involved in that dialogue.

At the same time, with growth rates of the American economy proving somewhat higher than those of the West European economies and nearly on a par with those of the Japanese economy, the illusion arose in the United States that it could stabilize and possibly recover its lost positions in the world economy. This was indeed an illusion, since American reckoning was based on the obsolete philosophy of a world community that was divided and steadily being further divided, and in which the struggle to advance selfish, separate interests was the rule.

Another reason this was an illusion is that, in reality, a drop in growth rates in a competitor country or group of countries no longer inevitably results in changing the relative positions of centers of power in the world capitalist economy. The real correlation of forces among the centers is neither exclusively nor even principally determined by these growth rates. In the age of the scientific and technological revolution, the constant improvement of the quality and efficiency of products used is taking the place of the quantitative increase in personal and production consumption. Therefore, in order to evaluate the United States' real place in the world economy, it is far more important to look at such factors as the rapid drop in its share of world trade in high-technology products; its negative foreign-trade balance in such products, which manifested itself for the first time in 1986; its growing imports of means of production; and the growing share of foreign products purchased with capital investments in U.S. industry, transportation, and communications. The unprecedented combination of a rise in imports and a drop in the exchange rate of the dollar sharply exacerbated the problem of the competitiveness of American goods on both the internal and external markets. The transformation of the United States into a debtor nation was also a new phenomenon.

The deterioration of the developing countries' economic situation also negatively affected the United States' world standing. Backwardness inevitably leads to social and political instability, creating dangerous hotbeds of conflict that take on an international dimension and draw states located beyond the region of conflict into their orbit. Backwardness—instability—conflicts—militarization—international tension—the slowing of development: such is the logical pattern of processes rooted in the poverty of peoples. The accumulation of tremendous debts reduces guarantees that they will be repaid, undermines the stability of the world currency and credit system, and may lead to unpredictable political decisions and economic consequences. The current deterioration in the developing countries' economic situation is automatically resulting in a reduction of their imports from the developed states, including the United States. In 1985 and 1986, U.S. exports to the African countries dropped by 5.8 percent and 22 percent, respectively; in the same two years, its exports to West Asia dropped by 12.8 percent and 13.3 percent; and in 1985 its exports to Southeast Asia dropped by 16.1 percent.

Finally, the U.S. policy established in the 1980s of exacerbating the U.S.S.R.'s economic problems and achieving its own military superiority also stemmed from the philosophy of the past. In practical terms, it caused a rise in international tension and in the real danger of nuclear war and the destruction of civilization. Today when you lay a trap for the other party you risk laying one for everyone, including yourself.

Thus, essentially two appraisals were formed of the changes and trends in world development that gave rise in the United States to the illusion of stabilizing the American power center. One of these appraisals, based on the traditional approach that entails protecting only one's own interests and strategic class goals, derives from the principle that the weakening of some is equivalent to the strengthening of others. According to the other appraisal, since we live in an interconnected and integral world, the weakening of some may mean the weakening of all, a threat to a region becomes a threat to the world as a whole, and an attempt to destroy one country may turn into the end of civilization. The first appraisal is an attribute of the neoconservative approach, while the second expresses the essence of the new thinking in international relations.

What does an interconnected and integral world mean to the United States? It means, first of all, a profound interdependence between the U.S. economy and the economies of other countries. We are talking about 1986 imports of $387 billion worth of products, including more than $26 billion worth of food; nearly $50 billion worth of mineral raw materials, including fuel; more than $50 billion worth of other materials; and $166 billion worth of machinery products. On the other hand, a substantial part of these imports are produced within the structure of U.S. transnational corporations or joint companies involving American capital, which simultaneously points up the exporting countries' dependency on the U.S. market. We are also talking about American business's use of manpower and raw materials in a large number of other countries. For the latter, in turn, that business is an extremely important source of industrial development, technology acquisition, and the training of indigenous personnel. We are talking about a process that has gone a long way and in which interdependence has become an obvious imperative. At the same time, the problems of establishing fair and just economic relations continue to be important, and the solution of such problems is becoming a matter of urgency.

Whereas the basis of economic relations between countries used to be trade, which led to the development of *interrelationships*, today that basis has come to be joint production, in which an absolutely different, qualitatively higher level of relations—relations of *interdependence*—is being attained in various forms, such as transnational corporations, joint ventures, shipping-line conferences in commercial shipping, intergovernmental agreements and programs. The standardization of products within the framework of such production is making it possible to create, in place of what were once autonomous markets, homogeneous markets spanning not only various countries but various continents. The leader among states that have created this sort of global production structure is the United States—its "second" economy is estimated at nearly $1 trillion. Those that have become involved in this structure (from states to physical and juridical persons), while trying to advance their own national, company, industry, and other interests, are simultaneously united by the interests of the structure itself. The establishment of appropriate international regulatory institutions and the growing complication of their functions reflect the new situation whose essence is that economic relations in today's world economy have increasingly become relations of interdependence. Of course, this phenomenon exists and develops in social forms that derive from the social nature of the subjects interacting in it, and from the correlation of forces between them. What is new, however, is that today it is impossible to view that correlation of forces outside the context of interdependence.

Analysis of this correlation of forces is also impossible apart from the idea of the integral nature of the present-day world. A weapon of mass destruction and the numerous fatal consequences of its use will not select their victims according to the criteria of membership in a particular socioeconomic system, level of economic development, or geographical situation. The effect of that weapon is global, and the differences in the degree and depth of its impact on regions that have been directly struck and those that have avoided the blow are only of short-term significance. In the final analysis, both will inevitably perish. This leads to a conclusion that is extremely important to Soviet-American relations: today they cannot be determined solely by national or class interests. The integral nature of world civilization and the objectives of preserving it and ensuring the security of all states in the world should take priority when it comes to the military aspect of those relations.

From 1941 to 1945 our countries cooperated in the name of ridding humanity of fascist aggression. In doing so, they were working to ensure humanity the right to peace, security, and life. Since that time, ideas about the spectrum of rights that should be guaranteed to both the present-day individual and the present-day state have expanded considerably. The cooperation of the U.S.S.R. and the United States in creating such guarantees would be an extremely important contribution to ensuring the integral nature of today's world, since the integral nature of the world community and the stability of law-based (rather than power-based) relations among its numerous components are reinforced through the universality of legal norms.

Of all aspects of the early 1980s' policy of global revenge, the most dangerous for humanity was proclamation of a crusade against the U.S.S.R. and socialism. Here the U.S. administration's policy increasingly took on the features of an apocalyptic movement based on the illusion of its own side's ability to survive a nuclear war. But in the 1984 elections it became obvious that that movement was evoking a growing sense of fear both among Americans themselves and among West Europeans. The prospects of global catastrophe had moved from the future to the present. The buildup of nuclear arsenals had reached not only a dangerous but a senseless point.

Tension in Soviet-American relations reached its highest point at the end of 1983, when the deployment of American medium-range missiles began in Europe. A crisis arose not just in bilateral relations but concerning the fate of human civilization. It was vitally necessary to seek a way out of that crisis and a real response to the cry "civilization in danger!" The campaign for revolutionary transformations in the U.S.S.R. that began with the CPSU Central Committee's April 1985 Plenum created the possibility of making that search.

The beginning of a new phase in Soviet-American relations was due primarily to the foreign-policy component of perestroika, which once again combined the philosophy of the two cornerstones of Leninist diplomacy, the Peace Decree, and the Treaty of Brest-Litovsk. The U.S.S.R.'s foreign policy in the past few years forced the West to recognize that the initiative had shifted to Moscow. People in the United States came to realize more and more clearly that the new Soviet approach and the Soviet leadership's specific steps reflected the U.S.S.R.'s intention to abandon the "reactive" model of behavior in the international arena that was being imposed on it, a model according to which reaction to one's adversary's actions dominates foreign-policy practice, raising the level of confrontation. The fact that the creative element was coming to prevail in Soviet strategy, when seen against the backdrop of the Reagan administration's rigid subordination of its policy to the obsolete concepts with which it had come to power, was causing increasing concern in the U.S. establishment.

The first major result of the new foreign-policy thinking was the effective policy of taking steps to remove the "obstructions" that had arisen in previous years both in Soviet-American relations and in key issues related to averting the world nuclear threat. The December 1987 summit provided the first real results on the path toward creating a comprehensive system of international security—the Treaty on the Elimination of Medium- and Shorter-Range Missiles. An agreement that just a short time before had been regarded in the United States, Western Europe, and many other countries as unattainable became a reality thanks to the new thinking, which embodied the fundamental philosophy of the Peace Decree and the "philosophy of action" that had been expressed in the Treaty of Brest-Litovsk. Now real preconditions were created for making progress in strategic arms reduction as well.

Today Soviet-American relations are entering a new phase. The U.S.S.R. and the United States are only at the very beginning of the latest stage in their relations, a point at which a great deal has not yet been clarified. The stage that is beginning will evidently be a transitional one. Its main content should consist of developing stable models of interaction between the two powers. A tremendous, probably even decisive, influence on the process of forming those models will be exerted by perestroika, which is already evoking a mixed reaction in the United States. This reaction contains on the one hand, elements of concern that the U.S.S.R. may become a more serious rival and competitor and on the other, disbelief that it will succeed in carrying out its plans. Both variant appraisals are already being seriously taken into account in creating a future model for the American stance toward the U.S.S.R. They have been receiving growing attention in the course of the 1988 election campaign. The successes of Soviet perestroika will have a tremendous influence on public attitudes in the United States and, consequently, on development of a concept for doing business with the U.S.S.R., a concept which might differ significantly from those to which the United States has previously adhered.

In addition to perestroika, a considerable influence on that process would be exerted by the Soviet Union's maintaining the foreign-policy initiative and taking steps that might bring about a radical change in Western ideas about alleged Soviet aggressiveness—ideas which form the political and philosophical foundation of NATO—and draw the United States and Western Europe more deeply into the détente process. In addition, the interrelated goals, means, and structure of Soviet-American cooperation require careful study. In particular, it would be of fundamental importance to define mutual interests in two spheres where the aspirations of the whole human race and prospects for the future especially require the support and responsible action of the two great powers. We are referring, in the first place, to universal human problems, and in the second place, to the problems of providing support in international law for global cooperation, of which humanitarian problems should be a part. One of the most important accomplishments of current Soviet foreign policy has been to single out, from the whole complex of Soviet-American relations, the issues that together form the common human agenda. Finally, a genuinely broad and long-term basis should also be found for economic cooperation between the two powers.

The foreign-policy principles and interrelationships that Lenin put forward in the first days following the October Revolution are being creatively enriched today in the socialist state's policies in the international arena. It is the Soviet Union that has discovered the possibility of proposing not just an impressive program for freeing humanity from the threat of self-destruction, but also specific ways out of existing impasses, including impasses created by the United States. The ability to think for all humanity and undertake unilateral steps for the sake of universal human goals is a property of socialism as a humanitarian system. This policy is one confirmation of the historic mission that socialism brings to the world.

Soviet-American Relations at a New Stage

By Georgiy Melorovich Sturua*

The normalization of Soviet-American relations ranks first among those events that have signified an easing of tension in the world. Never before in the history of these relations has there been such an intensive dialogue at the highest level. The fourth summit to take place in two-and-a-half years between General Secretary of the CPSU Central Committee M.S. Gorbachev and U.S. President R. Reagan ended in early June. In essence, this meeting completes the cycle begun in November 1985 in Geneva.

The Geneva debut brought encouraging results for both sides. After a prolonged period during which they returned to Cold War rhetoric and practices, the U.S.S.R. and the United States showed their ability to establish a dialogue based on realism. And despite the enormous importance of the subjective factor, there were objective reasons for this turn of events.

No matter how badly Soviet-American relations were going, both Moscow and Washington knew perfectly well, albeit in different ways, that the political imperative was the continuation of talks to curb the arms race. Their temporary suspension in 1984 made it clear that no alternative to talks is acceptable to public opinion on either side. Regardless of whether the talks were fruitful, their very continuation was a kind of guarantee against an uncontrollable deterioration of the strategic situation.

To make a comprehensive assessment of the first half of the 1980s, one should probably add this key observation: the current White House leadership is one of a small number of American administrations that have not threatened the use of nuclear weapons during a crisis.

And finally, Reagan's two terms as President will go down in history as a period in which the United States and the U.S.S.R. were not drawn into a direct confrontation in some new regional conflict.

---

*Candidate of history and head of a Section at the U.S.S.R. Academy of Sciences' Institute of World Economy and International Relations. This article appeared in the September 1988 issue of *MEMO*.

The first half of the 1980s made clear the limits to which the U.S.S.R. and the United States could afford to let relations deteriorate. Despite rhetorical excesses, these limits seem narrower than those that prevailed in the 1950s and 1960s. If one were to describe the recent period as the "Second Cold War," it would be marked, in comparison with the original model, by great rationalism, which, of course, does not make it any more acceptable.

The path toward increased cooperation was difficult for both sides. Much has been said and written about the evolution of the republican administration's foreign-policy views. The distance it has come is impressive. From the idea that talks with the U.S.S.R. are unacceptable in that they legitimize the continued existence of this "social aberration"—to the President's speech from the rostrum at Moscow State University, against a background of red flags, where he told Soviet students: "Your generation lives in one of the most exciting, hopeful periods of Soviet history." From its persistence in pushing through a plan to deploy medium-range missiles in Europe—to the ratification of the Treaty on the Elimination of Medium- and Shorter-Range Missiles. We will not rule out that the President wanted to conclude his term in the White House positively, especially in light of the smoldering Iran-Contra scandal. The popular theory that the president would like to leave his post with the image of a peacemaker oversimplifies the motives for his behavior in at least one respect: He is more likely to claim credit for the conclusion of an agreement in keeping with his plan (the "zero option") that, by breaking with "unacceptable tradition," really does ensure the United States' security through an asymmetrical reduction of its chief opponent's military might.

More important, however, is the acceptability—after such a difficult era in Soviet-American relations—of the very thought of capping one's presidency with a rapprochement with the "Soviets" and a visit to Red Square. It could emerge only from a particular alignment of political forces and "state of mind" in the United States. The wave of neoconservatism, with its pathological anti-Sovietism, is subsiding. The economic ills caused by the sharp jump in military expenditures are making themselves felt more clearly. Public sentiment in the United States is reaching a point where it rejects the bogus dilemma of "better dead than red." The results of opinion polls among ordinary Americans and the U.S. ruling elite have created favorable conditions for a positive change in the administration's policy in its relations with the U.S.S.R. President Reagan is called "the great communicator" precisely because he has sometimes been able to express the prevailing mood very accurately, and he has not only shaped it but followed it.

An interesting assessment of the transformation of U.S. political life and of the President himself was published in the American newspaper *Christian Science Monitor:* "The neoconservatives called Reagan their leader. . . . From the very beginning, the neoconservatives did everything in their power to keep agreements from being concluded with the Soviets. The fact that the Senate ratified the Treaty on Medium- and Shorter-Range Missiles by 93 votes to 5 was a cruel blow for them. The fact that this week their own hero, smiling, went to the walls of the Kremlin, and even took his wife with him, was the final shock for them. He is treating the leader of the Communist Party of the U.S.S.R. like a friend. He is doing this on the grounds that Gorbachev's regime has brought changes. The U.S.S.R. is changing, rather than being changed. And all this is causing the fundamental beliefs of the neoconservative movement to crumble. It has lost Ronald Reagan."[1]

The transformation of the administration's policy toward the U.S.S.R. has confirmed the predictions of Soviet Americanologists who, as far back as 1980, maintained that Reagan's conservatism would objectively put him in a better position to conclude an agreement with Moscow. But in their analysis, these experts could not yet take into account another key condition for the normalization of Soviet-American relations. As stated in the strategic survey for 1987-1988 prepared by the International Institute of Strategic Studies in London and published on the eve of the Moscow summit, the course of events in the Soviet Union was a key factor that elevated the world situation to a qualitatively new level.

Restructuring, which has brought so many changes and promises still more within the country, was the driving force behind the normalization of Soviet-American relations. Its epoch-making, historic importance to the world's future is recognized everywhere in both East and West, although it by no means always meets with satisfaction. With its powerful appeal to humanist, and therefore universal, principles, the policy of restructuring provides an escape from the quagmire of confrontation into which the international community was driving itself ever deeper.

The following proposition from M.S. Gorbachev's report to the 19th Party Conference is of fundamental importance in understanding the basic mechanisms of the international effects of restructuring: "in drawing lessons from the past, we have to admit that administrative-command methods also left their mark in the sphere of foreign policy. As it was, even the most vital decisions were made by a small circle of individuals, without collective, comprehensive review and analysis,

---

[1]*Christian Science Monitor*, June 1, 1988. [This quote could not be verified—*Eds.*]

and sometimes without even bothering to seek the necessary counsel of friends. This resulted in inappropriate reactions to international events and to the policies of other countries, and sometimes even in bad decisions. Unfortunately, the cost to the people or the possible outcome of this or that course of action were not always carefully weighed."

Efforts to overcome the administrative-command features of our political system are destroying the negative (and unfortunately, not always false) ideas about Soviet society. As noted at the 19th Party Conference, the outside world is "discovering" the Soviet Union anew. The image cultivated in the West of the Soviet Union as a closed, totalitarian society is in its death throes. Of course, we should not delude ourselves—it is still too early to speak of a total break with the stereotypes that were fostered by the establishment of the administrative-command system in our country, the crimes of the Stalin period, and the stagnation of the Brezhnev era. This system has begun to give ground, but as long as it continues to exist, so will favorable conditions for the Western propaganda machine, which can continue to create its "image of the enemy."

Another way in which restructuring has had a positive effect on the international situation is through the transformation of Soviet foreign policy. By distorting the socialist nature of our state, the administrative-command system could not help but influence its policy in the international arena as well. It was not sufficiently open to reasonable compromise, lacked flexibility and the ability to react quickly, and was to some extent informed by scholastic views of social progress and international relations. In order to justify its own failures and mistakes, it was predisposed to exaggerate the importance of external causes. In foreign-policy initiatives, the interests of Soviet society as a whole—which are defined as the consistent implementation of a policy of peace and disarmament—were gradually, and sometimes imperceptibly, replaced with the interests of ensuring the survival of the system itself. It must be noted that the incorrect understanding of the magnitude of the external danger and its basic elements also resulted from decision-making bodies' lack of carefully analyzed information. All this created a situation in which the priority of such strategic objectives as the decisive easing of international tension was objectively downgraded, regardless of the subjective intentions of particular individuals and organizations. It seems logical to conclude that the existence of the administrative-command system was an obstacle to the strengthening of world peace and strategic stability.

An awareness of the shortcomings of our previous foreign policy, together with apparent attempts to overcome rigid administrative-bureaucratic structures, lends dynamism to the U.S.S.R.'s actions in the international sphere and gives it a broader field in which to maneuver. Greater flexibility does not signify a deviation from socialist ideals, but, on the contrary, makes it possible to be more effective in defending the interests of the Soviet Union as both a socialist state and a great power.

The conclusion of the Treaty on Medium- and Shorter-Range Missiles was very important in this sense. It is based on the idea of the "zero option" that we repeatedly rejected in the past. Meanwhile, the Reagan administration's energetic attempts to make it look as if the United States, thanks to its concessions and its buildup of military might, was able to gain the upper hand on this question are not getting the anticipated response. The world public does not view the Treaty on Medium- and Shorter-Range Missiles as a unilateral strategic victory for the White House—even leaving aside the question of whether certain influential forces in the U.S. government really wanted to see an agreement signed on nuclear weapons in Europe. Moreover, the treaty is rightly regarded as a real achievement of Soviet restructuring. Outside the context of restructuring, the treaty—if it were even possible, which is rather doubtful—would appear to be a compromise that was forced on us, rather than an essential element of the long-term policy of disarmament being developed by Moscow in the latter half of the 1980s.

It should be emphasized that at the present time, with respect to modernization of the U.S.S.R.'s foreign policy, the empirical aspect still noticeably predominates over a scientific grasp of the methods and means used to resolve our country's problems and of the deeply rooted causes of our difficulties and failures. At the current stage it is quite natural for the "practitioners" to outstrip the "theoreticians," so to speak. Often simply common sense, as well as life itself, have required immediate action and shown the direction it had to take.

Among other things, an examination of the period of détente in the 1970s provides some rich food for thought. An analysis of this particular period served as the basis for many of the methodological propositions in the foreign-policy section of M.S. Gorbachev's report to the 19th Party Conference. When we compare this period with the course of events since the Geneva summit, we discover a number of striking differences. They give us grounds for asserting that what we are experiencing today is not the brief concurrence of two factors—the peace-loving policy of one side and the sober awakening of political leaders on the other (that is the superficial and flimsy explanation given for the current détente in some of our publications)—but the creation of a qualitatively new, more stable situation: the development of constructive and realistic Soviet-American cooperation.

The elevation of relations between the two countries to a higher plane and imparting to them a more civilized tone has been possible mainly because the Soviet Union has begun to revise approaches and dogmas that prevailed in the 1970s and made détente so short-lived.

First, this touches on the general philosophical question of the relationship between class struggle (in the form of the struggle between two systems—socialism and capitalism) and peaceful coexistence. The proposed solution seemed quite simple and logical: rather than clashing, we should nurture these phenomena in their corresponding spheres. One belongs to the sphere of relations between systems that are of an antagonistic nature, the other—to the sphere of relations between states that should be based on an understanding of the inevitability of coexistence, unless we and our political and ideological opponents wish to perish in a thermonuclear conflagration.

Paradoxical as it may seem, opponents of peaceful coexistence accurately noted the weakness of the above postulate and its metaphysical nature, if you will. The dialectical relationship between the struggle of opposing systems, on the one hand, and intergovernmental relations, on the other—that is the reality that cannot be erased by any clever theoretical maneuvers. Conservative ideologists in the United States hastened to open politicians' eyes: Look, the Russians themselves maintain that peaceful coexistence and détente should serve to promote the spread of socialism around the planet. Détente, they said, is no more than a sly trick of the Soviets, and there can be no mutually advantageous détente, because our interests are irreconcilable. Antagonism of interests was also the point of departure for those who saw in the possibility of détente the danger of class peace, the neglect of the working people's interests, and so forth.

The improvement of relations between the U.S.S.R. and the United States in the 1970s did not have far-reaching effects. Neither side ruled out the advisability of agreements to regulate the basic boundaries—and no more than that—of the arms race, but the foundation of new-style relations needed to begin the process of real disarmament was missing. Pathological distrust of the U.S.S.R. and fears that we were preparing to "temporarily exploit" the United States and avail ourselves of its technological resources to strengthen our own military machine created an insurmountable barrier to the expansion of trade and economic cooperation. The administrative-command system, which has an unhealthy reaction to anything that undermines the ideological guarantees of its existence, opposed genuine rapprochement between the two peoples, without which genuine peaceful coexistence is inconceivable. Affirmation of the principles of cooperation was hampered by the fact that U.S. ruling circles viewed the problem of rapprochement through the prism of "psychological warfare."

The problem with the détente of the 1970s was that it was approached as a zero-sum game: your victory is our defeat, and vice versa. This approach reflects not good or ill will on one side or the other, but the objective nature of Soviet-American relations and of the two systems' relations over the course of almost their entire history.

Today, by freeing themselves from the fetters of dogmatism, Soviet social scientists are reaching the conclusion that in today's world there are no classic models of socialism and imperialism as they were depicted in the 19th century and the first quarter of the 20th century. Their "environment" is fundamentally different than it was in that era. Today we understand better than ever that the joint "residence" of the two systems on one planet will continue for quite some time, so long as it is not interrupted by a disastrous third world war.

In other words, a situation has come about that was not foreseen and taken into account in the Marxists' theoretical constructs. At the same time, the works of K. Marx and V.I. Lenin provide a methodological key to the accurate assessment of the current stage of world civilization's development. The thesis of the priority of universal human interests and values over purely class interests, which was advanced by them and has recently come back into political use, is assuming a striking urgency. The sphere of universal human interests and values is gradually widening. The inclusion in that sphere of the activities of states that belong to opposing social systems is increasing the tendency of nations to influence one another.

I think today the concept of peaceful coexistence should take on a different meaning, one that is neither a simple enumeration of international legal norms and principles recorded in a series of international documents, nor an interpretation of the term to mean a specific form of class struggle which is unacceptable to the other side. (It is no accident that the political and psychological associations evoked by this term moved the American delegation to the Moscow summit to reject the insertion in the final document of a paragraph on the place and role of peaceful coexistence.) It would probably be more accurate to characterize peaceful coexistence as a process in which the states of different types influence one another, a process that depends on implementing in their practical actions the idea of an expanding commonality of interests.

Critics of détente in the United States have rejected it as an unsuccessful experiment either because, they claim, mutually acceptable rules for its implementation were never agreed on, or because the Soviet Union supposedly tried to impose its own rules. Without getting involved in the debate over whether it is possible to develop universal rules of détente, I find, in studying the 1970s version, a picture altogether different from the one painted by American critics of the improvement of Soviet-American relations in the past decade. The real substance of détente was largely in keeping with the "superpower" version put forward by the United States. As a result of the administrative-command system's flaws, the Soviet Union found itself unwittingly drawn into a tug-of-war that was not to its advantage. This was particularly obvious in the arms issue and in the approach to the Third World.

Both the United States and the U.S.S.R. entered into negotiations without fully developed concepts of arms limitation. Such concepts could be formed only as a result of direct contacts, when the two sides' specific positions were clarified. It must be admitted that the traditions of maintaining the utmost secrecy and privacy when making military and political decisions placed us in a less advantageous position than the United States, which had highly sophisticated strategic thinking that had been developed with considerable help from civilian specialists. The problems posed by arms limitation require a pooling of efforts by military men, diplomats, political scientists, economists, ecologists, and engineers. It was necessary to arrange a similar coordination among people of that kind in the Soviet Union and concurrently to open doors previously closed to them, first at the beginning of the talks and then in step with their rapid progression.

We entered a period of détente without jettisoning the baggage of outdated views. In 1969, the commander in chief of the strategic missile forces wrote: "Imperialist ideologists are trying to dull the vigilance of the world's peoples by resorting to the propaganda hoax that there can be no victor in a future thermonuclear war. . . . Victory in a war, if the imperialists succeed after all in unleashing it, will go to world socialism and to all of progressive humanity."[2] And in 1971, it was stated in the magazine *Kommunist vooruzhennykh sil* that "the CPSU's military-technical policy is aimed at creating and maintaining the socialist countries' military superiority over the forces of war and aggression."[3]

All this could serve as a partial explanation for the uncritical borrowing from the West the idea that the principle of parity is formally in keeping with the terms of détente. Another and, perhaps, more important reason that this principle was incorporated into our policy was the preference that the administrative-command system showed for military-technical means of ensuring security, an approach that apparently was more in keeping with its nature, since it relied on the use of pressure and power. As M.S. Gorbachev stressed in his speech at the conference: "In concentrating vast amounts of money

---

[2]*Sovetskaya Rossiya* [*Soviet Russia*], Aug. 30, 1969.
[3]*Kommunist Vooruzhennykh Sil* [*Communist of the Armed Forces*], No. 9, 1972, p. 12.

and attention on the military aspect of our opposition to imperialism, we have not always used the political opportunities that have presented themselves as a result of fundamental changes in the world to help guarantee our nation's security, ease tension, and foster mutual understanding among peoples. As a result, we have allowed ourselves to be drawn into the arms race, which could not help but affect the country's social and economic development and its international status."

Outwardly the principle of parity is simple: the country that adheres to it aims at maintaining rough equivalence with its opponent in the military sphere. The problems arise in the interpretation of what "rough equivalence" can mean. On the 25th anniversary of the Caribbean crisis, the American side stated that despite the United States' possession of a nuclear potential many times the size of ours, parity had already been established at that time, since, as was then believed, the U.S.S.R. could have responded with a nuclear strike after a U.S. first strike. Parity can also mean something else—quantitative equivalence in the basic parameters of strategic forces. Granted, a question arose: what parameters should we be guided by—the number of launchers or the number of warheads, for example? And further: should our strategic potential be equivalent to the corresponding potential of the United States or to the combined strategic power of all countries that oppose the U.S.S.R.? Parity can also be defined in terms of equivalence of strategic capabilities, including those that would otherwise not be called destabilizing.

In fact, from the very beginning we gravitated toward the interpretation of parity as rough quantitative equivalence, and considering that the scientific and technical revolution knows no bounds—toward equivalence of capabilities, as well. As a result, because it was the United States that initiated the majority of trends in the arms race, we found ourselves captives of a purely mechanical logic: we will respond to each of your new systems with one of our own. Naturally, in this atmosphere the relationship was more difficult. Even without the United States' prompting, our engineers were not sitting idle, but the emergence "in their camp" of the latest strategic weapons system was one of the key factors in the creation of something similar "in our camp."

The United States' intensive implementation of the "Star Wars" program most vividly demonstrated the weaknesses of the mirror-image method. According to this logic, we should have created our own space-based strike weapons, at extraordinary cost and at the risk of aggravating the strategic situation. The concern with maintaining parity, understood thus, ultimately drew us into an endless arms race, since our response was met by a counter-response that forced us to keep busy, as well. In this way we played into the hands of certain forces in the United States that were trying to exhaust us economically through this military rivalry and were cleverly using our efforts to maintain parity as proof that a "Soviet military threat" existed.

In all fairness, it should be noted that by adopting this simplified interpretation of parity, the U.S.S.R., albeit at a high cost, did achieve one positive result: the futility of the arms race and its disadvantages for the United States became increasingly obvious to American ruling circles as well.

It is also clear that drawbacks in the concept of parity in the context of détente were very difficult to detect in a speculative vein, without having actually lived it. The new thinking can only be reached through suffering. Unfortunately, it does not appear all at once, with the wave of a magic wand, so to speak, but arises from an awareness of contradictions, conflicts, and mistakes.

In the latter half of the 1970s and the early 1980s, the U.S.S.R. declared its fundamental doctrinal tenets: denial of any interest in military superiority, belief that victory is impossible in a nuclear war and that a new war will inevitably have ruinous consequences for civilization, and a pledge not to be the first to use nuclear arms. It is likely that we were not always in step with the times and that we did not always manage to act with foresight. Evidently, not until the latter half of the 1980s could we advance the proposition that the side dealing the first nuclear blow "dooms itself to an agonizing death—and not so much from a counterstrike as from the consequences of the explosion of its own warheads."[4] The maturing of the new political thinking, with its central idea of the impossibility of ensuring unilateral security, was encouraged by such events as the deployment of medium-range missiles in Europe, the U.S.S.R.'s departure from talks on the limitation of nuclear and space weapons, and Chernobyl.

Without renouncing the principle of parity in the latter half of the 1980s, Moscow gave it new substance, placing primary emphasis on the principle of reasonable sufficiency, which stipulates that military efforts not exceed the needs of defense, and that a nonoffensive defense be created. The new principle is better than the principle of parity for three reasons. First, it is basically aimed at the study of the objective needs of defense, not at blind reaction to the opponent's moves. Second, it is oriented to consideration not only of military-technological, but also political and economic aspects, which creates more room for compromise decisions. Third, its application gives us a chance to stop the spiraling arms race. Now we are faced with the

---

[4]*Pravda*, Aug. 19, 1986.

exciting stage in which we must build bridges from doctrinal tenets to actual practice.

I would like to express a few thoughts on this subject. If one follows formal logic, then the arrival in the second half of the 1980s at the principle of reasonable sufficiency means that in preceding decades we amassed certain "military surpluses" that we can now confidently dispense with. (Incidentally, this thesis is quite popular with both our friends and our opponents in the West.) At the same time, a number of very complex questions arise: what kind of "surpluses" are these, should we dispose of all of them, how should they be eliminated and in what period of time? Moreover, the conclusion that unilateral arms reductions are possible does not seem to give proper recognition to the inevitable conservativeness of military planning. Military officials responsible for maintaining a sound defense capability base their military construction and preparations on a worst-case scenario, or in other words, on the possibility that the situation could take a highly unfavorable turn. In principle, figures can always be produced to show that our military efforts are inadequate. As a matter of fact, that is what led to the conclusion that it is unrealistic to try to guarantee security by purely military means.

Under any circumstances, and especially when the Soviet Union has embarked on a path of new political thinking, there are restrictions that limit efforts in the military sphere (in the past, financial and economic resources were the most serious restriction). The kind of restrictions we might be dealing with today will probably become clearer if we obtain answers to the following questions in particular. What interests is NATO prepared to defend, and to what extent, through the aggressive use of armed force? Under what circumstances could a war begin between NATO and the Warsaw Pact? Is a protracted conventional war in Europe possible? How much nuclear potential is needed to guarantee the inevitability of retribution? What should be the minimum scope of such retribution? How will unilateral arms reductions affect disarmament talks? Obviously, the list of questions could go on. In answering them, we come closer to understanding the array of problems created by "military surpluses." Undoubtedly there can be no simple answers, but this only shows that, first of all, the principle of reasonable sufficiency does not presuppose automatic unilateral reductions—"surpluses" are easier to acquire than to dispose of—and second, any decisions to implement the aforementioned principle carry some risk.

With the advent of the 1970s, the Soviet Union made no move to revise its customary strategy of approaching events in the Third World primarily from the standpoint of Soviet-American relations, an approach that is one of the components of the American version of détente. We were deceived by our excessive optimism that the socialist model of development would spread throughout the developing countries and our overestimation of their ability to make progress on a noncapitalist path. In fact there was no real basis for this in the overwhelming majority of countries that were built on the ruins of colonial empires. Rather than making a thoughtful and impartial analysis of concrete facts and situations, we studied the self-appraisals contained in the socialist-style programs of parties and movements in Third World countries.

Our theoretical delusions caused us serious political embarrassments. The failure of attempts to realize socialist dreams was almost always explained with a saving reference to "imperialist intrigues," of which there were in fact many examples. Meanwhile, by one-sidedly focusing our attention on the export of counterrevolution to the Third World, we became involved in a confrontation with the United States and gave the West reason to accuse us of "exporting revolution."

The correct idea that détente does not cancel out the Soviet Union's support of the anti-imperialist movement was sometimes reduced to the level of considering it our international duty to all but automatically give military aid to any forces that had anti-imperialist aspirations. When the United States and its allies are sending tons of military cargo to the developing world and strengthening their interventionist potential, the problem of Soviet military shipments to patriotic forces remains relevant in many cases, but aid to the anti-imperialist movement must be substantially broader in both methods and forms, and probably not always so direct. The fact that Soviet arms subsequently ended up in the hands of dictatorial, antipopular regimes did nothing to create a positive impression of the Soviet Union's policy, either.

Confrontation with the United States in any part of the developing world led to the creation of prolonged regional conflicts. Antagonism between various groups relying, in their power struggles, on the U.S.S.R. and the United States turned into permanent armed struggle that placed a heavy burden on the local population and increased international tension.

No matter how the situation developed, the transformation of the Third World into a staging ground for Soviet-American confrontation meant gains for the United States. Above all, these clashes came to be regarded by one segment of public opinion as a cynical struggle between the "superpowers." Washington had to have been gratified to see us squander material resources in the Third World and divert them from our own needs.

I think the affirmation of the new political thinking is accompanied by a reassessment, as yet incomplete, of our views of the socioeconomic dynamic of the Third World. We are groping for ways to untie the knots of regional conflicts through the constructive idea of national reconciliation. It is still too early to say that the developing world has completely escaped the U.S.S.R.-U.S. confrontation. But the departure of Soviet troops from Afghanistan that is under way and the reduction in the size of the Vietnamese military contingent in Kampuchea indicate that regional conflicts are tending to lose their importance as a bone of contention between the great powers.

At one time many good things were said about the period of Soviet-American détente. And we need not renounce the majority of them—it was the first grandiose experiment in positive cooperation between the U.S.S.R. and the United States in the nuclear age. Nevertheless, it is now clearer than ever that we must understand why détente failed. I think détente—in the form in which it was understood by both sides—was doomed from the start. And here is why.

Washington hoped to keep the ship of the "American empire" afloat. Without abandoning their "imperial" goals and obligations, the Washington administrations assumed that détente would make it possible to withstand pressure for changes in the world that were unfavorable to the United States, changes that they believed the "Soviets" supported. As a result, according to the American leadership's plans, détente, by somewhat altering the terms of rivalry with the U.S.S.R. to the advantage of the United States, was supposed to reduce the burden of maintaining the "empire."

Détente did not assume any revolutionary change in political thinking from the Soviet point of view either. (In this respect the situation in the latter half of the 1980s stands in sharp contrast. In the words of M.S. Gorbachev: "not only an improvement, but a resolute renewal of foreign policy was required. To accomplish this, a new kind of political thinking was needed.") It goes without saying that the noble ideas of strengthening peace and curbing the arms race in large part defined the Soviet approach to détente. But it seems that limiting oneself to this conventional conclusion today means stopping halfway to the truth. The administrative-command system, having set our country on the road to a precrisis situation, naively tried to patch up the ever-widening rifts by exploiting the West's economic, scientific, and technical potential. It is hard not to see that this system, with its long-standing methods of conducting foreign affairs, ultimately revealed its helplessness, when a changed world insisted on a rethinking of the aims and priorities of foreign policy and the forms and methods of its implementation.

From all appearances, the chief lesson learned from the period of détente in the 1970s is that it is impossible to maintain stable cooperation between two great powers while preserving the United States' system of "imperial" pretensions and the administrative-command system in the U.S.S.R.

* * *

To launch ballistic missiles, a double-key procedure is used: two operators must insert keys into locks and turn them, whereupon the missile's launch mechanism is unblocked, and it takes off. For the long-term normalization of Soviet-American relations to take off, to make it irreversible, both powers have to take the appropriate actions. The Soviet Union has fulfilled its part of the common task and turned its "key" to improved relations between the two countries. The 19th All-Union CPSU Conference demonstrated its ability to find important solutions to problems, particularly those in Soviet-American relations, and to work out far-reaching compromises in the name of world peace and security.

But at the same time, one has the impression that the United States is slow in following the U.S.S.R.'s example completely. One still senses a certain confusion on the part of Washington's politicians, who do not seem to know how to react to Moscow's bold steps toward disarmament.

The administration's tactics at the Moscow summit bear witness to the absence of clear-cut criteria for choosing its entire strategic policy toward the U.S.S.R. in the age of restructuring. Like many other influential political forces in the United States, it is still a prisoner of outdated ideas that keep constructive principles from ultimately triumphing. The signing of the Treaty on Medium- and Shorter-Range Missiles and the accords on Afghanistan took the hard edge off stock accusations against the U.S.S.R., causing the administration to place emphasis on the issue of human rights "violations" in the Soviet Union.

Then again, it is quite possible to attribute the president's tactics to his desire to bridge the gap between the "old Reagan" and the "new Reagan," to his wish to please right-wing forces, and to the current election campaign. All this undoubtedly has a certain influence. At the same time, we are dealing with something more complicated and fundamental in this case.

At this point it is appropriate to quote the authoritative Western expert C. Bertram, former director of the International Institute of Strategic Studies in London, who writes: "Western unity during the postwar period . . . owes much to a shared sense that the threats to Western security are ambiguous. . . . Mr. Gorbachev's striking arms control initiatives suggest an attempt to move away from traditional Soviet military overinvestment. He is manifesting the Kremlin's desire to withdraw from exposed positions in the Third World. And his appeals for reform, 'democracy,' and public accountability all contribute to a less frightening image of Soviet power in the West. If it were only the 'Soviet threat' that held the alliance together, these would be worrisome prospects for Western cohesion."[5]

Bertram's judgment accurately notes the dilemma that, together with other factors, continues to hamper the pace of the Soviet-American dialogue. One of the cornerstones was knocked out of NATO and U.S. military-political strategy. The United States and the West as a whole have found it necessary to fundamentally revise their foreign-policy and strategic military views and to set their course not for a year from now, or five years, but for decades into the future. The very scope of the task and the lack of psychological preparedness for accomplishing it at this time, not to mention the long history of hostility and staunch anti-Communism, cannot help but impede the positive development of contacts between East and West. No doubt it took an "engineer" with just such a biography as Reagan's to begin braking the Cold War locomotive from the American side. But it is apparent that the train cars will have to be hooked up to another locomotive by leaders with different views, by a different administration. Incidentally, an idea that was mentioned more than once during the Moscow talks by P. Salinger, John Kennedy's former press secretary, seems productive: the continuity of the accelerating Soviet-American dialogue could be ensured by a new summit, during which Reagan could introduce the Presidential candidates George Bush and Michael Dukakis to Gorbachev.

The 19th All-Union CPSU Conference unequivocally supported the utmost intensification of the processes of restructuring and throughout its sessions convincingly demonstrated that the policy of democratization is not a tactical maneuver, but a long-term strategy that reflects the desires of all the Soviet people. It removed many of the doubts of our partners overseas, helped overcome negative ideas about the Soviet Union, broadened the basis for mutual understanding as a whole, and marked a qualitatively new stage for the international community.

The favorable prospects that are emerging for improving Soviet-American relations are just one of many options for the development of international life. One has to be able to take advantage of it. So where does the road lead after the Moscow summit? Today there is an increasing number of reasons for asserting that the answer to that question will be determined in large part by whether restructuring—this time American restructuring of U.S. foreign-policy thinking and military-political strategy—is to get under way, and if so, when.

---

[5]*Foreign Affairs*, Summer 1987, p. 945.

Deep Reductions in Strategic Arms

First Article

Aleksey Georgiyevich Arbatov*

This article, the conclusion of which will be published in the following issue of the journal, deals with the key problems in negotiations between the U.S.S.R. and the United States on a 50 percent reduction in strategic offensive arms. It analyzes the questions of preserving the ABM Treaty, and the role and place of an agreement on a period of nonwithdrawal from that treaty. It examines the prospects for a complete elimination of strategic arms and the attendant questions concerning disarmament and the strengthening of security. It also examines the principal aspects of the treaty that is being prepared on reducing strategic arms by half, including a consideration of those aspects in the context of strengthening the stability of the strategic military balance at lower levels of nuclear arsenals.

Since the Washington signing of the Treaty on the Elimination of Medium- and Shorter-Range Missiles, the question of a 50 percent reduction in strategic offensive arms (SOAs) has assumed first place on the disarmament agenda. From the standpoint of improving both Soviet-American relations and the whole international atmosphere, the importance of a treaty on significant reductions in the levels of the two major strategic potentials is obvious and requires no explanation. But the military-strategic aspect of the question is no less important.

For example, as is known, more than 20,000 nuclear weapons are now deployed in the strategic forces of the U.S.S.R. and the United States. A relatively small portion of them may be retargeted to cover targets in Europe and Asia that were previously threatened with a strike by the approximately 2,200 warheads on medium- and shorter-range missiles. Reducing strategic weapons by half would make such retargeting more difficult. Taking the makeup of the two powers' strategic forces into account, a 50 percent reduction itself would probably result in eliminating, for the U.S.S.R. and the United States together, more than 2,000 deployed missiles and planes, more than 70

*Doctor of history, head of the Department of Disarmament and Security of the U.S.S.R. Academy of Sciences' Institute of World Economy and International Relations [IMEMO]. This article, which is the first of two on the same subject, appeared in the April 1988 issue of *MEMO*.

nuclear-powered, ballistic-missile submarines, and more than 10,000 nuclear warheads. The further reduction of SOAs, in which more than 90 percent of the world's destructive nuclear force is concentrated, will be the central direction in the process of reducing and, ultimately, completely eliminating the nuclear threat.

A number of steps toward a new treaty were taken at the Washington meeting of Soviet and U.S. leaders. Both powers' representatives in Geneva were instructed to strive to complete the drafting of a treaty, if possible, by the following summit meeting in the first half of 1988. Specifically, the joint statement reflected certain new agreed-upon parameters of the future treaty, and it was decided to pay increased attention to other points.[1]

At the same time, many issues still await resolution. It seems important to dwell particularly on three points. First, there is the matter of expressing in mutually acceptable form an agreement on the observance of the ABM Treaty as an indispensable condition for the reduction of strategic arms. Second, there is the question of the ultimate goal of strategic-arms reductions. And finally, it is necessary to identify the root cause of the remaining disagreements on numerous issues directly connected with the stage of deep, 50 percent cuts that is under discussion.

In connection with the examination of these difficult problems, the time has evidently come to finally begin an open discussion of certain important methodological questions, as well. Among Soviet political scientists concerned with the problems of international security and disarmament, a latent debate has long been under way between two schools of thought. One school believes that the study of these subjects requires a thorough knowledge of military strategy, weapons systems, and the military balance of power. The other school claims that the main issue is politics, and the technical military details, the so-called "hardware," only divert analysis from the main issues. The disagreements between the "technocrats" and the "politicians," as the representatives of these two informal schools sometimes—not without sarcasm—call one another (evoking associations with debates on other issues between the so-called "physicists" and "poets" in the 1960s), have more than purely academic significance. Relying on different approaches, individual specialists at the Institute for the United States and Canada, IMEMO, and other research centers often reach different conclusions on the same problems.

The profound restructuring of Soviet foreign policy, and its unprecedented dynamism, which is especially apparent in the area of disarmament—where it has already produced its first positive

---

[1]See *Pravda*, Dec. 12, 1987.

results—naturally presuppose the existence of differing views, an open struggle among opinions, and constructive debate, including debate on the most important problems of disarmament, security, and military sufficiency. "There was a time when controversial topics were not touched on, and opinions, even harmless ones, that differed from the official opinions were not expressed," U.S.S.R. Minister of Foreign Affairs E.A. Shevardnadze has noted, "Now that time is past."[2]

That is the only way it is possible to develop a serious scholarly basis for practical activity. The great interest that the Soviet government's foreign-policy departments are now showing in the opinion of scholars confronts scholarship with increased demands.

The SDI Program and Observance of the ABM Treaty

Recent Soviet scholarly literature has examined in detail the destabilizing consequences of a possible large-scale antimissile system with space-based elements. It can negatively affect the prospects for preserving the ABM Treaty and the possibility of banning antisatellite weapons systems and other space strike systems. This bears directly on the stability of the military-strategic balance between the U.S.S.R. and United States, the possibility of deep reductions in SOAs, and the prevention of the development of third-generation nuclear weapons. The course of events will play an important role in reducing the economic costs of military rivalry. The international political situation in the broadest sense of the word, including the security of the great powers' allies and other countries, will depend on the state of affairs in this area.[3]

The December 10, 1987, joint statement sets the goal of achieving an agreement on observance of the ABM Treaty "in the form in which it was signed in 1972, in the process of carrying out research, development, and if necessary, testing that is allowed under the ABM Treaty." The sides will pledge not to withdraw from the treaty for an agreed-upon period. Three years before that period ends, intensive negotiations are supposed to begin, but if the sides do not agree otherwise, each will have the right to determine its own course of action. The

---

[2]*Bulletin of the U.S.S.R. Ministry of Foreign Affairs* [*Vestnik MID SSSR*], No. 2, Aug. 26, 1987, p. 33.

[3]See *Space Weapons: the Security Dilemma* [*Kosmicheskoye oruzhiye: dilemma bezopasnosti*], ed. by Ye. P. Velikhov, R.Z. Sagdeyev, and A.A. Kokoshin, Moscow, 1986; *SDI: The American "Star Wars" Program* [*SOI. Amerikanskaya programma "zvezdnykh voyn"*], U.S.S.R. Academy of Sciences' KSU-ISKAN-IKI [KSU: Committee of Soviet Scientists for Peace, Against the Nuclear Threat; ISKAN: U.S.S.R. Academy of Sciences' Institute for the United States and Canada; IKI: Institute of Space Research], Moscow, 1987; "SDI: Dangers, Illusions, Alternatives" (*Novoye vremya* [*New Times*], Special Supplement, 1987); and *Disarmament and Security Yearbook, 1986* [*Razoruzheniye i bezopasnost. 1986. Yezhegodnik*], Moscow, 1987.

nonwithdrawal agreement is supposed to have the same legal status as the treaty on SOAs, the ABM Treaty, and other agreements.[4]

The logic of a mutual pledge by the two powers not to exercise their right to withdraw from the ABM Treaty for a specific period (a right provided in Article XV, conditioned on a six-month notification) rests on the following considerations. Every state that is a party to any treaty has a sovereign right to withdraw from it under certain conditions, and no one has any intention of taking that right away from the United States or the U.S.S.R. with respect to the ABM Treaty. But if the sides agree on deep reductions of SOAs, then—in light of the objective, organic relationship between offensive and defensive weapons—additional guarantees are needed to make matters definite in such an important area. In other words, guarantees are needed that a large reduction in the levels of strategic potentials will take place under the conditions of a strict observance of the limitations on defensive systems. Otherwise, instead of strengthening stability, a reduction in strategic weapons might make it easier to upset that stability. This conclusion in based on the premise that the side that decided at some stage to withdraw from the ABM Treaty anyway and to create a large-scale antimissile system could make that system all the more effective, the fewer the targets—i.e., ballistic missiles and their warheads—there remained for it to cover.

The words concerning the observance of the ABM Treaty "in the form in which it was signed in 1972" are of key importance in the wording of the Washington joint statement. Their meaning, it seems, can only signify that the so-called "broad interpretation," according to which the treaty supposedly allows the testing in space of ABM components and systems based on new physical principles (lasers, microwaves, charged-particle beams), is wrong. For all intents and purposes, in Washington the sides put their signatures to the original and only true interpretation of the treaty, according to which ABM systems and components based on new physical principles can be tested only if they are stationary and land-based. And the deployment of them is supposed to be the subject of special agreement, in order to prevent violation of the strict quantitative, qualitative, and territorial restrictions specified in Article III of the treaty and the 1974 protocol to it (according to which there can be only one region of ABM deployment).

At the same time, the agreement not to withdraw for an agreed-upon period from the treaty, which itself has the status of unlimited duration, should not represent some sort of agreement that the treaty will virtually automatically expire at the end of that period. In accor-

---

[4]See *Pravda*, Dec. 12, 1987.

dance with Article XV of the treaty, one side cannot withdraw from it, for example, simply in view of its successful development of technical programs that create the prospect of establishing an effective ABM system covering its entire territory. Either side can do this only if it "decides that exceptional circumstances connected with the content of this treaty place its supreme interests in danger."[5] That means that the United States, for example, could withdraw from the treaty because the Soviet Union had violated it, or in connection with the latter's buildup of offensive nuclear forces.

But the U.S.S.R. has no intention of violating the treaty and is proposing that all disagreements on questions of its observance be settled to mutual satisfaction (that is the aim of the decision to freeze construction of the Krasnoyarsk radar for a year). In turn, strategic arms are to be cut by 50 percent and, after that, to even lower levels, which is to say that the threat of offensive nuclear weapons will be diminished—on the condition that the restrictions on the development of antimissile weapons remain firm.

It is therefore important to guarantee that opponents of the ABM Treaty cannot, in exchange for a pledge of nonwithdrawal for a limited period, predetermine the treaty's termination once that period ends, in spite of the letter and spirit of Article XV. Unfortunately, in the United States lately one increasingly encounters precisely that arbitrary interpretation of this approach. Moreover, one can conclude that the supporters of a spaceborne antimissile system, having been unable to break up the treaty with a frontal attack (as was demonstrated by Senator S. Nunn's 1987 report and the Congressional resolution that was adopted on its basis, which essentially rejected the "broad interpretation" of the ABM Treaty), are now increasingly placing their hopes on terminating it at the expiration of the nonwithdrawal period. They place their main emphasis on the phrase in the Washington summit's joint statement to the effect that "unless the sides agree otherwise, each will have the right to determine its own course of action." These circles are calculating that they will now be able to continue spaceborne ABM programs on the pretext of creating "trump cards" for negotiating "from a position of strength" on strategic relations between the U.S.S.R. and United States once the nonwithdrawal period expires. In particular, in January 1988 the American side submitted a draft "Treaty Between the United States and the U.S.S.R. on Certain Measures Facilitating the Transition, on the Basis of Cooperation, to the Deployment of a Future Strategic Defense Against Ballistic Missiles."[6] The aim is to thereby give a "second wind" to the SDI

[5]*Disarmament and Security Yearbook, 1986*, Vol. 2, p. 202.
[6]See *Pravda*, Jan. 24, 1988.

program, which in 1986 and 1987 came under increasingly sharp criticism concerning its technical and strategic soundness, and from whose appropriations Congress cut increasingly larger sums.

It seems that in a future Soviet-American agreement on observance of the ABM Treaty there should be perfect clarity on the point that the "right to determine its own course of action" by no means revokes the wording of Article XV, and that the nonwithdrawal period absolutely does not imply a limitation on the period in which this unlimited-duration treaty remains in effect.

These conclusions follow from a political analysis of the problem that takes into account both the treaty's role in Soviet-American relations and in the system and process of arms limitation, and the domestic political situation in the United States. However, without examining the strategic and military-technological aspects of the problem, such an analysis would plainly be incomplete.

Most experts agree with the view that, because of the "immaturity" of exotic spaceborne antimissile technology, the feasibility of a large-scale ABM system will not be clear before the mid-1990s, and full-scale testing of its components and the deployment of such a system could occur no earlier than the late 1990s to early 21st century. The difficulties that the U.S. plan for "early deployment" of a spaceborne ABM system encountered in 1987 provided yet another graphic confirmation of this. In the foreseeable future, until the deployment of a spaceborne ABM system comes onto the agenda, the key question in a technical and strategic sense is the interpretation of the restrictive provisions of the ABM Treaty with respect to specific antimissile and spaceborne weapons programs. And here it is important that Washington not attempt, in exchange for its formal pledge not to withdraw from the treaty, to revive, by hook or crook, the "broad interpretation" of a number of the treaty's articles. It is no secret that SDI proponents have been trying to claim that the implementation of related projects does not violate the terms of the ABM Treaty. To this end, they have attempted to pass off ABM components as "experimental models" and "subcomponents," to pass off tests as "experiments," and to represent experiments with spaceborne systems as tests in placing devices in space in suborbital ballistic trajectories, rather than in orbit. At the beginning of 1988 the U.S. delegation to the Geneva talks resumed attempts to defend the "broad interpretation" of the ABM Treaty, claiming that experiments and tests of a number of elements of SDI were supposedly allowed by the joint Soviet-American statement issued at the Washington summit.[7]

---

[7] *Ibid.*

Verifiable limits on such work that accord with the authentic interpretation of the terms of restriction on ABM systems would be an extremely important, realistic guarantee against a sudden spurt ahead by either of the two powers in the area of spaceborne antimissile systems. And in this connection it becomes extremely urgent to reach an agreement on the limits of allowable research in the area of ABM systems based on new physical principles, including agreement on the characteristics of devices that can be placed in space and the operations they can perform. Research and development in this area is a costly process that takes many years and is difficult to disguise. If agreed-upon limits turn out to be violated in the course of that process, the other side will have sufficient time to take military-technological, political, international, and other countermeasures. But if such restrictions do not exist, and programs of military-technological development and experiments progress far ahead in an undefined situation, the restrictive significance of the ABM Treaty may be gradually eroded, even without formal withdrawal. This would foreordain its termination once the nonwithdrawal period had ended.

Without by any means diminishing the political role of a pledge of nonwithdrawal from the treaty, one must not overlook the military-strategic aspects, either. As an international legal document, such a pledge would be as reliable as the military-strategic deterrent factors are strong. If they prove inadequate to prevent the denunciation or simply the treacherous violation of the ABM Treaty—the cornerstone of the whole international system of arms limitations—it is hardly possible that any additional pledge of nonwithdrawal will save the situation (especially since the American side is insisting on including reservations in the pledge that would permit renunciation of observance of the nonwithdrawal period under certain conditions).

The chief military-strategic factor having significant influence on plans for the creation of a global antimissile system on the basis of SDI is the likelihood of the other side's countermeasures. The Soviet Union has taken an optimal line in this regard, declaring that its countering steps will be asymmetrical to the SDI program, less costly, and will require less time.

It seems to us that the most effective such measure would be to develop a system for directly combating the space echelons of the ABM system using nuclear and kinetic-energy weapons and directed-energy systems, as well as electronic-warfare systems: land-, sea-, air-, and, if necessary, space-based. They would be intended not for destroying the U.S. population and material assets, but for disabling space strike weapons and disrupting the operation of U.S. observation, tracking, command, and communications systems. In addition, it would also be necessary to ensure a high degree of survivability for the systems used to counter a spaceborne ABM system and to give them sufficient protection against a strike from U.S. offensive nuclear weapons, as well as against the use of American spaceborne weapons.

Indisputably, from a political viewpoint, in and of itself the process of making deep reductions in strategic arms would weaken the support for SDI in the United States and reinforce the popularity of the ABM Treaty. It is natural, however, to ask whether a radical reduction in SOAs wouldn't facilitate the subsequent development of a more effective ABM system. Or, to put it simply, wouldn't a 50 percent reduction in strategic arms make eventual creation of a spaceborne antimissile system easier and less expensive? And in this case political analysis should be backed up by strategic and military-technological assessments.

First, considerable research persuasively demonstrates that, within a broad range of the correlation of forces, the effectiveness of a spaceborne antimissile system (including one utilizing directed-energy weapons) depends not only on the number of the other side's strategic missiles, but even more on their qualitative characteristics (in particular, the duration of the boost phase of the trajectory, the speed with which the warhead separates, the effectiveness of decoys), as well as on the means of basing, the tactics governing the strategic missiles' use, and the effectiveness of weapons used to directly attack the space echelons of the ABM system.[8]

Second, the components of an antimissile system being developed within the framework of the SDI program are intended to directly intercept existing types of Soviet land-based and sea-launched ballistic missiles and modifications that are anticipated in the foreseeable future. Taking into account the huge estimated cost of a multi-echelon ABM system, those who are carrying out the SDI program are banking on the assumption that the countermeasures will cost the Soviet Union relatively (or even absolutely) more. In this connection, they express the hope that the U.S.S.R. will take the most expensive and least cost-effective course of quantitatively building up its forces of existing types of missiles, and that that will divert its funds from qualitative improvement.

Third, the main calculation is that the Soviet Union, with its traditionally great stress on defensive weapons (expressed, in particular, in its maintenance of a large-scale antiaircraft system and of its one allowed ABM complex around Moscow) ultimately will not stick to the course of "asymmetrical countermeasures," and will get drawn into a competition

---

[8]See C. Gray, "Deterrence and Strategic Defense," in *The Strategic Defense Debate*, ed. by C. Snyder, Philadelphia, 1986, pp. 170-182.

in expensive space- and land-based systems. In that competition, the supporters of SDI hope, many geostrategic and mechanical disproportions will start to work against the U.S.S.R. In a certain sense, the tasks of an American ABM system would become substantially easier in that context: its effectiveness would be measured less in comparison to Soviet offensive weapons and countermeasures than in comparison to the Soviet antimissile system as such. An arms race in that sphere, moreover, would divert efforts and money away from systems intended to directly counter the spaceborne elements of the U.S. ABM system.

Thus, a 50 percent reduction really would have little impact on the effectiveness of a likely American ABM system in a technical sense. But at the same time, in a certain sense it would make it easier, if necessary, to adopt countermeasures in response to the U.S. deployment of an antimissile system. Finally, as a last resort, the possibility would always remain of building SOAs back up to current levels and higher if it were deemed advisable. Such a step could be implemented much faster and at a lower cost than the steps that would be required for the full-scale testing and deployment of a multi-echelon U.S. ABM system with space-based elements.

In addition, possible measures that have been examined for counteracting the development of new spaceborne antimissile systems along political and military-technological lines do not eliminate the need for special steps to ensure observance of the ABM Treaty. They would be necessary even in the event of an unequivocal U.S. renunciation of its "broad interpretation." An agreement on a period of nonwithdrawal from the ABM Treaty could be used in order to achieve, within the agreed-upon period, mutually acceptable agreements on these issues.

Progress in military technology creates a threat that the restrictive limits of the treaty will become increasingly blurred, and that the sides' mutual suspicions and fears will grow in connection with developments in related strategic and technological areas. Such areas might include antimissile defense for combating tactical ballistic missiles; new antiaircraft weapons; antisatellite weapons; new types of space systems for power supply, observation, tracking, communications, and battle management; land-based laser devices using spaceborne mirror-reflectors; and so forth. Many are not presently covered directly by the treaty but could lead to an erosion of its restrictive conditions from various directions. Some of these systems will objectively possess a certain potential for intercepting ballistic missiles, others will open the channels for improving technology to levels close to the requirements of a spaceborne antimissile system, and finally, still others will greatly complicate verification of treaty observance, the ability to distinguish between prohibited and permissible activities, and monitoring the observance of restrictions on the testing, and even deployment, of spaceborne antimissile systems.

The Problem of Eliminating Strategic Arms

An important subject of disagreement between the U.S.S.R. and the United States is the ultimate goal of strategic-arms reduction. The Soviet Union favors their complete elimination, possibly even within a 10-year period. The United States officially favors the elimination of ballistic missiles only, but not heavy bombers and cruise missiles. Granted, this position is not taken seriously even among American specialists. In the vast majority, these specialists, with various reservations, favor a certain reduction, but not the complete elimination of strategic arms, including ballistic missiles.

Political analysis persuasively demonstrates the insecurity and danger of a peace based on the confrontation between growing nuclear potentials for universal destruction. The political importance and constructiveness of the declared goal of completely eliminating strategic arms and all nuclear weapons are perfectly obvious. However, the enormity, multidimensionality, and complexity of this objective are even more evident in the military-strategic and military-technological context.

One can start with the fact that its accomplishment would mean (based on the situation as of Jan. 1, 1988) the dismantling by both sides of a total of 2,390 ICBM launchers and missiles themselves, 1,614 submarine ballistic-missile launchers, about 100 strategic-missile submarines, and 750 heavy bombers.[9] That means that the two states would each have to remove an average of 475 missiles and planes and 10 submarines from operational status annually. And that is on the condition that neither power would put a single new system, a single missile, or a single bomber into operation over a 10-year period. Otherwise, the dimensions of the reductions would have to be even greater to offset these additions. For comparison, let us recall that, under SALT-1 and SALT-2, over the course of 15 years (1972 to 1987) the two sides eliminated from their strategic forces about 900 ballistic-missile launchers and heavy bombers, and 26 nuclear-powered ballistic-missile submarines, that is, an average of approximately 60 planes and launchers, and two submarines a year.[10] It goes without saying that in this process a reliable barrier must be erected against space weapons. And evidently, the currently allowed ABM complexes and strategic components of antiaircraft systems would also be subject to elimination.

---

[9]*Pravda*, Nov. 8, 1988.
[10]Calculated on the basis of *Pravda*, Mar. 17, 1987.

But, for all their scope, the levels of the reductions are still not the most complex aspect of the problem. Considering the lengthy period of the development, construction (10 to 15 years), and active service (20 to 30 years) of strategic arms, an agreement on complete elimination of SOAs in such a short time would assume, for all intents and purposes, the simultaneous "freezing" of all programs for improving existing weapons systems and developing new ones (including a complete ban on nuclear testing), with appropriate methods and means of verification. The development of other types of weapons of mass destruction would also have to be barred, and existing stocks of them destroyed.

The political goal has been set and elicits no doubts among either specialists on international political problems, or experts on military-strategic matters who support the idea of ensuring security through political rather than military means, and who really desire the rapid reduction and, ultimately, complete elimination of the threat of nuclear war. But it is the duty of these specialists to work out specific steps for advancing toward this goal that take military and political realities into account, and to identify the interconnections and interdependence among various steps in this area. That is what M.S. Gorbachev has called for, stressing that "the politicians need scientific arguments and scientific conclusions in order to adopt decisions not just on domestic issues, but on international issues, as well."[11]

Strategic arms are not just a "superstructure" made of the most destructive weapons that sits atop present-day military arsenals and can be taken in isolation and cut back. SOAs are the core of the global strategic and politico-military situation, and they permeate all its objective interconnections. For example, if global-range weapons are eliminated, the significance of the geopolitical asymmetry of the respective positions of the U.S.S.R. and United States might again increase. It is perfectly obvious that it would be intolerable for the elimination of SOAs to return the world to the period of the 1940s and 1950s, when U.S. territory was effectively invulnerable to nuclear weapons because of the U.S.S.R.'s lack of intercontinental missiles, while Soviet cities were within the range of forward-based U.S. nuclear weapons. Consequently, arms of that sort should be subject to parallel destruction, and this means eliminating not just medium-range and shorter-range missiles, but also both powers' medium-range bombers and airfield- and carrier-based operational-tactical strike aviation.

---

[11]*Pravda*, Jan. 17, 1988.

Under such conditions, one could hardly leave tactical nuclear weapons and battlefield nuclear weapons outside of agreements.[12] If they were, the concepts of "limited" and "local" nuclear war, which are clearly insupportable today because of the inevitable escalation of a nuclear conflict into a global catastrophe, would gain serious reinforcement—especially in the eyes of a power that was more remote from an assumed theater of military operations.

By and large, the delivery vehicles of tactical nuclear weapons are so-called "dual-purpose" devices, and their range is being steadily increased, which would permit them to also be used for strategic nuclear strikes at great depth, including strikes against administrative and industrial targets (let us recall that the bombs that destroyed Hiroshima and Nagasaki were, by current classifications, tactical weapons in terms of their destructive power).

The elimination of tactical nuclear weapons would, in turn, result in the need to take major disarmament steps in the area of conventional arms and armed forces. First, the technical side of the question. Destruction of tactical nuclear munitions and prevention of the concealment of even a relatively small number of them are extremely difficult to verify. A more reliable guarantee would be the elimination of launch platforms and means of delivery, most of which are dual-purpose and are integrated into conventional armed forces.[13] This presupposes the dismantling of substantial components of current land forces and, to an even greater degree, of air, naval, and air-defense forces.

Second, the existence of tactical nuclear weapons and plans for their first use in the NATO armed forces have traditionally been justified on the grounds of the Warsaw Treaty's alleged "substantial superiority" in conventional arms and ground forces, especially armored and mechanized units. The Warsaw Pact countries justifiably link deep cuts in armed forces and conventional arms in Europe, and their restructuring according to highly defensive principles, to a reduction in dual-purpose systems and the subsequent elimination of tactical nuclear weapons. Thus, the inseparable connection between conventional armed forces and tactical nuclear arms is also obvious in strategic terms.

---

[12]This refers to missile systems in the "surface-to-surface," "surface-to-air," "air-to-surface," "ship-launched antiship," and "ship-launched surface-to-air" classes, as well as aerial bombs, depth charges, torpedoes, antisubmarine rockets, artillery shells, land mines, and mortars. At present, these systems total from 5,000 to 10,000 delivery vehicles and means of delivery, and more than 20,000 nuclear munitions.

[13]This refers to air-force operational-tactical strike aviation; land-based and carrier-based naval aviation; fighters and antiaircraft rockets; tactical missiles; large-caliber artillery belonging to ground forces; and large naval warships and submarines carrying dual-purpose missiles, torpedoes, and minelaying equipment.

And third, the reduction of strategic offensive arms themselves would, at a certain stage, raise the question of measures to deal with conventional or multipurpose weapons systems, the plans for whose use are directly connected with SOAs in an operational sense. This refers, first of all, to naval antisubmarine forces and weapons that are intended to combat nuclear-powered ballistic-missile submarines. A substantial, if not predominant, number of the combat missions of the surface, submarine, and air forces of the navies of the U.S.S.R., the United States, and a number of their allies are built around antisubmarine defense and combating the enemy's antisubmarine defense. The same is true of antiaircraft defense, whose radar detection and tracking systems, fighter-interceptors, and antiaircraft rocket complexes—not to mention medium bombers and dual-purpose operational-tactical strike aviation—are oriented, to a considerable extent, against heavy bombers and cruise missiles.

Thus, according to the logic of the objectively existing mechanism of strategic, operational, and technical relationships among the various elements of the global and regional military balance, the complete removal of such an important, central "block" of it as strategic offensive arms would inevitably give rise to a "chain reaction" in the disarmament area affecting an expanding range of nuclear and conventional elements. In essence, this would mean a radical restructuring of the entire world military-strategic situation, with elimination of its major components on land, on sea, and in the air.

However, in addition to this vertical "chain reaction," the elimination of SOAs and, in this connection, of medium-range, operational-tactical, and tactical nuclear weapons would raise the question of extending disarmament measures horizontally. Naturally, this refers first of all to dismantling all classes of the nuclear weapons of Great Britain, France, and the People's Republic of China, as well as to eliminating, according to the logic cited above, certain elements of their conventional armed forces.

These states regard nuclear weapons not just as a means of ensuring their national security in the narrow sense, but also as a factor in their political relations with the U.S.S.R. and United States, neighboring nonnuclear states (the Federal Republic of Germany, Japan), and the developing countries. It is most likely that these three powers' renunciation of nuclear status would be accompanied by a number of political conditions related to the restructuring of international relations on global and regional scales, as well as by the demand for additional disarmament measures and military guarantees pertaining to their neighboring countries.

In the study of these problems, scholars of the "political" school should speak their word. But this word will carry weight only if it is based on a thorough knowledge of military-strategic questions and their role and place in the political relationships among states. Such an approach requires a higher level of analytical art than do military-technological and military-strategic assessments alone. But without the latter, political analysis is just as impossible as higher mathematics without arithmetic.

In addition, the nuclear disarmament of the five aforementioned powers would require a drastic tightening of the procedures governing the nonproliferation of nuclear weapons. This would include monitoring the presence of the munitions in question, eliminating them when necessary, and providing guarantees against future development of nuclear weapons by such states as Israel, South Africa, Pakistan, Iraq, Libya, South Korea, Brazil, Argentina, and India (including turning the treaty banning nuclear testing into a multilateral treaty). The same thing applies to chemical, bacteriological, and other types of weapons of mass destruction. Obviously, the measures that have been mentioned cannot be some sort of joint, coercive action on the part of the five nuclear powers. That would be both politically unacceptable and impermissible in terms of international law; moreover, it obviously could not be carried out in practice. That means that the solution of this problem can be based only on appropriate negotiations and mutually acceptable agreements, and this presupposes, in turn, the settlement of a broad range of regional and internal political and economic problems.

Verification and monitoring measures represent a separate problem. They should encompass not only SOAs but also other nuclear and non-nuclear weapons and the armed forces of many states, those states' military activities, and their production and scientific and technological bases (including nuclear power engineering and enterprises that produce fissionable materials); and they should also be extended to include an extensive set of measures in the area of security and the settlement of international and internal conflicts.

In raising the question of the complete elimination of strategic weapons, the Soviet government unquestionably recognizes the full complexity and multifaceted military and political nature of such an action. Incidentally, the Jan. 15, 1988, Soviet program for the elimination of nuclear weapons provides for a comprehensive approach to solving the problem, an approach which has already begun to be realized in the Treaty on the Elimination of Medium- and Shorter-Range Missiles, and in various negotiations that are under way in the disarmament area.

At the same time, the vast majority of Western political leaders and military and civilian specialists—the people with whom it would be necessary to conduct direct negotiations on these issues—consider such radical steps to be unrealistic and unrealizable in the foreseeable future. But that does not mean that there is absolutely no basis for dialogue and interaction between the sides.

While differing in their vision of the ultimate goal of reducing SOAs, the sides have, in principle, a considerable area of agreement regarding the desirability and feasibility of the first major step along this path—a 50 percent reduction in delivery vehicles and nuclear warheads within the next several years.

By having in mind a perfectly definite ultimate goal for the negotiations, no matter how difficult it may presently seem to achieve, the Soviet Union possesses a fundamental advantage over the United States. But a clear goal, for all its importance, is still not everything. What is now on the agenda is the careful development, on the basis of the new thinking on security issues, of the whole path of progress toward that goal, and especially its first stage. Moreover, this stage should be delineated as clearly as possible not just from the standpoint of the quantity of arms to be reduced, but also in terms of the qualitative changes that should take place in the strategic correlation of forces, and in the firmness of guarantees against a first strike when nuclear potentials are at a lower level. It is obvious that strategic stability—which, according to widely accepted notions, has to do with the degree of probability that a nuclear war will be launched—is by no means necessarily automatically strengthened in proportion to a reduction in the quantity of arms. If the vulnerability of the weapons remaining after a reduction increases, an additional incentive for a preventive strike may arise, as a result of which the threat of nuclear war might hypothetically even increase.[14]

Specific measures for reducing SOAs by half should be incorporated into long-range plans that envisage successive stages of advancement toward the ultimate goal, and the timely preparation of accompanying disarmament measures and measures for strengthening political security. Such plans were mentioned above, and they go far beyond the framework of the Geneva negotiations on nuclear and space weapons. A clear ultimate goal is attractive primarily because it makes it possible to focus on political ways and means of ensuring security. That is, on the achievement of an orderly series of agreements to which both the diplomatic line in Geneva and current military programs should be subordinated.

The American approach suffers primarily from the vagueness of its ultimate goal for the process of reducing SOAs. If it envisages the

---

[14]See *Strategic Stability Under the Conditions of Radical Reductions in Nuclear Weapons* [*Strategicheskaya stabilnost v usloviyakh radikalnykh sokrashcheniy yadernykh vooruzheniy*], Moscow, 1987, p. 13.

termination of that process after the implementation of 50 percent reductions, or at some other, lower level, it thereby deliberately undermines the officially proclaimed goal of "strengthening the stability of the strategic balance." After all, no matter at what level the process of reducing SOAs is stopped, and no matter how stable the balance fixed by treaty initially is, scientific and technological progress in strategic systems and related areas inevitably will eventually erode that stability and create new methods and means of launching and waging nuclear war. The vagueness of its end goal dooms the U.S. line in Geneva to trailing after programs for improving SOAs. The American position in the negotiations, which has been very thoroughly thought out with regard to the stage of 50 percent reductions in SOAs, bears the clear imprint of short-range, highly pragmatic considerations, the pursuit of which could lead far afield from the main goal: reducing the probability of nuclear war.

What do advocates of the so-called political school who reject the need to study the military specifics have to say on this score? At the present stage there is no longer any need to try to convince anyone that there can be no victors in a nuclear war, and that agreements on deep cuts in SOAs are necessary. There is no need for lengthy arguments to the effect that the political path to ensuring security is preferable, and that individual disproportions in the strategic balance should not be turned into obstacles to agreements, whose importance to overall security is many times greater than the significance of individual asymmetries. The U.S.S.R.'s political leadership has not only unequivocally declared its views on these questions, but has demonstrated its determination to follow the principles of the new thinking in practice by achieving the signing of the Treaty on Medium- and Shorter-Range Missiles.

But does that mean that any terms of a 50 percent reduction in SOAs are acceptable to the Soviet Union, especially considering that there is not yet any mutual understanding between the sides regarding the next stage and the final goal on that path? Where is the boundary between allowable disproportions and serious distortions of equilibrium that undermine stability? This is the last stop for "political poetry"; this is where it starts to go around a closed circle of generalities. Further progress requires a professional analysis of numerous specific questions.

But can it be that the diplomats and military professionals should be put to dealing with the "hardware" and boring specifics, while scholars should be left to solve the really major problems, such as how much better peace is than war, how much preferable disarmament is to the arms race, and how much more important politics is than military hardware from the standpoint of security?

Most likely, such a division of labor would make the life of political scientists a great deal easier. But would it make it easier to work out a scientific basis for real steps to strengthen security? That is the question. Experience shows that as soon as one moves from abstract argumentation to specific ways and means of implementing ideas, one immediately has to talk about strategy, weapons systems, and the substantive content of the concepts of "equilibrium," "parity," "equal security," "stability," and so forth.

In such matters the scholars' responsibility, as well as their risk of error, is much higher than in the discussion of lofty "political" matters. But it is here that the importance of serious scholarly analysis and a firm theoretical basis is greater than anywhere else. However, that basis should not consist of well-turned formulations that are suitable for all occasions in life and beautiful in their infallibility and uselessness, but rather should rely on a knowledge of the extremely complex specifics in all of their contradictory and ambiguous nature, and on broad conceptual thinking that takes the new philosophy of security as its point of departure and is not limited by everyday routine and bureaucratic details. This is precisely what statesmen are at present demanding of the scholars and experts who are being enlisted in the development of foreign policy.

But do the representatives of our academic community always prove to be on top of these demands at the present time, when practice, so to speak, has turned its face directly to science? We must admit that they do not always prove to be so in every respect. The years of stagnation, divorce from life, and artificial isolation and self-isolation show up in this sphere, as in others. That applies, to one degree or another, both to international political science as a whole and, specifically, to the areas of it that concern politico-military and disarmament matters. Theoretical thought in that field was covered for many years by thick deposits of propaganda and started to lose the capacity for independent, critical analysis.

Naturally, this has not gone unnoticed in the West, where our scholarly publications are followed closely, and conclusions are drawn from discussions with representatives of Soviet scholarship. Here, for example, is what the American specialist S. Meyer, a director of the Center for International Studies of the Massachusetts Institute of Technology, and a Pentagon consultant, has written by way of explaining why he does not use our scholars' works in researching the U.S.S.R.'s politico-military policy: "In the areas under analysis here, these writers have little information beyond that published daily in Western in newspapers, journals, and books (which are the 'classified' sources to which they have access). Moreover, as academics of the state, it is explicitly their job to justify state policy, to place it in the proper—that is, best political and ideological light."[15]

There is no denying that it is an offensive judgment. One would like very much to reject it as slander that simply reflects the author's personal ill will. Indeed, such characterizations are too sweeping and are inapplicable to many Soviet scholars, who even in former times defended their own points of view to the extent that it was possible, and who now have actively involved themselves in the accomplishment of urgent practical tasks. Other American experts are more objective in their assessments. In particular, R. Legvold, director of Columbia University's Averell Harriman Institute for Advanced Study of the Soviet Union, notes that certain subdivisions of the U.S.S.R. Academy of Sciences' Institute of World Economy and International Relations and Institute for the United States and Canada, in close cooperation with government departments, concern themselves with far more important matters than simple propaganda.[16]

But unfortunately, the first opinion also contains its share of truth. Of course, not everything depends on scholars. One thing that does not, for example, is a substantial expansion of the publication of our own data, facts, and estimates, without which scholarly analysis lacks a basic foundation and is doomed to one-sidedness and detachment from real life. But even the representatives of the academic world are not always prepared to comprehend that information and integrate it into a system of concepts that have been thought through in depth.

In the Soviet Union people understand this, openly discuss it, and propose the task of radically changing the former state of affairs. Of course, not in order to satisfy S. Meyer and his ilk—their statements are the least of our problems. But in order, above all, that our theory do a much better job of meeting the needs of Soviet foreign policy. As E.A. Shevardnadze has pointed out, that "is not just an idle demand, but an iron necessity. An excessively active practice that gets ahead of sluggish theory, or a sluggish, flaccid theory that is concerned with serving practice as adroitly as possible, has sometimes cost us considerably."[17]

---

[15]*Hawks, Doves, and Owls*, ed. by G. Allison, A. Carnesale, and J. Nye, Jr., New York, 1985, p. 169.

[16]See *The Harriman Institute Forum*, Jan. 1988, p. 7.

[17]*Vestnik MID SSSR*, No. 1, Aug. 5, 1987, p. 19.

Deep Reductions in Strategic Arms

Second Article

ALEKSEY GEORGIYEVICH ARBATOV*

In the first article, in connection with an analysis of the problem of preventing a race in space weapons, preserving the ABM Treaty, and radically reducing and eliminating strategic offensive arms (SOAs), mention was also made of the methodological debate between the two schools of Soviet political scientists concerned with questions of disarmament and international security. It would be incorrect to understand the arguments between those two schools, loosely called the "politicians" and the "technocrats," as disagreements between theoreticians and practitioners, or as a debate between the representatives of basic and applied research.

The subject of disagreement between the two is more on the order of what sort of theory is needed here, how it should be developed, and how closely it should be tied to practice. By and large, the "technocrats" favor the inductive method, that is, movement from the particular to the general, the discovery of laws, and the development of theoretical concepts by relying on analysis of practical experience in all its complexity and contradictions. They seek the political "philosophers' stone" in the problems of international security by proceeding from studying the connection between progress in military technology and the evolution of strategic concepts; the reciprocal influence between strategic doctrines and international politics (especially from the standpoint of the danger of war); the clash between military programs and arms limitation negotiations; and finally, to close the circle, the connection between disarmament measures and the reduction of the threat of war in political relations among states.

Representatives of the "political" school adhere for the most part to the deductive method, that is, they proceed from the general theory of international relations to its politico-military aspects, and on this

---

*Doctor of history, head of the Department of Disarmament and Security of the U.S.S.R. Academy of Sciences' Institute of World Economy and International Relations [IMEMO]. This article, which is a sequel to the preceding article on the same subject, appeared in the May 1988 issue of *MEMO*.

basis they try to draw conclusions applicable to specific questions of security, disarmament, and the military situation.

On Political Ends and Military Means

Here, for example, is what E.A. Pozdnyakov, a Soviet specialist in the theory of international relations, writes: "No matter how great the influence of means on policy at times may be, they are nonetheless subordinate to it. If that were not the case, one would have to part forever with the hope not only of complete nuclear disarmament, but even of partial arms limitation. In actuality, missiles do not create themselves merely as the result of the simple 'logic' of development of military technology, just as they are not deployed of their own accord in various spots on the globe. Both are the result of the policy of states, which itself is determined to a significant extent by the political relations that exist among them. A given level of arms *is the direct result of the corresponding policies of states* (my emphasis—A.A.) and political relations among them. Consequently, in order to eliminate the effect, one must start by eliminating the causes that have produced that effect. The causes, however, are always political and cannot be otherwise."[1]

The basic propositions in the article cited seem entirely well-founded, but the statement that has been quoted is highly characteristic of the "political" school and therefore deserves more detailed analysis. The merit of the syllogism cited is that it is perfectly indisputable, but only on a very high level of generalization. Its shortcoming, on the other hand, is that when one attempts to give it the least bit of specific content, much less draw practical conclusions from it, numerous questions immediately arise.

First, what is meant by the policy of states that results in the creation and deployment of missiles? If what is meant are diplomatic, economic, and strategic-technological considerations in the process of making decisions on major military programs, everything here is clear. They, in fact, are the object of study by the "technocrats."[2] But if what is meant are more fundamental aspects of political relations among states, linking them directly to levels of armaments not only elicits theoretical objections in a number of cases, but leads straight to an impasse from the standpoint of practical recommendations.

In actuality, is there even one political conflict between the U.S.S.R. and the United States that would justify the accumulation of

---

[1]*MEMO*, No. 10, 1987, pp. 31-32.
[2]Among those "technocrats," incidentally, so-called "case studies" are very popular; they involve the examination of the process of decision making on major military programs in light of all factors influencing decisions, including the rivalry among government departments.

approximately 50,000 nuclear warheads and the continued buildup of destructive potentials capable not only of destroying those two states many times over, but of destroying all civilization and, possibly, even life on the planet? Is there even one intelligible explanation of the political reasons that would lead the Warsaw Pact or NATO to decide to attack one another? But groupings of the two alliances' armed forces numbering 3 million men, some 80,000 tanks, and 6,000 tactical strike airplanes confront one another on the continent.[3]

Another practical aspect of the problem is closely connected to this. If, as the author writes, a given level of arms "is the direct consequence" of political relations among states, it is simply impossible to hope for disarmament agreements without changing those relations. But since it is commonly acknowledged that the arms race today is, in and of itself, one of the most serious sources of mutual distrust and contradictions among states, changing their political relations without curbing the arms race is also hardly possible. The result is a closed circle; without breaking out of it, it really is impossible to hope for complete, or even for partial, arms limitation. When the issue is put this way, the basis for practical steps is lost, and all that remains is a subject for endless discussions and mutual accusations.

It seems that there is only one way out of that circle. It must be admitted that, although political conflicts in relations among states really do lie at the original basis of the arms race, in the past 40 years the military rivalry between the major powers, especially in the area of nuclear arms, has considerably outgrown the political contradictions that initially gave rise to it and has largely become separate from them.

The arms race has acquired a powerful momentum, formed its own, exceptionally complex mechanism of reproduction, and established its own laws and cycles. That which E.A. Pozdnyakov considers a transient, temporary effect of the "reverse action" of means on policy, an "optical illusion" leading to an exaggeration of the "dimension and significance" of the means,[4] is precisely the key problem today, and a long-range problem at that.

The military sphere is not unique in this regard. It is sufficient to look around to see, in practically every area of society's life, immense problems created because effects have turned into causes, tactics have turned into strategy, and means have become ends in themselves and are generating their own logic of development, leaving the original ends far behind.

---

[3]See *Disarmament and ·Security Yearbook, 1986* [*Razoruzheniye i bezopasnost 1986. Yezhegodnik*], Vol. 1, pp. 191, 220.
[4]*MEMO*, No. 10, 1987, p. 31.

These patterns only stand out especially distinctly in the military area. The dynamics of the arms race are fed by the energy of gigantic military-industrial, bureaucratic establishments, the powerful impetus of the scientific and technological revolution, and the tireless refinement of strategic thinking. Multiply this by the solid curtain of secrecy behind which lack of oversight and irresponsibility in the expenditure of vast resources are often concealed, by jingoistic slogans that hide chauvinism and narrow-minded ideas about other peoples, and by a fear, which paralyzes rational thought, in the face of boundless destructive might in the hands of other powers against which there is no defense, and the driving momentum of this flywheel appears in a scale that is closer to reality.

Its ever-faster revolutions have not only long since become divorced from their initial political motivation, they have even outgrown any minimally rational military considerations. (For example, what sort of actions could nearly 200 NATO and Warsaw Treaty divisions conduct in Europe if the two alliances' 7,000 to 8,000 units of tactical nuclear weapons were put to use, which would make the continent permanently uninhabitable?) From every indication, the levels of military confrontation, military programs, and strategic concepts themselves have turned into an extremely important, although highly specific, area and form of expression of the political relations among states. This area is becoming increasingly isolated from other aspects of international politics, but it represents for those politics the danger of the most destructive and irreparable consequences, consequences with which no disputed issue in contemporary international life is commensurate.

But it is precisely because military-strategic reality is a special form of expression of political relations among states that it is open to political influence; moreover, that influence is also exerted in a specific form of relations: through disarmament negotiations and corresponding agreements. And for major advances to be made along this path, it is not necessary to wait until the political first causes of the arms race are eliminated. Disarmament efforts and steps themselves, which enjoy increasingly wide support from world public opinion, are changing the political relations among states and actively and positively affecting as important an area of those relations as military-strategic relations.

In this connection it seems that the example of the Treaty on the Elimination of Medium- and Shorter-Range Missiles that is cited by E.A. Pozdnyakov is precisely evidence against his thesis, rather than for it. The treaty, of course, has drastically changed military-strategic relations between the U.S.S.R. and the United States, and the situation in Europe and Asia; and the overall world political situation has also unquestionably improved. The treaty was necessarily preceded by significant changes in attitudes and views in both the Soviet Union and the United States. But no political first causes of the arms race were eliminated in advance, and the remaining military programs proceed at full pace. (If anyone has proof to the contrary, I would be interested and glad to hear it.)

The example of the treaty confirms precisely the other point of view. And in that sense it is symptomatic that this agreement, which is in many respects unprecedented, was signed with the Reagan administration—the same administration that in preceding years had done a great deal to revive the Cold War, which served as the first cause of the modern-day arms race (modern-day in terms of its participants and the classes of weapons involved). At the same time, it is obvious that if a pause in the disarmament process sets in during the next few years, and the fast pace that has been set is lost, the arms race will once again prevail and will "make up for lost time" even without any additional political causes.

To prevent such a development of events, many problems must be solved—not just practical problems, but some very serious theoretical ones, as well.

The Problem of Strategic Stability

One such problem is the relationship between the objective military-technological possibility and the political probability of nuclear war. Negotiations on arms reductions influence mainly the former, although agreements in that area unquestionably improve overall political relations among states, and that contributes, in turn, to peaceful settlement of international conflicts whose escalation might lead to a nuclear war. It seems that the link between the physical possibility and political probability of a nuclear war is provided by the degree of stability in the military-strategic situation.

The concept of stability has to do with how easy it is to remove a given object from its existing state, and how difficult it is to return it to that state. Consequently, as research by the Committee of Soviet Scientists in Defense of Peace and Against the Nuclear Threat has shown[5] with respect to military-strategic equilibrium—the main objective factor in preventing nuclear war—the concept of stability, should have to do with how great the probability and danger of launching a nuclear conflict are in terms of the given correlation of the sides'

---

[5]See *Strategic Stability Under the Conditions of Radical Reductions in Nuclear Weapons* [*Strategicheskaya stabilnost v usloviyakh radikalnykh sokrashcheniy yadernykh vooruzheniy*] (Committee of Soviet Scientists in Defense of Peace and Against the Nuclear Threat), Moscow, 1987.

strategic weapons. More specifically, the most important aspect of stability evidently is the extent to which the constituent elements of the given strategic correlation of forces increase or decrease the possibility of delivering a first strike in a situation of acute crisis, that is, the way in which those elements affect the material aspect of the danger of launching a thermonuclear war.

In this connection, of course, it would be wrong to turn the significance of purely military factors into an absolute. In a conflict, the political prerequisites and goals of states have been and continue to be the determining factors, and their relation to the purely military situation has always been of an extremely complex, dialectical nature as to the danger that a crisis will turn into a war. Under present conditions, however, the influence of military-strategic factors on the development of potential crisis situations substantially increases.

This is due, first of all, to destructive power that has grown beyond all precedent, to the speed and range of the weapons, and to the catastrophic consequences of their use—and, at the same time, to the unprecedented increase in the technical and organizational complexity of military mechanisms. They are geared to previously planned and fine-tuned interaction among a tremendous number of elements and performers that are coordinated to the minute, even the second, and that encompass the land, the sea, and the air—and lately, more and more, outer space as well. This turns the contemporary armed forces of the principal powers, and especially their strategic nuclear "aggregates," into a powerful factor weighing on the choice of steps in a crisis, and increasingly forcing on politicians a special logic of action with a powerful mixture of strategic, operational, and tactical determinants.

Selection of criteria for evaluating the stability of the correlation of forces as the result of different options for reduction of SOAs is dictated to a critical extent by determining what strategic goals an opposing side might pursue in delivering a nuclear first strike.

According to Soviet strategic views, the most probable and primary objective of nuclear aggression might be to reduce retributive might, that is, to prevent a retaliatory strike, or to substantially reduce the damage it would cause.[6]

It should be noted that reducing the damage in a nuclear clash, while a permissible military goal, can hardly be accepted as a state's political goal in a war. After all, the most reliable means of reducing the damage to any state would be to prevent the unleashing of a nuclear conflict in the first place. Nonetheless, a nuclear cataclysm could

---

[6]D. F. Ustinov, "Avert the Threat of Nuclear War" (*Pravda*, July 12, 1982); *For the Sake of Peace on Earth: the Soviet Program for the '80s in Action* [*Radi mira na zemle. Sovetskaya programma dlya 80-x godov v deystvii*], Materials and Documents, Moscow, 1983, p. 184.

evidently be the continuation of a certain military strategy that had gotten out of the control of politics and was acting according to its own laws. The political goals of states can clash and result in a military conflict, including one involving their direct use of conventional armed forces and weapons against each other. It is precisely in that situation, when both the stakes and the losses in the course of a conflict have already become substantial, and when the leaders of the hostile states cannot stop the escalation of military actions and settle the conflict by peaceful means, that strategic logic threatens to prevail over common sense.

As noted by the late, prematurely departed V.I. Gantman, a major Soviet scholar and one of the founders of our theory of international relations, "after arising as a political relation, an international conflict acquires a certain independence and a logic of its own development, and it becomes capable on its own of influencing, in various ways, other relations that develop in the context of the given conflict, and even of influencing the nature of the contradictions on which that conflict is based and the means of resolving them."[7] In a case in which a strategic nuclear strike by the other side seems inevitable or very probable, and in which the estimated difference in damage sustained from a first strike and a second strike is relatively high, an incentive may arise to deliver a preemptive nuclear strike in the calculation that the retaliatory strike will be of less force than it would be under other conditions.

In such a situation, regardless of the states' original political motives and goals, it is precisely the condition of the strategic correlation of forces—the existence of equilibrium or, to the contrary, the superiority of one side—that can be a decisive factor capable of tipping the balance in one direction or another. Negotiations on SOAs should mainly serve the purposes of reducing the probability of a nuclear disaster by strengthening stability at reduced levels of strategic equilibrium.

Both the theoretical and practical importance of the scientific study of the problems of strategic stability is obvious. And it is equally obvious that no progress will be made here without a detailed analysis of the dynamics of the military balance, strategic doctrines and concepts, and the specifics of arms reduction negotiations.

A 50 Percent Reduction in Strategic Offensive Arms

During the Washington summit meeting the sides were able to bring their positions significantly closer in order to prepare joint

---

[7]*International Conflicts of the Present Day* [*Mezhdunarodnyye konflikty sovremennosti*] (principal editor, V.I. Gantman), Moscow, 1983, p. 18.

wording regarding the key elements of the first stage in the reduction of SOAs. In particular, they reaffirmed the previous principles of a 50 percent reduction in SOAs to the level of 6,000 nuclear warheads and 1,600 delivery vehicles for each side. They also agreed on a limit of 154 units for heavy ICBMs and 1,540 for nuclear warheads on them. A new development was setting a sublevel of 4,900 units for warheads on land- and sea-based ballistic missiles. The joint statement also reflected an agreement that, as the result of reductions, the total throw-weight of Soviet ICBMs and SLBMs [submarine-launched ballistic missiles] would be reduced by 50 percent, and that level would not be exceeded by either side. Rules for counting warheads on ICBMs and SLBMs were agreed on. A decision was recorded to focus attention on the rules for counting air-launched cruise missiles (ALCMs), and on limiting long-range sea-launched cruise missiles (SLCMs) with nuclear warheads to a separate ceiling above the aforementioned limits of 6,000 and 1,600 units for nuclear warheads and delivery vehicles, respectively. Measures for verifying and monitoring fulfillment of a future agreement on SOAs underwent considerable development on the basis of the experience gained with the Treaty on the Elimination of Medium- and Shorter-Range Missiles.[8]

At the same time, substantial differences remain between the two powers. The essence of the disagreements between the sides on the reduction of SOAs is rooted in the Soviet Union's and the United States' substantially different approaches to the essence of military-strategic equilibrium and strategic stability.

The concept of strategic stability on which U.S. policy is based postulates that land-based ICBMs are destabilizing, since they are best suited to a first strike against the other side's strategic forces (especially their analogous component) for the purpose of weakening them, and at the same time are themselves most vulnerable to such a strike by the enemy. This supposedly creates a dual incentive for their preemptive use. And submarine-launched missiles and bombers carrying cruise missiles are supposedly intended only for a retaliatory strike (the former are insufficiently accurate and have undependable communications with their headquarters, and the latter require many hours of flight time to their targets). Consequently, the more strictly ICBMs are reduced and limited, the less the likelihood of a first strike, and the greater the strategic stability.

Relying on its own understanding of stability, the United States has endeavored to achieve agreement terms that would change the structure, qualitative makeup, and consequently, military capability of the Soviet Union's strategic forces. From the time of the Reykjavik

---

[8]See *Pravda*, Dec. 12, 1987.

meeting, the American side, in defining ICBMs as the most "destabilizing" type of strategic weapon, has insisted on a treaty's including sublevels that would additionally limit the number of warheads on certain components of the strategic triad (combined ICBMs and SLBMs, and ICBMs separately), and even on certain specific types of land-based ballistic missiles. These terms presuppose a substantial restructuring of the traditional composition of Soviet strategic forces, a composition which stems from the specific features of the Soviet Union's geostrategic situation, its military organizational and technical development, and the history of the development of its military doctrine and strategy.

According to the American proposals, in addition to quantitative sublevels, strict qualitative limits should be placed on heavy ICBMs—traditionally the key element of Soviet SOAs—since it would be forbidden to produce, test, or deploy modernized versions, or to carry out the modification or conversion of their launchers. Another condition would be banning and dismantling mobile land-based ICBMs. It is directed simultaneously at two Soviet programs: the RS-22 (SS-24) ICBM systems with multiple reentry vehicles (MRVs), and modernized single-warhead ICBMs of the RS-12M (SS-25) type.[9] The Soviet Union would thereby be deprived of the possibility of improving the survivability of its strategic missile forces in the face of deployment of new U.S. systems (the MX, the Trident-2, cruise missiles) that have greater capability of striking hardened stationary targets such as ICBM silos.

The U.S. condition banning mobile ICBMs is officially based on the difficulties of verification, particularly verification of a ban on the capability to rapidly reload ICBM launchers. It is obvious, however, that given the comprehensive verification methods, including on-site inspection currently being discussed by the two powers, perfectly reliable guarantees could be provided against the possibility of reloading the launchers of mobile land-based ICBMs. It is instructive that this point in the official U.S. position has drawn serious criticism from both the U.S. "strategic community," including its conservative representatives, and from Congress.

The administration has demonstrated a diametrically opposite attitude toward issues of verification where American programs are concerned. The United States is by no means arguing for restrictions on long-range sea-launched cruise missiles, despite the understanding in principle about them reached in Reykjavik. Yet sea-launched cruise missiles are a plainly destabilizing weapon system. They possess heightened accuracy and the capability of destroying highly hardened

---

[9]*Disarmament and Security Yearbook, 1986,* Vol. 1, p. 26.

targets, and their launching and flight are difficult to detect using space and ground early-warning systems, which creates a threat to the other side's strategic forces, as well as to its command and communications system.

The United States is planning to deploy about 4,000 sea-launched cruise missiles of the Tomahawk type in 10 various modifications, with nuclear and conventional warheads, on multipurpose nuclear submarines of the Los Angeles and Sturgeon type (altogether, on 93 nuclear submarines by the mid 1990s), as well as on large guided-missile ships of the New Jersey, Virginia, California, Ticonderoga, and Burke type (altogether, about 100 existing and planned ships). It is characteristic that in this case the problem of verification does not worry the U.S. administration, and it refuses to discuss limitations on sea-launched cruise missiles, except for one type that carries a nuclear warhead, although it is practically impossible to distinguish the individual versions of that system on the basis of external features.

One cannot fail to note one circumstance of a general nature. Even without any sublevels and qualitative limitations, a 50 percent reduction in SOAs to ceilings of 6,000 warheads and 1,600 delivery vehicles would affect the Soviet Union's strategic forces and programs rather substantially. The point is, first, that the United States has a more balanced distribution of delivery vehicles and warheads among the three components of its strategic triad. Second, in the arms race the U.S.S.R., by and large, has responded to U.S. actions with an average lag of five years in the phases of deploying systems. The Soviet strategic forces have more single-warhead delivery vehicles than the U.S. strategic forces. In 1987 single-warhead missiles and bombers without cruise missiles constituted 49 percent of the U.S.S.R.'s delivery vehicles and 41 percent of those of the United States.[10] At the same time, the Soviet multiple-warhead ICBMs, SLBMs, and heavy bombers (with cruise missiles) are about five to seven years "younger" than the American ones, and the U.S.S.R.'s most expensive military units (figured in terms of the cost of a prototype), i.e., nuclear-powered submarines carrying missiles with MRVs, are, on the average, 15 years younger than their American counterparts.

This means that the Soviet Union would have to carry out its 50 percent reduction by eliminating systems that are much less obsolete, especially with respect to submarines. The removal of relatively old single-warhead missiles and planes would provide a substantial reduction in delivery vehicles (more than 50 percent), but a very small reduction in warheads (13 percent). By eliminating obsolete single-warhead missiles, multi-warhead delivery vehicles, and old

---

[10]*Pravda*, Feb. 8, 1988.

submarines, the United States theoretically could more painlessly reduce its SOAs by 60 percent of its delivery vehicles and 65 percent of its warheads (based on the counting rules).[11] That would provide its 50 percent reduction and create a certain additional "reserve" allowing the deployment of a new generation of strategic systems.

As previously noted, at the Washington meeting a compromise sublevel of 4,900 units was agreed on for the total number of warheads on ICBMs and SLBMs. Knowing the counting rules,[12] it is not difficult to calculate that with the deployment, say, of up to 3,300 warheads on ICBMs, the Soviet Union could have a maximum of 1,600 warheads on SLBMs, that is, it could have five Typhoon-type submarines with SS-N-20 missiles, and 9 to 10 submarines carrying SS-N-23 SLBMs (or, as an option, eight Typhoon-type nuclear-powered, ballistic-missile submarines alone, or some combination based on the rate of three submarines of the second type in place of one Typhoon-class submarine).

In any variation, the Soviet Union would have to remove more than 50 ballistic-missile submarines from its SOAs, including some relatively new nuclear-powered ballistic-missile submarines that have been launched since the late 1970s, as well as at least 500 old single-warhead ICBMs of the SS-11, SS-19, and SS-18 types (designated in the U.S.S.R. as RS-16s, RS-18s, and RS-20s), which have come on line since 1975.[13]

As for the U.S. strategic forces, by virtue of the objective circumstances that have been noted, they would be affected somewhat more "mercifully." With the removal of 28 obsolete submarines (built from 1962 to 1967) carrying Poseidon and Trident-1 SLBMs, 260 old B-52 bombers (made in the late 1950s and early 1960s), and 770 Minuteman-2 and Minuteman-3 ICBMs (1965 to 1975), the United States would be able to refit its SOAs with the latest systems with relatively less difficulty. As one possible course within the limits of the aforementioned sublevels, it would have the option of deploying, for example, 17 Ohio-type submarines carrying Trident-2 SLBMs, 50 to 80 B-1B heavy bombers carrying cruise missiles,[14] and 130 Stealth-type penetration bombers, as well as 100 new MX ICBMs, while keeping about 180 Minuteman-3 missiles with new MK-12A warheads (or, as an option, by building 50 MX missiles, it could keep all 300 Minuteman-3 ICBMs in this modification, or have 180 of them and deploy an additional 500 new Midgetman mobile missiles).

---

[11]*Pravda*, Mar. 17, 1987.
[12]*Pravda*, Dec. 12, 1987.
[13]Calculated on the basis of *Pravda*, Dec. 12, 1987; *Pravda*, Feb. 8, 1988; and *Where Does the Treat to Peace Originate?* [*Otkuda iskhodit ugroza miru*], Moscow, 1982, pp. 7-8.
[14]Depending on what sort of counting rules are agreed on, that is, on how many air-launched cruise missiles are counted for every heavy bomber, the number of bombers could be even greater.

"Why do we need all these mind-boggling calculations?" ask some supporters of the "political" school. "After all, the political meaning of reducing arms arsenals is much more important." Granted, that is indisputably the case. The treaty will improve Soviet-American relations and the entire world political climate. But just what does that mean, to put the question more specifically? How do you measure the positive changes, how do you weigh the potential negative consequences, and how do you eliminate them? Obviously, the chief political essence of the treaty is that it should help reduce the threat of nuclear war. And that requires more appreciable and stable changes than a good mood among the world public (although that too, of course, plays no small role). These changes should be expressed in a reduction of the material possibility and, therefore—all else being equal—political probability of a first nuclear strike in a hypothetical crisis situation—a first strike that could launch a nuclear war. And here you will not get by with general discussions. You have to calculate, analyze, and formulate well-founded concepts of the sort of strategic goals an adversary might pursue in launching a first strike, the factors in the military balance that contribute to that, the factors that discourage it, and how the relationship between them might change as the result of any given draft treaty.

As noted above, the sublevels and other limitations proposed by Washington are based on a detailed concept of "strategic stability." This concept was developed and widely discussed in the United States over the course of two decades among specialists, politicians, and representatives of the mass media. Although the concept is not monolithic and has a number of variants in the United States, its general propositions provide the basis for both the U.S. negotiating line and its strategic programs as complementary elements of a single policy of "providing security."

In actuality, it has many vulnerable points and has been subjected to serious criticism in Soviet scholarly literature.[15] But since strengthening strategic stability occupies such an important place in negotiations between the U.S.S.R. and the United States, it is obvious that the Soviet approach to this issue requires more detailed and comprehensive explanation in the context of the disclosure of the U.S.S.R.'s defensive military doctrine. After all, at the present stage, until nuclear arms are eliminated, both the U.S.S.R.'s armed forces and its policy of achieving radical disarmament agreements serve a single goal—preventing nuclear war.

---

[15]See Strategic Stability Under the Conditions of Radical Reductions in Nuclear Arms; A.G. Arbatov, A.A. Vasilyev, and A.A. Kokoshin, "Nuclear Weapons and Strategic Stability" (SshA: ekonomika, politika, ideologiya [The United States: Economics, Politics, Ideology], Nos. 9 and 10, 1987).

Where it has not yet been possible to reach agreement, the balance must be maintained through military programs that provide deterrence [sderzhivaniye] through the potential for a retaliatory strike. It is advisable to measure that potential according to the principle of reasonable sufficiency, taking into account the other side's forces and programs. But where it is possible to limit U.S. forces through agreements, the need for certain of the Soviet Union's nuclear weapons is eliminated, and they can be given up as part of those agreements. The decisions of the 27th CPSU Congress, which emphasized political means of strengthening security, call for priority to be given to precisely that course. In speaking at the 42nd session of the U.N. General Assembly, V.F. Petrovskiy, U.S.S.R. deputy minister of foreign affairs, emphasized: "We proceed from the premise that movement toward a nuclear-free world can be accomplished in stages, in terms of both the participants involved and the weapons covered, and at each stage and over the course of this entire process, there should be a steady strengthening of security and enhancement of strategic stability. At the intermediate stages of that movement, agreements should be reached at least on what constitutes reasonable sufficiency in both nuclear and conventional arms, and on maintaining strategic stability at the lowest possible level of that sufficiency."[16]

A comprehensive explanation of the Soviet concept of stability would persuasively show how our strategy of preventing war and orienting entirely toward a retaliatory strike determines the existing and future structure and the basic quantitative and qualitative characteristics of Soviet SOAs.

Greater glasnost regarding these matters cannot weaken security. After all, the principal aim in Soviet military doctrine (and consequently, in strategy, tactics, and military development) is to prevent nuclear war, and not to "surprise" an adversary, if he should decide to attack. Of course, in a number of respects a certain military uncertainty reduces the likelihood of aggression. The actual details of operational planning and the operation of the command, communications, and warning system, of course, should be kept secret (and incidentally, are kept secret not only by the Soviet Union but by America), so that the other side may not attempt to take advantage of such information to acquire the capability for a "decapitating" or "disarming" strike. Yet uncertainty proves absolutely counterproductive if the other side uses it to launch a campaign about the "Soviet threat" to justify new rounds of the arms race and to try to force inequitable agreement terms on the Soviet Union.

---

[16]*Vestnik MID SSSR* [*Bulletin of the U.S.S.R. Ministry of Foreign Affairs*], No. 9, Dec. 10, 1987, pp. 10-11.

The political approach to ensuring security presupposes major reductions in both old and new arms. The scholars of the "political" school correctly point out that there is no need to regret the anticipated removal of submarines, missiles, and airplanes from arsenals—that, after all, is the real disarmament process. But the stability of the strategic equilibrium should not be unsettled in the course of that process.

Since the sublevels presently being discussed, as pointed out above, would significantly limit the numbers of Soviet land-based ICBMs, SLBMs, and submarines themselves, we naturally cannot be indifferent to which new systems the United States will start deploying in the 1980s and 1990s within the framework of agreed-upon overall ceilings and sublevels. Cutting SOAs in half should result in strengthening stability and limiting U.S. counterforce potential (especially its ability to strike hardened targets and cover regions where land-based mobile missiles are deployed). That goal would be advanced by establishing certain additional sublevels or structural quotas on the strategic forces that will remain after a reduction.

For example, we are referring to limits on certain weapons systems within each of the components of the strategic triad. Let us recall that at the Washington summit, agreement was reached on a limit of 1,540 warheads for heavy ICBMs within a sublevel of 4,900 warheads on land-based and sea-launched ballistic missiles. In this connection, it seems, stability would be improved by also establishing special limits within the sea and air components of SOAs, in order to limit the deployment of destabilizing systems. This pertains to new SLBMs of the Trident-2 type (along with their technical analogues in the U.S.S.R., of course). Then, instead of deploying Trident-2 missiles on 17 Ohio-type submarines, the United States could deploy them on a smaller number of such boats, and the number of powerful and accurate counterforce weapons, which undermine stability and raise the threat of a first strike, would be reduced accordingly.

As for air-launched cruise missiles, the sublevel of 4,900 warheads (out of 6,000) on ICBMs and SLBMs presupposes the limitation of air-launched cruise missiles to a maximum of 1,100 units. By insisting on a larger number of them, the United States thereby erodes the significance of the 4,900 subceiling. After all, the other side could also put forward a proposal to raise that subceiling within the overall limits in order to increase the number of highly survivable retaliatory-strike weapons in other components of the triad. Since the United States insists on limiting ICBM warheads to 3,300 units (in October 1987 the U.S.S.R. proposed a version of that sublevel of 3,000 to 3,300 units), it would probably be useful to turn that sublevel into a limit on the concentration of warheads (i.e., 50 to 55 percent) in any one component of the triad, whether land, sea, or air.

As noted above, the U.S. terms for a 50 percent reduction assume a serious change in the traditional structure of Soviet SOAs. In this connection a question arises as to whether that structure is something sacred that will tolerate no changes. Obviously, that is not the case. Lately we have witnessed many traditions that once seemed unshakable undergoing revision for the overall good. And incidentally, even the structure of Soviet SOAs has historically changed quite substantially. For example, until 1967 the U.S.S.R. had absolutely no nuclear-powered ballistic-missile submarines, which both sides' specialists assign to the operational component of SOAs; when SALT II was signed (1972), sea-launched missiles accounted for approximately 20 percent of all Soviet warheads, while in 1986 they accounted for more than 30 percent.[17] The percentage of warheads on heavy bombers, which now amounts to about 5 percent, will increase (according to the sublevel of 4,900 units established in Washington) to nearly 20 percent, if the total number of the U.S.S.R.'s warheads is no less than the stipulated 6,000 after the 50 percent reduction.

So the question lies not in the unalterability of the structure, but in arranging matters in such a way that, within the limits of a 50 percent reduction in SOAs, the U.S.S.R.'s strategic forces are optimally suited to the performance of their main task: preventing an unpunished nuclear strike by relying on their readiness to deliver a retaliatory strike capable of causing unacceptable damage to an aggressor.[18] The principle of reasonable sufficiency, however, does not presuppose a restructuring of SOAs after the American model, toward which agreement terms are pushing us. On the contrary, the reasonable sufficiency principle would actually rule that out. After all, the structure and technical characteristics of the U.S. forces embody certain strategic concepts that are unacceptable to us ("counterforce disarming strike," for example, or "limited and protracted nuclear war"). Neutralizing these plans presupposes not the preparation of analogous plans and weapons, but maintaining the ability to perform the aforementioned task despite any new U.S. strategic arms. In addition, there are objective differences in the two sides' geostrategic situations and technical development.

Following the principle of ensuring security by political means, one could propose even further-reaching measures in a subsequent reduction of SOAs. For example, setting special, individual sublevels for the number of warheads on each side's systems that the other side considers to be destabilizing and the most dangerous. These subceil-

---

[17]Calculated on the basis of *Where Does the Threat to Peace Originate?* [*Otkuda iskhodit ugroza mira*], Moscow, 1987; p. 8; and *Disarmament and Security Yearbook, 1986*, Vol. 1, p. 39.
    [18]See D.T. Yazov, *Guarding Socialism and the Peace* [*Na strazhe sotsializma i mira*], Moscow, 1987, p. 34.

ings would encompass MX, Trident-2, and air-launched cruise-missile systems on the American side, and analogous systems, plus heavy missiles, on the Soviet. In that case, in addition to the reduction and limitation of a number of Soviet systems, substantial limits would be placed on dangerous new American weapons—with a considerable gain for the stability and security of both sides.

More radical steps are also possible, especially in light of the U.S.S.R.'s intention not to stop at 50 percent reductions. It makes no sense to put these steps off for long; after all, in the next five to seven years the deployment of new systems, even within lowered quantitative ceilings, could cost immense amounts of money, and that, in and of itself, will make subsequent, deeper reductions more difficult, not to mention the potentially destabilizing effect of a new generation of weapons. In this connection the Soviet scholar A.A. Kokoshin has put forward an important theoretical proposition, which is fully supported by experience: "As opposed to efforts to restore and maintain military-strategic parity," he stresses, "strengthening strategic stability unilaterally is much more difficult, and sometimes almost impossible. Hence an important feature of stability is the requirement that there must be reciprocity in order to achieve it" (that is, to achieve appropriate agreements—A.A.).[19]

Proceeding from considerations of improving the survivability of SOAs, to prohibit mobile land-based ICBMs[20] in the course of reducing strategic arms while ensuring adequate verification capability is absolutely unwarranted. Of course, sea-launched cruise missiles should be limited as one of the most destabilizing types of strategic weapons. If the United States is prepared to discuss limiting only sea-launched cruise-missiles with nuclear warheads, it should itself provide assistance in ensuring reliable verification by employing new technical means and on-site inspections. That is exactly the way it puts the question with respect to mobile land-based ICBMs and other Soviet systems. If verification measures and military programs come into conflict, it is the latter, not the former, that should be sacrificed for the sake of concluding more radical agreements. The political approach to ensuring security on the basis of the comprehensive analysis of both strategic and technical questions should also manifest itself here.

*   *   *

An analysis of the problems of a deep reduction in strategic arms also makes it possible to draw certain preliminary conclusions of a

---

[19]A.G. Arbatov, A.A. Vasilyev, and A.A. Kokoshin, "Nuclear Weapons and Strategic Stability (First Article)," (*SShA: ekonomika, politika, ideologiya*, No. 9, 1987, p. 10).

[20]The mobility of launching complexes makes it more difficult for the other side to target them with its weapons employing inertial guidance systems and programmed flight control, because of the uncertainty of the location of the targets, which in this case are ICBM launchers.

methodological nature. The dispute between the "politicians" and the "technocrats" (the latter-day "poets" and "physicists") usually lacks real grounds. In large part, it does not stem from different approaches to the problem, but reflects the desire of one side to avoid the systematic study of extremely complex military-strategic subject matter (which does not fit entirely within the traditional framework of the humanities and social sciences), and the readiness of the other to engage in this painstaking and endless work, sometimes starting with the very basics. However, life and work resolve these disputes quite clearly. When all the general (so to speak, "poetic") words have been spoken and it is necessary to move on to specific deeds, nothing can take the place of the professional and detailed study of military-strategic problems.

It is another matter that the problems of security or, to take an even narrower focus, the problems of disarmament—as one aspect of them—are by no means exhausted by the study of military-strategic and military-technological questions. They encompass a broad range of subjects in international politics, domestic policy, economics, and social psychology. For example, evaluation of the prospects for a 50 percent reduction cannot be reduced solely to the military-strategic, technological, and treaty-negotiation and legal aspects of the question. Here it is absolutely essential to also analyze the U.S. domestic political situation (including the results of the process of ratifying the Treaty on the Elimination of Medium- and Shorter-Range Missiles), the economic situation, the general development of Soviet-American relations, and the two powers' relations with their allies that affect the negotiations in Geneva. All these subjects require special study and for this reason are not dealt with in this article. Here it is the specialists in the appropriate fields who should have their say. But that should obviously be something perfectly concrete and entirely different from abstract arguments in favor of disarmament.

In general, one can express the view that the problems of disarmament are a specific, fully independent, new scholarly discipline. It lies at the juncture between the natural and exact sciences, between political and economic research, between military science and art, and between history and psychology. It is linked directly to practice in the form of diplomatic negotiations, is continually nourished by experience in those negotiations, and draws from that experience generalizations and laws that should serve as the basis for specific forecasts and recommendations. This discipline continuously undergoes a strict process of testing by practice. And, like any true scholarly discipline, it does not brook empty verbiage, careless formulas, or hasty ideas, and it exacts revenge for being dealt with arbitrarily.

For their part, the so-called "technocrats" should not, of course, turn into true technocrats in the negative sense of that word. Weapons systems, strategic concepts, methods of assessing the military balance, levels and sublevels of arms reductions—all that, of course, is not an end in itself, but only a means for implementing and a form for expressing policy that strengthens or, to the contrary, undermines security. This subordination should especially not be overlooked now, when the new philosophy of security presupposes a fresh view of the world, a view "without glasses and blinders," and the search for bold, nontraditional ways of curbing the nuclear threat.

The "politician" scholars who urge us not to be concerned with the "hardware" and to stay above the prosaic details are not contributing to the development of the scholarly base in the given field, a field where—there is no use denying it—for a variety of both objective and subjective reasons, the room for development is still much broader than it is most other fields of political science and economics. Believing that they are promoting the political approach, the "poets" are actually, without wanting to, reinforcing the truly technocratic point of view. In scholarly discussions, naturally, the representatives of that viewpoint do not take all that "poetry" seriously, but they often fail to encounter an alternative viewpoint that is elaborated in specific detail. Fine-sounding, rosy sentiments that lack any specific content often burst like soap bubbles when they come up against the sharp corners of military-strategic reality and negotiating practice. One can extol the political approach to one's heart's content, but that approach is nothing but rhetoric as long as it is not expressed in terms of levels of arms reductions, the conditions of their qualitative limitation, and alternatives to the evolution of the military balance and strategic conceptions. In addition, that approach must still be substantiated and defended in scholarly debate both at home and with foreign specialists.

Obviously, those are the sort of responsible opinions that practice is currently awaiting from scholarship. As the remarkable Russian historian V. O. Klyuchevskiy has written, "the price of all knowledge is determined by its connection with our needs, aspirations, and actions; otherwise, knowledge becomes the simple ballast of memory, suitable for reducing the rolling in life only of an empty ship that is sailing without any real, valuable cargo."[21]

---

[21]V. O. Klyuchevskiy, "Course in Russian History," *Works* [*Sochineniya*], Volume 1, Moscow, 1987, p. 60.

National, State, and Class Interests in International Relations

ELGIZ ABDULOVICH POZDNYAKOV*

What are national and state interests, and are state interests identical to the interests of the ruling classes? These and other questions remain without a clear answer. The answers that do exist in current scholarship cannot be deemed fully satisfactory, since they are often based on existing stereotypes and established dogmatic ideas. The author considers the notion of international relations as a sphere of class struggle to be a prime example of such dogmatic stereotypes. Without claiming to offer a comprehensive study of these problems, he analyzes several aspects of them that are important primarily for understanding the processes taking place in the area of states' foreign-policy activities and relations among them.

The success that perestroika is enjoying in the U.S.S.R., particularly its success in the area of social consciousness, depends to a considerable extent not only on the creative development of Marxist-Leninist theory, but also, and possibly to an even greater degree, on liberation from existing stereotypes and ossified dogmatic schemata and patterns, rote learning, and an array of commonplace quotations. Yet for many people these have all become a familiar and convenient means of seeing reality that frees them from the need to constantly interpret a rapidly changing world.

Today the process of rethinking domestic socioeconomic relations is proceeding rather rapidly and boldly. However, the study of foreign policy and relations among states has barely been touched. Above all, one feels the lack of theory—not that "limp, flaccid theory that is concerned with how to serve practice as adroitly as possible,"[1] but a harmonious and well-developed concept of the contemporary world based on Marxist-Leninist methodology and a profound understanding of what is going on. While Soviet diplomacy is putting forward far-

*Doctor of history, lead researcher at the U.S.S.R. Academy of Sciences' Institute of World Economy and International Relations [IMEMO]. This article appeared in the May 1988 issue of *MEMO*.
[1]See E.A. Shevardnadze's report at the May 3, 1987, conference in the U.S.S.R. Ministry of Foreign Affairs (*Vestnik MID SSSR* [*Bulletin of the U.S.S.R. Ministry of Foreign Affairs*], No. 1, Aug. 5, 1987, p. 19).

reaching and radical proposals and solutions that are changing, before our very eyes, ideas that have remained fixed for decades, the study of international relations still exists in relative tranquility, and sacred cows of dogmatism and orthodoxy continue to graze peacefully there, troubled by no one.

We have learned, not from theory but from life itself, that it is just as impermissible to treat the laws of economics arbitrarily as it is the laws of physics. We learned about the former from stagnant phenomena in our economy, and about the latter from Chernobyl. But the system of relations among states also has its own laws, and violating them, especially in our times, is fraught with the danger of a considerably broader-scale accident than an accident at a single nuclear reactor. Here, as in the economy, nothing can be done by relying solely on appeals, abstract formulas, and starry-eyed wishes. After all, we are talking about a self-regulating system of interaction among states that is distinguished by a high degree of interdependence. There are no isolated phenomena or processes in the system, nor, in principle, can there be—each of them affects the entire system of relations in one way or another and entails appropriate consequences both for the system itself and for individual states. The states, in turn, are guided in their activities by *interests* that are determined by many and diverse internal and external circumstances. To the extent that these circumstances differ for each state, their interests also differ, and frequently they can be opposed and antagonistic. At the same time, states live and act in a system of relations that is the same for all of them. The interaction of states within the framework of that system inevitably also gives rise to certain goals and objectives that are the same for all of them, and to a greater or lesser commonality of foreign-policy interests, which compels them, willy-nilly, to act together in many cases, especially in matters of maintaining and ensuring peace and security. Without that commonality of interests, relations among states would resemble a "war of all against all"; without it, cooperation among states and realization of the principles of peaceful coexistence would be impossible.

The fact that the objective basis of such commonality has expanded in our time does not, however, reduce the importance of the special, national interests of states, and consequently, does not eliminate differences and contradictions between them. As long as states exist, their special interests will also exist, and therefore so will clashes and rivalry both between them and between their national interests and the common interests. It is all a matter of degree. In former times the foreign-policy activities of states were directed primarily at securing only their own national interests, often at the expense of the interests of other states. If wars resulted from this, even when they were of the very broadest scale and greatest destructiveness, they did not threaten to destroy all humanity. But today, when the opposing sides have nuclear weapons that are capable of destroying all life, defending only their own interests and ignoring the close interdependence of all phenomena and processes in the system of relations among states may have fateful consequences and confront the world with the threat of annihilation.

The new situation also dictates a new logic of political thinking and a new content and new forms for the foreign-policy activities of states, especially those on which the fate of the world primarily depends.

In this connection, the theory of international relations is confronted with the task of more thoroughly investigating such key concepts as national and state interests, their relation both to one another and to class interests, and the relationship of national interests and the common interests of states.

National and State Interests

In the sense in which it is used, the concept "national interest" usually coincides with the concept "state interests," and usually serves as a synonym for it. At the same time, in both the specialized literature and the press one may encounter the "separation," and even the opposition, of these concepts. Who is not familiar, say, with the following expression from a newspaper analysis: "The foreign policy of such and such a state is not in keeping with its national interests"? On the whole, one can note that in everyday practice two interpretations of the concept "national interest" have established themselves—as a synonym for state interest, and as the interest of a nation, which not only differs from but, to a certain extent, stands in opposition to state interest. Which of these interpretations is correct? I think there is no simple answer here. Both are correct, and there is no contradiction in that: everything depends on the concrete historical circumstances (both internal and external) in which the state in question finds itself and which provide the grounds for judging whether the two sorts of interests coincide or diverge. Something else should be stressed. The fact that these interests may coincide in practice certainly does not mean that they are identical: under any conditions, they are just as different as the concepts "nation" and "state." Although the concept "nation" is used in political literature as a synonym for state just as frequently as the concept "national interests" is used as a synonym for state interests, this in no way means they are identical.

A distinction is drawn between the concepts "state" and "nation" mainly when people want to use the former to express the idea that a given people constitutes a political organism under a single government, and to use the latter to stress the internal unity of a state's population, and the homogeneity of its living conditions and traits. However, even that distinction is by no means always sustained—and not just in common usage but even in the specialized literature.[2]

The identity of national and state interests is especially obvious in matters pertaining to a state's foreign relations. State aspirations acquire the appearance of national aspirations, and in most cases that is how they are characterized. This is especially true of so-called nation-states, that is, states in which the entire population or the majority of it belongs to the same nationality. In such states, foreign-policy goals and interests often coincide with national goals and interests to such an extent that they can be distinguished only with difficulty.

Strictly speaking, foreign-policy interests and motives are undoubtedly state, rather than national, in nature. However, in political literature and the press (sometimes intentionally and sometimes out of habit, as a cliché) they are imprecisely called national interests. In theoretical research, on the other hand, it is obviously necessary to make a strict distinction between national and state interests, qualifying in every instance the special conditions under which the two may coincide. They can, of course, complement and reinforce one another, but they can also diverge sharply. Confusing these concepts or, much worse, deliberately identifying the one with the other results in distorted assessments of both sorts of interests. The urge, say, of some state for economic or political expansion, for expansion of its sphere of influence, or its desire to incorporate related population groups living on the territories of other states has often been called, and continues to this day to be called a "national aspiration" or "national tendency" toward unification, unity, and so on, whereas in actuality what is usually expressed here is much more the desire of a given state to expand the limits of its power or its economic sphere by relying on ageless national slogans.

But although foreign policy is conducted by the state, it cannot help reflecting, to one degree or another, general national interests pertaining first and foremost to questions of security, territorial integrity, and sovereignty, as well as people's related general attitudes and established stereotypes and ideas about the place and role of their state in the system of other states (attitudes and ideas which are usually shared, if not by a country's entire population, at least by its majority, regardless of internal social stratification). The nation [natsiya] (or people [narod]), as a historically established community, serves as the

---

2In his work, "Toward a Critique of the Hegelian Philosophy of Law," Marx reproached Hegel, in particular, for confusing two different concepts: the state as the aggregate, entire existence of the people, and the political state (see K. Marx and F. Engels, Works [Sochineniya], Vol. 1, p. 309).

basis on which any state regime relies in developing and implementing its foreign-policy activities. In order to enjoy "popular" support, these decisions and actions must at least outwardly accord with the perceptions, precepts, beliefs, and values—in other words, the world-view stereotypes—of a given nation.

Nation and state are engendered by the process of historical development, and the relationships between them change at various stages of that development. If, say, the national interest coincides with the state interest under certain given historical conditions, it by no means follows that this will always be the case.

State and Civil Society

So far we have viewed the national interest as something unified, as the interest of the entire nation on which the state regime presumably relies in its foreign policy. But is it correct, in principle, to say that the state's foreign-policy activities express the interests of the "entire nation" in whose interests the state supposedly acts, and does a unified national interest, the interest of the entire nation, actually exist?

If it is possible to acknowledge that the nation does exist as some sort of unity, as a community, with respect to the world outside it, it does not represent such a unity in and of itself. The nation is divided along many lines—class, political, economic, ideological, ethnic, religious, occupational, and others. Corresponding to them are various clashing, opposing, vying, or coinciding interests. And it is not so much the concept "nation" as the concept "civil society" that corresponds to that kaleidoscope of differing interests. And genuine interaction in both foreign and domestic matters takes place not between the state and the nation, but between the state and civil society.[3] Besides the nation, it unites within itself many other collectives, as well; besides national feelings, it encompasses feelings of a different sort that sometimes attain even greater force (for example, class feeling).

It is precisely the concept of civil society (or simply society), rather than the concept of nation, with which many realities of present and future world development are linked today. The *social* environment, *social* issues, *social* opinion [with this and certain other phrases

---

[3]The concept "civil society"—one of the basic concepts in the theoretical legacy of Marxism—was for a long time undeservedly forgotten in our political and philosophical literature and reduced to the concept "production relations." However, "civil society" is a broader and fuller concept than production relations. It includes the sum total of relations outside the framework of the political state—economic, national, religious, spiritual, moral, family, and cultural relations, among others—and it constitutes the real basis of the state. We note with satisfaction that this concept is regaining its "right of citizenship." In this connection, let us note A. Migranyan's profound and interesting article, "Relationships Among Individual, Society, and State in the Political Theory of Marxism, and the Problems of the Democratization of Socialist Society," which appeared in the journal *Voprosy filosofii* [*Problems in Philosophy*], No. 8, 1987.

in this list, "public" would be a better English rendering than "social" of the Russian adjective "obshchestvennyy" that is repeated here.— *Trans.*], *social* vices, *social* interests, and so forth—all these and many other concepts fully reflect the specific features of contemporary social development, at the basis of which lie *social* processes.

The social element is increasingly becoming the dominant element in the life of peoples and nations; it is penetrating every corner of life and sphere of activity, and it is breaking down national barriers and national limitations.

And this element assumes all the greater scope and importance in the life of a given people the more thoroughly it is encompassed by the process of democratization. Therefore, to be scientifically strict and objective, one must examine the relationship not between nation and state (not between national and state interests), but between civil society and state, and correspondingly—between social and state interests.[4]

According to Marxist doctrine, the state and civil society constitute a dialectical unity of form and content, in which the form is represented by the political state and the content by the civil society.[5] As a form, the state is an expression of commonality; the civil society, conversely, is the expression of difference. The state's goal is the general interest, and "without that goal the state is not a real state."[6] The state is "based on the contradiction between *social* and *private* life, on the contradiction between *common interests* and *private interests.*" Therefore, the relationship between the state and civil society is characterized by a covert or overt "conflict between the *common* interest and *private interest*, and a split between the *political state* and *civil society*"[7]—within the framework, however, of the indissoluble dialectical unity of the two. Closely interwoven, the two sides of the unity can turn for a certain time into a political commonality[8] in which the state element becomes indistinguishable from the social.

From these propositions it follows, first and foremost, that studying the state and its interests (be they domestic or foreign) independently of society and its interests and apart from them, and likewise, studying civil society and its interests independently of the state, are just as erroneous fundamentally as identifying the state and society. A science of the state that ignores civil society as the basis of any state will

---

[4]Since the concept "national interest" has already become familiar and is firmly established in the political lexicon, we will continue to use it, but in the sense of the interests of a given society as they relate to the interests of the political state, and we will specifically note cases in which it really does reflect the interests of a given nation.

[5]See K. Marx and F. Engels, *Works*, Vol. 1, pp. 253, 391-392; and Vol. 21, pp. 220, 310.

[6]K. Marx and F. Engels, *Works*, Vol. 1, pp. 233, 236.

[7]*Ibid.*, pp. 392, 440.

[8]See *Ibid.*, p. 402.

inevitably prove to be a science of the form of the state, rather than the science of its essence. On the other hand, a science of society that ignores the state must necessarily renounce actual reality, since society, at least modern-day society, lives and develops within the framework of the state, its organizational structure, its laws, and its administration. And the state itself, in Marx's definition, is nothing other than the organizational structure [ustroystvo] of society.[9]

The state as form must meet the internal requirements of the civil society, and as long as it meets those requirements, it is in keeping with the society. Without the state, civil society cannot achieve the free development of its forces; but without a society that freely develops under its aegis, the state gradually degenerates and loses its genuine meaning and purpose.[10]

Civil society as such lives not by common but by different, often opposing, interests. But therein lies the distinctive characteristic of societal life [obshchestvennaya zhizn]: Any given historically distinctive manifestation of it results not from the operation of one sort of interest, but from the interaction and struggle of diverse interests. For all the diversity of interests, however, there naturally also exist interests that are common to the society as a whole, since living and working together are impossible without a certain order. The state, as the form that society's organizational structure takes, embodies this commonality, thereby assuming the function of a kind of compromise among different social forces and their interests.[11]

Marx, for example, wrote that the activities of any exploitative state "encompass two aspects: both the fulfillment of common tasks that follow from the nature of any society, and specific functions that follow from the opposition between the government and the popular masses."[12] Engels, for his part, noted: "Society creates for itself an agency for the protection of its common interests against internal and external attacks. That agency is the state regime."[13]

---

[9]"From the political viewpoint," Marx wrote, "the state and the organizational structure of society are not two different things. The state is the organizational structure of society" (*Ibid.*, p. 439).

[10]I. Kant wrote about this: "Civil liberty . . . cannot be violated in any significant way without doing damage to all branches of the economy, especially to trade, and thus without weakening the forces of the state in its foreign affairs. . . .When a citizen is prevented from pursuing his happiness by his chosen means, so long as it is compatible with the freedom of others, all production is deprived of its viability, and thereby once again the forces of the whole are diminished" (I. Kant, *Works* [*Sochineniya*], Vol. 6, Moscow, 1966, pp. 19-20). See Engels' full characterization of the interaction between state and civil society in his famous letter to K. Schmidt of October 27, 1890 (K. Marx and F. Engels, *Works*, Vol. 37, pp. 416-421).

[11]The function of the state as the expression of commonality is dialectically combined with its role as the instrument of class domination. However, in our literature this combination is usually ignored, and consequently the property of commonality has either disappeared entirely or been preserved only with respect to the socialist state.

[12]K. Marx and F. Engels, *Works*, Vol. 25, Part 1, p. 422.

[13]K. Marx and F. Engels, *Works*, Vol. 21, p. 311.

Thus, civil society and the state are in constant, contradictory interaction and reciprocal influence, a condition whose nature depends to a great extent on the degree of development of the civil society and its institutions, and the ability of the latter to monitor the actions of the political regime. This point is especially important, considering the very nature of the state as regime, as external necessity with respect to civil society, and thereby, as an instrument of coercion of sorts. *External* necessity can only mean, Marx noted, that the "laws" and "interests" of society must, in the case of a clash, yield to the "laws" and "interests" of the state, that they are subordinate to it, and that its will and its laws take the form of necessity with respect to the "will" and "laws" of society.[14]

When the civil society is insufficiently developed, the state is capable of usurping its rights and privileges, with the result that an "inversion of the functions of the state and the civil society" may occur. In that case, the state not only assumes its own functions, but also appropriates the functions of society, sets society's objectives for it, and demands from it the unquestioning implementation of its own, the state's, decisions, believing that they most adequately reflect the interests of individuals and society as a whole.[15] And this applies equally to both domestic- and foreign-policy decisions. Such an inversion has its reasons. Without dealing with all of them, let us note one general reason: usually an inversion occurs in especially tense periods of a society's historical development, and once it has arisen, it has a certain historical duration, by dint of the independent movement of the form (the state regime). "At moments of an especially heightened sense of its power," Marx wrote, "political life strives to suppress its prerequisites—the civil society and its elements—and to constitute itself in the form of genuine, generic human life that is free of contradictions. But it can achieve that only by entering into *violent* contradiction with the conditions of its own life, only by declaring the revolution to be *continuous*, and therefore the political drama ends in the restoration of religion, private property, and all the elements of civil society with the very same necessity with which war ends in peace."[16] That idea naturally flows from the proposition that the civil society is the foundation of and prerequisite for the state, and therefore, as such, cannot fail to bring its form—the state—into conformity with itself sooner or later. Experience invariably confirms this truth.

And so the state, as form, as the organizational structure of society, and as the embodiment of commonality, also thereby expresses

---

[14]K. Marx and F. Engels, *Works*, Vol. 1, pp. 221, 222.
[15]For more details on this point, see *Voprosy filosofii*, No. 8, 1987, p. 79.
[16]K. Marx and F. Engels, *Works*, Vol. 1, p. 393.

certain common interests of the civil society as a whole. This conclusion is very important in analyzing the nature of so-called "national interests" and their relationship to the interests of the state. At the same time, it in no way contradicts the well-known Marxist proposition that the state is the political organization of the ruling class, and the "instrument" that it uses to protect its class interests. Nor does such a conclusion contradict the understanding of national interest as the interest of that same ruling class, which elevates its own particular interest to the level of the interest of the entire nation. No matter what the class nature of the state, it invariably retains the function of securing certain common "national" interests. The ruling class, Engels wrote, "by virtue of the very fact *that it is ruling*, bears responsibility for the condition of the entire nation and is obligated to look after its common interests."[17]

Thus, any state embodies both the common interests (the interests of the nation or society as a whole) and special interests (the interests of the ruling class). The relationship between the two sets of interests and their relative order of priority differ in different historical periods. The identification of that relationship requires concrete historical analysis in each instance.

Two Embodiments of the State

So far we have examined the state primarily in relation to its "own" civil society, or in other words, as "directed inward." But it has another, no less important side to its activity that pertains to its ties with the external world and with other states. The state, like Janus, simultaneously faces different directions and performs two interrelated, but different functions—internal and external.[18] These differences cannot help also being reflected in the evaluation of the relationship between the national, state, and class interests in the case of the state "directed inward" and those of the same state "directed outward."

The differences between these two "faces" of the state are unquestionably determined primarily by differences between the environments with which the state deals in each case: in the one case—the system of interstate relations, and in the other—the system of internal socioeconomic relations (or the civil society). And although one and the same state is acting in both instances, the difference between the

---

[17]K. Marx and F. Engels, *Works*, Vol. 2, p. 355.

[18]On the differences in content and form between the state's domestic-policy and foreign-policy activities, see E. Pozdnyakov, *Foreign-Policy Activities and Relations Among States* [*Vneshnepoliticheskaya deyatelnost i mezhgosudarstvennyye otnosheniya*], Moscow, 1986, Chapter 1.

internal and external environments of its activity places such an indelible imprint on both of its functions that it may sometimes create the impression that a different state is acting in each case.

The content of the state's domestic political function is determined mainly by the desire of the ruling class to strengthen its power, utilize it in its own interests, and consolidate social relations appropriate to it, using the state apparatus to this end. Here the ruling class, if one is speaking of class-antagonistic societies, has to deal with such domestic political and socioeconomic factors as the internal opposition, the struggle of classes and parties for power, various antigovernment movements, internal economic and social crises, unemployment, and more. It must simultaneously attempt to accomplish a dual task: advancing its special class interests and advancing common national interests having to do with developing the economy, strengthening defense capability and law and order, combating crime, ensuring the security of citizens).

The content of the foreign-policy function is different. The object of its attention is international relations, especially interstate relations. Here the state encounters phenomena and processes that are not subject to its control and jurisdiction, and it is surrounded by other states that are carrying out their own foreign-policy activities, which are often opposed, and even hostile, to it. What is involved in this case is not retaining or preserving the power of the ruling class in question, but ensuring the integrity, independence, and security of the state as such in the face of a real or supposed external danger, and creating favorable external conditions for the development of the economy, the performance of the domestic-policy function, and the accomplishment of other internal tasks.

In this case the state acts as the representative of the entire nation, the embodiment of the people's sovereignty, and the spokesman for the interests of the entire society.[19] This is contributed to by the fact that the nation (or the civil society) also appears in two embodiments, as it were: it is one thing when it is taken in and of itself—in which case it represents a *divided whole*—and another when it is taken in relation to the external world, where it acts as a *unified whole*.[20] If this "shared wholeness" of the nation in relation to the external world can, to a certain extent, be called illusory, it is no more illusory than the state itself is illusory in the sense of a shared wholeness. Yet embodied in the state's foreign policy and, accordingly, in its state interests, this gener-

---

[19]Hegel wrote: "One may speak of the *sovereignty* of the people in the sense that *in relation to the external world* the people is always something independent that constitutes a state of its own" (Quoted from K. Marx and F. Engels, *Works*, Vol. 1, p. 262).
[20]This assessment does not extend, of course, to critical periods in the lives of nations— periods which are often accompanied by internal divisions (revolutions, civil wars, etc.).

ality becomes perfectly real—hence the phenomenon of the coincidence of so-called national interests and state interests. Indeed, if the state is capable, through its dispositions and laws, of turning private goals into common goals and social consciousness into a social force internally,[21] it is even more capable of doing this with respect to its external aspirations.

It is by no means coincidental that even forces representing opposing classes within a state often enter into agreements and reconciliations where foreign-policy issues are concerned, while maintaining the polarity of their stands on domestic-policy issues. It would therefore be a big mistake, when assessing the attitude of a given state's population toward its foreign policy, to take only the factor of social and class stratification into account and not to consider, at the same time, what motivates that population, and such feelings as patriotism, a sense of connection to one's nation, a sense of homeland, and finally, a sense of loyalty to the state, which is expressed in a recognition that each citizen's life and well-being depend on the power and importance of his own state in the world, and on its economic and political might. These feelings are especially intensified in times of war or acute international conflicts. Ignoring them has led in the past, and continues to lead in the present, to serious mistakes in estimating various domestic and foreign situations. Let us recall how German and other social democratic literature on the eve of World War I claimed that the proletarian strata of various large nations, by virtue of their inherent internationalism, were natural allies, that national contradictions had no place amongst the proletariat, and that the working class's antinationalism would provide a reliable bulwark against a world war (K. Kautsky and others claimed this). However, the cruel war of European states among themselves led to the complete collapse of all these illusions. Not only were national disputes not suppressed by the dogmatically and simplistically conceived internationalism of the working class, but to the contrary, such disputes caught up the working class along with the others, and they did so with considerable help from the very social democratic leaders who only the day before had been proclaiming their loyalty to internationalism. The power of national feeling manifested itself—and it continues to manifest itself to this day—amongst not only the bourgeoisie but the working class as well.

One must not, of course, discount the fact that national feeling always has been and still is something that political demagogues of all stripes attempt to capitalize on, and a convenient tool in foreign-policy matters. Here the whole arsenal of political demagoguery is brought into play: appeals to people's sense of national pride and patriotism,

---

[21]See K. Marx and F. Engels, *Works*, Vol. 1, p. 103; and Vol. 16, p. 198.

the kindling of jingoism, chauvinism and enmity toward other peoples, and so forth. One must admit that all these means have their effect, especially since they fall on the fertile soil of national consciousness. Let us merely recall, in this connection, Washington's "Grenada action," or London's "Falklands operation," which were supported by the majority of the population in both countries, regardless of class affiliation. One could go on to cite other foreign-policy actions by various states in various periods of history when party (or class) interests yielded to common, national interests.

What has been said, however, should not be interpreted as meaning that state and national interests always coincide, and that the former are in all cases an expression of the latter, in regard to foreign affairs. Here, as in internal life, contradictions between the interests of the state and the interests of the civil society continue to exist, albeit in more veiled form. They come out in the open in cases where the state suffers failures in its foreign-policy actions, or where it thrusts the people into a prolonged, unpopular war (such as the U.S. war in Vietnam) that exhausts their human and material resources. The conflict between the state and civil society is expressed in various manifestations of society's discontent with its government's policy, acts of civil disobedience, the spread of defeatist or isolationist attitudes among the public, and—in extreme situations—the creation of a revolutionary situation within the country.

Interstate Relations and the Class Struggle

Regardless of whether state and national interests coincide outside a country, it is both methodologically and substantively mistaken to reduce either of them to class interests and identify them with the latter. The characterization of the state (and its interests) *only* as the instrument and expression of class domination is one-sided even when applied to internal relations between the state and civil society, and when applied to the state's foreign-policy activities and the sphere of its relations with other states, it results in erroneous judgments and irresolvable contradictions in both theory and practice.

One such judgment that has long been established in our scholarship is the opinion that interstate relations are an area of class struggle. The thesis concerning the class nature of interstate relations and their representing a sphere of class struggle (albeit in a special, specific form) stems mainly from an uncritical and essentially mechanical transfer of the laws of class struggle from the area of internal, social relations to interstate relations.

The emergence and establishment of this view in theory have their reasons. Here I think it is necessary to note two aspects. The first is the so-called epistemological aspect. The point is that, through the efforts of Marxist scholasticists and dogmatists, the class approach in our social science was in many cases turned into a kind of scientific superstition. It was made clear that any sphere of social relations, regardless of its specific nature, was to be examined solely from the viewpoint of class struggle, as an area of class relations. Consequently, the class approach, which in the hands of the founders of Marxism was a means of genuinely scientific, sociological analysis, was "successfully" transformed into a mindless faith, into vulgar social theorizing "à la Marxism" that was suitable for every occasion in life.

The second aspect, in our view, also involves a mechanical, uncritical application to relations among states of the well-known Marxist formula that every political struggle is a class struggle. The logic here is obvious: Since interstate relations are a sphere of political struggle, it follows that they are simultaneously an area of class struggle. But to apply formal logic in this case is simply to fail to understand the essence of Marxist doctrine concerning the class struggle. By political struggle the founders of Marxism meant (in all cases in which they used that formula) internal political struggle, since it is that struggle, regardless of the area in which it is waged, that is the more or less clear expression of the struggle among social classes, for its aim is the gaining or maintaining of political power by a given class.[22]

But it is not classes but states that are the actors in interstate relations. The class nature of the state is only one aspect of its characteristics as a social institution. Therefore, examining interstate relations as an area of class struggle betokens an obvious one-sidedness in treating the subject, and it leads, for all intents and purposes, to equating these relations with intrasocietal relations, and reducing the laws of the given sphere to the laws of class struggle.

Denying the thesis that interstate relations are a sphere of class struggle in no way means denying the operation of class interests in them. Naturally, states differ in their social-class nature, and these differences account for their having their own specific class interests. The place and role of the latter depend on concrete historical conditions, because of which it would be mistaken to accord priority to that group of interests in all cases (a priori). Indeed, at certain moments in states' historical development that are brought about by revolutionary reversals, class interests may emerge from the whole aggregate of foreign-policy interests and come to the fore, lending their color, as it were, to all other types of interests and contradictions, and creating what might be called the sociohistorical background. The revolutionary breakup of political, economic, and social relations within a state

---

[22]See K. Marx and F. Engels, *Works*, Vol. 4, pp. 427-444; and Vol. 21, pp. 220, 259, 309-310.

unavoidably affects foreign-policy ties as well, and brings about serious changes in them too. Consequently, foreign-policy contradictions take on a clearly expressed social-class nature and turn into interstate class conflict. Reflected "hot on the heels of events" in the minds of ideologists in the form of theoretical propositions, these notions of the class nature of the foreign-policy struggle continue their life by dint of inertia, eventually turning into dogma. The distinctive feature of any dogma is the ease with which it is assimilated; the ease of assimilation results in popularity; and broad popularity creates the appearance of truth.

The erroneousness of this thesis becomes especially obvious if one turns to the principle of peaceful coexistence on which the foreign-policy activities of the Soviet Union and the other socialist states are based. Equality, noninterference in each other's internal affairs, refraining from attack and repudiating encroachments on other states' territorial integrity, respect for sovereignty and national independence, and the strengthening of good-neighborly relations have nothing to do with class struggle as Marxism understands it. The principles of peaceful coexistence also mean acknowledgement of peoples' right to decide for themselves, without any imposition from outside, what sort of social system they want to have (which also does not fit into the concept of class struggle).

In our time the thesis concerning class struggle in the international arena means, in practice, admitting that the capitalist and socialist systems cannot coexist; inherent in it is the idea that it is permissible to "export" revolution and, by the same token, to "export" counterrevolution; it creates the dangerous illusion that the contradiction between socialism and capitalism can be overcome by foreign-policy means, including war. Admitting such a thing means subscribing to the thesis that war (including thermonuclear war) between socialism and capitalism is inevitable, rendering any activity aimed at preventing war pointless, and depriving people of all hope for the future.

Here, I think, we are dealing with mutually exclusive positions: Either we regard interstate relations as an area of class struggle—and then the principles of peaceful coexistence are inapplicable to it; or, conversely, we consider the principles of peaceful coexistence to be universal in relations among states—and then the view of interstate relations as a sphere of class struggle is unacceptable.

It may be objected that class struggle in the international arena has acquired its genuine and clear meaning only in the period since 1917, i.e., since the establishment of the world's first socialist state, which brought states with opposite class natures into direct conflict. However, in our opinion this argument does not withstand criticism.

Class struggle has been going on in the world for millennia, as has the struggle among states—including states of differing social-class natures. Therefore, to propose that the thesis which holds that interstate relations are an arena of class struggle correctly applies only to the last 70 years means forcing Marxism to conform to familiar views and models. In their analysis of international relations, the founders of Marxism always proceeded from realities and the laws that were proper to that area, and they never attempted to apply laws to it that belonged, in principle, to another sphere, i.e., the laws of class struggle. As an example, let us cite Engels's 1890 article, "The Foreign Policy of Russian Czarism," where he noted that the existing situation in Europe was determined by three factors: (1) Germany's annexation of Alsace-Lorraine, (2) czarist Russia's designs on Constantinople, and (3) the struggle between the proletariat and the bourgeoisie that was flaring up with increasing intensity in all countries. "*The first two facts* (our emphasis—E.P.)," he continued, "derive from the present division of Europe into two great military camps. The German annexation has turned France into Russia's ally against Germany, and the czarist threat to Constantinople is turning Austria and even Italy into Germany's allies. Both camps are preparing for a decisive struggle, for a war the likes of which the world has never seen. . . ."[23]

If one proceeds from the laws of class struggle, it is impossible to explain the emergence of an alliance between bourgeois, republican France and semifeudal, monarchist Russia, just as it is impossible to explain many other examples that one encounters in international practice of alliances between states with different, even diametrically opposite, social systems. In the example cited, Engels builds his analysis on realities, on a study of the correlation and alignment of forces in Europe that naturally existed at that time, i.e., on the basis of those material factors that from time immemorial have formed the basis of states' foreign-policy activities and been responsible for the creation or breakup of alliances. That is precisely why Engels's analysis and forecast were so brilliantly confirmed 25 years later.

In the prenuclear era the view of international relations as an arena of class struggle (although erroneous in essence) was still not as dangerous as it is now, in the age of nuclear missiles. Humanity faces a choice: either the continued buildup of tension and confrontation, or constructive efforts to reach mutually acceptable accords. Such an approach is also dangerous because it is based from the very outset on the unacceptability of all agreements with "imperialism," on a dogmatic refusal to compromise, on a belief in the truth of one's own viewpoint alone, and on a kind of "presumption of infallibility" in one's

---

[23]K. Marx and F. Engels, *Works*, Vol. 22, p. 48.

assessment not only of domestic political phenomena and processes, but of international ones as well.[24]

Without question, class interests primarily manifest themselves in the sphere of ideological struggle between states. Any social struggle, whether between classes, estates, and parties, or between states in the form that it has taken place in history up until now, has always been waged with the help of ideologies. However, it has always been a struggle for real, material interests. And ideas and interests may not coincide. In interstate relations, by virtue of their specific nature, such a discrepancy between ideas and interests is more the rule than the exception. But, as K. Marx noted, *"ideas"* have invariably disgraced themselves as soon as they have been detached from *"interests."*[25]

One must assume that they disgrace themselves even more when they enter into direct contradiction with interests. Consequently, there is nothing left to do but give up either the idea or the interest— an option quite often encountered in interstate relations. And since the outward-directed activities of a state are still based on the aggregate of its foreign-policy interests, it usually gives preference to precisely those interests. Anyone who cared to could find an abundance of examples in both history and the present day to illustrate the idea of the priority of state foreign-policy interests over ideological and philosophical interests.

Let us touch, in this connection, on the question of states' belonging to the same social-class type, and the role of this class similarity in interstate relations. In addition to such characteristics as "commonality of class interests" and "class solidarity," this fact of belonging to the same class type sometimes serves as virtually the main argument used to explain the foreign-policy unity of a given group of states. Such characteristics stem, once again, from the view of interstate relations as an arena of class struggle and the corresponding treatment of the class and ideological aspects of those relations as absolutes. Thus, in our political literature the foreign-policy unity of the imperialist states in their struggle with the socialist countries, like the centripetal tendency in their relations, is often attributed largely to their belonging to the same social-class type. When this is done, one little "detail" is overlooked: a half-century ago the fact that they belonged to the same social-class type in no way prevented the imperialist states from waging war against each other and launching World War II, which began precisely as an interimperialist war.

The U.S.S.R. and China, and China and Vietnam are also states of the same class type. However, in and of itself this circumstance by no

---

[24]See Ye. Primakov, "A New Philosophy of Foreign Policy" (*Pravda*, July 10, 1987).
[25]K. Marx and F. Engels, *Works*, Vol. 2, p. 89.

means eliminates serious disagreements and contradictions (and there have even been conflicts) between them with respect to a number of international issues.

If states' real interests in interstate relations derive from an aggregate of many specific factors and circumstances (starting with their geopolitical situations and ending with the existing system for maintaining the balance of power in the world, the corresponding system of military alliances and groupings, and states' related commitments with regard to collective or individual security), applying to this sphere the concepts of "belonging to the same social-class type" and "class solidarity" diverts one from studying and understanding the real causes of complex phenomena and processes in international life and leads one to the area of the most general, vulgar-sociological argumentation or commonplace propaganda.

Since interstate relations are not a sphere of class struggle, the role in them of the ideological factor as the expression of class interests has its own specific features. As previously stated, states' foreign policy is largely determined by interests connected with the functioning and development of the system of interstate relations as an external environment. Ideology, on the other hand, is based on a given world view, expressed in a system of specific values. Ideology is less changeable and more conservative than the system of interstate relations, which constantly changes under the influence of various world processes. Consequently, foreign-policy interests—"material" interests—constantly come into contradiction with ideological interests.

The excessive influence of ideological considerations on practical policies and on the sphere in which states' foreign-policy interests interact often distorts the real content of those interests and deforms them. That is precisely the cause of the so-called "ideologization" of foreign policy. The essence of it is that a kind of inversion of the role of political and ideological interests takes place, like the inversion that sometimes occurs in relations between the political state and the civil society: Ideological interests turn into a kind of end in themselves, while "material" foreign-policy interests become their "handmaidens."

Such ideologization of foreign policy frequently becomes an obstacle to development of normal relations among states based on a balance of real interests, serves to kindle enmity, suspicion, and mistrust among them, and gives rise to persistent stereotypes of the "external enemy," thereby preventing rapprochement and mutual understanding among different peoples.

"It is precisely the transfer of ideological contradictions and struggle to the area of international relations, especially to the process of peace negotiations, that is a pattern of the old political thinking,"

V. Bil'ak, a leader of the Czechoslovak Communist Party, has right-fully stressed.[26] Indeed, the subordination of foreign policy to the demands of ideology would represent the worst sort of idealism in foreign-policy practice.

The idea of the impermissibility of confusing, much less equating, foreign-policy and ideological elements in the international activities of states is not really anything new. Back in 1983 the Political Declaration of the Warsaw Treaty Member States noted that "in their policies the socialist countries strictly separate ideological questions from the problems of interstate relations, and build their relations with the capitalist states on the basis of peaceful coexistence.[27]

Today this idea is not only being reaffirmed but undergoing further development. The impermissibility of transferring ideological differences to the sphere of interstate relations and subordinating foreign policy to them is stated in no uncertain terms in M.S. Gorbachev's book, *Perestroika: New Thinking for Our Country and the World*. This same idea is also behind the rejection of the previous formula for peaceful coexistence among states with differing social systems, a formula which regarded it as a "specific form of the class struggle."

In all these propositions, a clear line is drawn between the sphere of interstate relations (and the principles of peaceful coexistence that are appropriate to it) and the sphere of class struggle (and the ideology that is appropriate to it). Confusing or equating the two, or mechanically transferring the laws of one to the other inevitably leads to mistakes in both theory and practice. However, that is not the only point. The correctness of the proposition that it is impermissible to transfer ideological disagreements to interstate relations, and likewise, the correctness of replacing the previous formula for peaceful coexistence can be recognized only if one also recognizes that interstate relations themselves are not an area of class struggle. If they really were such an area, any changes of formulas would be simply absurd, since the laws of class struggle are objective and, consequently, not subject to willed decisions. A willed decision or replacement of formulas can change only an incorrect notion about a given area of objectively existing relations, but not those relations themselves. If interstate relations were really a sphere of class struggle, ideological disagreements would be an inalienable property of such relations, and peaceful coexistence would be a form of class struggle and nothing else. Consequently, in rejecting the previous formula for peaceful coexis-

---

[26]V. Bil'ak, "Our Common European Home" (*Problemy mira i sotsializma* [*Problems of Peace and Socialism*], No. 8, 1987, p. 4).
[27]See *Pravda*, Jan. 7, 1983.

tence, we thereby also reject the former notion of interstate relations as a sphere of class struggle.

In the past, erroneous ideas were obscured and intensified by many circumstances of both an internal and external nature. Today the problem of survival that faces mankind, like the fact that the world has come to a dangerous frontier in its development, to the brink of disaster, is forcing people to rethink many propositions that had once seemed true and to reject ossified dogmas and look at the world with different eyes that are free from accumulated prejudices and false stereotypes.

Today the antagonism between the two social systems is developing under conditions in which the universal human interest cannot help but take priority over class interest. While the Marxist proposition that "the interests of social development are higher than the interests of the proletariat," and "the interests of all" are higher than the interests of one's own nation alone[28] has always been true, today it is becoming an imperative.

The contemporary world continues to be divided by deep contradictions, and too much prejudice, mistrust, fear, and enmity have accumulated in it. The inertia of the old, "traditional" political thinking and political action, and the approach to dealing with international affairs through force continue to operate.

However, even in this area gratifying changes for the better are occurring. Objective processes taking place in international relations are helping change the style of political thinking. The growing political and economic interconnection and interdependence of states and peoples, the internationalization of production, the threat of the annihilation of humanity, environmental problems—these are all leading to a great overlapping of interests and a multiplication of points of contact among states on various issues, and are objectively giving rise to a commonality of interests among them.

This commonality is an extremely important political prerequisite for the development of cooperation among states with differing social systems, a prerequisite for their concerted action.[29] However, although commonality is an essential condition for the development of normal relations among them, it is not a sufficient condition. Any politics is realistic to the extent that it takes the interests of other sides into account. As the Soviet scholar V.F. Petrovskiy rightfully notes, "conducting a realistic foreign policy in our day is impossible without taking into account both one's own interests and capabilities, and those

---

[28]See V.I. Lenin, Complete Works [Polnoye sobraniye sochineniy], Vol. 4, p. 220; and Vol. 30, pp. 43, 44-45.
[29]"Where there is no commonality of interests," Engels wrote, "there can be no unity of goals, not to mention unity of actions" (K. Marx and F. Engels, Works, Vol. 8, p. 14).

of other states. A balance of mutual interests is the basis on which the political solution of international problems should be built."[30]

Seeking out elements of commonality and taking them into account presuppose mastery of the art of compromise. Today it is no longer possible to achieve anything through threats and force—they lead only to the destruction of trust among states. Consequently, the great art of living together on the basis of peaceful coexistence is built on the equally great art of political compromise. Uncompromising politics is an antipolitics that is unwarranted even under exceptional, extreme conditions. On the other hand, sensible compromise in politics means searching for and finding the general in the particular, the common in the different. Without this, all efforts to achieve agreement among states, whether in matters of ensuring mutual security, or in the establishment of mutually advantageous, equitable economic relations, are doomed to failure. "After all, if every state," M.S. Gorbachev has noted, "pursues only its own interests and is not capable of meeting its partner halfway, seeking points of contact, and cooperating with that partner, it will be difficult to bring about an improvement of international relations."[31]

A good deal of experience has been accumulated in achieving compromise-based, mutually acceptable solutions between socialist and capitalist states. This has become possible, to no small extent, thanks to the breaking down of former ideas about the principles of interaction among states, and to a change in established stereotypes pertaining to the assessment of priorities between national and universal human interests, state and class interests, ideology and foreign policy. The changes that are taking place reflect the process of the development of a new political thinking that is free of fixed, abstract ideas and oversimplified views of the world and one's own role in it, and free of claims to possess a monopoly on the truth.

---

[30]*Twentieth-Century Europe: Problems of Peace and Security* [*Yevropa XX veka: problemy mira i bezopasnosti*], Moscow, 1985, pp. 207-208.
[31]*Vestnik MID SSSR*, [Bulletin of the U.S.S.R. Ministry of Foreign Affairs] No. 1, Aug. 5, 1987, p. 6.

The Confrontation of Conventional Forces in the Context of Ensuring Strategic Stability

ANDREY AFANASYEVICH KOKOSHIN AND VALENTIN
VENIAMINOVICH LARIONOV*

In May 1987 the Berlin session of the Political Advisory Committee adopted a document entitled "On the Military Doctrine of the Warsaw Pact States." The basic content and orientation of the military doctrine adopted consists of rejecting both nuclear and conventional war and in securing the socialist countries and defending them against encroachment from outside. The cutting edge of the Warsaw Pact's military doctrine is directed not toward preparation for war, but against war and toward strengthening the foundations of international security. This is the first time that the tenet on preventing war has figured in the Warsaw Pact's military doctrine so emphatically. The Pact's military activities included strenuous efforts to prevent war in the past as well, but this issue has now moved to the forefront in the doctrine and become the main, determining task.[1] The conclusion that victory is impossible in a nuclear war, and the task of preventing war, both nuclear and conventional, are emphasized in the joint statements issued by the top Soviet and American leadership in Geneva, Reykjavik, and Washington. All of this compels a new look at several traditional, long-established approaches to the accomplishment of purely military tasks.

I.

Many prominent political and military figures, specialists, and scholars in the West, have been making statements with increasing

---

*Kokoshin is a corresponding member of the U.S.S.R. Academy of Sciences, deputy director of the Institute for the United States and Canada, and vice chairman of the Committee of Soviet Scientists for Peace and Against Nuclear War. Maj. Gen. Larionov is a doctor of history and professor at the General Staff Academy. This article, which appeared in the June 1988 issue of *MEMO*, is an excerpt from the authors' book, *The Problem of Preventing War* [*Problema predotvrashcheniya voyny*], which at the time the article appeared was being prepared for publication in Russian and English at Progress Publishing House.
[1]See D.T. Yazov, *Guarding Socialism and Peace* [*Na strazhe sotsializma i mira*], Moscow, 1987, p. 27.

frequency, particularly of late, on the need for a purely defensive stance in the activities of the opposing military alliances. In the West there have been repeated calls for the United States, France, and Great Britain to follow the example of the U.S.S.R. and the People's Republic of China in pledging no first use of nuclear weapons. Operational concepts of a destabilizing nature are being more vigorously criticized, including such concepts as "air-ground operations (battles)," "attack on the second echelon and reserves" (the "Rogers Plan"), the U.S. naval strategy formulated in the 1980s that is associated with the names of former U.S. Navy Secretary John Lehman and Admiral Watkins, and others. Moderate political circles, with the increasingly active participation of high-ranking military professionals, are persistently advancing and fleshing out the so-called alternative military ideas and concepts of "nonprovoking defense," "nonoffensive defense," "nonoffensive containment," and so forth.

One of today's central issues is how policy directives for preventing war and bolstering strategic stability will be reflected in the military-technical component of military doctrines: in strategic and operational concepts, in the makeup of the armed forces and their disposition, in industrial mobilization plans, and so on. How will the transformation and development of the military-technical component of military doctrines be effectuated in the arms limitation and disarmament process?

In this article we shall examine in order four hypothetical variants for the two sides' confrontation in the area of general purpose forces and conventional arms. Each of these variants is rather tentative and sketchy and is offered as a stimulus to research.

In many respects the nature of the confrontation and the criteria and conditions for ensuring strategic stability in this sphere differ significantly from those at the level of strategic nuclear forces. At the same time we must always keep in mind the high concentration of unit-level nuclear weapons in the general-purpose forces—those at the disposal of each side's ground forces, air forces, and navies. This brings up the need for a radical solution to the problem of decreasing the numbers of dual-purpose armaments.[2]

It goes without saying that the variants presented here by no means exhaust the conceivable forms of this confrontation—one can imagine them in various combinations, for example. However, the studies conducted by the authors allow the claim that the four proposed variants can be regarded as one of the analytic tools for dealing with the problems of bolstering strategic stability in Europe and in Warsaw Pact-NATO relations.

---

[2]See A. Arbatov, "Deep Reductions in Strategic Weapons," *MEMO*, No. 4, 1988, p. 18 [the first installment of a two-part article translated at page 435 in this collection].

Variant one. The essence of this variant is that each side, in case of war (attack by the other side), is geared to immediate counteraction—to conducting strategic offensive operations. Military operations under such conditions would be decisive and uncompromising. We can assume that under this alternative each side would seek to move military operations into the enemy's territory and airspace as quickly as possible, among other reasons, to prevent subjecting its own territory to excessive destruction and radioactive contamination.

This variant conforms to deeply rooted traditions in military thought, expressed in the idea that only decisive offensive operations and efforts to seize the strategic initiative lead to victory, and that victory, in turn, consists of conclusively routing and destroying the enemy's forces. This tradition took shape most distinctly in the 19th century during the Napoleonic Wars and dominated military and political thinking alike during both world wars.

Psychologically, offensive strategic and operational concepts have always been highly attractive for a number of reasons. Even today many consider them indispensable to the maintenance of high morale in the armed forces. Traditionally, such ideas are popular with a significant portion of the public, which has a poor grasp of military realities.[3]

To all intents and purposes, this kind of confrontation from the outset of military operations gears both sides to a series of head-on engagements. These are traditionally considered among the most complex of all military operations, demanding especially great skill in directing troops. Under modern conditions directing operations of this kind is growing immeasurably more complex.

Readiness for head-on engagements raises the tension in the military-political situation and increases mutual suspicion. The reason is that this orientation requires the highest degree of combat readiness and constant large-scale troop and staff-training exercises. This variant of confrontation assumes an appropriate force and resource structure and manpower levels for head-on attacks and retaliatory strikes. Under such conditions it is exceptionally difficult to determine which resources are intended for preemptive offensive operations from a defensive posture and which are solely for repulsing attack.[4]

---

[3]See A.A. Svechin, *The History of the Art of War* [*Istoriya voyennogo iskusstva*], Moscow, 1922, part 1, pp. 31, 46.

[4]Reconnaissance-attack (missile-controlled) missile launch systems may become basic combat weapons in the future. In these systems the launch-to-impact process is carried out within the system's range (up to several hundred kilometers) by guided (self-guided) missiles and projectiles along the entire flight trajectory or separate segments thereof. Control and operation of the elements of these systems are based on extensive use of electronics, laser technology, and computers; they are quite sensitive to jamming and vulnerable to high-explosive fragmentation rounds. Timely destruction of appropriate headquarters and communications and control centers

Second operating echelons and deep reserves play a vital role in this confrontational variant. This, in turn, presumes a high probability that second echelons will become the object of powerful long-range attacks (including attacks during the earliest stage of the armed conflict) by both aviation and surface-to-surface missiles, as well as by advanced reconnaissance-attack systems. In this way the battle may, from the outset, spread far beyond the limits of the forward battle line.

Under this confrontational variant the beginning of armed conflict immediately leads to the movement of great numbers of troops, giving rise to the most complex combinations in regrouping them. Returning them all to their original positions and reestablishing peace would be exceptionally difficult. That is, it should be assumed beforehand that a military conflict of growing intensity and scale is irreversible, and allowance should be made for unavoidable difficulties in maintaining control—and even for loss of control—on the part of the political leadership and the higher military command.

The combination of many factors—the fast-paced nature of military operations, the sudden changes in the operational situation, the simultaneous envelopment of large areas of several European countries by military operations, the intentional destruction of communications channels, and the conduct of military operations at any time of day or night and in any kind of weather—could, in all probability, lead to a situation where, for lack of time and information, the political leadership and the higher military command would be unable to control events fully. In extreme cases this could result in an irreversible escalation of military operations, right up to the use of tactical nuclear weapons. The crossover from military operations employing only conventional weapons to operations employing weapons of mass destruction can be sudden and unpredictable, and this leads to a tendency to maintain one's nuclear resources in a heightened state of readiness, which, in turn, substantially increases the danger of touching off and escalating a nuclear war.[5]

Variant two. Each of the sides orients its strategy and tactics toward intentionally renouncing attack in the initial stage of the conflict, intending to conduct only defensive operations. In this case

---

makes it possible to sharply reduce the effectiveness of such systems. The high operating speed of these systems will require attacking them immediately upon detecting their characteristic reconnaissance indications. That is, in the aggregate of preventive measures against such systems, the decisive role will belong to preemptive nuclear and artillery strikes, capturing (putting out of commission) their individual elements, and electronic suppression of their automated control systems, as well as interdicting reconnaissance. See M.A. Gareyev, *M.V. Frunze—Military Theoretician* [*M.V. Frunze—voyennyy teoretik*], Moscow, 1985, pp. 244-245; Yu. Molostov, "Defense Against High-Accuracy Weapons," *Voyennyy vestnik* [*Military Herald*], No. 2, 1987, pp. 83-84.

[5]See V. Shabanov, "'Conventional' War: New Dangers," *Novoye vremya* [*New Times*], Nov. 14, 1986, p. 8.

reliance would be placed on a deeply echeloned, well-engineered positional defense site and on forces prepared beforehand for counterattack. After repulsing the attack in the course of a defensive battle that allows for retreat and for surrendering a certain amount of territory, the defensive force retains the capability, using reserves brought up from the rear, to mount a decisive counterattack (and, if necessary, to mount a general offensive) right up to a complete rout of the enemy on its own territory. Counterattacks can be conducted both on an operational scale (armies, groups of armies, fronts, flotillas, and fleets) and on a strategic scale (groups of fronts and fleets in a theater of military operations.)

The basic ideas and concepts of such a defense, the principles for constructing and equipping it, the disposition of forces and resources, and what it means to conduct a defensive battle can be seen in broad outline from the example and historical experience of the battle of Kursk in the summer of 1943.[6] It goes without saying that there can be no direct analogy between the battle of Kursk and the forms of confrontation in present-day conditions. The defense around Kursk was organized in the course of a war and was motivated by completely different political and strategic considerations than are modern armed forces and strategies, with their primarily nonoffensive structure and their peacetime operational plans, which are oriented toward preventing war.

In evaluating the merits and shortcomings of the second variant of confrontation it can be noted that, from the standpoint of strengthening strategic and international political stability, it is first and foremost interesting for the idea of intentional defense. The actual nature of the troops' operational deployment and the engineering details of the defensive line would have to be the subject of detailed comparative studies and joint discussions by the two sides' representatives. These discussions could also include such issues as density of the defense, disposition of forces to the rear, and how positional and active defense are combined.

This variant of confrontation appears to be more stable than the preceding one. Its shortcoming is the difficulty in differentiating and verifying the capabilities (training) of each side for counteroffensive or preemptive offensive operations, although the difference between them will in any case be more distinct than under the first alternative.

The likelihood of a conventional war growing into a nuclear one under this variant of confrontation (especially when the sides maintain the capability for counteroffensive operations that can evolve into a

---

[6]For more detail see A. Kokoshin and V. Larionov, "The Battle of Kursk in the Light of Modern Defensive Doctrine," *MEMO*, No. 8, 1987, pp. 32-40.

general invasion on a strategic scale) remains just as high as under the first variant.

The difficulties for the higher political and military leadership in controlling and overseeing events as they unfold will be quite significant in this scenario, although establishing oversight will be easier than under the first variant.

Variant three posits for each side only the capability to defeat the enemy's invading forces on the territory being defended, without mounting a cross-border counteroffensive.

The essence of such a defense is that military operations are not carried into the territory of the side that started the war. As a result, the defender's active efforts are directed only toward restoring the situation that existed before the start of military operations (the *status quo ante bellum*). The operational scale—the capability for counterattack (army group, army)—limits each side's possibilities for conducting active operations on a reciprocal basis. Correspondingly, the notion of victory is possible only on an operational and tactical scale, but is ruled out on the strategic scale.

With a number of qualifications, the rout of Japanese troops that had committed an act of aggression against the Mongolian People's Republic in 1939 in the Khalka River region can serve as a military-historical analogy for such operations. During August 21 to 30, 1939, the First Army Group of Soviet and Mongolian Forces under Corps Commander G. K. Zhukov, in a brilliant operation to surround and cut off the invading troops from the border, crushed the Sixth Japanese Army in the Mongolian desert.[7] The Soviet Air Force's success in winning air supremacy in the course of this operation (in the early stages of the armed conflict the Japanese had enjoyed air supremacy) played an extremely important role in the victory.

The aggressor was taught a stern lesson. But no invasion was mounted on the territory from which the aggression was launched, although certain purely military opportunities existed for an "operation retribution." The enemy asked for a truce. In view of the combination of factors determining the military and political situation in both Asia and Europe, the Soviet leadership decided not to retaliate with military actions against Japanese-occupied China. As a result of negotiations between the U.S.S.R. and Japan, military operations were terminated on September 16, 1939. In the final analysis the rout of the

---

[7]The composition of each side's forces prior to August 20, 1939, gives an idea of the scale of the military operation: the Soviet and Mongolian forces numbered 57,000 troops with 542 artillery pieces, 498 tanks, 385 armored vehicles, and 515 aircraft; the Japanese forces had 75,000 troops, 500 artillery pieces, 182 tanks, and over 300 aircraft. They had no armored vehicles. Thus, the Japanese side had the advantage in numbers of troops, but they were not as well equipped, especially with tanks and motorized vehicles.

Japanese in the Khalka River region significantly stabilized the situation there.

The war in Korea, or rather, one of its stages, may serve as another, relatively fresher example. We refer to the tacit agreement of both sides not to cross a certain boundary (demarcation line) and not to broaden the scale of military operations in the fourth stage of the war after the situation had stabilized.

As is known, the war in Korea was the first large-scale local conflict after 1945. From July 10, 1951, until July 27, 1953, that is, until the signing of the Panmunjon armistice, military operations between the two sides had the character of a fluid defense with episodic battles in regions adjacent to the 38th parallel. The limited scale of military operations was expressed in the tacit agreement by both sides to refrain from steps that could ignite a large conflagration: troops of the Korean People's Democratic Republic's armed forces and the Chinese people's volunteers did not penetrate deeply into the territory of South Korea south of the 38th parallel, and the U.S. Air Force refrained from bombardment of targets inside the People's Republic of China.

Under modern conditions the difficulty in implementing this defensive variant lies in determining what losses of territory, with whatever resources are situated therein, each side agrees to react to only by reestablishing the *status quo ante bellum*, suppressing the desire for revenge, and what losses each side agrees not to react to in that way. Second, how are we to measure the amount of compensation for the losses of the party subjected to attack? Third, when will that side deign to stop: just with the elimination of the invading forces, or will it go further? In the Khalka River region the Mongolian territory that the Japanese invaded was a desert, and during military operations losses among the civilian population and property losses were almost nil.[8]

Variant four assumes that each side, on an agreed-upon basis or on the basis of mutual example selects, on a strategic and operational scale, an exclusively defensive operational alternative without the material resources to conduct offensive or counteroffensive operations.[9] A high degree of mobility would be agreed upon mutually only for tactical combat units that could be used to mount a counterattack (battalions, regiments, at most divisions).

---

[8]In his memoirs G. K. Zhukov notes the absence of a civilian population in the combat zone as a factor that complicated intelligence gathering. See G. K. Zhukov, *Reminiscences and Reflections* [*Vospominaniya i razmyshleniya*], Moscow, 1984, Vol. 1, p. 204.

[9]A number of prominent West European (including West German) specialists believe that under conditions of the balance achieved between Warsaw Pact and NATO forces and the palpable relaxation of tensions in the international situation, the West could allow itself to take major unilateral steps toward changing over to exclusively defensive strategic alternatives in the hope that they would evoke similar reciprocal steps from the Warsaw Pact.

This type of grouping obviously does not require that the sides possess strike aviation, surprise attack weapons (like reconnaissance-strike systems), high mobility and strike power (tank and air assault divisions), or have forces and resources for deep strikes at their disposal. In a word, defense of this kind could completely become "non-offensive defense," although two of the three alternatives set forth above have that property to some degree or another. Accordingly, the notion of victory in this variant is retained only on the tactical scale. On the strategic and operational level the notion of victory is ruled out.

II.

In examining the above alternatives, as well as all other variants of the confrontation between the two sides in the area of general-purpose forces and conventional weapons, we must consider all possible conditions under which military operations may develop, and the entire range of their consequences.

Under massive employment of conventional weapons, intentional or inadvertent attacks on the enemy's nuclear or chemical resources are not out of the question, including attacks on nuclear- or chemical-weapon stockpiles, launch facilities, storage-transporters for nuclear warheads and missiles, transporter-launchers, and other such targets. In terms of consequences, that may turn out to be equivalent to employing the corresponding means of mass destruction, and may disrupt the balance in tactical nuclear arms and evoke unpredictable retaliatory actions. Strikes by conventional weapons under certain conditions are also capable of destroying the numerous European atomic power stations and generating facilities. The result would, for all intents and purposes, be equivalent to a nuclear attack, and the consequences would be felt considerably more than those of the Chernobyl accident.[10]

By and large, the industrially developed countries, with their many enterprises employing the latest technology, may turn out to be the most vulnerable in a military conflict. This applies first to Europe, the scene of the Warsaw Pact-NATO confrontation. The destruction of a large chemical plant or oil storage facility, even with the use of a conventional weapon, would lead to explosions and fires comparable in overall output of heat to a medium-yield nuclear explosion. The release of chemically or biologically active substances into the atmosphere in connection with the destruction of industrial enterprises could have the same consequences for the population living nearby as would military operations employing chemical or biological weapons.

---

[10]See *Novoye vremya*, Nov. 14, 1986, p. 8.

The destruction of atomic power plants by conventional means is tantamount to using a radiological weapon.[11]

In comparing all four of the confrontation variants in the domain of general purpose forces and conventional arms we can conclude that the first variant is the least stable. The fourth variant appears most appropriate to the idea of bolstering strategic stability and reducing the two sides' military potential to the limits of sufficiency, as dictated solely by the requirements of defense in a form carried to its logical conclusion.

One of the real problems in bolstering strategic stability is that the task of preventing both nuclear and conventional war should not, it would appear, be limited only to the period of time preceding the onset of military operations proper—"D-Day." It is necessary to think through, and include in the mechanism of the opposing sides' relations, elements that would make it possible to localize any armed conflict that might arise should political and diplomatic safety valves fail to function. The task seems just as complicated as its resolution is imperative. Once again, the fourth of the variants examined meets this requirement most completely.

The task of localizing armed conflict as it applies to the use of battlefield tactical nuclear weapons is an especially difficult one. On one hand, the concepts of "limited" nuclear war are destabilizing in this context, while on the other, the absence of mechanisms that could prevent the use—including the unsanctioned use—of a single nuclear weapon from escalating into an uncontrollable, all-out nuclear war is also dangerous. In this connection, it is worth emphasizing once more the abnormality of having large numbers of nuclear resources permanently assigned to general-purpose forces. In this regard, it is exceptionally important that each side's higher political leadership and military command have full control over nuclear weapons and that this control be ensured by organizational and technical means.

Proceeding from the need to reject rigid formulations—either complete peace or catastrophic war—in resolving the problem of preventing war, it is important to seek mutually advantageous agreements, considering each positive step as useful. The difficulty of achieving a truly nonoffensive defense should not rule out agreement on other, albeit less stable, variants of confrontation that nonetheless represent movement toward an optimally stable balance.

All these defense variants may be taken as a subject for strategic analysis only in the case of a contiguous confrontation or one along some kind of widely spaced, agreed-upon demilitarized corridor, but once again only on land. Still other factors must be taken into account

---

[11]See L. Feoktistov, "Constructive Actions for Ending the Arms Race and Averting the Threat of Nuclear War," *Mir Nauki* [*World of Science*], No. 3-4, 1987, p. 19.

when dealing with the forces and resources stationed deep within the countries' and the coalitions' territory. For example, the parties might work out the principles of the confrontation of ground forces, taking into account all forces along the border, as well as those that would tend to be drawn into the joint accomplishment of military tasks together with ground forces, up to an agreed-upon distance inside the border. But independently from whatever events are taking place on land (hypothetically there could be complete calm), an aggressor is capable of a surprise attack from the air, through space, or from the sea. So the issues of endowing the navies, air forces, and space resources with a nonoffensive character should be resolved based on principles of equal and mutual security.

The proposals contained in the documents of the June 1986 Budapest session of the Political Consultative Committee of the Warsaw Pact member-states are in fact working in the direction of realizing the fourth variant. The conference documents propose working out a procedure for reducing armed forces and conventional armaments, under which the reduction process would lead to decreased danger of surprise attack and would serve to bolster strategic stability on the European continent. To that end they propose agreeing from the outset to significant cuts in each military-political alliance's tactical strike aircraft in Europe, as well as to decreases in the concentration of troops along the line of contact between the sides. To this same end, additional measures would be worked out and implemented, measures capable of increasing the confidence of the Warsaw Pact, NATO, and all European countries that no surprise attack will be mounted against them.

One should be aware of the fact that the two sides' switch to a nonoffensive defense variant entails very considerable difficulties and the need to discuss with unprecedented frankness and to resolve jointly many exclusively military issues that are becoming political issues before our very eyes. Among them are evaluating which armaments to consider defensive and which offensive, what kinds of operational-training and combat-training methods can be used, and other issues.

Excluding certain existing types of armed forces and armaments from both sides' future defensive military structure poses a range of serious political, military-technical, doctrinal, and other questions.[12] Determining the defensive and offensive capabilities of division-size, front-size, and smaller units appears to be no simple thing.

---

[12]Thus, renouncing nuclear weapons (first and foremost tactical nuclear resources) puts in doubt the efficacy of the entire "flexible response" strategy, which was adopted by NATO in 1967.

It is exceptionally difficult to work out some kind of single criterion for comparing the quantitative and qualitative parallels of armed forces and weapons. Nevertheless, a number of features and characteristics permit placing this or that weapons system or resource into a predominantly offensive or predominantly defensive class (category) with a significant degree of exactitude.[13] Moreover, the sides can agree on some quantitative limit, which, if exceeded, would be seen as a departure from a defensive concept and as an acquisition of offensive capabilities.

Tactical and technical characteristics seem to be important qualitative indicators of weapons systems that allow differentiation, within certain limits, between offensive and defensive resources. The list of such qualitative characteristics might include speed, mobility, the capabilities of the system for multipurpose use, the degree of its defensibility and invulnerability, what equipment it has that enables it to conduct military operations under any weather conditions and at night, and others. The sides may determine and agree upon the relative balance of offensive and defensive characteristics for each large weapons system.

As these examples attest, even weapons systems with different basic missions possess certain general qualitative indicators, and differentiating their defensive and offensive capabilities seems completely feasible. The biggest difficulty here lies in weapons systems with multiple roles. This problem can be resolved by combining a system's qualitative characteristics with other factors, such as the nature of force deployment, the distance from the front lines, the number of systems available, and so forth. Even the most obviously offensive weapons system appears less dangerous in combination with such limiting factors as a small quantity, disposition far from the region of possible military actions, and so on.

For military specialists, an important, and sometimes decisive factor, that determines the nature and result of combat operations is the manpower problem: the number of soldiers, the level of their training and morale, the skill of the commanders, as well as the organizational structure of the armed forces, unit strength levels, mobilization plans for force deployment, the condition of the reserves, and the methods of preparing and training troops. All of these factors can be examined with reference to offensive and defensive capabilities.

---

[13]A number of Soviet and Western specialists see several systems as predominantly defensive resources, including antitank guided missiles, portable surface-to-air missile systems, land mines, various defensive structures, self-propelled artillery systems, and low speed air support aircraft with no aerial refueling capabilities.

Reducing the number of large-scale military exercises and maneuvers, and even more so, abandoning them altogether, can be considered a graphic demonstration of the sides' defensive intentions. Increasing the period for advance notification and limiting the number of participants in exercises that do not require advance notification serves the same goal.[14]

New agreements in this area could include, in the very near future, limits on exercises in terms of numbers of troops, aircraft, and naval forces, and in their thrust, operational scale, and the corresponding extent and location of the areas where they are conducted. Subsequently, agreement should be reached on reducing exercises to a tactical scale. And they should be conducted in such a way that defensive operations, such as holding on to occupied positions and mounting counterstrikes and counterattacks, would be evident.

The transfer of regular units to the reserve ranks can be one of the elements in the shift to a nonoffensive defense.

The issues indicated above require detailed and thoroughgoing elaboration by military and civilian specialists on both sides, on the basis of the criteria and conditions of a stable strategic military balance.

---

[14] Under modern conditions narrowing the differences between exercise conditions and combat conditions is becoming increasingly difficult; as the development of forms and methods of operational and combat training shows, the difference between training and combat increases as the means of waging an armed conflict are improved and their destructive properties increase.

Regional Conflicts and Global Security

ANDREY IGOREVICH KOLOSOVSKIY*

The dialectics of the connection between regional conflicts** and the general state of international affairs, the level of world tension, and the general atmosphere in East-West relations, is an important element of the interdependence of the contemporary world. Regional situations and the state of affairs in the world arena, and the interests of large and small states interact on the most diverse planes, merging into a single system of international relations.

To put the question in the broadest terms, one cannot speak about any sort of all-embracing global security if it does not mean security in the direct sense for everyone. If people feel at ease living in European homes, but are under a constant threat of death, destruction, or deprivation living in Asian, African, or Latin American homes, that is only European security. And it is quite a relative security at that.

Postwar history shows that a crisis with any degree of seriousness, even in the most remote corner of the globe, can quickly cause repercussions—sometimes substantial ones—in Soviet-American and inter-bloc relations, and can also determine the attitude of the world community, or part of it, toward one of the great powers.

The experience of détente in the 1970s confirmed that it is impossible to achieve a stable normalization of relations between the U.S.S.R. and the United States, and between the Warsaw Treaty Organization and NATO, by dealing only with the issues of arms control and the establishment of bilateral cooperation. Granted, there were apparently certain internal reasons contributing to the break with détente. Steps were taken in military development that caused tension and destabilized the situation. The relations between the two systems are an internally contradictory process with inherent ebbs and flows. At the same time, the most important catalyst—and I do mean catalyst,

---

*Expert on problems in multilateral diplomacy. This article appeared in the June 1988 issue of *MEMO*.

**The concern here is primarily with conflict situations, crises, and wars in the Third World, in which either developing countries only, or both developing and developed—socialist and Western—countries may be involved. The subject also includes tension that arises in some part of the Third World in connection with a crisis within a given country.

Considering the particular timeliness of the problem, the editors intend to continue its discussion in upcoming issues.

and not pretext—of the sharp deterioration in Soviet-American relations in the late 1970s and early 1980s, of the increase in East-West tension, and of the transformation of the image and prestige of the great powers in the eyes of governments and public opinion was the development of regional crises and the behavior of the two sides with regard to those crises.

Now, as we are rethinking a great many things, we are working persistently to establish nonconfrontational forms of interaction with the West, proceeding from the premise that a real strengthening of security is possible only if we resolve the entire range of problems existing between the two blocs, including regional conflicts. That is the only correct path that reflects the objective interweaving of interests, events, and processes in the contemporary world.

Every region of the Third World has close political, economic, military, ideological, historical, and cultural ties to states that are militarily and economically powerful. At the same time, it would be wrong to depict relations between the major powers and these regions according to the "subject of action—object of action" pattern, as though the various powers were merely pursuing their own goals in the regions, while encountering more or less resistance in the process. Both the peoples and governments of developing countries have long since had their own specific interests, and by taking advantage of interbloc and other contradictions, they have repeatedly managed to realize those interests, sometimes plainly to the detriment of the interests of the great powers close to them.

When a crisis begins or develops, the entire established system of relations, balances, interests, and influences starts shifting either slowly or quickly, and sometimes very rapidly and chaotically. The reaction of each individual state or bloc depends, of course, on many factors, but especially on the general approach that has been taken at the given moment to relations with the Third World, and to processes taking place in the region of liberated states.

The correct interpretation of real interests and of the ways in which they are perceived by the parties involved is a critical element in the resolution of regional crises. This is of fundamental importance both for finding a formula for compromise between the parties directly involved in the conflict, and for establishing cooperation among third countries, especially the great powers, in connection with that compromise. Many interests are intertwined in various conflict situations, but in each concrete case those interests are very specific for the direct parties to the conflict. Interests of third countries are more universal in nature, and the approach of those countries to circumstances that outwardly are totally different is determined by the relationship among factors that are approximately the same.

Economic considerations, in particular, exert a powerful and fairly stable influence on the determination of long-term approaches both to conflict situations in general and to specific crises. Economics often does not come to the fore as the motive for given actions when there is an abrupt development of events, but its demands are always there in some latent form, and they are taken into consideration in the normal process of policy making, when that process is not based on a subjective, arbitrary approach.

It is unlikely that anyone would dispute the contention that the Western economy today cannot exist without the closest, day-to-day relations with the developing world. For a long time now these have not been relations based on the old colonial model, when the main activity was the removal of riches from the colonies. Today the Third World is not only a source of raw materials, but also an extremely important market, which, naturally, would not exist if it were denied the means for development. It would also be a distortion to claim that these relations are based entirely on diktat and one-sided gain, rather than on reciprocity. The developing countries also need the Western economy—which represents money, technology, and technological skills, as well as a market for their goods.

Just how fairly and equitably the relations between them are organized, and how they might be reformed, is another matter. This question is now being answered and will be answered in the future in a difficult, intense struggle on a bilateral and multilateral basis, but we can be confident that an absolute majority of the participants will not try to introduce any sort of serious crises into the established system of West-South economic relations. One indicator of the validity of this thesis is the widespread positive reaction to the Soviet statement, made at the highest official level, that our goals do not include undermining the established system of economic relations between capitalist and developing countries.

Unquestionably, the Soviet Union and the other states in the socialist commonwealth have their own economic interests in the Third World; they have an interest in commercial and economic ties with the developing countries. However, because of their geographical situation, the structure of their natural resources, the level of their economic development, and the extent of their involvement in the world economy, it would seem that these relations are not vitally important to them. One can suppose that they will eventually have a greater economic need to expand economic relations with the developing countries, and to participate in a more active division of labor and economic integration. But that is not a question for the immediate future. From an economic standpoint, it is evidently more important for us today simply to have normal economic cooperation with the developing countries that is mutually beneficial. That means we need, first and foremost, solvent partners or partners that have resources and products we need.

The classical thesis that policies should be acutely attuned to economic requirements lest they redound to the harm of their creators remains valid today.

The developing countries' exceptional importance to the economy of the West is the primary factor determining the close, sometimes even morbid, political attention the West pays to what is going on in those countries, what sort of crises are developing there, and how the other pieces on the world chess board are behaving toward them. It is also important, in our opinion, to state that today the West strives to protect its economic interests in the Third World mainly through economic and political-economic methods. Of course, there are still quite a few remnants of open colonialism and of approaches that rely on military force, especially in U.S. policies. But the more than cool reaction to such actions on the part of the United States' West European and other allies shows that this tendency is not the prevailing one.

It would be an intolerable oversimplification to claim that the West's policy toward regional conflicts is determined by economics alone, or that political interests are just translations of economic interests—although it does sometime happen that economic interests can be seen quite plainly in political positions. Consider, for example, Japan's attitude toward the Mideast conflict or the Iran-Iraq conflict, or the Western powers' approach to the situation in South Africa and Namibia. Usually everything is much more complicated, and numerous contradictory and overlapping factors affect the formation of policy.

Among them, one of the most important and difficult to analyze is the class or ideological factor. The reality of today's world is such that evaluations by the East and West of events in the Third World are inevitably influenced by the factor of class sympathies or antipathies, and relationships to accepted ideological precepts and social and political ideals and stereotypes. This is a powerful factor in attitudes both toward crises associated with social and political changes in some country, or with the national liberation struggle, and toward more classical interstate or international conflicts.

It would not be a great exaggeration to claim that over the course of several decades it has been precisely the ideological approach—developed, moreover, in terms of the classical "socialism-capitalism" dilemma—that has largely been the determining factor in the choice of policies in the Third World, including policies toward conflicts. As experience has shown, the result of this approach has been an acute, sometimes simply dangerous, confrontation with the United States, and an analysis of trends in the development of that group of states that has not always been appropriate to the processes that were actually taking place. This is not a matter of denying the existence of class interests or different social orientations in the developing countries, or of casting doubt on the legitimacy of the national liberation struggle or the reality of contradictions between the United States and other Western countries, on the one hand, and the developing world, on the other. All these things do exist and will exist, just as the attitude toward these phenomena that is based on our ideology does and will exist. The categories enumerated here, however, do not provide a picture of the complete reality of the Third World. That reality is much more varied and contains many more components, many of which do not fit into the "socialism-capitalism" scheme, and do not yield to an ideological analysis built around that contradiction. Therefore, we need a view of the developing countries that is to a considerable degree de-ideologized, and that recognizes the uniqueness of the processes at work there, and their independence of the rivalry between the two socioeconomic systems.

In addition, it is of fundamental importance to determine, in the spirit of the new political thinking, what, from the standpoint of our domestic tasks and foreign policy goals, and the demands of world socialism, corresponds to our class interests. Does a struggle, a confrontation, always mean that they are truly being defended?

In our practical and scientific circles, and especially in our propaganda, the concept that defines class interest in terms of elementary confrontational logic used to be common (and, from every indication, has still not been totally overcome). Reduced to the simplest formula possible, this concept interprets everything that happens, especially Third World conflicts, as follows. If the course of events is detrimental to U.S. interests and creates difficulties for the United States, if anti-American slogans and moods are present there, then that is automatically good, regardless of all other components. Just as in a children's game, everything is divided into "ours" and "theirs," and the map of the world is seen as some sort of abacus on which the countries are like counters that move from the American side to the Soviet side.

Such a view of the world—oversimplified, inaccurate, unproductive, and dangerous—is, incidentally, quite widespread (only with the labels reversed) among rightist imperialist circles.

Historical experience and, what's more, the contemporary political map of the world demonstrate clearly that by no means does every regime that has quarreled with the Americans follow a course of social progress, justice, and democracy; provide development and peace for its people; and contribute to the strengthening of regional and international security. By no means does every regime that counts on support in a conflict with other countries pursue its own legitimate interests, or is prepared to take into account the interests of others, the norms of international law, and the disposition of world public opinion.

In assessing the behavior of parties in conflicts, and events in the Third World, it is important to rely on criteria that have been carefully weighed and checked against our fundamental tenets and tasks in all areas of world policy, and that do not diverge from our overall, highest-priority foreign-policy goals.

The main causes of regional crises and social upheavals in the Third World are processes taking place in those countries and regions themselves, and that are determined by the stage of their development, the alignment of political forces, and the specific features of their history, traditions, and so forth.

It follows from this that attempts made from the outside either to stop or reverse naturally occurring changes, or to urge them on in an effort to upset the social and political status quo, no matter how anachronistic it may seem, are equally illegitimate. It also follows that the processes developing in those countries or in relations among them will be the more natural, lasting, and organic to their peoples, the less that third countries are involved in them. The involvement of third countries in conflicts and crises that arise on local soil inevitably leads to the internationalization of those conflicts, to the introduction of what are usually alien ideological criteria borrowed from the arsenal of East-West debates, and to a hardening of the positions of the parties directly involved, which cease to act according to the local balance of forces and interests, and strive to forcibly tilt the balance in their own favor by relying on outside support. This sort of aggravation of a conflict is usually difficult to reverse, since it significantly increases the resources that continue to feed the conflict, and also creates new dimensions that cannot be altered by its direct participants.

Finally, it follows from this that one needs to evaluate a conflict in the Third World (no matter what kind of conflict it may be, whether between states or within a state) primarily within the local system of reference point, without closing one's eyes to the interests of all the parties involved, rather than transferring it into the ideologized system of East-West relations. It will be considerably better for the immediate parties to the conflict and for international relations as a whole if a crisis is kept as long as possible outside the plane of East-West relations, and not used as an arena for East-West confrontation.

At the same time, living in an interconnected system of international relations in which there is a certain logic to the behavior of the parties involved, it is difficult to expect that regional conflicts will take place in laboratory-like isolation, without drawing in outside forces to some degree or another. The question is whether such involvement should be viewed as a desired goal, or as a necessary step that requires caution, a careful consideration of one's own and others' interests, a constant measuring of concrete situations against the more general imperatives of strengthening global security, an effort to overcome confrontation, and an orientation toward universal human values.

If principles and proclaimed objectives are applied selectively, rather than universally, and are reinterpreted in some specific way in each situation, they are devalued and become their own antitheses. A great power can and must avoid interfering in internal events in other countries and regions, but it is difficult to be neutral and not to show one's attitude toward what is happening. Our sympathies, it seems, cannot be separated from the image of the socialism that we have now started to create. Therefore, our concrete actions should correspond in reality to the conviction that peace is the highest value, that disputes and problems should be resolved through peaceful rather than military means, and that law should prevail over force. It should become an indisputable truth that, in addition to one's own interests, others' interests exist and are taken into consideration; that policies are carried out not for one's own sake, but for the sake of a genuine, tangible improvement in the living conditions of the masses and of each individual; and that no goals can justify terrorism, genocide, and the death of totally innocent people.

As a result of its difficult history, our country has gained through suffering an understanding that socialism without democracy, without respect for the human being and his rights and freedoms, is impossible. The image of socialism will become immeasurably more attractive when the outside world sees that the criteria of democracy and respect for human rights are invariably present in our evaluation of events in other regions, and in our choice of friends and allies, and that our condemnation of terrorism and our orientation toward political rather than military means of solving problems are not just declarations, but actual policies.

In short, the new political thinking, the theory of the balance of interests, recognition of the right of every people to arrange its life independently, the unconditional orientation toward the peaceful solution of problems, and the firm belief in the importance of democratic values, rather than a view of the world as a theater of hostilities where beachheads of influence must be won—that is the basis for ideologically evaluating conflicts and crises, and the actions of their participants, in our time. Fortunately, the contemporary world has reached such a stage of development, such a recognition of realities, and such a wide state of democratic consciousness that these criteria are becoming more and more universal. Voting in the United Nations and in other international forums, and outbursts of public opinion in various countries, including the United States and Western Europe, show that the world community reacts sharply to situations in which the actions of the parties, particularly the great powers, are dominated by selfishness, an unwillingness to reckon with the will of other peoples, and disregard for international law; and it clearly expresses its negative attitude toward such politics. One could say that a certain type of universal human solidarity has developed, the boundaries of which ignore bloc barriers, and often go against them, but coincide with the goals of preserving peace on earth and ensuring the right of every people to independent development, without violating the rights of others.

To be among the leaders of this process, soberly recognizing one's own interests, guided by the need to find a balance between these interests and the interests of others, and concerned primarily with the search for ways to prevent, settle, or de-escalate a crisis—that, in accordance with socialist ideology, is the fitting role of a great power with regard to regional conflicts.

The great powers' military presence and military strategy considerations play no small role in regional dramas. This is one of the factors capable of drastically altering the balance of power in a regional conflict, aggravating the situation, and shifting the crisis onto the plane of interbloc confrontation. Military rivalry is a constant element in decisions that are made, and protection of national security is a widespread public justification for involvement in regional events.

In speaking of the great powers' military activities with regard to various regions, it would evidently be a good idea to distinguish between actions that are connected with their own interests and those of their bloc allies, and actions that support the parties directly involved in the conflict.

The security of the U.S.S.R. vis-à-vis the United States and of the Warsaw Treaty Organization vis-à-vis NATO, and vice versa, is ensured today, as we know, by parity in nuclear weapons in the context of the alignment of forces that has developed historically in other areas of military rivalry. The mountains of weapons that both sides have amassed have reached such a height that the military potential of practically any other figure acting in the international arena simply cannot be compared to them and cannot pose any serious military threat to them. The concept of ensuring the security of the nuclear powers and their allies in the context of a radical reduction of nuclear weapons aimed at their ultimate elimination is not based on a buildup of military strength in other areas, but on political and legal measures, the establishment of an arms balance that is not perceived as a threat to either side, and the introduction of trust, openness, and predictability in relations between the blocs. At the same time, naturally, guarantees will have to be made that threats to them, including nuclear, chemical, and others, will not arise from third parties.

Under current conditions and in the foreseeable future, it seems incorrect to assert that regional conflicts and crises represent any sort of real military threat to the national security of the great powers, and therefore may require military action in response, no matter how close to their own territory these events take place. It is another matter that regional complications may threaten the political and economic interests, prestige, and other interests of the great powers, and may take an undesirable turn for them from an ideological standpoint. But one can hardly say that any sort of military action is legitimate and justified in order to defend national security against such "threats," and to secure interests that have nothing directly to do with defense.

Any military actions—from direct participation to the supply of weapons—in the interest of any of the parties to a conflict are also extremely dangerous from the standpoint both of the preservation of world peace, and of the development of specific situations. These kinds of action cause the greatest anxiety among the other great powers, the other bloc, and have the potential to rapidly escalate regional tension into global tension. They force the other parties involved in the conflict to also seek military assistance; they lead to an even greater polarization and hardening of positions; they weaken the influence of factors that might encourage a settlement, such as natural economic, political, and moral fatigue from hostilities; and they make it more difficult for the parties not only to achieve a lasting settlement, but even to return to their original positions. Massive military assistance ultimately leads to the militarization of the regime receiving that assistance, with all the ensuing consequences, to a change in the balance of forces in the region, and to a resulting increase in tension and unleashing of an arms race. The power providing the military assistance itself gradually becomes a hostage to it—it has become so involved in relations with the receiving side that it is forced to be governed in the conflict by that party's goals and interests, rather than by its own. In time, the hope of obtaining great economic benefits from the military aid also reversed. As experience shows, countries exhausted by a conflict sooner or later may turn into unreliable debtors, and the country that helps them reach such a state ends up having to help pay to get them out of it.

The conclusion from the premises cited here is obvious: a maximum reduction in the great powers' military activities in the Third World is needed. This will benefit both the international situation as a whole and the regional conditions. Naturally, some sort of military activity related to the requirements of strategic opposition and to helping allies among the developing countries will remain, but it is important to ensure that it be steadily reduced. This will not be easy to achieve, especially since this aspect is far from the top of the disarmament list. But armed with firm political will and a realistic assessment of the current state of affairs, we should be able to move things off dead center here, too. All the paths—both negotiated decisions and unilateral steps based on the principle of rational sufficiency—are open to this goal. Here it is also necessary to establish trust and a belief in the predictability of the other side's actions. In any case, when decisions are made that involve military activities in the Third World, the determining factors should be the endeavor for restraint, and fear, lest some clumsy move rock the boat of regional and global stability.

Both the development of regional conflicts and the global, international situation depend to a great extent on the behavior of the great powers, especially the United States and the U.S.S.R., with regard to these conflicts, and on their correct understanding of their interests and the intentions of others. There will be no significant progress toward a world free of constant confrontation and an escalating arms race, no progress toward a truly secure world, if we do not succeed in establishing cooperation in these matters. The issue here is not dividing the world up into spheres of influence, or prolonged negotiations aimed at working out a code of conduct on paper. The issue here is the need to understand the interests of others, to realistically assess one's own needs and actions, to overcome long-established stereotypes in evaluating the positions of parties involved in a conflict, and to aim for joint actions in the name of preventing, localizing, and settling crises.

In the final analysis, the direct parties to a conflict are the only ones that can achieve a lasting settlement. Each has its own goals and interests, its own history of hostility, and its own framework for political maneuvering. Their desire for a settlement is by no means a foregone conclusion: it happens, and fairly often, that a constant state of crisis is politically advantageous to certain governments, political forces, and leaders. But the threat to peace that the conflict creates, and the deprivations it brings on the peoples involved are not lessened by this fact.

This makes the international environment in which a conflict develops all the more important. It can either feed and prolong it, or it can do everything possible to lessen the crisis, refuse to provide resources for its continuation, and help induce the parties to seek out rational compromises. A crisis, particularly an armed conflict, must be viewed as a dangerous anomaly in international life that the efforts of all states should be focused on preventing and eliminating. There needs to be widespread understanding that any regional conflict is a threat to universal security and represents the death and suffering of thousands of people, and that the only proper response to it is not unilateral interference and confrontation, but joint, coordinated actions by forces representing all poles on the present-day political map of the world.

The key to progress in the matter of settling conflicts is a change in the approach of the world community, particularly that of the great powers, to the problem, and the application of new political thinking in this area.

Just as the task of curbing the arms race requires a renunciation of selfish attempts to ensure security for oneself alone, the settlement of regional conflicts dictates the need to overcome the outmoded approach that views them through the prism of strengthening influence, penetration, the protection of strategic interests, and the ideological, regional, or religious solidarity of individual states.

Using regional crises for one's own selfish purposes and determining one's position by something other than the interests of a fair settlement is just as immoral as building security on nuclear terror.

The imperative of our time is to introduce into international political thinking an orientation toward mandatory settlement of conflicts and creation of the conditions for lasting peace, and not just polemical debates about the situation in a given region. It is fairly indicative that in the Security Council, at sessions of the U.N. General Assembly, and at forums of the Nonalignment Movement, items on the agenda pertaining to regional issues are usually formulated simply as the discussion of the situation in some part of the globe. It would be more logical to focus attention on the question of what sort of formula there should be for a fair—in the sense of taking the interests of all the parties into account—and lasting settlement, and what sort of practical measures are necessary for its implementation.

One should not conclude that it is possible to work out some magical plan that will enable us to find a solution to all conflict situations in a short time. In each case, the concrete mechanism for reaching a settlement must take into account the internal workings of the given conflict, its history, the national psychology of the parties involved, and so on. The settlement of crises that have been particularly neglected will always be complicated and will require persistent and purposeful efforts. It is important to try to get started and to take at least the first steps. The de-escalation of a conflict, and the beginning of a partial settlement represent a better option than the endless maintenance of a conflict in expectation of an all-encompassing resolution.

Today there are enough international legal principles to form a universal foundation for the settlement of regional conflicts. They are set down in the U.N. Charter, in the Declaration on the Principles of International Law, and many other documents. A conflict, properly speaking, arises from situations in which one or several of these principles are violated, and the essence of a settlement lies in working out a formula according to which the situation can be brought into line with the basic norms of international law and the interests of all the parties involved.

This formula is different in each individual case, but it must always be based on a recognition of the principle of peaceful coexistence and consideration of the legitimate interests of all the parties.

The principle of peaceful coexistence should be considered not just as the basis of relations between the two systems, but as the universal basis for relations among all states, a basis which assumes respect and tolerance for the political and economic system and the specific ideological, religious, and other features of other countries, and for their legitimate interests.

Consideration for the interests of all the forces involved in a conflict (governments, the population, individual national and religious groups, and so forth) should be given priority over the identification and punishment of the aggressor, the sorting out of historical rights, or other such factors. Practically all present regional conflicts have a long history of mutual claims, attacks, infringements on legitimate interests, and violations of the norms of international law on the part of all the parties to the conflict. Experience clearly shows that concentrating on identifying and condemning the "guilty party" often means, in practice, blocking a settlement. Therefore, the settlement process should be aimed first and foremost at working out a balance of the interests of all parties, and at eliminating the factors that could lead to the use of force or threat of its use in the future.

The settlement process itself should be based on a renunciation of the use of force as a method for resolving conflicts, and on the principle of settling them through peaceful, political means. This means that none of the parties should initiate an armed phase of any dispute, conflict, or crisis. But it also means that if an armed struggle has broken out, once it ends the victim should view force as an extremely undesirable method for regaining its positions.

The methods and concrete paths for a political settlement can be extremely varied. Life itself gives rise to new forms that have never been used before. The promising nature of the method of national reconciliation, and the originality of the settlement process in Central America are living proof of this.

Any wars are dangerous in the nuclear-space age, and they should be totally ruled out. Moreover, the history of regional conflicts shows that a series of armed clashes usually does not lead to a fair settlement, or even to a stable resolution in favor of any of the parties.

The principle of settling conflicts peacefully will remain useless in practice, and will even be used to actually consolidate the results of the use of force, if it is not combined with decisive, including compulsory, measures on the part of the international community to eliminate the results of the use of force and to achieve a stable settlement.

We need to revive the idea of collective security that is presented in the U.N. Charter, understood not simply as actions to stop aggression and punish the aggressor, but as a set of measures, including compulsory ones, providing for the prevention and settlement of conflicts, and creation of the conditions for lasting peace.

Naturally, the United Nations should play the central role in developing the principles and concrete dimensions of settlements, and in implementing measures to bring about any particular settlement. Despite the fact that the U.N.'s successes in resolving regional crises are far from brilliant, it has worked out a set of basic principles that are applicable to all major conflicts, and it has gained unique experience in peacekeeping operations. Energetic U.N. efforts in this area based on the cooperation of the great powers and all states would mean implementation of the concept of comprehensive security. Naturally, the stronger the will of the parties to a conflict to find ways to normalize relations with one another, the greater the success will be here. The U.N.'s diplomatic efforts should be aimed primarily at involving the parties to conflicts in a negotiating process. At the same time, it seems that the world community should involve itself in settlement efforts regardless of whether all parties want to participate in this process. Refusal to participate should mean not that international settlement efforts are halted, but only that the interests of the absent party will be less well known and less well taken into account.

In determining our approach toward regional conflicts, we must proceed firmly from the premise that maintaining peace and stability in all regions, while observing the right of all peoples to determine their own course of development, is in keeping with the highest interests of our state. For Third World countries, both near and far, the Soviet Union cannot fail to be a symbol of justice and of the struggle for peace and security for all. It must be obvious that we propose and support realistic settlement formulas and mechanisms that take into account the interests of all parties involved, and not just those that are close to us, and that we disapprove of any illegal actions.

In the long run, such a policy will strengthen the prestige and influence of the state much more than blind support for allies, which often are not seeking a settlement. In any conflict it is possible to maintain contacts with all the parties, and to act as a force that is realistically capable of serving as an intermediary.

By acting in this way, we can become a pioneer of the new political thinking in the area of settling regional conflicts, as elsewhere, and can demonstrate in this field that the priorities of our foreign-policy activities are determined by universal human values and the interests of global security.

Reflections on the Fate of Europe

Yuriy Antonovich Borko and Boris Sergeyevich Orlov*

In studying Western European social-science literature of the past 10 to 15 years, one cannot fail to notice the recurring motifs of alarm. Here are but a few titles of books and articles: "The Crisis of Europe"; "In Defense of a Europe That Is Becoming Degraded"; "The Decline of Europe Need Not Be Considered Irreversible"; and "To Revive Europe." Needless to say, there is a degree of a deliberate dramatization in these titles. However, it is a question of degree, not essence. In other words, there are real grounds for the alarmed questions about trends in Europe's development and prospects and its place and role in the world community of the 21st century now at our doorstep. And this also affects our country directly.

The problems of European development are the subject of a discussion between Doctor of Economics Yuriy Antonovich Borko, head of a department of the U.S.S.R. Academy of Sciences' Institute of Social-Science Research Information, and Doctor of History Boris Sergeyevich Orlov, head of a section of the Institute.

Borko: So much has been written and said about Europe and its past, present, and future that there's a danger of repeating what's already been said. Let's try to take a fresh look at our subject and to avoid established stereotypes.

Orlov: I agree. And without wasting the precious lines of this journal, let us pose the first question: What is the reason for our interest in Europe and its future? Only a few years ago, we would have had to cite a host of arguments to justify this interest. Today we are significantly relieved of that need. Our approach to Europe is summed up in the most succinct and at the same time pregnant formula: "Europe is our common home." Incidentally, how does this formula compare with other ideas of European community—for example, with de Gaulle's famous formula of a "Europe from the Atlantic to the Urals"?

Borko: That is a reasonable question, and I will try to answer it; but first I would like to speak about another reason for our interest in

---

*Borko is a doctor of economics and senior research associate of the U.S.S.R. Academy of Sciences' Institute of Social-Science Research Information. Orlov is a doctor of history and head of a section at the same institute. This article appeared in the September 1988 issue of *MEMO*.

Europe. It is the only region where, for the past 40 years, the two social systems have developed side by side in peaceful conditions. Time is changing our perceptions of the past, changing the criteria for our assessments—as well as the assessments themselves. Today we apply a different yardstick to both the achievements and the failures of real socialism—in our country and in those of our friends. We can also assess in a new light the various large-scale experiments conducted in Western Europe and aimed at effecting reformist transformations in capitalist society.

Orlov: I agree with you, but I must point out that we are very late in examining this experience, having wasted many years identifying mainly the negative aspects of Western European development. And only at some point in the mid-1970s did the situation start to change. And in the process of examining this experience, we must bear in mind that we have only just set out on this path. Western Europe has amassed experience that we will find instructive in the most varied areas of life and thought. This subject is worth returning to later. But for now, back to de Gaulle and his formula. What did he have in mind?

Borko: When Charles de Gaulle proposed this formula in the mid-1960s, some of our journalists and political scientists saw it as all but a strategy for the restoration of capitalism in the countries of Eastern Europe. Such were the costs of the propaganda battles of the Cold War era. In reality, de Gaulle sought to restore to France an independent role in world politics, and as a result he came to understand the need for détente and cooperation on the European continent, a détente prompted by the interdependence of the European peoples' destinies and, consequently, by a certain community of interests. In this respect, the formula of a "Europe from the Atlantic to the Urals" is akin to the idea of a "common European home."

In my view, however, the formula is significantly narrower in content. The French president thought in traditional categories of geopolitics, and it is hardly correct to see him as a forerunner of the new political thinking.

Orlov: Nor could such thinking possibly have been formulated at that time. It would be another 20 years before one could take a fresh look at the world and at Europe and appreciate the interdependence of the modern world and the inevitable alternative: either live together, or die together.

Borko: Yes, therein lies the essence of the new political thinking, which spawned the idea of the common European home that Soviet diplomacy proposed in the mid-1980s. The common European home is a *qualitatively different condition from mere political and military détente and normalization of economic relations*. It refers to the attainment of a degree of mutual understanding and a level of comprehensive and intensive cooperation such that Europe truly becomes a peaceful community of the peoples living here and an extremely important factor for peace throughout the world.

Orlov: And if Europe is our "common home," we must carefully look at what is happening on its various "floors" and in its various "apartments," at what representatives of Western Europe think about European development, and at how they interpret the idea of "wholeness." The question is of purely practical significance. For only with a full appreciation of our Western European partners' views and arguments for and against can creation of a common European home be a realistic and successful undertaking. And here we must examine the following phenomenon: exactly why have the Europeans reflected on Europe's fate so actively in recent years?

Borko: In my view, there are two sources of concern. One of them is a sobering up from the euphoria occasioned by the successes of the European capitalist countries' economic and social development in the 1950s and 1960s. Under the new economic and social conditions that arose in the 1970s, these achievements are threatened. I am referring not only to the deterioration of Western Europe's position in the world capitalist economic system. Also in doubt is the fate of the postwar "social experiment," i.e., the strategy, pursued since the late 1940s, of promoting the social and political stabilization of Western European capitalism through partial reforms and class compromises. So there are ample grounds for alarming thoughts.

But that is only an internal source. There are global sources of alarm as well, such as the threat of nuclear catastrophe, the mounting destruction of man's environment, and the famine and poverty afflicting hundreds of millions of people in the developing countries. In my view, it is the Europeans in particular who are most aware of the scope and consequences of these threats today.

Orlov: I would add that Europeans' concern is compounded by a keen awareness of the loss of historical leadership. After all, for many centuries Europeans considered themselves (and not without some justification) to be at the center of world development. This gave rise to the world outlook that would come to be called "Eurocentrism." Since the Renaissance and the times of the great geographical discoveries, Europe had been the most dynamic continent. Its productive potential developed at a rapid pace. It was the world's industrial engine and science laboratory. It was the setting for the leap in intellectual and cultural development that put the individual at the center of development. In short, all the things the authors of the Communist Manifesto observed in characterizing capitalism had their origins in Europe. But then came the First and then Second World Wars, separated by a brief interlude of two decades, and fascism and its defeat. And then there was Europe in the role of sick man, a sick man the Americans would try to put back on his feet through the Marshall Plan. And the upshot was the loss of leadership.

Borko: Yes, but that was followed by a rather lengthy period of rapid economic growth, social reforms, the establishment and development of the European Community, and the strengthening of Western Europe's international positions.

Orlov: Nevertheless, since the mid-1970s, the theme of Western Europe's lagging behind and its becoming a backward peripheral area has been sounded once more. That raises the question of what lessons Europe has drawn from its history, especially its history in the 20th century.

Borko: It is difficult to overstate the drama of European history in the first half of this century. Indeed, it is the history of two world wars, the history of the most acute social conflicts and revolutionary battles, the history of the short-lived triumph and then crushing defeat of fascism. European capital was shaken to its foundations. The peoples of Europe paid for these lessons with millions of deaths and crippled lives. It seems to me indisputable that since 1945, Western Europe has drawn the most serious conclusions from the experience of the preceding decades, and that these conclusions encompass the realm of both social relations and relations among states.

Orlov: Can you briefly describe the essence of those conclusions?

Borko: Their essence consists in a realization of the need for regulation—regulation of social processes and regulation of relations among states, regulation based on the principle of compromise and effected through institutional mechanisms. And this is not theory, much less propaganda—as it was presented to us in the past. It has become practice, real experience that is constantly studied and analyzed by Western researchers.

Orlov: I agree with you. Specifically, this is reflected in the way Western Europeans view social issues.

Borko: In my opinion, this is the most important aspect. Had they not embarked on the path of regulating their internal social problems, the Western European states would not have been able to regulate their relations with one another.

Orlov: And the principal regulating mechanism is the social-welfare state, a state that resulted from a compromise between the dominant classes and the organizations representing the interests of working people. Its formation began in the final decades of the previous century (let us recall the policies of Bismarck). However, it did not fully manifest itself in the form of the welfare state until after the Second World War. Insisting on the implementation of social reforms, the parties representing the workers' interests—above all the social democrats—essentially assumed the function of effecting a social correction in the market mechanism. In this connection, it should not be forgotten that this reformist strategy rested on the might of the entire leftist movement, including the communists, who constantly criticized the social democrats for inconsistency in pursuing reforms and who put forward their own alternative strategy.

Borko: But didn't the bourgeois parties participate in implementing this policy? It seems to me that the long-term orientation toward social compromise represented a most important shift in the dominant class's political ideology and political practice.

Orlov: That is true. Nevertheless, there was and is a difference between the social strategies pursued by the bourgeois parties and the leftist parties. To oversimplify somewhat, the social reformism of the bourgeoisie was aimed at stabilizing capitalist relations. For the social democrats, it was simultaneously a means of improving the lot of the working people in the specific situation and a stage in the movement toward a society of "democratic socialism."

Borko: I would like to stress that this social policy had a solid economic base. It is especially clear today that, from the first postwar decades right up to the early 1970s, there existed in Western Europe exceptionally favorable conditions for rapid economic growth. But even those conditions would probably have had far less of an impact had not the West Europeans created a well-developed system of state regulation of the economy based on Keynesianism. The most important component of this Keynesianism is a broad-based social policy that has enabled capitalism to catch its second wind, so to speak.

Orlov: But as subsequent events have shown, the mechanism of social regulation has begun to break down. What do you see as the cause of this phenomenon? Let us say that, on the political level—or to be more precise, the political-ideological level—the causes are as follows. The neoconservatives—it is they who play the role of chief critic—contend that the social democrats have overburdened the state with social outlays; that excessive intervention in the economy has sapped its dynamism and robbed it of its flexibility; that the bureaucracy has burgeoned; that the working class is living beyond its means and "consuming" investments in production; and that the social state has in general become a kind of social keeper, spawning a free-ride mentality in society.

Borko: Generally speaking, where there's smoke, there's fire. Some of the phenomena that conservative ideologists and economists have cited have indeed taken place, such as the excessive bureaucratization of the state regulatory system, its relative inefficiency, and its sluggishness. But these phenomena are secondary in nature. Most important, in my view, are radical changes in the basic conditions of the development of the capitalist economy that took place in the 1970s. These changes have been thoroughly analyzed in Soviet and foreign economic literature, and there's no need to dwell on them. In the context of our dialogue, it is important to emphasize their outcome—a shift from high rates of economic growth to very moderate rates, the reemergence of massive unemployment, and reduced possibilities for social maneuvering.

Orlov: Are you saying, then, that the trouble lies not with mistakes or errors on the part of various politicians but with established objective conditions?

Borko: Well, that would be an oversimplification. I simply want to emphasize that the social and political situation of the 1970s and 1980s must be analyzed from the standpoint of a clear deterioration of the basic conditions for capitalist expansion.

As for mistakes, I would single out two. But the blame for the first lies not so much with politicians as with European business, which missed the start of a new stage of the scientific and technical revolution and of industrial restructuring. You will recall that the terms "Europessimism" and "Eurosclerosis" suddenly appeared in the literature. Western Europe took its loss of scientific and technical leadership—above all in such fields as microelectronics and biotechnology—especially hard, although talk of a "Eurosclerosis" is groundless, in my view. In many so-called high-tech fields (aerospace, precision machinery and machine-tool manufacturing, optics, chemicals, and so on), Western Europe continues to hold leading positions. But facts are facts: Western Europe faces the task of making substantial progress in the fields in which it has lagged behind the United States and Japan and of restructuring its industry as quickly as possible. The Western European countries cannot do this individually, and hence the creation of a "European technological community" has become a key avenue for the further development of integration.

Orlov: Perhaps this accounts for the recent emergence of yet another concept—"Euro-optimism." But you spoke of two errors. What is the second one?

Borko: The second mistake is that the social democratic and bourgeois-reformist parties that were in power in the preceding decades missed the moment when they should have taken stock of the new situation and the new economic conditions and revised their theory and practice of economic and social regulation. They were too late, and then the neoconservatives, with their criticism and alternative, took political center stage.

Orlov: But I think it important to point out that radical programs are one thing, but political realities are another. On coming to power in a number of Western European countries and embarking on a policy of limiting state intervention in the economy and encouraging entrepreneurial activity, the conservatives left the system of the social state as such virtually untouched. The social budgets of the states in which they are in power attest to that.

Borko: That is understandable. Even the conservative wing of the bourgeoisie realizes that there is currently no alternative to the policy of social compromise.

Orlov: And not just now. The bourgeoisie is convinced that confrontational models of social development are fraught with unforeseen consequences. Its flirtation with German fascism taught it an unforgettable lesson. Incidentally, even the term "social revenge," in my view, fails to convey the essence of modern neoconservative policy. The entrepreneurial circles have a stake first of all in maintaining a consensual climate in society; it is not in their interest to aggravate social conflicts. It is another matter that the social policies they pursue are oriented toward the individual, thereby destroying the atmosphere of collective solidarity.

Borko: Even so, social tensions have increased with the coming to power of bourgeois-conservative forces. There is a logic of actions that is stronger than the logic of intentions. The economic situation of the past 10 to 15 years has dictated a "hard-line" social policy—and dictated it to social-democratic and socialist governments alike in a number of Western European countries. The conservatives are putting social policy on a market footing, shattering not only collectivist solidarity but also the social and political consensus established since the war.

Orlov: I don't entirely agree. The problem lies not in the destruction of consensus as such but in the search for a new consensus, one that takes into account the stratification of society into two-thirds people who are fairly well off and one-third marginals who are completely dependent on social entitlements. The stability of that consensus is another matter, not to mention the humanitarian aspect of the problem. In any case, the neoconservatives are devising their own strategy of social maneuvering, and for the present it has brought them success, as voter support attests.

Borko: Yes, you're probably right. Your clarification takes into account the level achieved in the formation of a civil society—one of the Europeans' chief accomplishments in their political history. I think that, while rightly criticizing the shortcomings and limited character of bourgeois democracy, we have at the same time underestimated its positive role in the Western European countries' social and political development. In this connection, I would pose the question, isn't our assessment of the theory and practice of "pluralist democracy" one-sided?

Orlov: I think that we must indeed take a closer look at this question. Ideological and political pluralism in Europe was not granted to or by the bourgeoisie; it is the result of an acute struggle waged in Western Europe for centuries (the medieval city was the first cradle of democracy in the new era).

Borko: But without going so far back in history, we doubtless have a right to say that, at all the stages of capitalist development, every step on the path of establishing and broadening political democracy has been linked with the growth of the organized workers' movement.

Orlov: Yes, that is precisely how the eight-hour workday, universal suffrage, certain social guarantees, and the right to form trade unions and political organizations were won. And all this gave living meaning to what political scientists have subsequently termed pluralist democracy. This democracy eventually enabled the bourgeoisie to gradually occupy commanding positions in European society. But this same democracy enabled the leftist political parties to form—above all the social democratic and communist parties. The influence of the workers' parties and labor unions grew to such an extent that the dominant class could no longer ignore them. And in the late 1960s and early 1970s, the social democratic parties completely set the tone of political life in the countries of Western Europe. This was the "golden age," so to speak, of social democracy. The multiplicity of interests and positions, the autonomous existence of civil society, the regulation of conflicts on the basis of social and political compromise—these trends were developed in Western Europe, especially after many countries of the European continent experienced first-hand the nightmares of Hitler's totalitarian regime.

And so the creation and maintenance of the institution of the social-welfare state, the regulation of the economy, and political diversity—all these have been conceptualized and developed by Western Europe in the past few decades. But the lessons of the two world wars go beyond that. Western Europe has demonstrated unique experience in the establishment of state-to-state relations. Let us ask a very simple question: What has prompted the Western Europeans to pursue integration?

Borko: First, a desire to put a stop to intra-European wars once and for all. The speech that Winston Churchill delivered in the American city of Fulton in March 1946 is well known, a speech that might be called the "cold war manifesto." But in September of that same year, Churchill gave a brief speech in Zurich on the occasion of his receipt of an honorary doctorate from Zurich University. In this speech, he recalled the old slogan of a "United States of Europe," saying that only such an arrangement could overcome French-German antagonism and other conflicts between states, prevent new wars, and create conditions for the restoration of Europe's position in the world. In my view, this speech is even more important than the Fulton address in European political history.

Orlov: But the accepted view is that integration was based on economic processes and considerations.

Borko: Yes, Western European integration is indeed based on the internationalization and integration of capitalist production. I observed only that the first powerful political impetus for a "united Europe" was the desire to put an end to the conflicts between states that had led to two world wars. Without this, integration could not have assumed the required dynamism or won mass support, including the support of a majority of the democratic forces.

Orlov: Integration processes have been developing for almost 40 years now (if we take the unveiling of the famous Schuman Plan as the starting point), and we have witnessed all these years a constant and bitter struggle within the European Community over the most varied issues. But the community has not collapsed. Moreover, it has gone from the Six to the Nine, to the Ten and, finally, to the Twelve. What accounts for this, when it would seem that the admission of new members would complicate the effort to reconcile interests? Aside from all else, this question also interests me from the standpoint of understanding the maturity of Western European political culture.

Borko: Indeed, at first glance the European Community would seem to be acting to its own detriment, since the development of integration in terms of breadth undoubtedly impedes its development in terms of depth. But let's talk about this for a moment. Economic integration is an extraordinarily lengthy process. In the modern world, meanwhile, a country has to defend its economic and political interests in the present, on a day-to-day basis. Hence the drive for political consolidation, for a situation in which Western Europe would speak with one voice and act as an autonomous political player in the world arena. For this reason, the political advantages of broadening the Community outweigh, in a certain sense, the financial and economic losses that such action entails. And this being the case, the process of reconciling interests and the need to fashion compromises are inescapable. Consensus based on compromise is the cornerstone of integration, so to speak. The entire tremendously complex mechanism through which the European Community functions is based on it.

Orlov: In this context, how are we to assess the new level of integration that is to be achieved by 1992?

Borko: I am not convinced that the Community will reach that level on schedule. I would add that the Community itself is not convinced of it, and that from a legal standpoint, 1992 is an agreed-upon deadline, not a treaty obligation. The fact is that the creation of a truly common market in goods, services, capital, and labor is to be completed by that time. But the difficulties and divergent interests are so great that they can hardly be fully overcome in the remaining four years. Nevertheless, we must proceed on the assumption that Western European integration will continue to develop.

Orlov: Has the process affected the tenor of relations among the Community member countries?

Borko: Without a doubt. But for my part, I would like to ask this question: What has integration changed in French-West German relations?

Orlov: Something has happened that nobody could have imagined 30 or 40 years ago. A process of intensive rapprochement is under way in the most diverse spheres—political, economic, and military. French-West German consultations at the widest range of levels have become common practice. But it is one thing for politicians to meet, and another for rapprochement to occur between peoples. Let us recall that for centuries the French regarded the Germans as an enemy and potential aggressor. The Germans felt the same way about the French. The feeling of mutual enmity was all but genetically encoded. Today the nature of relations between the Germans and French has changed considerably. The image of the enemy has disappeared. A culture of Western European intercourse is forming before our very eyes. For the West Germans and French are not the only peoples who are behaving in a new way. But the example of France and the Federal Republic of Germany is especially impressive because relations between these two neighbors were the most antagonistic in Europe.

Borko: I agree. Moreover, the new culture of Western European intercourse seems to me to be an element without which the Community would find it impossible to attain the new level of economic and political integration. One of the strongest impressions I brought back from trips to France and Belgium concerns the intensity of integration in the fields of education, science, culture, student exchanges, and the development of tourism. In my view, all these things are elements of what I would call the integration of national cultures and societies.

Orlov: Yet we also see an opposing process in which national cultures and the identity of ethnic minorities are being upheld.

Borko: Yes, and an important condition for the development of integration consists in the optimal combination of these two processes.

Orlov: And so let us sum up the initial findings. Europe has learned lessons from the two world wars, carried out substantial social and economic transformations on the basis of consensus, and created an integration mechanism. But it has also faced the task of ensuring its security under peaceful conditions.

Borko: If we consider the entire postwar period, we can distinguish two alternative ways of accomplishing this task: the Cold War and détente.

Orlov: I would put it differently. The Cold War did not serve the Europeans' interests. They faced a different problem—that of how to ensure their security. On a national or collective basis? By relying on their own forces or on the Americans' support? And they joined in the Cold War because it was the foundation on which the political and military conception of NATO was built.

Borko: It goes without saying that the Cold War did not serve the Europeans' interests. For what people's interests could be served by a cold war? Nevertheless, the Western European states chose NATO, military confrontation, and a policy based on dealing from a position of strength, though this was apparently a choice dictated by the actual correlation of forces between the United States and Western Europe and between Western Europe and the Soviet Union. It is clear that the class positions of the dominant circles and, at the same time, traditional stereotypes of foreign policy behavior played an enormous role in that choice. By the 1960s, however, it had become obvious to the more farsighted and realistic statesmen of Western Europe—such as de Gaulle, Willy Brandt, and Harold Wilson—that security and peace could not be ensured in Europe in this way.

Orlov: Yes, and that is precisely when the term "Ostpolitik" arose, and one of its chief results was the Conference on Security and Cooperation in Europe, which concluded in Helsinki in August 1975. It was essentially a unique phenomenon.

Borko: Indisputably. The Helsinki Conference was without precedent in world history. The Final Document was essentially the first document in which states with different social systems agreed in a single text on certain basic principles on which society is based, on rules of mutual behavior, and on a program of cooperation encompassing the entire region.

Orlov: In my view, this was a reflection of the high level of European political culture. It seemed that Europe had entered a period of completely new relations. As we know, however, in the late 1970s the Helsinki process of detente essentially became deadlocked and was supplanted by a new exacerbation of the international situation, including in Europe. To what can we attribute that setback today?

Borko: As for the underlying causes of what happened, I see the explanation as follows. The modern world develops in a rapid and contradictory fashion. Hotbeds of conflict arise in the most varied points of the globe. And all this takes place against the backdrop of increased interdependence of peoples and states, opposing social systems and ideologies, and, finally, the existence of nuclear weapons, which are capable of destroying all life on earth at any moment. All this demanded a radical rethinking of old ideas about the balance of national and global imperatives, class interests, and the interests of mankind as a whole. In other words, it essentially demanded new political thinking. In the late 1970s and early 1980s, not one of the states that participated in the Helsinki process, including the United States and the Soviet Union, proved capable of reaching a new level of understanding. Therefore, Helsinki was a first step—a step that was constructive but insufficient. And when this became clear, a new round of reflection and search began.

Orlov: An important feature of that search is that the most varied forces—from communists to social democrats to neoconservatives—have followed their own paths to understanding the same truth—the inevitability of creating a mechanism to prevent thermonuclear war. Among the first to embark on this path were the social democrats, who proposed the concept of "joint security." This represents a new view of realities that—and I see this as extremely important—has coincided with our new approach, as reflected in the concept of new political thinking. Such an approach could become a conceptual framework for both the process of détente initiated at Helsinki and the formula of a "common European home."

Borko: But aren't the Helsinki process and the common European home one and the same thing?

Orlov: As I see it, they have some things in common, but there are also differences. The Helsinki process represents the formulation and observance of a code of behavior of the European states in conditions of peaceful coexistence, as well as of continuing confrontation between the two different social systems. The common European home is a process of further rapprochement, a process of forming a kind of wholeness in conditions of continuing differences. This is a prospect that all the European peoples must work on and that could result in some new level of European community.

Borko: I would express that thought differently. The Final Act in Helsinki is a political platform whose aim is to create a stable system of security and cooperation in Europe. The idea of a common European home is of a historical-philosophical character, in that it reminds us of the many centuries of intellectual and material ties among the European peoples and of their interwoven historical destinies. At the same time, this idea is oriented toward the future as well as the past, for it implies the full restoration and further development of ties on a basis of common human values and with due regard for the traditions of European culture. That said, I would like to point out that some Western political scientists claim that the notion of Europe altogether excludes the Soviet Union, which is said to represent a distinctive, Eurasian type of civilization.

Orlov: The proponents of that viewpoint could even cite Blok. Recall his words: "Yes, we are Scythians, yes, we are Asiatics." Indeed, just who are we?

Borko: The question is not a simple one, needless to say. It is not simple if only because the Soviet Union is a community of many dozens of peoples who inhabit a gigantic territory that encompasses a sizable part of Europe and a sizable part of Asia. In any case, the question of whether the Eastern Slavic peoples are Europeans betrays a deliberate prejudice that is dictated by certain ideological and political positions. I don't think we need try to prove the obvious fact that the Slavs are part of the European community. Suffice it to cite such an authority as John Paul II. In 1985 he released his encyclical "Slavorum apostoli" (Apostles of the Slavs), in which Cyril and Methodius are called heralds of the integration of the European peoples. Needless to say, the point is not to cite the authority of the head of the Vatican but to recall the fact that the intellectual and material ties of the Slavic and other European peoples date back to times beyond the bounds of human memory.

Orlov: That is true. But our opponents often cite the following argument. The Soviet Union is a great power, while Europe is a community of medium-sized and small states. The U.S.S.R. acts according to its own logic, which does not coincide with the logic of the Western Europeans' behavior and their aspirations. Though an equal member of a "common European home," the U.S.S.R. will still have its global interests to consider, and hence will introduce in overall European politics emphases that are of little concern to, say, the British, the French, or the Italians.

Borko: There is no doubt that differences remain. After all, differences exist between the Americans and the Western Europeans in the Atlantic alliance, but that doesn't stop them from talking about their common Western civilization. As for globalism, Western Europe also has global interests and interests having to do with securing supplies of raw materials or markets on which to sell its products. My personal view is that the Western Europeans' global interests coincide with our country's interests in the most important respect—in preserving the peace, sharply reducing the weapons burden, and channeling the funds thus freed into efforts to accomplish pressing tasks, including the provision of aid to the developing countries, where there exists a truly explosive situation that threatens all mankind.

Orlov: In analyzing the character of relations between the U.S.S.R. and the countries of Western Europe, we seem to have left out the socialist countries of Eastern Europe.

Borko: You're right. These countries have their own special voice in the "common European concert."

Orlov: And even different voices, in view of the distinctive national policies of the Poles, the Bulgarians, the Hungarians . . .

Borko: Different within the framework of their common socialist orientation.

Orlov: Which is by no means easily realized, considering the political crises that some of these countries have experienced.

Borko: Yes, that's true. The problem of reaching a qualitatively new level confronts all the socialist countries of Europe, which are grappling with the need to modernize the entire system of social relations. But I would like to stress something else. The period of establishing the new society in these countries is long since past; they have multiplied their economic and cultural potential and amassed great political experience, which has enhanced the autonomous role that each of them plays, both within the socialist commonwealth and in overall European affairs. An understanding of this was especially apparent during Gorbachev's visit to Poland in the summer of 1988.

Orlov: Also important is the fact that the time when we tried to demonstrate "complete unanimity" is behind us. Consequently, we have embarked on a normal path of developing relations with the other socialist countries of Europe, a path that implies both compromise and a desire to reach consensus, both within the Council for Mutual Economic Assistance and outside it, as in relations with Yugoslavia, for example. Let us say frankly that we had a much more difficult time reaching such a "consensual" level of relations with the other socialist countries of Europe than we did with the Western European countries, just as it is sometimes harder to reach agreement with a close relative than with a neighbor.

Borko: Here is another indication of the fact that Europe is a continent that demonstrates exceptional diversity and, at the same time, an ability to promote that diversity to one another's benefit. I want to cite what I regard as another important aspect of European life. I am referring to the talks on establishing official relations between the European Community and the CMEA, which finally concluded with the signing in June 1988 of a corresponding document, as well as the talks between the European Community and the U.S.S.R. Rather broad prospects are opening up for economic, scientific, and technical cooperation between the two integrating associations. But this is just the beginning. Implementation of the plans for restructuring our economy, for revamping its mechanisms and structures, will open up truly colossal possibilities for trade, industrial cooperation, and joint assistance to the developing countries.

Orlov: But that is only one aspect of the matter, albeit a very important one. By virtue of its logic, restructuring affords fundamentally new possibilities for the creation of a different climate of relations between the different parts of Europe. The policy of glasnost gives free rein to dialogue, to the establishment of deeper mutual understanding between people as well as political organizations and public movements. Take the following example. Everybody knows how difficult our relations were with the social democrats, relations seemingly burdened by intractable ideological conflicts. And who could have imagined only 10 years ago that representatives of the communist and social democratic parties would sit down at the same table for their first exchange of views on pressing issues, and that this would take place in the course of celebrations of the 70th anniversary of the October Revolution in Moscow. Ideological differences remain, as do disagreements on many other issues. At the same time, however, a desire has been demonstrated to jointly discuss modern-day global problems—among them the problem of preventing thermonuclear war.

Such a meeting could be held only under glasnost. And take cultural and intellectual contacts. They have increased severalfold. And intellectual ties in particular constitute the invisible but very firm foundation that has united the peoples of Europe in its most difficult times.

Borko: Good, we've been discussing restructuring in our country. But isn't West European society in need of a certain restructuring? And what implications could such restructuring have for overall European relations?

Orlov: What are you suggesting?

Borko: The Western Europeans have a number of "sore spots," a number of problems that demand solutions. These solutions could be different, since the political forces prepared to, or trying to, solve them are different. But the solutions will determine what path the West European countries' development takes, and hence the shape of their relations with us. Moreover, the struggle is not yet over between the old and the new approaches to overall European relations. What is your view of this?

Orlov: We need to bear in mind the fact that, in the immediate future—say, up to the year 2000—great changes are going to occur in living and working conditions in Western Europe as a result of the "microelectronics revolution." The changes will be marked by shifts in the social structure of society, in mass psychology, and in value orientations. As for the basic trends, they will likely consist of the following. Individualist sentiments will grow, while collectivist ties of solidarity will weaken. Another trend will be polarization, with the highly skilled and rather well-paid segment of the population that is employed in the various sectors of social activity on one side, and growing numbers of "redundant" people and marginals on the other. And all this will take place on the foundation of the social institutions that continue to function in Western European society as a result of the many years of effort by the organizations that represent the interests of wage workers.

Borko: In other words, on the basis of the social reforms that have been won—reforms that have now become an integral part of the life of society?

Orlov: Precisely. By the younger generation of West Europeans, these things are already taken for granted. And so the parties that reflect these trends most adequately and that propose their own ways of solving the problems will likely dominate West European political life. In my view, the neoconservatives owe the stability of their positions not only to the fact that they encourage entrepreneurial activity on the most varied of scales, and not only to the fact that their individualist credo strikes a chord among those who have come to attach greater importance to individual self-affirmation. The neoconservatives are supported by many so-called ordinary people who are weary of the excessive regimentation and hassles of big cities and large organizations and tired of bureaucracy—both local and national—and who no longer need to demonstrate for the sake of a piece of bread. But society is not simply the sum total of separate individuals who are concerned solely with their purely personal happiness. It needs ties of solidarity, collective ties, the setting of major intellectual objectives, and constant reflection on the destiny of man and mankind. This, in my view, is the most vulnerable spot in the neoconservatives' political philosophy. Conversely, it is the strong point of the social democrats and the organizations of the leftist movement.

Borko: In view of these circumstances, what course might events take?

Orlov: It appears that the neoconservatives will continue to ride the "individualist wave" for a few more years. But they will eventually be pressed by the parties of leftist orientation—provided, of course, that they do not oversimplify their opponents' position by reducing the whole matter to "social revenge," and that they offer their own response to the age-old problem of the "individual versus society" in the specific context of contemporary Western Europe, which has entered the age of the "microelectronic civilization," with all its social and intellectual achievements and costs.

Borko: Your prognosis for the political development of Western Europe seems quite probable: The needle on the scale of voter preference could indeed swing from the conservatives to the social democrats again. But Western Europe is comprised of some 20 states, and they exhibit not a trace of uniformity! And so there can be different variants of political development—for example, the revival of centrist coalitions of social democrats and bourgeois-liberal parties. Generally speaking, it sometimes seems to me that, in the West European countries, it's not so much a matter of what a party is called or what place it is traditionally assigned in the spectrum of political forces, as it is a question of which party is the first to seize on the "spirit of the times," on changes in the social and political climate, and in the mood and outlook of the "man on the street"—i.e., the average voter. Incidentally, let's remain true to our purpose here: Our reflections are intended more to raise questions than to provide exhaustive answers to them.

And at this point I would like to touch on one other "sore spot," one that we are somewhat reluctant to address but that exists and is actively discussed all the same. I am referring to the prospects for the "German community." There are various points of view as to what is taking place. Some feel that the German question is closed once and for all, and that we needn't return to it—in any case not in the foreseeable future. There are politicians who try to predict what might happen were Germany to be reunited, and what role its productive, scientific, and, not least, military potential would play under such circumstances. The following viewpoint is expressed as well: harmony is impossible in Europe unless harmony is achieved in the German question. As a German expert, what is your position?

Orlov: A realistic one—a position that takes into account the fact that the problem of the future of their national community continues to be a concern to the Germans. To close our eyes to this fact would be to ignore the realities and, moreover, to encourage those forces and trends that will support revanchist sentiments and attempts to solve the problem by force. If we want to build a "common European home" on a firm foundation—and we have declared our intention to do so— we must take all these trends into consideration, and not shut ourselves off from them by recalling the revanchist past. It must be said honestly and openly: The establishment of two German states began not in Berlin but in Bonn, and not on our initiative but on the initiative of the Western allies. And the nature of the German community in the future is now a matter for the two German states to decide, and to decide in such a way that the shape of that community is in accordance with the interests of their neighbors, both East and West. Consequently, processes having to do with a German sense of community can develop only in an atmosphere of complete trust, firm guarantees, and a fundamentally new, truly common European climate.

Borko: In my opinion, such an approach is justified. I simply want to emphasize that the German community, in whatever form it develops, can be a derivative of the European community, not the other way around. Europe has only just begun to build a tremendously complex engineering structure—a bridge from distrust to trust, and the German community is one of the spans of this bridge.

Orlov: And a final question: Europe and the future of world civilization. That the world is becoming increasingly interconnected and increasingly a single whole is rather obvious. In this world concert of countries, peoples, and continents, each has his own contribution to make. Europe can exert an influence through the example of its own existence, which is based on tolerance for different views, a high level of intellectual and political culture, and the combination of diversity and community.

Borko: We have come back to the subject of the intellectual foundations of the European community. What an alluring and incredibly complex subject for reflection! Just what is this intellectual foundation? And is there any unequivocal answer to that question? After all, for the French "new right," for example, even Christianity with its sermon of equality is somewhere outside the fundamental principles of European intellectual culture. One could cite other examples of a highly unique interpretation of European civilization, of "Europe-ism." And yet we have surrendered this field of dialogue and discussion without a fight, so to speak. Moreover, some West European researchers have undertaken to defend the proposition that we belong to Europe and to European culture.

We thank them, of course, but we could well have something to say on this score ourselves. Moreover, we are virtually immune to the danger of supplanting the idea of European community with "Eurocentrism." Russian social thought has long concerned itself with the subject of spiritual ties between East and West. We have been led to do so by our historical past, and by our multinational makeup. And today this subject merits our attention all the more. We are entering an age of planetary thinking whose chief characteristic is the priority it attaches to common human values. Europe can make a contribution to the development of this new approach.

Part Five

The Third World

The New Thinking and Problem of Studying the Developing Countries

RACHIK MAMIKONOVICH AVAKOV*

In publishing this article by R.M. Avakov, a prominent Soviet specialist on the economics and politics of the developing countries, we recognize that one article cannot encompass every problem of any consequence pertaining to the development of the states of Asia, Africa, and Latin America, especially every possible approach toward, and position on, the problems of that group of countries. At the same time, we hope it may serve as a basis for fruitful discussion of the controversial issues of studying the Third World, issues which have not been adequately dealt with.

Some research topics do not fit into the rigid "classical" framework of articles in the press. The topic offered to readers here is evidently one of them. A different form of exposition is required—something on the order of reflections with an invitation to discussion: reflections on the state of affairs in the study of the developing countries, on the "sore spots" in this area of scholarly exploration, which are making themselves felt more and more strongly, and on the need to extend to this particular area of scholarship the process of restructuring of the social sciences that is developing in our own country. In the study of Third World sociopolitical, economic, cultural, and other problems, there is also a good deal that needs rethinking, fresh examination, and updating, not to mention the need to abandon certain obsolete, erroneous, and dogmatic ideas.

It is all the more appropriate to raise this question now, in a period when the problems of Soviet society are being critically analyzed and it is undergoing a positive restructuring, a period of returning to the ideals and traditions of Great October, whose 70th anniversary [celebrated the month this article was published—*Trans.*] serves as a kind of appeal for the revival of genuinely humanistic principles in socialist society, for realization of the slogan "more socialism and democracy,"

*Doctor of economics, head of the Department of the Economics and Politics of the Developing Countries at the U.S.S.R. Academy of Sciences' Institute of World Economy and International Relations [IMEMO]. This article appeared in the November 1987 issue of *MEMO*.

and for letting the purifying spirit of criticism, glasnost, and truth penetrate to every sphere of life without exception, and without bypassing scholarly research on the problems of the Third World.

In the heated debates that characterize turning points in a society's development—and socialism is currently going through such a period—one finds a good many negative phenomena, particularly a tendency to dart back and forth from one extreme to the other. I am referring to cases in which the struggle against exaggerations and extremes of the past is itself waged from extreme positions, in which a tendency develops to all but totally reject previously achieved scholarly results, to indiscriminately rehabilitate phenomena that received a negative appraisal, and conversely, to revise anything that was previously declared to be in some way positive. But scholarship needs a creative spirit, not the destructive, all-negating spirit of Goethe's Mephistopheles, whose credo the great poet expressed in the following words:

> I am the spirit that endlessly negates.
> And rightly so: Nothing is necessary.
> There is nothing in the world worth sparing,
> The creation is fit for naught.

These extremes are especially unacceptable with respect to research on the Third World, much of which has been done with a genuinely scholarly, creative approach. The achievements of Soviet scholars in this area of research are indisputable. They have dealt with a number of fundamental problems pertaining to the social development of the Asian, African, and Latin American countries—such problems as the distinctive features of national-liberation revolutions and the course of the contemporary revolutionary process; the developing countries' place in the world capitalist economy and the international division of labor; the role of these countries, and the nonaligned movement in particular, in world politics; the relationship between economic growth and social progress; the influence of the scientific and technological revolution on the development of the Third World; the specific features of industrialization and industrial development; the critical analysis of colonialism and neocolonial relations; the sociopolitical structure of a developing society and the role of the army; the specific features of "peripheral capitalism," and many others. Special mention should be made of Soviet scholars' contribution to elaboration of the theory of Third World development. They have worked out the concepts of a multistructural society [mnogoukladnost], of dependent development, of interdependence, of the specific formational features of developing societies, and of the synthesis of the modern and the traditional.

But today, when we need to mobilize scholars' creative efforts to the utmost for participation in the processes of the restructuring of Soviet society, it is impossible not to take a look back over the path that has been covered, and to critically interpret it from the standpoint of today's tasks. Positive criticism could help overcome everything that is extraneous and erroneous in scholarly research on the problems of the Asian, African, and Latin American countries; help formulate the most important topics that require in-depth study; and stimulate the development of modern forms of cooperation among scholars, practicing specialists, and research institutions. Effective ways must be found to deepen connections with practice and expand scholars' participation in the restructuring processes. It must be acknowledged that today such ties and such cooperation are usually of a coincidental, sporadic nature. A poor job is being done of implementing the idea of joint studies, not to even mention the delays that have occurred in forming up-to-date, dynamic interinstitute groups to carry out programs and projects with the enlistment of practicing specialists.

Third World Studies as a Scholarly Discipline

The social-science discipline concerned with the developing countries is a relatively young branch of scholarship that is establishing itself as "Third World studies," with its own methodological approach, conceptual apparatus, and objectives. In contrast to Oriental studies, African studies, and Latin American studies, the new discipline is concerned not with regional problems or the problems of individual countries, but with the developing world as an integral whole that encompasses more than half the world's population, and at the same time, is highly contradictory in its diverse characteristics.

It is a discipline concerned with the social development of the Third World, the specific sociopolitical and economic features of the developing society, and its place in world economics and politics.

With the collapse of imperialism's colonial system and the emergence of dozens of independent countries, and as the process of decolonialization and the formation of developing countries as a global international political and social entity grew, Third World studies expanded the sphere of its activities and honed its methods and analytical tools. Its place in the system of the social sciences thereby became more clearly defined. It is not an ordinary discipline but a comprehensive one that synthesizes elements, methods, and approaches of many different disciplines. And the very object of its investigation is a complex, conglomerate social formation that consists of more than a hundred components with strongly expressed sociopolitical, economic, cultural, and historical differences. But these are, if one may put it this way, "Third World" differences, that is, they characterize countries belonging to one and the same group, not one of which has been able to, or is yet in a position to, overcome the barrier of underdevelopment and "rise" to the ranks of the developed states.

Third World studies did not develop in a vacuum. Like any discipline, it has its own prehistory. We have in mind, for example, Oriental studies, which, of course, did not disappear with the new discipline's emergence, but, having created a solid foundation for it, continues to develop independently, using the achievements of its scholarly partner in the process. "Relations" between the two disciplines are fairly complicated, and in many respects the two are interwoven, but it is hardly possible, at least today, to equate them: the boundaries that separate them at present are generally fairly clear.

Indeed, the subject of Third World studies is broader. It includes not only Asia but also the African continent, in which classical oriental studies initially showed no interest, as well as Latin America. In addition, in studying its own set of problems, Third World studies has a tendency not to go beyond the boundaries of the recent past. After all, the developing world took shape within the past few decades, and that circumstance has put its imprint on the scholarly and political goals of the discipline, which is decidedly oriented toward the present day. It needs the historical element to the extent that it makes it possible to understand the present in greater depth. As we also know, a number of areas of scholarship that are specific to Oriental studies, such as linguistics, literary studies, and so forth, do not lie within the sphere of interests of Third World studies, although that situation may change in the future. Finally, the new scholarly discipline is characterized by a global approach, within the framework of which the developing world is viewed in the context of world development as a kind of "unity in diversity," to use the expression that was originated by Aristotle to characterize the democratic state (democratic by the standards of the ancient world) in his debate with Plato, who denied the significance of diversity in the state structure.

With the global approach, not only are the differences (including fundamental differences) among countries and regions belonging to the Third World group not ignored, but, to the contrary, emphasis is placed on the existence of those differences—more than that, on the deepening of differences in the course of the sociopolitical differentiation of the Third World, a social formation which is unique in its specific features and its place in the processes of world historical development.

Thus, in a certain sense Third World studies is both broader and narrower than Oriental studies. Along certain lines they intersect and coincide, and in that case the close connection between them manifests itself most vividly. Along other lines they diverge, developing autonomously and parallel to one another, as it were, although they do not lose the connections between them. What has been said about Oriental studies also pertains, to one degree or another, to the relationships between Third World studies and African studies and Latin American studies. It is impossible for us to speak in greater detail about the connections and differences among all these scholarly disciplines, the relationships among them, and their objects of study. A great deal here is still unclear, and for all intents and purposes, scholars and specialists in the Third World have not yet defined themselves in terms of the discipline. They are usually distinguished from one another more in traditional terms—as economists, historians, and so forth, rather than as representatives of Third World studies. To standardize the matter and introduce some clarity in it, it would evidently be a good idea to distinguish general Third World studies, a short characterization of which is given above, from the area-studies branches of that discipline—Oriental studies, African studies, and Latin American studies.

From the very outset, Third World studies developed under special conditions. During the period in which it was formed, Soviet social science was in a complicated situation.

First, by that time the negative tendency to turn it into a scholastic, didactic discipline had already appeared and continued to grow. While Soviet social science had the great teaching of Marxism-Leninism as its theoretical and methodological foundation, to a significant extent it lost this advantage. One could cite numerous instances of how the social-science disciplines concerned themselves less with the scholarly, objective investigation of trends in socioeconomic, political, and cultural development, than with the selection of quotations for the "correct" evaluation of some given phenomenon, or with the study of that phenomenon solely from the standpoint of confirming the "correctness" of a given quotation. In this sense the specific nature of Third World studies consisted in its having greater difficulty with quotations, since it had not inherited special, fundamental works on the national-liberation movement; moreover, today this movement looks a great deal different than it did in the previous century and at the beginning of the present one. Granted, this gave Third World studies a certain opportunity to avoid didacticism and dogmatism. To a certain extent, it took advantage of that opportunity, but it still did not manage to break out of the general tendency that overwhelmed the social sciences, especially such fundamental ones as philosophy, political economy, and sociology.

Second, the situation that existed in the social sciences was characterized, to put it bluntly, by absolutely abnormal relations between scholarship and politics. An idea of their relations is provided by the eastern proverb that says, "The camel has its own plans, but its route is dictated by the plans of the driver." Social science, of course, cannot help being related to politics. But the connecting link between them must be the truth and only the truth, which scholarship is called on to ascertain and place at the disposal of politics. For social science—like any other scholarly discipline, incidentally—performs essentially one function and one function only: the search for and discovery of truth. This is a fundamental principle, and in following that principle it asserts itself as a scholarly discipline. In turn, it is only through the purposeful and steadfast pursuit of truth that scholarship demonstrates its usefulness and its value, stimulates progress, and renders assistance to practice and politics in solving specific problems of social development. Any deviation from this principle can damage both scholarship and politics. Deviation from the truth dooms social science to creative sterility and politics to blind subordination to transient, ephemeral interests, to a narrowing of its outlook, and to arriving at impasses.

Colonialism, Neocolonialism, and the National-Liberation Revolution: Extremes in Assessments

Soviet scholars have given much attention to the national-liberation movement and its prospects, and they have made a comprehensive analysis of colonialism and its consequences for the peoples of the oppressed countries and for world development as a whole. From their original, frequently oversimplified approaches, they have ultimately arrived at a characterization of this contradictory phenomenon that is fairly precise and accords with historical reality. The topic, of course, has not been exhausted. New facts that make it possible to add to and deepen the treatment of colonialism are still appearing and will possibly continue to appear. But a general picture of colonialism has already been drawn in fairly faithful colors. And there is nothing surprising in that it is dominated by dark tones that symbolize, as it were, the unsightliness of the system of colonial oppression. Doubtless, it is precisely this historical misfortune that is the decisive external reason for the backwardness and underdevelopment of the former colonies and semicolonies. Of course, certain internal factors also contributed to these negative phenomena. One might also recall that colonial conquests helped draw the enslaved countries into the world market and the processes of international development, and into contacts with more developed states and with other cultures.

On the whole, today there is neither historical nor ideological and political need to return to the fairly clear question of the historical responsibility of colonialism and neocolonialism in relation to the peoples of the developing countries. It is well known that economic partitioning and repartitioning of the world, whether carried out in colonial or neocolonial form, cannot but have a retarding effect on development. In this connection, it is hardly fruitful, for example, to contend that the South was previously unable to work out a suitable economic and sociopolitical mechanism, although there was supposedly no forcible restraint on its development, and that present North-South economic differences are attributable "simply" to the fact that the North spurted ahead, because it had managed, unlike the South, to create the required mechanism. Assertions of that sort can justifiably be regarded as attempts to rehabilitate colonialism.

In recent years, when the barrage of the national-liberation movement razed the bastions of the colonial empires, Soviet scholarly literature advanced the thesis that the anticolonial revolution would turn into a social, socialist revolution. Frequently this process was viewed in an oversimplified fashion. It was said to be inevitable, and that the transition from one type of revolution to the other would occur immediately, all at once, without intermediate stages, encompassing one country after another. These ideas were in many respects the result of euphoria following the victorious march of the national-liberation movement, which gave rise to illusions and a desire to pass off wishes for reality. We therefore now unquestionably need to correct our scholarly ideas.

In critically reviewing those earlier forecasts and assessments, though, we should not forget that they nonetheless have been confirmed to a significant extent, not just with respect to a handful of people, but with respect to more than a billion inhabitants of the former colonial and dependent world: the peoples of China, Vietnam, the People's Democratic Republic of Korea, and Cuba have chosen the socialist path of development, and now it has been opened for a number of other peoples. Consequently, in a historical sense it is hardly correct to judge socialism's prospects in the Third World, as is sometimes done, solely on the basis of the fact that states of socialist orientation presently account for a relatively small part of the developing countries' population. If one is speaking of the present situation, it is true that they account for less than 10 percent of that population. But can one claim that the sociopolitical situation in the Third World has already been fully determined, and that fundamental changes in that percentage cannot be foreseen?*

Changes taking place in the developing countries and current trends in their development attest more to something else—to the growth and deepening of social contradictions that reflect the disastrous situation of hundreds of millions of people in many of the liberated states, and to the growth in discontent among broad segments of their populations in connection with the failure to solve vitally important problems. As a result, one sees an intensification of sociopolitical tension there that is causing concern not just in the Third World itself but in other countries as well. The woeful plight of the developing countries is justifiably regarded as one of Today's most acute global problems.

Under these conditions, it would be an error, if not scholarly blindness, to suppose that 10 percent is the limit alloted for countries of socialist orientation. That clearly underestimates the level of conflict in the Third World's social development, the potential for change, and the explosive nature of the political situation.

Here we are coming to another aspect of the problem, the scholarly evaluation of contradictory trends seen in the developing world—anti-imperialist and revolutionary trends, on the one hand, and reactionary and antisocialist trends, on the other. One still finds many hackneyed observations and obsolete ideas on this question in scholarly literature. Many conclusions and assessments, based on an analysis of the causes and sources of the powerful upsurge in the national-liberation movement that occurred in the decade and a half or two decades following World War II, continue to migrate from one scholarly article or book to another, although fundamental changes—and in the case of certain trends, radical changes—have occurred in the world situation and in the national-liberation movement itself.

That was the period in which the thesis was developed that the national-liberation movement constituted a powerful reserve for socialism and was one of the principal revolutionary and anti-imperialist forces in the modern world. The proposition that world capitalism could not count on the nationally independent developing countries as a reserve and source of rejuvenation gained a solid footing in scholarly studies. And even today, many people regard practically every action by the developing states against some imperialist state as a manifestation of anti-imperialism and a revolutionary attitude, while they invariably seek a reactionary and even antisocialist principle in any action

---

*G. Mirskiy's article "On the Question of the Developing Countries' Choice of Path and Orientation" (*MEMO*, May, 1987) looks at this problem from a somewhat different perspective, from the standpoint of the extent to which the prerequisites for socialism are formed in both the base and the superstructure of society in the developing countries.—*Ed.*

that runs contrary to the interests of the U.S.S.R. or other socialist countries. Such ideas can no longer satisfy us—can no longer satisfy either scholarship or politics. The national-liberation movement and the developing world are exceptionally complex social phenomena, too complex for a one-dimensional characterization, especially in the form of fine-sounding slogans.

Let us take a somewhat more detailed look at these issues.

It has been stated above that in a number of countries national-liberation revolutions have turned into socialist revolutions, while in others regimes of socialist orientation have emerged. Understandably, world socialism has drawn and continues to draw strength for its growth and development from these revolutions, although it currently does so on a somewhat narrower scale.

At the same time, in the process of national liberation dozens of states have emerged in which capitalism is developing, and in many of them it has become the dominant structure and is being formed as the method of production. One can, of course, avoid using the expression "reserve of capitalism," or "rejuvenation of capitalism," but the fact remains that in the Asian, African, and Latin American countries development of capitalism started proceeding at a faster pace once they had won their political independence than it had during the colonial era. The highest level of economic, scientific, and technological progress in the Third World has been reached in states in which capitalist relations have advanced further than in others. The group of so-called "newly industrialized countries" has emerged from among such states; the countries in this group have achieved substantial success in the industrialization and diversification of their economies, and in establishment scientifically and technologically advanced production processes. Membership in this group is expanding, and its second and third echelons have already appeared. In a number of liberated states, national monopolies have long since ceased to be a rarity, and their number is increasing. The first transnational corporations have also sprung up there. All this is capitalism, and it is developing not in opposition to world capitalism, but within its framework, with its assistance and its cooperation. Of course, the relationship and interaction between Third World capitalism, on the one hand, and imperialism, on the other, are marked by contradictions and conflicts. But these contradictions and conflicts do not imply that the developing countries are not contributing to the development of world capitalism, and that they are simply waiting to be turned toward socialism.

The question of the liberated countries' revolutionary and anti-imperialist potentials also must be approached from a new perspective. Indisputably, their development takes place in constant struggle with the imperialist states. Nor can one deny that they have contradictory and complicated, sometimes conflicting, relations with the socialist countries, as well. But should one always equate this with anti-imperialism or revolutionary attitudes in the first case, and with anti-socialist tendencies in the second? In my view, such an equation is mistaken. It indicates a confusion of interstate relations with ideological relations. Unquestionably, developing countries' struggle with a given Western state differs fundamentally, and even in principle, from the interimperialist struggle (although there are sometimes exceptions). However, the attitudes of states in the former group toward the states in the latter do not necessarily take on an anti-imperialist shading. Sometimes they contain ideological contradictions, but in many cases what happens is something else—a conflict between the state interests of two partners. And when this occurs the weakness of one partner, the developing country, does not necessarily represent an ideological confrontation.

In our time, the political importance of correctly assessing the anti-imperialist and revolutionary potential of the developing countries is especially great. Exaggerations in this respect can have undesirable consequences in politics, especially if one considers that anti-imperialist slogans are sometimes used for demagogic purposes, in order to appear "suitable" in political relations with the Soviet Union. It would be wrong to evaluate the prospects for Third World development and its role in world economics and politics, and consequently, our own positions and policies toward the developing countries, solely or even chiefly in terms of the extent of their anti-imperialism and revolutionary stance, especially since these traits do not always lend themselves to unambiguous appraisal.

The Problems of Socialist Orientation

These problems are among those accorded the highest priority in Soviet scholarly and political-propaganda literature. Numerous works have been devoted to them. Scholars and specialists have put forward a good many ideas that merit attention and have served us well; moreover, the theory itself of noncapitalist development and socialist orientation represents a fundamental contribution to Marxist-Leninist social science. At the same time, to limit oneself here, in evaluating this scholarly concept, to the statement that by no means everything is in order would be just another cliché. Unfortunately, one must admit that this is probably the weakest area of Third World studies. The number of articles and books on the problems of socialist orientation is inversely proportionate to the level and quality of the research. Here schematicism and triviality feel especially free and unrestrained. It has become practically a ritual to substitute such sacramental phrases as "they have encountered difficulties," "they have had to overcome the resistance of the internal reaction and the consequences of colonialism," and so forth, for real analysis of crises and other negative processes occurring in the countries of socialist orientation, including failures in their economies and their domestic and foreign policies. Difficulties, reactionary resistance, and imperialist intrigues, of course, all exist. But there are other phenomena that require objective study—such as contradictions inherent in development along the path of socialist orientation, internal party struggle, degeneration of leadership and regimes, violations of the norms of good-neighborliness and international law, and so forth.

Under past conditions of extremely limited glasnost and democracy, the absence of genuinely scholarly, that is, objective research on many aspects of the problems of socialist orientation could still in some way be explained, though not always justified. Now in this sphere of research that is exceptionally important not just for scholarship but for politics, scholars have immense work to do in opening up "prohibited zones," in clearing away hackneyed ideas, unsupported assertions, and impressive-sounding but empty statements, and in deepening theoretical and political analysis.

The countries of socialist orientation are countries friendly to us, which imposes special responsibility on the study of their problems. This is a responsibility, above all, to show the true state of affairs. Otherwise, our enemies will serve up the truth in a specially prepared and falsified form. Thus, there can be absolutely no justification for the fact that open, objective studies are not being conducted, and no in-depth scholarly books or articles exist, for example, on the Afghan question. Policy makers can hardly count on the effective solution of given problems if scholarship does not take part in explaining its essence and complexities to the public, and in actually creating public opinion concerning that problem, public opinion which is based on detailed, comprehensive research. In exactly the same way, the Soviet reader has not been clearly informed about many aspects of the domestic political situation in Nicaragua; about various aspects of Syria's policy in the Middle East, including its policy toward Lebanon; or about the foreign-policy attitudes of the Libyan leadership—on the question of Chad, for example. And how is the reader to understand that Somalia, which was once considered one of the promising countries of socialist orientation, was immediately demoted to a different sociopolitical rank as soon as the military conflict with Ethiopia began?

But the problem is not merely the existence of "prohibited zones," and not just that relations between scholarship and politics in this case are far from optimal, as mentioned above. Another, no less important aspect needs to be stressed: the theoretical and methodological aspect.

Socialist orientation is not only a subject of Third World studies, but also belongs to the area of scholarship that analyzes the problems of world socialism. That would seem to be obvious. However, judging from the works of Soviet authors, socialist orientation is studied only within the context of research on the developing world, while, to all intents and purposes, it does not figure at all in theoretical works on socialism. And if one adds to this the fact that a number of socialist countries that grew out of national-liberation revolutions—China, Vietnam, Cuba, the Korean People's Democratic Republic, and Laos—are, in turn, excluded from Third World studies, both the methodological confusion and the disconnected nature of research on the problems of socialist orientation become understandable.

This methodological defect may be partly attributable to the fact that socialist orientation is regarded only as a transitional form of social relations. Yet societies of socialist orientation have existed for decades now. In our fast-moving age, that is an entire era. And there are quite probably many generations in the countries of socialist orientation that are still not destined to see the end of the transition and the full establishment of socialism in those countries. As they see it, their society is something permanent and stable. In my view, it should be regarded not just as some sort of phase in the movement toward socialism, but also as a certain type of society with its own variations.

The analysis of those variations would not only make it possible to systematize our knowledge of socialist orientation, better understand its nature, and study trends in the development of the countries in question in greater depth. Such analysis is also needed to identify differences between progressive variations of socialist orientation and variations under which negative tendencies dominate, or even reactionary tendencies arise. Something of the sort happened, for example, in the Cambodia of the Khmer Rouge, where a barracks-style, police, terrorist regime was established. As we see, the degeneration of a regime of socialist orientation also has more than one variation and may take different directions.

Historically things have developed in such a way that it has mainly been the less developed countries that have embarked on the path of socialist orientation. That is noteworthy in and of itself, however, it has not yet been persuasively explained in a theoretical sense, and in a political sense it leads one to serious reflections. These countries are at such a low level of development that their choice of the more radical methods of development offered by socialist orientation is perfectly logical. But besides the logic of their choice, which may be made because of the strength of socialism's "demonstration effect," there is also the logic of objective conditions. If objective conditions are not ripe, even the most radical methods may not produce the desired results, or may even have undesirable consequences.

The countries of socialist orientation, the African countries in particular, could not help encountering such problems in their development. When they are compared to sub-Saharan states whose ruling circles made a different choice, an interesting picture emerges. In relation to Togo, Chad, and the Central African Republic, for example, the countries of socialist orientation have demonstrated their advantages. At least, they do not look worse in terms of the indicators of development. A different picture results from comparing them to Senegal, the Ivory Coast, Kenya, and other countries. In short, the path of socialist orientation has yet to demonstrate its fundamental superiority. Not one of the countries that has made such a choice has been able to even break out of the category of least developed. This model has not become sufficiently attractive for dozens of liberated countries.

What has been said, of course, by no means indicates the failure of the model of socialist orientation, and cannot serve as grounds for excessively pessimistic conclusions about its prospects. In this connection, the question of the influence of perestroika in the U.S.S.R. and the decisive democratization of Soviet society on the regimes of socialist orientation and on the future of socialist orientation as an option is of exceptional interest. This is a new area of Third World studies whose significance cannot be overestimated. Research in this area is just getting under way. In my view, today we can no longer evaluate the prospects of socialist orientation from the standpoint of its past failures. Thus, under conditions in which the international significance of perestroika is being confirmed more and more clearly, I find dubious the opinion one hears expressed in debates to the effect that the noncapitalist path or the path of socialist orientation will scarcely become a persuasive alternative on the periphery of the world capitalist economy in the foreseeable future. And it is absolutely incomprehensible why this rather categorical assessment is linked with the fact that in the perestroika process our own notions of socialism will become increasingly remote from actual social relations in most countries of socialist orientation. Among scholars, these notions have always been fairly remote from those relations. The question is what sort of conditions and possibilities do countries of socialist orientation have for their own perestroika, and whether they recognize the necessity of it. The path of social renewal and general improvement of social structures is open to them, too.

Debates About the Prospects of 'Peripheral Capitalism'

Another fundamental subject in Third World studies is the set of specific features of capitalism in the developing countries, its place in the world system of capitalist relations, and its prospects. It seems that compared to works on problems of the development of socialism in the Asian, African, and Latin American countries, research on the problems of "peripheral capitalism" has been conducted on a higher scholarly and theoretical level. However, we can no longer be satisfied with it today. Here, too, there are serious omissions, and one senses the fear of new ideas and encounters obsolete views. Thus, Third World studies has not yet been able to identify and elaborate a detailed picture of the specific features of capitalism in the developing countries as a Third World phenomenon. Criteria have not been developed for determining its level and maturity as a socioeconomic formation. Argumentation often comes down to the rule of contraries: states that do not fit into the concept of socialist orientation are readily assigned to the group of countries that are following a capitalist path.

Such logic, which at first glance seems impeccable, stems from a dichotomous vision of the sociopolitical structure of the world. Moreover, the content of the concept "following a capitalist path" is not revealed, evidently on the grounds that it is self-evident. However, just what specifically is meant by that concept? An established capitalist socioeconomic structure [uklad]? And if so, it is state capitalism or private capitalism? A dominant capitalist socioeconomic structure? Capitalism that has been fully formed as a method of production? The sociopolitical orientation of the ruling circles, regardless of the level to which capitalism has developed? Or can it be that something else is meant?

Let us look at another example. No one has yet refuted the thesis that one important criterion for established capitalism is the "proletariat-bourgeoisie" opposition, which is considered the fundamental contradiction of that society. Have social contradictions attained that level of development in many of the liberated countries? Finally, yet another example. Research shows that in sub-Saharan African countries capitalism is very weakly developed, and is still far from becoming the dominant socioeconomic structure. Yet our research also includes many of these countries in the group that is following the capitalist path.[1]

---

[1]In this connection, I would like to make one clarification. It is perfectly possible that most of the developing countries really are following the capitalist path. But is it not clear that such a conclusion should be supported by specific analysis, which, in particular, should contain answers to the questions that have been raised, and should be based on elaborated criteria for the development of capitalism under Third World conditions? The general arguments and approximate assessments often encountered only confuse the picture, or even serve to evade complicated problems.

What are the reasons for the existing situation in this area of Third World studies?

Of course, one can cite its youthfulness, and the fact that it has not yet had time to cover all the questions: many fundamental problems remain unsolved, or more accurately, untouched. That would be true, but only half-true. The problem also lies in certain stereotypes, especially in the methodology of analysis, that impede the in-depth study of the problems under discussion; it lies, in particular, in the preservation of Eurocentric ideas in studies of Third World capitalism—or, for that matter, in Third World studies as a whole.

It is customary to consider European capitalism (not all countries, of course) to be capitalism of the first echelon. From a scholarly standpoint, it is perfectly acceptable to compare it to capitalism of the third echelon, which encompasses the developing countries of capitalist orientation. But the fact that results obtained in this manner are often passed off as the specific features of Third World capitalism draws objections. Is that correct? After all, the content of a social phenomenon, in this case capitalism, can be disclosed, as it was by Marx, only by analyzing its "pure" model, while the specific features of one variant of the phenomenon in question can be analyzed only by comparing it to that model. European capitalism is obviously the closest to that "pure" model. But it is also true that it cannot be equated with it, and that is precisely the approach that is taken in the study of capitalism in the Third World. Yet the deviations of the Third World variant of capitalism from the European variant merely indicate the differences between them; they say nothing about the specific features of either variant.

But this methodological flaw is not the only point. Eurocentrism has led to a situation in which, in the study of the developing countries—including capitalism in those countries—research tools are being used that were developed on the basis of different historical material. That not only fails to contribute to a more correct orientation of analysis methods, it has also become a reason that Third World studies has shown carelessness with regard to its conceptual apparatus. As a result, today it has virtually no scholarly tools that adequately take the specifics of its object of investigation into account.

Yet another complexity lies in the fact that the study of Third World capitalism, especially theoretical and methodological aspects of the problem, relies to a considerable extent on an inadequately developed concept of world capitalism as a system. In this concept, the developing world as a source generating capitalism is clearly inadequately represented, even in a formal sense—as a kind of appendage to the world capitalist system that changes nothing about its essence or its qualitative characteristics. Moreover, in the study of that system, world capitalism is essentially identified with the capitalism of developed countries.

In reality, research indicates that the role of developing countries' capitalism in the world capitalist economy is changing qualitatively. Not only is "peripheral capitalism" being more deeply drawn into that economy, but something more fundamental is occurring—it is being integrated into and, in some sense, even dissolved in it. It is being increasingly drawn into the world capitalist economy, not as a unified, integral mass with its own specific features, but as numerous individual parts that exist at different levels of economic integration. Thus, contradictions in the world capitalist economy are being formed not just between the developed and the developing states that belong to it, but also between national capitalisms, and even between various multinational groups of capitalists. That is why the problem of the developing countries' economic independence appears in a different light today. It is not a question, as was recently claimed, of their breaking out of the world capitalist economy, but a question of their achieving equal participation and partnership in it.

In this connection, a more precise approach also needs to be taken to the quantitative evaluation of the developing countries' role in the world economy, and to the question of the gap in level of development between them and the developed capitalist countries. In my view, works by Soviet economists considerably exaggerate both the Third World's share of the nonsocialist countries' total GNP and industrial production, and the extent to which that gap has been narrowed. Their calculations evidently fail to take into account such points as differences in the structure of GNP and of industry, especially the processing industry, between the two groups of countries, or the fact that the Third World countries' statistics include the results of transnational corporations' production activities and other activities, not to mention the fact that those statistics are unreliable. In other words, what frequently happens, in essence, is that incomparable magnitudes are compared. And if such calculations and evaluations were rid of the errors mentioned above, as well as others, the picture would look less optimistic. Not only is the gap not narrowing, it is actually increasing, especially from the standpoint of quality of development; and for various indicators the developing countries' proportional contribution underwent no substantial changes from 1950 to 1985.

It might be said that integration within the framework of the world capitalist economy, which has been proceeding at a rapid pace, in the most diverse forms, and at various levels, has been a kind of reaction on the part of developed capitalism to the demand for the establishment of a new international economic order. World capitalism has managed to recover from the blow delivered by the collapse of the colonial system. Therefore, it can hardly be said that imperialism has failed to achieve sociopolitical revenge for that defeat.[2] Integration has become one of the means to expand and to consolidate its positions, for integration makes it possible to bind the various interests of different partners together with the tightest bonds, which are economic ties, into a single organism—albeit, let us repeat, one that is extremely contradictory and fraught with conflicts: the world capitalist economy. Even the foreign-debt crisis, which has created extreme tension between the developed capitalist countries and the developing countries, is, on the whole, contributing to integration by consolidating it in the extremely important currency and credit sphere.

In the world capitalist economy, foreign economic relations have always developed not only between states and through the state, but also directly between economic agents—enterprises, companies, and so forth. The distinctive nature of the present situation is that direct ties are increasingly coming to the fore; on the other hand, it is primarily organizational functions and implementation of nationwide measures, such as creating conditions for economic cooperation, and providing guarantees of normal operations that are being concentrated in the hands of the state. However, this area of research remains untouched, although it is assuming great scholarly and practical importance, especially for developing and deepening of our economic cooperation with the developing countries.

Problems of Cooperation Between the U.S.S.R. and the Developing Countries

I would like to stress from the outset that these problems are one of the central lines of connection between Third World studies and Soviet foreign economic practice. Just how they are studied from now on, and how practical organizations react to the results of those studies will become a kind of litmus test determining the extent and effectiveness of the new thinking's penetration into Third World studies, into the sphere of the country's foreign economic relations, and into the relationship between scholarship and practice. As for the past and—to a somewhat lesser degree—the present, that litmus test fairly clearly and fairly frequently yields results that are less than encouraging.

---

[2]It should be made clear that, first, the collapse of the colonial empires was a blow mainly to the mother countries. In the final analysis, American, and even Japanese and West German, imperialism came out ahead. Second, from the perspective of the present day, one can say that the elimination of the colonial system was the "sacrifice" that world capitalism had to undertake to save itself as a system.

Another preliminary observation: in research on the problems of the U.S.S.R.'s economic cooperation with the developing countries, published works (books, brochures, scholarly articles) are particularly inferior in content, results, and quality to special scholarly studies that have been prepared on commission from state economic organizations and institutions to address practical issues. Judging from studies of the latter sort, it would be no exaggeration to say that scholarship is clearly out ahead of the practice of our economic and scientific-technological cooperation with the developing countries. That is perfectly normal and natural: Theory, by definition, should lead the way. What is abnormal is something else—the fact that until recently Soviet foreign-economic practice reacted in an extraordinarily weak and highly conservative fashion to many recommendations and proposals by scholars, and if it accepted them at all, it did so with great delay. To give one example: the idea of creating joint ventures was proposed approximately 15 years ago, but only now has it become a part of our strategy of foreign economic relations. Moreover, the primary task—the basic work to implement the idea—still lies ahead.

Under the conditions of perestroika and glasnost, Third World studies face an important and, I would say, gripping task—to restructure itself in the name of maximum participation in perestroika, particularly in the study of the problems of the U.S.S.R.'s cooperation with the developing countries.

How, specifically, can that participation be expressed? This is a complicated question that has many aspects. I will limit myself to examining a few of them.

The *first* aspect is the quantity, depth, and intensity of foreign economic relations between the U.S.S.R. and the developing countries, and the extent of the interpenetration and interdependence of their economies. By these indicators, our country is substantially behind the developed capitalist states. We have already spoken above about the rapidly advancing process of the developing countries' integration into the world capitalist economy. Let us add that economic relations with the developed capitalist states are also helping to maintain and deepen involvement of the socialist-oriented countries in the world capitalist system. Meanwhile, the U.S.S.R.'s economic relations have not attained the integration level even with that group of liberated countries, whose involvement in the world socialist economy can only be detected as a weakly expressed tendency.

Of course, a great deal in economic relations between states depends on whether their economies are of the same type. A great deal, but not everything. Thus, the question of the autonomy of enterprises and of direct ties between them is not strictly dependent on the type of economies. I do not think that the capitalist economy alone possesses the features or conditions without which the effectiveness of foreign economic relations declines drastically. But we are only now coming to that idea and its practical implementation, since for decades our foreign-economic and foreign-trade practice found itself in the iron embrace of His Majesty Monopoly, which is perfectly acceptable in certain periods of a country's development, but if maintained for a long time can result in stagnation, and even decay. Yet at present, when the ideas of cost accounting, the autonomy of enterprises, and direct ties between enterprises form the basis of economic reform in the U.S.S.R., this important area of research, especially with regard to foreign economic relations, remains largely outside the field of scholars' vision.

The *second* aspect is the strategy of cooperation. The discussion here will not be about the general principles of the Soviet Union's political and economic relations with the developing countries. Those principles are well known and are the strong and attractive side of our cooperation with them. What causes concern is the tendency in the 1970s and early 1980s toward a relative decline in the level of the U.S.S.R.'s foreign economic relations with Third World countries. Moreover, in comparison to the developed capitalist states, that amount is extremely small. Why is this? It can be said that our published works do not even touch on this major scholarly and political problem. At any rate, from every indication, no special studies are being conducted on this matter.

The general impression is that the U.S.S.R.'s political cooperation with the Third World states has a broader scope and broader prospects than its economic cooperation, although it is difficult to measure and draw comparisons here. Whereas our strategy in foreign political affairs is aimed at establishing and maintaining friendly relations with all the developing countries, in foreign economic relations it is more oriented toward the fairly narrow group of socialist-oriented states and certain other friendly countries. In the first case, the strategy is perfectly understandable and in keeping with the spirit of the times and the interests of the peace and security of nations. As for the economic policy in which political motives so dominate, there is no certainty that it is effective.

What is the problem here? A lack of resources? That, of course, must be reckoned with. But in my view the main problem lies elsewhere—in a concept of foreign economic relations that gives preference to the country, rather than to the market and to the formation of interstate and intercompany economic complexes. Such an approach can result in a loss of interest in other countries, the abandonment of the search for mutually beneficial clients, and a general inertia in an area that demands a high degree of dynamism and a steady improvement of the forms and methods of operation, the maintenance and enhancement of competitiveness, and the improvement of the quality of export goods. When economic relations are narrow, are kept at a low level, and their forms are undeveloped, this can have a negative effect on the country's political positions over the long run.

The policy of developing commodity-money relations and utilizing the market is creating a new situation and new opportunities. It is intended to strengthen economic levers and incentives in the sphere of foreign affairs, as well as domestically, and to orient Soviet producers toward the criteria of products' competitiveness in the world economy and the developing countries' markets. That is especially important insofar as the expansion of market economies in those countries and the rise in their level of economic and technological development are bringing the criteria of quality and competitiveness to the fore for them, too. The study of this set of questions with respect to conditions in the developing countries is becoming especially important considering that foreign economic cooperation is expected to play a large role in restructuring the Soviet Union's national economy.

The *third* aspect is the influence of global problems on relations between states—between the U.S.S.R. and the developing countries, in particular. The number of problems in this area is growing steadily, and many of them are arising directly in the zone of the liberated states. In the political lexicon this process is expressed by the well-known formula, "an interconnected and interdependent world," a world tied together by the bonds of global problems. The essence of these problems is clear—they affect, directly or indirectly, the interests not just of individual countries or regions and continents, but of all humanity and all groups of contemporary states—socialist, developing, and developed capitalist.

Global problems are occupying an increasingly large place in relations among states. However, whereas specific negotiations are being conducted on issues of disarmament, the situation is different when it comes to other global problems, especially those that have a Third World coloring. In many respects that is the result of (and, simultaneously, a cause of) the fact that Third World studies has still not seriously concerned itself with these problems. Yet these problems have firmly established themselves on the agenda of bilateral and, especially, multilateral cooperation, including cooperation in the sphere of foreign economic relations with the developing countries. Third World studies should be prepared to answer both theoretical and practical questions that arise here.

* * *

The increasingly strong critical bent of Soviet scholarship with respect to negative trends in the development of our own society is opening up new horizons for better studying and understanding other countries and peoples, and for the movement of Third World studies to a new, higher level of research, so that the new thinking firmly establishes itself as the discipline's genuine driving force. At the same time, the objective study of the developing world and Third World society can provide a good deal of material for use in elaborating the theory and practice of socialist perestroika, and in enriching the new social and political-economic thinking.

The new thinking in scholarship is an orientation toward objective research, rather than biased research, toward real knowledge, rather than predetermined knowledge, and toward creative debates, rather than grinding set formulas in a scholastic mortar. Like any scholarly discipline, Third World studies aims not at obligatory unanimity, and not at the victory of one viewpoint over another, but at research results that accord with the real state of affairs and real prospects for the future. Scholarship, dialectical thinking, and the politics of dynamism—or dynamism in politics—cannot, by definition, accept the concept of unanimity. Genuine scholarly ambition consists not in scoring blows against and defeating one's opponent, and not in striving, as people have continued to do since the time of the Sophists, to impose and assert one's opinion, but in following the method that originated with Socrates and not being afraid to cast doubt on the veracity of one's own results, to compare various views, and to search and work together toward the establishment of truth. In other words, not individual opinion, but doubt and final results are what count in scholarly debates.

"The revival of the creative spirit of Leninism" is asserting a new vision of the world-historical process as the possibility, at each given moment, of moving in different directions, the vector of which will ultimately depend on the activities of all the participants in that process. The developing world is one of the participants in world history. The study of that unified and diverse world can provide an additional creative impetus for the development of Soviet social science.

Liberated Countries: The Present Stage in the Struggle for Development

NIKOLAY ALEKSANDROVICH KARAGODIN AND
ANATOLIY YAKOVLEVICH ELYANOV*

The deep cyclical and structural crises that shook the world capitalist economy in the last decade and a half, intensifying its overall instability, has had an especially negative and, to a great extent, destabilizing effect on the developing countries' economies, which had not yet become firmly established. The deterioration of the world economic situation, which exposed the weakest areas and profound imbalances in the economies of the liberated states, has helped aggravate the socioeconomic and, particularly, currency and financial problems of those countries, and contributed to a slowdown in the pace of their development.

Under the conditions that have emerged, developing states have been forced to take steps to conserve their scarcest resources. Current developments also demand reconsideration of a number of principles of economic strategy, not to mention current economic policies. A heated battle has developed around these issues, a battle in which not only various social and political forces in the liberated states themselves, but also such international organizations as the International Bank for Reconstruction and Development [World Bank] and the International Monetary Fund (IMF), have been taking part. On the whole, as was stressed at the 27th CPSU Congress, "a slow, difficult, but unstoppable process of social and economic transformations is taking place in the lives of peoples who comprise the majority of humanity. It is a process that has brought quite a few fundamental changes, but has also encountered quite a few difficulties."

The authors see their task as identifying the sources, scale, and nature of the problems that former colonial and dependent countries have encountered at the present stage of development, as well as examining the measures being taken to solve those problems. In this

*Karagodin is a candidate of economics and senior research associate at the U.S.S.R. Academy of Sciences' Institute of World Economy and International Relations [IMEMO]; Elyanov is a doctor of economics and head of a section at the institute. This article appeared in the February 1987 issue of *MEMO*.

article analysis focuses on the countries that have been developing along the path of capitalism. Naturally, the problems being discussed here also affect, in one way or another, those countries with a socialist orientation. However, the manifestation of these problems, as well as the methods for solving them, in states of that type are highly specific to them, and they deserve to be examined separately.

Successes and Difficulties in Economic Growth

To better sort out the existing situation, one needs to take a broad, retrospective historical look at the process of the liberated countries' economic development. If the beginning of the 1950s is taken as a starting point, then one can see that despite immense objective difficulties, and a number of indisputable errors and miscalculations, the former colonies and semicolonies have managed, on the whole, to achieve significant economic successes in their economies. Between 1950 and 1985 their combined GNP grew by more than 440 percent, their agricultural production by 160 percent, and their industrial output by 670 percent, including an increase of approximately 880 percent in processing-industry output.[1] The most significant growth in agriculture was achieved by countries in Latin America, while the greatest growth in the processing industry was achieved by states in the Middle East (a 19-fold increase), and in South, Southeast, and East Asia (a more than 12-fold increase).

Substantial changes also occurred in the structure of the developing countries' economies. Whereas in the early 1950s agriculture accounted for almost 3.3 times as much of the GNP of these countries as the processing industry (38.3 percent as opposed to 11.7 percent), by the mid-1980s the processing industry accounted for almost 1.2 times as much of the GNP as agriculture (21.2 percent as opposed to 18.4 percent).[2] They made especially marked progress in the development of heavy industry, the total production of which grew by 160 percent from 1970 through 1984, with its share in the output of industrial goods rising from 47.8 percent to 51.8 percent.[3]

As a result, from 1950 through 1985 the "peripheral" countries' share in the GNP of the nonsocialist world rose from 17 percent to 23 percent; their proportional share of production rose from 48 percent to 58.7 percent in agriculture and from 13.2 percent to 21.9 per-

---

[1]Calculations and estimates by B. M. Bolotin (in 1982 prices and at official exchange rates), based on *Yearbook of National Accounts Statistics* and *Monthly Bulletin of Statistics*, for the corresponding years.
[2]*Ibid.*
[3]Calculated (in 1980 prices and official exchange rates) on the basis of: *Statistical Yearbook 1982*, United Nations, New York, pp. 22-23; *Monthly Bulletin of Statistics*, Feb. 1986, pp. XVIII-XIX.

cent in industry (extractive and processing industries and electrical power engineering), including a climb of from 8.6 percent to 18.6 percent in the output of manufactured goods.[4]

In most of the countries, the increase in production was accompanied by diversification and increased complexity in their economic structures, a strengthening of the material and technical base of their economies, especially of industry, the development of interbranch and intrabranch integration of basic economic subdivisions, and an expansion and consolidation of domestic markets. In the course of these processes, the foundations of national mechanisms for expanded reproduction were formed and improved, and the necessary material prerequisites were created both for achieving and strengthening the former colonies' economic independence, and for their more thoroughgoing and diversified inclusion in a system of the international division of labor that was being modified under the influence of scientific and technological progress.

The 1970s, which were marked by an increase in the developing countries' role in the world capitalist economy, are particularly noteworthy from this standpoint. In addition to an increase in their relative contribution to the nonsocialist world's combined GNP, this growth was also associated with a consolidation of the liberated states' forces and a marked acceleration in their economic and political activity in the international arena, which was aimed at compensating for their obvious lack of overall economic might. It was in the 1970s that OPEC made its presence felt, managing to achieve a substantial increase in oil prices. Also during that time, in 1974, with the support of the socialist-commonwealth countries, the liberated states succeeded in getting the U.N. General Assembly to adopt the Declaration and Program of Action on the Establishment of a New International Economic Order, which was aimed at improving external conditions for their development. The economic and political consequences of the changes that have been noted were far from uniform. But on the whole they contributed to the expansion and deepening of various ties between the central and peripheral zones of the world capitalist economy.

Changes in the structure of their exports and, correspondingly, in their position on the world capitalist market were an important indicator of the positive changes in the developing countries' economies during that period. For example, from 1971 through 1980, when the foreign trade of countries in the "peripheral" group underwent especially vigorous development, their exports of industrial goods rose by 820 percent in terms of monetary value, which was second only to

[4]Calculated (in 1982 prices and official exchange rates) on the basis of: *Yearbook of National Accounts Statistics* and *Monthly Bulletin of Statistics*, for the corresponding years.

the increase in exports of fuel oil, whose rise in value was due primarily, if not exclusively, to the sharp leap in oil prices. It is typical that the percentage of industrial goods in the exports of these countries, excluding oil, rose by a factor of more than 1.5 (from 36 percent to 55.8 percent), with a 3.7-fold increase in the percentage of machinery and equipment (from 3.8 percent to 14.2 percent).[5]

At the same time, the developing countries' proportional contribution to the total exports of the nonsocialist world grew by a factor of more than 1.5. And the sharp rise in oil prices was not the only reason for this. Other goods accounted for 35 percent of the total increase in the value of exports from these countries during those years, with 22.2 percent of that increase coming from a rise in the export of industrial products. As a result, their proportional share of the nonsocialist world's industrial exports rose from 7.2 percent to 11.7 percent, including a rise from 1.8 percent to 6.6 percent in their share of exports of machinery and equipment. These percentages continued to rise in subsequent years, reaching 14.5 percent for general industrial exports and 9.6 percent for machinery and equipment in 1984. The rapid growth in industrial exports was, to all intents and purposes, evidence that part of local industry was rising to a qualitatively new, higher level of development, which brought public recognition of its results not only in the domestic market, but in the world market as well.

As a result of the changes that have been noted in the development of exports, as well as a marked increase in the flow of financial resources into the liberated countries (a considerable part of which was associated with the recycling of petrodollars, which increased the total mass of "free" liquid assets in the world capitalist economy), the importance of these countries' markets increased considerably. From 1970 through 1981 their proportional share in the nonsocialist world's total imports rose by a factor of almost 1.4, approaching 29 percent of the total value of those imports; in 1981 their share of machinery and equipment imports reached 35.3 percent, which was 1.4 times as high as the 1970 figure.[6]

All of this, combined with the liberated countries' higher rate of economic growth (in the past decade the average annual growth rate has been 5.8 percent, as opposed to 3.2 percent in the developed capitalist states),[7] gave rise for a period of time to certain illusions regarding the possibilities for their further development and, correspondingly, a possible increase in their role in the world economy in the

---

[5]Based on: *Statistical Yearbook 1979/80*, United Nations, New York, 1981, pp. 448-476; *Monthly Bulletin of Statistics*, May 1986, pp. XXXIV-LIII.
[6]*Ibid.*
[7]Calculated in terms of 1982 prices and official exchange rates.

1980s. A reflection of these illusions was the scenario drawn up by experts from the United Nations Conference on Trade and Development (UNCTAD) for world development for the current decade, in which the dynamic economic growth of the group of "peripheral" countries was seen as all but the primary driving force, supposedly capable of "shaking up" and pushing forward the entire world capitalist economy through a system of direct and reciprocal relations.[8]

However, the significant expansion of ties between developing countries and the world capitalist economy in the 1970s was based, to a large extent, on an inadequate economic foundation. The increase in their share in world capitalist trade, together with a significant influx of foreign borrowed funds, was still mainly due to the change in price proportions in the course of the energy and raw-materials crisis. Evidence of this can be seen, in particular, in the contradictory dynamics of the developing countries' contribution to the nonsocialist world's total exports when calculated in current and constant prices. In current prices, this figure rose by more than half in the 1970 to 1980 period, while in constant prices it declined by almost a third.

When prices for raw materials—for mineral and agricultural raw materials at first, and then later for energy raw materials—started to drop, it was discovered that their previous growth had not eliminated, but only camouflaged and postponed the arrival of a deep crisis that had been developing earlier in the structure of local exports, thereby intensifying the subsequent effect of that crisis. It became clear that the diversification of the liberated countries' exports and the improvement of their commodity structure as a whole lagged significantly behind rapidly changing conditions and demands of the world market. And they were lagging behind not just because of objective factors associated with difficulties in restructuring local economies, or because of miscalculations in the economic policies of the developing countries themselves, but to a great extent, because of resistance on the part of imperialist states and their monopolies, which did not want to part with the privileges they had seized earlier in the spheres of production and international trade.

Concealed behind the aggregate figures for the developing world, which show a growth in its overall economic potential, are huge differences in the achievements of individual countries and groups of countries, and a deepening socioeconomic differentiation among them. From 1960 through 1982 the total increase of 66.4 percent in their combined GNP, including a 68.1 percent increase from 1970 through 1982, was for all practical purposes achieved by two groups of countries—the major oil exporters and the so-called newly indus-

---

[8]See *Trade and Development Report 1981*, Geneva, 1981, pp. 89-99.

trialized states, which account for only 28.8 percent of the Third World's population. The share of these groups of countries in the GNP of all the liberated states rose from 44.6 percent in 1960 to 48.8 percent in 1970, and 64.5 percent in 1982. If we examine this phenomenon through the prism of the level of development that has been achieved, we will see that countries that had an average annual per capita income higher than $1,500 in 1980 (19.8 percent of the developing countries' total population) accounted for 55.4 percent of the total increase in the Third World's GNP from 1960 to 1970, and 62.5 percent of that increase from 1970 to 1982.

Equally, if not more, significant are the differences among liberated countries in the extent to which they have overcome narrow agrarian and raw-materials specialization within the framework of the international capitalist division of labor (one indicator of this is the increase in the percentage of industrial goods in their exports). According to data from the United Nations Industrial Development Organization (UNIDO), from 1970 through 1982 just 12 countries accounted for more than half of the total exports of industrial products from the developing world, and their share showed a marked tendency toward growth.[9] Thus, the aforementioned rise of some of local industry to a qualitatively new, higher level took place predominantly in those countries. On the other hand, the vast bulk of them had not yet begun the development of industrial exports, or had taken just the very first steps in that direction. But even in the countries that have made the greatest strides forward, this still applies mainly to industries with well-developed and widely used technologies, such as textiles, clothing, shoes, steel, pulp, plywood, home electronics products, motor vehicles, and ship building. In the export of research-intensive products, where the possibilities for technology suppliers to dictate their own terms are considerably greater, the developing countries' successes have been much more modest.

The expansion and strengthening of these countries' export sector must take into account the structural reorganization of economies in the developed capitalist states, and they depend to a considerable extent on the nature of relations with those states. A rapid and painless solution of the problems that are arising in this connection is hardly likely. But their gradual solution seems fairly realistic. The new round of economic transformations that has begun in the developing countries, and their growing resistance to imperialist policies of discrimination and diktat are not the only factors that tend to support such a conclusion. Other evidence can be seen in the ability of the developed capitalist countries to make certain concessions and compromises,

---

[9]*Industry in the 1980s. Structural Change and Interdependence*, New York, 1985, p. 6.

which, despite the intense nature of their current conflicts with the liberated states, may somewhat expand the Third World countries' possibilities for maneuvering and development.

The prospects for strengthening a developing country's positions in the world markets, as well as the extent of the benefits realized by using the present system of economic relations with the leading capitalist states, depend to a huge extent on the economic, scientific, and technological potential of each country taken individually, and on the economic policies that it pursues. The more developed a country is and the larger its domestic market, the greater competition there is among foreign corporations in that country; and in principle, the possibilities for it to defend its own economic interests are accordingly broader.

At the same time, its ability to take advantage of existing possibilities depends considerably on the nature of the sphere in which its economic relations with the West are carried on. In industries with technologies of low and average complexity that are oriented toward the mass consumer, where competition is especially strong, such possibilities are realized more fully and readily than in industries where the latest science-intensive and unique goods are produced, and the market is controlled by a limited number of corporations. The specific stage of the life cycle of a given technology that has been developed in the West also plays a significant role. The developing countries' ability to achieve favorable conditions for themselves increases to the extent that that technology becomes more fully mature and widely adopted.

It is not surprising that the less developed Third World states encounter the greatest difficulties in their relations with Western companies. The weakness of national industry and the production infrastructure, a narrow domestic market, and a poor-quality labor force limit the ability of these countries to influence potential investors, suppliers, and creditors, not to mention their ability to optimize the terms of cooperation with them and to organize effective supervision of their operations. All this confirms the idea, which has been repeatedly expressed by Soviet scholars, that raising the level of the liberated states' development is critically important to their overcoming their unequal status in the world capitalist economy.[10]

This does not mean, of course, that the less developed states are in a hopeless situation. First, as a rule, various progressive transformations being carried out in those countries are helping them to make progress. Second, the general factors forcing imperialism to adapt to

---

[10]See, for example, L. V. Stepanov, *The Problem of Economic Independence* [*Problema ekonomicheskoy nezavisimosti*], Moscow, 1965; *Developing Countries in the Contemporary World. Unity and Diversity* [*Razvivayushchiyesya strany v sovremennom mire. Yedinstvo i mnogoobraziye*], Moscow, 1983.

changing conditions in the Third World are, indisputably, also affecting those countries, although to a lesser extent. Because of a kind of chain reaction, concessions wrung out of transnational corporations by the more developed liberated countries are eventually often granted, to òne degree or another and in one form or another, to the less developed countries as well. A vivid example of this can be seen in the changes that have taken place in the past 15 or 20 years in the mining industry on the periphery of world capitalist economy as a result of the complete or partial nationalization of Western companies' property. At the same time, the situation with respect to the less developed states confirms once again the fact that external conditions of development, superimposed on the domestic situation in various liberated countries, contribute to a deepening of the differences in their social and economic conditions.

The liberated states' adaptation to the extraordinarily complicated and, in many ways, unusual conditions of the 1970s and 1980s has largely proceeded in tandem with the existing and increasingly pronounced differentiation among them in terms of the dimensions and levels of development of their national economies, the degree and depth of their economies' adoption of industrial production methods, the speed and scope of their assimilation of current scientific and technological advances, and the forms and types of their integration into the world economy.

A Change in the Foreign Economic Situation

This decade and the previous one have in many ways marked a turning point in the economic history of the developing countries. It is in this period that the processes of structural reorganization in the world capitalist economy began to accelerate, and the instability of the international commodities and financial markets rose sharply. The economies of the former colonies and semicolonies, which were relatively inefficient, burdened by numerous imbalances and acute social problems, and often not managed skillfully enough, found themselves unable to react promptly to the change in the world economic situation, and consequently suffered sizable losses from the overall deterioration of conditions on world markets. The stubborn contradiction between the demands made on liberated countries by the development of the world capitalist economy, on one hand, and their continuing socioeconomic backwardness, on the other, has become increasingly evident.

Since the increase in developing countries' share in international trade in the 1970s·was based primarily on such transient factors as rising prices and a substantial increase in the influx of foreign financial

resources, their seemingly strong positions in the world market have
wavered considerably.

The deep cyclical recession that occurred in the main centers of
capitalism between 1980 and 1982 dealt a serious blow to the liberated
countries' economies. In the current decade the developing countries
have started to feel the full consequences of the structural reorganization of the Western economy that developed under the influence of a
new round of scientific and technological revolution, and that was
stimulated by the acute outbreaks of the energy and raw-materials
crisis. These consequences have included a relative decline in demand
for the developing countries' raw materials, a slowdown in the shifting
of a number of labor-, energy-, and materials-intensive production
processes from the center to the periphery of the capitalist economy,
and an intensification of protectionist tendencies in the West.

Under existing conditions, the immense weight of the burden
placed on the economies of the many developing countries that have
been drawn into the arms race has become particularly obvious.
According to estimates by SIPRI [Stockholm International Peace
Research Institute], approximately 15 to 20 percent of their foreign
debt, which grew rapidly over the past 10 to 15 years, was connected
directly to payments for the delivery of Western arms.[11]

The deep and unusually prolonged deterioration in trading conditions on raw-materials markets in the first half of the 1980s significantly
increased imbalances in the liberated states' foreign economic sectors.
Added to the consequences of the 1970s rise in oil prices, it contributed to a colossal swelling of their foreign debt. The increase in
payments on the foreign debt, a process which particularly picked up
speed after the leap in credit costs in the early 1980s, as well as growing
protectionism in Western markets, have worked in this same direction. One can get an idea of the magnitude of the disproportions that
have arisen in the liberated states' foreign transactions by looking at
the increase in the oil-importing countries' balance of payments deficit
for current operations, which rose from an average of $10.8 billion in
1970 to 1972 to $73.8 billion in 1980 to 1982. The large positive
balances that the group of oil-exporting countries showed in the 1970s
have also been replaced by significant deficits in the current decade.

The decline in the influx of foreign financial resources has had
equally serious consequences for the developing countries. In the
previous decade the attraction of large loans, primarily from private
banks, made it possible for the more developed liberated states to
somehow "absorb" external shocks without resorting to any substantial
reduction in imports, investments, and consumption. Starting in 1982,

---

[11]*World Armaments and Disarmament. SIPRI Yearbook 1985*, London, 1985, p. 448.

access to the bank-loan market became seriously restricted for most of them. [12] The net influx of foreign financial resources[13] into oil-importing countries, which accounted for an average of 2.7 percent of their GNP (or approximately 10 percent of gross accumulation) in the 1970s, was replaced by a net outflow after 1981.

The situation that has developed in the area of foreign financing is unlikely to change significantly, at least in the medium-range future. Considering the size of the debt accumulated by the developing countries, and the extraordinary caution with which Western banks have approached the matter of lending to them since 1982, it seems quite unlikely that the net influx of funds from external financing will be revived on any significant scale. At the same time, there is no reason to assume that a reduction in new bank loans can be offset by an influx of aid and direct investments.

The decline in the influx of financial resources from abroad has apparently put an end to the period when the liberated countries were able to make fairly wide use of borrowed funds from abroad, thereby expanding the possibilities for acquiring foreign currency to support their economic growth. To lessen their dependence on foreign financing sources, the overwhelming majority have been forced to take measures to reduce their balance of payments deficit for current operations. The African and Latin American countries have achieved significant results in this area (the ratio of African countries' total balance of payments deficit to their exports of goods and services dropped from 30 percent of exported goods and services in 1981 to 17 percent in 1984, while the ratio for Latin American countries dropped from 35 percent in 1982 to 6 percent in 1985). [14] It is noteworthy that these were primarily the countries that depended mainly on commercial sources of financial resources, while those that received funds through aid channels still have sizable deficits.

Thus, whereas in the 1970s the access of the more developed liberated countries to private bank loans enabled them to reduce the dependence of import growth on export growth, thereby somewhat expanding the boundaries of their accumulation and consumption, the change in the world economic situation in the current decade has forced them largely to return to depending on their own resources. In addition, a sharply increased outflow has turned some of them into net

---

[12]This was connected with a sharp deterioration in the financial and economic condition of many debtor countries, which undermined confidence in their solvency.

[13]Net influx here means the difference between the total volume of capital and "aid" received and the reverse outflow of funds in the form of payments on debts and profits on direct investments.

[14]Calculated on the basis of: *World Economic Outlook*, Apr. 1985, pp. 240-241; and *International Financial Statistics*, Jan. 1986, p. 423.

"donors" to the developed capitalist countries. This has required economic and social sacrifices.

To achieve the necessary balance in foreign transactions, the majority of developing countries have been forced to resort to a substantial reduction in imports, which play a vitally important role in maintaining the conditions for economic growth. Combined with the drop in the value of their exports, this has led to a rapid decline in their share in the nonsocialist world's total foreign trade (see table below).

The Developing Countries' Share of the
Nonsocialist World's International Trade
(percentages)

	1970	1981	1984
Exports	19.7	30.5	27.5
Imports	22.0	31.6	26.1

Calculated on the basis of: *Statistical Yearbook 1979/80*, United Nations, New York, 1981, pp. 448-476; *Monthly Bulletin of Statistics*, May 1986, pp. XXXIV-LIII.

Thus, in just three years the developing countries' share of the nonsocialist world's total imports declined by more than one sixth, and their share of exports by almost one tenth. Under these conditions, naturally, predictions of their rapid economic growth, much less predictions that they would play a leading role in stimulating an overall upsurge in the capitalist economy, proved unfounded.

The deterioration in developing countries' currency and financial situation negatively affected the overall course of the investment process. From 1980 through 1984 the overall accumulation rate declined by approximately one tenth in this group of countries. At the same time, largely due to the shortage of foreign currency funds, the import component of that rate also declined (to 26.9 percent in 1982, as opposed to 33.7 percent in 1975). A deterioration in the technical and economic characteristics of investment resources also occurred.

In the final analysis, all this caused a sharp slowdown in the pace of economic development in the liberated states, a slowdown which in a number of countries, including those that had previously been the most prosperous, resulted during 1982 and 1983 in an absolute decline in total production (in Brazil, Mexico, Nigeria, etc.). From 1980 to 1985 the average annual increase in the GNP of Third World countries dropped to less than one fourth of what it had been—to 1.5 percent, down from 5.8 percent in the previous decade.[15]

At the same time the process of the structural reorganization of the developing countries' economies in favor of technically more com-

---

[15]Calculation and estimates by B.M. Bolotin in 1982 prices and official exchange rates.

plicated production operations ground to a halt, and in a number of areas it even started to reverse. For example, heavy industry's share in the total output of the local processing industry dropped to 48.4 percent in 1984, down from 51.8 percent in 1980. It is characteristic that even when production output is calculated in current prices, heavy industry's share of total output declined during these years, though less significantly so.[16]

In a situation of steady demographic pressure, the deterioration in the economic situation led to an aggravation of the employment problem and a substantial decline in average per capita income. In connection with the growing shortage of many producer and consumer goods, production costs rose, the efficiency of the investment process declined, and inflation grew. It assumed particularly dangerous dimensions in Latin America (where the average annual increase in retail prices from 1981 through 1985 was 91.4 percent). All of this had an extremely unfavorable effect on the situation of the working people, as well as on the development of the liberated countries' domestic markets and technical and economic potential.

The changes in the world economic situation affected individual liberated states and groups of states differently. A significant and growing socioeconomic heterogeneity was distinctly manifested among the bulk of the developing countries, while clear differences also showed up in their abilities to counter unfavorable outside influences—whether they were spontaneous processes or the policies of imperialist powers and international monopolies, which tried to shift most of the burden of both the cyclical crises and the technical restructuring of the economy that had been launched in the West onto the liberated states. The stormy events of the past decade and a half have served as a sort of "endurance test" for the economies and development strategies of individual countries. From this standpoint, one can identify three basic groups of liberated states.

The first group includes the principal oil exporters. In connection with the change in the conditions on the market in energy raw materials, the defects in the structure of their economies, especially the inadequacy of their export base, became especially noticeable. Efforts made in the oil-exporting countries during the past decade to diversify their economies and exports proved to be clearly insufficient for a significant reduction in their dependence on the export of liquid fuel. What is more, the "golden rain" that poured down on these countries in many cases made conditions worse for their enterprises that

---

[16]Calculated on the basis of: *Monthly Bulletin of Statistics*, Feb. 1986, pp. XVII-XIX; *Statistical Yearbook, 1973*, United Nations, New York, pp. 28-29; *Statistical Yearbook, 1978*, pp. 28-29; and *Statistical Yearbook, 1982*, pp. 22-23.

exported nonpetroleum products, and in some instances even slowed the process of industrialization as a whole. Broad access to foreign technology and imported goods depressed the development of the production of producer goods, especially machinery and equipment, and weakened incentives for the formation of a national scientific and technological potential.[17]

To maintain the living standard and level of economic activity they had achieved, some of the oil-exporting countries (Saudi Arabia, the United Arab Emirates, and several others) resorted to using foreign assets that they had accumulated earlier. Most of these countries, however, did not have assets of this nature and were forced to cut back substantially on their imports, freeze many investment projects, and reduce social expenditures. The difficulties they are experiencing are aggravated by the fact that they have to bear the burden of huge debts that developed during the period of high prices for energy raw materials. Mexico, Nigeria, and Venezuela are among the countries with the most complicated debt situation.

The second group includes the petroleum-importing countries that have more or less actively adapted to the new energy situation that emerged in the world in the 1970s. This group includes the relatively developed countries and territories of Southeast Asia and the Far East, Brazil, and several other countries that have a fairly diversified economic structure and significant manpower and technical potential. The "oil shocks" of the 1970s pushed these countries to strengthen their self-sufficiency in energy resources, and they also stimulated efforts aimed at developing the investment complex and strengthening the export sector (primarily by orienting some of the industry being created there toward foreign markets). In the 1960s and 1970s the countries in this group created foreign-currency and tax regulations favorable to the development of exports. An important role in the accomplishment of these tasks was played by an improvement in the mechanisms for mobilizing domestic savings, as well as by the use of foreign credits to modernize the structure of the national economy and of exports.

Progress in the expansion and diversification of exports (relying both on industrial goods and services and on raw materials enjoying increased demand), as well as in the development of the means of production, have made it easier to adapt to the unfavorable financial and market conditions in the current decade, and have enabled countries in this group largely to maintain (and in some cases restore) relatively high rates of economic growth.

------

[17]See *World Development Report 1984*, Oxford, 1984, p. 27.

India can also be counted among the group of oil importers that have successfully withstood unfavorable foreign economic changes. The relative stability of its economy during the tumultuous period of the 1970s and 1980s is attributable not so much to the development of exports, as to its consistent policy of reducing its dependence on imports and foreign capital, and also to the opportunity it had to meet its need for foreign financial resources primarily through favorable loans provided as part of "aid" programs.

The third and largest group is comprised of oil-importing countries that were not able to adapt satisfactorily to the changing world economic situation. This group includes primarily states with a poorly diversified economic structure and exports based on a narrow range of raw materials, or often, on just a single commodity. Because of their limited economic possibilities and, often, miscalculations or unsound economic policies, these countries' adaptation to the new energy situation and other crisis-related phenomena in the world capitalist economy took the form primarily of attempts to increase their export of traditional types of raw materials and to obtain foreign loans to cover constant deficits in their balance of payments. Their efforts to mobilize additional domestic savings, as well as to restructure their economies and exports proved relatively ineffective. This sort of situation is especially typical of countries in tropical Africa. This group also includes some of the relatively developed countries of Latin America and Asia (Argentina, Chile, the Philippines, etc.), where considerable borrowing of foreign loan funds in the 1970s was not accompanied by effective enough measures to mobilize domestic savings, increase the efficiency of the economy, and develop new foreign markets.

The Complicated Process of Adjustment

The difficult financial and economic situation in which the majority of the liberated states have found themselves in this decade has forced them to seriously rethink many elements of their national economic strategies. Pressure from foreign creditors, especially the IMF and the World Bank, have also contributed to this. The IMF and World Bank actively intervene in the development and implementation of economic reforms in dozens of liberated countries, especially in Africa and Latin America. The most important elements of the prescriptions that the West's two leading financial institutions propose for overcoming crises are: providing maximum incentives for exports, increasing the "openness" of economies with respect to imports and the influx of foreign investments, reducing state budget deficits and restricting the economic functions of the state as a whole, cutting back on social programs carried out by the state, reducing the national consumption level and encouraging savings, redistributing funds in favor of agriculture, and so on.

In giving a Marxist assessment of the programs that the IMF and World Bank propose for developing countries, one must note that these programs are aimed primarily at preserving and strengthening capitalism in its weakest, peripheral links. As the West's largest financial institutions, which operate in the interests of the developed capitalist states as a whole, the IMF and World Bank substantially base their recommendations on the need to rapidly eliminate disproportions that have arisen in the liberated states' economies and that threaten the stability of local capitalist institutions. Having no direct ties to the interests of specific privileged groups of the developing countries, the IMF and World Bank are often more consistent than local ruling circles both in their analysis of the reasons for the economic difficulties those countries have encountered in this decade, and in the development of measures to resolve them. It is no coincidence that the probourgeois circles that hold power in many liberated states took steps to implement a number of long-overdue reforms (for example, in the area of providing incentives for agricultural production and small-scale industry) only after strong pressure from their creditors.

At the same time, the recommendations imposed on the developing countries by the international financial organizations are based on theoretical constructs of bourgeois economics that were worked out primarily with reference to the reality of developed capitalist states, and often clearly fail to give due consideration to the specific features of the Third World countries' socioeconomic situation. Specifically, liberalization of the price, foreign-currency, and credit policies required by IMF and World Bank experts, who put their trust in the "magic of the market," is incapable, by itself, of providing a stable economic upswing—even in developed capitalist countries. It is especially unrealistic for countries where the private sector is still relatively weak and, without state assistance and support, incapable of resisting pressure from international monopolies and the unfavorable consequences of unregulated market forces. In addition, such recommendations, based to a significant extent on monetaristic concepts, emphasize the modification of current economic policies, whereas what the liberated states need most is long-range programs for economic restructuring that are aimed at strengthening the national production base and that require major additional capital investments.

One must also note that, despite all the claims of objectivity, IMF and World Bank recommendations to a great extent bear the imprint of the selfish interests and demands of transnational banks and corporations. From a social-class standpoint, it is especially important that the programs for the "rationalization" of local capitalism that come from the Western financial organizations depend largely on cutting back the income and social gains of the working people.

Many developing countries are trying to counter the policies of the IMF and World Bank with their own programs for getting out of their crisis. While recognizing the need for serious structural changes in their economies and for a revision of their national development strategies, they are trying to preserve their right to choose the measures needed to accomplish this, and the order in which they are carried out. At the same time, the liberated states are proceeding on the premise that any program of economic reform should provide economic growth and take the social needs of the population into account. Since the notions of the debtors and the creditors about the areas and methods of the necessary economic restructuring nearly always differ seriously, the reforms being carried out with the participation of the IMF and World Bank are usually the result of a difficult compromise, and their content is determined to a great extent by the actual, developing balance of forces.

The reconsideration of economic strategy that began in the Third World in the first half of the 1980s is aimed primarily at improving the relative position of export-oriented branches of the economy. The point is that until recently most countries that were unable to adapt to the new economic situation typically employed systems of currency exchange rates, import quotas, tax and other advantages that put the processing industries producing for the domestic market in a clearly privileged position compared to other sectors of the local economy.

In principle, the policy of protecting and encouraging industry that serves the domestic market has an extremely important role to play in the process of the liberated countries' industrialization, and without such a policy it is practically impossible for new types of production to appear and develop. However, in many countries, such a policy having lost over time the necessary flexibility and balance has resulted in preserving the uncompetitiveness of those types of production and thus hindered the diversification and growth of exports.

In order to correct disproportions that have arisen and to encourage exports, most countries in tropical Africa, as well as Mexico, Peru, Bolivia, and Indonesia, among others, have devalued their national currencies and simultaneously increased direct financial and technical support for exporters. The goal of increasing nontraditional exports has become a key element in the economic-development programs of many liberated countries. Mexico, Peru, India, Turkey, the Ivory Coast, Liberia, Morocco, and a number of other countries have started to implement or outline plans for making the protectionism system more rational in order to weaken the protection of national enterprises and encourage them to increase their international competitiveness. With that same goal, tariffs are being selectively reduced, administrative restrictions on the import of technology and competing products are being eased, a higher level of direct foreign investments is being allowed, and so forth. In India, for example, in the first half of the 1980s quantitative restrictions on the importation of a significant number of industrial goods were lifted, and the procedures for authorizing license purchase and financial cooperation with foreign firms were simplified, among other things.

At the same time, most of the liberated states are approaching the "open-economy" policy so heavily promoted by the West with extreme caution. When local industrial structures are weak, complete openness to imports (combined, moreover, with a decline in the role of the state) contains a latent threat that many vitally important branches of local industry will be destroyed, and that a narrow raw-materials specialization within the framework of the international division of labor will be reinforced. When a relative decline in the demand for raw materials occurs as a result of scientific and technological progress, an excessive increase in exports of raw materials carries a real possibility that there will be a drop in prices and a corresponding decline in foreign-currency revenues. Stabilization of the developing countries' foreign economic positions requires an upgrading of their exports, primarily by increasing the proportion of industrial goods. This is impossible without an active state policy aimed both at protecting and strengthening local industry, and specifically, at stimulating industrial exports.

Practically all the countries that ran into financial difficulties in the first half of the 1980s have planned a revision of their investment strategies. Capital-investment plans place greater emphasis on projects that are supposed to provide an increase in exports and a savings in imports. At the same time, allocations have been cut for the construction of enterprises of secondary importance that require a high level of imports and have inadequate sources of raw materials and insufficient markets for their products. The infatuation with "grandiose" (and often economically unsound) projects so characteristic of the petroleum-producing countries and a number of other liberated countries in the 1970s has started to give way to an orientation toward the development of substantially less capital-intensive and import-intensive small- and medium-scale production facilities.

Measures aimed at development of agriculture have become an important element of adjustment programs in many liberated countries. That is especially true of countries in tropical Africa, where until recently insufficient attention was given to the economic and social needs of rural areas. In the 1970s per capita agricultural output in the African region declined by an average of 1.1 percent annually, including a 0.9 percent drop in food production. The dependence on food imports, which rose by 7 percent a year between the early 1960s and late 1970s, reached dangerous proportions. The stagnation of agriculture also had a negative effect on African exports, a substantial portion of which are agricultural products. In order to improve the situation, in the first half of the 1980s most countries in the region made decisions to raise purchase prices for agricultural commodities, increase the amounts of financial and technical resources allocated to the countryside, and so forth.

The drop in the influx of financial resources forced the liberated states to focus special attention on strengthening national savings mechanisms. In the 1970s a decline in the effectiveness of these mechanisms, combined with a rapid rise in social and investment expenditures in many Latin American and African countries, helped intensify dependence on foreign financing and aggravate the debt problem. To encourage savings, state control over bank interest rates has been relaxed in Brazil, Argentina, Bolivia, Kenya, and many other countries during the current decade. This sort of control, introduced in the interests of national industry, often undermined the attractiveness of bank deposits for people with disposable funds. When the cost of credit is restricted under conditions of high inflation, the real interest rate for depositors often turns out to be negative. This contributed to a large-scale outflow of capital abroad. From 1974 through 1982, according to estimates by the World Bank, this outflow, for example, equaled $32.7 billion in Mexico (whose increase in indebtedness over the same period was $82.6 billion), $15.3 billion in Argentina (with a debt increase of $32.6 billion), $10.8 billion in Venezuela (with a debt increase of $27.0 billion).[18]

Steps have also started to be taken to make adjustments in the financial activities of the state. The measures that have been adopted are aimed, in particular, at reducing the state budget deficit, which in the 1970s and early 1980s rose to dangerous levels in many liberated countries. In 1981, for example, the state budget deficit equaled 7 percent of the GNP in Mexico, 9 percent of the GNP in Argentina, 13 percent in Sri Lanka, 14 percent in Zambia. Since these deficits are covered mainly by foreign loans or by increasing the amount of money in circulation, they stimulated an increase in indebtedness and an intensification of inflationary tendencies.

The effort to put state finances in order is being carried out both by reducing expenditures and by increasing the revenue side of the budget through improvements in the tax system, higher prices for the products of state enterprises, and so on. A number of countries, for

---

[18]*The World Bank Research News*, No. 1, 1985, p. 6.

example (Egypt, Nigeria, Mali, and others), are attempting to cut back an excessively swollen administrative apparatus, whose maintenance costs represent one of the main expenditure items in the state budget.

The role of foreign borrowed funds in economic development has also been seriously reevaluated. In the 1970s the view that foreign bank loans were a readily accessible, relatively inexpensive source of foreign currency resources free of foreign control became quite widespread. This contributed to a slackening of demands that these funds be put to effective use. In many cases the attraction of foreign loans essentially served as a convenient alternative to difficult measures to restructure the economy in accordance with changing external circumstances, and it failed to provide an increase in the foreign-currency resources needed to repay debts. The dramatic change in the situation in the world credit market in the early 1980s graphically demonstrated the danger of the strategy based on growing indebtedness. It forced even those developing countries that still enjoyed the trust of banks to take a more cautious approach to attracting borrowed funds on commercial terms, and to carefully monitor the use of such funds.

Financial difficulties and the desire to overcome their growing technical lag also forced the majority of liberated states to take steps to increase the influx of direct foreign investments. A number of countries liberalized regulations governing the activities of foreign companies—in particular, they expanded such companies' sphere of operations, relaxed restrictions on the extent of ownership, and so on. Changes in legislation have mainly involved export branches and technically complicated branches of the economy, where the developing countries' own capabilities are extremely limited.

Changes have also affected the activities of the state sector. With the deteriorating economic situation in the first half of the 1980s, many liberated countries placed stricter demands on the economic aspect of the operations of state enterprises, and cut their expenditures and staffs. A number of countries (Bangladesh, Brazil, Pakistan, Liberia, and others) sold or are planning to sell certain enterprises to private owners (mainly those enterprises whose profitable operation has been impossible to maintain within the framework of the state sector). For example, Mexico is planning to turn 236 companies over to private hands. Tanzania is planning to privatize sisal plantations, Pakistan intends to privatize the power-distribution and banking networks, Malaysia will privatize airlines and medical institutions, and so on.

In most countries stronger emphasis has been placed on private business (primarily small and medium-sized businesses). This policy, like that of privatizing some state enterprises, reflects the desire of right-wing circles of the developing countries' now stronger bourgeoisie, in alliance with conservative Western forces, to restrict the role of the state in the economy. To justify this they refer to the relative inefficiency of state enterprises. A number of studies conducted by the World Bank, for example, note that state corporations have not made effective use in every instance of the huge sums they obtained in the form of loans and increased oil revenues. Having concentrated considerable economic power in their hands, the managers of many of these corporations have often ended up effectively outside of governmental or public control. Consequently, in a number of countries corruption and nepotism have increased, and the efficiency of state enterprises has declined.

Criticism of several unsound methods for state regulation of the economy that were used in capitalist-oriented developing countries in past decades is also being energetically used to undermine confidence in the state. Administrative regulation of many aspects of economic life, including the price of key goods, the allocation of loans among branches and companies, the setting of terms for such loans, the number and size of enterprises operating in a given sphere of the economy, and so on, distorted actual monetary-value proportions, often lowered the efficiency with which available resources were used, and contributed to monopolization of the market, development of shortages, and price increases. Moreover, in countries with inadequately developed institutions of public oversight, administrative regulation was sometimes used to redistribute the national income in favor of influential social groups, in whose support the ruling circles had an interest.

In the present situation, when the requirements for economic efficiency in the developing countries have sharply increased, the rejection of a number of methods of administrative intervention in economic life, and the broader use of economic methods of management could help invigorate overall business activity and mobilize local resources more fully. At the same time, it must be stressed that the interests of the liberated countries require neither restriction of the economic activity of the state, nor, especially, its reduction, which is what the West is insisting on, but rather a search for and development of more rational forms of state intervention in the economy while maintaining the state's leading role in the development process.

Deterioration in the financial and economic conditions has had an extremely painful effect on the state's social policy, as well. In countries that are experiencing financial difficulties, a reduction in state budget deficits has largely been carried out by cutting expenditures on education, health care, and other social needs, and by reducing price subsidies for many essential goods and services. (Subsidies of this kind became particularly widespread in the 1970s.) At the same time, a reduction in subsidies is usually accompanied by a sudden rise in prices. Thus, in 1984, following the adoption of a budgetary economy program in Bolivia, the prices of inexpensive varieties of bread doubled, and the price of kerosene, the fuel used by poor people, quadrupled.

The IMF and World Bank are exerting serious pressure on to developing countries to limit subsidies. This policy is being conducted under the banner of ensuring "more efficient" distribution of state funds. In this connection, use is being made of the fact that in past decades it was mainly the residents of cities, where the income level is significantly higher than in rural areas, who realized gains from state subsidies, and it was by no means only people in the poorest groups who enjoyed the benefits. For example, in Egypt in 1979 about half of all the subsidies for electric power and food went to the upper half of the urban population in terms of income.

The cutback in programs for distributing food at subsidized prices that was carried out, under IMF pressure, by a number of debtor countries proved especially painful. Generated by a desire to speed up industrialization and relax social tensions in the cities, these programs not only swallowed up considerable budget funds, but also often undermined incentives for the development of farming and encouraged mass migration from rural areas. Food handouts to the poorest urban residents almost always covered up ruling circles' unwillingness to seriously tackle urgent social and economic problems, especially in the agrarian sector—in particular, to support and strengthen the huge mass of small and tiny peasant farms where people were scraping out a miserable existence, in order to help them be included in the development process.

At the same time, one cannot help but see that, in the absence of real opportunities to provide "productive employment,"[19] the IMF-imposed drastic reduction in the "social feeding" of the poorest segments of the population is fraught with the danger of causing the social and physical degradation of millions of inhabitants of developing countries, and of further increasing social and political tension. Therefore, it is perfectly possible that such measures may result not in strengthening capitalism in these countries, as the IMF and World Bank are striving for, but on the contrary, in increasing social and political instability there. It is no coincidence that attempts to reduce food subsidies have invariably given rise to mass protests, which in a number of cases have turned into real revolts (Egypt, the Dominican Republic, Morocco, and others).

---

[19]What is meant here are those forms of economic activity from which the income can provide at least a living wage.

Thus, the economic restructuring currently going on in the developing countries is aimed, for all intents and purposes, at strengthening local capitalist structures. It implies a redistribution of resources among the most important sectors of the economy and various segments of the population. In countries that succeed in carrying out this restructuring, one can expect a certain "pulling up" of agriculture, as well as accelerated growth in other branches that contribute directly to reducing imports or that are oriented toward exports. In social respects this restructuring would lead to a strengthening of the relatively high income and medium income peasant strata of the rural population, to an expansion of the base of capitalism in cities through the creation of more small- and medium-sized businesses, and to a strengthening of the positions of foreign capital, as well as of those groups of the local bourgeoisie whose activities involve high-priority branches of the economy. At the same time, the situation of the poorest segments of the population (especially in the cities) would grow worse. The concrete distribution of the benefits and costs of reforms in individual states depends to a great extent on the alignment of forces within the ruling bloc, as well as on the social and political activeness of broad segments of the working people.

*   *   *

The developing countries' search for their own answers to the questions facing them in this decade is far from over. Changes in the world capitalist economy, while erecting especially difficult obstacles along the development path of these countries, are also thereby forcing them to move toward a more complete mobilization and rational utilization of both external and internal factors of economic growth. The attainment of this goal in many respects requires nonstandard approaches to the solution of problems that arise. The states that have suffered the most from the world economic disturbances (primarily African and Latin American states) evidently still need considerable time to achieve more or less stable social and economic progress.

In the coming years the liberated countries will doubtlessly have to depend more on their own financial and production resources than they have in the past. This means that they will have to make unflagging efforts to improve national systems for mobilizing savings and increasing the effectiveness with which they are used. Success here depends to a great extent on the economic-organizational activity of the state, and on its ability to rationally combine state forms of economic activity with private forms, market stimuli with state regulation, and protection for new economic branches with the maintenance of a certain level of "openness" to the foreign market.

In the new world economic situation, incentives for growth that are linked to the development of national markets are coming to play a greater role. In particular, there is a growing need to increase labor productivity and income among those segments of the population that still remain outside the contemporary market economy. In the majority of countries, realization of this goal is hardly possible without a deepening of agrarian reforms, particularly the redistribution of the basic means of production—land—in favor of the direct producers, mainly the poor and poorest segments of the peasantry, and the provision of genuine financial and technical support to them, as well to small-scale producers in other sectors of the economy.

In connection with the relatively unfavorable conditions in the developed capitalist countries' markets, trade and economic cooperation among the developing states themselves will evidently receive a new impetus. One can expect significant changes in mutual trade among the most developed liberated countries, and in their trade relations with the less developed countries.

At the same time, the developing countries' search for "nontraditional" ways to resolve contradictions that arise in relations with developed capitalist countries is being expanded. In particular, increasingly insistent demands are being made for the West to ease the burden of payments on the foreign debt and to link the debt question with the problem of eliminating protectionist barriers. A number of developing countries have succeeded in obtaining long deferments (up to 14 years) of payments on the principal of their loans. In many cases Western banks have, in effect, been forced to agree to an incomplete repayment of the interest on debts, covering it with new loans to the insolvent borrowers. The volume of such "involuntary" loans has totaled tens of billions of dollars in recent years. In the future, Western creditors will apparently have to reconcile themselves more and more to a situation in which debt obligations are actually repaid only to the extent that such repayment is compatible with the maintenance of socially acceptable rates of economic growth for the borrower countries.

The likelihood of such an approach is linked to the fact that the degree of interdependence between the centers and periphery of the world capitalist economy has grown considerably in the past decade and a half. Economic disarray and a sharp aggravation of social and political tension in large developing borrower countries that represent important markets, spheres for the application of capital, and sources of raw materials and other commodities for the West threaten to disrupt the normal functioning of the entire world capitalist system.

At the same time, the existing situation provides evidence that the extremely complicated economic problems that developing countries are presently encountering cannot be solved on the basis of individual concessions by developed capitalist states. The solution of these problems requires a broad set of measures on both national and international levels aimed at easing the situation and strengthening the foreign economic positions of the liberated countries. Implementing the program that was proposed by the 27th CPSU Congress for creating a comprehensive international security system could be an important contribution to the accomplishment of this task.

Extremism, Terrorism, and Internal Conflicts in the Third World

By Georgiy Ilyich Mirskiy*

Extremism and terror are rather closely related phenomena, but there is no automatic link between them. While it is true that every terrorist is an extremist, since he resorts to the most extreme methods of struggle, it would not be correct to suppose that every extremist is a terrorist. Needless to say, as a particular kind of mind-set, extremism logically leads to a justification of terror, but it by no means necessarily goes that far. As for armed conflicts, they cannot necessarily be considered a manifestation of extremism; sometimes forces that do not subscribe to political extremism come into conflict under pressure of circumstances.

Nevertheless, certain common traits enable us to view these three diverse phenomena on the same plane. They are violence (the desire to forcibly impose one's position on an opponent, to suppress or even destroy him) and rejection in principle of the idea of compromise, of seeking to resolve a disputed question by reconciling different viewpoints. The political extremist in the true sense of the word is a person who considers only himself to be right, who is convinced that only his position is just, and who rejects his opponent's arguments in principle. This approach is not unique to extremists, of course, but it is invariably typical of them.

I.

These three phenomena have been known from time immemorial. No era has been without violence and bloodshed. But the 20th century, as compared to the 19th, for example, has brought something new: terrorism not only "from below" but "from above" as well—state terrorism that goes to the point of concentration camps and genocide; or purposeful, deliberate terror against the civilian population, including the taking of hostages. Elements of all that have existed in the past

*Doctor of history and chief research associate at the U.S.S.R. Academy of Sciences' Institute of World Economy and International Relations [IMEMO]. This article appeared in the August 1988 issue of *MEMO*.

as well, but the massive scale of the phenomenon in question is characteristic of the present century.

Revealing the roots of the extremely widespread use of violence in our times is the task of history and social psychology. But the fact remains that economic and social development, the successes of the scientific and technical revolution, and progress in public health and education are not necessarily accompanied by a more humane, tolerant, and gentler society or, as we customarily put it, by a more "conscious" society. Together with the growth of criminality, including gangsterism and mafia-type crime, political violence fed by extremism is becoming widespread.

This is by no means uniquely characteristic of the Third World. Extremism is on the rise in the so-called civilized countries as well, and the potential for conflict is growing, whether it be the terrorist activities of the Red Brigades in Italy, the Basque separatists in Spain and the Corsican separatists in France, the Catholic and Protestant extremists in Northern Ireland, or the as yet bloodless but dangerous confrontation between the Flemings and the Walloons in Belgium.

Setting aside social extremism that is unrelated to nationality problems (ultrarightist and ultraleftist groups), then nationalism would have to be deemed the principal and most salient cause of political violence. This phenomenon has proven much stronger than one might have thought. Josip Broz-Tito said at one point in the 1970s, when nationalist sentiments had surfaced in Croatia and other republics of the Socialist Federal Republic of Yugoslavia, that if anyone had predicted, during the war of liberation, that 30 years hence Yugoslavia would be encountering problems of nationalism, he would have been a laughing stock—but lo and behold, nationalism had become a fact.

The phenomenon in question is far more inherent in the Third World than in Yugoslavia.

In speaking of the problem of nationalism in Asia and Africa, we have generally had in mind the anti-imperialist nationalism of peoples freeing themselves from colonial oppression. The "progressive nationalism" of the oppressed became the banner of the liberation struggle, and independence was won under its slogans. And to this day, certain Third World conflicts are based on precisely that kind of nationalism, i.e., a desire to get rid of foreign rule and achieve national independence. The most vivid example of this is the Palestinian Arabs' struggle against the Israeli occupation. However, national and ethnic conflicts of a different sort predominate in Asia and Africa today, conflicts that essentially involve national minorities inside a sovereign multinational state that are unhappy with their subordinate and unequal status and the discrimination against them.

The Ibo uprising in Nigeria, which became a regular war after Biafra was founded; the Kurds' many years of incessant warfare against the Iraqi and Iranian authorities; the separatist movements of the southern Sudan's non-Arab-speaking tribes and of Sri Lanka's Tamils, the protracted feuds and conflicts among ethnic groups in Ruanda, Burundi, Kenya, and Zimbabwe; the wars of the West Saharans against Morocco and of the Eritreans against the Ethiopian central government; the uprising of Bengalis in Pakistan that led to the formation of Bangladesh; and finally, the exceptionally complex and explosive ethnolinguistic situation in India that is spawning conflicts which threaten the country's geographic integrity—all these are merely the best-known and most apparent conflicts of that sort.

Conflicts on religious grounds must be added to the list. Suffice it to recall the situation of the Sikhs in India and the multilateral conflicts in Lebanon. In a certain sense, such conflicts can also be viewed as belonging to the same category as the nationality-ethnic type conflicts. After all, in both cases we are dealing with the problem of self-affirmation and self-definition, the problem of finding their own unique identity and place in the world that is faced by ethnic or religious groups that formerly had been "stewed" in a common colonial pot, and that had made common cause with similar groups in a joint protest against colonial oppression, but that subsequently—in the context of an independent state—felt themselves unfairly treated. They develop a kind of "inferiority complex" that they can dispatch only by self-assertion, which almost always presupposes a struggle against other groups that occupy a dominant, or at least a privileged, position in the new state.

Economic motives are often behind such an inferiority complex. The fact is that the relative importance of particular groups in the national economy is not always in keeping with their sociopolitical status. For example, the Ibos in Nigeria and the Sikhs in India have sufficient grounds for considering themselves better developed in the economic sense (and in the cultural and educational sense, as well) in comparison to other groups, and consequently the Ibos' and the Sikhs' economic contribution to the "common pot" is greater, in proportion to their numbers, than that of their neighbors. As they see it, however, that does not give them equivalent political standing; in their opinion, they are inadequately represented in the state apparatus, and so forth. On the other hand, certain ethnic or religious groups may regard others with envy and malice—those who are wealthier, better educated, cleverer, and more capable in commercial dealings and in business matters in general, and who use long-established ties and a traditional "specialization" to bolster their monopoly position in some area or other of economic life. That is noticeable, for example, in the attitude of Moslems toward Christians in Lebanon, or in the difficult relations among certain peoples in India and Pakistan.

II.

There is yet another important factor that reflects the legacy of the colonial era. It is that, in their system of governing a country, the colonial powers generally gave preference to certain local groups to the detriment of others. In the subsequent "transfer of power," the privileged status of the former groups was maintained, which could not but evoke protests from the latter groups. This is obvious from the way that armed forces and local police were recruited, among other things.

For example, in British West Africa the officer corps of the Royal Border Troops was basically formed from the most culturally developed population of the southern coastal areas of Nigeria and Ghana, while the rank-and-file troops were recruited in the backward northern areas. When Nigeria attained independence, 92 percent of the officers were from the coastal regions (principally Ibos), while 62 percent of the privates were from the far northern regions. In Kenya there were practically no Kikuyus in the enlisted ranks, since that ethnic group had played the dominant role in fighting the colonial power, and the British did not recruit them as soldiers. They made up less than 10 percent of the police. In Uganda the percentage of soldiers from the most numerous tribe, the Buganda, was minuscule. In the Pakistani Armed Forces, by a tradition that dates to the period of British rule, Punjabis hold the dominant position. Similar instances can be cited from an analysis of the makeup of the state apparatus in the countries in question.

This could not help but cause friction and tension. Yet our scholarship, with its emphasis on the role of class factors, has shed no light on Asian and African peoples' internal ethnic and religious diversity.

Indians, Syrians, Kenyans, Nigerians, and other peoples have each been regarded as a single whole, as it were, in that respect, with the stress being placed on class contradictions. In real life, however, the Indians, for example, figure as such only to the external world, whereas inside their own country they regard one another first as Bengalis, Marathas, Tamils, and so forth, second as representatives of some caste or other, and only then do class differences come into play. Apart from Arab solidarity vis-à-vis the enemy, the Arabs see one another as Syrians or Egyptians, Iraqis or Lebanese, and as Copts, Sunnis, Shiites, Alawites, and so forth. Things are even more complex in tropical Africa, with its multitude of peoples and tribes.

Relations between all these ethnic, national, and religious groups are often far from idyllic. Things were that way before, as well, but after independence these relations became immensely strained. For independence ushers in that "place in the sun" that has previously belonged to foreigners: a state apparatus is formed, local businesses grow, a bourgeoisie takes shape, and finally, the peoples and ethnic groups that had previously had no intelligentsias of their own see them develop at a rapid rate.

The latter deserves particular note. It is precisely the intelligentsia, including the rapidly growing numbers of students, that is commonly the repository of nationalist ideology. The following chain of events is typical, for example. A group's native language is cultivated and enriched; ancient traditions are preserved, restored and multiplied; and the historical and cultural achievements of the given people or group are emphasized. Educated people lay claim to fitting positions in administrative agencies and in education, but the number of such places is naturally limited. Pretensions and vanity grow, grievances pile up, and complexes of all sorts intensify. The most energetic, dynamic, and active segment of the ethnic or religious group (the educated young people, as a rule) demands radical solutions. Movements spring up with the goal of seeing that the group in question attains higher status in the framework of the state hierarchical system.

However, the realization of these movements' and groups' aspirations is blocked by a barrier that is difficult—and more often than not, virtually impossible—to surmount, such as an authoritarian system that does not permit pluralism and real opposition. This authoritarianism, which is attributable not only to historical and traditional factors but also to circumstances involving the need for accelerated modernization, bolsters and affirms the dominant role of certain groups at the expense of others that are deprived, to all intents and purposes, of legal means to change the existing—and from their standpoint, unjust—system. It seems quite logical for opposition groups and currents to switch to forcible, "subversive," and "unconstitutional" methods of struggle, to the tactics of conspiracy and coups d'état. Insofar as it is almost impossible to overthrow a government without the armed forces' participation, every effort is made to take advantage of discontent in some part of the army and police. Under these conditions, the role of the military increases immeasurably—it finds itself at the center of sociopolitical life, and the role of political violence grows accordingly.

Thus, an atmosphere is created in which few people believe in the possibility of bloodless, constitutional change. Everybody knows that the government, upon discovering the opposition's "subversive activities," will crush its opponents in a totally merciless fashion, and if the occasion presents itself, will not hesitate to fabricate a "conspiracy" in order to bring down the full force of repression on the opposition;

and the opposition forces will repay in kind if they overthrow the government. "Winner takes all is the rule in African politics," the London *Economist* wrote. "Second prizes are as rare as balanced budgets. More often than not, the vanquished either knuckle under or get clubbed down."[1]

By the mid-1980s there had been 56 successful and 65 attempted military coups in tropical Africa; from 1948 through 1985, 68 heads of state and government were forcibly removed, of whom 20 were either assassinated or executed. Every coup is not only the succession of one elite or ruling leadership by another, but also a complete or substantial replacement of the apparatus. The new leaders bring their own people in with them, place them in soft jobs, and ensure that members of their own ethnic group or clan predominate at all echelons of power.

Patronage-clientele relationships are ubiquitous, and where ethnic origin plays no role, it is precisely those relationships that figure as the leading element in the political struggle. People follow their "patron," often with little understanding of his program, goals, and stands on the issues.

The bloody events in South Yemen in January 1986 were typical in that respect. The thousands who perished in a few days of exceptionally fierce civil strife belonged to one and the same people, to the same classes and social strata, and to one and the same party; they had been trained in the same educational institutions and held identical views. There were neither national, religious, nor class differences. The split came over personal devotion and loyalty to one or the other leader, and sometimes (though not always) that also coincided with traditional intertribal relations and had to do with which province the leader of a given group was born in. Even before the battles began, it was generally known which military unit or party organization supported which contender—Abdel Fatah Ismail, Ali Nasser Mohammed, or Ali Antar. There were political differences among the three leaders, of course, and there were differing views on the ways and means of developing the society and building socialism. It is hardly likely, however, that the majority of those driving tanks, flying aircraft, and shooting automatic weapons in the streets had a precise understanding of those differences. It was simply known from the outset that "one's own" patron was in the right and his opponents were the enemy (the enemy of revolution and socialism). And with equal conviction in the rightness of their cause, the young soldiers and party functionaries exterminated each other in the streets of Aden.

---

[1]*The Economist*, Jan. 30, 1982, p. 57.

III.

Thus, we can conclude that Eastern society is literally suffused with latent, potential conflict on national, ethnic, religious, clan, and patronage-clientele grounds. It is precisely this latent tension, which constantly threatens to erupt and creates a permanent atmosphere of violence that is always ready to get out of control, that is at the basis of the extremist mind-set readily leading to terrorism in practice. Of the three elements that figure in the title of this article (extremism, terrorism, and conflict), the primary and most basic factor, the principal link in this chain, is precisely the last—the potential for conflict that is rooted in the nature of society. Extremism and terrorism are derivative factors.

The potential for conflict, which is organic, rooted in tradition, and based on ancient tribal, religious, and clan enmity, is immeasurably strengthened, assumes a new quality, and becomes more threatening as a result of processes that take place after independence is won, and that end in the profound disenchantment of society with the results of independent development. The "revolution of rising expectations" and the "revolution of dashed hopes" lead to bitterness, anger, political apathy, cynicism and, among a certain segment of the population—particularly active young people—to extremist sentiment.

A correspondent for the Paris newspaper *Le Monde* writes of Africa: "There is certainly no respect for the constitution and human rights in the majority of African countries, where tribalism and nepotism reign. Political power has been usurped; the inhabitants, both powerless and indifferent, observe the bloody wars among the clans and the succession of coups without seeing reforms of any significance whatsoever. . . . The word 'development' has become an empty sound; there is corruption and the black market." Shifting to the topic of the widespread tendency toward violence in Africa, the journalist continues: "One has only to shout 'Stop thief' or 'Help' for a crowd to jump the suspect in unison and lynch him if the police don't arrive in time to provide protection."[2]

The situation is no better in many countries of Asia. It is enough to remember the pitiless extermination of hundreds of thousands of people of leftist convictions in Indonesia in 1965, the bloody intercommunal conflict in Sri Lanka, the chronic bloodletting of intercommunal clashes in India and Pakistan, the systematic, cold-blooded destruction of "dissidents" in Iran under the "Islamic Republic" and in Iraq under the Baathists. Political violence has become an integral, organic fea-

---

[2]J. de Barrin, "Le retour des sorciers," *Le Monde*, Dec. 11, 1987.

ture of public life; extremism and individual and state terrorism are common, widespread phenomena.

It is impossible to foresee when the wave of violence will begin to subside. Doubtless that will require a long period of developing social institutions and establishing a civil society. The rate of progress of this process will depend to an immense degree on the rate and nature of economic development, which, in turn, is connected with the state and dynamism of the world economy, with the international situation, and so forth. In any case, for the foreseeable future, even if there is fundamental improvement of the situation along the East-West axis (above all, between the U.S.S.R. and the United States), and the world enters an era of deconfrontation and disarmament, it would be naive to expect this to affect the nature of internal social relations in the Third World, much less affect them immediately. Apparently, violence will long remain an integral part of the political life of developing countries, and there is little the world is able to do about it.

At the same time, there is an aspect of the problem about which something can be done. I have in mind international terrorism or, to be more precise, the component of that terrorism rooted in internal conflicts in Third World states or in situations connected with the national-liberation struggle. In simple terms, in view of the fact that in the future that sort of terrorism could, if allowed to develop with relative impunity, spread like wildfire, reach the point of using atomic devices, and even turn against Soviet citizens (recall the Soviet diplomats who were taken hostage in Lebanon), I believe it would be correct to condemn it unconditionally, even if that were to damage our image for a certain time among adherents of the Third World's leftist and revolutionary movement.

It is time we abandoned our established position, based (apparently by analogy with the concept of just and unjust wars) on the notion of the need to make a distinction between the violence born of national or social oppression, and that which is practiced by the ruling classes or powers. In and of itself, this notion is a correct one, but correct precisely insofar as it concerns wars, uprisings, and revolutions—not, however, terrorist activities. The time has now come to think about saving mankind, and about saving it not only from a thermonuclear catastrophe but from a host of other ills as well—including the threat of international terrorism.

After all, in time, we may even see terrorists take groups of schoolchildren, if not whole kindergartens, hostage in order to make absolutely certain that their demands are met. And what government can permit itself to be charged with sacrificing children's lives for the sake of principle?

If we proclaim the principle that in this day and age universal human interests should take priority over all others, including class interests, then it is logical to extend that approach to the problem of combating terrorism, regarding it as an epidemic that must be treated through the combined efforts of interested parties, including our fundamental ideological opponents.

The preceding brief analysis of the reasons that create the potential for violence and generate a psychology of violence and extremism in the Third World was intended to show that these phenomena are long-term in nature and are not amenable to rapid elimination, that they will inevitably give rise again and again to terrorism, which is spreading across state borders today and threatening the safety of innocent people in the most varied parts of the globe. To assume that the resolution of some particular international or intercommunal conflict or other, and the elimination of present-day "hot spots" on the globe will end international terrorism is, in my opinion, a dangerous illusion.

New conflicts will take the place of the old, and new "hot spots" will inevitably arise. After all, the Third World is seething; it is living through a period of chronic instability and painfully contradictory development. In many cases, people fighting for their community's self-affirmation and for the demise of a regime that they consider unjust and oppressive (and a profusion of such situations will arise in the Third World in the future as well) will stop at nothing to achieve their aims, including terrorism on an international scale. One can sympathize with those goals, but if we do not give thought in advance to developing coordinated measures, on an equally international scale, for putting a stop to the wave of terrorism—especially today, when it will soon be possible to hide not just bombs but atomic devices in suitcases and attaché cases—the consequences may be catastrophic.

Nicaragua: Some Distinctive Features of the Transitional Period

TATYANA YEGENYEVNA VOROZHEYKINA*

I.

The 10-year experience of implementing revolutionary transformations in Nicaragua is one of the most interesting and unusual in the social development of the Third World in the 1980s. Indeed, in terms of its origins, the Sandinista revolution differs substantially from all the other popular-democratic processes in the developing world, since it triumphed not in a society with a diversity of socioeconomic structures, but in a capitalist one. In "genetic" respects, the Nicaraguan revolution is closest to the Cuban revolution: in both countries a new regime arose as a result of a grass-roots, popular movement that destroyed the repressive military apparatus of pro-American dictatorial regimes, and with it the political foundations of bourgeois rule. At the same time, the postrevolutionary development in Nicaragua proceeded along an utterly distinctive course: Nicaragua, contrary to the predictions, did not become a "second Cuba."

The July 26 Movement [in Cuba] was not a Marxist organization at the time that power was won, and it developed ideologically along with the revolution. However, the socialist nature of the revolution in Cuba was declared two years after the dictatorship was overthrown, at the time that the armed aggression of imperialism was repulsed; this corresponded to the actual dynamics of the revolution's development in the socioeconomic sphere and realm of political psychology, and at the same time it became one of the most important factors in mobilizing the masses, which two years previously had been anticommunist in their attitudes.

In contrast, the Sandinista National Liberation Front (FSLN), which arose under the direct influence of the triumph and progress of the Cuban revolution, was formed from the very outset as a Marxist-Leninist organization whose platform (in the 1960s and 1970s) included

*Research associate at the U.S.S.R. Academy of Sciences' Institute of World Economy and International Relations [IMEMO]. This article appeared in the January 1989 issue of *MEMO*.

a provision concerning the (ultimately) socialist nature of the future revolution. But, having won power under democratic and anti-imperialist slogans, the Sandinistas declared a course aimed at preserving national unity and at economic and political pluralism. Foreign political and economic factors played an important role in the adoption of this line: They included the desire to expand the number of the Nicaraguan revolution's allies abroad to the greatest extent possible, and to ensure that a number of Western European and Latin American governments, as well as international social democracy, would look on the revolution favorably, which became especially important after the Reagan administration came to power in the United States. This orientation did not change, however, when favorable external conditions came to an end under the extremely difficult conditions of military aggression, an aggression which in duration and scale cannot even be compared to the 1961 Bay of Pigs invasion.

Only after the passage of nine years did the Sandinista leadership consider it possible to talk about the socialist prospects for the development of the revolution, while simultaneously stressing that they were talking about socialism under which protection of the interests of workers and peasants would be integrated with reliance on a mixed economy and political pluralism.[1] In other words, the social, economic, and political line adopted by the FSLN, which at first appeared to be strictly tactical, increasingly acquired the features of a long-term strategy oriented toward seeking out the Sandinistas' own course for building a new society in a backward country with a dependent economy.

The model of a transitional society worked out by the FSLN assumes the long-term existence of state and private sectors in industry and agriculture (including large-scale production), and accordingly, allows for continuation of the bourgeoisie as a social and political force, including its political parties and mass media.

In proposing this model, the Sandinistas proceeded on the premise that the monopoly of political power they had won meant that they did not have to try to push social and economic changes too fast, and that they could ensure the dominant position of the state and state sector in the economy by relying on the nationalized property formerly owned by the Somoza clan and families close to it. They believed that under these conditions the bourgeoisie would act mainly on the basis of its own economic interests. Assessments of this sort and the logic of their arguments were, to a considerable extent, reinforced by the fact that throughout the country's history the Nicaraguan bourgeoisie had been subordinate to the dictatorship both economically and politically.

---

[1]See *Barricada*, July 20, 1988.

The bourgeoisie had never played the role of a genuine political force under Somoza, and therefore, according to the Sandinistas' logic, in the new political situation it would not aspire to political power. On the other hand, an expansion of the possibilities for economic activity (liberalization of credit, various types of subsidies, and other incentives) would, in theory, compel the Nicaraguan bourgeoisie, which under Somoza had been crushed in effect by the clan that had monopolized all the profitable spheres of the economy, to once and for all put strictly economic interests above all others, including political interests. Stepping up the economic activity of the bourgeoisie and expanding its capital investments in production accorded with the new regime's goals for economic revival and overcoming backwardness.

An important role in the development of production, particularly agricultural production, was assigned to the cooperative sector. Thus, the system of economic pluralism was envisioned as an analogue of the New Economic Policy (NEP): A mixed economy was expected to function as a single unit under the aegis and coordination of the state, which would occupy the commanding position.

In the first stage the practical implementation of the Nicaraguan model (until the beginning of massive intervention in 1983) took place under fairly favorable conditions. Revolutionary Nicaragua maintained good relations with many Latin American governments, and it received loans from international financial organizations, and considerable economic assistance from a number of West European countries. Within the country the FSLN received direct political support from the majority of the people, and no one realistically challenged the Sandinistas' right to power. The rest of the political parties were weak and could not propose any alternatives, and the potential counterrevolution was demoralized by the collapse of the Somoza regime.

As a result of the nationalization of Somoza's property, a large state sector was created, composed of about 30 percent of industrial production and 20 percent of all the agricultural land under cultivation. These lands were not distributed among the peasants: the expropriated estates, some of which of were agroindustrial complexes oriented toward exports, were turned into state farms. Later on, in 1981, the first agrarian reform law was adopted; it called for confiscation, in the most densely populated Pacific coast region, of holdings of more than 370 hectares in size that were being neglected or were not being farmed efficiently, and for the confiscation of similar holdings of more than 740 hectares in size in the rest of the country. However, while the implementation of this law did substantially reduce the amount of landlords' [latifundistas'] property in the country (from 40 percent of the total area of agricultural land in 1978 to 12 percent in 1984), it failed, practically, to change the situation of the landless peasants and those with very small holdings. Once again, for the most part state farms were created on the confiscated lands, and the peasants generally received land only on condition that they enter cooperatives. Until 1985 the preservation of private ownership of efficient farms, including large farms and even the very largest ones, remained a basic principle of the FSLN's agrarian policy.

By 1983 the Sandinistas had succeeded in substantially improving the working people's living standard by redistributing income, raising wages, providing various sorts of benefits and price subsidies for food products, and increasing government expenditures on health care and education. These measures could not but sharply increase the expenditure side of the budget and raise the budget deficit. On the whole, however, Nicaragua's economic development from 1979 through 1983 was successful: In many branches of the economy the level of production that had been reached in 1977 and 1978 was restored, and in some it was even exceeded.[2] Despite the worldwide economic crisis, Nicaragua maintained relatively high growth rates (approximately 4.5 percent per year) while most Latin American countries were experiencing a decline in growth rates. A vital factor that enabled the Sandinistas to combine economic growth with a social policy aimed at improving the living conditions of a significant proportion of the population was foreign financing and Nicaragua's broad access to international loans and aid.

During this period the political strategy of the FSLN had two main goals: ensuring the efficient functioning of a mixed economy and, at the same time, preserving and strengthening the potential of the popular movement that had built up during the campaign against the dictatorship and was the Sandinista regime's principal source of support. The national unity policy being followed in Nicaragua deprived the FSLN of the most effective means of mobilizing mass support (a means which had previously been used successfully in Cuba)—the direct class struggle of the workers and peasants. What is more, starting in late 1979 the Sandinistas had already been forced to put a stop to repeated attempts at the spontaneous seizure of enterprises and land holdings. Objectively, therefore, one of the front's most important political tasks should have been the search for other paths, forms, and—most importantly—goals of the mass struggle. Initially, however, the Sandinistas followed the fairly traditional course of creating (usually from the top down) their own mass organizations—trade-union, youth, peasants', and women's; and Sandinista Defense Com-

---

[2]At the same time, the prerevolutionary level of the GNP was not restored in 1983, partly due to a decline in prices for goods exported by Nicaragua. There was a corresponding decline in the per capita GNP: from $1,113 in 1977 to $745 in 1983 (in constant 1980 prices).

mittees—and of carrying out large, mass campaigns (to eliminate illiteracy, to mobilize people for the coffee harvest, to clean up and beautify city neighborhoods, and so forth). The easiest, superficial forms of mass organization were thus exhausted fairly quickly. The most important and, essentially, the only, mobilizing factor in the first three or four years of the Nicaraguan revolution continued to be the momentum of the antidictatorial struggle. This unquestionably ensured the FSLN, particularly in combination with the political effect of its social policies, the support of the overwhelming majority of the people. However, the absence of other, equally effective impulses toward mass struggle that would not die out, but rather grew, could not help having negative consequences that emerged at subsequent stages of the revolution.

At the same time, the proclamation of political pluralism under the conditions of the actual social and political hegemony of the FSLN created a fairly complicated and internally contradictory situation. Most opposition political parties had little influence, and as mentioned above, none could offer any real alternative to FSLN policies. In this connection, there was a danger from the outset that political pluralism would turn into an illusion, while the Sandinistas' real interest lay precisely in having the political parties, rather than economic pressure and the military counterrevolution, become the means for expressing the political interests of the bourgeoisie. That is why the Sandinistas wanted to maintain the bourgeois parties' access to the mass media, and ensure their integration into the political mechanism that was taking shape (the creation of the Council of State, where the majority of political parties were represented, and the inclusion of bourgeois politicians in the government). The operation of this mechanism, however, was not intended to affect (and this was discussed bluntly during the first years following the triumph of the revolution) the main accomplishment—the totality of the real power that the FSLN had won in the armed struggle against the dictatorship.

This situation fundamentally modified the economic functioning of the private sector in Nicaragua. The problem was not just the scale of state regulation and state ownership, but above all, the very existence of a regime that was antibourgeois by its sociopolitical nature.

Under these conditions—and contrary to the Sandinistas' desire—economic power did become the most important means that the Nicaraguan bourgeoisie had at its disposal to exert real pressure in the political sphere.

II.

The model of economic and political pluralism was geared toward a long-term prospect of peaceful development, and at the same time it was supposed to create the conditions for that development. The Sandinistas tried to avoid a situation in which the beginning of social and economic transformations created stimuli to mobilize the counter-revolution, which until then had been demoralized by the fall of the overthrown regime. The moderation of the Sandinistas' socioeconomic line, combined with the totality of the political power they had won, and the maximum possible consideration of the interests of various social classes and groups, were aimed at preventing consolidation of an armed counterrevolution. From the standpoint of the internal align-ment of forces, it seems, such a prospect was entirely realistic, but for all the flexibility of their domestic and foreign policies, the Sandinistas were not able to prevent the export of counterrevolution. What is more, it was the very novelty of the Sandinista plan, which opened up a new channel of the national liberation revolution on the continent and thereby gave it a "second wind," that was largely responsible for the particular aggressiveness of American imperialism toward Nicaragua.[3] The Reagan administration's single-minded policy played a decisive role in escalating the war in that country. Neither the creation and arming of the contra army, nor its survival as a fighting force, nor the duration and scope of the war would have been possible without the constant and growing U.S. support. But even though it was imported from the outside, under the conditions of the developing revolutionary process, the war became the chief factor shaping the economic and political situation in the country and altering the behavior of all partici-pants in the social and political conflict.

The war put the viability of the Nicaraguan model to the test. First, a genuine need to concentrate resources arose, which led, contrary to the Sandinistas' original intentions, to greater centraliza-tion of the economic system, and to an increase in state interference. Second, and this seems more important, the emergence of a real alternative to the Sandinista regime, in the person of the U.S.-backed contras, substantially reduced the objective possibilities for economic and political cooperation between the Sandinista government and the bourgeoisie. Under these conditions, the bourgeoisie's willingness to

---

[3]A joint study by Latin American and American scholars stresses that "yet another socialist revolution, developing in accordance with a model that assumes a one-party system, universal state ownership of property, and association with the Soviet bloc, would be very easily isolated, and no 'self-determination' of any kind would be able to take root in such a situation. The Reagan administration, correctly assessing the effectiveness of the Nicaraguan model as a contemporary alternative for the continent, where peasants and the economically marginal urban population predominate, openly turned Nicaragua into its ideological enemy" (*La transicion dificil: La autodeterminacion de los pequenos paises perifericos*, Managua, 1987, p. 22). And although not only the effectiveness, but even the feasibility of the Nicaraguan model still remain to be proven in practice, this argument seems to be correct in principle and to confirm that it was by no means only geopolitical considerations that lay at the heart of the Reagan administration's intransigent attitude toward Sandinista Nicaragua.

accept the proposed rules of the game (that is, to contribute to the economic strengthening of a politically alien regime), became even more problematic than during peacetime. On the contrary, the economic deterioration and the aggravation of the new regime's difficulties corresponded as fully as possible to the interests of that part of the Nicaraguan bourgeoisie that was still holding on to the hope of returning to power. So, with the expansion of military actions, the most influential organization of Nicaraguan business owners—the Private Sector Confederation, which maintains political ties with the contras— took an increasingly hard line toward the FSLN. In time most bourgeois political figures who in one way or another had cooperated with the FSLN during the first years of the revolution ended up among the opposition, and some of them, directly in the camp of the armed counterrevolution.

Nevertheless, not all of the Nicaraguan bourgeoisie have taken an obstructionist stand toward the Sandinista government. What was said above refers primarily to the urban bourgeoisie. Rural businessmen, including some exporters whose capital is invested primarily in land holdings, have by and large followed a policy of cooperating with the government, without which they would be unable to sustain the reproduction process: Loans, farm machinery and the agricultural infrastructure, and the sale of export products are controlled entirely by the state.

The war drastically worsened Nicaragua's economic situation and very rapidly wiped out gains made in reviving the economy from 1979 through 1982. Starting in 1983 the Sandinistas were increasingly forced to subordinate their economic policies to defense tasks. Military expenditures, which accounted for between 40 and 50 percent of the national budget, the diversion of a sizable part of the ablebodied population into the army, the destruction of production capacity and infrastructure, the drop in exports (military operations were launched in the country's main coffee-growing regions), and the disruption of domestic economic relations that had been weak anyway—all led to spasmodic increases in the budget deficit and became an additional powerful factor contributing to inflation (in addition to the FSLN's social measures mentioned above). This effect was intensified by the unfavorable foreign-economic conditions, especially the continuing drop in prices for Nicaraguan exports.

The war also inevitably brought adjustments in the political model. In 1983 to 1984 the Sandinistas periodically imposed restrictions on political and personal freedoms (in particular, on assemblies and demonstrations), imposed press censorship on reports of a military nature, and repeatedly suspended the publication of the main opposition newspaper *La Prensa*, as well as the activities of antigovernment radio stations, including those operated by the church. During this period, however, restrictions on civil liberties were partial and, as a rule, temporary, and on the whole they did not violate the rules of the political game that had been established in peacetime, that is, all opposition parties and mass media that wanted to take part in political life could do so. The main confirmation of the seriousness of the Sandinistas' intentions and of their desire to maintain political pluralism, even under the conditions of war, was the November 1984 presidential and parliamentary elections. They were conducted under international supervision; all the parties that were registered to take part in them, as well as, incidentally, those that followed the line of the American administration and called for a boycott of the elections, were given the opportunity to campaign.

Without question, the elections played a role in splitting the forces opposing the FSLN, and the Sandinistas succeeded in preventing the bulk of the political opposition from uniting with the military counterrevolution. However, the primary goal of the elections—legitimization of the regime—was not a domestic-policy goal, but a foreign-policy goal. The idea was to retain the support of European social democratic governments and parties, as well as the support of Latin American countries, under conditions in which pressure on them from the United States had grown sharply. Within the country, in the eyes of the majority of the people, the legitimacy of the FSLN regime continued to be based on its prestige' the force that had overthrown Somoza and was now standing up to foreign invasion. The willingness of the Sandinistas to hold elections in an extraordinary situation was due to their confidence that they had the support of the majority of the population.

While confirming the FSLN's predominant political influence in the country, the elections showed at the same time that the actual scope of this influence was somewhat narrower than had been assumed. One third of the voters came out against the FSLN in one way or another. The most graphic indicator of trouble was the voting by some of the peasants. This occurred precisely in the areas where military operations were going on, that is, where the Sandinistas' power was being openly disputed. Under these conditions, the flaws in the Front's social policy with regard to the peasants were revealed, especially its miscalculations in implementing agrarian reform. Up to 1985 the reform, as previously mentioned, made virtually no change in the situation of the landless peasants and those with small land holdings. The Sandinistas tried to prevent the breakup of large land holdings into miniature estates, believing that the stage of small-scale peasant production could be bypassed by creating state farms and cooperatives on expropriated lands. The poorest peasants' unrealized hopes of receiving land, and their discontent with what was essentially the forced organization of farming into cooperatives (land was allocated on the condition that a peasant would join a cooperative), became joined with the fears of the more prosperous landowners who had witnessed the expropriation of Somoza's property and of the large estates. The latter move was perceived as the beginning of a campaign against private ownership of land. As D. Ortega stressed on June 19, 1988, the violation of the peasants' interests led to the creation of a social base for counterrevolution in some regions of the country,[4] creating a danger that the intervention would turn into a civil war.[5]

However, the situation involving the peasants was just part of a more general problem stemming, on the one hand, from the specific nature of the Nicaraguan model, and on the other, from shortcomings in the mass political work done by the Front. In 1983 and 1984 the Sandinistas proceeded on the assumption that the very scale of the external threat ("several Bays of Pigs daily") was such a strong factor in uniting and mobilizing the masses that it more than made up for the weakness of the popular movement's social impulses. In addition, all mass organization activities were carried out in accordance with instructions handed down from above, and leaders of the lower-level units felt accountable only to higher agencies. This resulted in the bureaucratization of the entire system of mass organizations—the Sandinista Defense Committees, the peasants' organizations, and the trade unions—all of which proved insensitive to the actual needs of the masses who comprised their membership. The reaction of the people quickly made itself felt: by 1984 the influence of these organizations began to fall sharply, and membership in them declined or became strictly a formality.

In effect, the FSLN was confronting a situation tantamount to a political crisis, and the Front's chief source of power—its vital and direct tie to the people, its deep roots among the masses—was in danger. The war forced the Sandinistas to evaluate this danger fairly rapidly, and in 1985 they started to reorganize their work in the mass movement. The primary goal of this reorganization was to make the masses really feel, through day-to-day experience, that it was *their* revolution and *their* power, and to this end, to give them the opportunity to exercise that power themselves at the lower level and to make decisions that would affect the actual conditions of their lives. Thus, what was involved here was moving to self-government in mass organizations, and turning them into a channel for the expression of real

---

[4]*Barricada*, July 20, 1988.
[5]According to the Sandinistas' estimates, up to one third of the peasants in the three zones of the country most affected by the war supported the contras in 1983 and 1984.

popular initiative, rather than of proposals that had actually been handed down from above. With this aim, elections were held in all the mass organizations, during which people nominated directly by residents of a certain neighborhood, by workers at a specific enterprise, or by members of a given agricultural cooperative became the leaders of the organizations. As a result, the lower-level units of the mass organizations became the key elements in solving the most important problems of production, supply, urban improvement, and so on.

At the same time the Sandinistas set the goal of turning the lower-level committees of the FSLN into real vehicles of the decentralization process, into one of the genuine centers of grass-roots power (in addition to mass organizations). With this aim, elections of lower-level FSLN committees, which in the past had often consisted of little-known functionaries, started to be held directly at enterprises, while the candidates for these committees were nominated by the working people themselves. All this laid the foundation for the process of radical democratization, for democracy from below, which is the only means of turning the power of the people into a tangible reality for the people themselves. In the course of this process a new basis was created for mobilizing the masses, for overcoming their passivity and the weakness of the mass struggle's social impulses. Thus the gap between the regime and the masses that showed up in 1983 to 1984 is being overcome successfully.

Of course, the significance of this process should not be exaggerated. On the one hand, so far we are talking mainly about Managua (although this in itself is no small number: the capital has about a half million residents, of the country's population of 3.5 million). On the other hand, there are also some objective obstacles in the path of realization of this trend. The principle of vertical, rigidly centralized organization of the FSLN, which is connected to its origins as a politico-military organization and which inevitably grows stronger during a war, contradicts this trend. What is more, this process has drawn resistance from government agencies and ministries, which perceived it as interference in their affairs, and as an attempt to create an alternative authority.

A series of problems also exist at enterprises: Genuine self-management assumes that people view an enterprise as their own, which they can imagine when a state enterprise is involved, but not when a private enterprise is involved. In the latter case, of course, this can be realized through a form of worker control. However, if the principal objective task dictated by the serious economic situation is a maximum increase in production and labor productivity, with a consequent rise in the owner's profits, then it is unrealistic to expect that workers will totally identify their interests with those of the enterprise, and that they can—when the owner is alive and well—feel that they are in charge. In any case, that would require some additional conditions.

But the main problem, it seems, lies in that age-old passivity, submissiveness, and at the same time, dependent attitude toward any sort of authority, be it the government, an owner, or a village chief [cacique]—inclinations which developed over centuries of oppression and dependent development, which permeate the society from the bottom to the top, and which are being eliminated very slowly. But even with these flaws, the experience in the exercise of grass-roots, popular democracy in Nicaragua, which as yet has no analogues, deserves the most serious attention.

Along with restructuring the activities of mass organizations, the FSLN made radical changes in its policies toward the peasants. In 1985 mass allocation of land to individual peasants was begun, first in areas with the highest rate of landlessness, and later throughout the country. In 1985 the distribution of land was carried out mainly by confiscating landed estates, and by dividing up some state farms. At the beginning of 1986 a new agrarian reform law was adopted according to which the size limit for land holdings not subject to confiscation was cut to one tenth of what it had been in 1981 (from 370 hectares on the Pacific coast and 740 hectares in the rest of the country, to 37 and 74 hectares, respectively). As a result of these measures, the Sandinistas were able to strengthen their social base and curb the trends in the peasants' behavior that the counterrevolution had begun to use to its advantage. But at the same time these measures led to a sharp drop in the production of a major export crop—cotton, since cotton plantations accounted for a significant share of the lands distributed among the peasants. Cotton producers, afraid of further confiscations, cut back their plantings of this crop, which requires large capital investments and, at the same time, considerable labor expenditure.

Maintaining a balance between the production of export crops, which provide foreign currency for imports, and the production of grain crops intended for domestic consumption, has become one of the most complicated problems in the FSLN's agricultural policy. From 1979 through 1984 the ban on free trade and low state purchase prices for grain consumed within the country led to a drop in the production of basic food products. At the same time, priority incentives, including incentives built into pricing policy, were provided for the production of export crops. Radicalizing the agrarian reform, especially allowing free trade in corn and beans in 1986, made it possible to rectify the situation fairly quickly and substantially improve the supply of goods to the population. However, the violation in 1985 to 1986 of the principle proclaimed earlier of maintaining efficient privately owned operations caused discontent among the rural bourgeoisie and soon affected exports (although the policy of providing incentives for them continued, including payments in hard currency). Therefore, the Sandinistas are now trying to leave the private sector alone as much as possible in terms of expropriations, and to provide land to those who need it mainly by drawing on state property, which in the past year was reduced almost to half.[6] On the whole, the Sandinistas believe that although there are still landless peasants in the country, most of the transformations in the countryside have already taken place, and the remaining private landowners fully support the revolution.[7]

Still, despite the carefully weighed nature and flexibility of the Sandinistas' agrarian policy, it is apparently based on a certain duality connected with the contradictions of reality. The export of four or five agricultural crops is the foundation of Nicaragua's economy, and will continue to be so for a long time. Hence the Sandinistas' continuing effort to make the agrarian transformations as painless as possible and not to undermine the efficient large farms. At the same time, the peasants who own medium-sized and small farms, and the agricultural workers are the FSLN's primary political support in the countryside.

The economic expediency of preserving large farms producing agricultural products for export, be they in private or state form, is obvious. The history of agrarian reform in Nicaragua, however, clearly shows that attempts to "surmount" the political logic of the revolutionary process in the name of economic efficiency, and to ignore (as contradicting the objectives of socioeconomic development) the peasantry's demands embodied in the slogan, "Land to those who work it!" are fraught with the potential of serious political complications for the revolutionary regime.

III.

The Sandinista government's relations with the peasantry, on the one hand, and with mass organizations on the other, are just specific

---

[6]The share of the state sector in farming dropped from 22 percent in 1985 and 1986 to 12 percent at the end of 1987 (*Barricada,* January 2, 1988).

[7]As of the beginning of 1988 the private sector accounted for 61 percent of the farming in Nicaragua. The greatest reduction had occurred in landed estates (holdings of more than 350 hectares), whose share of agriculture dropped from 36 percent in 1978 to 9 percent in 1987. The share of agriculture represented by large commercial farms (between 140 and 380 hectares) had also declined somewhat—from 16 percent in 1978 to 12 percent in 1987. The share represented by medium-sized farms (between 35 and 140 hectares), which include most of the exporters, remained unchanged at 30 percent. The share represented by peasant farms of between 7 and 35 hectares had been cut in half—from 15 percent in 1978 to 7 percent in 1987. This apparently was the result of the movement of large masses of peasants from areas of military operations to cities, and it was also partly due to organization of farms into cooperatives. The share of agriculture represented by small farms (smaller than 7 hectares) also remained unchanged at 2 percent. At present, various types of cooperatives own 22 percent of the land, and 12 percent, as already mentioned, belongs to the state; 5 percent of the available land has fallen into neglect (*Barricada,* January 2, 1988).

manifestations of a problem common to all revolutions—the relationship between politics and economics. In a society that emerges out of a revolution, politics is the leading, most dynamic sphere, and it "cannot help having preeminence over economics."[8] The preeminence of the political sphere is also associated with the specific characteristics of revolutions that take a country beyond the limits of immature, poorly developed capitalism, with what Lenin noted was a different order of development, with the shift to a different approach "to creating the basic premises of civilization."[9] Under such conditions, political power is the main instrument for carrying out social and economic transformations. Therefore, the central task of the revolutionary vanguard, which comes before all others is strengthening that power, and a key element of that strengthening is expanding and deepening its social base. Thus, at the first stage, political logic inevitably becomes the dominant element of postrevolutionary strategy, including one of its most important components—economic policy. And not economic laws, but political necessity forms the basis of that policy's main components, such as meeting the basic needs of the working people, maintaining their real income at a minimum level, expanding employment, and turning over land to the peasants. The entire complex of economic problems generated by backwardness, as well as by the revolutionary transformation of the socioeconomic sphere itself, cannot be solved successfully using economic methods alone, without taking into account the refracting effect of the political sphere on all economic processes, without exception.

Another point that is equally important: unlike the economy, where strict objective limitations operate, the political sphere gives the revolutionary regime much greater possibility for maneuvering that allows it to mitigate and neutralize the inevitable economic difficulties.[10]

But the "compensating" possibilities provided by the political sphere are by no means unlimited. The more time that passes, the more the results of economic policies affect the political will of the working people. Implementation of socioeconomic transformations intended to take place over a long period of time should be coordinated with an effective short-term economic policy, since over time (if, of course, mass noneconomic coercion is not used), the latter becomes the most important element in strengthening the hegemony of revolutionary forces in society.[11] Of course, there is an objective contradiction here, the resolution of which is one of the main difficulties that a

---

[8]V. I. Lenin, *Complete Works*, [*Polnyye sobrannyye sochineniya*], Vol. 42, p. 278.
[9]V. I. Lenin, *Complete Works*, Vol. 45, p. 380.
[10]See *La transicion dificil* . . . , p. 88.
[11]*Ibid.* pp. 258-259.

revolutionary regime faces: To be effective, economic policies should be based first on economic laws, whose violation will lead sooner or later to an undermining of consensus and, thus, of the regime's social base. At the same time, such a violation is practically unavoidable because of the objective primacy of political logic over economic logic in the transitional period, as noted above.

It must be pointed out that we are talking here about a political logic whose essence is the mobilization of the forces that constitute the revolution's social base. Politics and political methods, including the political component of economic policy, are not identical and cannot be reduced to administrative-command methods, although there is no doubt that here, in the primacy of the political sphere, lie the objective roots of state-bureaucratic distortions, and the danger that the autonomy of politics can be perceived (as it is often perceived) by the revolutionary vanguard as an opportunity for completely arbitrary rule of the economy.

Evidently, for every stage of the revolutionary process there is a certain balance of political and economic components. A disruption of this balance in one direction or another always carries with it a threat to the revolutionary regime. In postrevolutionary Russia the attempt to move from war to peace along the course of further strengthening political (War-Communism) methods of economic management resulted in a political crisis in the spring of 1921, for which the New Economic Policy was the solution. Conversely, in Nicaragua in 1983 to 1984 an imbalance in the direction of the strictly economic components of the FSLN's economic policy, which from the very outset was based on the principles of the NEP, led under wartime conditions to a disruption of the political consensus and to the threat of a crisis. Predictably, reinforcing the strictly political aspects of all of the Front's activities, particularly giving a political cast to the agrarian reform, provided a way out of this situation.

All this does not mean that the relationship between economics and politics in the transitional period is rigid and predetermined. On the contrary, the transition from immature capitalism to a new socioeconomic formation in the long-range future entails the gradual elimination of the predominance of political logic, and the growth of elements of economic self-regulation. It seems that this was precisely the basis of Lenin's concept of NEP as an *economic* policy, as management of the economy predominantly by economic means and on the basis of economic laws, although—according to Lenin—the most important prerequisites for this sort of transition are the decisive *political* gains of the revolution: the overthrow of the bourgeois political regime and establishment of public ownership of the means of production.[12] The primacy of the political sphere can be fully overcome only at the conclusion of the transitional period, when the new system is based on a self-regulating economic foundation. The existence of such a foundation is also evidently the criterion for judging whether the transitional period has been completed.

These problems are even more complicated under the conditions found in Nicaragua, where the FSLN has proclaimed a policy of slow, gradual socioeconomic transformation, which presupposes the organic incorporation not just of elements, but of whole blocks of the previous structure into the new system, and, consequently, the maximum possible preservation of the previous economic logic based on regulation by the market.

IV.

The country's economic situation has deteriorated sharply since 1985: The effect of a new factor—an embargo imposed by the United States in May 1985—was added to the increasingly serious consequences of the war and to the structural shifts in the world capitalist economy.[13] The blockade was an especially serious blow to the Nicaraguan economy because of the extremely weak ties among the individual branches of its economy, most of which depended on corresponding production in the United States to supply what could not be produced domestically, and because of Nicaragua's dependence on the importation of raw materials, equipment, and energy resources. This forced the Sandinistas, in essence, to abandon the policy of reconstruction and economic development that they had proclaimed in previous years, to curtail the majority of their economic projects, and to move to a policy of "survival." In 1985 they carried out a set of measures aimed at adapting the economy to the situation that had developed: subsidies for consumers were eliminated, the monetary unit was devalued, a parallel currency market was legalized, and state social expenditures were cut back. Meanwhile, the wage freeze was lifted to maintain their purchasing power, and a new pricing policy was introduced that was to compensate producers for their expenditures and ensure them a certain level of profit. The peasants and hired workers in the material-production sphere received priority in the supply of essential goods. These measures, according to the Sandinistas, made it possible to implement a more realistic economic policy and, while preserving the

---

[12]See V.I. Lenin, *Complete Works*, Vol. 45, pp. 373, 376.

[13]To maintain a constant volume of imports, Nicaragua has to produce twice as much now as it did ten years ago (*La transicion dificil* . . . , p. 269).

mixed nature of the economy, to prevent a decline in the working people's living standard.

The decisive effect of external factors on Nicaragua's economy makes it impossible to evaluate objectively the effectiveness of the Sandinistas' economic strategy. There is no question, however, that the reasons for the present economic difficulties are not just the war, crisis, and blockade, since internal problems are becoming increasingly obvious, along with the contradictions of the original economic model and the related miscalculations and errors in economic policy.

The first of these obvious problems is the set of relations between the state and the private sector. Throughout recent years, which have been the most difficult in economic respects, the Sandinistas have repeatedly reaffirmed the long-range nature of the economic model they adopted. Enterprises in the private sector in Nicaragua operate under the same conditions as those in the state sector; the policies involving subsidies and loans are the same for both sectors. What is more, in reality the privately owned enterprises are subsidized to the same extent as state-owned enterprises, since until 1988 the profitability of both types of enterprises was ensured through financial levers—the pricing mechanism described above, a higher exchange rate for the national currency (for importers), and the use of a number of different exchange rates in export and import operations.

At the same time, Nicaragua has not found the optimal balance between state regulation and the market, a balance that would enable the state to maintain the commanding heights in the economy while providing the necessary room for private initiative. This problem is aggravated by the fact that, despite the initial orientation toward economic pluralism, the Sandinistas have not succeeded in avoiding establishment of monopolies by various ministries (in particular those controlling foreign and domestic trade, the distribution of resources, construction, and transportation), which have developed their own interests. Management of the actual economic process has become fragmented into individual sectors that are subordinate to various departments, and this has generally worked to the detriment of producers, both state and private.

The Sandinistas tried to solve this problem by creating a special department to coordinate the activities of all the economic ministries. At first this was the planning ministry, headed by a member of the national leadership; then, starting in 1985, it was the secretariat for planning and budget under the president of the republic. Experience showed, however, that under the conditions in Nicaragua it was impossible to carry out current or long-range planning in any detail, especially planning that translated into administrative directives. Not a single annual or three-year plan has been fulfilled yet. Of course, the main reason for this is the war, but that is evidently not the whole problem. It is extremely difficult, in general, to plan realistically the development of a small and relatively unstable economy that depends critically on external market conditions. And, as the socialist countries' experience shows, centralized planning does not protect an economy from domination by the interests of the various economic departments. In all likelihood, under Nicaragua's conditions introduction of a rigid planning system (if this were possible) would only aggravate the majority of economic problems, especially those associated with the functioning of the private sector.

In actuality, the task of coordinating the Nicaraguan economy came to rest within the financial system. Credit and monetary policy became the main lever for state regulation. From 1985 to 1987 the main instrument of this policy was the system of prices and subsidies (through differences in exchange rates) for private and state enterprises, a system which, according to the Sandinistas' plans, was to stimulate an increase in production. In practice this meant that a price set by the state was supposed to compensate the producer for an increase in expenditures and provide a profit rate that was set each time through negotiations between business owners and the appropriate ministry. The idea was that with this sort of mechanism, inflation, which actually was planned, would stimulate production activity, which in turn would make it possible to solve the basic social problems and, most importantly, would provide employment. The constant price increases would be offset by wage increases, and it seemed that this would make it possible to increase production without sacrificing the people's living standard.

Indeed, for some producers, especially those who were involved in raising agricultural crops with a short capital turnover cycle—sorghum, corn, beans—this sort of system was beneficial. Moreover, under these conditions all the enterprises became profitable, although this profitability was essentially fictitious, since it was achieved exclusively by manipulating financial levers, and not by increasing production efficiency.[14]

On the whole, this policy had fairly severe economic consequences. The proper relationships among prices were upset, which made it impossible for the government to influence the economy in the required direction. The artificial reduction of prices for imported goods resulted in increasing unproductive consumption and scattering funds among many different projects with long recoupment periods. Some private business owners and managers in the state sector devel-

---

[14]See *Barricada*, December 14, 1987; February 1, 1988.

oped distorted, exaggerated notions about the economy's real capabilities. The state budget deficit grew by leaps and bounds, and currency emissions became the main source for covering the deficit (70 percent of it). An unrestrained rise in prices began, and inflation went out of control over a three-year period, reaching 1,500 percent by the end of 1987, and reducing to zero the would-be advantages of this course. As a result, by 1987 the national monetary unit had ceased to be the principal means used for transactions. The country's economy was effectively based on dollars, which was partly due to its open nature and to the policy of the government, which paid bonuses to exporters in hard currency. The dollar became virtually the only real means to gain access to most material goods. Under such conditions, the most profitable sphere of activity was not production, but speculation.

All this could not help affecting the situation of the working people. Inflation undermined the purchasing power of wages, which, despite constant increases, no longer provided a minimal living. The government tried to prevent a decline in the living standard by subsidizing the basic consumer "shopping basket," creating supply centers for workers directly at enterprises, and so on. On the whole, however, these measures turned out to be relatively ineffective, since subsidizing the basic array of consumer goods created additional pressure on the entire economic system and stepped up inflation even more. A significant percentage of products left the standard distribution network for the parallel market, and the resale of goods purchased at state prices became one of the easiest ways to derive an income, which was sometimes two or three times as much as normal wages.[15]

These processes have resulted in accelerated growth of the so-called informal sector, on which significant numbers of urban working people rely to carry out their own "strategy for survival." This sector also includes large-scale operators who make large amounts of money by smuggling food and essential goods from other Central American countries. However, the vast majority of dealers, most of whom are women, are the wives and relatives of people who are receiving wages. Often it is the sale of homemade goods and small-scale speculation that provide the main source of a family's income.

Chaos in the financial system and inflation have given rise to a number of negative processes in the social sphere. First, what is already a weak and small working class in Nicaragua has been undergoing mass deproletarization. Second, the existence of an unofficial sector, together with the war, has become one of the main reasons for the influx of rural residents into Managua. This flow was somewhat

---

[15]See *La transicion dificil* . . . , pp. 268-269.

reduced after the decision in 1986 to allow free trade in some grain products. However, until recently, living off the buying and selling of goods has appeared to be easier than peasant labor, and therefore the capital continued to be a magnet for many rural migrants, who became members of the marginal population there and were forced to exist under very difficult conditions. And third, the presence of a parallel economy has inevitably led to the spread of corruption.

These processes, which have affected primarily the strata of the population that comprise the social base of the revolution, inevitably weaken the mass organizations supporting the Sandinista Front, since the most important thing for the working people under present conditions is the struggle for survival. The unofficial sector has become one of the most important objects of ideological work by the church hierarchy, the FSLN's most dangerous and far-sighted political opponent.[16] The government's repeated attempts to combat speculation through administrative methods generally failed to produce any economic effect, and even turned out to be politically harmful, since in reality there is no distinction between a hired worker and an "unofficial" worker. Many of the "speculators" and "antisocial" elements against whom the government attempted to mobilize public opinion only recently had been workers and peasants, that is, the people who provide the FSLN's main base of support.

All this indicates, in our opinion, that specific economic problems—inflation, the purchasing power of wages—sooner or later inevitably become the most important political issues. So far, not one of the forces opposing the Sandinistas has been able to capitalize on the growing dissatisfaction with the economic situation. The decisive obstacles to this have been the people's memory of the recent Somoza past, the foreign threat, the policy of democratization from below that has been carried out recently, and apparently, the fact that both the working people and business owners sense that the government is trying to take their economic interests into account.

The agreements on ways to reach a political settlement of the Central American conflict signed in August 1987 in Guatemala gave the Sandinistas the opportunity to rescind some of their emergency measures and return to the original model of political pluralism. At the end of 1987 La Prensa went back into publication, and opposition radio stations resumed their operations. Under these conditions, it was especially important for the Sandinistas not to overlook the point at which complaints about economic difficulties started to grow into mass political protest. The political need for a reform that would solve the main problems involved in the functioning of the mixed economy

---

[16]*Ibid.*, p. 265.

became obvious. What sort of mechanism can be fashioned for protecting the working people's living standard that will not turn into a factor contributing to inflation? How can the commanding heights be maintained in the economy without turning state control into a brake on private initiative? What sort of system should there be for state regulation that will stimulate real production growth, rather than an increase in producers' expenses?

In 1988 the Sandinista government is carrying out a radical turnaround in its economic policies, whose main goal is stabilization of currency. In principle, the Sandinistas have rejected state price controls and centralized wage increases, granting producers themselves the right to set prices for their goods and to make additional payments to workers on the basis of an enterprise's profitability. The system of inexpensive loans for production has been eliminated (as a rule, the loans were not paid back to the banks anyway), and there has been a sharp rise in bank interest rates, which now should change according to the level of inflation. The government has announced that it will support genuine parity between the cordoba and the dollar in order to put an end to the policy of inexpensive imports and to stimulate exports.

The Sandinista leadership believes that economic reform is a necessary step to prevent a breakdown of the economy and to provide protection for the revolutionary regime under conditions in which hopes for an end to the war in the near or not-too-distant future seem fairly unrealistic.[17] The measures that have been taken apparently represent the only possible way out of the existing situation, and in principle, it seems that they open up real paths toward stabilization and improvement of the economy. On the one hand, the private sector, which until now has developed under the hothouse conditions of practically free credit, inexpensive imports, and numerous state subsidies, is now forced to be responsible for its own efficiency, proceeding from the actual possibilities of the economy. On the other hand, the rejection of universal nominal wage increases (on the condition that price increases are halted or slowed down) should ensure that wages earned by working people employed directly in production retain their purchasing power, without which it is impossible to maintain labor productivity in vitally important spheres of the economy (the production of food products, other sectors of the processing industry, and the export sector).

On the whole, however, these measures have led to an unavoidable reduction in demand that has been extremely painful for the majority of the population. The most vulnerable have proved to be

---

[17]See *Barricada*, Edicion especial, June 17, 1988.

employees in the so-called nonproduction sphere—teachers, physicians, and state employees, who have no additional sources of income. In addition, the reform, which sharply cut back the amount of money in circulation, has dealt a serious blow to the unofficial sector, which actually was one of the Sandinistas' intentions. But the possibilities of "individual survival" have also thereby been substantially reduced for a significant number of the working people.

All this could not help but affect the social and political situation in the country. The government quickly ran into clearly expressed concern among the most politicized segment of the people who in an ideological sense had been its most reliable supporters—teachers and medical personnel, who demanded that they be provided with a living wage.[18] And what is especially important here is that pro-Sandinista trade union organizations became spokesmen for their interests—a fact which provides clear evidence of the real nature of the process of democratization described above. Representatives of industrial workers, who supported the government's rejection of centralized wage controls, called for expanded rights for trade unions, and for their direct participation in drawing up enterprises' plans and in distributing profits.[19] On the whole, the program for the liberalization of the economy was supported by the producers of basic export goods and food products. But on the other hand, private business owners, united in the Private Sector Confederation, spoke out against the reform, which was clearly advantageous to them economically and which included most of their traditional demands. Besides the obvious preeminence of the political interests of the bourgeoisie, this reaction also apparently reflects its justifiable concern that the steps taken by the FSLN could lead in principle to a situation in which the Sandinista state would no longer be responsible for all the economic difficulties, and the economic demands of the working people would be addressed not to the government, but to the business owners themselves.

Just a month after the economic reform began, the opposition tried to take advantage of the situation and put the Sandinista regime to the test by organizing a demonstration in the town of Nandaime calling for the creation of a "national rescue" government. Both the harshness of the Sandinistas' reaction (arrest of the most active participants in the demonstration, temporary closing of the opposition radio stations and newspaper, deportation of the American ambassador) and, to a certain extent, the very proclamation of the socialist nature of the Sandinista process on the ninth anniversary of the revolution indicate that the new economic policy, while stabilizing the economic situation, is

---

[18]See *Barricada*, June 19, 1988.
[19]See *Barricada*, May 14, 1988.

complicating the political situation. This means that the Sandinistas must search for new, nontraditional ways to mobilize the people politically that can compensate for inevitable dissatisfaction with the economic situation and make it possible to put up successful resistance to the offensive of the church and opposition political parties.

*   *   *

In 1979 the Sandinistas led the Nicaraguan revolution to victory along the same path that had been followed by the July 26 Movement, confirming all the basic lessons provided by Cuba's experience. There seemed to be every reason to believe that the further course of events in Nicaragua would also correspond to laws deduced from past experience, especially since worldwide socialist development had not provided a wide range of alternatives. However, first by dint of circumstances, and later because of the political will of the leadership, as well, the Nicaraguan revolution followed its own particular course, offering its own variations for the resolution of basic problems arising from backwardness and dependence.

The future will show whether the direction chosen by the FSLN is a real alternative to the course that has been followed by the majority of socialist countries and Third World countries with a socialist orientation; whether this direction corresponds to the underlying laws governing the transitional period in the developing world; and whether the choice made by the FSLN is the first harbinger of overdue changes in the understanding of those laws, or whether Nicaragua will remain an exception. At the same time, one can already draw certain conclusions from the Nicaraguan experience.

First, the fundamental possibility of preserving and developing a democratic, pluralistic system under the conditions of war and an extremely grave economic situation has been demonstrated. The most important thing, in our opinion, is not so much the existence of opposition parties, but rather the attempts to democratize society from the bottom up; the adoption of decisions, including economic decisions, with the consensus of the masses; the consideration of their real economic and political demands; and efforts to encourage their initiative in every way possible. Granted, it should be said that this trend is reversible. The greatest threat to its development is the war: the longer it lasts, the greater the number of low- and middle-level political leaders who will be inclined toward authoritative methods. The masses' extremely low level of political sophistication, their passivity, and their conformist attitude toward authority also contribute to this.

Second, the Sandinistas have shown that rigid centralization and the predominance of War-Communism methods in economic management can be avoided, even in the situation of a civil war. One can easily see the drawbacks of the Nicaraguan economic system, which provides virtually no administrative control over the distribution of extremely limited resources. It is also obvious that certain blocs of an administrative-command system (reflecting the special interests of government [economic-management] departments) are nonetheless being formed, and the Sandinistas apparently recognize that this danger exists. In the past nine years, however, the economy has not become the domain of the state; since the nationalization of Somoza's property, the private sector's share in the economy (about 60 percent in agriculture and 50 percent in industry) has remained practically unchanged, and state enterprises are managed primarily by economic methods.

Third, the stability of Nicaragua's economic development will depend to a great extent on how successfully the private sector is integrated into the transitional economy. As it is, its nine-year existence demonstrates only the possibility of such integration, while a stable mechanism for accomplishing it has not yet been created. In all probability, long-term cooperation with the Sandinista regime (if the contras stop being a real politico-military alternative) is the only acceptable option for the Nicaraguan bourgeoisie. That does not mean that it will restrict its activities to the economy. Economic power independent of the state will inevitably give rise to a desire to expand the political space allotted to the bourgeoisie. In this situation the Sandinistas face the task of averting, on the one hand, the danger that their power will be eroded (through corruption, degeneration of personnel, and so on), and on the other hand, the tendency toward a complete state takeover of property, a tendency which is always going to exist in their own ranks.

Brazil and Argentina in the Modern World

Ye. N. Grekov, one of our readers in Moscow, asks the follow-ing question: Isn't it about time that Brazil and Argentina were included in the category of developed capitalist countries? The editors sought an answer to this question from Irina Nikolayevna Zorina and Viktor Leonidovich Sheynis, research associates at the USSR Academy of Sciences' Institute of World Economy and Inter-national Relations [IMEMO] who are well-known Soviet specialists on the economic and political problems of developing countries. We have recorded their discussion, which we now present to our readers.*

Zorina: The reader raises an interesting question, once again calling attention to a problem that has been discussed in scholarly circles for quite some time with mixed success, so to speak. Several years ago, soon after the Falklands (Malvinas) conflict of 1982, I myself wrote an article titled "To Which 'World' Does Argentina Belong?" Granted, the article was never published in its original form, since the implication that the question was open to debate was frowned on by many Latin American specialists.[1]

But now this question is being asked, as it was then, by many Argentines themselves—politicians, scholars, and simply ordinary Argentine citizens. Similarly, for Brazil, for its business and political circles, and for rank-and-file Brazilians, defining their country's place in the modern, interconnected, and rapidly changing world is a critical issue. Will Brazil be a "great power" by the end of our century, as its president promises? Will it be able to repeat—in its own way, of course—the Japanese phenomenon by getting into the forefront of scientific and technical progress? Do Argentina and Brazil still belong to the developing world, occupying its upper strata, or are they surging further ahead—Brazil developing at a more dynamic pace than Argen-tina—"hot on the heels" of the rear guard group of industrially devel-

---

*Zorina is a candidate of history and leading research associate at IMEMO; Sheynis is a doctor of economics and chief research associate at the institute. This article appeared in the August 1987 issue of *MEMO*.
    [1]The reflections and discussions of those days resulted in our jointly written article "Argen-tina at a Historical Turning Point" (*MEMO*, No. 5, 1984).

oped countries? Are there really any insurmountable barriers to development that can keep them from catching up to the group of industrially developed capitalist states that have far outstripped them, and from eventually joining the "club of rich nations"? Or will backwardness and dependency be their lot forever?

As we see, there are many questions, and they can be answered in different ways. First of all, we should probably look at the world capitalist economy and the global community, decide how the role of our subject-countries in it has changed, turn to concrete statistics that enable us to determine the level of development of productive forces, the economy as a whole, social relations, and political culture, and make clear the general dynamics of change using all these parameters. How shall we begin, Viktor Leonidovich?

Sheynis: Before we start I'd like to make a few comments of a general nature that will enable us to define the subject and the points of reference of our discussion.

First, I think it's time to abandon excessively rigid methods of contrast that break down our modern, very complex and diverse world into opposites: black and white, dependence and independence, developed and developing countries. No analytical work is needed to detect in the world capitalist economy—and that is precisely what we are discussing here today—two basic groups or, to be more exact, two types of countries: developed and developing. As a first approximation, this dividing line is quite necessary: without it the general picture of the nonsocialist world would look like an immense mosaic. But if we stop there, we overlook the great dissimilarities among both the developed, and especially the developing, subsystems of the world economy, and also—let us stress this from the beginning—the conditional nature of the boundary drawn between them.

Some 10 years ago the Soviet scientists L. Gordon, V. Tyagunenko, L. Fridman, and their fellow mathematicians presented convincing evidence that groups of typologically similar countries are like "nuclei," with "bridal trains" that extend in all directions and eventually merge with each other in the border zone.[2] Turning the boundary between them into an absolute is like looking for a grid of geographical parallels and meridians not on a globe, but on a patch of earth. Like our reader who asks about Brazil and Argentina, we could as well ask: Should Ireland, Portugal, and Malta be ranked as developed countries? By the way, this is commonly done, though, without a second thought.

---

[2]See *The Typology of Nonsocialist Countries* [*Tipologiya nesotsialisticheskikh stran*], Moscow, 1976.

But a boundary, although it can be drawn in different ways, is at the very least a useful tool. The "barrier of underdevelopment" you mentioned—a concept popularized, I believe, by the leftist radicals and defended by some of our scientists, and one that is definitely loaded—is another matter. When developed and developing countries are separated by a barrier, the boundary appears, if not closed, as we used to say in our country 50 years ago, then in any case almost insuperable in the course of evolutionary development.

The question, incidentally, is applicable not only to Argentina and Brazil. It could just as well be asked of Mexico and a number of small and medium-sized countries in Latin America and Eastern Asia. In the intermediate zone there exist, albeit in different positions, at least two or three dozen states that are usually included in the developing world. According to my estimates, they account for roughly half of the world's global social product and one sixth of its population.

But let us return to the two countries of interest, especially since they are quite representative of the intermediate zone and—a fact that is also of no small importance—occupy an important place in the nonsocialist world as a whole because of the absolute size of their economic potential. Suffice it to say that in the size of its gross national product, Brazil ranks eighth in the world, immediately after the leading "Seven" major capitalist nations. By 1990 it could overtake Italy and Canada.

But these facts don't exhaust the issue of level of development. Indeed, what are the criteria used to categorize countries as developed or developing? After all, they too change with time. From an economic standpoint, not so long ago—in the first half of this century—industrial nations were considered developed countries, while agrarian societies were regarded as undeveloped countries. The establishment of capitalism as the dominant means of production in the economy as a whole was viewed as crucial proof that a country was "developed." The same criterion was applied to the set of social indicators. Today, in the era of the scientific and technical revolution, when a scientific-industrial system of productive forces is taking shape and capitalist relations are rapidly spreading throughout the majority of Third World countries, the standards of "development" are higher. This is probably the approach we should take to Argentina and Brazil—their historical path and their present state.

Zorina: I'm in complete agreement with this approach. I would just like to add some political nuance. During the postwar years many people saw the international structure as bipolar: two "superpowers," each heading its own military-political bloc of allies, and a seemingly vast, inactive "Third World"—the battlefield for capitalism and socialism. These ideas, oversimplified even for that era, were refuted by a richer and more complex reality. In the capitalist world, the United States' unconditional leadership has been questioned: New economic and political centers have taken shape—the uniting states of Western Europe and Japan. Neutral and nonaligned European nations have become more active, and the foreign policy of Canada, Australia, and New Zealand have become more autonomous.

The world as a whole and the developing world, in particular, have become far more complex and interdependent, while at the same time polycentrism has grown stronger not only in economics but in politics. The role played by India and China in international affairs has increased many times over. Rapid processes of differentiation have been under way in the Third World, which have led to formation of various regional and intercountry alliances, and regional centers of political activity have themselves emerged. I would particularly like to stress that in addition to the factor of power and the possession of strategic weapons, the factor of moral and political power has also increased, particularly in the past few years; the influence of the nonaligned movement in international politics has grown considerably.

Just what position do Brazil and Argentina occupy in this complex modern world, where, I agree, it is difficult (yes, and apparently useless) to establish insurmountable "barriers" between the constantly changing levels of development of various countries? In the political literature both Argentina and, especially, Brazil are sometimes ranked among the "rising powers of the developing world" and singled out as new regional centers of power and the economic leaders of the developing countries, especially the "Group of 77" developing countries.

Do you agree with this classification, Viktor Leonidovich? After all, you've done a great deal of work on the subject of the differentiation of typology of Third World countries.

Sheynis: It seems that Argentina, like Brazil, can be included in the intermediate zone of the world capitalist economy. In this zone they occupy leading positions in terms of a number of key economic and social indicators, surpassing not only many Latin American countries, but some south European states, as well. Although both countries share a number of distinguishing features with the majority of Third World nations (I won't dispute that in the least), they are far removed not only from its "lower stratum"—the least developed countries—but from the main group that includes India, Indonesia, Egypt, Nigeria, and many others. During the discussions of the 1970s I was asked: What are you doing, putting Argentina on an equal footing with the United States? No, I am not, but if you want to use the term "footing," then in my view, Argentina is closer to the West European countries than to Nigeria or Pakistan, for example.

Zorina: I think that Argentina and Brazil themselves are different in many respects. To call Argentina a "newly industrialized state" would be inaccurate, first, simply because it became industrial-agrarian at the beginning of the 20th century, or in other words, a long time before today's "newly industrialized states" entered world markets. Second, it is of no small importance that the key sector of its economy is still large-volume agricultural exports, which are based on a system of highly concentrated land ownership and the political power of the "Pampas bourgeoisie"—the cattle-breeding and farming oligarchy.

Sheynis: You're quite right, Irina Nikolayevna, but at the same time let's not belittle Argentina's level of industrial development. Agriculture's contribution to both countries' gross national product in the first half of the 1980s was roughly the same, about 10 to 13 percent. But when it comes to industry's contribution, especially that of manufacturing, Argentina considerably surpassed Brazil—by 5 to 10 percent. But in terms of the technological level and branch structure of industry, and in the quantity and competitiveness of its industrial exports, Brazil ranks much higher, of course. In 1973 both countries exported roughly the same amount, in monetary terms, of means of production, whereas in 1982 Brazil exported 5.5 times more than Argentina.[3]

Zorina: Finally, I would like to take special note of Argentina's sizable economic and political role in both Latin America and the world, a role that was defined as far back as the late 19th century. It was with good reason that V.I. Lenin singled out Argentina as one of the transitional types of states of his time, as an example of those countries that "have political independence in the formal sense, but in fact are entangled in nets of financial and diplomatic dependence."[4]

Sheynis: Argentina was, or rather, became a developed country by the standards of the time no less than 100 years ago. According to estimates made by the well-known British economist A. Maddison, in 1870 Argentina's per capita social product, in 1965 prices, totaled $412, while Mexico's figure at roughly the same time was $120; Japan, $209; Italy, $379; Russia, $226; the United States, $503. By that measure, Argentina was approximately at the level of France and Germany at the time.[5] It is no accident that beginning in the mid-19th century, an enormous number of European immigrants headed there. The wealth of the pampas and the state of the world market, which

---

[3]*Comercio exterior*, No. 5, 1986, p. 432.

[4]See V.I. Lenin, *Complete Works* [*Polnoye sobraniye sochineniy*], Vol. 27, p. 383.

[5]See A. Maddison, *Economic Progress and Policy in Developing Countries*, London, 1970, p. 18.

offered Argentina exceptional export opportunities—all this played a role, but even more important was the social and ethnic element that shaped the Argentine nation at a time when the country had ceased to be a poor and sparsely populated backwater of South America. The first wave of immigrants that formed the European component in the majority of Latin American nations consisted mainly of descendants of the knighthood, the absolutist bureaucracy, and the medieval clergy and the "lumpen" products of the disintegrated feudal system in the Pyrenean countries. In the 19th and 20th centuries, when Argentina, as well as Brazil, was swept by a second, ethnically more hetero-geneous wave, the prevalent groups were socioeconomically active elements that were bourgeois or oriented to bourgeois values. Accord-ing to W. Rostow's data, from 1856 to 1932 over 6.4 million people migrated from Europe to Argentina, while from 1821 to 1932 more than 4.4 million went to Brazil (during the same period 5.2 million migrated to Canada and 34.2 million to the United States).[6]

Reynolds, an American author who analyzed the economic history of 41 developing countries, states that the "turning point" in Argen-tina's economic development came in 1860, and in 1880 in Brazil's (specifying, of course, that this change was confined mainly to the Sao Paulo zone).[7] The distinction, however, lies not so much in Brazil's later transition to modern economic growth, which involves extensive, rather than enclave-type development of capitalism, as in what hap-pened in subsequent decades. After creeping up to the foot of the economic Olympus, Argentina, for reasons that would require a sepa-rate discussion, began "eating up" its wealth, while Brazil, with brief interruptions, steadily increased its rate of economic growth. Even before the war, during it, and during the first postwar decade (1928 to 1955), Brazil moved considerably ahead of Argentina in its rate of growth of per capita social product: an average 2.5 percent annually, compared with 0.5 percent, and from 1950 to 1980 the corresponding figures were 4.0 percent and 1.4 percent.[8] In general, one could say that Argentina was a country with a slowly developing economy, while Brazil had a rather rapid rate of development, which narrowed the gap in their levels.

Zorina: Yes, Argentina, although it was developing, and growing more modern to some extent, provides an instructive example—and not only for the developing world—of how a country can gradually lose its former advantages. The wealth it accumulated during the "years of

[6]W. W. Rostow, *The World Economy. History and Prospect*, London, 1978, p. 19.

[7]See L. G. Reynolds, *Economic Growth in the Third World. 1850-1980*, New Haven, 1985, pp. 10, 32, 85-98.

[8]The data for 1928 to 1955 is from L. G. Reynolds, *op. cit.*, p. 90; for 1950 to 1980—our estimates, based on national and international statistics.

prosperity" and the resources that flowed into the country were not used productively and to a great extent were simply plundered by foreign capital and local ruling groups and their incredibly vast social clientele. In regard to Brazil, you probably know that in the view of the well-known Japanese economist S. Okita, that country began its economic modernization in about 1950, being at that time at roughly the level of Japan in 1900.[9]

Sheynis: S. Okita was very optimistic in his assessment of Brazil's economic prospects. The future will show to what extent he is right. But let's look at how the situation has developed up to now. Let's turn first to the most aggregate and synthetic index of the level of economic development—the per capita social product. To get a clearer picture, let's compare the relevant indicators for Argentina and Brazil with the average levels of the developing and developed capitalist countries in each of the years shown below. The calculation was done in two ways. Since the conversion of national currencies into American dollars can result in serious errors, we also cite alternative figures on the basis of the currencies' purchasing power, using the methods of the research group composed of I. Kravis, R. Summers, and their colleagues. This method is not infallible, either, but it is being more and more widely used in U.N. publications and I think that in this instance it more accurately reflects the real dynamics. So we invite our readers to take a look at the following table—the result of my recent calculations.

These data enable us to make at least three observations. First of all, both countries are considerably above the average level of the developing countries (not to mention the overwhelming majority of them). Second, the gap between Argentina and the developed capitalist states has stabilized or is widening, whereas the distance between Brazil and those countries is gradually narrowing, but still quite significant. Third, the historical advantage that Argentina has had over Brazil since mid-century is steadily waning.

Zorina: I too participated in the discussions of the 1970s, and I recall that our opponents responded to these calculations with a counterargument: socially the Latin American countries are far closer to the Afro-Asian nations than to Western Europe and North America. What's important, they said, is quality, not quantitative indicators.

Sheynis: If we compare countries by their levels of economic and social development and their place in the world economy, a discussion without indicators is like counting on one's fingers, and then no one can

---

[9]S. Okita, *Japan in the World Economy*, Tokyo, 1972, p. 182.

TABLE 1
Per Capita Production of GNP (percentages)

	Based on official exchange rates					Based on comparable purchasing power of currencies			
	1950	1960	1970	1980	1985	1950	1960	1970	1980
Developing countries = 100									
Argentina	518	437	436	571	507	376	324	327	277
Brazil	167	182	208	211	218	129	144	151	202
Developed capitalist countries	1,058	1,088	1,315	1,018	1,166	509	528	599	563
Developed capitalist countries = 100									
Argentina	49	40	33	56	43	74	61	55	49
Brazil	16	17	16	21	19	25	27	25	36

Calculations made by author on basis of international and national statistics.

prove anything to anyone else. In this instance, I am on the side of the mathematicians who assert that quality is an unknown quantity.

Zorina: I'm reminded of the words of Leonardo da Vinci, "No human study can be called real knowledge unless it has been proven mathematically." These words are probably an exaggeration, a completely understandable reaction of the titan of the Renaissance to the literary scholasticism of the Middle Ages, but in this case it's true.

Sheynis: Precisely. And as to social development per se, here too Brazil—following Argentina—has advanced quite rapidly from backwardness to more developed forms of social life. Both countries—and this too distinguishes them from the majority of Third World states— have already transformed themselves from agrarian-peasant societies into nations whose industrial and service sectors also play the leading role in the structure of employment (and not only in global social product), from societies dominated by traditional socioeconomic structures to societies of the bourgeois type, from rural societies to urban societies. The level of public education has increased, as well.

Once again we must burden our readers with numerical data: When organized in a table, they give us a clearer idea of the social situation in 1980 or thereabouts. (See Table 2).

As we can see, in all the important social indicators, both Brazil and—especially—Argentina have a serious lead over the majority of developing countries. Some of the benefits of modern-day civilization have become rather widespread. Nevertheless, both countries lag considerably behind the majority of developed capitalist states.

TABLE 2

Indices of social development	Argentina	Brazil	Developing Countries	Developed Capitalist Countries
Demographic				
Life expectancy (years)	65	55	44	70
Infant mortality (per 1,000 births)	45	77	94	11
Time required for population to double (at 1980-1983 growth rates; years)	45	31	29	112
Social structure				
Percentage of employees:				
in agriculture	13	31	59	7
in industrial branches	39	30	19	43
in services sector	48	39	22	50
Percentage of hired employees:				
in economy as a whole	71	65	37	82
in industrial branches	75	84	65	***
Urbanization				
Percentage of urban population	82	68	33	76
Education				
Percentage of literates in population over age 15	93	76	55	99
Percentage of corresponding age contingents in school:				
elementary school[1]	107	99	88	109
secondary school	57	34	31	79
postsecondary school	23	12	7	30
Development of means of communication and transportation (units per 1,000 inhabitants):				
automobiles	72	50	14	357
television sets	185	123	28	450
radios	379	169	113	1,086
daily newspapers	95	45	32	331
Health care and nutrition				
Number of inhabitants per physician	521	1,700	5,706	554
Calories per capita (percentage of requirements)	125	109	102	134
Protein per capita (grams per day)	108	61	59	99

[1]Indices exceeding 100 percent reflect a situation in which the number of pupils in elementary school includes some belonging to older age groups.

Sources: *World Bank. World Tables, 1984*, Washington, 1985, vol. II, pp. 5, 13, 148, 149; *World Population Data Sheets*, Washington, 1984; *Handbook of International Trade and Development Statistics, 1984*, UNCTAD, New York, pp. 466-470; *Statistical Yearbook, 1985*, UNESCO, Paris, 1985, pt. III.

Zorina: This lag becomes particularly impressive when one recalls what is virtually the most critical problem facing these two countries, one that is especially typical of Brazil—the social disintegration of society. Large segments of the marginal population do not participate (or participate to a very slight extent) in the process of consumption of modern goods and services, or in the whole modern way of life—economic, social and political.

The socially polarizing model of development that was practiced during the rule of military-authoritarian regimes and even earlier in both Brazil and Argentina hampered the expansion of the domestic market and fragmented it. This limited the consumer demand not only of the dangerously expanded mass of socioeconomically marginal people, but of large strata of the working people. The problems of disparities in the levels of development of certain regions were aggravated. According to the authoritative testimony of J. Sarney, Brazil's current president, Brazil is outstripping many of the developing countries in the growth of hunger and poverty. Here are figures cited by France's *Le Monde*: 40 percent of Brazilians cannot satisfy their need for food, and another 25 percent cannot afford to buy anything but food products.[10]

Sheynis: All this is very serious, of course. But let's not forget that in nearly every country in sub-Saharan Africa, those figures are probably higher. Moreover, the statistical average of 109 percent of the norm for calories per Brazilian and 125 percent per Argentine cannot be obtained merely by resorting to the old trick of comparing a mountain and a molehill. The kinds of foods that make up these calorie counts and the way that affects the nation's health is another matter. All the same, in such instances I am always reminded of Marx's oft-quoted remark, "Hunger is hunger, but hunger that is satisfied with boiled meat, eaten with a knife and fork, is different from the hunger that a man satisfies by devouring raw meat with his hands, fingernails and teeth."[11] Incidentally, the statistically average Argentine "eats" over 100 kilograms of meat annually. (The average consumption per capita in developing countries is less than 13 kilograms.)

Zorina: But the Brazilian pauper doesn't compare his situation with that of the African!

Sheynis: Yes, he's more apt to compare himself to the European and the North American. The mass media have seen to that. We note, however, that people in Latin America are far more aware of what the European consumes than of how he works.

---

[10]*Le Monde*, Apr. 18, 1986.
[11]K. Marx and F. Engels, *Works* [*Sochineniya*], Vol. 12, p. 718.

Zorina: Even more important are the striking contrasts within the Latin American countries: outrageous, parasitical luxury coexists with the most extreme poverty. I glanced through the latest publication of the International Bank for Reconstruction and Development [World Bank]. Not one of the more than 40 developed capitalist nations and developing countries on which data is given has such a drastic difference in incomes as Brazil: In the mid-1970s the poorest 20 percent of the population received only 2 percent of the country's total income, while the upper 10 percent of the population pocketed over 50 percent of that income. Things are somewhat better in Argentina, but the distribution of wealth is still more unequal there than in the developed countries.[12] While visiting Mexico City in 1985, I saw for myself how every day the capital's Eastern Bus Terminal discharged into the city hundreds of confused, desperate people who were prepared to do any kind of work or semblance of work, no matter how dirty or how temporary, that yielded even a little money. I saw scenes in the city's streets whose commonness made them all the more dreadful. If a red light stopped the vast flow of cars, which sometimes seemed like a veritable parade of modern technology, before them there immediately appeared, as if springing from the earth itself, dancers dressed in feathers and Indian costumes or, far more often, "fire-eating" boys who earn their living with this physically dangerous pastime.

Sheynis: There is no question, Irina Nikolayevna, that it is precisely the depth of social contrasts and the existence of huge numbers of uprooted and impoverished people that constitute the most noticeable watershed between European and Latin American countries, although probably not all of them: I believe that Buenos Aires is somewhat different. But then economic growth and social modernization have never proceeded evenly or embraced all of society at once, especially in places where they have developed rapidly. This gives rise to the complex social and political problem of the forced coexistence in one country of a "society of consumption" and a "society of poverty." The distinguished Argentine scholar R. Prebish often spoke of this. In the history of different countries, this problem has been resolved in various ways.

Zorina: Unfortunately, there are limited possibilities for pursuing a broad social policy—particularly the redistribution of income in the interests not only of the middle class, but of a segment of the workers, especially skilled workers, not to mention material support for the socioeconomically marginal people flooding into the cities, and reduced polarization of incomes. And this is also the problem of providing a more stable social base for the new regimes that have

---

[12]See *World Development Report. 1986*, World Bank, New York, 1986, pp. 226-227.

replaced military rule. Even in Brazil, where the economic boom of the early 1970s enabled the bourgeoisie to somewhat expand the scope of social policy, to announce a policy of "national integration" and begin involving workers in "profit-sharing" by allocating stock, the crisis of the early 1980s narrowed possibilities for social maneuver. Granted, the situation then began to change. But the problem of foreign debt, which has no quick solution and shows that both Argentina and Brazil are strongly dependent on the centers of the world capitalist economy, will aggravate the resolution of social problems, won't it?

Sheynis: Generally speaking, all this is true, of course. But I wouldn't dramatize the debt situation. Brazil (which is over $100 billion in debt) ranks first and Argentina (over $50 billion) ranks high on the list of debtors. For this reason, one hears a great deal of concern expressed both within these countries and abroad. The situation is not determined solely by the absolute sum of indebtedness, however. First, it is important to know what the loans were used for, and whether they helped increase production potential. This seems to have been done with greater effectiveness in Brazil than in Argentina.

Second, debt payments are always a burden, but they don't necessarily fetter the economy. After a prolonged crisis, Brazil's economy began to improve in the latter half of 1984. The increase in the gross national product in 1984 was 4.4 percent; in 1985, 8.3 percent; and in 1986, about 7 percent. It is just as important that the set of financial and economic measures known as the "cruzado plan" (referring to the new monetary unit) made it possible to drive down inflation. The balance of payments improved.

Third, both governments, relying on the real, albeit asymmetrical, interdependence of debtors and creditors, conducted a rather flexible policy and were by no means defenseless against outside pressure. Brazil and Argentina repeatedly tried to get deferments, revision of terms, and refinancing of their debt and, moreover, completely rejected IMF requirements that they considered unacceptable for their countries. Sarney's government, in particular, rejected the switch to "zero economic growth," limited debt payments to 2 to 2.5 percent of the country's global social product—a sum that leaves the necessary reserve for domestic capital investments—and in February of this year announced a temporary suspension of interest payments on all loans from private foreign banks. Granted, the economic situation, although it improved considerably, is still not quite stable. According to A.P. Karavayev, the Soviet authority on Brazil, the main driving force of economic growth between 1984 and 1986 was the increase in consumption, not capital investments.

Things are getting worse in Argentina. After all, the economic growth that began there after 1982 was considerably weaker and by 1985 had already given way to a new decline. In 1985 Argentina's gross national product at best matched the level of 1975, and when calculated per capita, was less than it was in 1970.[13]

Zorina: Argentina is in a different situation than Brazil. It has to not only solve its crisis, but change its longstanding historical tendency toward economic and social stagnation, raise stagnating sectors of the economy to the modern-day technological level, and make the economy more flexible and capable of swiftly reacting to the demands of the scientific and technical revolution and the world market. We know how difficult this is, and not only from Argentina's experience. All this will probably take a great deal of time.

As for Brazil, the economic growth of the past few years has already produced certain social results and served as the basis for even more far-reaching plans. It has proclaimed a program to "eradicate absolute poverty." In the state budget, social expenditures have been increased: more money for education and public health, subsidies for the production and import of certain types of foodstuffs, and more funds for irrigation and the development of urban public transport. The social sections of the program for economic development for 1986 to 1989 call for the creation of 6.6 million new jobs (the total number of employed in 1980 was about 43 million, and of officially registered unemployed, 900,000),[14] the vocational training of 18.2 million workers and office employees and the regular distribution of free milk to children from the poorest families. A total of $100 billion will be spent on the plan's implementation, and about half of that sum is devoted to the war against poverty.[15]

Sheynis: The future will show how successfully this plan can be implemented. I hope that consideration is given to the main recommendation made by the authors of a report prepared at the government's request and titled "Brazil in the Year 2000": efforts should be made to distribute national wealth more equitably and to lessen, not deepen, social contrasts. Otherwise the democratic political structures being restored with such difficulty, and the reviving, still struggling institutions of a civil society might be destroyed. And it is not all that important who does the destroying—the extreme right-wing forces that are trying to restore authoritarian regimes, or the leftist extremists

---

[13]Based on figures from: *Yearbook of National Accounts Statistics, 1981*, New York, Vol. 1, pt. I, p. 20; *Monthly Bulletin of Statistics*, Jan. 1987, p. 325; *Industrie et développement international*, No. 394, 1986, pp. 523-524.

[14]*Yearbook of Labour Statistics, 1984*, Geneva, 1984, pp. 54-55.

[15]*Industrie et développement international*, Paris, No. 392, 1986, pp. 408-412.

who are provoking that turn of events. What is your view, as a political scientist?

Zorina: Yes, the new civilian regimes in both countries are currently faced with an extremely difficult task. They must not only complete in Argentina and secure in Brazil the changeover to stable economic development and adapt to the restructuring that is under way in developed capitalist states; at the same time they must also promote social modernization and the integration of society. Only by completing this set of tasks can Brazil and Argentina truly reach a level comparable to that of the industrially developed countries.

Perhaps the most difficult problem is that of establishing the well-developed political system of a modern-day society. In the specific conditions that exist in Argentina and Brazil, it would ensure the development of a democratic process—including the practice of making social compromises, something that both the bourgeoisie and the organized workers could learn to do by studying the example of opposing classes in developed capitalist countries. Only the stabilization of a democratic political system in which there is increasing participation by the masses could guarantee development and social progress within the framework of a multiparty parliamentary system, while cutting off and isolating extremist forces.

Many countries that are belatedly undergoing capitalist development are experiencing a more or less lengthy historical phase of rule by authoritarian regimes. This does not mean, however, that there is a strong link between the level of economic development and the political system. Let us note that the majority of West European states already had well-developed institutions of a civil society and had multiparty parliamentary systems (granted, with restricted voting rights) in the 19th century, despite having considerably less developed capitalist economies than do present-day Argentina and Brazil. Both countries, slowly and painfully, with continual setbacks and relapses into either military regimes or dictatorships with populist overtones, are fighting their way into the democratic mainstream of world historical progress.

Let's be cautious. Under conditions of social instability—which, apparently, is continuing and at certain stages might even increase—in the process of economic restructuring and general modernization, and in the absence of well-developed democratic structures and historically established mechanisms that would ensure development on the basis of a consensus of all politically active forces that observe democratic procedure, both the dominant classes and the opposition in these countries might repeatedly feel tempted to resort to violent methods of rule and struggle. Therefore the phase of authoritarianism might not be completely over in the contemporary history of these countries. Argentina still has powerful antidemocratic, oligarchical forces that during the years of unchecked power tasted the "sweetness" of impressive material privileges and lofty social status. The recent heated battle over the law on national defense showed that there are influential forces trying to bring back the era of military dictatorship.

This was also evident during several dramatic days in April of 1987, when some military units were involved in an open revolt against the democratic regime and its policy of "settling accounts with the past." The revolt failed, but the government also failed to secure the unconditional capitulation, arrest, and immediate trial of the conspirators. "The military can no longer do whatever it wants, but the democracy still isn't strong enough, either," was the assessment of C. Gabetta, editor of the Argentine weekly *El Periodista*.

In Brazil the dismantling of the authoritarian power structure was begun as a "reform from above," proceeded for a time in accordance with the schedule devised by moderate members of the former regime, and only during its final stage did the opposition, which had been joined by some of that regime's former supporters, take the political initiative and come to power with a program of broad reforms. Here, however, the military regime was not discredited as it was in Argentina after exposure of the junta's unlawful acts and its military defeat in the Falklands. The former state apparatus is still largely intact, particularly the army, the police, and the security agencies. The leaders of the new government were forced to abandon the idea of retribution for the crimes committed in the early years of the military regime. The army, which has retained several means of unofficially interfering in political life, reacts unfavorably to any attempts to make the military leadership's crimes against its own people the subject of an open investigation.

The latifundistas staunchly resist the government's attempts to implement, at long last, an agrarian reform. This is the reef on which the democratization process has foundered in more than one country. "The agrarian problem is bathing Brazil in blood," said Tancredo Neves, who was elected President of the country in 1985 but never took office due to his premature death. It created a genuine war in the forests and on the savannas. Many regions were transformed into something akin to the American "Wild West."

All the same, I would like to conclude on a more optimistic note. R. Alfonsin's government in Argentina has held its "Nuremberg"—a public trial of former rulers who have besmirched themselves with bloody repressions and are guilty of the "disappearance" of 12,000 people (that's the official figure—30,000 is the unofficial estimate), torture, and suppression of democratic freedoms. For virtually the first time in Latin American history, the men who not long ago proclaimed themselves "saviors of the nation" have disappeared, not behind desks to write their memoirs while drawing a generous pension, but behind bars. This is a lesson not only in the political, but in the moral cleansing of society—and probably not for Argentina alone.

Today the struggle to settle accounts with the authoritarian past and to ensure Argentina's democratic future has been focused on the recently adopted law on "obediencia debida" ["following orders under constraint"], which absolves many military officers (who held the rank of lieutenant colonel or lower during the years of the dictatorship) of legal responsibility for their crimes. The constitutional government is clearly striking a compromise with the military caste and with the many supporters of the former regime. The unshaken power of the reactionary military and the continuing conflict between the armed forces and civilian institutions are a ticking time bomb underneath the democratic structures that are being built with such enormous effort. In Argentina and countries like it, one of the most difficult problems is that of establishing a developed democratic political system and form-ing a civil society under conditions of social instability that, to all appearances, is continuing and at some stages could even increase in the process of economic restructuring and general modernization. "Democracy has ceased to be a timid wish and has now gone into action," said R. Alfonsin in congress recently. "Argentine society is aware of its power and knows that the government is relying on it."

The democratic process is also growing stronger in Brazil, which during its military dictatorship did not experience the bloody terror that swept Argentina. The transition to a "New Republic" will be completed this year with the adoption of a new Constitution. It will probably stipulate measures for improving the condition of the poorest strata, grant the right to strike, provide for a sovereign foreign policy, and so forth.

Sheynis: I fully share both your fears and your hopes, Irina Nikolayevna. Of course, it would be naive to think that the social antagonisms that have been manifested repeatedly in Brazil and Argentina would develop without occasionally being exacerbated. But in today's world, when highly effective means of destruction can readily be used, and any internal conflict can transcend national bor-ders, it is especially important to keep these flare-ups within the bounds of civilized social behavior.

The chief danger of social disintegration lies in the fact that many opposing forces, each defending its own interests (and in the majority of cases—its version of modernization, rather than the preservation of social structures), periodically feel tempted to bring into play their reserve capacity for lending support and applying pressure, a move that can easily get completely out of control, paralyze economic life and still not firmly constituted democratic institutions, produce professional squads of terrorists, push people into bloody violence and pogroms, and provoke the establishment of more or less rigid dictatorships, for which a weary and demoralized society pays an enormous price by sacrificing democratic, independent institutions for the sake of restoring "order."

Brazilian Communists are justified in stressing that "social protest in a society with weak traditions of political organization and class struggle also creates the prerequisites for reactionary political trends. . . . It is most important," they say, "that the Constitution guarantee political democracy," because "until today political crises in Brazil have always been resolved with the use of force." This is a common problem in the Third World, but I would like to think that both Argentina and Brazil have already felt the full consequences of these events and will not return to the past.

Zorina: Viktor Leonidovich, I believe I hear the voice of our opponents. You see, you yourself admit that the multiparty parliamentary system in Brazil and Argentina is not firmly established and that a return to authoritarian forms of rule is possible; this is what puts them in the same category as other Third World countries.

Sheynis: Well, first of all, we never said that in terms of their political culture the Latin American countries have already become part of the developed world (which is itself certainly not beyond reproach in this respect, to put it mildly). We have discussed only the positive changes of the past few years, which are in many ways similar to the processes that began a bit earlier in the countries of Southern Europe, which are moving further and further away from right-wing authoritarian regimes and closer to democratic ones. Second, and this is my main point, there is a considerably sharper division between the most developed Latin American states and the majority (although not all) of Afro-Asian and certain other Latin American countries. And it's not just a question of certain attributes of democracy, which, in undergoing a more or less prolonged period of historical strengthening, cease to be a mere formality. After all, at the root of all this is the level of civic involvement, people's sense of justice, and their beliefs about the value of every human life and the individual's freedom in society.

Zorina: Yes, comparing the people's level of law consciousness in different countries is difficult, but it can be done, and Latin American countries—although violence is a longstanding tradition in their societies—are still ahead of many Eastern countries. We should remember how Argentine society was shaken by the military rulers' crimes. The trial of the junta was a public event, a kind of catharsis, rather than an episode accompanying the "changing of the guard," of which history has known many. Many Asian and African countries, on the other hand, have been swept, in the recent and more remote past, by waves of dreadful terror in which tens and hundreds of thousands of people perished, yet few people recall those tragic events today. Even in modern-day Turkey there is a desire to conceal the truth about the genocide of the Armenian people in 1915 to 1916. What countries' political cultures have made room for a true settling of accounts with the past?

Sheynis: You know, I recall an ironic remark from one of F. Iskander's last stories. "Progress is when people still kill each other, but no longer cut off each other's ears." In the Central African Republic, cannibal and former "emperor" Bokassa I was condemned for treating himself—in the literal sense of the word—to some of his political opponents.

But to speak seriously, the settling of accounts with the past that you mentioned, if it is indeed being done, unquestionably shows that a country that has experienced a phase of authoritarianism is rising to a higher level of political development. It is not enough to condemn the organizers and perpetrators of arbitrary acts—the severity of the retribution can only satisfy the pride of the victors, and the spiral of violence begins again. It is far more important that the whole society and all of its vital forces acknowledge their responsibility for what has happened and that they be filled with resolve to prevent any "repetition of the past." This is a long and difficult path. The word "repentance" is now heard everywhere—its meaning is not religious, but deeply moral and political. I think that a critical view of the past is an integral element of the new political thinking that is entering the modern world.

Zorina: I don't think a discussion of Argentina's and Brazil's place in the world would be complete without pointing out their increasing role in international relations and their foreign policy. Both countries are leaders in the "Group of 77" and often represent not only Latin American, but all developing states in the struggle for a new international economic order, the democratization of international relations, and a just solution to the problem of indebtedness, and in their support of the "disarmament-and-development" process. Since 1973 Argentina has been a full-fledged member of the nonaligned movement, while Brazil prefers to maintain the status of an observer. The activity of both countries, particularly Argentina, has sharply increased, which was clearly evident at the Eighth Conference of the Heads of State and Government of the Nonaligned Countries held in Harare (in September of 1986). Both countries are members of the "support group" of the Contadora process and favor a peaceful political solution of the

Central American crisis. Argentina, as a member of the "Delhi Six," is participating in important initiatives aimed at averting a thermonuclear disaster, achieving disarmament, and ensuring humanity's survival.

Sheynis: Add to this Brazil and Argentina's apparent tendency to economic integration, the 1986 agreement whose stated goal is the creation of a trade and customs alliance, joint investment projects—all this could provide the economic basis for one of the new centers of power that are emerging in the world.

Do you think we should sum up our remarks?

Zorina: Hardly. In presenting our general position, we don't seem to have avoided some sharp edges and controversial formulations. The discussion, which didn't begin yesterday, will continue, naturally. And the processes that we have spoken of can admit only of interim assessment where their very essence is concerned. It's clear that development will continue, and that it will pose new problems and new questions.

Sheynis: That's a kind of conclusion. You have painted an optimistic picture in at least one respect: we'll have reason to continue our conversation in a few years' time.

A Retrospective

Let Bygones Be Bygones

SOMETHING FROM *MEMO* BEFORE PERESTROIKA:

Accommodating the publisher's wishes, we are presenting American readers with excerpts from a number of issues of MEMO published over the past 30 years. As one can readily see, along with substantive and interesting articles, certain opinions, assessments, and formulations that clearly reflected the stereotyped ideas of the era of stagnation, and the spirit of the Cold War and confrontation—in short, the "commonly accepted" style of thinking at that time—sometimes found their way into the journal.

We would like to hope that the following selection of excerpts will help readers see more clearly the tendencies and approaches that are developing in the intellectual life of Soviet society in connection with perestroika and the new political thinking. All it takes to do so is to compare the following excerpts with the preceding articles in this book.

* * *

"Over the next 15 years the Soviet Union will attain first place in the world both in overall production volume and in per capita production, and the material and technical basis of communism will be created in the U.S.S.R.; at the same time, this will signify a great victory in the competition with the most developed capitalist countries. . . .

"The fulfillment of the majestic assignments of the seven-year plan will be a new crushing blow to bourgeois ideology and to international reformism and revisionism. Now it is becoming clear to all unprejudiced people that it is socialism and not capitalism that is holding high the torch of human progress. The great growth in world socialism and, along with it, the accelerating decline of world imperialism—that is the direction of the course of events in the modern era. . . .

"The main element in the seven-year plan consists in the sort of mighty economic development and rapid improvement in the people's well-being that will turn the Soviet Union in the next 10 to 12 years into the country with the highest living standard in the world. That will represent the world-historical victory of socialism in the worldwide competition with capitalism. . . . There can be no doubt that the successful fulfillment . . . of the grandiose program of economic development will raise the world communist and workers' movement to a new stage, reduce reformist and revisionist "theories" to ashes, and bring much closer the time of humanity's final liberation from capitalist exploitation and imperialist oppression. . . .

"A new stage has begun in the general crisis of capitalism; socialism has become a worldwide system; the sphere of capitalism's domination has narrowed; imperialism's colonial system is in the process of collapse; the unevenness in the development of the capitalist countries' economies has become increasingly acute; and the process of the decay of capitalism has intensified. . . . War and the militarization of the economy are organically inherent in modern capitalism. . . . Dying capitalism can have no strictly cyclical rhythm, just as a gravely ill person cannot experience normal breathing." (*MEMO*, No. 12, 1958)

* * *

". . . Imperialism, and especially U.S. imperialism, having encountered serious shocks and failures in its domestic and foreign policy, is organizing politico-military adventures and channeling increasing efforts into the subversive political and ideological struggle against the socialist countries and the communist and democratic movement. . . . The ideologists and politicians of contemporary capitalism are striving to give the EEC a very definite politico-military function—to split up the socialist commonwealth and draw the socialist countries, one by one, into the integrated capitalist system, and to change the status quo in today's Europe by either 'peaceful' or military means." (*MEMO*, No. 10, 1968)

* * *

"The militarization of the economy serves as a concentrated expression of the decay of capitalism in the era of imperialism. . . . The forward movement of the world capitalist system . . . is proceeding within the framework of the general crisis of capitalism, which, having once begun, is continuing to intensify.

". . . It is noteworthy that the capitalist world's most developed country, the United States, having grown extraordinarily rich in the course of two world wars, is steadily losing its positions in economic competition with the Soviet Union. This shows one of the main distinctive features of the crisis of world capitalism at the present stage.

". . . Never before have the tasks of struggling for peace, democracy, and socialism been so closely intertwined as they are in our time. And that is also a manifestation of the exacerbation of the crisis of world capitalism—an exploitative system with no historical future.

"The principal feature of the present day, and the main content of our era has become the transition from capitalism to socialism, which is being carried out by peoples on a worldwide scale . . . Yet foreign propaganda is proclaiming that the Marxist assessment of contemporary capitalism is obsolete, and that present-day capitalism is entirely different from what it was a half-century or century ago." (*MEMO*, No. 11, 1968)

* * *

"As is known, within NATO there is one state, the Federal Republic of Germany, that still dreams of redrawing the political map of Europe. Revanchist designs and militarism, like birth marks, betray the true nature of Bonn's present foreign-policy course. It can plainly be seen through the coating of verbal cosmetics called the 'Ostpolitik.' . . . As we can see, West German revanchism is not losing hope that the new Wehrmacht will grow nuclear teeth. . . . The American conductor's baton is no longer able, as it was in former times, to elicit nothing from the NATO orchestra but melodies that are soothing to Washington's ear. Sometimes it also has to listen to solo numbers in which national motifs can distinctly be heard. . . . For many years the strongest power in the imperialist world trampled its allies underfoot." (*MEMO*, No. 6, 1969)

* * *

"The experience of the U.S.S.R. has fully demonstrated the great advantages of the socialist state and of socialist democracy in the area of nationality relations. . . . The superiority of socialist federalism over any form of bourgeois federalism stems from the superiority of socialist democracy over bourgeois democracy.

". . . In the character of a representative of Soviet society, the national element withdraws to the background, as it were, giving way to the common, the socialist, and the internationalist element. The main thing is not whether a given person is an Uzbek or a Belorussian; the main thing is that he is a citizen of the Soviet Union. . . . While constituting one of the Soviet people's greatest achievements, the resolution of the nationalities question in the U.S.S.R. simultaneously represents an important landmark in the social progress of all humanity.

". . . L.I. Brezhnev vividly and accurately disclosed the remarkable dialectic of the international and the national in his report. . . . 'The unity of the multinational Soviet people,' he noted, 'is as strong as a diamond. And as a diamond's facets shine with many colors, so the unity of our people shines with the diversity of the nations that make it up, each of which is living a rich, full-blooded, free, and happy life.'

". . . State-monopoly capitalism, with its tendency toward reaction along every line, intensifies every sort of oppression, including nationality oppression. . . . Guided by the immortal ideas of Marxism-Leninism, and breaking down the fierce resistance of the exploiters and oppressors, all of multinational humanity will take the road of struggle and labor toward a common radiant and happy life, toward communism.

"The crisis in bourgeois political economy began approximately a half-century before the general crisis of capitalism. The appearance of *Das Kapital* dealt it a mortal blow. . . . A kind of collapse of bourgeois political economy is taking place. . . . Nearsighted bourgeois economists, incapable of rising in their theoretical concepts above one-dimensional empiricism and narrow pragmatic considerations, celebrated the fact that 'Ford beat Marx'. . . ." (*MEMO*, No. 12, 1972)

*   *   *

". . . After October 1917 the main class contradiction of the era, that between the working class and the bourgeoisie, was extended directly to international relations. The dominant factor in world politics became the existence, interests, and struggle of state-organized antagonist classes, of states representing opposing socioeconomic systems. . . . It is precisely in the very nature of the recognition of the dangers of the nuclear age, the very approach to the extremely urgent, universal human task of preventing nuclear war (as to other global problems), and in foreign-policy strategy and practice that the antitheses of the class nature and class interests of the socialist and capitalist states, of progressive and reactionary political parties and politicians, manifest themselves in full force." (*MEMO*, No. 4, 1985)

*   *   *

"In the 1970s the internal contradictions of capitalist reproduction once again became sharply exacerbated, which attests to a further deepening of the general crisis of capitalism. . . . The combination of a growth in productive forces with the processes of economic decay is a typical contradiction of contemporary capitalism. . . . The anti-humane nature of the capitalist application of the accomplishments of the scientific and technological revolution, and the ruinous socioeconomic and ecological consequences of that application are manifesting themselves more and more vividly. It is not difficult to recognize new forms of decay in that.

". . . Under the conditions of imperialism, decay stems from the very domination of the monopolies, whereby 'to a certain extent, the motivations for technological progress and, consequently, for all other progress disappear.' . . . Along with the innovation process, a tendency toward decay, engendered by the monopolistic nature of contemporary capitalism, operates like inexorable fate.

". . . The monopolistic bourgeoisie is increasingly becoming a parasitical growth on the social organism, feeding on its juices . . . and increasingly manifesting its uselessness and parasitical nature.

". . . Imperialism is the final stage of capitalism, the stage of its dying away. . . . The real, actual transition to socialism is accomplished through the revolutionary breakup of the capitalist order. This takes place, as historical experience shows, through the successive defection of individual countries or groups of countries from the capitalist system." (*MEMO*, No. 5, 1985)

About BNA

The Bureau of National Affairs, Inc. (BNA) is a leading publisher of print and electronic news and information services, as well as books, reporting on developments in business, economics, law, taxation, labor relations, environmental protection, and other public policy issues. It is headquartered in Washington, with a staff of editors and reporters in the United States and throughout the world.